The Student's Introduction to *Mathematica*®

A Handbook for Precalculus, Calculus, and Linear Algebra

Second edition

Bruce F. Torrence
Eve A. Torrence

CAMBRIDGE
UNIVERSITY PRESS

CAMBRIDGE
UNIVERSITY PRESS

University Printing House, Cambridge CB2 8BS, United Kingdom

Cambridge University Press is part of the University of Cambridge

It furthers the University's mission by disseminating knowledge in the pursuit of education, learning and research at the highest international levels of excellence.

www.cambridge.org
Information on this title: www.cambridge.org/9780521717892

First published 1999
Second edition 2009
5th printing 2014

© B. Torrence and E. Torrence 2009
Page design and composition: Paul Wellin

Printed in the United Kingdom by TJ International Ltd, Padstow, Cornwall

A catalog record for this publication is available from the British Library

ISBN 978-0-521-71789-2 Paperback

For

Alexandra and Robert

Contents

Preface

The mathematician and juggler Ronald L. Graham has likened the mastery of computer programming to the mastery of juggling. The problem with juggling is that the balls go exactly where you throw them. And the problem with computers is that they do exactly what you tell them.

This is a book about *Mathematica*, a software system described as "the world's most powerful global computing environment." As software programs go, *Mathematica* is big—really big. We said that back in 1999 in the preface to the first edition of this book. And it's gotten a good deal bigger since then. There are more than 900 new documented symbols in version 6 of *Mathematica*. It's been said that there are more *new* commands in version 6 than there were commands in version 1. It's gotten so big that the documentation is no longer produced in printed form. Our trees and our backs are grateful. Yes, *Mathematica* will do exactly what you ask it to do, and it has the potential to amaze and delight—but you have to know how to ask, and that can be a formidable task.

That's where this book comes in. It is intended as a supplementary text for high school and college students. As such, it introduces commands and procedures in an order that roughly coincides with the usual mathematics curriculum. The idea is to provide a coherent introduction to *Mathematica* that does not get ahead of itself mathematically. Most of the available reference materials make the assumption that the reader is thoroughly familiar with the mathematical concepts underlying each *Mathematica* command and procedure. This book does not. It presents *Mathematica* as a means not only of solving mathematical problems, but of exploring and clarifying the concepts themselves. It also provides examples of procedures that students will need to master, showing not just individual commands, but sequences of commands that together accomplish a larger goal.

While written primarily for students, the first edition was well-received by many non-students who just wanted to learn *Mathematica*. By following the standard mathematics curriculum, we were told, the presentation exudes a certain familiarity and coherence. What better way to learn a computer program than to rediscover the beautiful ideas from your foundational mathematics courses?

What's New in this Edition?

The impetus for a second edition was driven by the software itself. The first edition coincided with the release of *Mathematica* 4. While version 5 introduced a few notable new commands, much of the innovations in that release were kept under the hood, so to speak. The algorithms associated with many well-used commands were improved, but the user interface underwent minimal changes. *Mathematica* 6 on the other hand is a different beast entirely. Perhaps the most fundamental innovation is the introduction of dynamic user interface elements with commands such as **Manipulate**. It is now possible to take essentially any *Mathematica* expression and add sliders or buttons that permit a user to adjust parameters in real time. The second edition was re-written from the ground up to take these and other changes into account. Virtually every section of every chapter has undergone extensive revision and expansion. This edition reflects the software as it exists today.

The organization of the book has not changed, but there are two notable new additions:

The second edition has exercises, several hundred in fact. These provide a means for experimenting with and extending the ideas outlined in each section. They also provide a concrete and structured framework for interacting with the software. It is through such interactions that familiarity and (ultimately) competence and even mastery will be attained. Complete solutions are freely available online, as discussed in the next section.

In addition, a new chapter has been added (Chapter 8) to address the fundamental aspects of programming with *Mathematica*. While this topic is far too expansive to cover thoroughly in a single chapter, many of the fundamentals of programming are conveyed here. It is a fact that many of the new features of version 6 require a working knowledge of pure functions and other ideas that fit naturally into this context. You are likely to find yourself reading a section of this chapter here and there as you explore certain topics in the earlier chapters. Think of it as a handy reference.

How to Use this Book

Of course, this is a printed book and as such is perfectly suitable for bedtime reading. But in most cases you will want to have the book laid open next to you as you work directly with *Mathematica*. You can mimic the inputs and then try variations. After you get used to the syntax conventions it will be fun.

The first chapter provides a brief tutorial for those unfamiliar with the software. The second delves a bit deeper into the fundamental design principles and can be used as a reference for the rest of the book. Chapters 3 and 4 provide information on those *Mathematica* commands and procedures relevant to the material in a precalculus course. Chapter 5 adds material relevant to single-variable calculus, and Chapter 6 deals with multivariable calculus. Chapter 7 introduces commands and procedures pertinent to the material in a linear algebra course.

⚠ Some sections of the text carry this warning sign. These sections provide slightly more comprehensive information for the advanced user. They can be skipped by less hardy souls.

Beginning in Chapter 3, each section has exercises. Solutions to *every* exercise can be freely downloaded from the website at www.studentsmathematica.com.

Mathematica runs on every major operating system, from Macs and PCs to Linux workstations. For the most part it works exactly the same on every platform. There are, however, a few procedures (such as certain keyboard shortcuts) that are platform specific. In such cases we have provided specific information for both the Mac OS and Microsoft Windows platforms. If you find yourself running *Mathematica* on some other platform you can be assured that the procedure you need is virtually identical to one of these.

Acknowledgments

Time flies. When we wrote the first edition of this book Robert and Alexandra were toddlers who would do anything to get our attention and wanted to sit on our laps while we worked. Now they are teenagers who just want our laptops. Like *Mathematica* our kids have grown up. They have become our best friends and terrific travel buddies. This project has again disrupted their lives and we thank them for their attempts at patience. To quote Robert, "You guys aren't going to write any more books, are you?" Don't worry kids, at this rate you'll both be in college.

Special thanks go out to Paul Wellin at Wolfram Research, who handled the page design and who dealt tirelessly with countless other issues, both editorial and technical. We would like to thank Randolph-Macon College and the Walter Williams Craigie Endowment for the support we received throughout this project. And we thank Peter Thompson, our editor at Cambridge, for his professional acumen and ongoing encouragement and support.

1
Getting Started

1.1 Launching *Mathematica*

The first task you will face is finding where *Mathematica* resides in your computer's file system. If this is the first time you are using a computer in a classroom or lab, by all means ask your instructor for help. You are looking for "Spikey," an icon that looks something like this:

When you have located the icon, double click it with your mouse. In a moment an empty window will appear. This is your *Mathematica notebook*; it is the environment where you will carry out your work.

The remainder of this chapter is a quick tutorial that will enable you to get accustomed to the syntax and conventions of *Mathematica*, and demonstrate some of its many features.

1.2 The Basic Technique for Using *Mathematica*

A *Mathematica* notebook is an interactive environment. You type a command (such as $2 + 2$) and instruct *Mathematica* to execute it. *Mathematica* responds with the answer on the next line. You then type another command, and so on. Each command you type will appear on the screen in a **boldface** font. *Mathematica*'s output will appear in a plain font.

Entering Input

After typing a command, you *enter* it as follows:

- On a machine running Windows: Hit the combination SHIFT-ENTER, or hit the ENTER key on the numeric keypad if you have one (usually in the lower right portion of the keyboard).
- On a Mac: Hit the ENTER key (usually in the lower right portion of the keyboard), or hit the combination SHIFT-RET.

1.3 The First Computation

For your first computation, type

   2 + 2

then hit the [SHIFT][ENTER] combination (Windows) or the [ENTER] key (Mac OS). There may be a brief pause while your first entry is processed. During this pause the notebook's title bar will contain the text "Running..."

In[1]:= **2 + 2**

Out[1]= 4

The reason that this simple task takes a moment is that *Mathematica* doesn't start its engine, so to speak, until the first computation is entered. In fact, entering the first computation causes your computer to launch a second program called the MathKernel (or kernel for short). *Mathematica* really consists of these two programs, the Front End, where you type your commands and where output, graphics, and text are displayed, and the MathKernel, where calculations are executed. Every subsequent computation will be faster, for the kernel is now already up and running.

1.4 Commands for Basic Arithmetic

Mathematica works much like a calculator for basic arithmetic. Just use the +, −, *, and / keys on the keyboard for addition, subtraction, multiplication, and division. As an alternative to typing *, you can multiply two numbers by leaving a space between them (the × symbol will automatically be inserted when you leave a space between two numbers). You can raise a number to a power using the ^ key. Use the dot (i.e., the period) to type a decimal point. Here are a few examples:

In[1]:= **17 + 1**

Out[1]= 18

In[2]:= **17 − 1**

Out[2]= 16

In[3]:= **123 456 789 * 123 456 789**

Out[3]= 15 241 578 750 190 521

In[4]:= **123 456 789 × 123 456 789**

Out[4]= 15 241 578 750 190 521

In[5]:= **123 456 789 ^ 2**

Out[5]= 15 241 578 750 190 521

In[6]:= **9.1 / 256.127**

Out[6]= 0.0355292

In[7]:= **34 / 4**

Out[7]= $\dfrac{17}{2}$

This last line may seem strange at first. What you are witnessing is *Mathematica*'s propensity for providing exact answers. *Mathematica* treats decimal numbers as approximations, and will generally avoid them in the output if they are not present in the input. When *Mathematica* returns an expression with no decimals, you are assured that the answer is exact. Fractions are displayed in lowest terms.

1.5 Input and Output

You've surely noticed that *Mathematica* is keeping close tabs on your work. Each time you enter an expression, *Mathematica* gives it a name such as In[1]:=, In[2]:=, In[3]:=. The corresponding output comes with the labels Out[1]=, Out[2]=, Out[3]=, and so on. At this point, it is enough to observe that these labels will appear all by themselves each time you enter a command, and it's okay:

In[1]:= $\left(\dfrac{1}{2}\right)^6$

Out[1]= $\dfrac{1}{64}$

You've surely noticed something else too (you'll need to be running a live session for this), those brackets along the right margin of your notebook window. Each input and output is written into a *cell*, whose scope is shown by the nearest bracket directly across from the respective input or output text. Cells containing input are called *input cells*. Cells containing output are called *output cells*. The brackets delimiting cells are called *cell brackets*. Each input–output pair is in turn grouped with a larger bracket immediately to the right of the cell brackets. These brackets may in turn be grouped together by a larger bracket, and so on. These extra brackets are called *grouping brackets*.

At this point, it's really enough just to know these brackets are there and to make the distinction between the innermost (or smallest, or leftmost) brackets which delimit individual cells and the others which are used for grouping. If you are curious about what good can possibly come of them, try positioning the tip of your cursor arrow anywhere on a grouping bracket and double click. You will *close the group* determined by that bracket. In the case of the bracket delimiting an input–output pair, this will have the effect of hiding the output completely (handy if the output runs over several pages). Double click again to open the group. This feature is useful when you have created a long, complex document and need a means of managing it. Alternately, you can double click on any output cell bracket to *reverse-close* the group. This has the effect of hiding the input code and displaying only the output.

Since brackets are really only useful in a live *Mathematica* session, they will not, by default, show when you print a notebook. Further details about brackets and cells will be provided in Section 2.2 on page 27.

One last bit of terminology is in order. When you hit the `SHIFT`+`ENTER` combination (Windows), or the `ENTER` key (Mac OS) after typing an input cell, you are *entering the cell*. You'll be seeing this phrase quite a bit in the future.

1.6 The BasicMathInput Palette

There may already be a narrow, light gray window full of mathematical symbols along the side of your screen. If so, you are looking at one of *Mathematica*'s palettes, and chances are that it is the BasicMathInput palette:

The BasicMathInput palette

If you see no such window, go to the Palettes menu and select BasicMathInput to open it.

The BasicMathInput palette is indispensable. You will use it to help typeset your *Mathematica* input, creating expressions that cannot be produced in an ordinary one-dimensional typing environment. Palettes such as this provide you with a means of producing what the designers of *Mathematica* call *two-dimensional* input, which often matches traditional mathematical notation. For instance, use the ▪□ button in the upper left corner of the palette to type an exponential expression such as 17^{19}. To do this, first type **17** into your *Mathematica* notebook, then highlight it with your mouse. Next, push the ▪□ palette button with your mouse. The exponent structure shown on that button will be pasted into your notebook, with the 17 in the position of the black square on the palette button (the black square is called the *selection placeholder*). The text insertion point will move to the placeholder in the exponent position. Your input cell will look like this:

      17▪

You can now type the value of the exponent, in this case 19, into the placeholder, then enter the cell:

In[1]:= **17^{19}**

Out[1]= 239 072 435 685 151 324 847 153

> ⚠ Another way to accomplish the same thing is this: First hit the palette button, then type 17 into the first placeholder. Next hit the ⟨TAB⟩ key to move to the second placeholder (in the exponent position). Now type 19 and enter the cell. This procedure is perhaps a bit more intuitive, but it can occasionally get you into trouble if you are not careful with grouping. For instance, if you want to enter $(1 + x)^8$, and the first thing you do is push the ▪□ button on the palette, then you must type **(1+x)** with parentheses, then ⟨TAB⟩, then 8. By contrast, you could type **1+x** with or without parentheses and highlight the expression with your mouse, then hit the ▪□ palette button, and then type 8. The parentheses are added automatically, if needed, when this procedure is followed.

If you don't understand what some of the palette buttons do, don't fret. Just stick with the ones that you know for now. For instance, you can take a cube root like this: type a number and highlight it with the mouse, then push the √▪ button on the BasicMathInput palette, then hit the ⟨TAB⟩ key, and finally type 3. Now enter the cell:

In[2]:= **$\sqrt[3]{50\,653}$**

Out[2]= 37

This is equivalent to raising 50653 to the power 1/3:

In[3]:= **$50\,653^{1/3}$**

Out[3]= 37

And of course we can easily check the answer to either calculation:

In[4]:= 37^3

Out[4]= 50653

Entering Input

Speaking in general terms, the buttons on the top portion of the BasicMathInput palette (in fact all buttons containing a solid black placeholder ■ on this and any other palette) are used this way:

- Type an expression into a *Mathematica* notebook.
- Highlight all or part of the expression with your mouse (by dragging across the expression).
- Push a palette button. The structure on the face of the button is pasted into your notebook, with the highlighted text appearing in the position of the solid black square.
- If there are more placeholders in the structure, use the ⌷TAB⌷ key or forward arrow (or move the cursor with your mouse) to move from one to the next.

The buttons on the middle portion of the BasicMathInput palette have no placeholders. They are used simply to paste into your notebook characters that are not usually found on keyboards. To use them, simply position the cursor at the point in the notebook where you want the character to appear, then push a palette button.

For instance, the $\leq$ symbol can be used to test if one number is less than or equal to another:

In[5]:= $\sqrt{50653} \leq 225$

Out[5]= False

In[6]:= $\sqrt{50653} \leq 226$

Out[6]= True

The special symbol == is used to test if one quantity is equal to another. It has the same meaning as the equal sign in standard mathematical notation:

In[7]:= $\sqrt{50653} == 50653^{1/2}$

Out[7]= True

1.7 Decimal In, Decimal Out

Sometimes you don't want exact answers. Sometimes you want decimals. For instance how big is this number? It's hard to get a grasp of its magnitude when it's expressed as a fraction:

In[1]:= $\dfrac{17^{19}}{19^{17}}$

Out[1]= $\dfrac{239\,072\,435\,685\,151\,324\,847\,153}{5\,480\,386\,857\,784\,802\,185\,939}$

And what about this?

In[2]:= $\sqrt[3]{59\,875}$

Out[2]= $5\,479^{1/3}$

Mathematica tells us that the answer is 5 times the cube root of 479 (remember that a space indicates multiplication, and raising a number to the power $1/3$ is the same as taking its cube root). The output is exact, but again it is difficult to grasp the magnitude of this number. How can we get a nice decimal approximation, like a calculator would produce?

If any one of the numbers you input is in decimal form, *Mathematica* regards it as approximate. It responds by providing an approximate answer, that is, a decimal answer. It is handy to remember this:

In[3]:= $\dfrac{17.0^{19}}{19^{17}}$

Out[3]= 43.6233

In[4]:= $\sqrt[3]{59\,875.0}$

Out[4]= 39.1215

A quicker way to accomplish this is to type a decimal point after a number with nothing after it. That is, *Mathematica* regards "17.0" and "17." as the same quantity. This is important for understanding *Mathematica*'s output:

In[5]:= $\sqrt[3]{59\,875.}$

Out[5]= 39.1215

In[6]:= $\dfrac{30.}{2}$

Out[6]= $15.$

Note the decimal point in the output. Since the input was only "approximate," so too is the output. Get in the habit of using exact or decimal numbers in your input according to the type of answer, exact or approximate, that you wish to obtain. Adding a decimal point to any single number in your input will cause *Mathematica* to provide an approximate (i.e., decimal) output. A detailed discussion on approximate numbers can be found in Section 8.3 on page 392.

1.8 Use Parentheses to Group Terms

Use ordinary parentheses () to group terms. This is *very* important, especially with division, multiplication, and exponentiation. Being a computer program, *Mathematica* takes what you say quite literally; tasks are performed in a definite order, and you need to make sure that it is the order you intend. Get in the habit of making a mental check for appropriate parentheses before entering each command. Here are some examples. Can you see what *Mathematica* does in the absence of parentheses?

In[1]:= $3*(4+1)$

Out[1]= 15

In[2]:= $3*4+1$

Out[2]= 13

In[3]:= $(-3)^2$

Out[3]= 9

In[4]:= -3^2

Out[4]= -9

In[5]:= $(3+1)/2$

Out[5]= 2

In[6]:= $3+1/2$

Out[6]= $\dfrac{7}{2}$

The last pair of examples above shows one benefit of using the BasicMathInput palette instead of typing from the keyboard. With the two-dimensional typesetting capability afforded by the palette there is no need for grouping parentheses, and no chance for ambiguity:

In[7]:= $\dfrac{3+1}{2}$

Out[7]= 2

In[8]:= $3 + \dfrac{1}{2}$

Out[8]= $\dfrac{7}{2}$

The lesson here is that the order in which *Mathematica* performs operations in the absence of parentheses may not be what you intend. When in doubt, add parentheses. Also note: you do not need to leave a space to multiply by an expression enclosed in parentheses:

In[9]:= **25 (2 + 2)**

Out[9]= 100

Note also that only round brackets can be used for the purpose of grouping terms. *Mathematica* reserves different meanings for square brackets and curly brackets, so never use them to group terms.

1.9   Three Well-Known Constants

Mathematica has several built-in constants. The three most commonly used are π, the ratio of the circumference to the diameter of a circle (approximately 3.14); e, the base of the natural logarithm (approximately 2.72); and i, the imaginary number whose square is -1. You can find each of these constants on the BasicMathInput palette.

In[1]:= π

Out[1]= π

In[2]:= $\pi + 0.$

Out[2]= 3.14159

Again, note *Mathematica*'s propensity for exact answers. You will often use π to indicate the radian measure of an angle to be input into a trigonometric function. There are examples in the next section.

It is possible to enter each of these three constants directly from the keyboard, as well. You can type ESC p ESC for π, ESC ee ESC for e, and ESC ii ESC for i.

△   You can also type **Pi** for π, **E** for e, and **I** for i. The capitalizations are important. These do not look as nice, but it illustrates an important point: it is possible to type any *Mathematica* input using only the characters from an ordinary keyboard. That is, every formatted mathematical expression that can be input into *Mathematica* has an equivalent expression constructed using only characters from the keyboard. Indeed, versions 1 and 2 of *Mathematica* used only such expressions. These days, the keyboard, or **InputForm**, of an expression is used when you include a *Mathematica* input or output in an email message (say, to a friend or to your professor). If you copy a formatted expression such as $\pi^{1/3}$ from *Mathematica* and paste it into an email or text editor, you'll find that it becomes Pi^(1/3) (or just π^(1/3) if the editor has the π symbol available). The point is that it is exceedingly simple to include formatted *Mathematica* expressions in plain text environments. Note that you can display any input cell in **Input· Form** from within *Mathematica* by clicking on its cell bracket to select it, and going to the Cell menu and choosing ConvertTo ▷ InputForm.

In[3]:= **Pi == π**

Out[3]= True

1.10 Typing Commands in *Mathematica*

In addition to the basic arithmetic features discussed earlier, *Mathematica* also contains hundreds of *commands*. Commands provide a means for instructing *Mathematica* to perform all sorts of tasks, from computing the logarithm of a number, to simplifying an algebraic expression, to solving an equation, to plotting a function. *Mathematica*'s commands are more numerous, more flexible, and more powerful than those available in any hand–held calculator, and in many ways they are easier to use.

Commands are typically typed from the keyboard, and certain rules of syntax must be strictly obeyed. Commands take one or more *arguments*, and when entered transform their arguments into output. The typical syntax for a command is:

Command[*argument*] or **Command**[*argument1, argument2*]

> Rules for Typing Commands
>
> When typing commands into *Mathematica*, it is imperative that you remember a few rules. The three most important are:
> - Every built–in command begins with a capital letter.Furthermore, if a command name is composed from more than one word (such as ArcSin or FactorInteger) then each word begins with a capital letter, and there will be no space between the words.
> - The arguments of commands are enclosed in square brackets.
> - If there is more than one argument, they are separated by commas.

When you begin typing a command, the individual characters will be blue. They will change to black as soon as they match the name of a built–in command. This syntax coloring mechanism is designed to help you spot typing errors. If you were to type **Arcsin** instead of **ArcSin**, for example, it would remain blue, indicating that it's not right.

Here are some examples of commonly used commands:

Numerical Approximation and Scientific Notation

The first command we will introduce is called **N**. You can get a numerical approximation to any quantity *x* by entering the command **N**[*x*]. By default, the approximation will have six significant digits:

In[1]:= **N[π]**

Out[1]= 3.14159

Very large or very small numbers will be given in scientific notation:

In[2]:= **17^{30}**

Out[2]= 8 193 465 725 814 765 556 554 001 028 792 218 849

In[3]:= **N[17^{30}]**

Out[3]= 8.19347×10^{36}

In[4]:= **N$\left[\dfrac{1}{2^{50}}\right]$**

Out[4]= 8.88178×10^{-16}

If you were wondering, yes, typing **17.^{30}** has the same effect as typing **N**[17^{30}]. But the command **N** is more flexible. You can add an optional second argument that specifies the number of significant digits displayed in the output. Type **N**[*x*, *m*] to get a numerical approximation to *x* with *m* significant digits:

In[5]:= **N[17^{30}, 20]**

Out[5]= $8.1934657258147655566 \times 10^{36}$

In[6]:= **N[π, 500]**

Out[6]= 3.14159265358979323846264338327950288419716939937510582097494459230781640`.
62862089986280348253421170679821480865132823066470938446095505822317253`.
59408128481117450284102701938521105559644622948954930381964428810975665`.
93344612847564823378678316527120190914564856692346034861045432664821339`.
36072602491412737245870066063155881748815209209628292540917153643678925`.
90360011330530548820466521384146951941511609433057270365759591953092186`.
11738193261179310511854807446237996274956735188575272489122793818301194`.
91

Trigonometric Functions

All trigonometric functions require that their argument be given in *radian* measure. The command names themselves and the square brackets are most easily typed directly from the keyboard, while many arguments (such as $\frac{\pi}{4}$) are best typeset with the BasicMathInput palette. Note carefully the placement of capital letters in these commands. You can choose from **Cos**, **Sin**, **Tan**, **Sec**, **Csc**, **Cot**, **ArcCos**, **ArcSin**, **ArcTan**, **ArcSec**, **ArcCsc**, and **ArcCot**:

In[7]:= $\mathbf{Cos}\left[\dfrac{\pi}{4}\right]$

Out[7]= $\dfrac{1}{\sqrt{2}}$

In[8]:= $\mathbf{Sin}\left[\dfrac{\pi}{12}\right]$

Out[8]= $\dfrac{-1+\sqrt{3}}{2\sqrt{2}}$

In[9]:= $\mathbf{ArcSin}\left[\dfrac{-1+\sqrt{3}}{2\sqrt{2}}\right]$

Out[9]= $\dfrac{\pi}{12}$

In[10]:= $\mathbf{Tan}\left[\dfrac{\pi}{12}\right]$

Out[10]= $2-\sqrt{3}$

In[11]:= $\mathbf{Sec}\left[\dfrac{\pi}{12}\right]$

Out[11]= $\sqrt{2}\left(-1+\sqrt{3}\right)$

In[12]:= $\mathbf{Csc}\left[\dfrac{\pi}{12}\right]$

Out[12]= $\sqrt{2}\left(1+\sqrt{3}\right)$

If you wish to use degrees, enter the degree measure multiplied by the degrees-to-radians conversion factor of $\frac{\pi}{180}$. This will simply convert your degree measure to radian measure. For instance, the sine of 45 degrees is found as follows:

In[13]:= $\mathbf{Sin}\left[45 * \dfrac{\pi}{180}\right]$

Out[13]= $\dfrac{1}{\sqrt{2}}$

Alternatively, you can use the built-in constant **Degree**, which is equal to $\frac{\pi}{180}$. Either type **Degree** or push the ⬚° button on the BasicMathInput palette. Both of these have the effect of reading nicely, although in reality you are simply multiplying the argument by $\frac{\pi}{180}$:

In[14]:= $\mathbf{Sin[45\,^\circ]}$

Out[14]= $\dfrac{1}{\sqrt{2}}$

In[15]:= $\mathbf{Sin\big[45\,Degree\big]}$

Out[15]= $\dfrac{1}{\sqrt{2}}$

In[16]:= $\mathbf{N}\left[\dfrac{\pi}{180}\right]$

Out[16]= 0.0174533

In[17]:= $\mathbf{N[^\circ]}$

Out[17]= 0.0174533

Logarithms

Type **Log[x]** to find the natural logarithm of x:

In[18]:= $\mathbf{Log[e]}$

Out[18]= 1

In[19]:= $\mathbf{Log\big[e^{45}\big]}$

Out[19]= 45

Note that it is possible to build up input by nesting one command inside another. Before long you'll be doing this sort of thing without giving it a second thought:

In[20]:= **N[Log[π], 30]**

Out[20]= 1.14472988584940017414342735135

To find the base *b* logarithm of *x*, type **Log[*b*, *x*]**. Here is a base 10 logarithm:

In[21]:= **Log[10, 1000]**

Out[21]= 3

And here is one in base 2:

In[22]:= **Log[2, 512]**

Out[22]= 9

Of course you can always check an answer:

In[23]:= **2^9**

Out[23]= 512

Factoring Integers

You can factor any integer as a product of prime numbers using the command **FactorInteger**. Type **FactorInteger[*n*]** to obtain the prime factorization of *n*:

In[24]:= **FactorInteger[4 832 875]**

Out[24]= {{5, 3}, {23, 1}, {41, 2}}

The output here needs interpretation. It means that 4,832,875 can be factored as $5^3 \times 23 \times 41^2$. Note the form of the output: a list whose members are each lists of length two. Each list of length two encloses a prime number followed by its exponent value. Again, it is easy to check the answer:

In[25]:= **$5^3 * 23 * 41^2$**

Out[25]= 4 832 875

⚠ You may wonder why the output to **FactorInteger** appears in a form that at first glance is somewhat cryptic. Why isn't the output just $5^3 * 23 * 41^2$? The rationale is subtle, but important. The designers of *Mathematica* put the output in the form they did to make it easier for the user to work programmatically with the output. That is, it is easy to extract just the primes 5, 23, and 41, or just the exponents 3, 1, and 2, from this output, and to input those values into another command for further analysis. Remember that *Mathematica* is a sophisticated programming language that is used by experts in many disciplines. In this and in many other cases, commands are designed to allow their output to be easily operated on by other commands. It makes the task of assembling many commands into a single *program* much simpler for the user. For the beginner, however, these advantages may not be immediately obvious.

Factoring and Expanding Polynomials

Mathematica is very much at home performing all sorts of algebraic manipulations. For example, you can factor just about any imaginable polynomial by typing the command **Factor[***polynomial***]** (recall that a polynomial is an expression consisting of a sum of terms, each of which is the product of a constant and one or more variables each raised to a nonnegative whole number power). Typically, lowercase letters such as x or t are used to represent the variables in a polynomial. Here's an example that you could probably do by hand:

In[26]:= **Factor$\left[t^2 - 9\right]$**

Out[26]= $(-3 + t)(3 + t)$

But here's one that you probably couldn't do by hand:

In[27]:= **Factor$\left[64 - 128\,x + 48\,x^2 + 144\,x^3 - 292\,x^4 + 288\,x^5 - 171\,x^6 + 61\,x^7 - 12\,x^8 + x^9\right]$**

Out[27]= $(-2 + x)^6\left(1 + x + x^3\right)$

Note that you do not need to type a space between a number and a variable to indicate multiplication as long as the number is written first; *Mathematica* will insert the space automatically in this case.

You can also have *Mathematica* expand a factored polynomial by typing **Expand[***polynomial***]**. Below we confirm the output above:

In[28]:= **Expand$\left[(-2 + x)^6\left(1 + x + x^3\right)\right]$**

Out[28]= $64 - 128\,x + 48\,x^2 + 144\,x^3 - 292\,x^4 + 288\,x^5 - 171\,x^6 + 61\,x^7 - 12\,x^8 + x^9$

The commands **Factor**, **Expand**, and a host of others that perform various algebraic feats are explored in Chapter 4, "Algebra."

Plotting Functions

Mathematica has a variety of commands that generate graphics. One of the most common is the **Plot** command, which is used for plotting functions. **Plot** takes two arguments. The first is the function to be plotted, the second is something called an iterator, which specifies the span of values that the independent variable is to assume. It is of the form

{*variable, min value, max value*}

Here's an example. Note that we view the function on the domain where the variable x ranges from -3 to 3. *Mathematica* determines appropriate values for the y axis automatically:

In[29]:= $\text{Plot}\!\left[x^2 - 1, \{x, -3, 3\}\right]$

Out[29]=

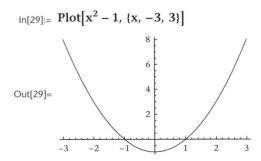

Here's a more interesting example:

In[30]:= $\text{Plot}\!\left[x\,\text{Cos}\!\left[\dfrac{10}{x}\right], \{x, -2, 2\}\right]$

Out[30]=

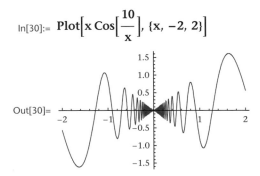

The **Plot** command is explored in greater depth in Section 3.2 on page 53.

Manipulate

Version 6 of *Mathematica* introduces the **Manipulate** command, which allows the user to create a dynamic interface (with sliders or buttons that can be manipulated in real time). Like **Plot**, **Manipulate** takes two arguments. The first is the expression to be manipulated, the second is an iterator which specifies the span of values that the controller variable is to assume. Here's an example:

In[31]:= $\text{Manipulate}\!\left[x^2 - 1, \{x, -3, 3\}\right]$

Out[31]=

x   ⊙

8

You can now move the slider with your mouse to control the value assumed by x, and watch as the value of $x^2 - 1$ is displayed in real time. This is far more interesting to play with than it is to read about, so be sure to try it! Click on the ⊞ button to the right of the slider to reveal a more sophisticated user control panel:

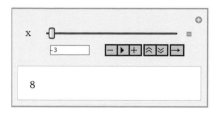

As you mouseover each button on the panel, a tooltip message will display on screen with a brief explanation of that button's function. Go ahead and try each button in turn to get a feel for what you can do. You can even type a value for the variable **x** into the input field and hit Return (Mac) or Enter (Windows PC) to see the value of $x^2 - 1$ in the display area.

Here's a more interesting example:

In[32]:= $\mathbf{Manipulate}\left[\mathbf{Plot}\left[a\ x\ \mathbf{Cos}\left[\dfrac{10}{x}\right],\ \{x,\ -2,\ 2\},\ \mathbf{PlotRange} \to 2\right],\ \{a,\ -2,\ 2\}\right]$

Out[32]=

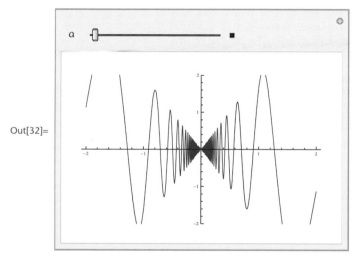

As you type this input, be sure to leave a space between the a, the x, and **Cos**. The setting **Plot·. Range→2** has been added after the second argument in the **Plot** command to fix the viewing rectangle between -2 and 2 in both the x and y directions. This is needed so that the scaling on the y axis does not change as the slider moves. You can find the → symbol on the BasicMathInput palette. **Manipulate** is explored in greater depth in Section 3.4 on page 76.

Square Root Function

Here you have two choices. You can use the square root button on the BasicMathInput palette:

In[33]:= $\sqrt{144}$

Out[33]= 12

Or you can forgo the palette approach and type **Sqrt[*x*]** to get the square root of *x*:

In[34]:= **Sqrt[144]**

Out[34]= 12

⚠ It is a fact that every palette button with a placeholder (such as the square root button) has an equivalent syntax that may be typed entirely from the keyboard. In most cases you will find the palette version of the command easier to use. However, if you are a good typist and use *Mathematica* frequently you may find it easier to work from the keyboard more rather than less. If you ever want to know the name of the *InputForm* of a palette command, follow this procedure: First use the palette version of the command to create an input cell. Then use a single click of your mouse to highlight the cell bracket for the cell. Go to the Cell menu and select Convert to ▷ InputForm from the pop-up menu. You will see the two-dimensional formatted command replaced by its **InputForm** alternative. In the future, you can just type the **InputForm** of the command directly instead of using the palette.

Real and Imaginary Parts of Complex Numbers

Every complex number is of the form $a + bi$, where i represents the square root of -1. The real part of the number is a, and the imaginary part is b. You can extract the real and imaginary parts of complex numbers with the commands **Re** and **Im**.

In[35]:= **Re[2 + 3 *i*]**

Out[35]= 2

In[36]:= **Im[2 + 3 *i*]**

Out[36]= 3

In[37]:= **Re$\left[(2 + 3\,i)^6\right]$**

Out[37]= 2035

Extracting Digits from a Number

The command **IntegerDigits** will produce a *list* of the digits appearing in an integer.

In[38]:= **IntegerDigits[2010]**

Out[38]= {2, 0, 1, 0}

The output is a *list*; it is comprised of items (digits in this case) enclosed in curly brackets and separated by commas. Lists such as this are a fundamental data structure in *Mathematica*. Many commands will produce lists as output and accept lists as input. Lists are so ubiquitous that many operations that work on numbers will automatically be distributed over lists. For instance, we can add 1 to every member of a list like this:

In[39]:= **1 + {2, 0, 1, 0}**

Out[39]= {3, 1, 2, 1}

FromDigits will take a list of digits and assemble them back into a number.

In[40]:= **FromDigits[{2, 0, 1, 0}]**

Out[40]= 2010

Programming

The real utility of commands such as these lies in the ability to take the output of one and use it as the input to another. Putting commands together in a way that does something useful is known as *programming*. *Mathematica* is, among other things, a rich programming environment. Here we take a number and form a new number by adding 1 to each of the original number's digits:

In[41]:= **FromDigits[1 + IntegerDigits[2010]]**

Out[41]= 3121

Think about how little code is required to do that, and then think how you might accomplish the same task in some other programming language, or in Excel.

The following input illustrates this embedding of commands, one within another, but taken to another level:

In[42]:= **ArrayPlot[NestList[Function[x, IntegerDigits[Floor[$\frac{3}{2}$ FromDigits[x, 2]], 2]],**

{1, 0}, 200], Background → Gray]

Out[42]=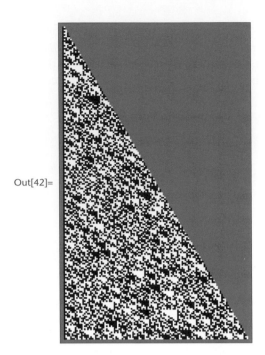

While what's happening here is far beyond what one needs to know at this early stage, it is possible, with a bit of perseverance, to see what is going on. We read from the inside out: starting with x, which represents the base–2 digit sequence of a number, it multiplies the number (**FromDigits**[x, **2**]) by $\frac{3}{2}$, rounds down if the result is not a whole number, then displays its **IntegerDigits** base–2. This is invoked successively, starting on the number 2 (i.e., the number whose **IntegerDigits** are {1, 0}), and then on the result, and then on the result of that, a total of 200 times. So beginning with 2, one next gets $\frac{3}{2}$ of 2, i.e., 3, then $\frac{3}{2}$ of 3 (rounded down), or 4, then $\frac{3}{2}$ of 4, i.e., 6, and so on. The numbers are displayed in base–2, one above the other as successive rows in an array, with zeros represented by white squares and ones represented by black squares. Chapter 8 presents the basic commands used here in more detail.

Naming Things

It is easy to assign names to quantities in *Mathematica*, and then use those names to refer to the quantities later. This is useful in many situations. For instance, you may want to assign a name to a complicated expression to avoid having to type it again and again. To make an assignment, type the name (perhaps a lowercase letter, or a Greek character, or even an entire word), followed by =, followed by the quantity to which the name should be attached. For example (look for θ in the BasicMathInput palette):

In[43]:= $\theta = \dfrac{\pi}{6}$

Out[43]= $\dfrac{\pi}{6}$

Now whenever you place θ in an input cell, *Mathematica* will replace it with $\frac{\pi}{6}$:

In[44]:= θ

Out[44]= $\dfrac{\pi}{6}$

In[45]:= **Sin[θ]**

Out[45]= $\dfrac{1}{2}$

In[46]:= **Sin[2 θ]**

Out[46]= $\dfrac{\sqrt{3}}{2}$

In[47]:= **Tan[4 θ]**

Out[47]= $-\sqrt{3}$

You can (and should) clear an assignment when you are done. This is accomplished with the **Clear** command:

In[48]:= **Clear[θ]**

No output will be produced when you enter the **Clear** command. You can check that no value is attached to the symbol θ by typing it into an input cell:

In[49]:= θ

Out[49]= θ

For a second example, we can assign to **p** the value of π rounded to 39 decimal places (the 3 followed by 39 decimal places makes a total of 40 significant digits):

In[50]:= **p = N[π, 40]**

Out[50]= 3.141592653589793238462643383279502884197

Using this approximation of π, we can approximate the area of a circle of radius 2:

In[51]:= $\mathbf{p} * \mathbf{2^2}$

Out[51]= 12.566370614359172953850573533118011536679

Note how *Mathematica*, in performing a calculation involving an *approximate* number **p** and an *exact* number 2^2, returns an approximate number with the same number of significant digits as **p**.

In[52]:= $\mathbf{Clear[p]}$

For a final example, we'll assign values to words. Each word is treated as a separate entity. The terms **miles** and **hour** are not given values, but **distance** is assigned the value 540 **miles**, and **time** is assigned the value 6 **hour**:

In[53]:= **distance = 540 * miles**

Out[53]= 540 miles

In[54]:= **time = 6 * hour**

Out[54]= 6 hour

In[55]:= $\mathbf{rate = \dfrac{distance}{time}}$

Out[55]= $\dfrac{90\ miles}{hour}$

We can clear all of these assignments in one shot with the **Clear** command—just put a comma between each successive pair of names:

In[56]:= **Clear[distance, time, rate]**

Since all built-in *Mathematica* objects begin with capital letters, it's a good practice to make all your names lowercase letters, or words that begin with lowercase letters. This practice assures that you will never accidentally assign a name that *Mathematica* has reserved for something else. The only Greek character that has a built-in value is π. All others make perfectly good names. You'll find these characters in the Special Characters palette.

It is also permissible to use numbers in your names, provided that a number is not the first character. For instance, you might use the names **x1** and **x2**. It is not alright to use the name **2x**, for that means $2 \times x$.

1.11 Saving Your Work and Quitting *Mathematica*

Say you want to save a notebook that you created. Let's suppose that it is a freshly created notebook that has not been saved previously. Go to the File menu and select Save. You will be prompted by the computer and asked two things: What name do you want to give the notebook, and where would you like the computer to put it? Give it any name you like (it is good form to append the suffix ".nb" which stands for "notebook"), and save it to an appropriate location. The details of this procedure vary somewhat from one platform to the next (Mac OS, Windows, etc.), so ask a friendly soul for assistance if you are unfamiliar with the computer in front of you. Keep in mind that the saving and naming routine isn't a *Mathematica* thing; it's a process that will be similar for every program on the computer you are using. Anyone who is familiar with the platform will be able to help.

⚠ The file size of a *Mathematica* notebook tends to be quite small unless the notebook contains lots of graphics. Notebook files are also portable across computer platforms, as the files themselves are plain text (ascii) files. The *Mathematica* front end interprets and displays notebook files in much the same way that a Web browser interprets and displays HTML files. For information on the structure of the underlying notebook file, select Documentation Center from the Help menu, type "notebooks as *Mathematica* expressions" in the text field, then read the tutorial Notebooks as *Mathematica* Expressions.

If you have created a large notebook file, and want to shrink its file size (for instance to make it small enough to attach to an email) do this: Open the notebook and delete the graphics cells. To do this, click once on a graphic's cell bracket to select it, then choose Cut in the Edit menu. Do *not* cut out the input cells that generated the graphics. Now save the notebook. When you open the notebook next time, you can regenerate any graphic by entering the input cell that created it. An even simpler approach is to select Cell ▷ Delete all Output, and then save your notebook. When you open the file later, select Evaluation ▷ Evaluate Note–book to re-evaluate every input cell in the notebook.

After a notebook has been saved once, the title bar will bear the name you have assigned. As you continue to work and modify the notebook, you can and should save it often. This is easy to do: choose Save from the File menu. This will write the latest version of the notebook to the location where the file was last saved. Should the power fail during a session, or should your computer crash for some reason, it is the last saved version of your notebook that will survive. Many hardened souls will save every few minutes.

To end a *Mathematica* session, select Quit from the application's main menu. If you have modified your notebook since it was last saved, you will be prompted and asked if you care to save the changes you have made since it was last saved. Answer Save or Don't Save as appropriate.

1.12 Frequently Asked Questions About *Mathematica*'s Syntax

Why Do All Mathematica Command Names Begin with Capital Letters?

Mathematica is case-sensitive, and every one of the thousands of built-in *Mathematica* commands begins with a capital letter. So do all built-in constants, built-in option settings, and so on. In fact, every built-in *Mathematica* symbol of any kind that has a name begins with a capital letter (or the **$** or \ characters). Taken together, there are over 3000 such objects.

In[1]:= **Length[Names["*"]]**

Out[1]= 3043

Why capital letters? The main reason is that you will find yourself assigning names to quantities, such as x = 3 or pi = 3.14. Since you don't know the name of every built-in object, there is a danger that you may choose a name that coincides with the name of a built-in command or constant. Without getting into the technicalities, that would be bad. But it can be avoided if you simply stick to the convention of beginning all your assignment names with lowercase letters. By doing this you guarantee that you will never choose a name that conflicts with any existing *Mathematica* symbol.

Why Does My Input Appear in Color as I Type?

Mathematica is ruthless in its demand for precise typing. Syntax coloring is an aid to help you navigate these perilous waters. Symbols that are not in the system's memory appear in blue. So as you type a command such as **Factor**, it will be blue until the final **r** is added, at which point it turns black. If it doesn't turn black—oops, you mistyped it. When you use = to define your own symbols, they too will turn black upon being entered. Brackets need to come in pairs, with each opening bracket having a matching closing bracket somewhere down the line. An opening bracket appears brightly colored, and turns black only when its mate has been appropriately placed. If your input has any brightly colored brackets it's not ready for entry. If you close a bracket too early, you may see a disturbing red caret. For instance:

In[2]:= **Plot[x$_\wedge$]**

    Plot::argr : Plot called with 1 argument; 2 arguments are expected. ≫

Out[2]= Plot[x]

The caret indicates that you forgot something; **Plot** needs two arguments (a function and iterator), and here we did not add the iterator. The caret points to where you need to type something.

Why Are the Arguments of Commands Enclosed in Square Brackets?

The numerical approximation command **N** is an example of what a mathematician calls a function; that is, it converts an argument *x* to an output **N**[*x*]. In *Mathematica*, all functions enclose their arguments in square brackets [ ], always.

You may recall that in our usual mathematical notation, we often write $f(x)$ to denote the value of the function f with argument *x*. This won't do in *Mathematica*, for parentheses ( ) are reserved for grouping terms. When you write $f(12)$, for instance, it is not clear whether you intend for a function named f to be evaluated at 12, or whether you want the *product* of a variable named f with 12. Since parentheses are routinely used for these two very different purposes, the traditional notation is ambiguous. You and I can usually flesh out the meaning of the notation $f(12)$ from its context, but a computer needs unambiguous instructions. Hence in *Mathematica*, square brackets are used to enclose function arguments, while parentheses are used to group terms.

When working with *Mathematica*, never use round parentheses for anything other than grouping terms, and never use square brackets for anything other than enclosing the arguments to functions.

What Happens If I Use Incorrect Syntax?

If you want to find the natural log of 7.3, you must type **Log[7.3]**, not **log(7.3)**, not **Log(7.3)**, not **log[7.3]**, not **ln[7.3]**, and not anything else.

What happens if you slip and muff the syntax? First of all, don't worry. This *will* happen to you. The computer won't explode. For example, behold:

In[3]:= **Log[7.3**

Here our input is close enough to the correct syntax that *Mathematica* suspects that we goofed, and tells us so. Upon entering an incomplete or erroneous input, version 6 and higher will show a warning flag in the expression's cell bracket, and will often highlight the offending part of the input. Click once on the warning flag and any relevant warning messages will be displayed.

In[3]:= **Log[7.3**

    Syntax::bktmcp : Expression "Log[7.3" has no closing "]".

    Syntax::sntxi : Incomplete expression; more input is needed.

You will certainly generate messages like this at some point, so its good to acquaint yourself with some. Error messages are somewhat cryptic to the new user, and are rarely a welcome sight. But do read the text of these messages, for you will often be able to make enough sense out of them to find the source of the problem. In this case we left off the closing square bracket. Note that as you type your input, each opening bracket will appear brightly colored until the corresponding closing bracket is added, at which time both brackets will turn black. This makes mistakes of this type easy to spot. If an expression has one or more brightly colored brackets, it is incomplete and should not be entered.

But worse than getting an error message or input flag is getting neither. It is not difficult to enter syntactically correct, but meaningless input. For example, consider this:

In[4]:= **ln (7.3)**

Out[4]= $7.3 \ln$

No warning is given (other than the command name ln appearing in blue before the cell is entered), but the output is *not* the natural logarithm of 7.3. *Mathematica* has instead multiplied the meaningless symbol **ln** by the number 7.3 (remember round brackets are for grouping only). *Always* look carefully and critically at your output. There will certainly be times when you need to go back and edit and re-enter your input before you get the answer you desire.

2
Working with *Mathematica*

2.1 Opening Saved Notebooks

You can open any *Mathematica* notebook file by double-clicking on its icon with your mouse. It will appear on your screen exactly as it was when it was saved. You can open two or more notebooks at the same time if you wish.

2.2 Adding Text to Notebooks

Text Cells

Mathematica has an integrated word processor that is simple to use once you are familiar with the cell structure of a *Mathematica* notebook (see Section 1.5, "Input and Output," on page 3 for a discussion of input and output cells). To add text to a notebook, you need to create a *text cell*. To do this, first go to the Window menu and select Show Toolbar. A toolbar will appear across the top of your notebook window. Now position your mouse *between* any two cells in your notebook (or below the last cell in the notebook, or above the first cell) where you want to add text. The cursor will change from a vertical bar to a horizontal bar. Now click. You should notice a horizontal black line that runs completely across your notebook window. Next, use your mouse to select Text from the pull-down menu on the toolbar, and start typing. As soon as you do, a new text cell will be inserted in your notebook at the position of the horizontal black line, and it will contain the text you type. It is common practice to use a new text cell for each paragraph of text. Note that using the key combination OPTION-RET at the end of a paragraph will create a new text cell under the current one, so it's easy to write paragraph after paragraph as if you were using a dedicated word processor.

Mathematica's text environment is a joy to use. It wraps lines for you within each text cell. You can use any palette to paste a mathematical symbol or expression into your text, just as you paste into an input cell. There is a full-featured spell checker—just place the cursor where you want to start spell checking and choose Check Spelling… in the Edit menu. We'll soon see that it is highly adept at formatting complex mathematical expressions. For these reasons, you may find yourself using *Mathematica* as your word processor of choice for technical papers. You can also highlight portions of text with your mouse and cut, copy, or paste (look in the Edit menu for these and other features). You can change the size, face, font, and color of highlighted text by choosing the appropriate item in the Format menu. There are buttons on the toolbar to control the centering and justification of your text. Use these features to make your notebook a masterpiece.

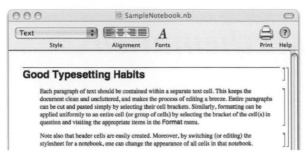

A Notebook with the Toolbar Displayed

You can cut, copy, paste, and format entire cells or groups of cells. You *select* a cell or group of cells by positioning the tip of the cursor arrow on a cell bracket or grouping bracket along the right side of the notebook window. The bracket becomes highlighted. Now choose Cut or Copy from the Edit menu, position the mouse where you wish to paste the selection (in the current notebook or in any other notebook that is open), click once, and select Paste from the Edit menu. Similarly, the commands in the Format menu will be applied to the text in any cell or group of cells whose bracket is selected.

Mathematica's cell structure makes it easy to organize your notebook into collapsible sections. You simply add preformatted title or section headings. To do this, click between existing cells (or below the last cell in the notebook, or above the first cell), and then go to the pull-down menu in the toolbar and select Title, or Section, or Subsection, or the like, and start typing. Upon adding a title to a notebook, you will notice a gigantic grouping bracket on the far right of your notebook window that spans the entire notebook. Place the cursor anywhere along this bracket and double-click to *close the group*. You will see the title, but the rest of the notebook will disappear. Don't worry, it's still there; double-click again on the bracket to *open the group*. When you create sections or subsections, grouping brackets will appear to show their respective domains, and these too can be toggled open or closed with a double-click on the appropriate grouping bracket. These features allow you to keep your work organized, and minimize the amount of scrolling needed to navigate a large document.

If you click between cells in a notebook and then start typing, you will by default create a new input cell. This makes it easy to enter input during a *Mathematica* session; as soon as you get output from one computation, you can just start typing to generate a new input cell. You only have to specify cell type (Text, Title, Section, etc.) when you want to create some type of cell other than input. By the way, you can forgo the toolbar if you want, and select your cell types from the pop-up menu that appears when you select Style in the Format menu.

If you accidently start typing text in an input cell, don't despair. The fix is simple: click once on the cell's bracket to select it, then use the toolbar (or go to the Format menu) to change the cell to a text cell.

Adding Mathematical Expressions to Text

If you wish to place a mathematical expression (such as $f(x) = x^2$) within a sentence of text, there is a simple means for doing so. However, be aware that typesetting mathematics is inherently a tricky business whose subtleties can only be appreciated by those who have attempted it. That said, *Mathematica* is an excellent environment for producing beautifully typeset mathematics. Its prowess in this regard far exceeds that of standard word processing programs such as Word, and rivals that of specialty programs such as LaTeX, while being much easier to use. We advise you to read carefully the procedure outlined below, as the method for adding mathematical expressions to text, while not difficult, is not obvious.

Suppose that you wish to place a mathematical expression in the middle of a sentence of text. Begin by creating a text cell (as outlined in the previous section) and typing the text that will precede the mathematical expression. When you are ready to insert the math, from the menus select Insert ▷ Typesetting ▷ Start Inline Cell. Or from the keyboard hit CTRL-9 (for both Mac OS and Windows). The state of the cursor will change to a placeholder within a lightly colored box. This colored box delimits what is called an *inline cell*. Now type your mathematics, using palettes if you like, being careful not to exit the inline cell as you add the mathematics (if you exit the colored box, use the backarrow to get back into it). When you are finished typing the mathematical expression, hit the forward arrow to exit the inline cell. You can also exit the inline cell by hitting CTRL-0. It's easy to remember these keyboard shortcuts as CTRL-(to start a mathematical formula and CTRL-) to end it.

When you are typing your mathematics within an inline cell, you'll notice that what you type is displayed differently than ordinary text. For instance: any single letter will be italicized, a hyphen will change subtly to a minus sign, and spacing will be different. For example, here is an equation typeset *without* using an inline cell: **f(x)-x=0**. And here is what is produced by the same keystrokes when typeset within an inline cell: $f(x) - x = 0$. The difference is striking, and clearly illustrates the advantage of using inline cells to display mathematics.

Modifying the Stylesheet

You can change the look of an entire notebook by changing the *stylesheet*. A stylesheet contains different formatting parameters for each cell type. One stylesheet might render all input cells with purple backgrounds; another might render all titles, sections, and subsections in Helvetica font with a gray background, and 12-point Times Roman as the default text font. By choosing a new stylesheet your notebook will take on a completely new look. Go to Format ▷ StyleSheet to select a new stylesheet for your notebook; there are several from which to choose.

Note that whenever you switch stylesheets, the items in the Format ▷ Style menu will change to reflect the cell styles available in that stylesheet. Note also that stylesheets can be used to control both the on-screen and print versions of notebooks, and even to make each look different from the other if you wish. Stylesheets may also be used to change what the default cell style is in a particular notebook (the type of cell that will be created if you just start typing). In order to see just how powerful these concepts are, try this: Open a new blank notebook, and switch to the Format ▷ Stylesheet ▷ Utility ▷ Correspondence stylesheet. Now pay attention: you are going to write a formal letter. First type your name and address, using carriage returns to create new lines. It appears in a special "Sender" cell, complete with a gray label to remind you of that fact. Now hit the *down-arrow* on the keyboard to jump to the insertion point for the next cell. Immediately start typing. This time a "Date" cell will be created, so type today's date. Again, when you're done hit the down-arrow. Now type the recipient's name and address. Down-arrow. Type a salutation, such as "Dear Stephen." Down-arrow. Now type the body of your letter, using the carriage return to create new paragraphs. Down-arrow. Type your closing, such as "Sincerely" or "Cheers." Down-arrow. And finally, add your signature. Now print it. All the gray cell labels do not appear in the printed version; the formatting is just right. If you have to write a lot of letters, this stylesheet streamlines your workflow. That's exactly what a stylesheet should do. *Creating* a sophisticated stylesheet like this one takes a bit of work, but *using* it takes almost none. And if you just wish to modify an existing stylesheet to better suit your purposes, well that's a breeze. Read on…

Suppose you wish to modify an existing cell style, for instance, to change the look of the "Section" headings. Or suppose you wish to create an entirely new cell style, say a custom text cell that puts a light-gray background color behind your text. To do this you add a local modification to an existing stylesheet (the principle is that of a *cascading stylesheet*, which is common in web design). This is the best way to ensure that you produce a document with consistent style parameters; it prevents you from having to apply the desired style features one by one onto each relevant cell in your notebook. Here's how to set it up: create a notebook using one of the included stylesheets. Choose Format ▷ Edit Stylesheet…, and a stylesheet notebook will appear. At the top of this notebook you may either choose an existing style to modify (if, for instance, you just want to change the default text font), or type the name of a new style you would like to create (if, for instance, you want to keep the default text style, and add a second text style for some other purpose). In either case, a cell will appear in this new notebook, and its cell bracket will be selected. Go directly to the Format menu and apply the formatting changes you desire to this selected cell. You can change the font, the font size, the font slant, the font color, the background color, the alignment, etc. When you are finished, close the stylesheet window, and return to your notebook. If you created a new style, its name will appear at the bottom of the Format ▷ Style menu, so you may easily apply it to any cell in your notebook at any time. If you modified an existing style, all cells of that style in your notebook will now reflect that change.

2.3 Printing

As long as your computer is properly hooked up to a printer, and the printer is turned on, you can print your current notebook by going to the File menu and choosing Print…. If your notebook contains graphics or two-dimensional input using special math fonts, it may take a moment to start printing, so be patient.

You can also select one or more cells to print, rather than printing an entire notebook. This can save vast quantities of paper, so we repeat: You don't have to print the entire notebook. To print a single cell or any group of cells delimited by a grouping bracket, position the tip of the cursor arrow on the cell or grouping bracket and click once. This *selects* the cell or group. Now go to the File menu and choose Print Selection….

To select several adjacent cells when there is no grouping bracket, hold down the SHIFT key and click on their cell brackets one by one. They will all become selected. To select several nonadjacent cells, hold down the ⌘ key (Mac OS), or the CTRL key (Windows), while clicking on cell brackets. You can then print your selection as above: Go to the File menu and choose Print Selection….

Printing a notebook that has graphics can sometimes lead to less-than-optimal page breaks. It is easy to add more page breaks, but it can be tricky to force pages not to break. To add a page break, simply click between the cells where the break should occur and select Insert ▷ PageBreak. To remove a break above or below a graphic, try resizing the graphic. It is often the case that when printed, smaller graphics look better, so this may be a good idea in any event. If this does not help, or if the unwanted page break is not adjacent to a graphic, select the bracket of the first cell to appear after the unwanted break, then summon the Option Inspector by visiting Format ▷ Option Inspector…. Make sure that the first pull-down menu reads **Selection** (which it should by default). Now type "PageBreak" into the text field. Change the **PageBreakAbove** setting for the selected cell to **False**. Repeat as necessary for nearby cells. If you are working on a Mac, be sure to make use of the Preview button in the Print dialog before committing your notebook to paper.

It is possible to control what is printed in the header and footer areas on each page of a printed notebook. By default, the header is comprised of the filename of the notebook and the page number. To change this, go to the File menu and select Printing Settings ▷ Headers and Footers…. The resulting dialog box gives you the option of not displaying any header on the first page, which is handy if you have a nicely typeset title page. There are also text fields for the content of the left, right, and center portion of each header and footer. What appears by default in some of these fields will look complex, but don't worry. You may replace the content of any of these fields with any text you like enclosed in double quotation marks, and you'll be good to go. The complex structures appearing by default are needed only if you wish to place page numbers or other such non-constant values into your headers. Look up any of the command names appearing in these fields in the Documentation Center for further information.

⚠ Each text field for the left, right, and center portions of a header or footer will accept a complete **Cell** expression. This ensures total control over the style of the header, and allows you to include CounterBoxes (for page numbers), and other such objects. To create a styled text heading in any one of these locations, type **Cell**["*your header text*", "**Header**"] in the text field. The first argument of the **Cell** command is your header text wrapped in double quotes. The second argument is a cell style name, also in double quotes. Other common style names for headers include "**PageNumber**", "**Footer**", or any other style name that appears in the Format ▷ Style menu. You can modify styles with a third argument, such as: **Cell**["*your header text*", "**Text**", **FontSlant** → "**Italic**"]. If you don't like the look of the page numbers that appear in the default headers, the most simple means of manually putting a page number into one of the text fields is to type

$$\textbf{Cell}\big[\textbf{TextData}\big[\{\textbf{CounterBox}[\text{"Page"}]\}\big], \text{"Header"}\big]$$

where you may change the second argument from "**Header**" to "**PageNumber**" or to any other style name that appears in the Format ▷ Style menu.

2.4 Creating Slide Shows

Most people are familiar with PowerPoint presentations. A Slide Show in *Mathematica* is a similar type of presentation environment. Making a Slide Show is easy. While the transition effects are not as polished as those in a dedicated presentation program such as PowerPoint or Keynote, a *Mathematica* Slide Show has the added feature of allowing live computations during your presentation. You can wow your audience with a **Manipulate** or take a surface for a spin in real time. This is possible because a Slide Show is really just a live *Mathematica* notebook with some special display features.

To get started simply grab the SlideShow palette from the Palettes menu. The top button, New Template, will open a new notebook with three pre-formatted generic slides. You are not bound to this format, it is just to give you an idea of what a very simple Slide Show looks like. You can delete everything in these slides and fill them with any *Mathematica* content, but before you do that let's take the generic one for a quick drive.

At the bottom of the palette there are two buttons labeled Normal and Slide Show. You can edit your slides in either environment. The Normal environment shows all your slides at once with cell brackets grouping the content of each slide. This is handy for cutting and pasting content into several slides. The Slide Show environment shows one slide at a time. You can toggle back and forth between the two environments as often as you wish.

In the Slide Show environment you can advance your slides by pushing the buttons in the toolbar at the top of the window or the small gray arrows at the bottom right. If you don't want the gray arrows at the bottom of a slide you can delete that cell when you are in the Normal environment. The leftmost arrow button among the four in the toolbar takes you to the beginning of the Slide Show while the one on the right takes you to the end. Hit the button in the far top left corner of the toolbar in order to toggle into full-screen presentation mode. Push it again to toggle out of full-screen mode.

Now you are ready to create your own Slide Show. You can use any format to add content to a slide. You can even change the Stylesheet. If you want to add another slide go to the Normal environment, position your cursor between the slides where you want to add a slide and click once to make a horizontal bar appear, then click the New Slide button in the palette.

Push the Table of Contents button and you get a window listing all your slides. Finally, the Convert Notebook button will convert any notebook into a Slide Show.

You can cut and paste content from other programs, such as photos from the web or sketches from Geometer's Sketchpad, into your *Mathematica* Slide Show. Once you get started you'll find it is very simple and intuitive to work in the Slide Show environment.

2.5 Creating Web Pages

If you would like to save a *Mathematica* notebook as an HTML (Hypertext Markup Language) document so that it can be posted as a web page, simply go to the File menu and select Save As..., then choose Web Page (*.html) in the Format pop-up menu near the bottom of the resulting dialog box. Your notebook will be converted, and any graphics or mathematical expressions will be saved as separate files (in the gif format).

We know of a student who was getting nowhere trying to explain a mathematics problem over the phone to a fellow student. He then typed the equations he was thinking of into *Mathematica*, saved the notebook as HTML, posted it to his website, and had the fellow student go to the freshly minted page. This seems a bit extreme, but if you maintain a web site and are handy with posting web pages, it's nice to know that it's a simple matter to compose in *Mathematica*.

2.6 Converting a Notebook to Another Format

Mathematica notebooks are highly structured documents, and as such it is possible to convert them into a variety of other formats (such as HTML, as outlined in the previous section). By choosing Save As... in the File menu and inspecting the Format options in the resulting dialog box, you can see exactly which formats are supported. For example, if you save your notebook as a PDF file, you'll be able to read it and print it out from a computer that does not have *Mathematica* installed.

2.7 *Mathematica's* Kernel

When you enter a command in *Mathematica*, it is processed by a separate program called the MathKernel, or kernel for short. This program is launched automatically when the first command is entered. It takes a moment to launch this program, and that is why there is a perceptible lag during the first computation. The kernel usually runs on the same computer that you are using, but this need not be the case. It can be located on another, perhaps more powerful, computer. Many web sites take user input and forward it to a *Mathematica* kernel, and then display the result as a web page (see, for example, the Integrator at http://integrals.wolfram.com). If you are running the kernel on your local computer, when you quit *Mathematica* the kernel quits as well. Each time you start *Mathematica* and enter your first command a new kernel is launched.

When you launch *Mathematica* by opening an existing notebook, the kernel is not needed. You can scroll through the notebook and view and even edit the contents. It is only when you place the cursor on an input cell and enter the cell, or type a new command line and enter it, that the kernel will be launched.

Numbering Input and Output

The command lines entered to the kernel and the outputs delivered by the kernel are numbered. They are numbered in the order that they are received by the kernel. After the *Mathematica* program is launched, the first command entered will be labeled In[1]:=, and its output will be labeled Out[1]=. The next input will be labeled In[2]:=, and so on.

Be mindful that the numbering is determined by the sequential order in which the commands are received by the kernel, and not necessarily by the order in which commands appear in the notebook. For instance, if you were to start a *Mathematica* session by opening an existing notebook, then scroll through to some input cell in the middle of that notebook, click on that cell and enter it, it would be labeled In[1]:=.

Reevaluating Previously Saved Notebooks

When you first open a previously saved notebook, you will notice that none of the inputs or outputs will be numbered any more. That's because the numbering refers to the order in which input cells were sent to the kernel and in which output cells were delivered from the kernel. When you save a notebook, this information is lost. You are now free to click on any input cell and enter it. That cell will acquire the label In[1]:=, and its output will be called Out[1]=.

It is important to realize that when you start a new *Mathematica* session by opening an old notebook, you should not enter any input cell that makes reference to another cell (or variable, or anything you created) that has not been entered in *this* session. For instance, suppose you opened a notebook that contained the following input and output cells (they are not numbered, since they have not been entered in this session):

$a = 90$

90

a^2

8100

What would happen if you were to click on the second input cell (containing the text a^2) and enter it? Mathematica would be unaware of the cell containing the assignment $a = 90$ since that cell has not been entered in the current session. The resulting notebook would look like this:

$a = 90$

90

In[1]:= a^2

Out[1]= a^2

In practice this means that when reopening an old notebook to continue work that you started in a previous session, you should reenter, one by one, all the cells to which you will refer later in the session.

You can automate this procedure if you like. After opening a previously saved notebook, go to the Evaluation menu and select Evaluate Notebook. This will instruct the kernel to evaluate every cell in the notebook, in order, from top to bottom. It's a handy way to pick up your work where you left off. Alternately, you may OPTION–click on the cell bracket of any cell (Mac OS), or ALT–click (Windows), to select *all* cells of that type the notebook. Do this to an input cell, and all input cells will be selected. Now go to the Evaluation menu and choose Evaluate Cells.

⚠ Many notebooks contain certain input cells that will be evaluated each time the notebook is used; this is often the case with notebooks created for students by teachers. Such notebooks utilize special types of input cells called *initialization cells*. When a cell is an initialization cell, it will be automatically evaluated before any other input cells in the notebook. Typical initialization cells will define a special command to be used throughout the notebook, or load a *Mathematica* package (more on packages later in this chapter). When you send your first input to the kernel from a notebook containing one or more initialization cells, you will be prompted and asked if you want to automatically evaluate all initialization cells in the notebook. If you ever see such a prompt, answer "Yes." Moreover, if you want to make an input cell in one of your own notebooks an initialization cell, select the cell by clicking once on its cell bracket (or SHIFT–click on several cell brackets), then go to the Cell menu and choose Cell Properties ▷ Initialization Cell.

You will notice that the cell bracket gets a little vertical tick mark at the top. Now when you reopen this notebook in the future, the cell (or cells) that are initialization cells can be automatically processed by the kernel. When you first save a notebook containing one or more initialization cells, you will be prompted, "Do you want to create an Auto Save Package?" Answer "No." This feature is for programmers who are creating *Mathematica* packages.

2.8 Tips for Working Effectively

Referring to Previous Output

In a typical *Mathematica* session you will enter a cell, examine the output, enter a cell, examine the output, enter a cell, examine the output, and so on. There are numerous little tricks that make it easier to deal efficiently with *Mathematica*'s input-output structure. Perhaps the most important is the percentage sign. When you need to use the output of the previous cell as part of your input to the current cell, just type %. *Mathematica* interprets % as the output of the last cell processed by the kernel (i.e., % represents the contents of the output cell with the highest label number):

$$\text{In[1]:=} \quad \frac{21^{20}}{20^{21}}$$

$$\text{Out[1]=} \quad \frac{278\,218\,429\,446\,951\,548\,637\,196\,401}{2\,097\,152\,000\,000\,000\,000\,000\,000\,000}$$

$$\text{In[2]:=} \quad \mathbf{N[\%]}$$

$$\text{Out[2]=} \quad 0.132665$$

If you want to keep the old input and output cells, click below the old output cell and select Insert ▷ Output from Above from the menu. It will paste the contents of the output cell that resides *directly above* the position of the cursor into a new input cell, regardless of when that cell was processed by the kernel. You can then edit the new input cell and enter it.

Referring to Previous Input

You will often enter a cell and later want to enter something very similar. The simplest way to deal with this is to click on the former input cell and edit it, then reenter it. The cursor can be anywhere in the input cell when you enter it; it need not be at the far right. Once the cell is entered, its label number will be updated (for example from In[5]:= to In[6]:=). The old output will be replaced with the output from the edited input cell.

If you want to keep (rather than overwrite) the old input and output cells, click below the old output cell, go to the menu, and select Insert ▷ Input from Above. The old input cell will be copied into a new input cell, which you can then edit and enter.

Another option is to use your mouse to copy and paste text from one cell (input or output) to a new input cell. You can highlight text with your mouse to select it, then choose Copy from the Edit menu, click to position the cursor where you want the text to appear, and finally choose Paste from the Edit menu.

Postfix Command Structure

The typical structure for *Mathematica* commands is:

$$\textbf{Command}[argument] \quad \text{or} \quad \textbf{Command}[argument1,\ argument2]$$

We've seen examples such as $\textbf{Sin}[\frac{\pi}{4}]$ and $\textbf{Log}[10, 243]$. When a command has only one argument, another way to apply it is in *postfix form*. The postfix form for a command is:

$$argument\ //\textbf{Command}$$

This form is useful when the command is applied to an existing expression as an afterthought. For instance, if you copy the contents of an earlier input or output cell into a new input cell, you can easily apply a command in postfix form to the entire copied expression. Here are some examples:

In[3]:= $\textbf{Sin}\left[\dfrac{\pi}{12}\right] // \textbf{N}$

Out[3]= 0.258819

This is equivalent to entering $\textbf{N}\left[\textbf{Sin}\left[\frac{\pi}{12}\right]\right]$.

In[4]:= $(x - 1)(2 + 3\,x)(6 - x)\ //\ \textbf{Expand}$

Out[4]= $-12 - 4\,x + 19\,x^2 - 3\,x^3$

This is equivalent to entering $\textbf{Expand}[(x\text{-}1)(2+3\,x)(6\text{-}x)]$.

Prefix Command Structure

When a command accepts a single argument, it can also be given in *prefix* form. The prefix form for a command is:

$$\textbf{Command}@argument$$

Like the postfix form, this form can useful when the command is applied to an existing expression as an afterthought. It allows you to apply the command without worrying about adding the closing square bracket. Here are some examples:

In[5]:= $\textbf{First} @ \{2,\ 4,\ 6,\ 8\}$

Out[5]= 2

This is equivalent to entering $\textbf{First}[\{2, 4, 6, 8\}]$.

In[6]:= **TraditionalForm @ Sin[x]^2**

Out[6]//TraditionalForm=

$$\sin^2(x)$$

This is equivalent to entering **TraditionalForm$\left[\text{Sin}[x]^2\right]$**.

Undoing Mistakes

If you make a bad mistake in typing or editing, the kind that makes you say, "I wish I could undo that and return my notebook to its former state," chances are you can. Look for Undo in the Edit menu. It will reverse the previous action. The catch is that it will only undo the most recent action, so use it immediately after making your mistake.

Another option is to close your notebook (choose Close in the File menu), and answer Don't Save when you are prompted. You can then reopen your notebook (choose Open Recent in the File menu). You will find your notebook in the state that it was in when it was last saved. Of course you should only do this if you have saved the notebook recently.

A more frightening scenario is entering an input cell and finding that *Mathematica* appears to be stuck. For a long time you see the text "Running…" in the notebook's title bar, but no output is being generated. You may have inadvertently asked *Mathematica* to perform a very difficult calculation, and after a few minutes you may get tired of waiting. How can you make it stop? Go to the Evaluation menu and select Abort Evaluation. Depending on the situation, it may halt immediately or you may have to wait a minute or two before it stops. Be patient. If more than a few minutes pass with no response, refer to Section 2.11, "Troubleshooting" on page 47.

Keyboard Shortcuts

If you have quick fingers you may find it easier to type characters than make repeated trips to the menus with your mouse. Next to many menu items you will find keyboard shortcuts for accomplishing the same task. We summarize some of the most common in Table 2.1.

Typesetting Input—More Shortcuts

We have seen that a typical input cell contains symbols and structures both from the keyboard and from palettes (such as the BasicInput palette). As you get more familiar with *Mathematica*, you will want to find the easiest way to typeset your input. It is helpful to know that there are ways to get many symbols and structures directly from the keyboard without invoking the use of a palette at all. Table 2.2 shows some of the most often used. You can find others by opening the SpecialCharacters palette. If a character has a keyboard entry sequence, it will be displayed on the palette when you select it.

Task	Mac OS	Windows PC
Save your notebook	`CMD` `S`	`CTRL` `S`
Cut	`CMD` `x`	`CTRL` `x`
Copy	`CMD` `c`	`CTRL` `c`
Paste	`CMD` `v`	`CTRL` `v`
Undo an editing or typing mistake	`CMD` `Z`	`CTRL` `Z`
Copy input from above	`CMD` `l`	`CTRL` `l`
Copy output from above	`SHIFT` `CMD` `l`	`SHIFT` `CTRL` `l`
Complete a command	`CMD` `k`	`CTRL` `k`
Make a command template	`SHIFT` `CMD` `k`	`SHIFT` `CTRL` `k`
Abort an evaluation	`CMD` `.`	`ALT` `.`
Quit	`CMD` `q`	`ALT` `F4`

Table 2.1 **Keyboard Shortcuts.** When reading this table, `CMD` `q` means hitting the command key and the q key at the same time. On a Mac, the command key is marked ⌘.

Type	to get
`ESC` p `ESC`	the symbol π
`ESC` ee `ESC`	the symbol e
`ESC` ii `ESC`	the symbol i
`ESC` inf `ESC`	the symbol ∞
`ESC` deg `ESC`	the symbol ° (for entering angles in degrees)
`ESC` th `ESC`	the symbol θ (no built in meaning, but often used)
`ESC` * `ESC`	the symbol $\times$ (for multiplication)
`CTRL` ^ or `CTRL` 6	to the exponent position
`CTRL` /	into a fraction
`CTRL` 2	into a square root
`CTRL` `SPACE`	out of an exponent, denominator, or square root
`TAB`	from one placeholder to the next

Table 2.2 **Keyboard Shortcuts for Typesetting.** When reading this table, `CTRL` `2` means hitting the control key and the 2 key *at the same time*, while `CTRL` 2 means hitting the control key *followed by* the 2 key.

For instance, you can produce the input

$$\pi^2 + \frac{x}{y}$$

by typing the following key sequence:

`ESC` p `ESC` `CTRL` 6 2 `CTRL` `SPACE` + `CTRL` / x `TAB` y

And you can produce the input

$$\frac{\pi^2 + x}{y}$$

by typing the following key sequence:

[CTRL]/ [ESC] p [ESC] [CTRL]6 2 [CTRL][SPACE] + x [TAB] y

Of course if you consider yourself a poor typist, you may want to use palettes more rather than less. Check out the BasicMathInput palette (in the Palettes menu). It contains buttons that will paste templates of commonly used commands into your notebook. This keeps your typing to a minimum, and helps you remember the correct syntax for commands. Whichever approach you take, you'll eventually find the way to typeset *Mathematica* input that works best for you.

Suppressing Output and Entering Sequences of Commands

There will be times when you don't want *Mathematica* to produce output. For instance, suppose you need to carry out several calculations involving the quantity $\frac{\pi}{12}$. Rather than type this expression each time it is needed, you can assign its value to a letter and type this letter instead. When you make this assignment and enter it, *Mathematica* will display the value as its output:

In[7]:= $x = \dfrac{\pi}{12}$

Out[7]= $\dfrac{\pi}{12}$

Here the output is not necessary. If you would like to suppress the output of any input cell, simply type a semicolon ; after typing the contents of the cell:

In[8]:= $x = \dfrac{\pi}{12}$;

You can enter a sequence of several commands in a single input cell by putting semicolons after all but the final command. Only the output of the final command will be displayed. When you are typing, you can use the character return key ([RET] on a Mac or [ENTER] on a PC) to move to a new line in the same input cell, or you can keep it all on one line if it will fit:

In[9]:= $x = 3$;
$\text{Expand}\left[(x - y)^8\right]$

Out[10]= $6561 - 17\,496\,y + 20\,412\,y^2 - 13\,608\,y^3 + 5670\,y^4 - 1512\,y^5 + 252\,y^6 - 24\,y^7 + y^8$

In[11]:= $\text{Clear}[x]; \text{Expand}\left[(x - y)^8\right]$

Out[11]= $x^8 - 8\,x^7\,y + 28\,x^6\,y^2 - 56\,x^5\,y^3 + 70\,x^4\,y^4 - 56\,x^3\,y^5 + 28\,x^2\,y^6 - 8\,x\,y^7 + y^8$

A different means for suppressing output is the **Short** command. This command is useful if you generate output that is just plain too long. If you enter a cell and produce screen upon screen of output, append the text //**Short** to the input and reenter it. You will get the very beginning and end of the total output, with a marker indicating how much was chopped out of the middle. Here's an example that makes use of *factorials*. The factorial of a positive integer n is the product of n with every other positive integer less than n. So the factorial of 5 is equal to $5 \times 4 \times 3 \times 2 \times 1 = 120$. The common mathematical notation for the factorial of n and the *Mathematica* notation agree: type **n!**:

In[12]:= **1000! // Short**

Out[12]//Short=
$$402\,387\,260\,077 \ll 2544 \gg 000\,000\,000\,000$$

Here *Mathematica* tells us that there are over 2500 digits missing from the output.

If you want to find out whose computer is faster, or if you want to know how long it takes *Mathematica* to arrive at an answer, use the **Timing** command. Wrap any input with this command, and the output will be a list containing two items (they will be separated by a comma). The first item in the list is the number of seconds that it took the kernel to process your answer (it doesn't include the time it takes to format and display the answer), and the second item is the answer itself. If the input to the **Timing** command is followed by a semicolon, the second item in the list will be the word **Null** rather than the answer. This is useful when the output is large:

In[13]:= **20! // Timing**

Out[13]= {0., 2 432 902 008 176 640 000 }

In[14]:= **1 000 000!; // Timing**

Out[14]= {0.985, Null}

2.9 Getting Help from *Mathematica*

Getting Information on a Command whose Name You Know

Type **?** followed by a *Mathematica* command name, and then enter the cell to get information on that command. This is useful for remembering the syntax for a command whose name you know, and for seeing the various ways in which a command can be used. For example:

In[1]:= **? N**

N[*expr*] gives the numerical value of *expr*.

N[*expr, n*] attempts to give a result with n-digit precision. $\gg$

You can click on the ≫ symbol at the end of this output to get more detailed information in the Documentation Center.

Command Completion

Mathematica can finish typing a command for you if you provide the first few letters. This is useful if the command has a long name; it saves time and guarantees that you won't make a typing mistake. Here's how it works: After typing a few letters choose Complete Selection from the Edit menu. If more than one completion is possible, you will be presented with a pop-up menu containing all of the options. Just click on the appropriate choice. Try it—type **Cos** in an input cell and attempt the completion. You will find that there are four *Mathematica* commands that start with these letters: **Cos**, **Cosh**, **CosIntegral**, and **CoshIntegral**.

Command Templates

If you know the name of a command, but have forgotten the syntax for its arguments, type the command name in an input cell, then choose Make Template from the Edit menu. *Mathematica* will paste a template into the input cell showing the syntax for the simplest form of the command. For example, if you were to type **Plot**, and then choose Make Template, the input cell would look like this:

$$\textbf{Plot}[f, \{x, x_{min}, x_{max}\}]$$

You can now edit the cell (replacing f with the function *you* want to plot, x_{min} with the lower bound for *your* domain, etc.).

Command templates and command completions work well together. Type a few letters, complete the command, then make the template. It's an easy way to avoid syntax errors. See Table 2.1 for keyboard shortcuts.

The Documentation Center

The Documentation Center is the most useful feature imaginable; learn to use it and use it often. Go to the Help menu and choose Documentation Center. In a moment a window will appear displaying the documentation home page. The documentation window is modeled after a web browser. You may either type a keyword in the text field, or follow links from the home page. Every one of the more than 3000 built-in symbols has its own individual help page. For example, if you type "Plot" into the text field (with a capital P), the help page for the **Plot** function will appear. In the large yellow box the basic syntax for the command is explained. In the far upper right corner there are links to related tutorials, a very useful feature. Under the main yellow box showing a command's syntax structure there is a button labeled "More Information." Push it and all the dirty details of your command will be revealed. Below all this are usage examples.

One could spend the rest of his or her natural life wading through the documentation center; it's a big place.

2.10 Loading Packages

Mathematica comes with over 3000 built-in commands and symbols. Nevertheless, there will inevitably come a time when you will seek a command that is not built into the system. In such cases it is possible to create or simply use a suite of custom-designed *Mathematica* commands designed for a particular application. A *Mathematica package*, or *add-on*, is a file that activates additional commands that are not ordinarily available. When you *load a package*, the commands in that package become available for you to use. *Mathematica* comes with a few dozen "standard" packages, and there are many more in use around the world.

⚠ If so many packages are "standard" and ship with the software, why does one have to load them separately? Why are they not just built-in? The reason is two-fold. On the one hand, keeping these packages on the shelf, so to speak, until needed makes *Mathematica* leaner and more nimble. If a user will not need these commands in most sessions, keeping them out of the system means that there will be more resources available for everything else. The user simply loads packages as they are needed. On the other hand, the design of packages allows for the possibility that the same command name could have one meaning in one package, and an entirely different meaning in another. Common mathematical terms such as "tensor," for instance, have different meanings in different mathematical contexts, and indeed there are different packages available that define the command **Tensor** differently. Thus packages allow the user flexibility to customize *Mathematica* to suit the purpose at hand.

To understand in a very basic way how packages work, it is necessary to understand that the built-in commands have a "full name" and a short name. So far we have only mentioned the short name. The full name of a built-in command can be had by attaching **System`** to the front of it. For instance, the full name of **Plot** is **System`Plot**. We say that the **Plot** command lives in the **System** *context*. The commands found in a package, by contrast, have a context other than **System**. For instance, below we give examples from the **Units`** package. The command whose short name is **Convert** is defined in this package; its full name is **Units`Con**‑**vert**. One can always call a command by typing its full name, but this is almost never done. It is only necessary if two commands have the same short name, a situation that we generally try to avoid. When a package is loaded, its context is recognized, so that calls can be made to the short name of any command defined in the package.

Hundreds of additional packages are available to download (for free) from the web site http://library.wolfram.com. At this site, type a topic of your choosing in the search field, and search within "MathSource." A listing of hits is displayed, each with a brief summary, a link, and the date on which it was posted (recent dates are generally better than old). It is a simple matter to follow a link, then download and install the relevant package. Package files are identical regardless of which operating system your computer uses. To install a package, simply place the package file (ending in .m) into the ~/Library/Mathematica/Applications folder in your home directory (Mac OS), or the Documents and Settings*username*\\Application Data\\Mathematica\\Applications folder (Windows).

The following input can be used to get a listing of the standard packages included in your installation of *Mathematica*. It looks rather complicated, but it simply instructs *Mathematica* to look in the appropriate directory on your computer and report the names of the files that are stored there. Note that it is possible to do this with slightly shorter input, but the following (redundant but simple) input will work on *all* platforms (Mac, PC, etc.):

In[1]:= **SetDirectory[$InstallationDirectory];**
SetDirectory["AddOns"];
SetDirectory["Packages"];
FileNames[]

Out[4]= {ANOVA, Audio, BarCharts, Benchmarking, BlackBodyRadiation, Calendar,
Combinatorica, Compatibility, ComputationalGeometry, ComputerArithmetic,
Developer, EquationTrekker, ErrorBarPlots, Experimental, FiniteFields,
FourierSeries, FunctionApproximations, Geodesy, GraphUtilities, GUIKit,
HierarchicalClustering, Histograms, HypothesisTesting, LinearRegression,
MultivariateStatistics, Music, NonlinearRegression, Notation, NumericalCalculus,
NumericalDifferentialEquationAnalysis, PhysicalConstants, PieCharts, PlotLegends,
PolyhedronOperations, Polytopes, PrimalityProving, Quaternions, RegressionCommon,
ResonanceAbsorptionLines, Splines, StandardAtmosphere, StatisticalPlots,
Units, VariationalMethods, VectorAnalysis, VectorFieldPlots, WorldPlot, XML}

It is highly likely that you will at some point need to load a package into *Mathematica*. To do so, the **Needs** command is used. Suppose that you wish to use a package, and either it is a standard package or you have already downloaded it and placed it in the Applications directory. For example, there is a standard package called **Units** that allows you to easily convert units of measurement. To load it, enter a cell containing the text:

In[5]:= **Needs["Units`"]**

This must be typed with perfect precision. The argument to **Needs** is a **String**, that is, it is enclosed in double quotation marks. And the package name will invariably contain one or more *backquote* characters ` (look in the upper left portion of your keyboard for the backquote character. Do not use an apostrophe '). If the cell is entered properly, there will be no output. If you get an error message, chances are good that you didn't type the input exactly right; fix it, then reenter the cell. Under no circumstances should you attempt to use the commands in the package until it has been properly loaded. You can check that the package loaded properly by typing and entering

In[6]:= **$Packages**

Out[6]= {Units`, ResourceLocator`, DocumentationSearch`,
JLink`, PacletManager`, WebServices`, System`, Global`}

The output shows all currently loaded packages; your output may be slightly different. What you need to look for is the name of the package you tried to load. Since **Units`** appears in the output, all is well. If your package does not appear in the list, try using the **Needs** command again until it does.

Once the package has loaded you can use the commands it contains just as if they were ordinary *Mathematica* commands. The Units package contains the command **Convert**, which allows the conversion of just about any imaginable pair of measurement units. The syntax is:

Convert[_from_, _to_**]**

For example, how many miles are there in a light year? How many teaspoons in a 16 gallon tank of gas? Bartenders take note: How many jiggers in a 1.75 liter bottle?

In[7]:= **Convert[LightYear, Mile]**

Out[7]= 5.87863×10^{12} Mile

In[8]:= **Convert[16 Gallon, Teaspoon]**

Out[8]= 12 288. Teaspoon

In[9]:= **Convert[1.75 Liter, Jigger]**

Out[9]= 39.4497 Jigger

Note that all units of measurement are given in the singular, so you should type **Foot** rather than **Feet** and **Mile** rather than **Miles**. Note also that you may arithmetically combine basic units of measurement; for instance, you can convert miles per hour to feet per second like so:

In[10]:= **Convert[90 Mile / Hour, Foot / Second]**

Out[10]= $\dfrac{132 \text{ Foot}}{\text{Second}}$

You can deal in thousands with the prefix **Kilo**, which is simply equal to 1000. For instance there is no unit named Kilometer. Rather, you should use the product (note the space) **Kilo Meter**.

This brings a natural question to mind: How do you find out what commands are available in a given package? For instance, what units of measurement are available in the Units package? To find out, use the **Names** command (do this _after_ loading the package). The syntax for **Names** is just like that of the **Needs** command, except that you need to place an asterisk between the last backquote and double quote (the asterisk is the "wild-card" symbol common in many computer applications and operating systems). You can save yourself some typing by clicking once under the input cell containing the **Needs** command, and from the menus choosing Insert ▷ Input From Above. Then edit the new cell, adding the asterisk and changing **Needs** to **Names**. To save space below, we **Take** only the 40th through 70th names from over 250 names in the package.

In[11]:= **Names["Units`*"] // Short**

Out[11]//Short=
{Abampere, ≪274≫, Zetta}

In[12]:= **Take[Names["Units`*"], 40 ;; 70]**

Out[12]= {BTU, Bucket, Bushel, Butt, Cable, Caliber, Calorie, Candela,

Candle, Carat, Celsius, Cental, Centi, Centigrade, Centimeter, Century,

CGS, Chain, ChevalVapeur, Cicero, Convert, ConvertTemperature,

Cord, Coulomb, Cubit, Curie, Dalton, Day, Deca, Decade, Deci}

Here we see that there are a host of objects defined in the package. Most of them are units of measurement, but two of them, **Convert** and **ConvertTemperature**, are commands. You can now find out about any of these names in the usual way:

In[13]:= **? Butt**

Butt is a unit of volume. »

In[14]:= **? ConvertTemperature**

ConvertTemperature[*temp*, *oldscale*, *newscale*] converts

temperature *temp* from temperature scale *oldscale* to scale *newscale*. »

In[15]:= **ConvertTemperature[212, Fahrenheit, Celsius]**

Out[15]= 100

There is an important thing you need to know about packages. If you accidentally attempt to use a command defined in a package *before* the package has been loaded (you'll know if you've done this because the command won't work; the output will simply match the input), you'll create a bit of a challenge for both yourself and for *Mathematica*. Suppose, for instance, that you tried to use the **Convert** command *before* loading the **Units`** package. By calling the **Convert** command prematurely, you have inadvertently created a symbol of that name. *Mathematica* notes that **Convert** is now a recognized symbol, albeit a symbol that has no meaning. The next logical step is for you to realize that you forgot to load the package, and proceed to load it. Now here's the rub: As *Mathematica* goes about loading all the new symbols in the package it will encounter *two* symbols with the name **Convert**, the one in the package and the meaningless one you (inadvertently) created. This will lead to a warning message as the package loads. It will also lead to the symbol **Convert** being displayed in red when it is typed, to flag it as a symbol with conflicting meanings. However beyond this rather disturbing red display, nothing bad will happen. The package definition takes precedence over your meaningless one, and everything will work as it should.

You can avoid these issues by simply loading the package before calling any commands in it. And if you do inadvertently call a command prematurely (this is known as premature evaluation), and would rather not see the command displayed in red, simply type **Remove[Convert]** (or whatever command you accidentally called) before loading the package. This will purge the offending symbol from the system registry so that there will be no conflict upon loading the package.

Exercises 2.10

1. How many gallons are in a butt? Load the Units package and investigate. Make a joke out of the answer.

2.11 Troubleshooting

The most common problem with learning *Mathematica* is adapting to a system in which spelling and syntax must be perfect. What happens if your syntax is wrong (say you typed a period instead of a comma, or forgot to capitalize a command name)? Usually you will get an error message. Don't panic. Most error messages can be traced to a simple typing mistake. Just go back to your last input cell, edit it, and reenter it. If you can't find your mistake, ask a friend or your instructor. You may also want to try the online help features discussed earlier.

In any event, if your input is either generating error messages or not generating the output you want, look first for spelling or syntax problems. If you are reasonably certain that the command has been entered correctly, there are a few other things you might try. If *Mathematica* beeped when you attempted to enter your input cell, you can go to the Help menu and select Why the Beep?.... This will provide you with an explanation that may be quite helpful. Another tactic that cures a common source of problems is to clear the names of any variables appearing in your input, then try reentering the cell. For instance, if your current input involves a variable called *x*, and somewhere long ago you typed **x = 3**, then *Mathematica* will substitute 3 for *x* every chance it gets for as long as the current kernel is running. You may have forgotten that you made such an assignment, and no longer want it. Type and enter **Clear[x]** to remove any previous assignment to *x*, then reenter your input cell (you will need to clear the values of all expressions that have been assigned values in *your* current session; such expressions may or may not be called *x* in *your* notebook). Get in the habit of clearing variable names as soon as you are done with them.

Another reality that you may encounter at some point is that your computer can *crash*. This occurs only *very* rarely under ordinary usage on a computer of recent vintage, but it's good to be able to recognize one should it occur.

Recognizing a Crash

When you enter a command to *Mathematica*'s kernel, the title bar to the notebook window will display the text "Running...." This label will vanish when the output appears. It is *Mathematica*'s way of telling you that it is working on a calculation. Some calculations are fast, but some are slow, and some are *very* slow (hours, days, even weeks). How much time a calculation will require depends on the complexity of the calculation and the type of computer being used. If you have entered a command and nothing seems to be happening, don't despair. It is likely that you have simply asked a difficult question (intentionally or not) and it will take *Mathematica* a bit of time to answer.

If you don't have time to wait and just want *Mathematica* to stop, read on.

Or if (heaven forbid) the cursor does not respond when you move the mouse, and the keyboard does not seem to work, it is likely that a crash has occurred. Don't panic, and don't pull the plug just yet. Read on…

Aborting Calculations and/or Recovering from a Crash

Under ordinary circumstances (the computer hasn't crashed), simply select Abort Evaluation from the Evaluation menu. This will usually work, but not always. Wait a minute or two and take a deep breath. Relax. If all goes well you should eventually see the message **$Aborted** in your notebook window where the output would ordinarily appear. Mission accomplished.

If nothing happens when you attempt to abort, you will have to take slightly more decisive action: You will have to quit the kernel. To do this, go again to the Evaluation menu, but this time select Quit Kernel (you then have to select the kernel that is running, usually the local kernel), then hit the Quit button when it asks if you *really* want to quit the kernel. The only consequence here is that if you wish to continue working, you will have to start a new kernel. This will happen automatically when you enter your next input. Remember that the new kernel will not be aware of any of your previous calculations, so you may have to reenter some old cells to bring the new kernel up to date (if your new commands make reference to any of your previous work).

Now for those of you who have lost control of the mouse and keyboard due to a crash, none of the above is possible. Ideally, you would like to be able to quit *Mathematica* without losing any of your unsaved work. It's not always possible; this is why it's a good idea to save your work often.

The action that you should take depends to some extent on what type of computer you are using. Let's proceed by platform:

Mac OS Procedure

First, try simultaneously hitting ⌘ and . (that's the period key). This is just the keyboard equivalent of selecting Abort Evaluation from the Evaluation menu as described above. It probably won't work, but give it a try. We've seen instances in which the mouse failed in the middle of a long calculation. No crash, just a worn mouse that died at an inopportune time.

If that doesn't work, try simultaneously hitting ⌘Q. If this works you will be presented with a dialog box asking if you wish to save your work. Answer "Yes." In this case, the result will be quitting the entire *Mathematica* program (front end and kernel).

If that doesn't work, simultaneously hit the ⌘ OPTION ESC keys. A dialog will appear asking which application you wish to Force Quit. Choose *Mathematica*. This is almost always effective. The front end and kernel will quit, but you will not have an opportunity to save your work.

As a last resort, you will have to turn off your computer manually. Any unsaved changes will be lost. If the computer has a reset button, use it. Otherwise find the "off" button (often on the back of your computer) and use it. Wait a few seconds and restart the computer in the usual way.

Windows Procedure

First, try simultaneously hitting ⌑ALT⌑ and . (that's the period key). This is just the keyboard equivalent of selecting Abort Evaluation from the Evaluation menu as described above. It probably won't work, but give it a try. We've seen instances in which the mouse failed in the middle of a long calculation. No crash, just a worn mouse that died at an inopportune time.

If that doesn't work, simultaneously hit the ⌑CTRL⌑ALT⌑DEL⌑ keys. This is usually effective. You should be presented with a dialog box. Hit the Task Manager button, then look under the Applications Tab for *Mathematica*. Select it, and hit the End Task button to quit *Mathematica* altogether. It may be possible to save your notebook before quitting. You should restart your computer before launching *Mathematica* again. This will decrease the likelihood of another crash.

As a last resort, you will have to restart your computer. Again, any unsaved changes will be lost.

Running Efficiently: Preventing Crashes

Mathematica can make heavy demands on your computer's resources. In particular, it benefits from large amounts of random access memory, or RAM. You should be aware of this so that you can help it along. Here are some tips to consider if you find yourself pushing your system's resources:

First, quit other programs (such as your web browser) when using *Mathematica*. Other programs also require RAM, so running them at the same time steals valuable memory from *Mathematica*. Also, even though it is possible to have multiple notebooks open at one time, avoid having more notebooks open than necessary. Each open notebook will consume memory. You should also save your notebooks often. Doing so will allow *Mathematica* to store part of it on your computer's hard drive, rather than storing all of it in RAM. Finally, if you work on your own computer and are in the habit of leaving *Mathematica* running for days or weeks at a time, quit the kernel from time to time to flush out any symbols that are not being used.

3

Functions and Their Graphs

3.1 Defining a Function

A *function* is a rule that assigns to each input exactly one output. Many functions, such as the natural logarithm function **Log**, are built in to *Mathematica*. You provide an input, or argument, and *Mathematica* produces the output:

In[1]:= **Log[1]**

Out[1]= 0

You can define your own function in *Mathematica* like this (use the BasicMathInput palette to type x^2; see Section 1.6, page 4):

In[2]:= **f[x_] := x^2 + 2 x − 4**

This function will take an input x, and output $x^2 + 2x - 4$. For instance:

In[3]:= **f[1]**

Out[3]= −1

In[4]:= **f[π]**

Out[4]= $-4 + 2\pi + \pi^2$

As a second example, here is a function that will return the multiplicative inverse of its argument (again, use the BasicMathInput palette to type the fraction):

In[5]:= **inv[x_] := $\dfrac{1}{x}$**

Let's try it:

In[6]:= **inv[45]**

Out[6]= $\dfrac{1}{45}$

You can also create functions by combining existing functions:

In[7]:= **g[x_] := N[inv[x]]**

In[8]:= **g[45]**

Out[8]= 0.0222222

> ## Defining a Function
>
> Follow these rules when defining a function:
>
> - The name of the function (such as f or inv) should be a lowercase letter, or a word that begins with a lowercase letter. This is because all built-in functions (such as Log and N) begin with capital letters. If your function begins with a lowercase letter, you will never accidentally give it a name that already belongs to some built-in function.
> - The function argument (in these examples x) must be followed by an underscore _ on the left side of the definition.
> - Use square brackets [ ] to enclose the function argument.
> - Use the colon-equal combination := to separate the left side of the definition from the right.

After typing the definition, enter the cell containing it. Your function is now ready for action.

⚠ The := operator (called the **SetDelayed** operator) used in defining functions differs in a subtle way from the = operator (called the **Set** operator) used for making assignments (the = operator was discussed in Section 1.10—see page 20). Essentially, when you use := the expression appearing to its right is evaluated anew by the kernel each time that the expression appearing to its left is called. The = operator, by contrast, evaluates the expression on its right only once, at the time the assignment is made. In many settings = and := can be used interchangeably; however, there are cases when one is appropriate and the other is not. Using **SetDelayed** for function definitions will work in virtually every setting, and we will use it consistently for that purpose throughout this book.

An illustrative example is the following: Type and enter **x = RandomInteger[100]; {x, x, x}**. Then change = to := and do it again. In the first case, **x** is set to be a single (randomly chosen) integer, so the output is a list in which that same number appears three times. In the second case, each **x** causes a new random integer to be chosen, so the output is a list of three (probably) distinct numbers.

For more information, go to the Documentation Center and type **SetDelayed** in the text field, then follow the link to the tutorial titled "Immediate and Delayed Definitions."

Clearing a Function

A word to the wise: Once you are finished working with a function, get rid of it. Why? One reason is that you may forget about the function and later in the session try to use the name for something else. But *Mathematica* won't forget, and all sorts of confusion can result. Another is that in getting rid of a function you will clear out a little bit of memory, leaving more room for you to work. To see if a letter or word has been defined as a function, use the **?** command just as you would for a built-in *Mathematica* command:

In[9]:= **?f**

Global`f

$f[x\_] := x^2 + 2x - 4$

This indicates that *f* is still retained in memory. You can use the **Clear** command to erase it, just as you would to erase the value of a constant:

In[10]:= **Clear[f]**

Now if you use the **?** command you will find no such definition:

In[11]:= **?f**

Global`f

> ⚠ To clear out *every* user-defined symbol from the current session, try **Clear["Global`*"]**. The asterisk is a wild-card symbol; this essentially says, "**Clear** all symbols defined in the **Global** context" (the **Global** context is the default location where user-defined symbols are stored).

3.2 Plotting a Function

We begin with a simple example:

In[1]:= **Clear[f];**
f[x_] := $x^2 - 2x + 4$

In[3]:= **Plot[f[x], {x, −1, 3}]**

Out[3]=

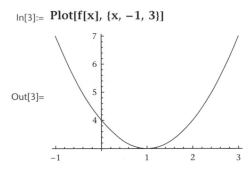

The **Plot** command takes two arguments, separated (as always) by a comma. The first (in this case **f[x]**) is the function to be graphed, and the second (in this case **{x,-1,3}**) is called an *iterator*. It describes the span of values that the variable x is to assume; that is, it specifies the domain over which the plot will be constructed. The curly brackets are essential in describing this domain. In fact, *Mathematica* uses this iterator structure in numerous commands, so it warrants a bit of discussion. The first item (**x**) names the variable, and the next two items give the span of values that this variable will assume (−1 through 3). Values in this domain are displayed along the horizontal axis, while the values that the function assumes are displayed along the vertical axis.

Note that the axes in this plot do not intersect at the origin, but rather at the point (0, 3). Every time you use the **Plot** command *Mathematica* decides where to place the axes, and they do not always cross at the origin. There is a good reason for this. As often as not you will find yourself plotting functions over domains in which the graph is relatively far from the origin. Rather than omit one or both axes from the plot, or include the axes together with acres of white space, *Mathematica* will simply move the axes into view, giving your plot a frame of reference. If you really want to produce a plot with the axes intersecting at the origin, you can. The details are provided in the next section of this chapter, "Using *Mathematica*'s Plot Options."

You can zoom in on a particular portion of a plot simply by editing the domain specified in the iterator, then reentering the cell. Let's take a close look, so to speak, at the function in the last example, this time with x values near 2. Notice how "flat" the graph becomes:

In[4]:= **Plot[f[x], {x, 1.9, 2.1}]**

Out[4]=

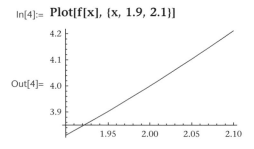

You could zoom in even more (say with a domain from 1.99 to 2.01) and get a more detailed view of the function's behavior near the point $x = 2$. In the plot below we show an extreme zoom (and make use of the lowercase Greek letter δ, which mathematicians often use to denote small quantities). Here we also employ the **With** command, a device that allows you to make *local* assignments; the assignment $\delta = 10^{-10}$ will only be utilized within the **Plot** expression, and will not be remembered by *Mathematica* later.

In[5]:= **With$\left[\{\delta = 10^{-10}\}, \text{Plot}[f[x], \{x, 2 - \delta, 2 + \delta\}]\right]$**

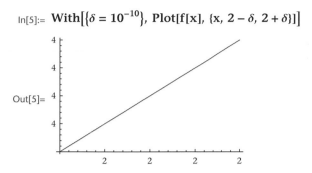

Out[5]=

Note that the numerical values on each axis display identically; this is simply because so many decimal places (ten in this case) are needed to distinguish them that there isn't room for their display. In principle you could keep zooming in forever, but in practice this is not possible. See Exercise 3 for a discussion on the limits of zooming.

Another little trick that's good to know about is how to resize a graphic. This technique is best learned by trying it, so get yourself in front of the computer and produce a plot. Position the cursor anywhere on the graph and click once. A rectangular border with eight "handles" appears around the graph. Position the cursor on a handle and drag (hold down the mouse button and move the mouse) to shrink or enlarge the graphic. It's easy; try it.

A plot often demands careful investigation:

In[6]:= **Clear[f];**

$$f[x\_] := \frac{x^5 - 4x^2 + 1}{x - \frac{1}{2}}$$

In[8]:= **Plot[f[x], {x, −3, 3}]**

Out[8]=

Something strange seems to be happening when $x = 1/2$ (see that vertical blip?). What's happening is this: the function is not defined when $x = 1/2$, since the denominator of f is equal to zero at this value of x. Think of there being an imaginary vertical line, an asymptote, at $x = 1/2$ through which the graph of f cannot pass. In order to understand *Mathematica*'s output it is important to understand how the **Plot** command works. **Plot** samples several values of x in the specified domain and numerically evaluates $f(x)$ for each of them. After refining its selection of sample points via an adaptive algorithm, it then plots these points and "connects the dots" with little line segments. There are so many that the graph appears in most places like a smooth curve. The important issue here is that *Mathematica*'s plots are not exact in a mathematical sense; they are only approximations. For instance, the vertical-looking segment that crosses the x axis near $1/2$ is not part of the true graph of f. As *Mathematica* plotted successively larger values of x, just to the left of $x = 1/2$, the function values got smaller and smaller. The last point that was plotted to the left of the true asymptote took a large negative value. The very next point plotted, just to the right of the true asymptote, took a large positive value. *Mathematica* then connected these two points with a line segment (so in fact that vertical-looking segment tilts ever so slightly from lower left to upper right). *Mathematica* had no way of knowing that in fact the true graph of f never crosses the vertical asymptote. Although technically inaccurate, this isn't a bad state of affairs. You can interpret the plot as the graph of f with the asymptote roughly drawn in. And an important lesson can be learned here: Never trust the output of the computer as gospel; it always demands scrutiny.

Beware also that vertical asymptotes (and other "narrow" features) in a plot will change in appearance as the specified domain changes. Asymptotes may disappear or become barely noticeable. For instance, here is another view of the function f, this time zoomed out to accommodate the domain from -10 to 10. The asymptote appears to have vanished:

In[9]:= **Plot[f[x], {x, −10, 10}]**

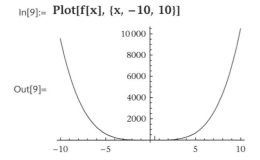

The asymptote is almost invisible because *Mathematica* (by chance) skipped over those values of x so close to the asymptote that $f(x)$ would return very large or very small values. The "true" graph of f still spikes up toward infinity just to the right of the asymptote and down to negative infinity just to the left of it. The point of all this is to make clear that the plots *Mathematica* produces are approximations. They may hide important features of a function if those features are sufficiently narrow relative to the domain over which the function is plotted. When it comes to finding a function's asymptotes, for instance, looking for them on a plot is not necessarily the best approach. We'll discuss better methods for finding vertical asymptotes (by finding explicit values of x for which the denominator is equal to zero) in the next chapter.

We note that if you do know the precise numerical position of a function's vertical asymptote(s), you can add these values between the lower and upper numbers in the iterator. *Mathematica* will omit such points from the resulting plot, and will hence produce a more accurate plot. In the next section, the **Exclusions** option will be introduced; this provides a sophisticated means of excluding points from a domain.

In[10]:= $\text{Plot}\left[\text{f[x]}, \left\{x, -1, \dfrac{1}{2}, 2\right\}\right]$

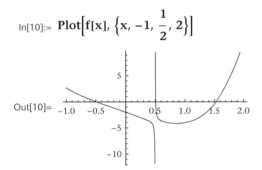

Out[10]=

A more subtle issue may arise from the manner in which *Mathematica* utilizes the complex number system. There are cases in which there are two potential definitions for a function: one which disallows complex numbers, and another which embraces them. *Mathematica* will always embrace them, and this can lead to some unexpected results. In particular, students in precalculus or calculus often work in a setting that opts to disallow non-real numbers. A classic example is the cube root function, $f(x) = x^{1/3}$. Here is a plot of this function on the domain $-8 \le x \le 8$:

In[11]:= $\text{Plot}\left[x^{1/3}, \{x, -8, 8\}\right]$

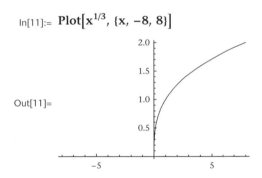

Out[11]=

The left side of the plot is empty. That seems odd; don't negative numbers have cube roots? We know that $(-2)^3 = -8$, so the cube root of -8 should be -2, shouldn't it? The issue is a subtle one. In the complex number system there are *three* numbers whose cube is -8, (they happen to be -2 and the two complex numbers $1 \pm \sqrt{3}\ i$). *Mathematica*, savvy as it is regarding the complex numbers, takes one of the *complex* numbers to be the cube root of -8. In a similar manner, it regards the cube root of every negative number to be complex. It can't plot a complex number, and so the left half of the plot is empty. A thorough discussion of why *Mathematica* chooses complex values as the cube roots of negative numbers can be found in Section 4.4 on page 162. Suffice it to say that there are very good reasons for doing so, but that it can be an annoyance to those who would like to study the real-valued cube root function (and remain blissfully ignorant of the complex number system).

If you would like to see the plot of the real-valued cube root function found in many precalculus and calculus texts (where the cube root of -8 is taken to be -2), one can define an alternative **Power** command, as follows:

In[12]:= **realPower[x_, p_] := If[x < 0 && Element[p, Rationals],**
    If[OddQ[Denominator[p]], If[OddQ[Numerator[p]],
        −Power[−x, p], Power[−x, p]], Power[x, p]], Power[x, p]]

A discussion of the **If** command can be found in Section 8.5. At this point it's okay to ignore the details of this definition, and to use it freely. It will modify the powers of negative numbers when those powers are rational numbers with odd denominator (powers such as 1/3). Here is how to use this alternate **Power** command to produce a plot of the real-valued cube root function:

In[13]:= **Plot[realPower[x, 1/3], {x, −8, 8}]**

Out[13]=

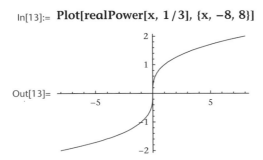

realPower will differ from the built-in **Power** command only if the power (1/3 in the example above) is a rational number. This will suffice for the types of power functions typically encountered in precalculus and calculus courses. Just be sure to enter an exact rational number (no decimal points) as the second argument to **realPower**.

Exercises 3.2

1. Plot the following functions on the domain $-10 \le x \le 10$.

   a. $\sin(1 + \cos(x))$

   b. $\sin(1.4 + \cos(x))$

   c. $\sin\left(\frac{\pi}{2} + \cos(x)\right)$

   d. $\sin(2 + \cos(x))$

2. One can zoom in toward a particular point in the domain of a function and see how the graph appears at different zoom levels. For instance, consider the square root function $f(x) = \sqrt{x}$ when x is near 2.

   a. Enter the input below to see the graph of f as x goes from 1 to 3.

   $$\text{With}\left[\{\delta = 10^0\}, \text{Plot}\left[\sqrt{x}, \{x, 2 - \delta, 2 + \delta\}\right]\right]$$

   b. Now zoom; change the value of δ to be 10^{-1} and re-enter the input above to see the graph of f as x goes from 1.9 to 2.1. Do this again for $\delta = 10^{-2}$, 10^{-3}, 10^{-4}, and 10^{-5}.

c. Use the last plot to approximate $\sqrt{2}$ to six significant digits. Check your answer using **N**.

d. When making a **Plot**, the lower and upper bounds on the iterator must be distinct when rounded to machine precision. Enter the previous **Plot** command with $\delta = 10^{-20}$. An error message results. Read the error message and speculate as to what is happening. The bottom line is that zooming has its limits.

3. Use the **realPower** command to plot the real-valued function $f(x) = x^{4/5}$ on the domain $-32 \le x \le 32$. What is the value of $f(32)$?

3.3 Using *Mathematica*'s Plot Options

Many of *Mathematica*'s commands accept *option settings*; you can type additional arguments into a command to modify the behavior of that command. In this section we'll see how to tweak the **Plot** command so that you get the most out of your graphs. For example, here is the plot of the function $100\cos(x) + e^{(x^2)}$:

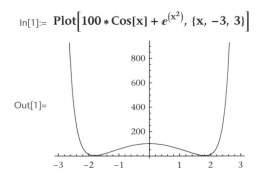

In[1]:= $\text{Plot}\left[100 * \text{Cos}[x] + e^{(x^2)}, \{x, -3, 3\}\right]$

Out[1]=

Notice how *Mathematica* only showed us a portion of what we asked for (the graph is not shown when $|x|$ exceeds 2.5 or so). This is because beyond the portion shown *Mathematica* observed no interesting behavior; the graph just kept going up on the left and on the right. The (boring) information near the edges was clipped off to give a better view of the middle portion of the plot. *Mathematica* will do this clipping by default.

The option **PlotRange** is set by default to an automated setting which will sometimes result in a graph with a truncated vertical scale. But suppose you really want to see the function over the *full* domain from -3 to 3. You can indicate this by adding **PlotRange → Full** as an additional argument to the **Plot** command. It must be placed after the two required arguments. The arrow → is found on the BasicMathInput palette; alternatively, it can be typed from the keyboard as a "minus" sign followed by a "greater than" sign: ->. After typing these two symbols one after the other, they will turn into the arrow on their own at the next keystroke.

In[2]:= $\text{Plot}\left[100 * \text{Cos[x]} + e^{(x^2)}, \{x, -3, 3\}, \text{PlotRange} \rightarrow \text{Full}\right]$

Out[2]=

Look at the output. The left and right sides of the plot now climb almost ten times higher, and as a result the detail in the middle is harder to surmise. It's a very different picture.

After exploring this function in the previous two graphs it is clear that the interesting behavior occurs above the *x*-axis and below $y = 250$. You can specify the exact range of values you wish to display using **PlotRange** $\rightarrow$ {*ymin*, *ymax*}. If your desired range is $-n$ to n, **PlotRange** $\rightarrow$ *n* will suffice.

In[3]:= $\text{Plot}\left[100 * \text{Cos[x]} + e^{(x^2)}, \{x, -3, 3\}, \text{PlotRange} \rightarrow \{0, 250\}\right]$

Out[3]=

In general, you type the name of the option, followed by $\rightarrow$, followed by the desired setting for the option. The philosophy of allowing commands such as **Plot** to accept options is simple: very little typing is required to allow the command to be used in its default form. But when the default output is not entirely to your liking you have the ability to tweak the default settings to your heart's content. There are over 50 options for the **Plot** command, several of which are discussed below. You may add several option settings to a command, and in any order you wish (provided each optional argument is listed *after* the required arguments); just use commas to separate them.

How to Get the Same Scaling on Both Axes

In order to get both sets of axes on the same scale use the option **AspectRatio** $\rightarrow$ **Automatic**:

In[4]:= $\text{Plot}\big[2\,(x-4)^2+1,\ \{x,\ 3,\ 5\},\ \text{AspectRatio} \to \text{Automatic}\big]$

Out[4]=

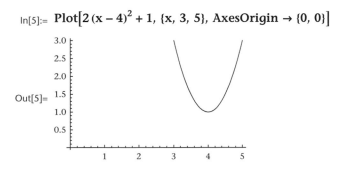

Be mindful that in many cases you definitely do not want your axes to have the same scale. You could, for instance, very easily ask for a plot that was a few inches wide and a few miles high. Imagine the plot at the beginning of this section if you are skeptical. That is why the default aspect ratio (the ratio of height to width) is set to a fixed value. In other words, by default **Plot** will scale the axes in such a way that the graph will fit into a rectangle of standard proportions. It's best to add the **AspectRatio → Automatic** option only after you have viewed the plot and determined that its use won't result in a plot that's too long and skinny.

Note that you can also set **AspectRatio** to any positive numerical value you like. The plot will have the *height* to *width* ratio that you specify. For instance, the setting **AspectRatio → 3** will produce a plot that is three times as high as it is wide. Widescreen televisions are advertised to have a 16 : 9 aspect ratio. In *Mathematica*, we can obtain these dimensions with the setting **AspectRatio → 9 / 16**.

How to Get the Axes to Intersect at the Origin
Use the option **AxesOrigin → {0, 0}**:

In[5]:= $\text{Plot}\big[2\,(x-4)^2+1,\ \{x,\ 3,\ 5\},\ \text{AxesOrigin} \to \{0,\ 0\}\big]$

Out[5]=

Note that the domain specified is $3 \leq x \leq 5$, yet the option setting extends the graphic beyond these values. You may need to adjust the **AspectRatio** as well if you end up with something too long and thin.

How to Display Mesh Points

To show the points delineating all the line segments generated in a **Plot**, use the option **Mesh → All**:

In[6]:= **Plot[Sin[x]², {x, 0, 2π}, Mesh → All]**

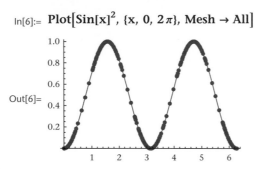

Out[6]=

Note that more points are generated in regions where the function bends sharply. The graph itself is comprised of line segments joining these points.

To show points whose x coordinates are regularly spaced, use the option **Mesh → Full** or **Mesh → n** where n is the desired number of points (not counting endpoints).

In[7]:= **Plot[Sin[x]², {x, 0, 2π}, Mesh → Full]**

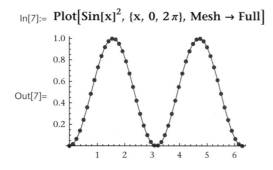

Out[7]=

In[8]:= **Plot[Sin[x]², {x, 0, 2π}, Mesh → 10]**

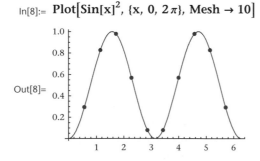

Out[8]=

⚠ One can display *any* finite collection of mesh points by setting **Mesh** to a *list* of x coordinates, such as **Mesh → {1, 2, 3}**. One can programmatically generate this list of x coordinates using

Range (for equally spaced x coordinates), or **Table** (see Section 3.5 for a discussion of the **Table** command). Even more control can be garnered by setting the **MeshFunctions** option, which specifies which function or functions are to be set to the list of **Mesh** values. Typically such functions are given as *pure functions* (see Section 8.4 for a discussion of the **Function** command). By default, **MeshFunctions** is set to {#1 &}, meaning that the list of **Mesh** values is a list of x coordinates. With the setting **MeshFunctions** → {#2 &}, the list of **Mesh** values becomes a list of y coordinates. See Exercise 5 for examples.

How to Add Color and Other Style Changes: Graphics Directives

It's not hard to make a plot any color you like using the **PlotStyle** option. The output below is shown in grayscale. It will appear red on your monitor:

In[9]:= $\text{Plot}\big[2(x-4)^2+1, \{x, 3, 5\}, \text{PlotStyle} \to \text{Red}\big]$

Out[9]=

You may use any standard color name; for a list of all colors go to the Documentation Center, type "Colors" in the search field, and navigate to the guide page of that name. You may also use a lighter or darker version of any color; just replace **Red**, for instance, with **Lighter[Red]**, or **Lighter[Red, .7]** or **Darker[Red, .2]**. The second numerical argument may be omitted. If present, it determines the extent of the lightening or darkening, and should be set to a value between 0 (no effect) and 1 (maximal effect).

In[10]:= $\text{Plot}\big[2(x-4)^2+1, \{x, 3, 5\}, \text{PlotStyle} \to \text{Lighter[Blue, .8]}\big]$

Out[10]=

You can also blend two or more colors. Setting **PlotStyle** to **Blend[{Blue, Red}, .3]** will produce a blend of 70% blue and 30% red. And one could nest these settings to create a custom color such as **Lighter[Blend[{Blue, Red}, .3], .4]**. Other color settings are discussed in Exercise 3.

These color settings are examples of *graphics directives*. The **PlotStyle** option may be set to any single graphics directive (such as the color directives outlined above), or simultaneously to several such directives. Multiple directives should be wrapped in the **Directive** command. For instance, one can apply the directives **Thick**, **Gray**, and **Dashed** as follows:

In[11]:= $\text{Plot}\!\left[2\,(x-4)^2+1,\,\{x,\,3,\,5\},\,\text{PlotStyle} \to \text{Directive}\!\left[\text{Thick, Gray, Dashed}\right]\right]$

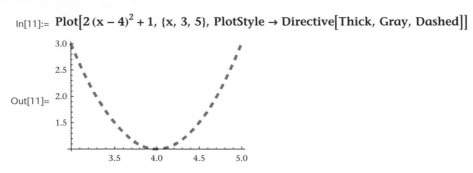

Out[11]=

Dashes may be fine-tuned by replacing **Dashed** with the directive **Dashing[Small]**, **Dashing[Large]**, or **Dashing[{.02, .01}]**. This last setting has the effect of breaking the plot into dashed segments each of which is 2% of the width of the entire graphic, and where the space between consecutive dashes is 1% of the width of the graphic. To fine-tune the thickness, try **Thickness[.01]**. This will adjust the plot's thickness to 1% of the width of the entire graphic.

Other common **Plot** options that accept graphics directive settings are **AxesStyle**, **Background**, **FillingStyle**, **FrameStyle**, and **MeshStyle**.

How to Remove the Axes or Add a Frame

To remove axes simply add the option **Axes → False**:

In[12]:= $\text{Plot}\!\left[2\,(x-4)^2+1,\,\{x,\,3,\,5\},\,\text{Axes} \to \text{False}\right]$

Out[12]=

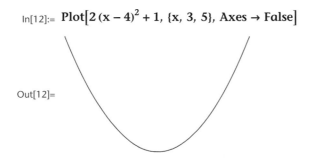

To replace the axes with a frame around the entire graph, add the option **Frame → True**:

In[13]:= $\text{Plot}\left[2(x-4)^2 + 1, \{x, 3, 5\}, \text{Frame} \rightarrow \text{True}\right]$

Out[13]=

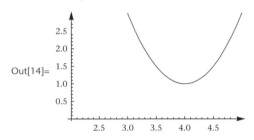

How to Place Arrowheads on the Axes

Add the option **AxesStyle → Arrowheads[0.05]** to put arrowheads on the top and right only, or **AxesStyle → Arrowheads[{−0.05, 0.05}]** to put arrowheads on both ends of each axis. The value .05 means that the arrowheads will be scaled to be 5% of the width of the entire plot.

In[14]:= $\text{Plot}\left[2(x-4)^2 + 1, \{x, 3, 5\}, \text{AxesStyle} \rightarrow \text{Arrowheads}[.05], \text{AxesOrigin} \rightarrow \{2, 0\}\right]$

Out[14]=

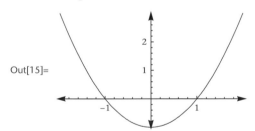

In[15]:= $\text{Plot}\left[x^2 - 1, \{x, -2, 2\}, \text{AxesStyle} \rightarrow \text{Arrowheads}[\{-.05, .05\}]\right]$

Out[15]=

When adding arrowheads, it may be desirable to manually increase the **PlotRange** for both axes to place the arrowheads farther from the center of your plot. This will allow room to display more tick marks on the axes.

In[16]:= $\text{Plot}\big[x^2 - 1, \{x, -2, 2\}, \text{AxesStyle} \to \text{Arrowheads}[\{-.05, .05\}],$
$\text{PlotRange} \to \{\{-3, 3\}, \{-2, 4\}\}\big]$

Out[16]=

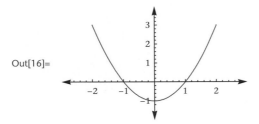

How to Add Grid Lines and Adjust Ticks on the Axes

To add a grid to your plot, as if it were plotted on graph paper, add the option
GridLines → Automatic.

In[17]:= $\text{Plot}\big[\text{Sin}[x]^2, \{x, 0, 2\pi\}, \text{GridLines} \to \text{Automatic}\big]$

Out[17]=

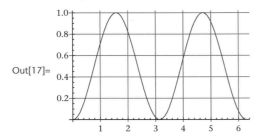

The appearance of the grid lines is controlled by the **GridLinesStyle** option, which can be set to any
graphics directive.

In[18]:= $\text{Plot}\big[\text{Sin}[x]^2, \{x, 0, 2\pi\}, \text{GridLines} \to \text{Automatic},$
$\text{GridLinesStyle} \to \text{Directive}\big[\text{Thin, Gray, Dotted}\big]\big]$

Out[18]=

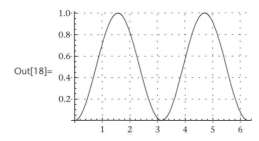

To adjust the placement of the grid lines, set **GridLines** to a list of two lists: the first consists of x
values indicating the positions of the vertical lines, and the second consists of y values indicating
the positions of the horizontal lines:

In[19]:= $\text{Plot}\left[\text{Sin}[x]^2, \{x, 0, 2\pi\}, \text{GridLines} \rightarrow \left\{\left\{\dfrac{\pi}{2}, \pi, \dfrac{3\pi}{2}, 2\pi\right\}, \{.2, .4, .6, .8, 1\}\right\}\right]$

Out[19]=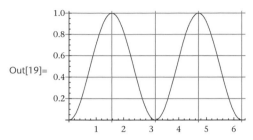

For fine grids, use **Range** to generate each of the x and y lists. **Range** is used to generate a list of evenly spaced numerical values. For example, **Range[0, 1, .1]** generates a list of numbers from 0 to 1 in increments of one tenth:

In[20]:= **Range[0, 1, .1]**

Out[20]= {0., 0.1, 0.2, 0.3, 0.4, 0.5, 0.6, 0.7, 0.8, 0.9, 1.}

In[21]:= $\text{Plot}\left[\text{Sin}[x]^2, \{x, 0, 2\pi\}, \text{GridLinesStyle} \rightarrow \text{Lighter}[\text{Gray}],\right.$
$\left.\text{GridLines} \rightarrow \left\{\text{Range}\left[0, 2\pi, \dfrac{\pi}{8}\right], \text{Range}[0, 1, .1]\right\}\right]$

Out[21]=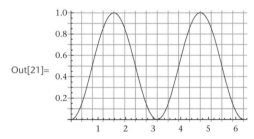

Numerical tick marks on the axes are controlled via the **Ticks** option, which works in a manner similar to **GridLines**. If you are happy with the default list of tick marks on one of the axes, just use **Automatic** instead of a specific list of values.

In[22]:= $\text{Plot}\Big[\text{Sin[x]}^2,\ \{x,\ 0,\ 2\pi\},\ \text{GridLinesStyle} \to \text{Lighter}\big[\text{Gray}\big],$

$\quad\quad \text{GridLines} \to \Big\{\text{Range}\Big[0,\ 2\pi,\ \dfrac{\pi}{8}\Big],\ \text{Range[0, 1, .1]}\Big\},$

$\quad\quad \text{Ticks} \to \Big\{\text{Range}\Big[0,\ 2\pi,\ \dfrac{\pi}{2}\Big],\ \text{Automatic}\Big\}\Big]$

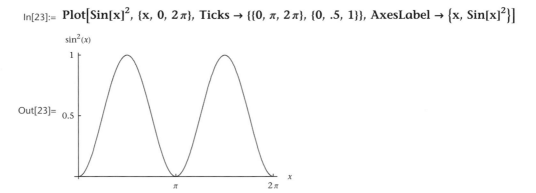

Out[22]=

How to Add Labels

Labels can be added to the axes via the option **AxesLabel**. By default, it will apply **TraditionalForm** to your label expressions. So, for instance, **Sin[x]**^{2} will be displayed using the traditional notation, $\sin^2(x)$.

In[23]:= $\text{Plot}\big[\text{Sin[x]}^2,\ \{x,\ 0,\ 2\pi\},\ \text{Ticks} \to \{\{0,\ \pi,\ 2\pi\},\ \{0,\ .5,\ 1\}\},\ \text{AxesLabel} \to \big\{x,\ \text{Sin[x]}^2\big\}\big]$

Out[23]=

You can put a label on the entire plot with the option **PlotLabel**.

In[24]:= **Plot[Sin[x]², {x, 0, 2π}, Ticks → {{0, π, 2π}, {0, .5, 1}},**
       AxesLabel → {x, y}, PlotLabel → Sin[x]²]

Out[24]=

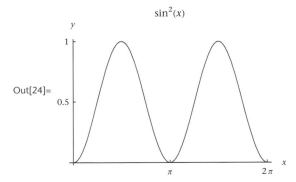

Labels that include operators (such as =), or that are comprised of more than one word, should be entered as a **String**, i.e., put in double quotation marks. In this case, the text between the quotation marks will be reproduced *exactly* as you write it. Below, for instance, we italicized the x and the y as we typed the label text.

In[25]:= **Plot[Sin[x]², {x, 0, 2π}, Ticks → {{0, π, 2π}, {0, .5, 1}},**
       AxesLabel → {x, y}, PlotLabel → "y = sin²(x)"]

Out[25]=

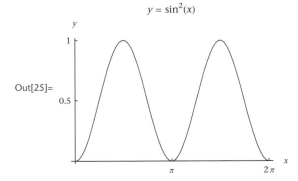

If one had not used double quotation marks, *Mathematica* would have actually made the nonsensical assignment $y = \sin^2 x$, possibly causing confusion later in the session. When in doubt, wrap your plot labels in double quotes.

An alternate means of labeling will work not only for plots, but for labeling any *Mathematica* expression. Simply wrap the expression to be labeled in the **Labeled** command, and add a second argument that specifies the text for the label. The label appears at the bottom by default, but if present a third argument may be given to specify the position of the label. Look up **Labeled** in the Documentation Center for information about micro-positioning the label text.

In[26]:= $p = \text{Plot}\left[\text{Sin}[x]^2, \{x, 0, 2\pi\}, \text{Ticks} \rightarrow \{\{0, \pi, 2\pi\}, \{0, .5, 1\}\}, \text{AxesLabel} \rightarrow \{x, y\}\right];$
$\quad\quad\text{Labeled}\left[p, \text{Text}\left["y = \sin^2(x)"\right], \text{Right}\right]$

Out[27]=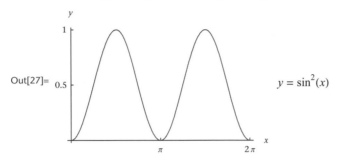

Exclusions and Vertical Asymptotes

As mentioned in the previous section, a single *x* value can be excluded from the domain of a plot by listing that value (or a few such values) within the iterator for the independent variable. Here, for instance, we let *x* span all values from 0 to 7, but in the second input we exclude the values 2 and 5 (where the function is undefined).

In[28]:= $\text{Plot}\left[\dfrac{(x-3)(x-4)}{(x-2)(x-5)}, \{x, 0, 7\}\right]$

Out[28]=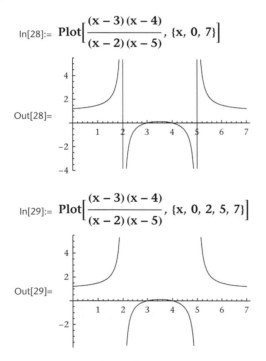

In[29]:= $\text{Plot}\left[\dfrac{(x-3)(x-4)}{(x-2)(x-5)}, \{x, 0, 2, 5, 7\}\right]$

Out[29]=

Even more control can be garnered using the options **Exclusions** and **ExclusionsStyle**. **Exclusions** can be set to a list containing an equation or equations whose solution(s) you wish to exclude. Use two equal signs back to back **==** when typing an equation. **ExclusionsStyle** specifies the directive(s) applied to the vertical line(s) through the points to be excluded, enabling you to include vertical asymptotes in your plot. Multiple directives should be wrapped in the **Directive** command, as was done earlier with **PlotStyle**.

In[30]:= $\mathbf{Plot}\left[\dfrac{(x-3)(x-4)}{(x-2)(x-5)}, \{x, 0, 7\}, \mathbf{Exclusions} \to \{x == 2, x == 5\}, \mathbf{ExclusionsStyle} \to \mathbf{Dashed}\right]$

Out[30]=

The benefit of expressing exclusions as *equations* is illustrated in the following example, where a single equation has many solutions in the specified domain:

In[31]:= $\mathbf{Plot}\Big[\mathbf{Tan}[x], \{x, 0, 4\pi\}, \mathbf{Exclusions} \to \{\mathbf{Cos}[x] == 0\},$

$\mathbf{ExclusionsStyle} \to \mathbf{Directive}[\mathbf{Gray}, \mathbf{Dashed}], \mathbf{Ticks} \to \Big\{\mathbf{Range}\Big[0, 4\pi, \dfrac{\pi}{2}\Big], \mathbf{Automatic}\Big\}\Big]$

Out[31]=

Note that **Exclusions** has little visible effect at a point unless there is an essential discontinuity there. See Exercise 4.

Putting a Logarithmic Scale on One or Both Axes

While **Plot** may use different scales on the horizontal and vertical axes, it will always put a uniform scale on each (in which there are equal distances between successive numbers). The commands **LogPlot**, **LogLinearPlot**, and **LogLogPlot** may be used to put a logarithmic scale (in which there are equal distances between successive powers of 10) on one or both axes. Each of these commands has the same syntactical structure as **Plot**, and will accept the **Plot** options discussed above.

To put a logarithmic scale on the vertical axis, use the command **LogPlot**:

In[32]:= **Plot[10ˣ, {x, 0, 3}]**

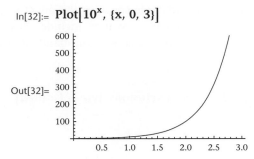

Out[32]=

The **LogPlot** of any exponential function will be linear since $\log(b^x) = x \log(b)$.

In[33]:= **LogPlot[10ˣ, {x, 0, 3}]**

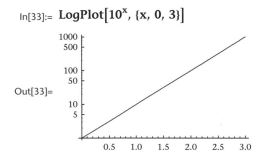

Out[33]=

To put a logarithmic scale on the horizontal axis, use the command **LogLinearPlot**:

In[34]:= **Plot[Log[10, x], {x, 1, 1000}]**

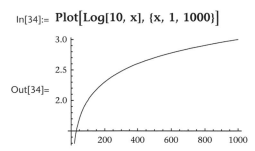

Out[34]=

LogLinearPlot will make logarithmic functions appear linear.

In[35]:= **LogLinearPlot[Log[10, x], {x, 1, 1000}]**

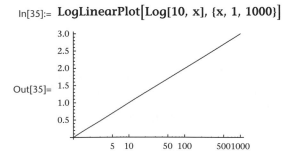

Out[35]=

To put a logarithmic scale on both axes, use the command **LogLogPlot**:

In[36]:= $\text{Plot}\left[x^{3/2}, \{x, 1, 100\}\right]$

Out[36]=

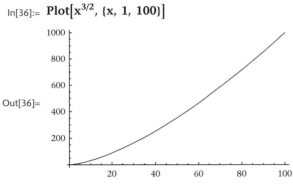

In[37]:= $\text{LogLogPlot}\left[x^{3/2}, \{x, 1, 100\}\right]$

Out[37]=

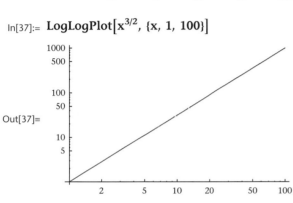

Exercises 3.3

1. Use the **GridLines** and **Ticks** options, as well as the setting **GridLinesStyle → Lighter[Gray]**, to produce the following **Plot** of the sine function:

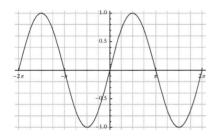

2. Use the **Axes**, **Frame**, **Filling**, **FrameStyle**, **PlotRange**, and **AspectRatio** options to produce the following plot of the function $y = \frac{\cos(15x)}{1+x^2}$:

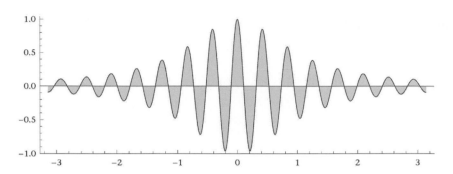

3. Color values such as **Red**, **Blue**, and **Orange** are easy to type and to remember, but they present you with a very limited color palette. Standard color spaces used in graphic design, such as RGB (for Red-Green-Blue) and HSB (for Hue-Saturation-Brightness), are supported. The command **RGBColor** take three arguments, each a number between 0 and 1. They represent the relative amounts of red, green, and blue, respectively, in the final color. **Hue** takes either one argument (the color setting), or three, where the second and third are saturation and brightness levels. Each is a number between 0 and 1. You may type in values yourself (such as **RGBColor[.2, .8, .8]** or **Hue[.6, .5, .5]**), or you may do this: type an option setting such as **PlotStyle →**, and with the cursor still at the tip of the arrow go to the Insert menu and select Color…. A dialog box appears, and you can use it any way you like to choose the color you're after. When you have it, hit the OK button. You'll find the appropriate **RGBColor** setting pasted in your notebook at the position of the cursor. Experiment with both methods, direct typing and using the menu, to custom-color the **Plot** of a function of your choosing.

4. **Plot** the function $f(x) = x^2$ on the domain $-2 \leq x \leq 2$, and set **Exclusions** to {x == 1}. Note that f has no vertical asymptote at $x = 1$. What happens?

5. In order to place mesh points on the graph so that their y coordinates are equally spaced, one may set the **MeshFunctions** option to {#2&}. This notation is explained in depth in Section 8.4 on page 403, but for our purposes it will suffice to understand that **#1** refers to x and **#2** refers to y, and that the ampersand character & is needed to make it a *function*. The mesh points will be displayed at the specified values for this function. For example, a numerical **Mesh** setting of 9 indicates that there should be 9 equally spaced values. A *list* of **Mesh** values indicates that the specific values in the list should be used as values for the function. For instance, consider the input and output:

In[38]:= Plot[x², {x, 0, 10}, Mesh → 9, MeshFunctions → {#2 &},
GridLines → {None, Range[0, 100, 10]}]

Out[38]=

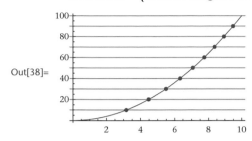

a. Replace the **None** in the input above with the appropriate of list of *x* values to add vertical **GridLines** that pass through these same mesh points.

b. Add a **GridLines** setting to the input below so that the output includes (equally spaced) vertical grid lines that pass precisely through the mesh points, and (unequally spaced) horizontal grid lines that pass through the same mesh points.

In[39]:= Plot[x², {x, 0, 10}, Mesh → 9]

Out[39]=

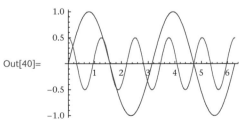

6. Add **Mesh** and **MeshFunctions** options to the input below so that the mesh points are precisely the points where the graphs of the two functions intersect.

In[40]:= Plot[{Sin[2 x], $\frac{1}{2}$ Cos[5 x]}, {x, 0, 2 π}]

Out[40]=

3.4 Investigating Functions with Manipulate

The **Manipulate** command is used to manipulate an expression in real time using the mouse (or even a gamepad controller; see Exercise 7). One of the most basic uses of **Manipulate** is to evaluate a function defined over an interval, say $1 \le x \le 10$. In such a case, the syntax is identical to that of the **Plot** command:

In[1]:= **Manipulate[x², {x, 1, 10}]**

Out[1]=

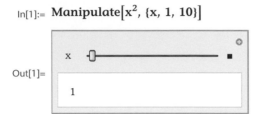

The controller, aptly called a *manipulator*, initially displays as a slider. Clicking on the ➕ button to the right of the slider, however, will reveal additional controls beneath:

Now operate the slider. It ranges over the values from 1 to 10 in this example, and the current value is displayed in the input field directly under the slider. The function value $f(x) = x^2$ is displayed below. Try it. As you position your mouse over any control button, a tooltip will appear that describes that button's function. For instance, the Play/Pause button ▸ is used to start and stop an animation, while the buttons on either side of it will advance it forward or backward one frame at a time. The double up and down arrow buttons are used to adjust the speed of the animation, and the direction button on the far right is used to determine whether the animation will play forward, backward, or oscillate (forward to the end, then backward to the beginning, and so on). You may also type a specific numerical value directly into the input field, followed by the ↵ key. Note that if you hit SHIFT-↵ (or ENTER on a Mac) after typing in the input field, you will generate a second output cell.

The **Manipulate** command in its most basic form takes two arguments, separated by a comma. The first (in this case **x²**) describes the expression to be manipulated. The second (in this case **{x,1,10}**) is an iterator. If you wish to have your variable increase in unit steps only, you can add a fourth element to the iterator that will specify the amount by which the variable will skip from one value to the next. For example, here we increment the variable x in steps of size 5. When the slider is moved, x jumps from 0 to 5 to 10, etc.

In[2]:= **Manipulate**$\left[x^2, \{x, 0, 50, 5\}\right]$

Out[2]=
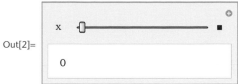

In the next example, we make a plot of the function $f(x) = x \sin(1/x)$, the right endpoint of which is controlled with a slider, while the left endpoint is fixed at 0. When the controller is moved to the left, the plot's domain narrows, and the user is afforded a zoomed-in view of the function's behavior near $x = 0$.

In[3]:= **Manipulate[Plot[x $*$ Sin[1/x], {x, 0, r}],**
        {r, .1, 2}]

Out[3]=
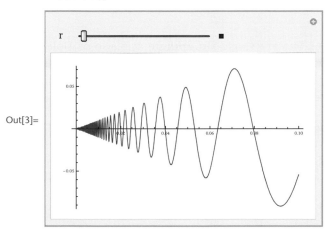

In cases such as this it would be nice to put a more descriptive label on the slider. This can be accomplished either by giving the controller variable a more descriptive name (e.g., one might use **xmax** or **rightEndpoint**), or by replacing the controller variable **r** in the iterator above by a *list* of the form {*var*, *init*, *label*}. Here *var* is the variable name, *init* is the initial value to be assumed by the variable upon evaluation, and *label* is the label you want to be displayed on the interface. For instance, below we generate the same output as above, except that we create a slider with the label right endpoint, and whose initial value upon evaluation will be 0.2.

In[4]:= **Manipulate[Plot[x ∗ Sin[1 / x], {x, 0, r}],**
$\quad$ **{{r, 0.2, "right endpoint"}, 10^{-10}, 2}]**

Out[4]=

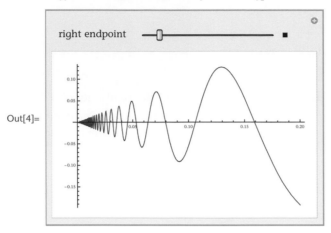

It is possible to place several controller variables in a single **Manipulate**. It is also possible to simultaneously animate all of them using their individual controls. Below we explore three directive settings for **PlotStyle**.

In[5]:= **Manipulate[Plot[x Sin[x], {x, −10, 10},**
$\quad$ **PlotStyle → Directive[Thickness[t], Dashing[{d}], Blend[{Red, Blue}, b]]],**
$\quad$ **{{t, .01, "Thickness"}, .001, .02}, {{d, .02, "Dash Size"}, 0, .04},**
$\quad$ **{{b, .5, "Percent Blue"}, 0, 1}]**

Out[5]=

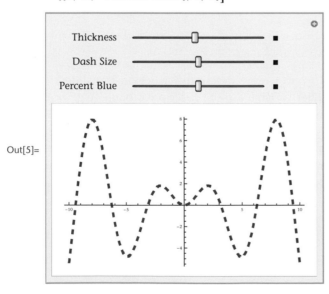

When manipulating a **Plot**, it is often desirable to include a **PlotRange** setting to maintain a fixed viewing rectangle as the controllers are moved. Here we use three controls to adjust some coefficients on a parabola:

In[6]:= **Manipulate[**
    Plot[a (x − b)^2 + c, {x, −5, 5}, PlotRange → 5, PlotLabel → "$y = a(x{-}b)^2{+}c$"],
    {a, −1, 1}, {{b, −1}, −3, 3}, {{c, 2}, −3, 3}]

Out[6]=

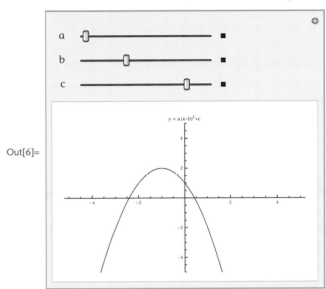

There are numerous control types available other than sliders. Below we force **Manipulate** to use a **SetterBar** (a row of buttons, only one of which can be selected at a time) simply by changing the syntax of the iterator. The values to be assumed by the controller variable are given explicitly as a list. This example is useful for exploring the roles of the **PlotPoints**, **MaxRecursion**, and **Mesh** options in producing a **Plot**. Note that the default setting for **PlotPoints** is 50, so most of the settings for this option below force *Mathematica* to produce a poor image.

In[7]:= **Manipulate[**
    Plot[Sin[4 / x], {x, −2 π, 2 π}, PlotPoints → pp, MaxRecursion → mr, Mesh → m],
    {{pp, 64, "PlotPoints"}, {4, 8, 16, 32, 64}},
    {{mr, 4, "MaxRecursion"}, {0, 1, 2, 3, 4}}, {{m, Full, "Mesh"}, {Full, All, None}}]

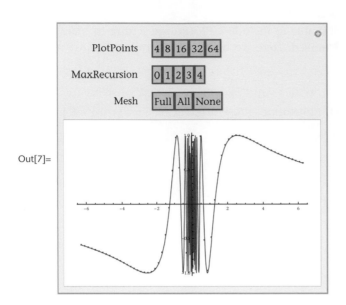

Out[7]=

The control type adapts to the syntax used in the iterator for that control. For instance, if a list of values associated with a controller variable contains six or more items, the controller will change from a **SetterBar** (as in the previous example) to a **PopupMenu**. While a **PopupMenu** is desirable if there is a *very* long list of choices, we prefer a simple **SetterBar** as long as there is room for it. In the next example we override the default behavior with an explicit **ControlType** option setting.

In[8]:= **Manipulate[**
   Plot[f[x], {x, 0, 4 π}, Ticks → {Range[0, 4 π, π / 2], Automatic}, PlotLabel → f[x]],
   {{f, Tan, "function"}, {Sin, Cos, Sec, Csc, Tan, Cot}, ControlType → SetterBar}]

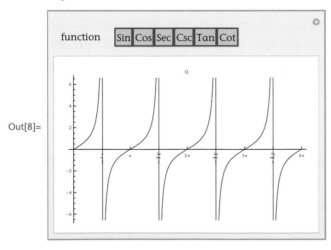

Out[8]=

There are many other useful controller types. For instance, you can produce the controller known as **Slider2D** by creating a **Manipulate** variable whose value is set to an *ordered pair* of the form {x,y} (i.e.

a point in the plane), and specifying its bounds as {*xmin,ymin*} and {*xmax,ymax*}. Below we illustrate this by letting the user manipulate the **AxesOrigin** setting with a two-dimensional slider:

In[9]:= **Manipulate[Plot[x Sin[x], {x, −20, 20}, AxesOrigin → pt, PlotRange → 20],**
     {{pt, {0, 0}, "Move the axes: "}, {−20, −20}, {20, 20}}, ControlPlacement → Left]

Out[9]=

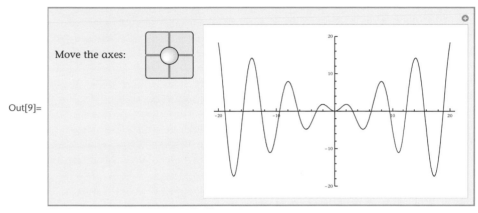

Another means of manipulating a point in a graphic is to use an iterator of the form {*var*,**Locator**}, as shown below. Drag the **Locator** icon with your mouse to move it directly across the graph, or simply click on the graphic to move the **Locator** to that location. The {**0,0**} in the input below specifies the initial position of the locator when the cell is first evaluated.

In[10]:= **Manipulate[Plot[x Sin[x], {x, −20, 20}, AxesOrigin → pt, PlotRange → 20],**
     {{pt, {0, 0}}, Locator}]

Out[10]=

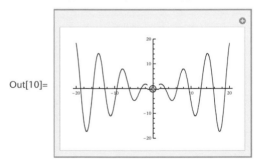

The simple iterator structure {*var*, *colorSetting*} will produce a color slider. You can drag over the color field with the mouse to adjust the color continuously in real time.

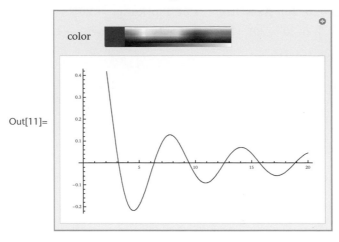

In[11]:= $\mathbf{Manipulate}\left[\mathbf{Plot}\left[\dfrac{\mathbf{Sin[x]}}{\mathbf{x}}, \{\mathbf{x, 0, 20}\}, \mathbf{PlotStyle} \to \mathbf{color}\right], \{\mathbf{color, Blue}\}\right]$

Out[11]=

A complete listing of permissible iterator syntax structures and their corresponding default controller types can be had in the More Information section of the documentation page for **Manipulate**. We summarize this information in Table 3.1.

Iterator Form	Default ControlType
$\{u, u_{min}, \infty\}$	Animator
$\{u, u_{min}, u_{max}\}$	Manipulator
$\{u, u_{min}, u_{max}, du\}$	discrete Manipulator with step du
$\{u, \{x_{min}, y_{min}\}, \{x_{max}, y_{max}\}\}$	Slider2D
$\{u, \{x_{min}, y_{min}\}, \{x_{max}, y_{max}\}, \{dx, dy\}\}$	discrete Slider2D with horizontal step dx, vertical step dy
$\{u, \text{Locator}\}$	Locator
$\{u, \{\text{True, False}\}\}$	Checkbox
$\{u, \{value_1, value_2, ...\}\},$	PopupMenu (or SetterBar if fewer than 6 items)
$\{u, color\}$	ColorSlider
$\{u\}$	InputField

Table 3.1 Iterator structures for Manipulate variables and the default control types they produce.

When making a **Manipulate** object it is important to put the right controllers in place for the task at hand. Options may be added to any of the iterator forms so that one may specify a controller other than the default. For example one might replace the **Manipulate** iterator $\{\mathbf{u, 0, 10}\}$ by $\{\mathbf{u, 0, 10, ControlType} \to \mathbf{VerticalSlider, ControlPlacement} \to \mathbf{Left}\}$. We summarize some valid **ControlType** settings for each iterator form in the Table 3.2 (with the default setting in bold).

Iterator Form	Valid ControlType Settings
$\{u, u_{min}, u_{max}\}$	Animator, InputField, **Manipulator**, Slider, Slider2D, VerticalSlider, None
$\{u, u_{min}, u_{max}, du\}$	Animator, InputField, **Manipulator**, PopupMenu, RadioButtonBar, SetterBar, Slider, Slider2D, VerticalSlider, None
$\{u, \{x_{min}, y_{min}\}, \{x_{max}, y_{max}\}\}$	InputField, Locator, **Slider2D**, None
$\{u, \{x_{min}, y_{min}\}, \{x_{max}, y_{max}\}, \{dx, dy\}\}$	InputField, Locator, **Slider2D**, None
$\{u, \text{Locator}\}$	**Locator**, None
$\{u, \{\text{True, False}\}\}$	Animator, **Checkbox**, CheckboxBar, InputField, Manipulator, Opener, PopupMenu, RadioButtonBar, SetterBar, Slider, VerticalSlider, None
$\{u, \{value_1, value_2, ...\}\}$	Animator, Checkbox, CheckboxBar, InputField, Manipulator, **PopupMenu**, RadioButtonBar, SetterBar, Slider, TogglerBar, VerticalSlider, None
$\{u, color\}$	ColorSetter, **ColorSlider**, InputField, None
$\{u\}$	**InputField**, None

Table 3.2 Valid control type settings for the various iterator structures used in Manipulate.

Other Dynamic Display Commands

While **Manipulate** is the single most flexible and powerful command for creating dynamic user environments, there are a number of other commands which produce dynamic output of some kind. For instance, one may use the command **Animate** to produce an animation. The syntax is identical to that of **Manipulate**.

Each of the commands **ListAnimate**, **FlipView**, **PopupView**, **OpenerView**, and **SlideView** accepts a list of expressions, and creates an environment in which the user can dynamically interact with the individual expressions. **OpenerView** accepts a list containing only two expressions: a header, and an expression to display when it is in the "open" state.

In[12]:= **OpenerView[{Style["click the triangle", "Text"], Style["Hah, you did it!", "Section"]}]**

Out[12]= ▶ click the triangle

The commands **MenuView** and **TabView** accept lists of the form $\{label_1 \rightarrow expression_1, label_2 \rightarrow expression_2,...\}$, and return a menu of labels or a collection of tabs, respectively, associated with their corresponding expressions.

In[13]:= TabView[{"sine" → Plot[Sin[x], {x, 0, 2π}], "cosine" → Plot[Cos[x], {x, 0, 2π}]},
    ImageSize → Automatic]

Out[13]=

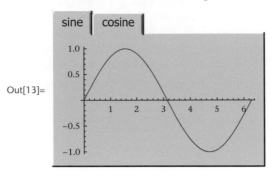

Exercises 3.4

1. The following simple **Manipulate** has two sliders: one for *x* and one for *y*. Make a **Manipulate** that also has output {*x,y*}, but that has a single **Slider2D** controller.

In[14]:= Manipulate[{x, y}, {x, 0, 1}, {y, 0, 1}]

Out[14]=

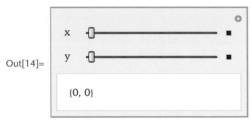

2. Make a **Manipulate** of a **Plot** where the user can adjust the **AspectRatio** in real time, from a starting value of 1/5 (five times as wide as it is tall) to an ending value of 5 (five times as tall as it is wide). Set **ImageSize** to {**Automatic, 128**} so the height remains constant as the slider is moved.

3. Make a **Manipulate** of a **Plot** where the user can adjust the **Background** in real time.

    a. Use the setting **Background → RGBColor[*r*, *g*, *b*]**, where *r*, *g*, and *b* are **Manipulate** variables that range from 0 to 1. They will control the relative amounts of red, green, and blue in the background, respectively. This allows you to interactively explore the RGB color space.

    b. Use the setting **Background → Hue[*h*, *s*, *b*]**, where *h*, *s*, and *b* are **Manipulate** variables that range from 0 to 1. They will control the values of hue, saturation, and brightness in the background, respectively. This allows you to interactively explore the HSBcolor space.

4. It is often the case that one wants to create a **Manipulate** that includes some sort of explanatory text that can be manipulated. A robust means of accomplishing this is to (1) transform any variable quantity in the text to a **String** using **ToString**, and (2) join together the static and variable text strings with **StringExpression**.

a. You can type ~~ between two text strings to sew them together into a single string. Technically, you are invoking the **StringExpression** command when you do this. Try it; type and enter the following. We use **FullForm** so that the double quotes will display.

> "This is a string" ~~ " and so is this." // **FullForm**

b. Now explain what's going on here:

In[15]:= Manipulate[Style["The square root of " ~~ ToString[x] ~~

" is " ~~ ToString[N[$\sqrt{x}$]] ~~ ".", "Subsubsection"],

{{x, 2}, 1, 10}]

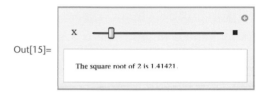

Out[15]=

c. Create a **Manipulate** showing a **Plot** of the sine function, with a **PlotLabel** that indicates the value of the function for any value of x between $-\pi$ and π. The user can control x with a slider.

5. The following input will create a useful interactive interface in which every available option for the **Plot** command appears in a popup menu. Select an option in this menu, and the usage message for that option is displayed. Try it (Courtesy of Lou D'Andria, Wolfram Research).

> Manipulate[
> ToExpression[SymbolName[option] ~~ "::usage"],
> {option, Map[First, Options[Plot]]}]

a. Modify the input above to create an option explorer for the **Grid** command, and use it to get information on the **ItemSize** option.

b. See if you can figure out how this **Manipulate** works. This will entail finding information in the Documentation Center on the commands **Map**, **First**, **Options**, **SymbolName**, **ToExpression**, and **StringExpression** (~~). Note that by replacing **Plot** (in the last line) by any other command that accepts options, an option explorer for that command can be generated.

6. Use **TabView** with two tabs to produce the output below. You'll have to find the answer to the riddle on your own, or look at the solution. (Riddle by Alexandra Torrence, age 10.)

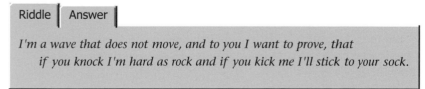

7. This exercise discusses the use of gamepad controllers to operate a **Manipulate** output. If you have a gamepad for your computer the first thing to do is to plug it in, select the cell bracket for a **Manipulate** and try it. In most cases it's plug and play. To bind a particular **Manipulate** local variable to a given controller axis, replace the iterator {*var*, *spec*} for that variable with *axisName* → {*var*,*spec*}, where *axisName* is the string name of the given controller axis. Typical axis names are given below. Create a **Manipulate** where you bind a specific local variable to a specific controller axis.

one-dimensional: "X1", "Y1", "Z1", "X2", "Y2"
two-dimensional: "XY1", "XY2"
buttons: "Button 1", "Button 2"

3.5 Producing a Table of Values

It is often handy to produce a table of function values for various inputs. Here is a table of the squares of the first ten positive whole numbers:

In[1]:= **f[x_] := x^2**

In[2]:= **Table[f[x], {x, 1, 10}]**

Out[2]= {1, 4, 9, 16, 25, 36, 49, 64, 81, 100}

Like **Plot** and **Manipulate**, the **Table** command takes two arguments, separated by a comma. The first describes the contents of each table entry, while the second (in this case {**x, 1, 10**}) is an iterator. Unlike **Plot** and **Manipulate**, however, the values of the variable will increment by 1 (by default) in a **Table**. As with **Manipulate**, a fourth number can be added to the iterator to specify the step size.

In[3]:= **Table[f[x], {x, 0, 50, 5}]**

Out[3]= {0, 25, 100, 225, 400, 625, 900, 1225, 1600, 2025, 2500}

You can also shorten the iterator to contain only two items—the name of the variable and a stopping number. When you do this, *Mathematica* starts at 1 and increments the variable in steps of 1 until the stopping number is reached. So for instance, using the iterator {**x, 10**} is the same as using the iterator {**x, 1, 10**}:

In[4]:= **Table[f[x], {x, 10}]**

Out[4]= {1, 4, 9, 16, 25, 36, 49, 64, 81, 100}

The output of the **Table** command is a basic data structure in *Mathematica* called a *list*. A list is comprised of an opening curly bracket, individual items (such as numbers) separated by commas, and a closing curly bracket.

Table will also accept a special iterator structure of the form {*var*,{*value$_1$*,*value$_2$*,...}}. In this case the variable will assume the explicit values in the given list.

In[5]:= **Table[f[x], {x, {1, 7, 12, 20}}]**

Out[5]= {1, 49, 144, 400}

One of the most useful applications of the **Table** command is producing something that actually looks like a table. We accomplish this by constructing a **Table** where the first argument is itself a list. The result is a list of lists. We then apply **Grid** to the result in order to create a two-dimensional display in which each inner list becomes a row. Here's an example where both the input value x and the output value $f(x)$ for a function are given in each row:

In[6]:= **data = Table[{x, f[x]}, {x, 5}]**

Out[6]= {{1, 1}, {2, 4}, {3, 9}, {4, 16}, {5, 25}}

In[7]:= **Grid[data]**

Out[7]=
```
1   1
2   4
3   9
4  16
5  25
```

Grid will display any list of lists in a two-dimensional format like this; each sublist appears as a separate row. Numerous options are available that allow all manner of presentation possibilities. But perhaps the most simple formatting tip is to apply **Text** to an entire grid. This will apply textual formatting to the individual items (numbers in this case) that occupy each grid cell. Here we use prefix form (@, see Section 2.8 on page 37) instead of square brackets when applying the **Text** command, and add the **Grid** option setting **Alignment → Right** to align each column to the right.

In[8]:= **Text @ Grid[data, Alignment → Right]**

Out[8]=
```
1   1
2   4
3   9
4  16
5  25
```

Another simple but valuable technique is to add headings to the columns of a table by *prepending* an additional row containing these headings to your table data. Typically each item in the header row is a *string*; this is accomplished by enclosing each item in double quotes.

In[9]:= **tableContents = Prepend[data, {"x", "x²"}]**

Out[9]= {{x, x²}, {1, 1}, {2, 4}, {3, 9}, {4, 16}, {5, 25}}

In[10]:= **Text @ Grid[tableContents, Alignment → Right,**
Dividers → {Center, {False, True}}, Spacings → 2]

Out[10]=

x	x^2
1	1
2	4
3	9
4	16
5	25

The **Spacings** option can be used to add a bit of space between successive columns. The **Dividers** option is used above to add dividing lines in a **Grid**. The setting is of the form {*vertical dividers,horizontal dividers*}. The **Center** setting specifies that there are no vertical lines on the far left or far right, only between the columns. The {**False, True**} specifies the horizontal dividing lines: there is no line above the first row, while there is one above the second row, and none for any subsequent rows. The following syntax may also be used for **Dividers**. It can be handy in cases like this where few dividers are required. It simply specifies that only the *second* vertical divider and the *second* horizontal divider will be rendered, and no others.

In[11]:= **Text @ Grid[tableContents, Alignment → Right,**
Dividers → {2 → True, 2 → True}, Spacings → 2]

Out[11]=

x	x^2
1	1
2	4
3	9
4	16
5	25

With these tools in hand, you can create tables to your heart's content. Here we use powers of ten as the values of the function variable, and the simple **Dividers → All** setting to put in all possible row and column dividers:

In[12]:= **Clear[data];**
data = Table[{10^n, f[10^n]}, {n, 0, 5}]

Out[13]= {{1, 1}, {10, 100}, {100, 10 000}, {1000, 1 000 000},
{10 000, 100 000 000}, {100 000, 10 000 000 000}}

In[14]:= **Text @ Grid[Prepend[data, {"x", "x^2"}],**
Alignment → Right, Dividers → All, Spacings → 2]

Out[14]=

x	x^2
1	1
10	100
100	10 000
1000	1 000 000
10 000	100 000 000
100 000	10 000 000 000

As a last example, here is how you can make a table that displays the values for multiple functions, in this case $f(x) = x^2$ and $g(x) = 2^x$:

In[15]:= **Clear[data];**
data = Table[{x, x^2, 2^x}, {x, 10}]

Out[16]= {{1, 1, 2}, {2, 4, 4}, {3, 9, 8}, {4, 16, 16}, {5, 25, 32},
        {6, 36, 64}, {7, 49, 128}, {8, 64, 256}, {9, 81, 512}, {10, 100, 1024}}

In[17]:= **Text @ Grid[Prepend[data, {"x", "x^2", "2^x"}],**
Alignment → Right, Dividers → {Center, {False, True}}, Spacings → 2]

Out[17]=

x	x^2	2^x
1	1	2
2	4	4
3	9	8
4	16	16
5	25	32
6	36	64
7	49	128
8	64	256
9	81	512
10	100	1024

The three most common types of brackets

Now is a good time to review the three most commonly used brackets in *Mathematica*. Parentheses ( ) are used to group terms in algebraic expressions. Square brackets [ ] are used to enclose the arguments of functions. And curly brackets { } are used to enclose lists.

Manipulating a Grid

Here is a grid with a header row, and a second row of content. The values in this second row can be manipulated. This gives a compact table that allows one to display the row of his or her choosing:

In[18]:= **Manipulate[**
      Text @ Grid[{{"x", "x²"}, {x, x²}}, Dividers → All, ItemSize → 5], {{x, 5.3}, 1, 10, .1}]

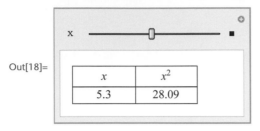

Out[18]=

The following shows a simple Celsius to Fahrenheit conversion tool:

In[19]:= **Manipulate[Text @ Grid[{{"C", "F"}, {c, 1.8 c + 32}}, Dividers → All, ItemSize → 5],**
      {{c, 0}, −40, 100, 1}]

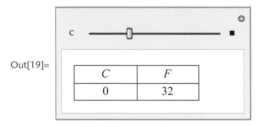

Out[19]=

The two examples above make use of the **ItemSize** option to the **Grid** command. When set to a single numerical value (as we did here) it specifies the width of each cell in the grid in *ems* (the width of the letter m). Other common settings for this option include **All** (which specifies that all cells have identical width and height values, determined by the content of the largest cells), or a list of two numerical values such as {5, 2} (which specifies the width of each cell in *ems* and the height of each cell in *line heights*, respectively). When manipulating a grid, it is a good idea to set **ItemSize** to a specific numerical value (or to a list of two such values) in order to keep the table dimensions steady as the controller is adjusted.

Exercises 3.5

1. The **Partition** command is used to break a single list into sublists of equal length. It is useful for breaking up a list into rows for display within a **Grid**.

    a. Enter the following inputs and discuss the outputs.

       Range[100]

Partition[Range[100], 10]

b. Format a table of the first 100 integers, with twenty digits per row. The first two rows, for example, should look like this:

1 2 3 4 5 6 7 8 9 10 11 12 13 14 15 16 17 18 19 20
21 22 23 24 25 26 27 28 29 30 31 32 33 34 35 36 37 38 39 40

c. Make the same table as above, but use only the **Table** and **Range** commands. Do not use **Partition**.

d. Make the same table as above, but use only the **Table** command (twice). Do not use **Partition** or **Range**.

2. The **Style** command is used to apply a particular style to an expression.

a. Enter the following inputs and discuss the outputs.

Style[4, Red]

Style[4, 72]

Style[4, "Section"]

Style[4, FontFamily → "Helvetica", FontWeight → "Bold"]

b. One can apply a particular style to *every* item in a **Grid** by using the entire **Grid** as the first argument to **Style**. Create an output that matches that below. The font is Comic Sans MS, and the text should be blue.

```
1   1    1    1
2   4    8    16
3   9    27   81
4   16   64   256
5   25   125  625
```

c. Alternately, one can apply style elements to an entire grid by selecting the cell bracket of the cell containing the grid, and visiting the Format menu. For instance, Format ▷ Text Color ▷ Blue will make all the text blue. Reproduce the **Grid** above, this time using the menu items to change the style.

3. A statement that is either true or false is called a *predicate*; in *Mathematica* a predicate is any expression that evaluates to **True** or **False**. In this exercise you will learn how to use predicates to apply **Style**s selectively.

a. There are many built-in predicate commands. Most end in the letter **Q** (for "Query"). Enter the following inputs and discuss the outputs.

? PrimeQ

? *Q

b. The **If** command is used to generate one output if a specified condition (i.e., a predicate) is true, and another if that condition is false. The predicate is the first argument to **If**. The next argument is what is returned if the predicate is true (**If** is discussed in Section 8.5). A third argument specifies the expression to be returned if the predicate is false. Enter the following input and discuss the output.

$$\text{Table}\big[\text{If}\big[\text{PrimeQ[n], Style[n, Red]}\big], \text{n}\big], \{\text{n, 100}\}\big]$$

c. Format a table of the first 100 integers, with ten digits per row. In this table, make all prime numbers red.

d. Format a table of the first 100 integers, with ten digits per row. In this table, make all *squarefree* numbers blue and underlined. Note: An integer is squarefree if none of its divisors (other than 1) are perfect squares.

e. Format a table of the first 100 integers, with ten digits per row. In this table, make all *prime powers* orange and italicized. Note: An integer is a prime power if it is equal to p^n, where p is prime and n is a positive integer.

4. The **Sum** command has a syntax similar to that of **Table**.

a. Use the Sum command to evaluate the following expression:

$$1^3 + 2^3 + 3^3 + 4^3 + 5^3 + 6^3 + 7^3 + 8^3 + 9^3 + 10^3 + 11^3 + 12^3 + 13^3 + 14^3 + 15^3 + 16^3 + 17^3 + 18^3 + 19^3 + 20^3$$

b. Make a table of values for $x = 1, 2, \ldots, 10$ for the function

$$f(x) =$$
$$1 + 2^x + 3^x + 4^x + 5^x + 6^x + 7^x + 8^x + 9^x + 10^x + 11^x + 12^x + 13^x + 14^x + 15^x + 16^x + 17^x + 18^x + 19^x + 20^x$$

c. Plot $f(x)$ on the domain $1 \leq x \leq 10$.

5. Comments can be inserted directly into your input code. Any text placed between the (* and *) tokens will be ignored by the kernel when an input is entered. Comments do not affect the manner in which your code is executed, but they can be helpful to you or someone else who has to read and understand the code later. Look at the *solution* to the *next* exercise to see an example in which comments are used to help a reader find each of four items in a somewhat complex two-by-two **Grid**.

6. Use a two-by-two **Grid** within **Manipulate** to create the interface below for zooming in on a graph of the sine function. The "Center" controller corresponds to a variable named **x0**, and the "Zoom Level" controller corresponds to a variable named δ. The iterator for the lower **Plot** is of the form {x0-δ,x0+δ}.

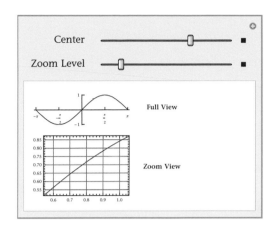

7. In this exercise you will explore the syntax for applying options to a **Grid**. Mastery of this syntax will allow you to construct stunningly beautiful tables. There are two common syntax forms that work for several options. To illustrate the possibilities we use the **Dividers** option, which specifies the placement and style of vertical and horizontal dividing lines in a **Grid**. First enter the input below to generate a 10×10 table of invisible data (each entry is simply a string comprised of a single space character). Note: The **Partition** command is discussed in Exercise 1.

> **emptyTable = Partition[Table[" ", {100}], 10];**

a. The simple setting **Dividers → All** will insert every possible line. But other single word settings such as **Gray** are permissible. Enter the inputs below, and discuss the outputs.

> **Grid[emptyTable, Dividers → Gray]**
>
> **Grid[emptyTable, Dividers → Dotted]**
>
> **Grid[emptyTable, Dividers → Thick]**
>
> **Grid[emptyTable, Dividers → Directive[Thin, Orange]]**

b. More control may be obtained with the syntax **Dividers → {*x setting*, *y setting*}**. Typically the *x* setting is a list of values relating to positions within a row, and is used to specify the style and placement of vertical items. Enter the input below. Here the *x* setting is **{Black, {Gray}, Black}**, and the *y* setting is **None**. What effect does this have?

> **Grid[emptyTable, Dividers → {{Black, {Gray}, Black}, None}]**

c. How would you produce the output below?

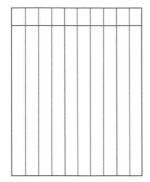

d. Take your last input and add the following option setting, then explain the output.

Background → {None, {Lighter[Gray, .7], {Lighter[Blue, .9], Lighter[Yellow, .9]}}}

e. Other options that utilize these syntactical conventions are **Alignment**, **Spacings**, **ItemSize**, and **ItemStyle**. Some simple but useful **Alignment** settings to try are **Alignment → Right** or **Alignment→"."** (to align numbers at the decimal point). Produce the following **Grid** using the options mentioned. The Helvetica font is used for the entries in the first column, while the default text font is used in the second. Once you can do this, you will be equipped to produce a rich assortment of useful tables.

10^{-5}	0.00001
10^{-4}	0.0001
10^{-3}	0.001
10^{-2}	0.01
10^{-1}	0.1
10^{0}	1
10^{1}	10.
10^{2}	100.
10^{3}	1000.
10^{4}	10 000.
10^{5}	100 000.

3.6 Working with Piecewise Defined Functions

Certain functions are defined by different rules over various disjoint pieces of their domain, so-called *piecewise defined functions*. For instance a function may be defined by the rule $f(x) = x$ when x is between zero and one, inclusive; by the rule $f(x) = -x$ when x is strictly between negative one and zero; and by $f(x) = 1$ for all other values of x. In standard mathematical notation we write:

$$f(x) = \begin{cases} x & 0 \le x \le 1 \\ -x & -1 < x < 0 \\ 1 & \text{otherwise} \end{cases}$$

Here "otherwise" means that either $x > 1$ or $x \le -1$. How can this be conveyed to *Mathematica*? It is a simple matter to enter a piecewise function directly from the keyboard in standard notation. To do so, first type **f[x_]:=**, then create the single bracket by typing ⌜ESC⌝pw⌜ESC⌝, and finally produce a grid to the right of the bracket by typing ⌜CTRL⌝ ,]. If more than two rows are needed, type ⌜CTRL⌝ ↵]. Each time you hit ⌜CTRL⌝ ↵] you will add one additional row. Now move the cursor to the first placeholder and type in a function expression, then use the ⌜TAB⌝ key to move to the adjacent placeholder and type a logical expression. This is typically an inequality such as $0 \le x \le 1$, but in all cases is an expression that evaluates to either True or False when x is a specific real number. Fill in the remaining pairs of placeholders; the first in each pair holds a function expression, the second a logical expression. The following example shows how one would enter the function above. Note that the logical expression in the final row can simply contain the expression **True**, which conveys the meaning that this rule is applied to all values of x for which the logical expressions in earlier rows are **False**; that is, it behaves like the word "otherwise" in the example above. When you're finished typing, enter the cell.

In[1]:= **f[x_] :=** $\begin{cases} \mathbf{x} & \mathbf{0 \le x \le 1} \\ \mathbf{-x} & \mathbf{-1 < x < 0} \\ \mathbf{1} & \mathbf{True} \end{cases}$

Once entered, this function behaves like any other. You may **Plot** it, **Manipulate** it, apply to it any transformations that you might apply to any other function. In short, it behaves exactly as it should. For instance:

In[2]:= **Plot[f[x], {x, −2, 2}]**

Out[2]=

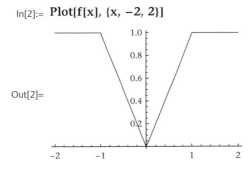

The underlying *Mathematica* command that is being utilized to create the function above is called **Piecewise**. In most cases it is easiest to use the syntax above, which has the effect of calling the **Piecewise** command. Equivalently, one can use **Piecewise** directly; the following example shows how to enter the function above using this syntax:

In[3]:= **f[x_] := Piecewise[{{x, 0 ≤ x ≤ 1}, {−x, −1 < x < 0}}, 1]**

This syntax can be useful when you are working with a function that has many "pieces," for you can then use the **Table** command to generate the first argument programmatically. See Exercise 3.

Regardless of how a piecewise function is entered, it is important to understand some syntactical conventions regarding the logical expressions (such as $0 \le x \le 1$) that specify when a function rule is applied. In particular, the logical connective **&&** can be used to mean "and," and **||** can be used to mean "or." The connectives allow complex conditions to be specified. Here's an example:

$$\text{In[4]:= } g[x\_] := \begin{cases} x^2 & (-2 \le x \le -1) \,||\, (1 \le x \le 2) \\ 1 & -1 < x < 1 \\ 4 & \text{True} \end{cases}$$

Here is an equivalent formulation, using the absolute value function:

$$\text{In[5]:= } g[x\_] := \begin{cases} x^2 & 1 \le \text{Abs}[x] \le 2 \\ 1 & \text{Abs}[x] < 1 \\ 4 & \text{True} \end{cases}$$

In[6]:= $\text{Plot}\big[g[x], \{x, -3, 3\}, \text{PlotRange} \to \{0, 5\}\big]$

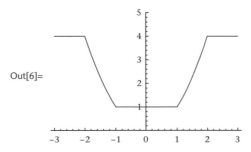

Out[6]=

Piecewise functions provide a rich setting in which to explore *discontinuous* functions. **Plot** is aware of discontinuities appearing at the boundary between regions, and excludes such points. This leads to accurate plotting of such discontinuous functions.

In[7]:= $\text{Plot}\Big[\begin{cases} 1 & x \ge 1 \\ -1 & x < 1 \end{cases}, \{x, -3, 3\}\Big]$

Out[7]=

The **ExclusionsStyle** option works as it should in such cases:

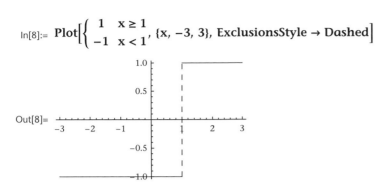

In[8]:= Plot$\left[\left\{\begin{matrix} 1 & x \geq 1 \\ -1 & x < 1 \end{matrix}\right., \{x, -3, 3\}, \textbf{ExclusionsStyle} \to \textbf{Dashed}\right]$

Out[8]=

Exercises 3.6

1. Show the second condition in the last example above could just as well be **True**.

2. Make a plot of the piecewise function below, and comment on its shape.

$$f(x) = \begin{cases} 0 & x < 0 \\ \frac{x^2}{2} & 0 \leq x < 1 \\ -x^2 + 3x - \frac{3}{2} & 1 \leq x < 2 \\ \frac{1}{2}(3 - x)^2 & 2 \leq x < 3 \\ 0 & 3 \leq x \end{cases}$$

3. A *step function* assumes a constant value between consecutive integers n and $n + 1$. Make a plot of the step function $f(x)$ whose value is n^2 when $n \leq x < n + 1$. Use the domain $0 \leq x < 20$.

3.7 Plotting Implicitly Defined Functions

An *implicitly defined function* is given as an equation relating two variables, such as $x^2 + y^2 = 1$ (which describes a circle of radius one). Here the y variable is not given *explicitly* as a function of the x variable, but rather the x and y terms are wrapped up in an equation; hence the term "implicitly" defined function. In order to plot an implicitly defined function, use the **ContourPlot** command. Use the implicit equation for the first argument (with a double equal sign == either typed from the keyboard or inserted via the BasicMathInput palette), and include two iterators: one for x, a second for y.

In[1]:= $\text{ContourPlot}\left[x^2 + y^2 == 1, \{x, -1, 1\}, \{y, -1, 1\}\right]$

Out[1]=

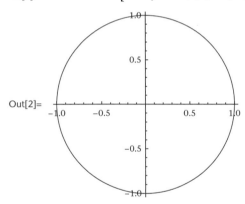

By default, a **ContourPlot** will display with a frame and no coordinate axes, but it is a simple matter to change this behavior.

In[2]:= $\text{ContourPlot}\left[x^2 + y^2 == 1, \{x, -1, 1\}, \{y, -1, 1\}, \text{Frame} \rightarrow \text{False}, \text{Axes} \rightarrow \text{True}\right]$

Out[2]=

Note that by default the **AspectRatio** of a **ContourPlot** will be set to 1, meaning that the coordinate axes will be scaled as necessary to produce a perfectly square plot. Such a plot can be misleading; for instance, the ellipse below looks like a circle!

In[3]:= **ContourPlot**$\left[x^2 + 4y^2 == 1, \{x, -1, 1\}, \{y, -.5, .5\}\right]$

Out[3]=

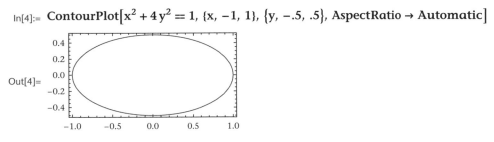

Set the **AspectRatio** to **Automatic** to give your axes a uniform scale. We do not recommend this as a default setting, however, as it is all too easy to ask for a plot that is thousands of times higher than it is wide. But in cases such as the ellipse above where a common scaling of axes is called for, this setting is important.

In[4]:= **ContourPlot**$\left[x^2 + 4y^2 == 1, \{x, -1, 1\}, \{y, -.5, .5\}, \textbf{AspectRatio} \rightarrow \textbf{Automatic}\right]$

Out[4]=

ContourPlot works in a fundamentally different way than **Plot** does, as there is no explicit expression to evaluate for each numerical value of x. Rather, it samples points in the rectangular region specified by the two iterators, and recursively applies an adaptive algorithm in an attempt to find a smooth curve (or curves) satisfying the given equation. It is possible that in some cases the default parameters governing the algorithm are insufficient to produce an accurate plot. For example, note the jagged appearance in some parts of the output below:

In[5]:= $\textbf{ContourPlot}\left[\textbf{Sin}\left[x^2\right] + y^2 == \textbf{Cos}[x*y], \{x, -10, 10\}, \{y, -1, 1\}\right]$

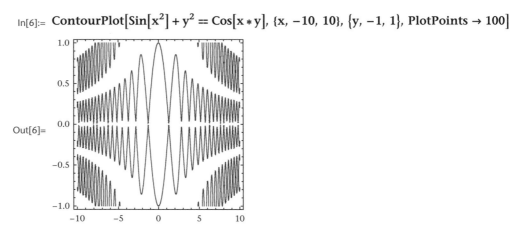

Out[5]=

To cure a case of the "jaggies," try setting the **PlotPoints** option to a large value such as 25, 50, or 100. **PlotPoints** controls how many points are initially sampled in the domain. Larger values tend to produce more accurate plots but may lead to significantly slower evaluation time, so use the lowest setting that produces a satisfactory plot.

In[6]:= $\textbf{ContourPlot}\left[\textbf{Sin}\left[x^2\right] + y^2 == \textbf{Cos}[x*y], \{x, -10, 10\}, \{y, -1, 1\}, \textbf{PlotPoints} \rightarrow 100\right]$

Out[6]=

Several implicitly defined functions can be simultaneously displayed by providing a *list* of equations as the first argument to **ContourPlot**. Mousing over a curve on the plot yields a tooltip displaying the equation corresponding to that curve, so it is easy to interpret the output when multiple equations are plotted.

In[7]:= **ContourPlot**$\left[\left\{2\,x^2 + y^2 == 1,\ 2\,x^2 - y^2 == 1\right\}, \{x, -1, 1\}, \{y, -1, 1\}\right]$

Out[7]=

As with the **Plot** command, the option setting **Mesh → Full** will reveal which points are sampled initially, while the setting **Mesh → All** will reveal the final points used to construct the curves after the algorithm has run. The following **Manipulate** is a useful aid for understanding how the options **PlotPoints** and **MaxRecursion** work in a **ContourPlot**. When **MaxRecursion** is set to 0, no iterations take place and the initial and final meshes are the same. We saw a similar example for **Plot** in Section 3.4 on page 79.

The three types of equal signs

Now is a good time to review the three types of equal signs that are used in *Mathematica*. Each is used for a separate purpose so it is imperative that they be used appropriately. A single equal sign = is used to assign a name to an expression, such as $a = 3$ or myPlot = Plot[2 x, {x, -2, 2}]. A colon-equal sign := is used to make a delayed assignment to an expression and is useful for defining functions, such as $f[x\_] := x^2$. A double equal sign == is used to express an equation, such as $2\,x^2 - y^2 == 1$.

In[8]:= **Manipulate[**
   ContourPlot[$2x^2 - y^2 = 1$, $\{x, -2, 2\}$, $\{y, -2, 2\}$,
      PlotPoints → plotPoints, MaxRecursion → maxRecursion, Mesh → mesh],
      $\{\{plotPoints, 4\}, \{2, 3, 4, 8\}\}$, $\{\{maxRecursion, 2\}, \{0, 1, 2, 3\}\}$, **{mesh, {Full, All}}]**

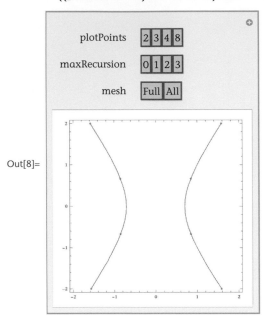

Out[8]=

Exercises 3.7

1. The option **ContourStyle** (not **PlotStyle**) is used to change the style of a **ContourPlot**. Plot the implicit function $x^2 - \sin(xy) == 3$ as a thick, blue, dotted line.

2. If you ever wish to simultaneously view contour plots of implicitly defined functions of the form $f(x, y) == z_1$, $f(x, y) == z_2$, $f(x, y) == z_3$, and so on, where z_1, z_2, etc... are constants, the following syntax will work. Suppose, for instance, $f(x, y) = x^2 - y^2$, and the z-values are -2, -1, 0, 1, and 2. Enter the following input to see overlaid plots of $x^2 - y^2 = -2$, $x^2 - y^2 = -1$, $x^2 - y^2 = 0$, $x^2 - y^2 = 1$, and $x^2 - y^2 = 2$.

   ContourPlot[$x^2 - y^2$, $\{x, -2, 2\}$, $\{y, -2, 2\}$,
      Contours → {-2, -1, 0, 1, 2}, ContourShading → False]

3. Piecewise functions may be implicitly defined. Let $f(x, y) = \begin{cases} x^2 - y^2 & x < y \\ 1 - \dfrac{x^2}{y^2} & x \geq y \end{cases}$. Make a **ContourPlot**

of the implicitly defined function $f(x, y) = \frac{1}{2}$ for $0 < x < 3$ and $0 < y < 3$.

3.8 Combining Graphics

So you want to combine two or more graphics together as one? There are many possibilities here, so we'll address each in turn.

Superimposing Plots

It is often desirable to view two or more plots together. If you simply want to plot several functions on the same set of axes, enter a *list* containing these functions as the first argument to the **Plot** command and you'll have it:

In[1]:= **Clear[f, g];**
　　　f[x_] := 1 − x;
　　　g[x_] := x²;

In[4]:= **Plot[{f[x], g[x], f[x] * g[x]}, {x, −1, 1}]**

Out[4]=

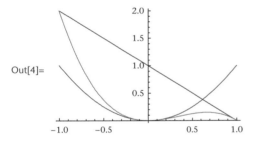

On your monitor the three functions are given three distinct colors. To better distinguish between them, one may wrap the list of functions with the **Tooltip** command. When you mouseover any curve in the resulting plot, a tooltip will pop up displaying that function's expression. Note that the output in printed form is indistinguishable from the prior output, so this feature is only useful in a live session.

In[5]:= **Plot[Tooltip[{f[x], g[x], f[x] * g[x]}], {x, −1, 1}]**

Out[5]=

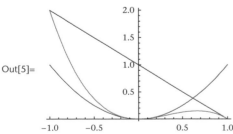

One may also use the **PlotStyle** option to change the appearance of the three functions. This is sometimes useful for printed output when using a black and white printer. Just set **PlotStyle** to a list of three directives. These will be applied to the functions (in the order listed).

In[6]:= **Plot[{f[x], g[x], f[x] * g[x]}, {x, −1, 1}, PlotStyle → {Gray, Black, Dashing[{.01}]}]**

Out[6]=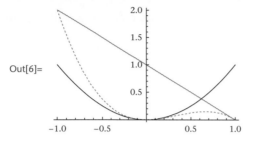

Finally, with a little extra work you can add a legend to the plot that will explain to the reader which function is which. You must first load the **PlotLegends** package. Be sure to type the double quotes and the backquote character.

In[7]:= **Needs["PlotLegends`"]**

In[8]:= **Plot[{f[x], g[x], f[x] * g[x]}, {x, −1, 1}, PlotStyle → {Gray, Black, Dashing[{.01}]},**
**   PlotLegend → {f[x], g[x], f[x] * g[x]}, LegendPosition → {1, −.5}]**

Out[8]=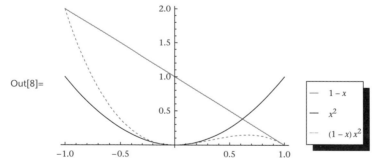

The option **PlotLegend** is set to the list of labels to be placed in the legend box. In this case we just used the functions themselves, but textual expressions or strings (expressions enclosed in double quotes) are also fine. The **LegendPosition** option specifies where the legend box is placed relative to the plot. To be more precise, it specifies where the *midpoint* of the *left side* of the legend box is placed. You will almost certainly want to change its default placement. To do this, set **LegendPosi·tion** to a coordinate pair where each coordinate ranges from −1 to 1. The setting {-1, -1} places the legend in the lower left corner, while {1,1} places it upper right.

Alternatively, it is a simple matter to build your own plot legend from scratch using the drawing tools (discussed in Section 3.9 on page 112); simply plot your functions, then click on the output image and use the drawing tools to place on it (for instance) some text and some lines to which the same directives used in the plot are applied. Finally, place a rectangle with opacity and a thick black edge on top of your text. For instance, here's a plot:

In[9]:= $\textbf{Plot}\big[\{\textbf{x}^2, \textbf{x}^4, \textbf{x}^6\}, \{\textbf{x}, .5, 1.5\}, \textbf{PlotRange} \rightarrow \{0, 3\},$
$\qquad \textbf{PlotStyle} \rightarrow \{\textbf{Black, Directive[Dashed, Black], Directive[Dotted, Black]}\}\big]$

Out[9]=

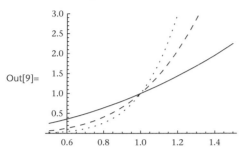

And here we've used the drawing tools to add a legend:

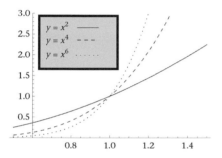

If you need to superimpose a large number of plots, you can use *Mathematica*'s **Table** command to generate the list of functions:

In[10]:= $\textbf{Plot}\big[\textbf{Table}\big[\textbf{n x}^2, \{\textbf{n}, -40, 40\}\big], \{\textbf{x}, -2, 2\}, \textbf{PlotRange} \rightarrow 50\big]$

Out[10]=

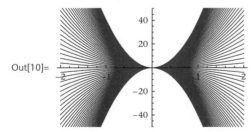

⚠ In cases like this where the expression appearing as the first argument to **Plot** is generated programmatically, it may be beneficial to wrap the expression with **Evaluate**. The necessity of the **Evaluate** command is a subtle business. Generally, **Plot** will hold the expression appearing as the first argument unevaluated, then evaluate it multiple times, once for each numerical value of x sampled in the domain. **Evaluate** forces **Plot** to first evaluate its initial argument before plugging in any values of x. In some settings this can lead to a plot that works versus one that does not. In other cases, **Evaluate** can reduce the time it takes to produce the plot. In the example above, the processing time is reduced (and curves become individually colored), if one replaces **Table$[n\,x^2$, {n, −40, 40}]** by **Evaluate[Table$[n\,x^2$, {n, −40, 40}]]**.

Producing Filled Plots

One can shade the region between a plot and the *x* axis as follows:

In[11]:= **Plot$\left[1 - x^2, \{x, -2, 2\}, \text{Filling} \to \text{Axis}\right]$**

Out[11]=

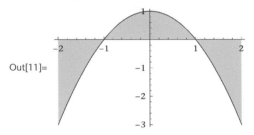

And one can shade the region between two curves like so:

In[12]:= **Plot$\left[\{\text{Sin}[x], 1 - x^2\}, \{x, -2, 2\}, \text{Filling} \to \{1\}\right]$**

Out[12]=

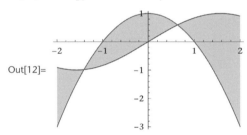

When there are more than two functions there are many ways to shade the various regions between them. Below, filling is added from the first function to the third, *and* from the second function to the top of the plot. Note that the filling is transparent, so the two filling styles can be layered one over the other. Look up **Filling** in the Documentation Center for more information.

In[13]:= **Plot$\left[\{x^2, x^4, \text{Sin}[20\,x]\}, \{x, 0, 1.5\}, \text{PlotRange} \to \{0, 1.5\}, \text{Filling} \to \{1 \to \{3\}, 2 \to \text{Top}\}\right]$**

Out[13]=

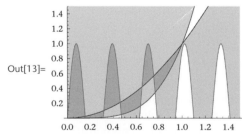

Superimposing Graphics

To overlay one graphic on top of another, simply feed the component images to the **Show** command. The individual images will be superimposed upon a common coordinate system. Below we demonstrate this by assigning names to the component images and suppressing their individual output with semicolons.

In[14]:= $p1 = Plot[Sin[x], \{x, 0, 2\pi\}, AspectRatio \rightarrow Automatic]$;

$p2 = ContourPlot\left[\left(x - \dfrac{\pi}{2}\right)^2 + y^2 == 1, \{x, 0, 3\}, \{y, -1, 1\}\right]$;

$Show[p1, p2]$

Out[16]=

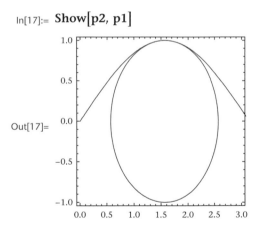

The plot domain, and option settings, such as **AspectRatio**, **Axes**, and so on will be inherited from their settings in the *first* image listed within **Show**. Changing the order of the graphics listed within **Show** may therefore change the appearance of the output:

In[17]:= $Show[p2, p1]$

Out[17]=

Note also that the order of the component images listed within **Show** is the order in which they are rendered. The first graphic is rendered first, with the next graphic overlaid *on top* of it, and so on.

In[18]:= **ellipse =**

$$\text{ContourPlot}\left[\frac{x^2}{3} + 2\,y^2 = 1, \{x, -2, 2\}, \{y, -1, 1\}, \text{ContourStyle} \to \text{Thickness}[.06]\right];$$

squiggle = Plot[Sin[10 x], {x, −2, 2}, PlotStyle → Directive[Gray, Thickness[.04]]];
Show[ellipse, squiggle]

Out[20]=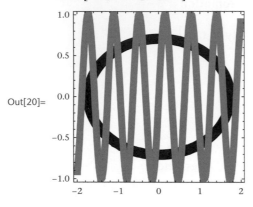

In[21]:= **Show[squiggle, ellipse]**

Out[21]=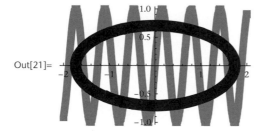

One may also include within **Show** any options accepted by **Graphics**. Such options can be used to override settings inherited from the component images.

In[22]:= **Show[squiggle, ellipse, Axes → False]**

Out[22]=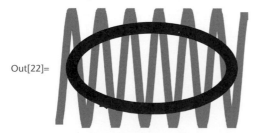

Keep in mind also that while **Show** is an extremely useful and versatile command, it is often not needed. To plot two functions together, for instance, recall that one can simply provide a *list* of the two functions as the first argument to **Plot**. One may also use the **Epilog** option in commands such as **Plot** and **ContourPlot** to overlay primitive graphic elements on a plot (the **Epilog** option is discussed in Section 3.9, on page 117).

Graphics Side-by-Side

A simple but rather primitive means of arranging graphics side-by-side is to simply create a *list* of graphics. Of course, the curly brackets enclosing the list will be displayed in the output, and there will be commas separating the images:

In[23]:= {Plot[Sin[x] + Cos[x], {x, −π, π}], Plot[Sin[x] − Cos[x], {x, −π, π}]}

Out[23]=

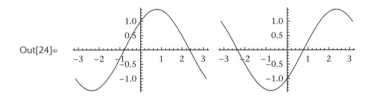

A better way to accomplish a side-by-side display is to use **GraphicsRow**. Its argument is a list of graphics. It will integrate this list of individual **Graphics** objects into a single conglomerate graphic that can, for instance, be moved or resized as a whole.

In[24]:= **GraphicsRow[%]**

Out[24]=

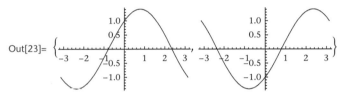

The **Frame**, **FrameStyle**, and **Dividers** options may be used to add frames around each item, or to place divider lines between some of them. The syntax for these options works as it does in a **Grid**. The list of graphics can be generated programmatically, using **Table** for instance:

In[25]:= GraphicsRow[Table[Plot[Sin[m * x], {x, 0, 2π}], {m, 3}],
            Frame → All, FrameStyle → Dotted]

Out[25]=

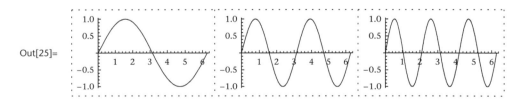

Graphics in a Grid

There is also a **GraphicsGrid** command to lay out graphics in a grid pattern. The syntax and many of the options are the same as for **Grid**.

In[26]:= **GraphicsGrid[{**
        Table[Plot[Csc[m * x], {x, 0, 2 π}, Axes → False], {m, 5}],
        Table[Plot[Sec[m * x], {x, 0, 2 π}, Axes → False], {m, 5}]},
        Frame → All, FrameStyle → Gray]

Out[26]=

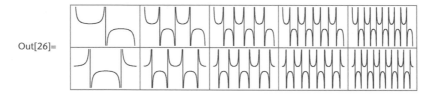

One could also use **Grid** instead of **GraphicsRow** or **GraphicsGrid**. The main difference is that the output of these latter commands is a *single* graphic that may be edited as such, for instance using the drawing tools. The entire output can be resized by selecting it and dragging a handle. In a plain **Grid**, only the *individual* component graphics can be edited.

Exercises 3.8

1. Name at least three strategies for determining which function is which in the graph below. You may alter the input and re-enter it.

In[27]:= **Plot[{x², x Sin[x]}, {x, −1, 1}]**

Out[27]=

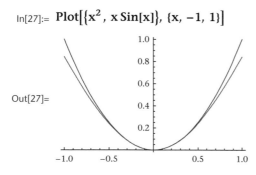

2. In this exercise you will examine the function $\frac{\sin(.4\,t)+\sin(1.6\,t)}{2\sin(t)}$ and the function $\cos(.6\,t)$.

  a. Simultaneously plot both functions on the domain $0 \le t \le 8\,\pi$ and describe what you find.

  b. Repeat for the functions $\frac{\sin(.3\,t)+\sin(1.7\,t)}{2\sin(t)}$ and $\cos(.7\,t)$. What do you find?

  c. How about for the functions $\frac{\sin(.2\,t)+\sin(1.8\,t)}{2\sin(t)}$ and $\cos(.8\,t)$?

d. Make a conjecture as to the value of $\frac{\sin(k\,t)+\sin((2-k)\,t)}{2\sin(t)}$ for any real numbers k and t, where t is not an integer multiple of π.

e. Enter the following, which illustrates the equivalence and allows the viewer to control k. Comment on the graphical implications of the fact that the third function is the sum of the other two. Note that in Exercise 2 in Section 4.6 we will return to this example and show why the equivalence holds.

In[28]:= **Manipulate[**

$\quad$ **Plot[** $\left\{ \dfrac{\text{Sin[k\,t]}}{2\,\text{Sin[t]}}, \dfrac{\text{Sin[(2-k)\,t]}}{2\,\text{Sin[t]}}, \text{Cos[(1-k)\,t]} \right\}$, **{t, 0, 8$\pi$}, PlotRange → 2,**

$\quad\quad$ **PlotStyle → {Darker[Gray], Darker[Pink], Directive[Thick, Black]},**

$\quad\quad$ **GridLines → {Range[0, 8π, π], {}}, Ticks → None,**

$\quad\quad$ **Filling → {1 → Axis, 2 → Axis}], {{k, .4}, 0, 2}]**

Out[28]=

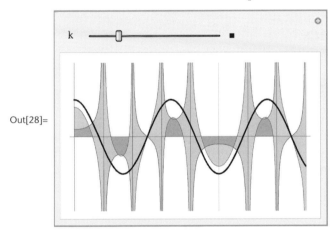

3. Make the following **Grid** showing the plots of power functions, i.e., functions of the form $f(x) = \pm p * x^n$, for real parameters p and n, with p positive and with domain $0 \le x \le 4$. Include text next to each plot indicating the values for the parameter n that will produce plots of the same general shape.

Plot of $p*x^n$ looks like:	When:	Plot of $-p*x^n$ looks like:	When:
	$n>1$		$n>1$
	$n=1$		$n=1$
	$0<n<1$		$0<n<1$
	$n<0$		$n<0$

3.9 Enhancing Your Graphics

The time will soon come when you feel the irresistible desire to add some sort of graphic enhancement to a plot. Maybe it will be something as minor as an arrow and some text. Maybe it will be a stick figure. Maybe it will be hundreds of circles, polygons, and lines. Whatever the need, the time will come. And if you read this section, you will be ready.

There are two basic ways to add information to an existing graphic: Use drawing tools and your mouse to interactively add the elements you desire, or use the **Graphics** command and primitive graphics elements to proceed programmatically. Each method has its advantages, and we'll address each in turn.

Drawing Tools

Drawing tools are found in the Graphics menu. The idea is simple and intuitive: elements are added to a graphic using the Drawing Tools and your mouse. This approach is appropriate when you are making a single image, or perhaps just a few, and when the placement of the elements on the graphic allows some leeway. It's great for adding labels with arrows pointing to items in a plot, for example.

Let's begin with a graphic produced by the **Plot** command.

In[1]:= $\text{Plot}\Big[\{\text{Sin}[x], \text{ArcSin}[x]\}, \Big\{x, -\frac{\pi}{2}, \frac{\pi}{2}\Big\}, \text{PlotStyle} \rightarrow \{\text{Automatic, Dashed}\},$

$\text{AspectRatio} \rightarrow \text{Automatic, AxesLabel} \rightarrow \{x, y\}\Big]$

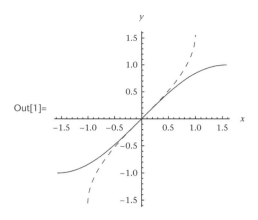

Out[1]=

Now go to the Graphics menu and select Drawing Tools. Begin by clicking once on the graphic you wish to modify; an orange border appears around it. Now the tools on the palette are bound to a target image. Explore the palette by mousing over its buttons. As you do, a tooltip will give a brief description of that tool's function. Generally speaking, click a tool button once to use that tool once, or double click it to keep it active. If you click only once, the Selection tool will become active immediately afterward. This is a good way to work in many cases; you push a palette button to activate a tool, use the tool to add an element to your graphic, then (without another trip to the palette) you can select and move or resize the new element. For example, in the graphic above let's add labels for the two curves and an arrow pointing from each label to the appropriate curve. Click on the graphic. Then push the arrow button on the palette (left column, half way down) to activate the arrow tool (or just type the letter "a" after clicking on the graphic). Now position the cursor over the graphic where you want the tail of the arrow to appear, and (left) click once. Holding the mouse button down, drag the cursor to where the arrowhead should be, and release. The arrow appears, with an orange bounding box around it. The palette has now resorted back to the default Selection tool (the cursor button in the upper right is now highlighted, not the arrow button). If you drag the edge of the orange box surrounding the arrow, you can move it. If you drag the handle by either its head or tail, you will move only that end of the arrow while the other end remains anchored. You really have to try this to get a feel for it. After you have finished, click outside the graphic. Note that you can continue to make adjustments on your arrow at any time in the future. Click once on the graphic to select it, then click again on any element to select that element. The orange bounding box appears, allowing you to move or resize it. Alternately, if you double click on an element, you can edit it. Finally, if you push the Inspector button at the bottom of the Drawing Tools palette, a second palette appears. Use this to fine-tune the appearance of any graphic element. Select any item, such as an arrow, and you can adjust its thickness, color, opacity (how transparent it is when overlaid on another element), and so on. With arrows you can easily adjust the size, shape, and position of the arrowheads.

The best way to learn about the drawing tools is simply to use them. You can create a new (empty) graphic by pushing the button in the upper left corner of the Drawing Tools palette, or by choosing New Graphic in the Graphics menu. Then play to your heart's content with the tools. Below we show a few simple labels added to our previously generated plot:

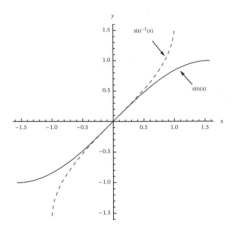

The Drawing Tools are a simple and powerful set of tools for creating all manner of creative and revealing information graphics. With no training whatever and in a matter of minutes, our 13 year old son Robert added the archer to the plot below:

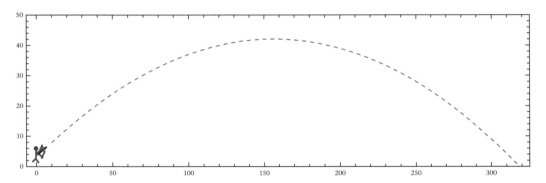

Detailed information on each drawing tool can be had in the Documentation Center. Type "Editing *Mathematica* Graphics" in the text field and follow the link to the *Mathematica* overview of that name. Some of the most commonly used keyboard equivalents for the drawing tools are given in Table 3.3.

Graphics Primitives

It is, of course, possible to forgo the freehand palette approach and work programmatically instead. This method is painstaking when you want to add a simple label with an arrow, as above, but it is absolutely essential when you have to add many elements, and at precise locations. We ask the reader to be patient here; this section will introduce ideas that take some practice and perseverance to master. The long term benefit, however, will be substantial.

Type	or click	to	Hold SHIFT to
CTRL-t		open the Drawing Tools palette	
CTRL-1		create a new graphic at the current selection point	
CTRL-i		open the Graphics Inspector palette	
o		activate the Select / Move / Resize tool	move horizontally / vertically, or resize preserving aspect ratio
l		activate the Line tool	make line horizontal or vertical
s		activate the Line Segment tool	make any segment(s) horizontal or vertical
a		activate the Arrow tool	make arrow horizontal or vertical
t	A≡	activate the Text tool	capitalize text
m	Σ≡	activate the TraditionalForm Text tool	capitalize text
g		activate the Polygon tool	make any segment(s) horizontal or vertical
c	○	activate the Disk / Circle tool	make a circle (aspect ratio 1)
q	□	activate the Rectangle tool	make a square (aspect ratio 1)
p	•	activate the Point tool	
f		activate the Freehand draw tool	

Table 3.3 Tools in the DrawingTools palette

Let's first meet the *graphics primitives*. These are the building blocks from which all two-dimensional *Mathematica* graphics are constructed. They are: **Point**, **Line**, **Rectangle**, **Polygon**, **Circle**, **Disk**, **Raster**, and **Text**. Let's look at a few of these on their own. Later, we'll show how to combine them into a single graphic. We note that three-dimensional versions of some of these primitives (and some new ones) exist as well; these will be discussed in Section 6.2 on page 276.

The most common elements you will use are points and lines. We will illustrate the ideas involved by drawing lines; the other primitives work in a similar manner. Let's first construct the line segments joining the points (0, 0), (1, 1), and (2, 0). To join any finite collection of points in the plane, feed a list of the Cartesian coordinates of the points as the sole argument to the **Line** command. Individual points, such as (2, 0), are input as lists of length two, like this: **{2,0}**.

In[2]:= **Line[{{0, 0}, {1, 1}, {2, 0}}]**

Out[2]= Line[{{0, 0}, {1, 1}, {2, 0}}]

Not too interesting yet. To *view* any primitive graphics element, wrap it in the **Graphics** command:

In[3]:= **Graphics[Line[{{0, 0}, {1, 1}, {2, 0}}]]**

Out[3]=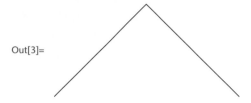

The visual appearance of any primitive object or objects can be tweaked using graphics directives (these were introduced in Section 3.3, in the subsection *How to Add Color and Other Style Changes: Graphics Directives* on page 63). Some commonly used directives are **Red**, **Thick**, **Opacity[.5]**, and **Dashed**. The syntax works like this: put the graphics primitive(s) in a *list* whose first item is the directive. If there is more than one directive, wrap them in the **Directive** command:

In[4]:= **Graphics[{Directive[Thick, Dashed], Line[{{0, 0}, {1, 1}, {2, 0}}]}]**

Out[4]=

Note that **Graphics** will accept many of the same options discussed for the **Plot** command:

In[5]:= **Graphics[{Directive[Thick, Dashed], Line[{{0, 0}, {1, 1}, {2, 0}}]}, Axes → True]**

Out[5]=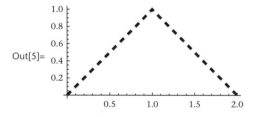

And combining primitive elements is as simple as putting them all into one big list within the **Graphics** command:

In[6]:= **Graphics[{**
          {Directive[Thick, Gray], Line[Table[{x, Sin[x]}, {x, 0, 6.3, .1}]]},
          {Directive[Dashed, Blue], Line[{{2, 0}, {2, Sin[2]}, {0, Sin[2]}}]},
          {Directive[PointSize[.02], Yellow], Point[{2, Sin[2]}]}
          }, Axes → True]

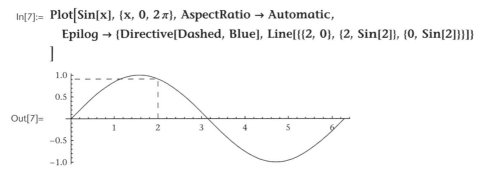

Note that the order in which the individual elements are specified matters. The first item is rendered first, and each additional item is placed "on top" of earlier items. The point above, for instance, would be obscured by the thick, gray sine curve had it been listed first.

Finally, it may be the case that you wish to include some primitive elements with the output of, say, the **Plot** command. There are a few ways to do this. One is to take advantage of the **Epilog** option in the **Plot** command. Set this option to any list of primitives that you could feed to the **Graphics** command. The effect is to overlay the primitives on top of the plot.

In[7]:= **Plot[Sin[x], {x, 0, 2π}, AspectRatio → Automatic,**
          Epilog → {Directive[Dashed, Blue], Line[{{2, 0}, {2, Sin[2]}, {0, Sin[2]}}]}
          ]

And now, at last, we demonstrate the true benefit of understanding **Graphics** primitives. Below we combine a (static) plot of the sine function with a dynamically controlled point that the user can adjust with **Manipulate**:

In[8]:= $\text{Manipulate}\Big[\text{Plot}\Big[\text{Sin[t]}, \{t, 0, 2\pi\}, \text{Ticks} \rightarrow \Big\{\text{Range}\Big[0, 2\pi, \frac{\pi}{6}\Big], \text{Sin}\Big[\text{Range}\Big[-\frac{\pi}{2}, \frac{\pi}{2}, \frac{\pi}{6}\Big]\Big]\Big\},$

$\text{Epilog} \rightarrow \{\{\text{Dashed, Line}[\{\{x, 0\}, \{x, \text{Sin}[x]\}, \{0, \text{Sin}[x]\}\}]\},$

$\{\text{Red, PointSize}[.015], \text{Point}[\{x, \text{Sin}[x]\}]\}\}\Big], \Big\{\Big\{x, \frac{2\pi}{3}\Big\}, 0, 2\pi\Big\}\Big]$

Out[8]=

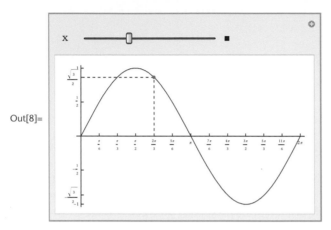

One final word is in order that pertains to printing. If you would like to produce a quality print of that *beautiful* graphic you spent hours getting just right, wouldn't it be nice to lose the cell label Out[117]= that appears to its left? There are two simple means of achieving this. First, you can highlight the cell label and hit the delete key. Mission accomplished. Alternately, wrap your input with the **Print** command, and the same output will appear but *without the label*. Note that **Print** will not send your output to a printer; rather, it "prints" an unlabeled cell in your notebook.

In[9]:= $\text{Print} @ \text{Plot}\big[\text{Sin}[x]^5 - \text{Cos}\big[x^5\big], \{x, -3, 3\}\big]$

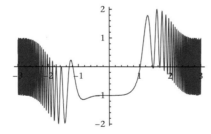

The same comment applies to that wonderful table you produced with **Grid**. One may use **Print[Style[Grid[⋯], "Text"]]** to generate a table with textual styling in an unlabeled cell, suitable for inclusion in the finest of publications.

Exercises 3.9

1. Make the following figure using the commands **Graphics**, **Rectangle**, and **Circle**, and including the **Graphics** option setting **Frame → True**. You will want to look up **Circle** in the Documentation Center to find out how to draw an ellipse. Do not use the Drawing Tools palette.

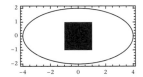

2. In this exercise you will explore various graphics directives using **Manipulate**.

   a. The following command will produce a red disk of radius 1 centered at the origin. Type and enter it:

   Graphics[{Red, Disk[]}]

   b. Replace **Red** by **Lighter[Blend[{Blue, Red}, .3], .4]**.

   c. Finally, make this into a **Manipulate**, replacing .3 and .4 above by the control variables **r** and **s**, respectively. Investigate the effects.

   d. Make two disks of radius 1 centered at (0, 0) and (1, 0) with the commands **Disk[]** and **Disk[{1,0}, 1]**, respectively. Make the first disk blue. Place them in a **Manipulate** with a single control variable that determines the **Opacity** of the second disk (with values that range from 0 to 1).

   e. Repeat the previous part, but make the second disk (the one with varying opacity) orange. If you are not a University of Virginia fan, feel free to use other colors.

3. Make a smiley face as follows:

   a. Create a **Manipulate** using **Circle[{0, 0}, {1, r}, {π, 2π}]** for $0.01 \le r \le 1$ and note the behavior.

   b. Using **Graphics** primitives such as **Disk**, create a yellow smiley face that can be manipulated.

   c. Add eyebrows that can be manipulated.

4. In this exercise we explore a family of ellipses.

   a. Using **Circle**, construct **Graphics** showing the ellipse $\frac{x^2}{4} + \frac{y^2}{9} = 1$ together with the coordinate axes.

   b. Construct **Graphics** showing together the family of ellipses $\frac{x^2}{\frac{k(n-k+1)}{n+2}} + \frac{y^2}{\frac{(n-k+1)(n-k+2)}{(n+1)(n+2)}} = 1$ with $n = 20$, and with k assuming integer values from 1 to 20. Note: A forthcoming paper by undergraduate Liza Lawson and Bruce Torrence shows that for any real number r, the roots of the kth derivative of $f(z) = (z - r)^n (z^2 + 1)$ will either be real or will lie on the kth ellipse in this family (where $z = x + iy$ in the complex plane).

   c. For one of the values of k above, the ellipse appears to be an honest circle. Is it? Find the value of k, and investigate.

d. For which value of k is the semimajor axis longest?

3.10 Working with Data

In situations where you have numerical data, you will want to enter the data into the computer to study it. How is this most easily accomplished with *Mathematica*? Here is an example. These data specify the temperature of a cup of coffee as it cools over time. The first column shows the number of minutes that have elapsed, while the second column indicates the temperature of the coffee, measured in degrees Fahrenheit:

$$\text{In[1]:= } \mathbf{data} = \begin{array}{c|c} 0 & 149.5 \\ \hline 2 & 141.7 \\ \hline 4 & 134.7 \\ \hline 6 & 128.3 \\ \hline 8 & 122.6 \\ \hline 10 & 117.4 \\ \hline 12 & 112.7 \\ \hline 14 & 108.5 \\ \hline 16 & 104.7 \\ \hline 18 & 101.3 \\ \hline 20 & 98.2 \\ \hline 22 & 95.4 \\ \hline 24 & 92.9 \\ \hline 26 & 90.5 \\ \hline 28 & 88.5 \\ \hline 30 & 86.6 \end{array};$$

When recording data a spreadsheet-type interface is desirable. To enter these data into *Mathematica*, first type **data** = (any name will do, but "data" seems convenient), then select Table/Matrix ▷ New... from the Insert menu. A dialog box will appear. In the top left portion select Table. To the right specify the number of rows (in this case 16) and columns (in this case 2). It is possible to add and delete more rows and columns later, so these numbers need not be exact. Ignore the remaining settings and hit the OK button. A rectangular array, a sort of mini-spreadsheet of the dimensions you specified, will appear in your notebook, and a very long, vertical, blinking cursor will appear to its right. Type ; so that when you eventually enter this cell the output will be suppressed. Now click on the placeholder in the upper left corner of your table (or hit the ⎆TAB key to jump there) and enter the first data value. When you are finished use the ⎆TAB key to move to the next placeholder. Continue to enter your data in this fashion. Additional rows or columns can be added at any time; just look in the Insert ▷ Table/Matrix menu for Add Row or Add Column. When all the data have been typed in, enter the cell.

When you enter data in this way, *Mathematica* stores it as a list of ordered pairs (one pair for each row in the table). Technically, it's a list of lists. If you don't put a semicolon after your data table, you will see it displayed in this form upon entering it. Or you will see it in this form if you ask for it by name:

In[2]:= **data**

Out[2]= {{0, 149.5}, {2, 141.7}, {4, 134.7}, {6, 128.3}, {8, 122.6}, {10, 117.4}, {12, 112.7}, {14, 108.5}, {16, 104.7}, {18, 101.3}, {20, 98.2}, {22, 95.4}, {24, 92.9}, {26, 90.5}, {28, 88.5}, {30, 86.6}}

You won't need to work with the data in this form, but it's good to see it once so you know how *Mathematica* interprets it.

The command for plotting such a list of ordered pairs is **ListPlot**:

In[3]:= **ListPlot[data]**

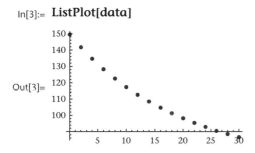

ListPlot takes a single argument: a list of two-tuples. Each two-tuple is interpreted as a point in the coordinate plane, and these points are then plotted. If your list of points is very short, you may find it easiest to type it directly into **ListPlot** rather than first making a data table:

In[4]:= **ListPlot[{{1, 1}, {2, 3}, {3, 2}, {4, 3}}]**

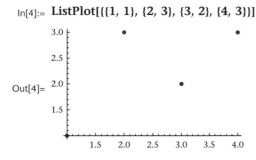

It is an annoying fact of life that **ListPlot** will often hide one or more of your points behind the coordinate axes. In the plot above, the point (1, 1) is at the intersection of the two axes! One way to alleviate this masking effect is to "connect the dots." The option **Joined → True** accomplishes this. Also, one may specify another symbol to indicate the data points using the **PlotMarkers** option. Here we used the ❀ symbol (from the Shapes and Icons portion of the SpecialCharacters palette).

In[5]:= ListPlot[{{1, 1}, {2, 3}, {3, 2}, {4, 3}}, Joined → True,
    PlotMarkers → ✳, AxesOrigin → {0, 0}, PlotRange → {0, 3.5}]

Out[5]=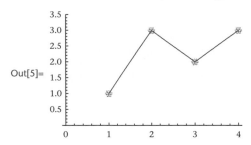

But **ListPlot** also accepts most of the options that the **Plot** command does, so it is a simple matter to produce as elaborate a graph as you desire. Here we assign the name *scatterplot* to our plot so that we can refer to it later. The *x* and *y* values in **AxesOrigin** were chosen just a bit smaller than the smallest *x* and *y* values appearing in the data; this pulls the axes off any data points. Finally, wrapping **Tooltip** around the data itself has the convenient effect of producing a tooltip showing a data point's exact coordinates when you mouseover that point (you'll have to try this to experience it).

In[6]:= scatterplot = ListPlot[Tooltip[data], AxesLabel → {"min", "temperature (°F)"},
    PlotStyle → Directive[PointSize[Small], Blue],
    Filling → Axis, AxesOrigin → {−1, 80}]

Out[6]=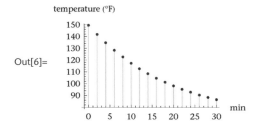

You can have *Mathematica* find the best-fitting polynomial for your data (according to the criteria of least squares) using the **Fit** command. Here is the best fitting linear function for the coffee cooling data. We assign it the name **fitLine**:

In[7]:= fitLine = Fit[data, {1, x}, x]

Out[7]= $141.332 - 2.03257\, x$

Here is the best quadratic:

In[8]:= fitQuadratic = Fit[data, {1, x, x²}, x]

Out[8]= $148.465 - 3.56107\, x + 0.0509498\, x^2$

The **Fit** command takes three arguments. The first is the data (a list of two-tuples). The second is a list of the terms requiring coefficient values in the polynomial. The last is the name of the variable, in this case *x*.

Once we have named these best-fit functions, we can view them against our data. A quick and dirty way to display the **Plot** of a function together with data points is as follows (the **Epilog** option is discussed in Section 3.9 on page 117):

In[9]:= **Plot[fitQuadratic, {x, 0, 30}, Epilog → Point[data]]**

Out[9]=

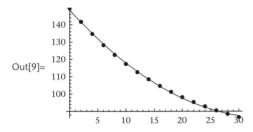

A more nuanced image can be had by using **Plot** and **ListPlot** to generate separate graphics, and then using **Show** to display them together:

In[10]:= **Show[scatterplot, Plot[{fitLine, fitQuadratic}, {x, 0, 30}, Filling → True]]**

Out[10]=

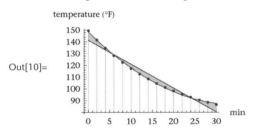

Here we display them individually:

In[11]:= **Show[scatterplot, Plot[fitLine, {x, 0, 30}], PlotLabel → Style[fitLine, 8]]**
Show[scatterplot, Plot[fitQuadratic, {x, 0, 30}], PlotLabel → Style[fitQuadratic, 8]]

Out[11]=

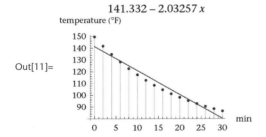

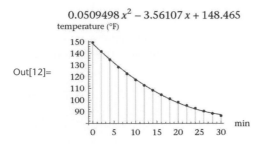

Out[12]=

A more efficient means of entering the input above, where we have a list of nearly identical **Show** items, is to use **Table** to generate the list:

In[13]:= **GraphicsRow[**

    Table[Show[scatterplot, Plot[f, {x, 0, 30}], PlotLabel → f],

      {f, {fitLine, fitQuadratic}}]

]

Out[13]=

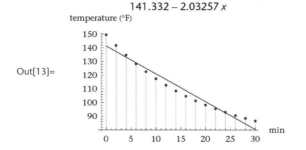
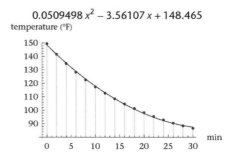

The **FindFit** command may be used in place of **Fit** when a more complex form of approximating function is sought than a polynomial (or sum of basis functions). For instance, while the quadratic above seems to fit the coffee cooling data rather well, a moment's thought tells us that this function will fare poorly if we use it to predict the coffee's temperature, say, when the time x is equal to 60 minutes. For quadratics with a positive coefficient on the x^2 term open upward, and so will eventually (for sufficiently large values of x) turn from decreasing to increasing functions. The coffee, on the other hand, is not going to get warmer as time progresses. It is a well known principle of physics that bodies cool *exponentially* toward the ambient temperature of the surrounding medium. Hence the form of the cooling function *ought* to be $f(x) = a + b * c^x$, where a, b, and c are positive constants with $0 < c < 1$, and where a is the ambient temperature of the room.

FindFit requires four arguments. The first is the data. The second specifies the *form* of the fitting function (in this case $a + b * c^x$), the third is a list of the parameters whose values we seek in this expression (in this case $\{a, b, c\}$), and the last is the independent variable (in this case x). Any or all of the parameters in the third argument may be given as an ordered pair of the form {*parameter*, *guess*}, where *guess* is a rough estimate of the correct value of that parameter. Below we use .5 as an initial guess for the decay parameter c, since we know that c is between 0 and 1. This helps *Mathematica* refine its search for optimal values of the parameters in question.

In[13]:= **FindFit[data, a + b * c^x, {a, b, {c, .5}}, x]**

Out[13]= {a → 69.348, b → 80.1489, c → 0.95015}

The output of **FindFit** is a list of *replacement rules* giving the values of the parameters. Replacement rules are discussed in Section 4.2 on page 153; for now we simply read off the values of the parameters, and note that the fit is excellent:

In[14]:= **Show[scatterplot, Plot[69.348 + 80.148 * 0.95015^x, {x, 0, 30}]]**

Out[14]=

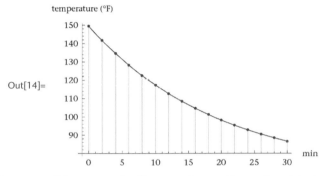

Moreover, this approach allows us to use the coffee data to determine that the ambient temperature of the room is approximately $a = 69.35\,°$ Fahrenheit.

Exercises 3.10

1. For the data given below, find the best-fitting line (according to the criteria of least-squares), and plot this line together with the data.

x	1	2	3	4	5
y	1.2	2.3	3.6	4.9	5.9

2. For the same data used in the previous exercise, find the best-fitting *power function*. That is, find the best-fitting function of the form $f(x) = p * x^n$ for real parameters p and n.

3. For the functions in each of the previous two exercises, find the *residuals*. That is, for each x-coordinate in the data, find the *difference* between the actual y value in the data and the value predicted by the fit function. Geometrically, these residuals indicate the vertical distance between a data point and the graph of the fit function. A residual is positive if and only if the data point lies above the graph of the fit function.

4. Enter the following input to create a command that will plot a collection of data, a fit-function, and the residuals for the data and the given function. Test the command on the data from the first exercise and the fit-function $f(x) = 3 - .25\,x + .125\,x^2$.

residualPlot[data_, function_, {x_, xmin_, xmax_}, opts___Rule] :=
  Show[ListPlot[{data, Table[{x, function}, {x, data[[All, 1]]}]}, Filling → {1 → {2}},
    FillingStyle → {Red, Green}, PlotMarkers → {"*", ""}, opts],
  Plot[function, {x, xmin, xmax}]]

5. When a **Manipulate** has a **Locator** controller, it's possible (and often desirable) to modify the **Locator**'s default appearance in the image pane. A simple way to do this is to display a **Graphics** object of your choosing at the position of the **Locator**, and add the option setting **Appearance → None** to the iterator for the **Locator** control. Enter the following input, explore the output, and then change things so that the **Locator** appears as a **Thick**, **Blue**, **Circle**.

Manipulate[
  Graphics[{Directive[PointSize[.03], Red], Point[pt]}, Axes → True, PlotRange → 1],
  {{pt, {0, 0}}, Locator, Appearance → None}]

3.11 Managing Data—An Introduction to Lists

You will often need to modify or transform the data with which you started. For instance, you might begin with a large table of data and wish only to work with a few rows or columns of it. Or you might wish to transform a particular row or column in a large table of data by applying the natural logarithm to each item in that row or column. In this section we introduce a few techniques to help with such tasks.

We mentioned in Section 3.5 that a *list* in *Mathematica* is a collection of items separated by commas and enclosed in curly brackets, such as {2, 5, 9, 7, 4}. Our first task will be to master the art of extracting one or more items from a list.

In[1]:= **myList = Table[2^k, {k, 10}]**

Out[1]= {2, 4, 8, 16, 32, 64, 128, 256, 512, 1024}

In[2]:= **myList[[5]]**

Out[2]= 32

If you type the name of a list followed by [[5]], you will extract the fifth part of the list. You can also use the ▪ button on the BasicMathInput palette (in the lower right portion of the top half of the palette) to produce **myList**$_{[5]}$, which has the same meaning. One may also type from the keyboard ESC [[ESC and ESC]] ESC to produce the double square bracket symbols ⟦ and ⟧, which also have the same meaning.

In[3]:= **myList**₍₅₎

Out[3]= 32

In[4]:= **myList[[5]]**

Out[4]= 32

We'll use this last notation throughout this section as it is easy to read, but remember that you may simply use double square brackets (which are easier to type). A negative number inside the double square brackets indicates an item's position relative to the end of the list. For instance, here is the second to last item:

In[5]:= **myList[[−2]]**

Out[5]= 512

To extract a sequential portion of a longer list, one may indicate a **Span** of positions as follows:

In[6]:= **myList[[1 ;; 4]]**

Out[6]= {2, 4, 8, 16}

The most commonly specified items in a list are the first and last. There are, for convenience, special commands to extract these items (although **myList[[1]]** and **myList[[-1]]** work just as well):

In[7]:= **First[myList]**

Out[7]= 2

In[8]:= **Last[myList]**

Out[8]= 1024

Most of *Mathematica*'s arithmetic operations have the **Listable** attribute. This means they will be "mapped over lists." In other words, each item in the list will be operated upon individually by these commands, and the list of results will be displayed. This is extremely handy. For example:

In[9]:= **{1, 2, 3, 4} + 1**

Out[9]= {2, 3, 4, 5}

In[10]:= **2 ∗ myList**

Out[10]= {4, 8, 16, 32, 64, 128, 256, 512, 1024, 2048}

In[11]:= **Log[2, myList]**

Out[11]= {1, 2, 3, 4, 5, 6, 7, 8, 9, 10}

⚠ To find out if a command has the **Listable** attribute, type ?? followed by the command name, and evaluate the cell. All the attributes of the command will appear (along with a brief description of the command and a list of its default option settings).

Recall that *Mathematica* stores a two-dimensional data table as a list of lists. That is, the data table is stored as one long list, the members of which are the rows of the table. Each row of the table is in turn stored as a list:

$$\text{In[12]:= } \mathbf{data} = \begin{array}{rl} 1 & 214 \\ 11 & 378 \\ 21 & 680 \\ 31 & 1215 \\ 41 & 2178 \\ 51 & 3907 \end{array}$$

Out[12]= {{1, 214}, {11, 378}, {21, 680}, {31, 1215}, {41, 2178}, {51, 3907}}

In[13]:= **data[[3]]**

Out[13]= {21, 680}

To extract the item in row 3, column 2, do this:

In[14]:= **data[[3, 2]]**

Out[14]= 680

To extract an entire column of a two-dimensional table, use **All** in the first position within the double bracket:

In[15]:= **data[[All, 2]]**

Out[15]= {214, 378, 680, 1215, 2178, 3907}

If your data happens to contain many columns, and you want to extract, say, only the second and fourth columns, type **data[[All, {2, 4}]]**.

The importance of these extraction commands manifests itself in situations that call for a transformation of the data. In most cases this will amount to performing some arithmetic operation on every item in a *column* of your data table. For instance, one column of a table may comprise the x coordinates of your data points, while another contains the corresponding y coordinates. You may want to subtract 70 from all the x coordinates, or take the logarithm of all the y coordinates. How can this be accomplished?

The simplest situation is one in which the same operation is to be applied to every member of a data table. The listable attribute of most operations makes this a one-step process. For instance:

In[16]:= **Log[data] // Grid**

Out[16]=
0	Log[214]
Log[11]	Log[378]
Log[21]	Log[680]
Log[31]	Log[1215]
Log[41]	Log[2178]
Log[51]	Log[3907]

If you wish to operate on just one of the columns, things are almost as simple. Suppose, for instance, that you want to take the logarithm of only the second column. One might proceed as follows (where we make a duplicate copy of the original data, then overwrite the second column in this copy):

In[17]:= **newData = data;**
newData[All, 2] = Log[data[All, 2]];
newData // Grid

Out[19]=
1	Log[214]
11	Log[378]
21	Log[680]
31	Log[1215]
41	Log[2178]
51	Log[3907]

Another method of accomplishing the same task invokes the useful **Transpose** command, which switches rows and columns in a two-dimensional table.

In[20]:= **Transpose[{data[All, 1], Log[data[All, 2]]}] // Grid**

Out[20]=
1	Log[214]
11	Log[378]
21	Log[680]
31	Log[1215]
41	Log[2178]
51	Log[3907]

This latter approach suggests a useful means of extracting a few columns from a larger table of data and applying transformations to them selectively. Here, for example, is a somewhat random collection of data:

In[21]:= **data = Table[{x, RandomInteger[10], RandomReal[10], RandomComplex[]}, {x, 6}];**
Grid[data, Dividers → Gray]

Out[22]=

1	4	1.96983	$0.201769 + 0.55101\,i$
2	10	8.8533	$0.388002 + 0.537243\,i$
3	7	1.79462	$0.873406 + 0.754408\,i$
4	7	8.99804	$0.338286 + 0.392776\,i$
5	0	5.90026	$0.903198 + 0.78486\,i$
6	7	1.71122	$0.610062 + 0.528001\,i$

And here is a new data table comprised only of the first column and the natural logarithm of the third column:

In[23]:= **newData = Transpose[{data[[All, 1]], Log[data[[All, 3]]]}];**
Grid[newData, Dividers → Gray]

Out[24]=

1	0.677946
2	2.18079
3	0.584791
4	2.19701
5	1.775
6	0.537204

So, for instance, one may now apply **ListPlot** or **Fit** to the **newData**, as discussed in the previous section.

Exercises 3.11

1. Suppose that **data** is input as a **Table** with 120 rows and 6 columns.

   a. What command could you use to extract only columns 2 and 6?

   b. What command could you issue to extract only the last 119 rows of columns 2 and 6 (for instance, imagine that the first row contains headings for the columns and not actual data)?

   c. What command could you issue to extract only the last 119 rows of columns 2 and 6, and then replace column 6 with the natural logarithm of its values?

3.12 Importing Data

The simplest means of bringing external data into *Mathematica* is by utilizing the "paclet" technology introduced in version 6. Many collections of data are curated regularly and stored on servers at Wolfram Research. *Mathematica* has built-in access to these data (provided your computer has internet access). That is, many built-in commands will simply call up these servers and deliver hot, fresh data paclets to your current *Mathematica* session.

An example is in order. The command **CountryData** is used to access data about countries, continents, and so forth. Like the other data commands, **CountryData** may be called with empty argument to produce a list of basic data objects. You will notice a slight delay before the output appears, but this will only happen the first time a data command is evaluated in a session; this is when the data is transferred from the central server to your computer.

In[1]:= **Short[CountryData[], 3]**

Out[1]//Short= {Afghanistan, Albania, ≪233≫, Zambia, Zimbabwe}

In[2]:= **CountryData[] // Length**

Out[2]= 237

Many of the data commands allow the single argument "**Properties**", which will list the properties available for each of the countries (or for the primary data objects of the data command you are using). At the time of this writing, there are 225 properties available for the country data:

In[3]:= **Short[CountryData["Properties"], 3]**

Out[3]//Short= {AdultPopulation, AgriculturalProducts, ≪222≫, WaterwayLength}

The typical usage of **CountryData** takes the form **CountryData["*tag*", "*property*"]**, where "*tag*" is a string (i.e., it is enclosed in double quotation marks) representing a country or group of countries (such as "**UnitedStates**" or "**G8**"), and "*property*" is a string representing the desired property for that country. A similar syntax applies to the other data commands. For instance:

In[4]:= **CountryData["UnitedStates", "Population"]**

Out[4]= 2.98213×10^8

One may specify a date or a range of dates for the property as follows. In the latter case the output is suitable for inclusion in the **DateListPlot** command:

In[5]:= **CountryData["UnitedStates", {"Population", 1970}]**

Out[5]= 2.10111×10^8

In[6]:= **DateListPlot[CountryData["Kuwait", {"Population", {1970, 2006}}]]**

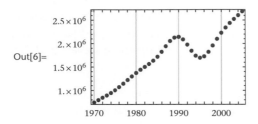

Out[6]=

Here is the gross domestic product of Germany, in US dollars, at the official exchange rate in place at the time of this writing:

In[7]:= **CountryData["Germany", "GDP"]**

Out[7]= 2.79486×10^{12}

Here is Greenland's oil consumption in barrels per day:

In[8]:= **CountryData["Greenland", "OilConsumption"]**

Out[8]= 3850.

And here we generate a list giving the name, gross domestic product, and oil consumption for every country. To accomplish this we use **Table**, where c ranges over the list of all possible countries. To save space, we use 〚1;;6〛 to take only the first six rows of data:

In[9]:= **Table[{c, CountryData[c, "GDP"], CountryData[c, "OilConsumption"]},**
{c, CountryData[]〚1 ;; 6〛}] // Grid

Out[9]=

Afghanistan	6.50383×10^9	5000.
Albania	8.53753×10^9	25 200.
Algeria	1.02257×10^{11}	246 000.
AmericanSamoa	3.338×10^8	4000.
Andorra	3.0909×10^9	Missing[NotAvailable]
Angola	2.88526×10^{10}	46 000.

Note the syntax used for missing data. With a bit of effort one can tweak the input above to produce a nicely formatted table. To save space, we again use 〚1 ;; 6〛 to take only the first six rows of data:

In[10]:= **Text @ Grid[**
     Prepend[
       Table[{c, CountryData[c, "GDP"], CountryData[c, "OilConsumption"]},
         {c, CountryData[][[1 ;; 6]]}],
       Table[Style[x, FontWeight → "Bold"],
        {x, {"Country", "Gross Domestic Product (US dollars)",
          "Oil Consumption (Barrels per day)"}}]
     ],
     Dividers → {Center, {False, True}}, Spacings → 2, Alignment → {{Left, Center}}]

Country	Gross Domestic Product (US dollars)	Oil Consumption (Barrels per day)
Afghanistan	6.50383×10^9	5000.
Albania	8.53753×10^9	25 200.
Algeria	1.02257×10^{11}	246 000.
AmericanSamoa	3.338×10^8	4000.
Andorra	3.0909×10^9	Missing[NotAvailable]
Angola	2.88526×10^{10}	46 000.

Out[10]= *(table above)*

In the exercises we illustrate how to **Sort** the rows of such a table, for instance by oil consumption, how to throw out rows containing missing data, and how to **Select** only rows, for instance, in which gross domestic product exceeds a certain value. In short, the commands **Sort** and **Select** are needed for such manipulations.

Here we make a **ListPlot** of the full data table above, showing each country's annual gross domestic product in U.S. dollars in the *x* coordinate, and that country's oil consumption in barrels per day in the *y* coordinate. A logarithmic scale is used on each axis. Missing data are simply not shown.

In[11]:= **ListLogLogPlot[Table[{CountryData[c, "GDP"],**
     CountryData[c, "OilConsumption"]}, {c, CountryData[]}]]

Out[11]=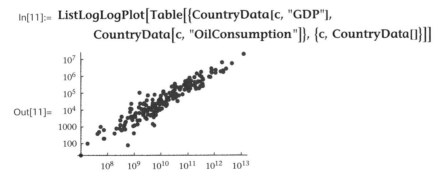

A slight modification allows us to add a **Tooltip** showing the name of each country as you mouseover its dot on the graphic. You'll have to experience this in a live session to appreciate it. Essentially, a tooltip such as this adds another dimension of content to your information graphic.

In[12]:= **ListLogLogPlot[**
     Table[Tooltip[{CountryData[c, "GDP"], CountryData[c, "OilConsumption"]},
       CountryData[c, "Name"]], {c, CountryData[]}]]

Out[12]=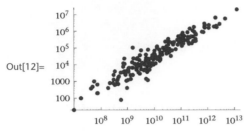

Many of the data commands can produce graphical content. One can easily produce a map of each country, for example:

In[13]:= **CountryData["Greece", "Shape"]**

Out[13]=

In[14]:= **GraphicsGrid[Partition[Table[CountryData[c, "Shape"], {c, CountryData["G8"]}], 4],**
     Dividers → All, ImageSize → 320]

Out[14]=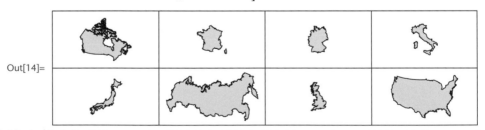

Many of the data commands load gigantic collections of data. **AstronomicalData**, for instance, which has information on over 100,000 celestial bodies, is astronomical in size. **ChemicalData** has information on over 18,000 chemicals. **FinancialData** has up-to-date information on over 186,000 securities. Each data command has its own unique syntax conventions, so the Documentation Center page for each such command is a must read. But there are also many similarities between commands; if you become familiar with one command, others will be easy to learn. For instance, after reading this section the input and output below should be self-explanatory, with only the units in need of explanation (in this case the units are *seconds*):

In[15]:= **AstronomicalData["Earth", "OrbitPeriod"]**

Out[15]= 3.1558149×10^7

Here we illustrate a pattern first deduced by Kepler—there is a mathematical relation between a planet's orbital period and its distance to the sun:

In[16]:= **data = Table[{AstronomicalData[p, "OrbitPeriod"],**
AstronomicalData[p, "SemimajorAxis"]}, {p, AstronomicalData["Planet"]}];

In[17]:= **ListLogLogPlot[data, AspectRatio → .3, ImageSize → 244]**

Out[17]=
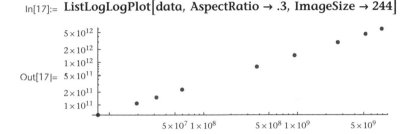

In[18]:= **FindFit[data, a * x^b, {a, b}, x]**

Out[18]= $\{a \to 1.496467 \times 10^6, b \to 0.6667315\}$

In[19]:= **Show[Plot[1 496 476 x^{2/3}, {x, 0, 10^{10}}], ListPlot[data]]**

Out[19]=
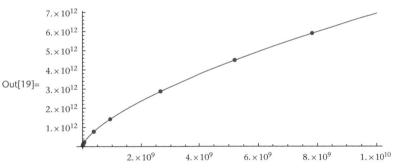

Hence orbital "radius" is proportional to $(\text{orbital period})^{2/3}$, or as Kepler put it, *radius*^{3} = *period*^{2}. The point is simply that facility with one data command makes the other data commands a quick study, and that facility with lists and data fitting makes the work of finding meaningful relations in data a snap.

In addition to built-in data commands, it is common practice to import data from other sources, such as a spreadsheet or text file, or directly from a web page. Suppose, for instance, you find a collection of raw data on a web page. For example, if you were to visit the URL http://www.census.gov/genealogy/names/dist.male.first you would find a collection of curated data from the 1990 United States census in which male first names are ranked by frequency. The web page is simply a plain text file containing four columns of data, with one or more spaces separating data values on each row, and with a return character at the end of each row. Use the **Import** command with a single argument, a string containing the URL for the web site, to bring the data into *Mathematica*.

In[20]:= **data = Import["http://www.census.gov/genealogy/names/dist.male.first"];**

There are over 1200 rows of data here. To save space we display only the top-ten list of male first names:

In[21]:= **Text @**
  Grid[Join[{{"Most Popular Male First Names from the 1990 Census", SpanFromLeft},
    {"Name", "Frequency (%)", "Cumulative Frequency (%)", "Rank"}},
    data[1 ;; 10]], Dividers → Gray]

Out[21]=

Most Popular Male First Names from the 1990 Census			
Name	Frequency (%)	Cumulative Frequency (%)	Rank
JAMES	3.318	3.318	1
JOHN	3.271	6.589	2
ROBERT	3.143	9.732	3
MICHAEL	2.629	12.361	4
WILLIAM	2.451	14.812	5
DAVID	2.363	17.176	6
RICHARD	1.703	18.878	7
CHARLES	1.523	20.401	8
JOSEPH	1.404	21.805	9
THOMAS	1.38	23.185	10

The **ListPlot** below shows the cumulative frequency distribution for the *entire* data set. Note that when a *single* list of numerical values is given as the argument to **ListPlot**, the *x*-coordinate values 1, 2, 3, … are used. This allows us to easily see that there are slightly more than 1200 data points. It also reveals that the 200 most popular male names account for over 70% of all males in the U.S.

In[22]:= **ListPlot[data[All, 3], Joined → True]**

Out[22]=

This same import technique works for many types of raw files that are found online, even graphic files:

In[23]:= **pic = Import[**
  "http://faculty.rmc.edu/btorrenc/bt–bikeclub/images/PoorFarm–ConesBW10–99.
  JPG", ImageSize → 180]

Out[23]=

The **InputForm** of this image reveals it to be a **Raster** of a matrix of pixel values. Once imported, one could apply a transformation to the matrix of numerical values to alter the image.

In[24]:= **Short[InputForm[pic], 3]**

Out[24]//Short=
  Graphics[Raster[{{255, <<679>>}, <<519>>}, <<3>>], <<3>>]

When the data you're after is found in a *formatted* table on a web page, add "**Data**" as a second argument to **Import**, like this: **Import["*URLstring*", "Data"]**. For instance, here we import a web page showing U.S. News and World Report's list of top liberal arts colleges.

  Import[
  "http://colleges.usnews.rankingsandreviews.com/usnews/edu/college/rankings/
  brief/t1libartco_brief.php", "Data"]

The output is rather large, so we don't show it here. One simply copies and pastes (and if necessary, edits) the list of data values from what is imported, and uses it as desired. Here, for instance, are the top few colleges from this page at the time of this writing; we copied the relevant data from the **Import** output, and pasted it into the **Grid** command below (evidently Carleton and Middlebury are tied, as are Pomona and Bowdoin):

In[25]:= **Text@Grid[{{"1.", "Williams College (MA)"},**
 {"2.", "Amherst College (MA)"}, {"3.", "Swarthmore College (PA)"},
 {"4.", "Wellesley College (MA)"}, {"5.", "Carleton College (MN)"},
 {"5.", "Middlebury College (VT)"}, {"7.", "Pomona College (CA)"},
 {"7.", "Bowdoin College (ME)"}, {"9.", "Davidson College (NC)"},
 {"10.", "Haverford College (PA)"}}, Alignment → {{Right, Left}}]

Out[25]=
1. Williams College (MA)
2. Amherst College (MA)
3. Swarthmore College (PA)
4. Wellesley College (MA)
5. Carleton College (MN)
5. Middlebury College (VT)
7. Pomona College (CA)
7. Bowdoin College (ME)
9. Davidson College (NC)
10. Haverford College (PA)

You may also **Import** data from a file on your local hard drive. Suppose you have a spreadsheet containing data that you want to analyze using *Mathematica*. The first step when importing a file is to tell *Mathematica* where to look for it. This is accomplished with the **SetDirectory** command. There are many ways to use this command. Its argument is a string representing the *complete* path of the directory (i.e., the folder) containing the file. Of course this can be tedious to type if the file is many levels from the top, and if the file is later moved, then its new path will be needed. Instead we advocate the following approach: save your notebook if you have not already done so, and then place the file you wish to import into the same directory containing your *Mathematica* notebook. Then type and enter the following into this notebook:

In[26]:= **SetDirectory[NotebookDirectory[]];**

This will set the current directory to be that of the notebook in which you are working. Even if you later move this directory (containing the *Mathematica* notebook and your data file) to another location, even to a different computer running a different operating system, the command above will still set the directory correctly.

Now you are ready to **Import** your file. Here we use an Excel spreadsheet that we downloaded from the data pages at the Math Forum maintained by Drexel University:

http://mathforum.org/workshops/sum96/data.collections/datalibrary/index.html.

We placed this spreadsheet into our notebook directory, as described above. The spreadsheet shows the 2005 National League baseball salaries. Note that **Import** recognizes the file-type by the suffix .xls, so no additional input is needed.

In[27]:= **baseballData = Import["NLBB.salaries.2005.xls"];**

Excel spreadsheets typically have multiple "sheets." *Mathematica* will import spreadsheets in the form {*sheet1, sheet2, sheet3,...*}, where each sheet is imported as a standard list of lists, suitable for display by **Grid**. In particular, if all of the data resides on the first sheet (a very typical scenario), there will be an extra set of curly brackets around your data. That is the case with this file, so we use **First** to access the first (and only) sheet, and display the top 20 rows of data:

In[28]:= **Text @ Grid[First[baseballData][[1 ;; 20]], Alignment → Left]**

National League Baseball Salaries (2005)

Team	Name	Salary	Position
Arizona Diamondbacks	Aquino, Greg	325 000.	Pitcher
Arizona Diamondbacks	Bruney, Brian	322 500.	Pitcher
Arizona Diamondbacks	Choate, Randy	550 000.	Pitcher
Arizona Diamondbacks	Cintron, Alex	360 000.	Shortstop
Arizona Diamondbacks	Clark, Tony	750 000.	First Baseman
Arizona Diamondbacks	Clayton, Royce	1.35×10^6	Shortstop
Arizona Diamondbacks	Counsell, Craig	1.35×10^6	Second Baseman
Arizona Diamondbacks	Cruz Jr, Jose	$4. \times 10^6$	Outfielder
Arizona Diamondbacks	Estes, Shawn	2.5×10^6	Pitcher
Arizona Diamondbacks	Gil, Jerry	318 000.	Shortstop
Arizona Diamondbacks	Glaus, Troy	$9. \times 10^6$	Third Baseman
Arizona Diamondbacks	Gonzalez, Luis	1.00833×10^7	Outfielder
Arizona Diamondbacks	Gosling, Mike	317 500.	Pitcher
Arizona Diamondbacks	Green, Shawn	7.83333×10^6	First Baseman
Arizona Diamondbacks	Halsey, Brad	317 500.	Pitcher
Arizona Diamondbacks	Hill, Koyie	318 000.	Catcher

Out[28]= (above grid)

A careful look at the data indicates that the actual data values begin on row 5, and that the last 3 rows are empty. Noting this, we can now make a histogram of all of the 2005 National League baseball salaries:

In[29]:= **Needs["Histograms`"];**

In[30]:= **Histogram[First[baseballData]〚5 ;; −4, 3〛]**

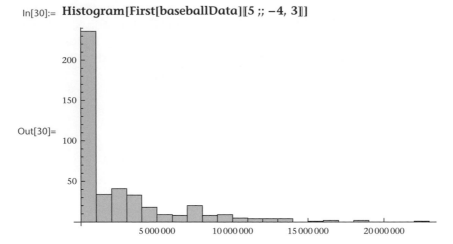

Out[30]=

We easily calculate that the mean salary exceeds a quarter million dollars, while the median is a paltry $800,000:

In[31]:= **Table[f[First[baseballData]〚5 ;; −4, 3〛], {f, {Mean, Median}}]**

Out[31]= $\{2.5858 \times 10^6, 800000.\}$

Import will work with over 120 file formats. File types are recognized by the suffix on the filename, so simply try **Import[*"filename"*]**, (where your filename includes the appropriate suffix) and chances are good that you will have success. Here is a quick list of formats that are recognized at the time of this writing:

In[32]:= **$ImportFormats**

Out[32]= {3DS, ACO, AIFF, ApacheLog, AU, AVI, Base64, Binary, Bit, BMP, Byte, BYU, BZIP2, CDED, CDF, Character16, Character8, Complex128, Complex256, Complex64, CSV, CUR, DBF, DICOM, DIF, Directory, DXF, EDF, ExpressionML, FASTA, FITS, FLAC, GIF, Graph6, GTOPO30, GZIP, HarwellBoeing, HDF, HDF5, HTML, ICO, Integer128, Integer16, Integer24, Integer32, Integer64, Integer8, JPEG, JPEG2000, JVX, LaTeX, List, LWO, MAT, MathML, MBOX, MDB, MGF, MOL, MPS, MTP, MTX, MX, NB, NetCDF, NOFF, OBJ, ODS, OFF, Package, PBM, PCX, PDB, PDF, PGM, PLY, PNG, PNM, PPM, PXR, QuickTime, RawBitmap, Real128, Real32, Real64, RIB, RSS, RTF, SCT, SDTS, SND, Sparse6, STL, String, SXC, Table, TAR, TerminatedString, Text, TGA, TIFF, TSV, UnsignedInteger128, UnsignedInteger16, UnsignedInteger24, UnsignedInteger32, UnsignedInteger64, UnsignedInteger8, USGSDEM, UUE, VCF, WAV, Wave64, WDX, XBM, XHTML, XHTMLMathML, XLS, XML, XPORT, XYZ, ZIP}

Exercises 3.12

1. This exercise makes use of the **ElementData** command.

   a. Construct a table with 118 rows and 3 columns. Each row should contain the name of an element, its atomic weight (in atomic mass units), and its molar volume (in moles, obviously). Use the first 118 elements listed in **ElementData**.

   b. Make a **ListPlot** of molar volume versus atomic weight for your data.

   c. Add a **Tooltip** to your **ListPlot** so that the name of each element is displayed as you mouseover it.

2. Visit the web site http://www.census.gov/genealogy/names/names_files.html.

   a. Find the file giving the distribution of *female* first names, and make a table of female first names, ranked by frequency.

   b. With male first names, we showed in the text that roughly 70% of all males had one of the top 200 names. What proportion of females have one of the top 200 names?

3. Visit the web site http://research.stlouisfed.org/fred2/data/FEDFUNDS.txt. It shows the effective federal funds rate each month from 1954 to the present. Like the census site in the previous exercise, this page contains raw data suitable for display in a **Grid**. Unlike the census site, however, the first 13 lines of text on this page describe the data that follows. That is, the file contains more than just the straight data.

   a. Use **Import** with the URL above as the first argument, and "**Table**" as the second argument.

   b. Extract the data (starting on line 12, so that the column headers are included), and name it **data**.

   c. Use **DateListPlot** and **Rest** to view the data.

4. The **Select** command will apply a function to each member of a list. The syntax is: **Select**[*list,function*]. It will return all items in the list for which the function returns the value **True**. Typically the function is given as a *pure function* (these are discussed in Section 8.4). For our purposes, just remember that the **Slot** character # represents the variable for the function, that is, the items in the list. Enter the input below to find all of the properties available to **CountryData** which contain the substring "**Product**":

   $$\text{Select}\big[\text{CountryData}\big[\text{"Properties"}\big],\ \text{StringMatchQ}[\#,\ \_\_\_ \sim\sim \text{"Product"} \sim\sim \_\_\_]\ \&\big]$$

5. Use **Select** to find all chemicals listed in **ChemicalData** that contain the substring "**ButylEther**".

6. How many cities in the U.S. have a population exceeding 100,000? Hint: Use the **CityData** command together with **Select** to produce a list of such cities, then use **Length** to get the answer.

7. There are two standard ways of removing **Missing** data values from a list. One is to use **Select**, and another is to use **Cases** together with **Except**.

   a. Enter the two inputs below to see an example of each.

$$\text{Select}[\{1, 2, \text{Missing}["NotAvailable"], 4\}, \text{NumberQ}[\#] \&]$$

$$\text{Cases}[\{1, 2, \text{Missing}["NotAvailable"], 4\}, \text{Except}[\text{Missing}[\_]]]$$

   b. List all countries in **CountryData** for which the **"OilConsumption"** property is given as numerical value (i.e., for which it is not **Missing**).

   c. List all countries in **CountryData** for which both the **"OilConsumption"** and the **"Popula‥ tion"** properties are given as numerical values.

8. The **Sort** command is used to rearrange the items in a list. With a list given as its argument, **Sort** will arrange the list in standard order (ascending order for a list of numbers, alphabetical order for a list of strings, etc.).

   a. Use **Sort** to put the list {10,7,9,8} in ascending order.

   b. A second argument may be added to **Sort**. It specifies the *sorting function* to use. This is typically given as a **Function** with two arguments, **#1** and **#2**. Pairs of list members are given as the two arguments, and the function should return **True** precisely if the item **#1** should precede **#2** in the sorting order. Enter the inputs below to sort the rows of a table according the values in the third column (by oil consumption). Note that we first remove missing values from the data as discussed in the previous exercise.

$$\text{Select}[\text{CountryData}[], \text{NumberQ}[\text{CountryData}[\#, "OilConsumption"]] \&\&$$
$$\text{NumberQ}[\text{CountryData}[\#, "Population"]] \&];$$

$$\text{Table}[\{c, \text{CountryData}[c, "Population"], \text{CountryData}[c, "OilConsumption"]\}, \{c, \%\}];$$

$$\text{Sort}[\%, \#1[\![3]\!] > \#2[\![3]\!] \&] // \text{Grid}$$

   c. Make a **Grid** with two columns. The first gives the name of a country. The second gives the oil consumption per capita, in units of *barrels per year per person*. Sort the rows of the table so that the countries with the greatest per capita oil consumption are listed first.

   d. Where does the U.S. rank in per capita oil consumption?

3.13 Working with Difference Equations

A *sequence* is a function whose domain consists of the positive integers. In other words, it is a function s whose values can be listed: $s[1]$, $s[2]$, $s[3]$, …. A more traditional notation for these values is $s_1, s_2, s_3, \ldots$.

It is often possible to define a sequence by specifying the value of the first term (say $s[1] = 3$), and giving a *difference equation* (also called a *recurrence relation*) that expresses every subsequent term as a function of the previous term. For instance, suppose the first term in a sequence takes the value 3, and each term that follows has a value twice that of its predecessor. We could express this via the difference equation $s[n] = 2\,s[n-1]$ for each $n > 1$. A sequence defined this way is said to be defined *recursively*. Computers make it easy to calculate many terms of recursively defined sequences. Here's a means for harnessing *Mathematica* for such a purpose:

In[1]:= **Clear[s, n];**

$$s[n\_Integer] := \begin{cases} s[1] = 3 & n == 1 \\ s[n] = 2 * s[n-1] & n > 1 \end{cases}$$

Let's walk through this carefully, as it makes nontrivial use of all three types of equal signs. First, the left hand side is of the form **s[n_Integer]**. This indicates that the variable *n* must be an integer in order for the definition that follows to be applied. This is a safety feature, as it will prevent the inadvertent use of the function *s* being applied, for instance, to *n* = .5 or to any other non-integer input. Next we see the **SetDelayed** operator :=. This indicates that the expression to its right will only be evaluated when the function *s* is called. We also see that the expression to its right is a **Piecewise** defined function, as described in Section 3.6 on page 94. There are two distinct definitions of *s* according to whether the input *n* is equal to 1 or greater than 1. These two conditions (on the far right) will, for any value of *n*, evaluate to either **True** or **False**. Note the double equal sign here; it is a condition to be tested, not an assignment being made to the symbol *n*, so the double equal sign is needed. Finally, what happens when *s[n]* is called with a specific value of *n*? Let's see:

In[3]:= **s[4]**

Out[3]= 24

Here is what is now stored in memory for the symbol *s*:

In[4]:= **? s**

Global`s

s[1] = 3

s[2] = 6

s[3] = 12

s[4] = 24

$s[n\_Integer] := \text{Piecewise}[\{\{s[1] = 3, n == 1\}, \{s[n] = 2\,s[n-1], n > 1\}\}]$

Here's what happened: $s[4]$ was evaluated as $2 \times s[3]$, which was in turn evaluated as $2 \times (2 \times s[2])$, which in turn was evaluated as $2 \times (2 \times (2 \times s[1]))$, which was finally evaluated as $2 \times (2 \times (2 \times 3)) = 24$, with the assignment **s[1]=3** being made. At this point, the intermediate assignments **s[2]=6**, **s[3]=12**, **s[4]=24** were made in turn. If you were to ask for $s[4]$ again, it would be a one-step process and the value 24 would be returned immediately, for at this point the assignment **s[4]=24** has already been made. This is very important, for if you were to then ask for, say, $s[5]$, it would be a quick calculation: $2 \times s[4] = 2 \times 24 = 48$. This is the reason for the **Set** operator = in each of the two lines of the **Piecewise** definition of *s*; it prevents long chains of calculations being repeated.

The only down side to this approach is that after, for instance, $s[20]$ is evaluated, the assignments **s[1]=3**, **s[2]=6**, ... , **s[20]=1572864** are all stored in memory. If $s[200]$ is called, you literally have hundreds of assignments stored in memory. Fortunately, they are all associated with the symbol **s**, and so can be **Clear**ed in one line:

In[5]:= **Clear[s]**

In[6]:= **? s**

Global`s

Here are three things you can do with a sequence: compute an individual value (such as $s[4]$ above), make a table of values, or make a plot. These are easy, and will be discussed below. More subtle is the task of trying to find a *solution* to a difference equation—an explicit representation of $s[n]$ as a function of n. For instance, the function in our example above has the solution $s[n] = 3 \left(2^{n-1}\right)$. The task of solving difference equations is addressed in Section 4.8 on page 189.

Let's use a different example to illustrate the remaining topics. It is vitally important that we **Clear** the symbol s when moving from one function to the next, as the myriad of intermediate assignments from an earlier definition could easily pollute calculations to be made with a newer definition. For this reason it's always a good idea to include a **Clear** statement when defining a function recursively.

In[7]:= **Clear[s];**

$$s[\text{n\_Integer}] := \begin{cases} s[1] = 2 & n == 1 \\ s[n] = 3\,s[n-1] - .05\,s[n-1]^2 & n > 1 \end{cases}$$

Finding individual values is simple. For instance:

In[9]:= **s[20]**

Out[9]= 37.0838

However, there is one subtlety. *Mathematica* has a safety mechanism in place to prevent calculations from falling into an infinite loop. It will not allow, by default, any recursively defined command from calling itself more than 256 times. In practice, this means that you cannot ask for $s[n]$ when n is more than 256 units greater than the largest n with which s was previously called. For example, if you want to know $s[1000]$, you can't just ask for it and receive an answer. But you can work up to it by evaluating $s[250]$, then $s[500]$, then $s[750]$, and *then* $s[1000]$:

In[10]:= **{s[250], s[500], s[750], s[1000]}**

Out[10]= {39.1038, 39.3646, 39.481, 39.5505}

⚠ The system parameter **$RecursionLimit** is by default set to 256. Another means of making more than this number of recursive calculations is to assign a new value to this parameter. For instance, you may simply type **$RecursionLimit = 1024**, or whatever value you need, prior to evaluating your sequence term.

Making a table of sequence values is accomplished exactly as it is for any other type of function:

In[11]:= **Text@Grid[Table[{n, s[n]}, {n, 10}], Alignment → {{Right, Left}}, Spacings → 2]**

Out[11]=

1	2
2	5.8
3	15.718
4	34.8012
5	43.8474
6	35.4125
7	43.5353
8	35.8398
9	43.2948
10	36.1624

ListPlot may be used as discussed in Section 3.10 for plotting the values of a sequence.

In[12]:= **ListPlot[Table[{n, s[n]}, {n, 50}],**
AxesLabel → {"n", "s_n"}, AxesOrigin → {0, 0}, PlotRange → All]

Out[12]=

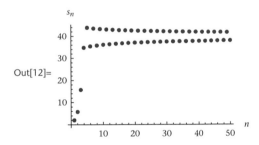

The option setting **Joined → True** will connect the dots. In this case, it helps to clarify the oscillatory nature of this sequence.

In[13]:= **ListPlot[Table[{n, s[n]}, {n, 50}], AxesLabel → {"n", "s_n"},**
AxesOrigin → {0, 0}, PlotRange → All, Joined → True]

Out[13]=

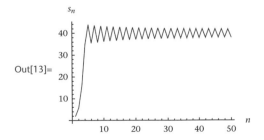

⚠ To generate several terms of a sequence defined by a first-order difference equation it is quite efficient to use **NestList** with a pure function as its first argument, rather than using **Piecewise** to define the sequence and **Table** to generate values. **NestList** is discussed in Section 8.7 and pure functions are discussed in Section 8.4. Here's an example showing how to generate the first ten terms of the sequence in the last example with only a few keystrokes. The first argument is a pure function that will generate a member of the sequence from the previous term. The second argument is the initial value in the sequence. The final argument is how many iterations you desire.

In[14]:= $\text{NestList}\left[3\,\# - .05\,\#^2\ \&,\ 2,\ 9\right]$

Out[14]= {2, 5.8, 15.718, 34.8012, 43.8474, 35.4125, 43.5353, 35.8398, 43.2948, 36.1624}

Exercises 3.13

1. Consider the sequence $s[n]$ with $s[1] = 100$, and with the remaining terms defined by the difference equation $s[n] = 1.05\,s[n-1]$.

   a. Enter this into *Mathematica*.

   b. Find $s[20]$.

   c. Make a **ListPlot** of the first 30 terms of the sequence.

   d. Assuming that the solution to this difference equation is of the form $s[n] = p * b^n$ for real parameters p and b, use **FindFit** and the data used in the **ListPlot** above to find a solution.

4
Algebra

4.1 Factoring and Expanding Polynomials

A *polynomial* in the variable x is a function of the form:

$$f(x) = a_0 + a_1\, x + a_2\, x^2 + \cdots + a_n\, x^n,$$

where the coefficients $a_0, a_1, \ldots, a_n$ are real numbers. Polynomials may be expressed in expanded or in factored form. Without a computer algebra system, moving from one form to the other is a tedious and often difficult process. With *Mathematica*, it is quite easy; the commands needed to transform a polynomial are called **Expand** and **Factor**.

In[1]:= **Clear[f, x];**
$$f[x\_] := 12 - 3\, x - 12\, x^3 + 3\, x^4$$

In[3]:= **Plot[f[x], {x, −2, 5}]**

Out[3]=

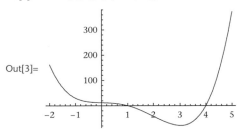

Here we see the graph of a polynomial that appears to have *roots* at $x = 1$ and $x = 4$ (that is, the function appears to assume the value 0 when $x = 1$ and $x = 4$). We can confirm this by factoring the polynomial:

In[4]:= **Factor[f[x]]**

Out[4]= $3\,(-4 + x)\,(-1 + x)\left(1 + x + x^2\right)$

Observe that when x assumes the value 4, the *linear factor* $(-4 + x)$ is zero, making the entire product equal to zero. Similarly, if $x = 1$, the linear factor $(-1 + x)$ is zero, and again the product is zero. Roots of a polynomial are often easily identified by determining the linear factors in the factored form of the polynomial.

The task of finding the roots of a given function f is a vitally important one. Suppose, for instance, that you need to solve an equation in one variable, say $-12 x^3 + 3 x^4 = 3 x - 12$. Equations such as this arise in a wide variety of applied contexts, and their solution is often of great importance. But solving such an equation is equivalent to finding the roots of a function—just subtract from each side of the given equation everything on the right hand side. In this case we get $12 - 3 x - 12 x^3 + 3 x^4 = 0$, so the solutions of this equation are the roots of the function $f(x) = 12 - 3 x - 12 x^3 + 3 x^4$, which we have just found (via factoring) to be 4 and 1. Solving equations and finding roots are essentially the same task.

You can expand a factored polynomial with the **Expand** command. This will essentially "undo" the factoring. One way to use this command is to open the AlgebraicManipulation palette (look for palettes in the Palettes menu). Use your mouse to highlight the factored output above, then push the Expand[■] button. Another way is to type:

In[5]:= **Expand[%]**

Out[5]= $12 - 3 x - 12 x^3 + 3 x^4$

The expanded form gives us different information about the function. The constant term (in this case 12) represents the y intercept of the polynomial's graph. It's simply the value of the function when $x = 0$. The leading coefficient (in this case 3, the coefficient of x^4) is positive. Since the $3 x^4$ summand will dominate the others for large values of x, a positive leading coefficient tells us that the function values will get large as x gets large.

It is important to note that some polynomials have real roots that will not be revealed by the **Factor** command:

In[6]:= $\text{Plot}\left[-1 + 3 x + x^2, \{x, -5, 3\}\right]$

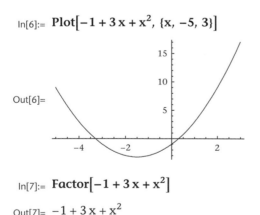

Out[6]=

In[7]:= $\text{Factor}\left[-1 + 3 x + x^2\right]$

Out[7]= $-1 + 3 x + x^2$

The graph clearly indicates two real roots, the x intercepts, yet there are no linear factors present in the factored form of the polynomial. Why? The **Factor** command will not extract factors that involve irrational or complex numbers unless such numbers appear as coefficients in the polynomial being factored. Since the coefficients in the above polynomial are all integers, only factors with integer coefficients will be extracted. To get *approximations* to the real roots, simply replace one of the integer coefficients in the original polynomial by its decimal equivalent by placing a decimal point after it. In doing this you are telling *Mathematica* that decimals are acceptable in the output:

In[8]:= $\text{Factor}\left[-1. + 3\,x + x^2\right]$

Out[8]= $1.\,(-0.302776 + x)\,(3.30278 + x)$

The real roots are approximately .302776 and -3.30278. You can easily check that this is consistent with the graph (and of course, you should).

Lastly, note that as always *Mathematica* makes a distinction between decimals and fractions when factoring:

In[9]:= $\text{Factor}\left[x^2 - 0.25\right]$

Out[9]= $1.\,(-0.5 + x)\,(0.5 + x)$

In[10]:= $\text{Factor}\left[x^2 - \dfrac{1}{4}\right]$

Out[10]= $\dfrac{1}{4}\,(-1 + 2\,x)\,(1 + 2\,x)$

Exercises 4.1

1. Let $f(x) = 1 + 5\,x + 2\,x^3 + 10\,x^4$.

   a. Use a **Plot** to estimate the real roots of $f(x)$.

   b. Use **Factor** to find the real roots of $f(x)$.

2. Factor the following expressions and explain the differences in the resulting factorizations.

   a. $1 + x^n + x^m + x^{n+m}$ and $1 + x + x^3 + x^4$

   b. $1 + x^3$ and $1 + x^n$

   c. $1 - x^4$ and $1 - x^{2n}$

4.2 Finding Roots of Polynomials with Solve and NSolve

The **Factor** command together with the **Plot** command are a powerful set of tools for discovering the real roots of polynomials. But there are a few shortcomings. Notice, for instance, that we can only *approximate* real roots that happen to be irrational (inexpressible as a quotient of integers). In addition, complex roots (involving the imaginary number i, the square root of -1) are completely inaccessible. For these reasons we introduce the **NSolve** and **Solve** commands.

Let's take another look at the polynomial $-1 + 3x + x^2$ from the previous section:

In[1]:= $\text{NSolve}\left[-1 + 3x + x^2 == 0, x\right]$

Out[1]= $\{\{x \to -3.30278\}, \{x \to 0.302776\}\}$

NSolve provides approximate numerical solutions to equations. It takes two arguments, separated as always by a comma. The first argument is an *equation*. Note that the double equal sign == is used for equations; this is because the single equal sign = is used to assign values to expressions, an essentially different operation. You may also use the $\boxed{==}$ button on the BasicMathInput palette. The second argument in the **NSolve** command (**x** in the example above) specifies the variable for which we want to solve. It may be obvious to you that you wish to solve for *x*, but it's not to the computer. For instance, there may be occasions when the equation you are solving involves more than one variable (we'll see an example later in this section). Lastly, the **NSolve** command can take an optional third argument which specifies the number of digits of precision that you desire:

In[2]:= $\text{NSolve}\left[-1 + 3x + x^2 == 0, x, 15\right]$

Out[2]= $\{\{x \to -3.30277563773199\}, \{x \to 0.30277563773199\}\}$

Now what about the output? First notice that it is in the form a *list* (a sequence of items separated by commas with a set of curly brackets around the whole thing). This is because there are typically numerous solutions to a given equation, so it is sensible to present them in a list. Now let's focus on the items in this list. Each is of the form {x → *solution*}. This looks strange at first, but it is easy enough to interpret. It is an example of a structure called a *replacement rule*, which will be explored later in this section.

You can smarten the appearance of the list of solutions by making a **Grid** of the results. As discussed in the last chapter (Section 3.5, see page 87) when **Grid** is applied to a such a list it will produce a neatly formatted column:

In[3]:= $\text{NSolve}\left[-1 + 3x + x^2 == 0, x, 35\right] // \text{Grid}$

Out[3]= $\begin{array}{l} x \to -3.3027756377319946465596106337352480 \\ x \to 0.3027756377319946465596106337352480 \end{array}$

Can *Mathematica* produce *exact* solutions to polynomial equations? The answer is sometimes. It is a mathematical fact that some polynomial equations involving powers of *x* that exceed 4 cannot be solved algebraically, period. However, if an equation can be solved algebraically, the **Solve** command is the ticket. Here are the precise roots of the polynomial above:

In[4]:= $\text{Solve}\left[-1 + 3x + x^2 == 0, x\right] // \text{Grid}$

Out[4]= $\begin{array}{l} x \to \frac{1}{2}\left(-3 - \sqrt{13}\right) \\ x \to \frac{1}{2}\left(-3 + \sqrt{13}\right) \end{array}$

Remember the quadratic formula? That's all that's happening here. In fact, if you ever forget the quadratic formula, you can have *Mathematica* derive it for you:

In[5]:= **Clear[a, b, c, x];**
Solve[a x^2 + b x + c == 0, x] // Grid

Out[6]=
$$x \to \frac{-b - \sqrt{b^2 - 4ac}}{2a}$$
$$x \to \frac{-b + \sqrt{b^2 - 4ac}}{2a}$$

Note the space between **a** and **x^2**, and between **b** and **x** in the last input line; they are needed to indicate multiplication. This example also makes it clear why the second argument to the **Solve** command is so important; this is an equation that could be solved for *a*, for *b*, for *c*, or for *x*. You have to specify the variable for which you wish to solve.

Let's look at a few more examples of these commands in action. We'll start with the **NSolve** command and later address some special considerations for using the **Solve** command:

In[7]:= **Plot[x + 3 x^2 + x^3, {x, −3, 1}]**

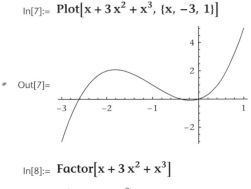

Out[7]=

In[8]:= **Factor[x + 3 x^2 + x^3]**

Out[8]= $x \left(1 + 3x + x^2\right)$

In[9]:= **NSolve[x + 3 x^2 + x^3 == 0, x]**

Out[9]= {{x → −2.61803}, {x → −0.381966}, {x → 0.}}

Note that the factor *x* corresponds to the root *x* = 0, but that the other roots are not revealed by the **Factor** command (although they would have been found had we replaced the **x** by **1.*x** in the polynomial). The **NSolve** command reveals all roots, always.

Now let's tweak things a little. We can shift the graph of this function up by one unit by adding 1 to its expression, and the resulting function should have only one real root (the dip on the right of the graph will be entirely above the *x*-axis):

In[10]:= $\text{Plot}\left[1 + x + 3\,x^2 + x^3,\ \{x,\ -3,\ 1\}\right]$

Out[10]=

In[11]:= $\text{Factor}\left[1 + x + 3\,x^2 + x^3\right]$

Out[11]= $1 + x + 3\,x^2 + x^3$

This didn't do a thing; the new function has no rational roots. What happens if we replace one of the integer coefficients with its decimal equivalent?

In[12]:= $\text{Factor}\left[1. + x + 3\,x^2 + x^3\right]$

Out[12]= $1.\,(2.76929 + x)\,\left(0.361103 + 0.230708\,x + x^2\right)$

This reveals a real root near $x = -2.76929$. But what about the quadratic factor?

In[13]:= $\text{NSolve}\left[1 + x + 3\,x^2 + x^3 == 0,\ x\right]$

Out[13]= $\{\{x \to -2.76929\},\ \{x \to -0.115354 - 0.589743\,i\},\ \{x \to -0.115354 + 0.589743\,i\}\}$

Mathematica is reporting three roots. The first root reported is the *x*-intercept that we see in the plot. The second two are complex numbers; they are each expressions of the form $a + bi$, where i is the imaginary number whose square is -1. They are purely algebraic solutions to the polynomial equation, bearing no obvious geometric relationship to its graph. Although you may not care to contemplate complex roots of equations, the **Solve** and **NSolve** commands will always display them if they exist. It is a fact that every polynomial whose highest power of *x* is *n* will have exactly *n* roots, some of which may be complex numbers (see the *fundamental theorem of algebra* in Section 4.4 on page 169). It is also true that any complex roots of a polynomial (whose coefficients are all real) come in *conjugate pairs*; one will be of the form $a + bi$, the other $a - bi$, as in the output above.

How can you extract one solution from a list of solutions? For instance, you may only need a real solution, or the context of the problem may dictate that only positive solutions be considered. You can extract a single solution from the list of solutions using double square brackets. This was discussed in Section 3.11 on page 126. Here's an example to illustrate:

In[14]:= $\text{sols} = \text{Solve}\left[x^2 - 225 == 0,\ x\right]$

Out[14]= $\{\{x \to -15\},\ \{x \to 15\}\}$

We have given the list of solutions the name **sols** (note the assignment operator = assigns the name **sols** to the output, while the equation operator == is used to produce equations). Here's how to extract the first element from a list (type ⎡ESC⎤ [[⎡ESC⎤ to get ⟦, or you may also just use two square brackets back to back):

In[15]:= **sols⟦1⟧**

Out[15]= {x → −15}

and the second element:

In[16]:= **sols⟦2⟧**

Out[16]= {x → 15}

This method works for any list:

In[17]:= **{a, b, c, d, e}⟦2⟧**

Out[17]= b

You may also use the ⎡■[□]⎤ button on the BasicMathInput palette to extract an item from a list.

To use one of the solutions provided by the **NSolve** or **Solve** command in a subsequent calculation, you need to understand the syntax of *replacement rules*. The symbol /. tells *Mathematica* to make a replacement. It is shorthand for a command called **ReplaceAll**. You first write an expression involving **x**, then write /. and then write a replacement rule of the form **x → *solution***. The arrow → is found on the BasicMathInput palette. You may type -> (the "minus" sign followed by the "greater than" sign) in place of the arrow if you wish:

In[18]:= **x^2 /. x → 3**

Out[18]= 9

This last input line can be read as "Evaluate the expression x^2, replacing x by 3."

Here's how you can use replacement rules to extract solutions generated by the **Solve** command:

In[19]:= **x /. sols⟦1⟧**

Out[19]= −15

In[20]:= **x /. sols⟦2⟧**

Out[20]= 15

In[21]:= **x^2 /. sols⟦2⟧**

Out[21]= 225

If you don't specify which solution you want, you will get a list where x is replaced by each solution in turn:

In[22]:= **x /. sols**

Out[22]= {−15, 15}

You can do all of this in one step, generating output that is a list of solutions rather than a list of replacement rules:

In[23]:= **x /. Solve$\left[x^2 - 225 == 0, x\right]$**

Out[23]= {−15, 15}

You may also use replacement rules to test whether an equation holds for a particular value of *x*:

In[24]:= **$x^2 - 225 == 0$ /. sols⟦1⟧**

Out[24]= True

In[25]:= **$x^2 - 225 == 0$ /. x → 10**

Out[25]= False

Replacement rules take some getting used to, but they are enormously convenient. Here, for instance, we plot a polynomial, and include an **Epilog** to place a **Point** at each of the roots (this will work when all roots are real):

In[26]:= **f[x_] := $12 + 4x - 15x^2 - 5x^3 + 3x^4 + x^5$**

In[27]:= **Plot$\left[$f[x], {x, −4, 3}, Epilog → {PointSize[.02], Point[{x, 0}] /. NSolve[f[x] == 0, x]}$\right]$**

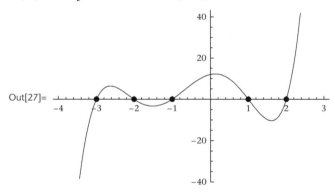

Out[27]=

Now let's look at the **Solve** command in greater detail. Note that you can find the exact roots (without any decimal approximations) for any polynomial whose degree is four or less:

In[28]:= **Grid$\left[$Solve$\left[x^4 - x - 2 == 0, x\right]$, Alignment → Left$\right]$**

$$x \to -1$$

$$x \to \frac{1}{3}\left(1 - 2\left(\frac{2}{47 + 3\sqrt{249}}\right)^{1/3} + \left(\frac{1}{2}\left(47 + 3\sqrt{249}\right)\right)^{1/3}\right)$$

Out[28]=
$$x \to \frac{1}{3} + \frac{1}{3}\left(1 + i\sqrt{3}\right)\left(\frac{2}{47 + 3\sqrt{249}}\right)^{1/3} - \frac{1}{6}\left(1 - i\sqrt{3}\right)\left(\frac{1}{2}\left(47 + 3\sqrt{249}\right)\right)^{1/3}$$

$$x \to \frac{1}{3} + \frac{1}{3}\left(1 - i\sqrt{3}\right)\left(\frac{2}{47 + 3\sqrt{249}}\right)^{1/3} - \frac{1}{6}\left(1 + i\sqrt{3}\right)\left(\frac{1}{2}\left(47 + 3\sqrt{249}\right)\right)^{1/3}$$

Wow, this is powerful stuff! But be careful when using the **Solve** command. If you just need an approximate decimal solution to an equation you will be better served using **NSolve**. In particular, if you want a numerical approximation to a solution generated by the **Solve** command, as you might with the output generated above, it is *not* a good idea to apply the **N** command to the result. In some cases, for instance, you may end up with complex numbers approximating real roots (try solving $x^3 - 15x + 2 = 0$; it has three real roots, yet applying **N** to the output of the **Solve** command produces complex numbers—see Exercise 2). The moral of the story: Use **Solve** to generate exact answers; use **NSolve** to generate numerical solutions to any required degree of accuracy.

Another consideration to be aware of when using the **Solve** command is that equations involving polynomials of degree 5 or more (i.e., where the highest power of x is 5 or more) may not have explicit algebraic solutions. This is a mathematical fact; there are equations of degree five with roots that cannot be represented in radicals. Here is what the output will look like in these situations:

In[29]:= **Solve$\left[x^5 - x + 1 == 0, x\right]$**

Out[29]= $\{\{x \to \text{Root}[1 - \#1 + \#1^5 \,\&, 1]\}, \{x \to \text{Root}[1 - \#1 + \#1^5 \,\&, 2]\}, \{x \to \text{Root}[1 - \#1 + \#1^5 \,\&, 3]\},$
$\{x \to \text{Root}[1 - \#1 + \#1^5 \,\&, 4]\}, \{x \to \text{Root}[1 - \#1 + \#1^5 \,\&, 5]\}\}$

The output here is comprised of **Root** objects, which are a means of cataloging the (in this case five) roots that cannot be expressed in algebraic form using radicals. When **Root** objects arise, it is always possible to apply **N** to the output to get numerical approximations. Alternately, **NSolve** can be used to get the same result:

In[30]:= **Grid$\left[\text{NSolve}\left[x^5 - x + 1 == 0, x\right], \text{Alignment} \to \text{Left}\right]$**

$$x \to -1.1673$$
$$x \to -0.181232 - 1.08395\,i$$
Out[30]= $x \to -0.181232 + 1.08395\,i$
$$x \to 0.764884 - 0.352472\,i$$
$$x \to 0.764884 + 0.352472\,i$$

After all this you may wonder why the **Solve** command is ever used, since **NSolve** seems to be more versatile and robust. The answer is that it depends on your purposes. For numerical solutions to specific problems, **NSolve** is probably all you need. But for exact algebraic solutions or the derivation of general formulae, **Solve** is indispensable. Here are two more examples to illustrate the power of this command. The first provides the general formula for the roots of a cubic equation of the form $x^3 + bx + c$, where b and c may be any numbers:

In[31]:= **Clear[b, c, x];**
Grid[Solve[$x^3 + bx + c == 0$, x], Alignment → Left]

$$x \to -\frac{\left(\frac{2}{3}\right)^{1/3} b}{\left(-9c+\sqrt{3}\sqrt{4b^3+27c^2}\right)^{1/3}} + \frac{\left(-9c+\sqrt{3}\sqrt{4b^3+27c^2}\right)^{1/3}}{2^{1/3}\,3^{2/3}}$$

Out[32]= $$x \to \frac{\left(1+i\sqrt{3}\right)b}{2^{2/3}\,3^{1/3}\left(-9c+\sqrt{3}\sqrt{4b^3+27c^2}\right)^{1/3}} - \frac{\left(1-i\sqrt{3}\right)\left(-9c+\sqrt{3}\sqrt{4b^3+27c^2}\right)^{1/3}}{2\,2^{1/3}\,3^{2/3}}$$

$$x \to \frac{\left(1-i\sqrt{3}\right)b}{2^{2/3}\,3^{1/3}\left(-9c+\sqrt{3}\sqrt{4b^3+27c^2}\right)^{1/3}} - \frac{\left(1+i\sqrt{3}\right)\left(-9c+\sqrt{3}\sqrt{4b^3+27c^2}\right)^{1/3}}{2\,2^{1/3}\,3^{2/3}}$$

The next example illustrates how **Solve** may be used to put a given formula into a different form. It is a rather trite computation, but it illustrates the versatility of the **Solve** command:

In[33]:= **Clear[e, m, c];**
Solve[$e == mc^2$, m]

Out[34]= $\left\{\left\{m \to \dfrac{e}{c^2}\right\}\right\}$

One last comment about the **Solve** command is in order. As you may expect, it will distinguish between decimals and fractions in the input, and adjust its output to match:

In[35]:= **Solve[$x^2 - 0.25 == 0$, x]**

Out[35]= $\{\{x \to -0.5\}, \{x \to 0.5\}\}$

In[36]:= **Solve[$x^2 - \dfrac{1}{4} == 0$, x]**

Out[36]= $\left\{\left\{x \to -\dfrac{1}{2}\right\}, \left\{x \to \dfrac{1}{2}\right\}\right\}$

Exercises 4.2

1. In Exercise 1 of Section 4.1 we used **Factor** to find the real roots of $f(x) = 1 + 5x + 2x^3 + 10x^4$.

   a. Use **Solve** to find the real roots of $f(x)$ and compare your solutions with the values you found in Exercise 1 of Section 4.1.

b. Use **NSolve** to approximate the real roots of $f(x)$ and compare your solutions with the values you found in Exercise 1 of Section 4.1.

2. Use **Solve** followed by **N** to approximate the roots of the polynomial $x^3 - 15x + 2$. Then find the roots using **NSolve**. Which gives the better approximation?

3. Fix two real numbers p and q, and consider the following quadratic equation in the variable z:
$z^2 - qz - \frac{1}{27}p^3 = 0$.

   a. **Solve** this equation in terms of p and q (use *Mathematica*, or work by hand using the quadratic formula).

   b. Consider the expression $\frac{z^2 - qz - \frac{1}{27}p^3}{z}$, which has the same roots as the quadratic above. Use replacement rules to replace z by w^3, then w by $\frac{1}{6}\left(3y + \sqrt{3}\sqrt{4p + 3y^2}\right)$, and then p by $\left(b - \frac{a^2}{3}\right)$ and q by $\left(\frac{-2a^3 + 9ab - 27c}{27}\right)$, and finally, y by $\left(x + \frac{a}{3}\right)$. **Simplify** the result and **Collect** the terms as ascending powers of x. What do you get?

   c. Use the information in parts **a** and **b** to develop a means of using the quadratic formula to solve the general cubic equation $x^3 + ax^2 + bx + c = 0$. That is, take the solution to the quadratic in part **a** and transform it into a root of the cubic $x^3 + ax^2 + bx + c$ using the transformations in part **b**. The idea to use these successive replacements for the purpose of solving a cubic was perfected in the 1500s by Italian mathematicians such as Cardano and Tartaglia.

   d. Compare the output to that of **Solve$\left[x^3 + ax^2 + bx + c == 0, x\right]$[[1]]**.

4.3 Solving Equations and Inequalities with Reduce

The **Reduce** command provides another means for solving equations. The input syntax is like that used for **Solve** and **NSolve**, but the output is expressed in a very different way.

In[1]:= **Reduce$\left[x^2 == 100, x\right]$**

Out[1]= $x == -10 \,\|\, x == 10$

The values of x are given as *equations* rather than as replacement rules. The double vertical bar $\|$ stands for the word "or." So the output here reads, "Either x is equal to -10, or x is equal to 10."

The reason for the different output format is that **Reduce** is designed to consider special conditions on all parameters appearing in an equation, whereas **Solve** will ignore conditions on any parameter whose solution is not explicitly being sought. For example, the solution below only makes sense when the parameter $a \neq 0$:

In[2]:= **Solve[a x == b, x]**

Out[2]= $\left\{\left\{x \to \frac{b}{a}\right\}\right\}$

Reduce takes into account the possibility that *a* could be zero:

In[3]:= **Reduce[a x == b, x]**

Out[3]= $(b == 0 \,\&\&\, a == 0) \,||\, \left(a \neq 0 \,\&\&\, x == \dfrac{b}{a}\right)$

Note that the double ampersand **&&** stands for the word "and," so this reads, "Either *a* and *b* are both equal to 0, or *a* is nonzero and $x = \frac{b}{a}$." The output syntax is designed to handle subtle expressions like this.

Another point where **Reduce** and **Solve** differ arises when an equation has an infinite number of discrete solutions, such as cos(*x*) = 0. We all know that the cosine function is equal to zero when its argument is of the form $2k\pi \pm \frac{\pi}{2}$, where *k* is any integer. **Solve** will not attempt to display them all. Rather it will send a warning message suggesting that you try **Reduce** instead:

In[4]:= **Solve[Cos[x] == 0, x]**

> Solve::ifun : Inverse functions are being used by Solve, so some
> solutions may not be found; use Reduce for complete solution information. ≫

Out[4]= $\left\{\left\{x \to -\dfrac{\pi}{2}\right\}, \left\{x \to \dfrac{\pi}{2}\right\}\right\}$

Okay, let's try it:

In[5]:= **Reduce[Cos[x] == 0, x]**

Out[5]= $C[1] \in \text{Integers} \,\&\&\, \left(x == -\dfrac{\pi}{2} + 2\pi\,C[1] \,||\, x == \dfrac{\pi}{2} + 2\pi\,C[1]\right)$

The output says precisely what it should, but we first need to understand the syntax. We said earlier that the solution set is comprised of all numbers $2k\pi \pm \frac{\pi}{2}$, where *k* is an integer. **Reduce** uses the generic name **C[1]** (rather than *k*) when it has to introduce a constant. It's a rather unsightly name, but something like this is necessary. For instance, in an output where fifty such constants are needed, they will be called **C[1]**, **C[2]**, and so on; the numerical piece guarantees that the notation is capable of handling arbitrarily many such constants. Next, we see the symbol ∈. This is standard mathematical notation; it reads "is an element of." Hence the output above says: "*C*[1] is an element of the set of integers, and $x = 2\pi\,C[1] \pm \frac{\pi}{2}$." The output concisely describes *all* of the roots of the cosine function.

Reduce is also effective at expressing inequalities:

In[6]:= **Reduce$\left[x^2 - 1 > 0, x\right]$**

Out[6]= $x < -1 \,||\, x > 1$

If you were asked to describe the natural domain (among all real numbers) for the function

$f(x) = \dfrac{x^2 - 7x + 3}{\sqrt{x^3 - 4x^2 + 2x - 1}}$, you would want to know for which values of x the polynomial

$x^3 - 4x^2 + 2x - 1 > 0$. **Reduce** can handle this:

In[7]:= **Reduce**$\left[x^3 - 4x^2 + 2x - 1 > 0,\ x\right]$

Out[7]= $x > \text{Root}\left[-1 + 2\#1 - 4\#1^2 + \#1^3 \ \&,\ 1\right]$

The solution is given in terms of a **Root** object, which at first glance may seem both intimidating and unhelpful. A careful inspection shows that **Root** simply writes the polynomial in the form of a pure function (see Section 8.4 page 403 for a discussion of these) for its first argument. The second argument gives an index number for the root in question. Essentially, **Root** objects are a means of cataloging roots of polynomials. What is important for us here is the fact that using **N**, we can numerically approximate any **Root** object with ease:

In[8]:= **Reduce**$\left[x^3 - 4x^2 + 2x - 1 > 0,\ x\right] \, // \, \mathbf{N}$

Out[8]= $x > 3.51155$

If an exact answer is preferred, one can specify for cubic or quartic polynomials that an explicit expression in radicals be given (instead of **Root** objects); just set the option **Cubics** (or **Quartics** in the case of a polynomial of degree 4) to **True**:

In[9]:= **Reduce**$\left[x^3 - 4x^2 + 2x - 1 > 0,\ x,\ \textbf{Cubics} \rightarrow \textbf{True}\right]$

Out[9]= $x > \dfrac{4}{3} + \dfrac{1}{3}\left(\dfrac{83}{2} - \dfrac{3\sqrt{321}}{2}\right)^{1/3} + \dfrac{1}{3}\left(\dfrac{1}{2}\left(83 + 3\sqrt{321}\right)\right)^{1/3}$

A plot is consistent with the result that $x > 3.51$:

In[10]:= **Plot**$\left[\dfrac{x^2 - 7x + 3}{\sqrt{x^3 - 4x^2 + 2x - 1}},\ \{x, 0, 5\}\right]$

Out[10]=

Note that *Mathematica* can also express the output generated by **Reduce** using standard notation from the field of mathematical logic. In this notation, the symbol $\wedge$ means "and" and the symbol $\vee$ means "or." If you have experience with this notation, you may find it easier to read. A constant is also represented as c_1 rather than **C[1]**. In all, it reads a bit more nicely. To get your output in this form, simply apply **TraditionalForm** to the output of **Reduce**.

In[11]:= **Reduce[Cos[x] == 0, x] // TraditionalForm**

Out[11]//TraditionalForm=

$$c_1 \in \mathbb{Z} \bigwedge \left(x = 2\pi c_1 - \frac{\pi}{2} \bigvee x = 2\pi c_1 + \frac{\pi}{2} \right)$$

Here is a more complicated example in which there are two constants. The symbol $\mathbb{Z}$ denotes the set of integers, as is traditional in mathematical notation.

In[12]:= **Reduce[Sin[1 + Cos[x]] == 1, x] // TraditionalForm**

Out[12]//TraditionalForm=

$$(c_1 \mid c_2) \in \mathbb{Z} \bigwedge \left(x = 2\pi c_2 - \cos^{-1}\left(\frac{1}{2} (4\pi c_1 + \pi - 2) \right) \bigvee x = \cos^{-1}\left(\frac{1}{2} (4\pi c_1 + \pi - 2) \right) + 2\pi c_2 \right)$$

While the output for **Reduce** *reads* very nicely, it is not obvious how one could work programmatically with it to perform some follow-up work. It is certainly possible to copy and paste portions of the output, but there are other ways. First note that just as you can extract parts from a **List**, you can extract parts from a logical expression like the one above:

In[13]:= **Reduce[Sin[1 + Cos[x]] == 1, x]〚1〛**

Out[13]= $(C[1] \mid C[2]) \in$ Integers

In[14]:= **ans = Reduce[Sin[1 + Cos[x]] == 1, x]〚2〛**

Out[14]= $x == -\text{ArcCos}\left[\frac{1}{2} (-2 + \pi + 4\pi C[1]) \right] + 2\pi C[2] \;\|\; x == \text{ArcCos}\left[\frac{1}{2} (-2 + \pi + 4\pi C[1]) \right] + 2\pi C[2]$

One can take this second part (or any other such logical combination of equations) and use **ToRules** to turn it into a list of replacement rules, suitable as input to other commands:

In[15]:= **{ToRules[ans]}**

Out[15]= $\left\{ \left\{ x \rightarrow -\text{ArcCos}\left[\frac{1}{2} (-2 + \pi + 4\pi C[1]) \right] + 2\pi C[2] \right\},\right.$

$\left.\left\{ x \rightarrow \text{ArcCos}\left[\frac{1}{2} (-2 + \pi + 4\pi C[1]) \right] + 2\pi C[2] \right\} \right\}$

Finally, one can replace the constants by numerical values, and hence obtain a usable list of replacement rules. **Flatten** is applied to this list to remove extra curly brackets.

In[16]:= **rules = Flatten[Table[{ToRules[ans]} /. {C[1] → 0, C[2] → k}, {k, −1, 1}], 1]**

Out[16]= $\left\{\left\{x \to -2\pi - \text{ArcCos}\left[\frac{1}{2}(-2+\pi)\right]\right\}, \left\{x \to -2\pi + \text{ArcCos}\left[\frac{1}{2}(-2+\pi)\right]\right\},\right.$

$\left\{x \to -\text{ArcCos}\left[\frac{1}{2}(-2+\pi)\right]\right\}, \left\{x \to \text{ArcCos}\left[\frac{1}{2}(-2+\pi)\right]\right\},$

$\left.\left\{x \to 2\pi - \text{ArcCos}\left[\frac{1}{2}(-2+\pi)\right]\right\}, \left\{x \to 2\pi + \text{ArcCos}\left[\frac{1}{2}(-2+\pi)\right]\right\}\right\}$

Here, for example, is a plot of the function $f(x) = \sin(1 + \cos(x))$ with the solutions to the equation $f(x) = 1$ shown as large points via the **Epilog**:

In[17]:= **Plot$\left[\text{Sin}[1 + \text{Cos}[x]], \{x, -10, 10\}, \text{Epilog} \to \{\text{PointSize}[.02], \text{Point}[\{x, 1\}] /. \text{rules}\}\right]$**

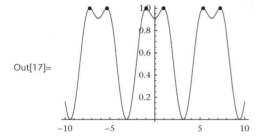

Out[17]=

As with **Solve** and **NSolve**, it may be the case that complex numbers are generated by **Reduce**.

In[18]:= **Reduce$\left[x^3 - x + 2 == 0, x, \text{Cubics} \to \text{True}\right]$**

Out[18]= $x == -\dfrac{\left(9 - \sqrt{78}\right)^{1/3}}{3^{2/3}} - \dfrac{1}{\left(3\left(9 - \sqrt{78}\right)\right)^{1/3}}$ ||

$x == \dfrac{\left(1 + i\sqrt{3}\right)\left(9 - \sqrt{78}\right)^{1/3}}{2 \cdot 3^{2/3}} + \dfrac{1 - i\sqrt{3}}{2\left(3\left(9 - \sqrt{78}\right)\right)^{1/3}}$ ||

$x == \dfrac{\left(1 - i\sqrt{3}\right)\left(9 - \sqrt{78}\right)^{1/3}}{2 \cdot 3^{2/3}} + \dfrac{1 + i\sqrt{3}}{2\left(3\left(9 - \sqrt{78}\right)\right)^{1/3}}$

In the next section we discuss a means for dispensing with non-real output.

Exercises 4.3

1. Find the largest possible domain in the real numbers for the function $f(x) = \frac{x^3 + 5x^2 + 4x + 5}{\sqrt{x^2 + 2x - 3}}$. Make a

   plot of f over a valid domain in the *positive* real numbers, along with the function

   $\sqrt{x^4 + 8x^3 + 20x^2 + 34x + 58}$. What do you notice?

2. **Reduce** can be used to solve *systems of equations*. A system of equations is a collection of several equations, each in several variables. A *solution* to such a system is a set of values for the variables for which all the equations are satisfied.

   a. A system of equations can be entered in several ways. One can either type a list of equations, or an equation of lists like the input below. Type and enter this input.

   $$\text{Reduce}[\{\text{Cos}[y]\,\text{Cos}[x\,\text{Cos}[y]], -x\,\text{Cos}[x\,\text{Cos}[y]]\,\text{Sin}[y]\} == \{0, 0\}, \{x, y\}, \text{Reals}]$$

   b. The output is a bit intimidating at first. This is unavoidable for the simple reason that the solution set happens to be rather complex. If we regard a particular solution (x_0, y_0) as a point in the xy plane, then this output is comprised of both discrete points and entire curves in the plane. Read the output carefully and identify the discrete points. **ListPlot** them in the plane.

   c. Use **ContourPlot** to sketch the solutions of both equations.

3. We can also use **Reduce** to solve a single equation with more than one variable. Use **Reduce** to

   find the set of points in the plane that are solutions of $\frac{8xy^2}{(1+y^2)^2} = \frac{4x}{1+y^2}$ and then use **ContourPlot** to

   graph the set of solutions.

4.4 Understanding Complex Output

You've noticed by now that complex numbers sometimes appear in *Mathematica*'s output. They can pop up in a variety of places, even when you don't expect them. In Section 3.2 on page 57, for instance, we saw that *Mathematica* regards the cube root of a negative number as a complex number.

In[1]:= $(-8)^{1/3}$ // N

Out[1]= $1. + 1.73205\,i$

In high school and early college courses it is more common to work with the *real-valued* cube root function, which would return the value -2 (instead of the complex number above) as the cube root of -8. Here are a few other instances where complex numbers can pop up in the context of a real computation:

In[2]:= **Log[−2]**

Out[2]= $i\pi + \text{Log}[2]$

In[3]:= **ArcSin[2.]**

Out[3]= $1.5708 - 1.31696\,i$

In[4]:= **Solve$\left[x^2 == -4,\ x\right]$**

Out[4]= $\{\{x \to -2\,i\},\ \{x \to 2\,i\}\}$

In[5]:= **Reduce$\left[1 + x + 3\,x^2 + x^3 == 0,\ x,\ \text{Cubics} \to \text{True}\right]$**

Out[5]= $x == -1 - \dfrac{\left(9 - \sqrt{57}\right)^{1/3}}{3^{2/3}} - \dfrac{2}{\left(3\left(9 - \sqrt{57}\right)\right)^{1/3}}\ \|$

$\quad x == -1 + \dfrac{\left(1 + i\sqrt{3}\right)\left(9 - \sqrt{57}\right)^{1/3}}{2\cdot 3^{2/3}} + \dfrac{1 - i\sqrt{3}}{\left(3\left(9 - \sqrt{57}\right)\right)^{1/3}}\ \|$

$\quad x == -1 + \dfrac{\left(1 - i\sqrt{3}\right)\left(9 - \sqrt{57}\right)^{1/3}}{2\cdot 3^{2/3}} + \dfrac{1 + i\sqrt{3}}{\left(3\left(9 - \sqrt{57}\right)\right)^{1/3}}$

Now this sort of output ought to make you hungry to learn about the complex numbers. If you are even a bit curious, ask your instructor about them. And even if you are not particularly interested in such matters be mindful that you are now using a grown-up software package, so you are going to have to deal with them from time to time. Let's deal with the inputs above individually. We'll discuss the cube root function at length later in this section. The next two inputs simply extend the domains of the logarithm and inverse sine functions beyond what we ordinarily allow. Doing so results in complex output. In a precalculus or calculus course, the likelihood of encountering complex numbers in this way is small. The next outputs, however, will be more difficult to avoid. We have already seen instances in which **Solve** and **NSolve** will find complex solutions to equations, even when every quantity appearing in those equations is real. Whereas **Solve** and **NSolve** are designed to always report complex solutions when they exist, the command **Reduce** allows one to specify that only real values are to be considered. Simply set the optional third argument of **Reduce** to **Reals**. If there are no real solutions, it will return **False**.

In[6]:= **Reduce$\left[e^x == -2,\ x,\ \text{Reals}\right]$**

Out[6]= False

In[7]:= **Reduce[Sin[x] == 2, x, Reals]**

Out[7]= False

In[8]:= $\textbf{Reduce}\big[x^2 == -4,\ x,\ \textbf{Reals}\big]$

Out[8]= False

In[9]:= $\textbf{Reduce}\big[x^3 == -8,\ x,\ \textbf{Reals}\big]$

Out[9]= $x == -2$

In[10]:= $\textbf{Reduce}\big[1 + x + 3\,x^2 + x^3 == 0,\ x,\ \textbf{Reals},\ \textbf{Cubics} \to \textbf{True}\big]$

Out[10]= $x == -1 - \dfrac{\left(9 - \sqrt{57}\right)^{1/3}}{3^{2/3}} - \dfrac{2}{\left(3\left(9 - \sqrt{57}\right)\right)^{1/3}}$

The lesson here is that if you are interested only in real solutions to equations, using **Reduce** with **Reals** as its third argument is a good strategy.

Another subtle issue that can arise from time to time is illustrated below:

In[11]:= $\textbf{Reduce}\big[x^3 - 15\,x + 2 == 0,\ x,\ \textbf{Reals},\ \textbf{Cubics} \to \textbf{True}\big]$

Out[11]= $x == \dfrac{5}{\left(-1 + 2\,i\,\sqrt{31}\right)^{1/3}} + \left(-1 + 2\,i\,\sqrt{31}\right)^{1/3}$ ||

$x == -\dfrac{5\left(1 + i\,\sqrt{3}\right)}{2\left(-1 + 2\,i\,\sqrt{31}\right)^{1/3}} - \dfrac{1}{2}\left(1 - i\,\sqrt{3}\right)\left(-1 + 2\,i\,\sqrt{31}\right)^{1/3}$ ||

$x == -\dfrac{5\left(1 - i\,\sqrt{3}\right)}{2\left(-1 + 2\,i\,\sqrt{31}\right)^{1/3}} - \dfrac{1}{2}\left(1 + i\,\sqrt{3}\right)\left(-1 + 2\,i\,\sqrt{31}\right)^{1/3}$

Here we have asked only for real roots, and yet **Reduce** has returned three expressions involving i. The output is correct; each of these numbers is indeed a real number (one could verify this with a plot of this cubic—its graph crosses the x-axis three times). But just as one can write the real number -1 as i^2, it is possible to express other real numbers in a manner that makes use of the complex number i. That's what has happened here. In some cases it is possible to algebraically manipulate such numbers so that all the i's go away. The command that can accomplish this is called **Complex·.Expand**. It will attempt to break a knotty complex number into its real and imaginary components. In this case, the imaginary part of each of the numbers above should be exactly zero. One could apply simply append //**ComplexExpand** to the previous input, but we will apply it just to the first root reported above to make the output easier to read:

In[12]:= **ComplexExpand**$\left[\dfrac{5}{\left(-1+2\,i\,\sqrt{31}\,\right)^{1/3}}+\left(-1+2\,i\,\sqrt{31}\,\right)^{1/3}\right]$

Out[12]= $\sqrt{5}\ \text{Cos}\left[\dfrac{1}{3}\left(\pi-\text{ArcTan}\left[2\,\sqrt{31}\,\right]\right)\right]+\sqrt{5}\ \text{Cos}\left[\dfrac{1}{3}\left(-\pi+\text{ArcTan}\left[2\,\sqrt{31}\,\right]\right)\right]+$

$i\left(\sqrt{5}\ \text{Sin}\left[\dfrac{1}{3}\left(\pi-\text{ArcTan}\left[2\,\sqrt{31}\,\right]\right)\right]+\sqrt{5}\ \text{Sin}\left[\dfrac{1}{3}\left(-\pi+\text{ArcTan}\left[2\,\sqrt{31}\,\right]\right)\right]\right)$

Notice the structure of the output; it is of the form $a+ib$. If this is indeed a real number, it had better be the case that $b=0$. Now your first impression upon seeing intricate output like this may be to both marvel at what *Mathematica* can do, and simultaneously to glaze over and fail to examine the output critically. Pause for a moment to take a good look at it, and focus your attention on the imaginary component b. You will find that b is indeed zero. It is of the form $\sqrt{5}\ \sin(c)+\sqrt{5}\ \sin(-c)$, and since $\sin(-c)=-\sin(c)$, the entire quantity is zero. In the next section the **Simplify** command will be discussed. It can be invoked to carry out this simplification as well:

In[13]:= **Simplify**$\left[\sqrt{5}\ \text{Sin}\left[\dfrac{1}{3}\left(\pi-\text{ArcTan}\left[2\,\sqrt{31}\,\right]\right)\right]+\sqrt{5}\ \text{Sin}\left[\dfrac{1}{3}\left(-\pi+\text{ArcTan}\left[2\,\sqrt{31}\,\right]\right)\right]\right]$

Out[13]= 0

Note also that the opposite issue can arise—certain non-real complex numbers may be expressed using only real numbers. At first glance they don't betray their complexity:

In[14]:= **Reduce**$\left[x^3==1,\ x\right]$

Out[14]= $x==1\ \|\ x==-(-1)^{1/3}\ \|\ x==(-1)^{2/3}$

Again, **ComplexExpand** is the ticket for putting a complex number into standard form:

In[15]:= **% // ComplexExpand**

Out[15]= $x==1\ \|\ x==-\dfrac{1}{2}-\dfrac{i\,\sqrt{3}}{2}\ \|\ x==-\dfrac{1}{2}+\dfrac{i\,\sqrt{3}}{2}$

⚠ *Real-valued Versus Complex-valued Rational Powers*

We have already noted that there are different definitions of the cube root function. In precalculus and calculus courses, where the complex number system is not utilized, one defines the cube root of any real number to be its real cube root. So, for instance, $(-8)^{1/3}=-2$. *Mathematica* uses a different definition, which we will discuss in this section. Under this definition $(-8)^{1/3}=1+i\,\sqrt{3}$.

In[16]:= **ComplexExpand**$\left[(-8)^{1/3}\right]$

Out[16]= $1 + i\sqrt{3}$

The reality is that when complex numbers are taken into account, there are *three* numbers whose cube is -8:

In[17]:= **Reduce**$\left[x^3 == -8, x\right]$

Out[17]= $x == -2 \,\|\, x == 1 - i\sqrt{3} \,\|\, x == 1 + i\sqrt{3}$

So in defining *the* cube root, one of these three must be chosen. *Mathematica* chooses the last of these. Note that the underlying command used to raise a number to a power is called **Power**:

In[18]:= x^p **// FullForm**

Out[18]//FullForm=
$\qquad$ Power$\left[x, p\right]$

It is the definition of this basic arithmetic operation that is at issue. When a negative number is raised to a rational power, and the denominator of that rational power is an odd number (e.g., 3, for the rational power $1/3$), you might like to have a power expression evaluate to a real number, as would be expected in a a precalculus or calculus course. In Section 3.2 on page 58 an alternate power command called **realPower** was defined that can be used to emulate the real-valued power functions commonly encountered in such a course.

We now discuss a topic that falls outside of the standard precalculus and calculus curricula: why on earth does *Mathematica* report that $(-8)^{1/3} = 1 + \sqrt{3}\,i$ when it would be so much simpler to say that the cube root of -8 is just -2? What possible reason could there be for such insanity? This will take a bit of careful thought, and a page or two of explanation, so make yourself comfortable before reading on. We'll see that there is indeed a compelling reason.

Let's suppose, for the sake of argument, that the cube root of -8 is -2. What consequences follow? Well, raising any negative real number to the power $1/3$ would, in a similar manner, produce a negative real number. In fact, raising any negative real number to the power $1/n$, where n is an odd positive integer, would produce a negative real number. Now suppose we raise this result to the mth power, where m is a positive integer; that is, our original negative number is raised to the rational power m/n. If m is *odd* the result is another negative number, while if m is *even* the result is a positive number (since squaring a negative number results in a positive number). To summarize: raising a negative number to a positive rational power with odd denominator produces a real number. This number is negative or positive according to the parity (odd or even) of the numerator. So far so good, but there's a problem.

Just as the exponential function $g(x) = 2^x$ is continuous, in a just world we would also expect the function $f(x) = (-2)^x$ to be continuous. What happens when x is a rational number with odd denominator? Are we to accept a state of affairs in which $(-2)^{311/99}$ is a negative real number, but $(-2)^{312/99}$ is a positive real number? The two exponents are very close to each other, yet they are producing values that are not close to each other (you can check this). Furthermore, noting that $\frac{311}{99} < \pi < \frac{312}{99}$, how would we define $(-2)^{\pi}$? It simply cannot be done when we operate under this convention that a negative number raised to a rational power with odd denominator is real.

And of course, under such a convention it does not even make sense to raise a negative number to a rational power with *even* denominator. For instance, using the power $1/2$, the square root of a negative number is ... what? It is certainly not a real number. That's a strong indication that one may need to consult the complex number system.

The complex numbers are in fact rather simple. They include the imaginary number i, which has the property that $i^2 = -1$. There are many other complex numbers whose squares are real. For instance, $(2i)^2 = 2^2 i^2 = -4$. Using multiples of i like this, one can find square roots of any negative real number. In general, a complex number has the form $a + bi$, where a and b are real. a is referred to as the *real* part of this complex number, and bi is its *imaginary* part. At this point, let's note that every complex number $a + bi$ can be represented as an ordered pair (a, b), and so can be geometrically identified with a point in the plane. The *complex plane* refers to this model of the complex numbers. The real number 1 has coordinates $(1, 0)$, and the complex number i has coordinates $(0, 1)$.

The *correct* definition of the powers of a negative real number necessarily entails the complex number system. Just as every positive real number has two square roots (one positive and one negative), every negative number also has two square roots. But neither of them are real numbers, both are complex. And just as we choose, for any positive real number a, *one* of its two square roots to be $a^{1/2}$ (we define $a^{1/2}$ to be the *positive* square root of a), we must also choose one of the two complex square roots of $-a$ to be $(-a)^{1/2}$. Which is *the* square root of $-a$? We choose the complex root whose argument is least, the so-called *principal* square root. That is, if one were to draw rays from the origin, one to each of the square roots of $-a$ in the complex plane, and for each measure the angle counterclockwise from the positive real axis to each ray (this angle is the *argument* of the complex number), the ray with the *smallest* angle corresponds to the principal root. Under this convention, for instance, $(-1)^{1/2} = \sqrt{-1} = i$.

Higher roots are even more subtle. In the complex number system, every nonzero number has three cube roots. One is real, and the other two are complex. The correct definition of *the* cube root of any real number a (that is, the definition of $a^{1/3}$) is the principal cube root, the one whose argument is smallest. When $a > 0$, this is the real cube root that we know and love. For instance, $8^{1/3} = 2$. The argument of 2 is zero radians after all, so it must be the principal cube root. But when $a < 0$, the real cube root is negative, and so its argument is π radians. It so happens that one of the complex roots has argument $\pi/3$. *This* is the principal cube root of a. *This* is the one that we designate to be $a^{1/3}$. So, in particular, working in the complex numbers as *Mathematica* does, $(-8)^{1/3}$ is *not* -2. Here is a graphic showing all three roots of -8 in the complex plane. Each is shown at the end of a ray projecting from the origin. The root in the first quadrant has the smallest argument. It is the principal cube root of -8, so it is $(-8)^{1/3}$.

In[19]:= **Graphics[{**
   {Thick, Blue, Line[{{0, 0}, {Re[x], Im[x]}}] /. NSolve[$x^3 == -8$, x]},
   {Red, PointSize[.03], Point[{Re[x], Im[x]}] /. NSolve[$x^3 == -8$, x]}},
   Axes → True, AxesLabel → {"real", "imaginary"}]

Out[19]=

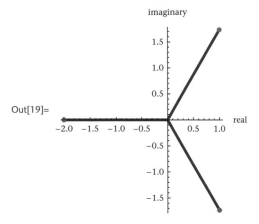

This notion of using the principal nth root as the proper definition of $a^{1/n}$ has long been accepted by the mathematical community. The most immediate benefit is the continuity of exponential functions, such as $f(x) = (-2)^x$. Note that for values of x that are close to each other, the values of this function, while complex, are also close to each other.

In[20]:= **N[{$(-2)^{311/99}$, $(-2)^{312/99}$}] // Column**

Out[20]= $-7.96732 - 3.79246\,i$
$-7.89809 - 4.07175\,i$

This means that it is possible to define powers with irrational exponents to be limits of powers with rational exponents. That is, for each irrational power (such as π), there is one and only one value of $(-2)^\pi$ that is consistent with nearby rational powers. For instance:

In[21]:= **N[{$(-2)^{311/99}$, $(-2)^\pi$, $(-2)^{312/99}$}] // Column**

Out[21]= $-7.96732 - 3.79246\,i$
$-7.96618 - 3.7974\,i$
$-7.89809 - 4.07175\,i$

It is easy, in fact, to witness the continuity (and the beauty) of the complex-valued function $f(x) = (-2)^x$ on the domain $-4 \le x \le 0$, by making a table of values for this function, and then produce a graphic of these numbers in the complex plane, joining adjacent values with line segments:

In[22]:= **pwrs = Table$\left[(-2)^x, \{x, -4, 0, .01\}\right]$;**

Graphics$\left[\text{Line}\left[\text{Table}[\{\text{Re}[z], \text{Im}[z]\}, \{z, \text{pwrs}\}]\right]\right.$,

Axes → True, AxesLabel → $\{$"real", "imaginary"$\}\big]$

Out[23]=
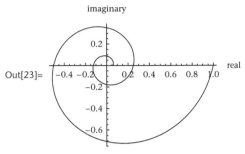

Note that the function assumes real values at precisely those points where this graph crosses the x-axis. You would be correct to speculate that it does so on this domain when the input variable assumes the *integer* values −4 through 0. Can you calculate the values of this function at those points?

One last word regarding the complex numbers is in order. If you've made it this far, you deserve to know one final fact. This fact is so important that it is commonly known as the *fundamental theorem of algebra*. We won't prove it, but we will tell you what it says. It states simply that *every* polynomial of degree n (with real or complex coefficients) can be factored completely over the complex numbers into n linear factors. It follows that for any positive integer n, and any real number r, the polynomial $x^n - r$ has n linear factors. It so happens that the factors will all be distinct in this case. In other words, every real number r has precisely n nth roots. This is why all real numbers have three cube roots. Letting $r = -8$, we reconstruct the polynomial $x^3 - r = x^3 + 8$ from the three cube roots of −8:

In[24]:= $(x - (-2))\left(x - \left(1 + \sqrt{3}\ i\right)\right)\left(x - \left(1 - \sqrt{3}\ i\right)\right)$ // **Expand**

Out[24]= $8 + x^3$

The fundamental theorem also explains why **Solve** and **NSolve** will always report n roots for a polynomial of degree n. Here is an example in which we display the eight roots of an eighth-degree polynomial as eight points in the complex plane (of which two happen to be real):

In[25]:= Graphics[{Directive[Red, PointSize[.02]], Point[{Re[x], Im[x]}] /.
NSolve[$x^8 + 9x^5 - x - 1 = 0$, x]}, Axes → True, PlotRange → 2]

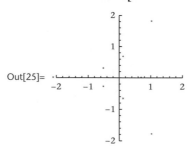

Out[25]=

Exercises 4.4

1. Use the following **Manipulate** to guess the value of c for which the polynomial $c - 6x + 8x^3$ has precisely *two* real roots. Test your guess. Note that by default, **TraditionalForm** is applied to the **PlotLabel** in any **Plot**.

In[26]:= Manipulate[Plot[$c - 6x + 8x^3$, {x, −1.1, 1.1},
PlotLabel → Reduce[$c - 6x + 8x^3 = 0$, x, Reals], PlotRange → {−4, 8}], {c, 0., 4}]

Out[26]=

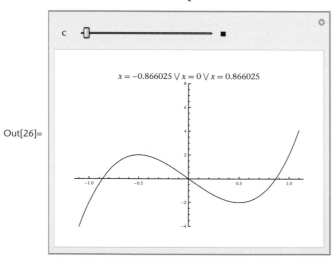

2. Use the command **realPower** defined in Section 3.2 on page 58 to produce the graph of the *real-valued* function $f(x) = x^{2/5}$ on the domain $-32 \le x \le 32$ shown below. What is $f(32)$?

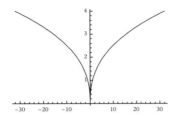

3. Use **Reduce** to find the roots of $f(x) = x^4 - x$,

   a. with the option setting **Quartics → True**.

   b. with the optional third argument **Reals**.

   c. Explain how it can be that there are no i's in the expressions representing the non-real roots.

   d. Re-do this problem with the polynomial $f(x) = x^4 - x - 1$.

4. Consider the following input and output, and use the fundamental theorem of algebra to formulate a plausible explanation for the apparent redundancy:

   In[27]:= **Solve**$[(x - 2)^3 == 0,\ x]$

   Out[27]= $\{\{x \to 2\},\ \{x \to 2\},\ \{x \to 2\}\}$

5. Make a **Manipulate** that displays the roots of a fifth degree polynomial $x^5 + ax^4 + bx^3 + cx^2 + dx + e$ in the complex plane. Make sliders for each of a, b, c, d, and e, which assume values from -2 to 2. Set the **PlotRange** to 4.

6. Make a **Manipulate** that displays the roots of the nth degree polynomial $x^n + 1$ in the complex plane, where there is a **SetterBar** displaying values of n from 1 to 10. These will be graphical depictions of all the nth roots of -1.

7. Make a **Manipulate** that displays a **Line** joining a **Table** of values for the function $(-k)^x$ on the domain $-4 \leq x \leq 0$ in the complex plane. Make a slider for k which assumes values from 0.1 to 4. Set the **PlotRange** to 2.

4.5 Working with Rational Functions

Solving Equations

The **Solve** and **NSolve** commands are built for polynomials, but they will also work for equations involving *rational functions* (quotients of polynomials). Essentially, the roots of the numerator that are not also roots of the denominator will be reported:

In[1]:= **Solve**$\left[\dfrac{(x + 3)(x - 1)}{(x - 1)} == 0,\ x\right]$

Out[1]= $\{\{x \to -3\}\}$

Thus all the remarks in Section 4.2 apply to equations involving rational functions as well to those involving only polynomials.

Simplifying Rational Expressions

When you are working with a rational function, you may want to use the **Simplify** command to, well ... simplify things:

In[2]:= **Simplify**$\left[\dfrac{1-x^5}{1-x}\right]$

Out[2]= $1 + x + x^2 + x^3 + x^4$

The **Simplify** command, like **Expand** and **Factor**, takes an expression as input and returns an equivalent expression as output. **Simplify** attempts a number of transformations and returns what it believes is the most simple form. In the case of rational functions, **Simplify** will cancel the common factors appearing in the numerator and denominator. In the example above, the linear expression $1 - x$ can be factored out of the numerator. You can easily check the result:

In[3]:= **Expand**$\left[(x-1)\left(1+x+x^2+x^3+x^4\right)\right]$

Out[3]= $-1 + x^5$

You can also guide *Mathematica* through such a simplification step by step. The best way to do this is by opening the AlgebraicManipulation palette (in the Palettes menu). Use your mouse to highlight a certain portion of an algebraic expression, and then feed that portion of the expression to one of the algebraic manipulation commands. This essentially allows you to drive *Mathematica* step by step through an algebraic manipulation. Here, for instance, is a rational function:

$$\frac{x^4 + 5x^3 + 8x^2 + 7x + 3}{3x^4 + 14x^3 + 18x^2 + 10x + 3}$$

Rather than simplify it in one go with the **Simplify** command, let's drive through it step by step. First, use the mouse to highlight the numerator, then push the $\boxed{\text{Factor[∎]}}$ button on the AlgebraicManipulation palette. The cell will then look like this:

$$\frac{(x+1)(x+3)\left(x^2+x+1\right)}{3x^4 + 14x^3 + 18x^2 + 10x + 3}$$

Now repeat the process to factor the denominator:

$$\frac{(x+1)(x+3)\left(x^2+x+1\right)}{(x+1)(x+3)\left(3x^2+2x+1\right)}$$

There is clearly some cancellation that can be done. Highlight the entire expression and push the $\boxed{\text{Cancel[∎]}}$ button:

$$\frac{x^2 + x + 1}{3\,x^2 + 2\,x + 1}$$

The results are the same as if you had simplified the original expression using the **Simplify** command. The difference is that you know exactly how the simplification took place:

In[4]:= **Simplify**$\left[\dfrac{3 + 7\,x + 8\,x^2 + 5\,x^3 + x^4}{3 + 10\,x + 18\,x^2 + 14\,x^3 + 3\,x^4}\right]$

Out[4]= $\dfrac{1 + x + x^2}{1 + 2\,x + 3\,x^2}$

This sort of interactive manipulation puts you in the driver's seat. You will sharpen your algebraic skills without falling into the abyss of tedium and silly mistakes (such as dropped minus signs) that can occur when performing algebraic manipulations by hand.

A rational function and the function that results from its simplification are identical, except that the original rational function will not be defined at those values of x that are roots of both the numerator and denominator. In the example above, the original function is not defined at $x = -1$ and $x = -3$, while the simplified function is defined at those points. For all other values of x the two functions are identical.

Formatting Output Using TraditionalForm

By default, *Mathematica* will always write a polynomial with ascending powers of x as you read it from left to right. It can be an annoyance reading $(-3 + x)$ rather than $(x - 3)$, but the former adheres to the ascending powers of x convention, and so that's what you will get.

In[5]:= **x − 3**

Out[5]= $-3 + x$

However, any expression produced by *Mathematica* can be displayed in several ways. Append //**Tradi**. **tionalForm** to any input, and it will be displayed using traditional notation (which, for a polynomial, means descending powers of x):

In[6]:= **x − 3 // TraditionalForm**

Out[6]//TraditionalForm=
$x - 3$

You can also convert an output into **TraditionalForm** by selecting its cell bracket with your mouse, and then choosing Cell ▷ Convert To ▷ TraditionalForm in the menus.

Vertical Asymptotes

Roots of the denominator that are not also roots of the numerator will yield vertical asymptotes in the graph of a rational function. Here, for example, is a function with vertical asymptotes at $x = 3$ and $x = -3$:

In[7]:= $k[x\_] := \dfrac{x^4 + 3x^3 - x^2 + 5x - 4}{x^2 - 9}$

In[8]:= $Plot\big[k[x], \{x, -10, 10\}, Exclusions \rightarrow \{x^2 - 9 == 0\},$
$ExclusionsStyle \rightarrow Directive\big[Gray, Dashed\big]\big]$

Out[8]=

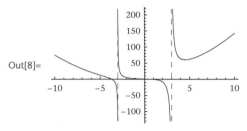

Long Division of Polynomials

Another manipulation that is useful when working with rational functions is long division. It can be done by hand, and you may have discovered that it is a tedious process. Every rational function $\dfrac{f(x)}{h(x)}$ can be expressed in the form $q(x) + \dfrac{r(x)}{h(x)}$, where $q(x)$ and $r(x)$ are polynomials, and $r(x)$ has degree less than $h(x)$. The term $q(x)$ is called the *quotient*, and the numerator $r(x)$ is called the *remainder*. When x gets sufficiently large, $\dfrac{r(x)}{h(x)}$ assumes values close to zero (since $r(x)$ has lesser degree than $h(x)$), so the rational function $\dfrac{f(x)}{h(x)}$ and the polynomial $q(x)$ are asymptotic to each other as x gets large. Here's how to get *Mathematica* to calculate the quotient and remainder:

In[9]:= $k[x\_] := \dfrac{x^4 + 3x^3 - x^2 + 5x - 4}{x^2 - 9}$

The commands **Numerator** and **Denominator** can be used to isolate the numerator and denominator of any fraction. You can then use these to find the quotient $q(x)$ and the remainder $r(x)$ with the commands **PolynomialQuotient** and **PolynomialRemainder**:

In[10]:= **num = Numerator[k[x]]**

Out[10]= $-4 + 5x - x^2 + 3x^3 + x^4$

In[11]:= **den = Denominator[k[x]]**

Out[11]= $-9 + x^2$

In[12]:= **q[x_] = PolynomialQuotient[num, den, x]**

Out[12]= $8 + 3 x + x^2$

In[13]:= **r[x_] = PolynomialRemainder[num, den, x]**

Out[13]= $68 + 32 x$

The commands **PolynomialQuotient** and **PolynomialRemainder** each take three arguments. The first and second are polynomials representing the numerator and denominator of a rational function, respectively. The third is the name of the independent variable. In this example we have computed that:

$$\frac{x^4 + 3x^3 - x^2 + 5x - 4}{x^2 - 9} = \left(8 + 3x + x^2\right) + \frac{68 + 32x}{x^2 - 9}$$

You can check that *Mathematica* has done things correctly. The following computation accomplishes this. Can you see why?

In[14]:= **Expand$\left[(8 + 3 x + x^2)(x^2 - 9) + (68 + 32 x)\right]$**

Out[14]= $-4 + 5 x - x^2 + 3 x^3 + x^4$

Here is a plot of *k* together with the quotient polynomial, which in this case is a parabola. We see that the graph of *k* is asymptotic to the parabola as *x* approaches $\pm\infty$:

In[15]:= **Plot$[\{k[x], q[x]\}, \{x, -15, 15\}$, Exclusions $\rightarrow \{x^2 - 9 == 0\}$,**
ExclusionsStyle $\rightarrow$ Directive$[$Gray, Dashed$]]$

Out[15]=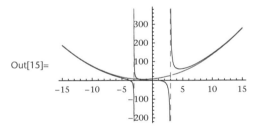

Partial Fractions

One final manipulation that is sometimes useful when working with rational functions is known as *partial fraction* decomposition. It is a fact that every rational function can be expressed as a sum of simpler rational functions, each of which has a denominator whose degree is minimal. The *Mathematica* command that can accomplish this decomposition is called **Apart**:

In[16]:= $\text{Apart}\left[\dfrac{x^4 + 3\,x^3 - x^2 + 5\,x - 4}{x^2 - 9}\right]$

Out[16]= $8 + \dfrac{82}{3\,(-3 + x)} + 3\,x + x^2 + \dfrac{14}{3\,(3 + x)}$

The command that puts sums of rational expressions over a common denominator (i.e., the command that does what **Apart** undoes) is called **Together**. Both can be found in the AlgebraicManipulation palette. If you take your mouse and highlight the output cell above, and then push the Together[■] button, an input cell will be created that will look like this:

$$\dfrac{-4 + 5\,x - x^2 + 3\,x^3 + x^4}{(-3 + x)\,(3 + x)}$$

Exercises 4.5

1. The rational function $\dfrac{-6 - 7\,x - x^2 + x^3 + x^4}{-2 - x + x^2}$ has no vertical asymptotes in its graph. Explain why.

2. The rational function $\dfrac{-6 - 7\,x - x^2 + x^3 + x^4}{-4 - x + x^2}$ has two vertical asymptotes in its graph. Identify them, and explain why. **Plot** this function along with the quadratic function to which it is asymptotic for large values of x. Use $-10 \le x \le 10$ as your domain, and used **Dashed** lines for the vertical asymptotes.

4.6 Working with Other Expressions

The commands found in the AlgebraicManipulation palette can be applied to all sorts of expressions other than polynomials and rational functions. Like **Expand** and **Factor**, the commands in this palette are given an algebraic expression as input, and return an equivalent algebraic expression as output. In this section we give examples how some of these commands can be used.

Simplifying Things

The **Simplify** command can handle all types of expressions as input. Any time you have a messy expression, it won't hurt to attempt a simplification. The worst that can happen is nothing; in such cases the output will simply match the input:

In[1]:= $\text{Simplify}\left[1 - (\text{Tan}[x])^4\right]$

Out[1]= $\text{Cos}[2\,x]\,\text{Sec}[x]^4$

In[2]:= **Simplify$\left[1 + (\text{Tan}[x])^4\right]$**

Out[2]= $1 + \text{Tan}[x]^4$

The **Simplify** command can also accept a second argument specifying the domain of any variable in the expression to be simplified. For instance, consider the following example:

In[3]:= **Simplify$\left[\text{Log}\left[e^x\right]\right]$**

Out[3]= $\text{Log}\left[e^x\right]$

This seems odd; you may recall having been taught that the natural logarithm function and the exponential function are *inverses* of one another—their composition should simply yield x. The problem is that this is not necessarily true if x is a complex number, and *Mathematica* does not preclude this possibility. To restrict the domain of x to the set of real numbers, do this:

In[4]:= **Simplify$\left[\text{Log}\left[e^x\right], \text{x} \in \text{Reals}\right]$**

Out[4]= X

The $\in$ character can be read "is an element of." It can be found on the BasicMathInput palette (in the same row with $\le$ and $\ge$). This paradigm in which **Simplify** is called with a second argument restricting the domain of one or more parameters is extremely useful. The second argument may also be an inequality, such as $x > 0$. In this case it is implied that x is a positive *real* number. That is, including a variable in an inequality means it is not necessary to state that the variable is real.

In[5]:= **Simplify$\left[\sqrt{x^2}\,\right]$**

Out[5]= $\sqrt{x^2}$

In[6]:= **Simplify$\left[\sqrt{x^2}, \text{x} > 0\right]$**

Out[6]= X

In[7]:= **Simplify$\left[\sqrt{x^2}, \text{x} < 0\right]$**

Out[7]= $-\text{X}$

It is also possible to restrict variables to the set of integers. To learn about other choices for this second argument, look up **Assumptions** in the Documentation Center.

Here is another example of how the **Simplify** command might be used. Note carefully the distinct uses of := (for defining functions), == (for writing equations), and = (for assigning names):

In[8]:= **Clear[f, x];**
      $f[x\_] := x^3 - 2x + 9$

In[10]:= **Solve[f[x] == 0, x]**

Out[10]= $\left\{\left\{x \to -2\left(\dfrac{2}{3\left(81-\sqrt{6465}\right)}\right)^{1/3} - \dfrac{\left(\frac{1}{2}\left(81-\sqrt{6465}\right)\right)^{1/3}}{3^{2/3}}\right\},\right.$

$\left\{x \to \left(1+i\sqrt{3}\right)\left(\dfrac{2}{3\left(81-\sqrt{6465}\right)}\right)^{1/3} + \dfrac{\left(1-i\sqrt{3}\right)\left(\frac{1}{2}\left(81-\sqrt{6465}\right)\right)^{1/3}}{2\,3^{2/3}}\right\},$

$\left.\left\{x \to \left(1-i\sqrt{3}\right)\left(\dfrac{2}{3\left(81-\sqrt{6465}\right)}\right)^{1/3} + \dfrac{\left(1+i\sqrt{3}\right)\left(\frac{1}{2}\left(81-\sqrt{6465}\right)\right)^{1/3}}{2\,3^{2/3}}\right\}\right\}$

In[11]:= **realroot = x /. %[[1]]**

Out[11]= $-2\left(\dfrac{2}{3\left(81-\sqrt{6465}\right)}\right)^{1/3} - \dfrac{\left(\frac{1}{2}\left(81-\sqrt{6465}\right)\right)^{1/3}}{3^{2/3}}$

When you plug a root of a function into the function, you had better get zero:

In[12]:= **f[realroot]**

Out[12]= $9 - 2\left(-2\left(\dfrac{2}{3\left(81-\sqrt{6465}\right)}\right)^{1/3} - \dfrac{\left(\frac{1}{2}\left(81-\sqrt{6465}\right)\right)^{1/3}}{3^{2/3}}\right) +$

$\left(-2\left(\dfrac{2}{3\left(81-\sqrt{6465}\right)}\right)^{1/3} - \dfrac{\left(\frac{1}{2}\left(81-\sqrt{6465}\right)\right)^{1/3}}{3^{2/3}}\right)^{3}$

Really?

In[13]:= **Simplify[%]**

Out[13]= 0

That's better.

The command **FullSimplify** works like **Simplify**, but it applies more transformations to the expression (and consequently it may take longer to execute). In certain instances, it will be able to reduce an expression that **Simplify** cannot.

Manipulating Trigonometric Expressions

There is a suite of commands specifically designed to deal with trigonometric expressions. They are **TrigExpand**, **TrigFactor**, **TrigReduce**, **ExpToTrig**, and **TrigToExp**. They really shine when you're working with trigonometric functions, and they're great for helping you remember your trigonometric identities:

In[14]:= **Clear[α, β, γ, x];**
TrigExpand[Cos[α + β]]

Out[15]= $\cos[\alpha]\cos[\beta] - \sin[\alpha]\sin[\beta]$

Of course we all know that identity. But what about this one?

In[16]:= **TrigExpand[Cos[α + β + γ]]**

Out[16]= $\cos[\alpha]\cos[\beta]\cos[\gamma] - \cos[\gamma]\sin[\alpha]\sin[\beta] - \cos[\beta]\sin[\alpha]\sin[\gamma] - \cos[\alpha]\sin[\beta]\sin[\gamma]$

Here are examples of some other commands:

In[17]:= **TrigFactor[Cos[α] + Cos[β]]**

Out[17]= $2\cos\left[\dfrac{\alpha}{2} - \dfrac{\beta}{2}\right]\cos\left[\dfrac{\alpha}{2} + \dfrac{\beta}{2}\right]$

In[18]:= **TrigReduce$\left[1 + (\text{Tan}[x])^4\right]$**

Out[18]= $\dfrac{1}{4}\left(3\,\sec[x]^4 + \cos[4\,x]\sec[x]^4\right)$

TrigExpand and **TrigFactor** are analogous to **Expand** and **Factor**, but they are designed to deal with trigonometric expressions. **TrigReduce** will rewrite products and powers of trigonometric functions in terms of trigonometric functions with more complicated arguments.

Any of the commands on the AlgebraicManipulation palette can be used in an interactive manner as explained in the previous section, where a method for individually factoring the numerator and denominator in a rational expression was discussed. Here's another example:

$$\cos[x]^2 + 2\cos[2\,x] + 3$$

Highlight the first summand, $\cos^2(x)$, with your mouse and push the TrigReduce[■] button on the AlgebraicManipulation palette. The cell will then look like this:

$$\frac{1}{2}(1 + Cos[2\,x]) + 2\,Cos[2\,x] + 3$$

There is now clearly some combining of like terms that can occur. Do it in your head, or else highlight the entire expression and push the $\boxed{\text{Simplify}[\blacksquare]}$ button. The cell will then look like this:

$$\frac{1}{2}(7 + 5\,Cos[2\,x])$$

You can keep manipulating an expression as much as you like. For instance, if you highlight the entire expression and push the $\boxed{\text{TrigExpand}[\blacksquare]}$ button you will have this:

$$\frac{1}{2}\left(7 + 5\,Cos[x]^2 - 5\,Sin[x]^2\right)$$

The point is that you have a great degree of control in manipulating expressions. You might continue to operate on an expression until it reaches a form that reveals some interesting property that was less than obvious before the expression was put in that form.

Here is an example where we will demonstrate why $\cos(\pi/9)$ is a root of the polynomial $f(x) = 8\,x^3 - 6\,x - 1$. First we state the (rarely seen) triple angle formula for the cosine function:

In[19]:= **Clear[a];**
Cos[3 a] // TrigExpand

Out[20]= $Cos[a]^3 - 3\,Cos[a]\,Sin[a]^2$

Next, use a replacement rule to manually replace $\sin^2(a)$ with $1 - \cos^2(a)$:

In[21]:= $\left(\textbf{Cos[3 a] // TrigExpand}\right) /.\ \textbf{Sin[a]}^2 \rightarrow \textbf{1} - \textbf{Cos[a]}^2$

Out[21]= $Cos[a]^3 - 3\,Cos[a]\left(1 - Cos[a]^2\right)$

Finally, expand this out and combine like terms:

In[22]:= $\left(\textbf{Cos[3 a] // TrigExpand}\right) /.\ \textbf{Sin[a]}^2 \rightarrow \textbf{1} - \textbf{Cos[a]}^2\ \textbf{// Expand}$

Out[22]= $-3\,Cos[a] + 4\,Cos[a]^3$

If $a = \frac{\pi}{9}$, then $\cos(3\,a) = \cos\left(\frac{\pi}{3}\right) = \frac{1}{2}$. Hence we have $4\cos(a)^3 - 3\cos(a) = \frac{1}{2}$. Multiply each side by 2, and we see that indeed, $\cos\left(\frac{\pi}{9}\right)$ is a root of the cubic $8\,x^3 - 6\,x - 1$. **Reduce** confirms this:

In[23]:= $\textbf{Reduce}\left[\textbf{8}\,\textbf{x}^3 - \textbf{6}\,\textbf{x} - \textbf{1} == \textbf{0},\ \textbf{x},\ \textbf{Cubics} \rightarrow \textbf{True}\right]\llbracket\textbf{2}\rrbracket\ \textbf{// ComplexExpand}$

Out[23]= $x == Cos\left[\dfrac{\pi}{9}\right]$

As useful as these commands are, it is important to realize that they are not a panacea. Most algebraic identities are at best difficult to uncover through blind application of the suite of commands provided in the AlgebraicManipulation palette. Rather, as in the previous example, they are best used when guided by a clear purpose. Here is another example. It is true that

$$\frac{\pi}{4} = \arctan\left(\frac{1}{2}\right) + \arctan\left(\frac{1}{3}\right)$$

yet no amount of manipulation of the right hand side using only the tools in the AlgebraicManipulation palette will produce the value $\frac{\pi}{4}$. How can these tools be used to explore, or to uncover, such an identity? The answer is subtle. First, recognize that they are only tools. They must be used carefully, with due deliberation and forethought. Owning a hammer doesn't make one a carpenter. That's the bad news. The process is much like traditional pencil-and-paper mathematics in that you pursue an idea and see if it bears fruit. The good news is that the pursuit is made less tedious with *Mathematica* working for you.

Let's explore the identity above. First, for sanity's sake, let's see if it can possibly be true:

In[24]:= $\mathbf{ArcTan}\left[\dfrac{1}{2}\right] + \mathbf{ArcTan}\left[\dfrac{1}{3}\right]$ **// N**

Out[24]= 0.785398

In[25]:= $\dfrac{\pi}{4}$ **// N**

Out[25]= 0.785398

Okay, it's believable. Now can we derive a general formula, for which the above identity is but a special case? As a first attempt, we might try commands such as **TrigExpand**, **TrigFactor**, and **TrigReduce** on the expression **ArcTan[a] + ArcTan[b]**. We find that none has any effect. For instance:

In[26]:= **Clear[a, b];**
ArcTan[a] + ArcTan[b] // TrigExpand

Out[27]= ArcTan[a] + ArcTan[b]

Now we are at a critical juncture in our investigation. We have made no progress, except to learn that *Mathematica* does not appear to have the magic command that will provide us with the type of formula we seek. It is at this point that we need to stop and *think*. What else might we try? Well, what if we took the tangent of the expression **ArcTan[a] + ArcTan[b]**, then tried to expand that? Believe it or not, this gets us somewhere:

In[28]:= **Clear[a, b];**

Tan[ArcTan[a] + ArcTan[b]] // TrigExpand

Out[29]= $\dfrac{a}{\sqrt{1+a^2}\ \sqrt{1+b^2}\ \left(\dfrac{1}{\sqrt{1+a^2}\ \sqrt{1+b^2}} - \dfrac{a\,b}{\sqrt{1+a^2}\ \sqrt{1+b^2}}\right)} +$

$\dfrac{b}{\sqrt{1+a^2}\ \sqrt{1+b^2}\ \left(\dfrac{1}{\sqrt{1+a^2}\ \sqrt{1+b^2}} - \dfrac{a\,b}{\sqrt{1+a^2}\ \sqrt{1+b^2}}\right)}$

In[30]:= **% // Simplify**

Out[30]= $\dfrac{a+b}{1-a\,b}$

This tells us that

$$\frac{a+b}{1-ab} = \tan(\arctan(a) + \arctan(b))$$

or, taking the inverse tangent of each side, that

$$\arctan\left(\frac{a+b}{1-ab}\right) = \arctan(a) + \arctan(b)$$

It is a simple matter to see that when $a = \frac{1}{2}$ and $b = \frac{1}{3}$, the left-hand side is equal to arctan(1), which is $\frac{\pi}{4}$, and so this reduces to the identity mentioned previously. This formula is a generalization of that identity. The final task is determining for which values of a and b the formula is valid. We leave this task to the reader.

Exercises 4.6

1. Use **TrigExpand** to examine patterns in the nth angle formulas for the sine function, i.e., identities for $\sin(n\,x)$.

2. Use the AlgebraicManipulation palette to derive the trigonometric identity
$\frac{\sin(a\,t)+\sin((2-a)\,t)}{2\sin(t)} = \cos((1-a)\,t)$.

3. Derive a quadruple angle formula for the cosine function, and use it to show that $\cos(\pi/12)$ is a root of $16\,x^4 - 16\,x^2 + 1$.

4.7 Solving General Equations

The **Solve** and **NSolve** commands are built for polynomials. They will also work for equations involving rational functions, and they will sometimes work with equations involving other types of functions. **Reduce** is even more inclusive, and can sometimes be used to describe solutions to equations when **Solve** fails. These are the commands to start with when you need to solve an equation. However, there are still a few things you can do if you don't get the answer you desire.

Often **Solve** and **NSolve** can be effectively used to solve equations involving powers that are rational numbers. For instance, since raising a quantity to the power $\frac{1}{2}$ is the same as taking its square root, equations involving square roots fall into this category:

$$\text{In[1]:= } \mathbf{Solve}\left[\sqrt{1 + x + x^2} == 2,\ x\right] // \mathbf{Grid}$$

$$\text{Out[1]= } \begin{array}{l} x \to \frac{1}{2}\left(-1 - \sqrt{13}\right) \\[2mm] x \to \frac{1}{2}\left(-1 + \sqrt{13}\right) \end{array}$$

$$\text{In[2]:= } \mathbf{Solve}\left[x^{\frac{1}{3}} == 4\,x,\ x\right] // \mathbf{Grid}$$

$$\text{Out[2]= } \begin{array}{l} x \to 0 \\[1mm] x \to \frac{1}{8} \end{array}$$

Solve and **NSolve** may be able to find solutions to simple equations with the variable appearing inside a logarithm or as an exponent:

$$\text{In[3]:= } x\ /.\ \mathbf{Solve}\left[400\,\mathbf{Log}[10,\ x] == 2,\ x\right]$$

$$\text{Out[3]= } \left\{10^{1/200}\right\}$$

$$\text{In[4]:= } x\ /.\ \mathbf{Solve}\left[200\,(1 + r)^x == 300,\ x\right]$$

> Solve::ifun : Inverse functions are being used by Solve, so some
> solutions may not be found; use Reduce for complete solution information. »

$$\text{Out[4]= } \left\{\frac{\mathbf{Log}\left[\frac{3}{2}\right]}{\mathbf{Log}[1 + r]}\right\}$$

Here we are warned that although one solution was found, there may be more. In fact, for this example no other real solution exists, but we have no way of knowing that on the basis of this output. Fortunately **Reduce** is effective here, working either over the complex numbers (which it does by default), or over the reals where we see that the solution above is indeed unique:

In[5]:= **Reduce[200 (1 + r)^x == 300, x]**

Out[5]= $C[1] \in \text{Integers} \ \&\& \ 1 + r \neq 0 \ \&\& \ \text{Log}[1 + r] \neq 0 \ \&\& \ x == \dfrac{2\, i\, \pi\, C[1] + \text{Log}\left[\frac{3}{2}\right]}{\text{Log}[1 + r]}$

In[6]:= **Reduce[200 (1 + r)^x == 300, x, Reals]**

Out[6]= $\text{Log}[1 + r] \neq 0 \ \&\& \ r > -1 \ \&\& \ x == \dfrac{\text{Log}\left[\frac{3}{2}\right]}{\text{Log}[1 + r]}$

On occasion these solving commands may come up empty, even when a unique solution exists:

In[7]:= **Solve[Sin[x] == 2 − x^2, x]**

Solve::tdep :

  The equations appear to involve the variables to be solved for in an essentially non−algebraic way. ≫

Out[7]= $\text{Solve}\left[\text{Sin}[x] == 2 - x^2,\ x\right]$

In[8]:= **NSolve[Sin[x] == 2 − x^2, x]**

Solve::tdep :

  The equations appear to involve the variables to be solved for in an essentially non−algebraic way. ≫

Out[8]= $\text{NSolve}\left[\text{Sin}[x] == 2 - x^2,\ x\right]$

In[9]:= **Reduce[Sin[x] == 2 − x^2, x]**

Reduce::nsmet : This system cannot be solved with the methods available to Reduce. ≫

Out[9]= $\text{Reduce}\left[\text{Sin}[x] == 2 - x^2,\ x\right]$

There are powerful numerical techniques for approximating solutions to equations such as this. **FindRoot** is the final equation-solving command that we introduce. It is your last line of defense. It is *very* robust, and adapts its methodology according to the problem it is fed. It's tenacious, but it's also old-school. To use it you must give it a numerical value as a starting point. Like a hound dog it will hunt down a single solution from this starting point, iteratively using its current position to zero in on it. It is likely to hone in to the solution nearest the starting point, so choosing a good starting point is key. A plot is helpful in this endeavor. A simple approach is to **Plot** two functions, the left side and right side of the equation you wish to solve. The solutions are the x coordinates of the points where the curves intersect. For instance, here's a view of the functions in the equation above:

In[10]:= $\text{Plot}\big[\{\text{Sin}[x], 2 - x^2\}, \{x, -2, 2\}\big]$

Out[10]=

We expect solutions near $x = -1.6$ and $x = 1$. To zero in on a solution once you know roughly where it is, use the **FindRoot** command like this:

In[11]:= $\text{FindRoot}\big[\text{Sin}[x] == 2 - x^2, \{x, -1.6\}\big]$

Out[11]= $\{x \to -1.72847\}$

In[12]:= $\text{FindRoot}\big[\text{Sin}[x] == 2 - x^2, \{x, 1\}\big]$

Out[12]= $\{x \to 1.06155\}$

The first argument of the **FindRoot** command is an equation, the second is a list whose first member is the variable to be solved for, and whose second member is a rough guess at the true root. To have all internal calculations performed with n-digit precision you can use the optional argument **WorkingPrecision**:

In[13]:= $x \, /. \, \text{FindRoot}\big[\text{Sin}[x] == 2 - x^2, \{x, 1\}, \text{WorkingPrecision} \to 400\big]$

Out[13]= 1.0615497746313838256020334035198993420588741783892414860849889358093253 6.
58078013681605147722169795200205523517584438182489915752386795185105198.
01898497141789694624781317887368590739943328390244768652889979635131820.
54066331171612084604692146632416602626438286949734162187208102212531109.
55046026055069360793013098705252533458512558323397412062383035427145357.
98284624484729386618537019854165883676711994

This technique of first estimating a solution with a plot and then using **FindRoot** to zero in on it is very robust in that it will work on almost any equation you wish to solve (provided that a solution exists). It does have several drawbacks, however. First, it is a strictly numerical command; it cannot be used when there are more variables than there are equations. For instance, it won't be able to solve $x + y = 1$ for x; the solution must a number (or a list of numbers if there are several equations). Second, it may be tedious to find an appropriate domain for a plot, one in which a point of intersection resides. Third, it is often difficult to discern whether or not other intersection points might be present to the left or right of those you have already found. And finally, for some equations the algorithm will fail altogether. For instance, **FindRoot** relies at times on a well-known algorithm, the Newton-Raphson method, to produce its solutions. It is also well known that this method doesn't work for all combinations of equations and initial guesses, even when a unique solution exists:

In[14]:= **FindRoot$\left[200\,(1.05)^x == 300, \{x, 2700\}\right]$**

> *FindRoot::cvmit : Failed to converge to the requested accuracy or precision within 100 iterations. ≫*

Out[14]= $\{x \to 650.407\}$

The output here is not correct (so the warning message is welcome). You can usually avoid this sort of thing if you make a reasonable initial guess. This sort of problem is unlikely if you follow our advice and make a few plots first, using the plots to generate reasonable initial guesses for **FindRoot**.

In[15]:= **Plot$\left[\{200\,(1.05)^x, 300\}, \{x, 0, 15\}\right]$**

Out[15]=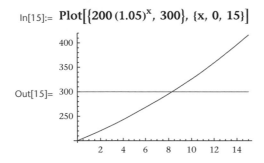

In[16]:= **FindRoot$\left[200\,(1.05)^x == 300, \{x, 8\}\right]$**

Out[16]= $\{x \to 8.31039\}$

Let's look at another example: solve the equation $\log(x) = x^3 - x$:

In[17]:= **Solve$\left[\text{Log}[x] == x^3 - x, x\right]$**

> *Solve::tdep :*
> *The equations appear to involve the variables to be solved for in an essentially non−algebraic way. ≫*

Out[17]= $\text{Solve}\left[\text{Log}[x] == -x + x^3, x\right]$

In[18]:= **NSolve$\left[\text{Log}[x] == x^3 - x, x\right]$**

> *Solve::tdep :*
> *The equations appear to involve the variables to be solved for in an essentially non−algebraic way. ≫*

Out[18]= $\text{NSolve}\left[\text{Log}[x] == -x + x^3, x\right]$

In[19]:= **Reduce$\left[\text{Log}[x] == x^3 - x, x\right]$**

> *Reduce::nsmet : This system cannot be solved with the methods available to Reduce. ≫*

Out[19]= $\text{Reduce}\left[\text{Log}[x] == -x + x^3, x\right]$

You shouldn't allow these outputs to let you to give up your hunt for a solution. **Solve**, **NSolve**, and **Reduce** may be unable to find a solution but that doesn't mean one does not exist. In your dealings with computers, you should live by the maxim made famous by Ronald Reagan: "Trust, but verify." In that spirit, we endeavor to make a plot and see what is going on:

In[20]:= $\text{Plot}\big[\{\text{Log}[x], x^3 - x\}, \{x, 0, 10\}\big]$

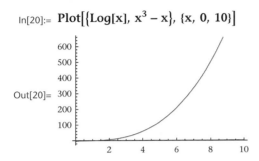

Out[20]=

One of the functions is barely visible. It is not uncommon for one function to dwarf another when viewed over certain domains. To make things clearer we render the **Log** function thick, dashed, and blue, and the cubic red.

In[21]:= $\text{Plot}\big[\{\text{Log}[x], x^3 - x\}, \{x, 0, 10\}, \text{PlotStyle} \rightarrow \{\text{Directive}[\text{Thick, Dashed, Blue}], \text{Red}\}\big]$

Out[21]=

Suspicion confirmed: the **Log** function is quite flat compared to the cubic on this domain. Perhaps they intersect over on the left, somewhere between 0 and 2. Try again: edit the iterator above, specifying the new plot domain, and reenter the cell:

In[22]:= $\text{Plot}\big[\{\text{Log}[x], x^3 - x\}, \{x, 0, 2\}, \text{PlotStyle} \rightarrow \{\text{Dashed, Red}\}\big]$

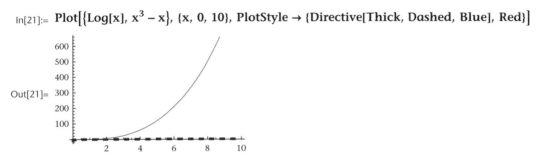

Out[22]=

Bingo! Let's see if **FindRoot** can find these solutions:

In[23]:= **FindRoot$\left[\text{Log}[\text{x}] == \text{x}^3 - \text{x}, \{\text{x}, 0.4\}\right]$**

Out[23]= $\{\text{x} \rightarrow 0.699661\}$

In[24]:= **FindRoot$\left[\text{Log}[\text{x}] == \text{x}^3 - \text{x}, \{\text{x}, 1\}\right]$**

Out[24]= $\{\text{x} \rightarrow 1.\}$

Is $x = 1$ an *exact* solution? Yes: plug it in by hand to the original equation, or do this:

In[25]:= **$\text{Log}[\text{x}] == \text{x}^3 - \text{x} \ /. \ \text{x} \rightarrow 1$**

Out[25]= True

It is worth noting that you can manipulate any equation into the form *expression==0* simply by subtracting the original quantity on the right from each side of the equation. Solving the resulting equation is then a matter of finding the roots of *expression*. The obvious advantages to this approach is that the roots are easy to read off of a plot, since they fall directly on the labeled x axis. Here is the graph for the last example when presented this way. Note that we still plot two functions, one of which is the x-axis. This guarantees that the x-axis will be included in the output graphic, even if you are unlucky enough to choose a domain on which there are no solutions.

In[26]:= **Plot$\left[\{\text{Log}[\text{x}] - \text{x}^3 + \text{x}, 0\}, \{\text{x}, 0, 2\}\right]$**

Out[26]=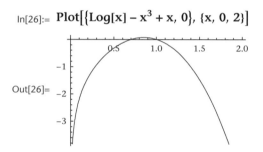

The roots, of course, are the same as the solutions we found earlier. **FindRoot** will report the same output regardless of whether you input the equation **$\text{Log}[\text{x}] == -\text{x} + \text{x}^3$** or the equation **$-\text{x} + \text{x}^3 - \text{Log}[\text{x}] == 0$**. In fact you can simply use **$-\text{x} + \text{x}^3 - \text{Log}[\text{x}]$** (and forgo the **==0**) when using **FindRoot**. The name "FindRoot" makes good sense in this light. You can use whichever approach seems easier to you.

Exercises 4.7

1. Approximate the solutions to the equation $1 - x^2 = \sin x$.

2. Approximate three of the solutions to the equation $e^{-x^2} = \sin x$.

3. Is it true that $e^{-\pi^2} = \sin \pi$?

4.8 Solving Difference Equations

Difference equations (also called recurrence relations) were discussed in Chapter 3 (Section 3.13, see page 142). Suppose we are given a difference equation for a sequence $a[n]$. Let's say that the nth term of the sequence is always twice the previous term, so the difference equation is $a[n] = 2\,a[n-1]$. How can we find an *explicit formula* for $a[n]$, not in terms of $a[n-1]$, but as a function of n? It is not difficult in this example to find a solution by hand, but how can *Mathematica* be employed for the purpose of solving this or any other difference equation? The command that you need is called **RSolve**.

```
In[1]:= Clear[a, n];
        RSolve[a[n] == 2 a[n – 1], a[n], n]
```

$$\text{Out[2]= } \left\{\left\{a[n] \to 2^{-1+n}\, C[1]\right\}\right\}$$

If no initial conditions are given (so the first argument is a difference equation and nothing else), one or more constant terms may be generated, as seen above. **C[1]** represents the constant in the output above. Any specific real or complex numerical value for this constant value will give, according to the previous output, a solution to the difference equation. The first argument may also be a list of equations. For instance, here we solve the same difference equation, but also specify the initial value $a[0] = 1/3$.

```
In[3]:= RSolve[{a[n] == 2 a[n – 1], a[0] == 1 / 3}, a[n], n]
```

$$\text{Out[3]= } \left\{\left\{a[n] \to \frac{2^n}{3}\right\}\right\}$$

RSolve is most useful when dealing with somewhat more complicated difference equations. Here we ask it to solve the difference equation that defines the Fibonacci numbers:

```
In[4]:= RSolve[{a[n] == a[n – 1] + a[n – 2], a[1] == 1, a[2] == 1}, a[n], n]
```

$$\text{Out[4]= } \{\{a[n] \to \text{Fibonacci}[n]\}\}$$

Yes, these are indeed the Fibonacci numbers:

```
In[5]:= Table[a[n] /. %[[1]], {n, 10}]
```

$$\text{Out[5]= } \{1, 1, 2, 3, 5, 8, 13, 21, 34, 55\}$$

Here is a logistic growth difference equation that **RSolve** cannot handle:

```
In[6]:= RSolve[a[n + 1] == 3 a[n] – .05 a[n]², a[n], n]
```

$$\text{Out[6]= } \text{RSolve}\!\left[a[1+n] == 3\,a[n] - 0.05\,a[n]^2,\, a[n],\, n\right]$$

And here's an example of a logistic growth equation that **RSolve** can handle:

In[7]:= **RSolve$\left[a[n+1] == 2\,a[n] - \dfrac{1}{3}\,a[n]^2,\ a[n],\ n\right]$**

Out[7]= $\left\{\left\{a[n] \to 3 - 3\,e^{2^n\,C[1]}\right\}\right\}$

Adding an initial condition forces it to use **Solve** internally, and in this case it is not able to determine if it has found a unique solution. We look at the first few values as a check:

In[8]:= **RSolve$\left[\left\{a[n+1] == 2\,a[n] - \dfrac{1}{3}\,a[n]^2,\ a[0] == 1\right\},\ a[n],\ n\right]$**

> *Solve::ifun : Inverse functions are being used by Solve, so some*
> *solutions may not be found; use Reduce for complete solution information. ≫*

Out[8]= $\left\{\left\{a[n] \to -3^{1-2^n}\left(2^{2^n} - 3^{2^n}\right)\right\}\right\}$

In[9]:= **Table[a[n] /. %[[1]], {n, 0, 3}]**

Out[9]= $\left\{1,\ \dfrac{5}{3},\ \dfrac{65}{27},\ \dfrac{6305}{2187}\right\}$

We can also look at the solution to the difference equation *without* the initial condition (three outputs ago), and do the solving ourselves:

In[10]:= **Reduce$\left[3 - 3\,e^c == 1,\ c,\ \text{Reals}\right]$**

Out[10]= $c == -\text{Log}\left[\dfrac{3}{2}\right]$

So $c = \ln\dfrac{2}{3}$, and the solution is $a(n) = 3 - 3\,e^{2^n\,\ln\left(\frac{2}{3}\right)} = 3 - 3\,(2/3)^{2^n}$. It is now clear from an algebraic viewpoint that this function will quickly approach the value 3. A plot confirms this:

In[11]:= **Plot$\left[3 - 3\,(2/3)^{2^n},\ \{n, 0, 5\}\right]$**

Moreover, using **NestList** to generate the first few terms of the sequence generated by the original difference equation, we see that it agrees with our solution. The use of **NestList** to generate terms of a sequence defined by a difference equation is discussed at the end of Section 3.13 on page 146.

In[12]:= $\text{NestList}\left[2\# - \frac{1}{3}\#^2 \&, 1, 3\right]$

Out[12]= $\left\{1, \frac{5}{3}, \frac{65}{27}, \frac{6305}{2187}\right\}$

In[13]:= $\text{Table}\left[3 - 3\,(2/3)^{2^n}, \{n, 0, 3\}\right]$

Out[13]= $\left\{1, \frac{5}{3}, \frac{65}{27}, \frac{6305}{2187}\right\}$

⚠ At times it may be helpful to note that the second argument to **RSolve** can be simply the symbol **a** (rather than **a[n]**), and the output will be a *pure function* expression for **a**. Pure functions are discussed in Section 8.4.

In[14]:= $\text{RSolve}[\{a[n] == 2\,a[n-1], a[0] == 1\}, a, n]$

Out[14]= $\left\{\left\{a \rightarrow \text{Function}\left[\{n\}, 2^n\right]\right\}\right\}$

Exercises 4.8

1. Suppose a \$30,000 car was purchased with no money down, using a five-year loan with an annual interest rate of 7%, compounded monthly. This means that each month interest is compounded at the monthly rate of $\frac{.07}{12}$, while the principle is reduced by the amount p of the monthly payment.

   a. Calculate the monthly payment.

   b. Make a table breaking down each payment as principle and interest for the 60 month loan period.

2. Suppose that the value of a new automobile is \$30,000, and that it loses 10% of its value each year. That is, at the end of each year it is worth only 90% of what it was worth at the beginning of that year. When will it be worth \$8,000?

4.9 Solving Systems of Equations

It is sometimes necessary to solve several equations simultaneously. For instance, what values of x and y satisfy both $2x - 39y = 79$ and $7x + 5y = 800$? To find out, use **Solve**, **NSolve**, or **Reduce** with a *list* of equations as the first argument and a list of variables to be solved for (such as {x,y}) as the second argument:

In[1]:= **Solve[{2 x − 39 y == 79, 7 x + 5 y == 800}, {x, y}]**

Out[1]= $\left\{\left\{x \to \dfrac{31\,595}{283}, y \to \dfrac{1047}{283}\right\}\right\}$

You can leave out the second argument entirely if you want to solve for *all* the variables appearing in the equations:

In[2]:= **Solve[{2 x − 39 y == 79, 7 x + 5 y == 800}]**

Out[2]= $\left\{\left\{x \to \dfrac{31\,595}{283}, y \to \dfrac{1047}{283}\right\}\right\}$

You can easily use generic coefficients to generate a general formula for solving similar systems:

In[3]:= **Clear[a, b, c, d, e, f, x, y];**
Solve[{a ∗ x + b ∗ y == c, d ∗ x + e ∗ y == f}, {x, y}]

Out[4]= $\left\{\left\{x \to -\dfrac{-ce+bf}{-bd+ae}, y \to -\dfrac{-cd+af}{bd-ae}\right\}\right\}$

The **Solve** command works very well for linear equations (like those above). It also does a good job with systems of polynomials. Here is an example showing the points of intersection of a circle and a parabola:

In[5]:= **ContourPlot[{x² + y² == 4, y + 1 == (x − 1)²}, {x, −2, 2}, {y, −2, 2}]**

Out[5]=

It turns out that there are two real solutions (you can see them on the plot) and two complex ones. One of the real ones is the point (2, 0). The other is:

In[6]:= $\text{Solve}\left[\left\{x^2 + y^2 == 4,\ y + 1 == (x - 1)^2\right\}\right][\![2]\!]\ //\ \text{Column}$

Out[6]=
$$y \rightarrow -\frac{2}{3} + \frac{1}{9\left(28-3\sqrt{87}\right)^{2/3}} + \frac{2}{9\left(28-3\sqrt{87}\right)^{1/3}} + \frac{2}{9}\left(28 - 3\sqrt{87}\right)^{1/3} + \frac{1}{9}\left(28 - 3\sqrt{87}\right)^{2/3}$$

$$x \rightarrow \frac{1}{3}\left(2 - \frac{1}{\left(28-3\sqrt{87}\right)^{1/3}} - \left(28 - 3\sqrt{87}\right)^{1/3}\right)$$

We won't list the complex solutions, as they're even nastier. Here's another example:

In[7]:= $\text{ContourPlot}\left[\left\{y == x^2,\ y^7 + 2x^2 == 1\right\},\ \{x,\ -2,\ 2\},\ \{y,\ -1.5,\ 4\}\right]$

Out[7]=
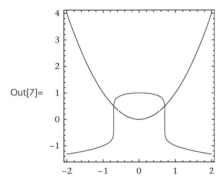

In[8]:= $\text{Reduce}\left[\left\{y == x^2,\ y^7 + 2x^2 == 1\right\},\ \{x,\ y\},\ \text{Reals}\right]$

Out[8]= $\left(x == \text{AlgebraicNumber}\left[\text{Root}\left[-1 + 2\#1^2 + \#1^{14}\ \&,\ 2\right],\right.\right.$
$\quad\quad \{0,\ -1,\ 0,\ 0,\ 0,\ 0,\ 0,\ 0,\ 0,\ 0,\ 0,\ 0,\ 0,\ 0\}\right]\ ||\ x == \text{AlgebraicNumber}\big[$
$\quad\quad \text{Root}\left[-1 + 2\#1^2 + \#1^{14}\ \&,\ 2\right],\ \{0,\ 1,\ 0,\ 0,\ 0,\ 0,\ 0,\ 0,\ 0,\ 0,\ 0,\ 0,\ 0,\ 0\}\big]\big)\ \&\&\ y == x^2$

This output, while potentially useful, may make you cringe. In such situations, applying **N** to the result will often provide a good numerical approximation:

In[9]:= $\{x,\ y\}\ //.\ \{\text{ToRules}[N[\%]]\}$

Out[9]= $\{\{-0.70448,\ 0.496292\},\ \{0.70448,\ 0.496292\}\}$

Similarly, **NSolve** can be used, but it will report both real and complex solutions.

In[10]:= $\text{Grid}\big[\text{NSolve}\big[\{y == x^2,\ y^7 + 2\,x^2 == 1\},\ \{x,\ y\}\big],\ \text{Alignment} \rightarrow \text{Left},\ \text{Dividers} \rightarrow \text{Gray}\big]$

Out[10]=

$x \rightarrow -0.978813 - 0.298975\,i$	$y \rightarrow 0.868688 + 0.585282\,i$
$x \rightarrow -0.978813 + 0.298975\,i$	$y \rightarrow 0.868688 - 0.585282\,i$
$x \rightarrow -0.73046 - 0.780978\,i$	$y \rightarrow -0.0763556 + 1.14095\,i$
$x \rightarrow -0.73046 + 0.780978\,i$	$y \rightarrow -0.0763556 - 1.14095\,i$
$x \rightarrow -0.268914 - 1.05489\,i$	$y \rightarrow -1.04048 + 0.56735\,i$
$x \rightarrow -0.268914 + 1.05489\,i$	$y \rightarrow -1.04048 - 0.56735\,i$
$x \rightarrow 0.268914 - 1.05489\,i$	$y \rightarrow -1.04048 - 0.56735\,i$
$x \rightarrow 0.268914 + 1.05489\,i$	$y \rightarrow -1.04048 + 0.56735\,i$
$x \rightarrow -0.70448$	$y \rightarrow 0.496292$
$x \rightarrow 0.73046 + 0.780978\,i$	$y \rightarrow -0.0763556 + 1.14095\,i$
$x \rightarrow 0.73046 - 0.780978\,i$	$y \rightarrow -0.0763556 - 1.14095\,i$
$x \rightarrow 0.978813 + 0.298975\,i$	$y \rightarrow 0.868688 + 0.585282\,i$
$x \rightarrow 0.978813 - 0.298975\,i$	$y \rightarrow 0.868688 - 0.585282\,i$
$x \rightarrow 0.70448$	$y \rightarrow 0.496292$

Just as there are single equations that can foil the **Reduce**, **Solve** and **NSolve** commands, there are systems of equations that can as well. In such situations one can use **FindRoot** to approximate a solution. Give as the first argument the list of equations. Follow that with an additional argument for each variable. Each of these arguments is of the form {*variable,guess*}, where the guess is your best estimate of the actual value for that variable. Use a plot to help you make your guess:

In[11]:= $\text{FindRoot}\big[\{y == x^2,\ y^7 + 2\,x^2 == 1\},\ \{x,\ 1\},\ \{y,\ 0.5\}\big]$

Out[11]= $\{x \rightarrow 0.70448,\ y \rightarrow 0.496292\}$

Exercises 4.9

1. Use a graph to estimate the solutions to the system of equations $y = x^2$ and $y = 4\sin(x)$. Then find a command that will find or approximate the real valued solutions.

5

Calculus

5.1 Computing Limits

An understanding of limits is fundamental to an understanding of calculus. Let's start by defining a few functions:

In[1]:= **Clear[f, g, x]**;

$$f[x\_] := \frac{Sin[x]}{x};$$

$$g[x\_] := \frac{1}{x}$$

Note that $x = 0$ is not in the domain of either of these functions. How do they behave as x approaches 0, that is, as x assumes values very close to 0? A plot is a sensible way to approach this question:

In[4]:= **Plot[f[x], {x, −10, 10}]**

Out[4]=

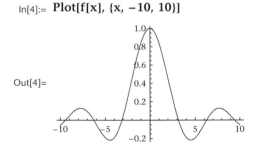

In[5]:= **Plot[g[x], {x, −1, 1}]**

Out[5]=

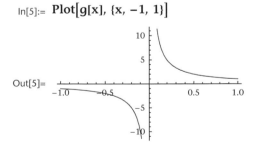

The two outcomes are strikingly different, and they illustrate the likely possibilities for similar investigations. The function $f(x)$ assumes values that approach 1 as x approaches 0. The function g has a vertical asymptote at $x = 0$; as x approaches 0 from the right, g assumes values that approach $+\infty$, while as x approaches 0 from the left, g assumes values that approach $-\infty$.

We can check this numerically by making a table of values. Here is a table of values for f as x approaches 0 from the right:

In[6]:= **data = Table[{N[10⁻ⁿ], N[f[10⁻ⁿ], 15]}, {n, 1, 5}]; Text@**

$\qquad$ **Grid[Prepend[data, {"x", "f(x)"}], Alignment → Left, Dividers → {Center, 2 → True}]**

Out[6]=

x	$f(x)$
0.1	0.998334166468282
0.01	0.999983333416666
0.001	0.999999833333342
0.0001	0.999999998333333
0.00001	0.999999999983333

The **Limit** command provides an easy way to investigate the behavior of functions as the independent variable approaches some particular value (such as 0):

In[7]:= **Limit[f[x], x → 0]**

Out[7]= 1

In[8]:= **Limit[g[x], x → 0]**

Out[8]= ∞

The first argument to the **Limit** command is the expression for which you wish to find a limiting value. The second argument ($\mathbf{x \to 0}$ in these examples) specifies the independent variable and the value which it will approach. You may use the → symbol from the BasicMathInput palette or the keyboard equivalent -> by hitting the "minus" sign followed by the "greater than" sign.

It is important to note that the **Limit** command by default computes one-sided limits, and these are limits *from the right*. That is, the expression is examined with x values chosen slightly to the *right* of the value that x approaches. In the limit for g as $x \to 0$, for instance, the output was ∞. You can take limits from the left by adding the option **Direction → 1**. You can think of this as the direction in which you need to move on a number line to get to the number 1 from the origin.

In[9]:= **Limit[g[x], x → 0, Direction → 1]**

Out[9]= $-\infty$

In a strictly mathematical sense, a limit exists if and only if the limits from the left and right agree. So the limit of the function g as x approaches 0 *does not exist* since the limit from the right is $+\infty$ while the limit from the left is $-\infty$. In *Mathematica*, the **Limit** command defaults to the limit from the right to increase the likelihood of being able to find a limiting value. It is crucial to check that the limit from the left matches the limit from the right before concluding that a limit exists. A plot is usually helpful in this regard. The only exception to this convention is a limit as x approaches infinity (where the **Limit** command will by default compute limits from the left).

In[10]:= **Limit$[g[x], x \to \infty]$**

Out[10]= 0

Taking another glance at the graph of g, you can see that as the value of x gets large, the value of $g(x)$ approaches 0. A table of values is also useful in this regard:

In[11]:= **data = Table$[N @ \{10^n, g[10^n]\}, \{n, 1, 5\}]$; Text@**
Grid$[$Prepend$[$data, $\{$"x", "$g(x)$"$\}]$, Alignment $\to$ ".", Dividers $\to$ $\{$Center, 2 $\to$ True$\}]$

Out[11]=

x	$g(x)$
10.	0.1
100.	0.01
1000.	0.001
10 000.	0.0001
100 000.	0.00001

Note that you may use the ∞ symbol from the BasicMathInput palette, or type **Infinity**. Note also that some functions will not have one-sided limits:

In[12]:= **Limit[Sin[x], x $\to \infty$]**

Out[12]= Interval[$\{-1, 1\}$]

The output here indicates that the sine function assumes values in the interval from -1 to 1 without approaching a single limiting value as x approaches infinity. This is consistent with our knowledge of the sine function; a plot provides additional confirmation:

In[13]:= **Plot[Sin[x], $\{x, 0, 30\}$]**

Out[13]=

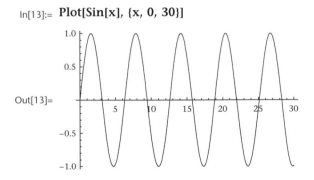

Piecewise functions provide the standard examples of functions for which the left and right directional limits differ.

In[14]:= $\text{Plot}\left[\left\{\begin{array}{ll} x^2 + x + 1 & x \le 0 \\ \text{Sin}[x] & x > 0 \end{array}\right., \{x, -1, 1\}\right]$

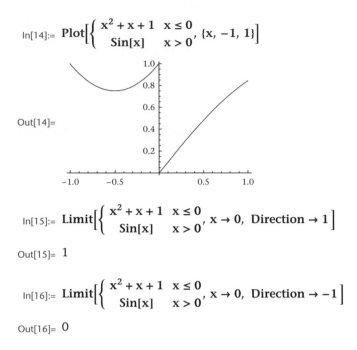

Out[14]=

In[15]:= $\text{Limit}\left[\left\{\begin{array}{ll} x^2 + x + 1 & x \le 0 \\ \text{Sin}[x] & x > 0 \end{array}\right., x \to 0, \text{Direction} \to 1\right]$

Out[15]= 1

In[16]:= $\text{Limit}\left[\left\{\begin{array}{ll} x^2 + x + 1 & x \le 0 \\ \text{Sin}[x] & x > 0 \end{array}\right., x \to 0, \text{Direction} \to -1\right]$

Out[16]= 0

In some cases there may be one or more parameters appearing in an expression other than the one whose limiting value we wish to determine. For instance, what happens to an expression of the form $\frac{1-x^n}{n}$ as $x \to 0$?

In[17]:= **Clear[x, n];**

$\text{Limit}\left[\dfrac{1 - x^n}{n}, x \to 0\right]$

Out[18]= $\text{Limit}\left[\dfrac{1 - x^n}{n}, x \to 0\right]$

This should be interpreted to mean that without some further assumptions regarding the value of the parameter n, it is simply impossible to determine the value of the limit. Assumptions can be specified using an optional argument of that name:

In[19]:= **Clear[x, n];**

$\text{Limit}\left[\dfrac{1 - x^n}{n}, x \to 0, \text{Assumptions} \to n > 0\right]$

Out[20]= $\dfrac{1}{n}$

In[21]:= $\mathbf{Limit}\left[\dfrac{1-x^n}{n}, \; x \to 0, \; \mathbf{Assumptions} \to n < 0\right]$

Out[21]= ∞

Exercises 5.1

1. Use the **Limit** command to find $\lim_{x \to 2} \frac{6x-12}{x^2-4}$ and $\lim_{x \to -2} \frac{6x-12}{x^2-4}$. Then use a graph to explain these answers.

2. Use a graph to examine the behavior of functions of the form $y = x \sin\left(\frac{b}{x}\right)$ for large values of b and use your graph to predict $\lim_{x \to +\infty} x \sin\left(\frac{b}{x}\right)$. Use the **Limit** command to confirm your answer.

3. The function $f(x) = \sqrt{x^2 + 2x + 3} - x$ has very different behavior as x approaches $+\infty$ and x approaches $-\infty$. Use the **Table** command to examine this function for large positive and negative values of x.

5.2 Working with Difference Quotients

Producing and Simplifying Difference Quotients

It is easy to simplify difference quotients with *Mathematica*. (Get the Δ character from the BasicMathInput palette, and do not put a space between it and x, for you are creating a new symbol whose name is Δx, rather than multiplying Δ by x.)

In[1]:= $\mathbf{Clear[diffquot, \; x, \; \Delta x]};$

$\mathbf{diffquot[f\_] :=} \dfrac{\mathbf{f[x + \Delta x] - f[x]}}{\mathbf{\Delta x}}$

This is much more fun to do than to read about, so if possible get yourself started in a *Mathematica* session. You first define a function, and then produce the difference quotient:

In[3]:= $\mathbf{h[x\_] := x^3};$

$\mathbf{diffquot[h]}$

Out[4]= $\dfrac{-x^3 + (x + \Delta x)^3}{\Delta x}$

You can now simplify it by typing and entering Simplify[%], but it's much more fun (and informative) to "drive" *Mathematica* through it step by step. First use your mouse to highlight $(x + \Delta x)^3$ in the last output, and then hit the Expand[■] button on the AlgebraicManipulation palette. You will then have this:

$$\frac{-x^3 + x^3 + 3\,x^2\,\Delta x + 3\,x\,\Delta x^2 + \Delta x^3}{\Delta x}$$

Now highlight the entire numerator, and hit the Simplify[■] button. The x^3 cancels with the $-x^3$, and Δx is factored out of the remaining three summands. You will have:

$$\frac{\left(\Delta x \left(3\,x^2 + 3\,x\,\Delta x + \Delta x^2\right)\right)}{\Delta x}$$

Lastly, select the entire output and hit the Cancel[■] button. The Δx's cancel and you are left with:

$$3\,x^2 + 3\,x\,\Delta x + \Delta x^2$$

That's it! You've just simplified an algebraic expression painlessly, with no dropped minus signs, and without skipping a step. We encourage you to do this for five or six functions of your choosing; you might even find it fun.

Average Rate of Change

Once you have entered the cell defining the **diffquot** command, you can work with specific values of x and Δx to find the *average* rate of change of a function as the independent variable ranges from x to $x + \Delta x$:

In[8]:= **Clear[f, x, Δx];**

$$\mathbf{f[x\_] := \frac{Sin[\pi\,x]}{x}}$$

In[10]:= **diffquot[f]**

Out[10]= $\dfrac{-\dfrac{Sin[\pi\,x]}{x} + \dfrac{Sin[\pi\,(x+\Delta x)]}{x+\Delta x}}{\Delta x}$

You can find the average rate of change of f from $x = 2$ to $x = 2.5$ as follows:

In[11]:= **diffquot[f] /. {x → 2, Δx → 0.5}**

Out[11]= 0.8

Recall from the last chapter (Section 4.2, page 153) that the replacement rule $/.\{x \to 2, \Delta x \to 0.5\}$ instructs *Mathematica* to replace x by 2 and Δx by 0.5. The average rate of change of f from $x = 2$ to $x = 2.1$ is:

In[12]:= **diffquot[f] /. {x → 2, Δx → 0.1}**

Out[12]= 1.47151

Here is a table of values for the difference quotient of f at $x = 2$ for various small values of Δx:

In[13]:= **data = Table[{Δx, diffquot[f]} /. {x → 2, Δx → N[10⁻ⁿ]}, {n, 1, 5}];**

$$\textbf{dataWithHeadings = Prepend}\left[\textbf{data, }\left\{\textbf{"}\Delta x\textbf{", "}\frac{f(2 + \Delta x) - f(2)}{\Delta x}\textbf{"}\right\}\right];$$

Text @ Grid[dataWithHeadings, Alignment → Left, Dividers → {Center, 2 → True}]

Δx	$\frac{f(2+\Delta x) - f(2)}{\Delta x}$
0.1	1.47151
0.01	1.56272
0.001	1.57001
0.0001	1.57072
0.00001	1.57079

Out[14]=

Instantaneous Rate of Change

The *instantaneous* rate of change at $x = 2$ is found by taking the limit as Δx approaches 0 of the difference quotient at $x = 2$:

In[15]:= **diffquot[f] /. x → 2**

Out[15]= $\dfrac{\text{Sin}[\pi(2 + \Delta x)]}{\Delta x\,(2 + \Delta x)}$

In[16]:= **Limit[%, Δx → 0]**

Out[16]= $\dfrac{\pi}{2}$

In[17]:= **N[%, 10]**

Out[17]= 1.570796327

Note that this result is consistent with the table that we computed above.

Exercises 5.2

1. Find the difference quotient for $f(x) = \frac{1}{x^2}$ and use the AlgebraicManipulation palette to simplify this expression.

2. Find the limit of the difference quotient for $f(x) = \frac{1}{x^2}$ as $\Delta x \to 0$.

3. Find the difference quotient for $f(x) = \sqrt{x}$ and use the AlgebraicManipulation palette to simplify this expression.

4. Find the limit of the difference quotient for $f(x) = \sqrt{x}$ as $\Delta x \to 0$.

5.3 The Derivative

Of course there is a simpler way to take derivatives than to compute the instantaneous rate of change as above. This is an instance where the *Mathematica* syntax matches that of traditional mathematical notation. For the function f defined above, the derivative can be found as follows:

In[1]:= **f'[x]**

Out[1]= $\dfrac{\pi \cos[\pi x]}{x} - \dfrac{\sin[\pi x]}{x^2}$

If you check this using the quotient rule, your answer may look slightly different. You can simplify the output above by highlighting it and pushing the $\boxed{\text{Simplify}[\blacksquare]}$ button on the AlgebraicManipulation palette, or by typing:

In[2]:= **Simplify[%]**

Out[2]= $\dfrac{\pi x \cos[\pi x] - \sin[\pi x]}{x^2}$

This is exactly what you would obtain if you worked by hand using the quotient rule. We can evaluate the derivative at any value of x:

In[3]:= **f'[2]**

Out[3]= $\dfrac{\pi}{2}$

A plot of a function and the tangent line to the function at a point (at $x = 2$, for example) can be produced as follows. The expression representing the line is obtained from the *point-slope* formula for a line, where the point on the line is $(2, f(2))$, and the slope of the line is $f'(2)$. You can zoom in (or out) by changing the bounds on the iterator. Try {x, 1.9, 2.1} to zoom in on the two graphs near $x = 2$.

In[4]:= **Plot[{f[x], f[2] + f'[2] ∗ (x − 2)}, {x, 1.5, 2.5}]**

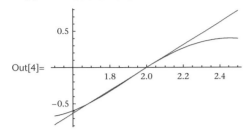

Out[4]=

You may also find it instructive to study the graph of a function and its derivative on the same set of axes. Here the graph of f is black, while its derivative is gray. Of course you can use your favorite colors.

In[5]:= **Plot[{f[x], f'[x]}, {x, 0, 3},**
PlotStyle → {Black, Gray}]

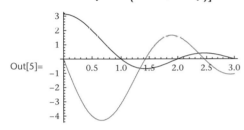

Out[5]=

There is another way to take derivatives of expressions with *Mathematica* that is useful in many situations. The command is called **D**, and it takes two arguments; the first is an expression to be differentiated, and the second is name of the variable with respect to which the differentiation is to be performed:

In[6]:= $D\left[\dfrac{Sin[\pi x]}{x}, x\right]$

Out[6]= $\dfrac{\pi Cos[\pi x]}{x} - \dfrac{Sin[\pi x]}{x^2}$

A palette version of the **D** command exists and is sometimes useful. Go to the BasicMathInput palette, and find the $\partial_{\square}\blacksquare$ button. Type and highlight the expression you wish to differentiate, *then* push this button. Now type **x** (as the subscript) to indicate that you wish to differentiate with respect to x:

In[7]:= ∂_x **Sin[x]**

Out[7]= **Cos[x]**

The palette approach is most useful when the expression you wish to differentiate already exists on your screen (as the output of some former computation, for instance). You can then highlight it and push the button.

A word of warning regarding the palette button is in order. If you *first* hit the palette button and *then* enter an expression to be differentiated in the position of the placeholder, you should put grouping parentheses around the expression. Here's an example of what can happen if you don't:

In[8]:= $\partial_x x^2 + x^3$

Out[8]= $2x + x^3$

You certainly don't want to report that the derivative of $x^2 + x^3$ is $2x + x^3$! With parentheses things are fine:

In[9]:= $\partial_x (x^2 + x^3)$

Out[9]= $2x + 3x^2$

When you first highlight the expression to be differentiated, and then push the palette button, *Mathematica* will add the grouping parentheses automatically.

D can be used to easily derive just about any differentiation rule. You just need to ask it to derive an expression involving "dummy" functions (functions which have been given no specific definition). Here is the product rule, for instance:

In[10]:= **Clear[f, g, x];**
         D[f[x] * g[x], x]

Out[11]= $g[x] f'[x] + f[x] g'[x]$

There are two points to remember about the **D** command. First, it is imperative that the variable (**x** in the example above) be cleared of any value before it is used in the **D** command. Second, if you plan to plot a derivative generated by the **D** command, you need to wrap it in the **Evaluate** command before plotting:

In[12]:= **Plot[Evaluate[{x², D[x², x]}], {x, −1, 1}]**

Out[12]=

As a general rule of thumb, **D** is useful for differentiating unnamed expressions and for deriving general formulae. For functions to which you have already given names (such as *f*), the "prime" command **f'[x]** is generally easier to use than **D**.

Exercises 5.3

1. Make a **Manipulate** that shows the tangent line to $f(x) = \cos(x)$ at the point $x = a$ as a assumes values from -4π to 4π.

2. Graph the derivatives of $f(x) = \sin(x^n)$ for $n = 2, 3, 4$ and look for patterns in the graphs that are reflected in the expressions for their derivatives.

5.4 Visualizing Derivatives

It can be instructive to create a dynamic visualization environment, using **Manipulate**, showing the derivative function as the limit of a difference quotient. Moving the slider in the **Manipulate** below demonstrates graphically that the derivative of $\sin(x)$ is $\cos(x)$. Note the iterator for Δx is backwards; it moves from a value of 2 when the slider is positioned on the left *down* to .01 when the slider is moved all the way to the right.

In[1]:= $\mathbf{Manipulate}\left[\mathbf{Plot}\left[\left\{\dfrac{\mathbf{Sin}[x + \Delta x] - \mathbf{Sin}[x]}{\Delta x}, \mathbf{Cos}[x]\right\}, \{x, -2\pi, 2\pi\}\right], \{\Delta x, 2, .01\}\right]$

Out[1]=

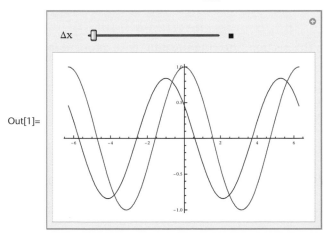

The equivalence of the instantaneous rate of change and the slope of the tangent line can be visualized by the following **Manipulate**. Here we see the graph of $f(x) = e^x$ and its tangent line at $x = 1$. As we move the slider we zoom down to the microscopic level where the curve and the tangent line become indistinguishable.

In[2]:= Manipulate[Plot[{Exp[x], Exp'[1] (x − 1) + Exp[1]}, {x, 1 − δ, 1 + δ},
    Frame → True, Axes → False, Epilog → {Red, Point[{1, Exp[1]}]},
    GridLines → {Range[0, 2, .05], Range[−1, 8, .2]}, GridLinesStyle → Gray,
    FrameTicks → None, Filling → {1 → {2}}], {{δ, 1, "zoom"}, 1, .01}]

Out[2]=
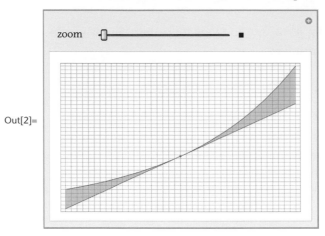

Exercises 5.4

1. Make a **Manipulate** like the first one in this section, showing the difference quotient for the natural logarithm function ln(x) converging to $\frac{1}{x}$ as $\Delta x \to 0$.

2. Modify the zooming **Manipulate** at the end of this section so that it includes a **Checkbox** control. The tangent line should display if the checkbox is checked, but not otherwise.

5.5 Higher Order Derivatives

In[1]:= **Clear[f, x];**

$$f[x\_] := \frac{Sin[\pi x]}{x}$$

The easiest way to take a second derivative is to do this:

In[3]:= **f''[x]**

Out[3]= $-\dfrac{2\pi\,Cos[\pi x]}{x^2} + \dfrac{2\,Sin[\pi x]}{x^3} - \dfrac{\pi^2\,Sin[\pi x]}{x}$

You must use two *single* quotation marks.

Third derivatives?

In[4]:= **f'''[x]**

Out[4]= $\dfrac{6\pi\,\mathrm{Cos}[\pi\,x]}{x^3} - \dfrac{\pi^3\,\mathrm{Cos}[\pi\,x]}{x} - \dfrac{6\,\mathrm{Sin}[\pi\,x]}{x^4} + \dfrac{3\,\pi^2\,\mathrm{Sin}[\pi\,x]}{x^2}$

Another way to take a third derivative is to use the **D** command as follows:

In[5]:= **D[f[x], {x, 3}]**

Out[5]= $\dfrac{6\pi\,\mathrm{Cos}[\pi\,x]}{x^3} - \dfrac{\pi^3\,\mathrm{Cos}[\pi\,x]}{x} - \dfrac{6\,\mathrm{Sin}[\pi\,x]}{x^4} + \dfrac{3\,\pi^2\,\mathrm{Sin}[\pi\,x]}{x^2}$

The **D** command is useful for producing general formulae as in the last section. For example, here is the (seldom seen) second-derivative product rule:

In[6]:= **Clear[f, g, x]**

In[7]:= **D[f[x] * g[x], {x, 2}]**

Out[7]= $2\,f'[x]\,g'[x] + g[x]\,f''[x] + f[x]\,g''[x]$

And here is a product rule for third derivatives. Note that the **StandardForm** notation for the third derivative of **f[x]** is $f^{(3)}[x]$. A similar notation is employed for all derivatives beyond the second.

In[8]:= **D[f[x] * g[x], {x, 3}]**

Out[8]= $3\,g'[x]\,f''[x] + 3\,f'[x]\,g''[x] + g[x]\,f^{(3)}[x] + f[x]\,g^{(3)}[x]$

Exercises 5.5

1. Use the **D** command to find a general rule for the second derivative of $y = \dfrac{f(x)}{g(x)}$.

2. Use a **Table** to look for patterns in the higher order derivatives of $\mathrm{Sec}\,(x)$.

5.6 Maxima and Minima

A function can only attain its relative maximum and minimum values at *critical points*, points where its graph has horizontal tangents, or where no tangent line exists (due to a sharp corner in the graph, for instance). For a differentiable function there is a unique tangent line at each point in the domain, so the critical points are all of the first type. To find a value of x for which f has a horizontal tangent, one must set the derivative equal to 0 and solve for x. Having experience with taking derivatives and solving equations with *Mathematica*, this shouldn't be too difficult. In many cases it's not. Here's an example:

In[1]:= **Clear[f, x];**
$$f[x\_] := x^3 - 9\,x + 5$$

In[3]:= **Reduce[f '[x] == 0, x]**

Out[3]= $x == -\sqrt{3} \;||\; x == \sqrt{3}$

In[4]:= **Solve[f '[x] == 0, x]**

Out[4]= $\left\{\left\{x \to -\sqrt{3}\right\}, \left\{x \to \sqrt{3}\right\}\right\}$

Recall from Section 4.2 on page 149 that the **Solve** command returns a list of *replacement rules*. Here is how to use that output to get a list of the two critical points, each of the form **{x, f[x]}**. These are the points in the plane where the graph of f assumes its extreme values:

In[5]:= **extrema = {x, f[x]} /. %**

Out[5]= $\left\{\left\{-\sqrt{3}, 5 + 6\sqrt{3}\right\}, \left\{\sqrt{3}, 5 - 6\sqrt{3}\right\}\right\}$

And here is a plot of f, with the extreme points superimposed as large dots. They will appear as large red dots on a color monitor:

In[6]:= **Plot$\left[\text{f[x], \{x, -4, 4\}, Epilog} \to \text{\{PointSize[0.02], Red, Point[extrema]\}}\right]$**

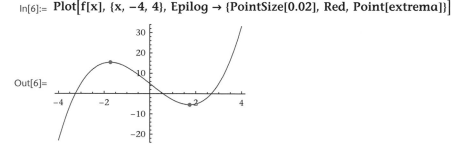

Out[6]=

The **Epilog** option can be used with any command that produces graphics, such as **Plot**. It allows you to overlay "graphics primitives," such as points, on the graphic after it has been rendered. In this case, the directive **PointSize[.02]** makes the points big (they are each 2% of the width of the graphic), the directive **Red** makes them red, and the **Point[extrema]** transforms the list of coordinate pairs into a **Graphics** primitive **Point** object.

In any event, that little bit of technical typing produces a satisfying plot, and allows you to verify visually that the points you found using the **Solve** command are really the extrema you sought.

We can confirm that an extreme point is a maximum or a minimum by using the second derivative:

In[7]:= $f''\left[-\sqrt{3}\,\right] < 0$

Out[7]= True

The function is concave down at $x = -\sqrt{3}$ and so has a maximum at $x = -\sqrt{3}$. Similarly, the second derivative confirms that f has a minimum at $x = \sqrt{3}$:

In[8]:= $f''\left[\sqrt{3}\,\right] > 0$

Out[8]= True

Returning to the task at hand, the strategy that we followed above will fail precisely when the **Solve** (or **NSolve**) command is unable to solve the equation $f'(x) = 0$, typically when f is something other than a polynomial of low degree:

In[9]:= $f[x\_] := \dfrac{Sin[\pi x]}{x}$

In[10]:= **Reduce[f'[x] == 0, x]**

Reduce::nsmet : This system cannot be solved with the methods available to Reduce. ≫

Out[10]= $Reduce\left[\dfrac{\pi\,Cos[\pi x]}{x} - \dfrac{Sin[\pi x]}{x^2} == 0,\ x\right]$

In[11]:= **NSolve[f'[x] == 0, x]**

Solve::tdep :

The equations appear to involve the variables to be solved for in an essentially non−algebraic way. ≫

Out[11]= $NSolve\left[\dfrac{\pi\,Cos[\pi x]}{x} - \dfrac{Sin[\pi x]}{x^2} == 0,\ x\right]$

This is a clue that you need to follow an alternate strategy. One approach is to stare hard at the equation $f'(x) = 0$ and see if you can find a solution by hand. There are rare occasions in which there is an obvious solution that *Mathematica* will miss (there's an example at the end of this section). Try a few values of x, such as 0 or 1, and see if they work. If the **Solve** (or **NSolve**) command does produce a solution, but warns you that inverse functions were used, work by hand to see if you can find other solutions. Bear in mind that this process of finding extrema cannot be reduced to a single, simple, automated procedure; you have to remain fully engaged at every step. If your efforts in solving $f'(x) = 0$ bear no fruit (as will probably be the case with the example above), don't despair. In such cases we resort to attacking the extreme points one at a time, using **Plot** and **Find·Root**, and settle for approximations to the actual extreme points.

The first step in this strategy is to produce a graph of f. In this example, we'll look at the graph of f between $x = 0$ and $x = 3$. If you are working on an applied problem, there is probably some specified domain. That would be a good choice for your plot.

In[12]:= **Plot[f[x], {x, 0, 3}]**

Out[12]=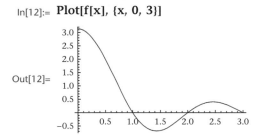

There appears to be a relative minimum near $x = 1.5$. Use that as an initial guess, and let **FindRoot** do the rest:

In[13]:= **FindRoot[f'[x] == 0, {x, 1.5}]**

Out[13]= $\{x \rightarrow 1.4303\}$

The coordinates of the relative minimum can be easily recovered using replacement rules:

In[14]:= **minpoint = {x, f[x]} /. %**

Out[14]= $\{1.4303, -0.68246\}$

Note that this is an approximate, rather than an exact solution. This is the best that *Mathematica* can do in such situations. Note also that when you use **FindRoot**, you can almost always get an answer, but you have to settle for one solution at a time. If you need to find six extreme points, you need to run **FindRoot** six times, each with a different initial guess (suggested by a plot).

Here's how to produce a plot with the relative minimum shown. It will appear as a red dot on a color monitor:

In[15]:= **Plot[f[x], {x, 0, 3}, Epilog → {PointSize[0.02], Red, Point[minpoint]}]**

Out[15]=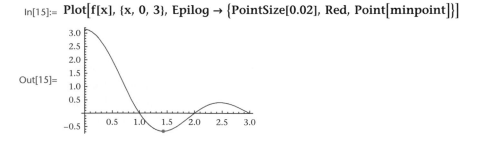

Be mindful that a plot of some sort is important. For although relative extrema for a function f must occur at values of x that satisfy $f'(x) = 0$, satisfying this equation is no guarantee that the point in question is in fact a relative maximum or minimum. This will often happen when the equation $f'(x) = 0$ has repeated roots:

In[16]:= **f[x_] := 8.01 + 12 x − 6 x^2 + x^3**

In[17]:= **NSolve[f'[x] == 0, x]**

Out[17]= {{x → 2.}, {x → 2.}}

In[18]:= **Plot[f[x], {x, 1, 3}, Epilog → {PointSize[0.02], Red, Point[{2, f[2]}]}]**

Out[18]=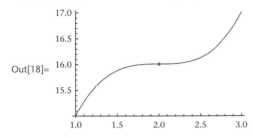

The plot suggests that even though f has a horizontal tangent when $x = 2$, f takes points immediately to the left of 2 to values smaller than $f(2)$, and f takes points immediately to the right of 2 to values greater than $f(2)$. In other words, f has no relative maximum or minimum at $x = 2$. Without a plot (or some careful mathematical reasoning) it is unclear whether a function f has extrema at those values of x satisfying $f'(x) = 0$. Note that the second derivative confirms that the function is neither concave up nor concave down at $x = 2$:

In[19]:= **f''[2]**

Out[19]= 0

We next give an example of a function f for which *Mathematica*'s **Solve** command cannot produce a real solution for the equation $f'(x) = 0$, but for which **Reduce** can. An exact solution can also be found by hand.

In[20]:= **f[x_] := Cos[π e^x]**

In[21]:= **f'[x]**

Out[21]= $-e^x \pi \, \text{Sin}[e^x \pi]$

In[22]:= **Solve[f '[x] == 0, x]**

> *Solve::ifun : Inverse functions are being used by Solve, so some*
> *solutions may not be found; use Reduce for complete solution information. ≫*

Out[22]= $\{\{x \to -\infty\}\}$

Solve is likely to fail when the function in question is a transcendental function without an inverse. We know from the expression for f that it will oscillate, and hence will have infinitely many local extrema. In fact, a moment's thought reveals that since the cosine function attains its extreme values when its argument is an integer multiple of π, this function will attain its extreme values when x is the natural logarithm of an integer. This is precisely what **Reduce** tells us, provided we instruct it to restrict x to the field of real numbers. It distinguishes between the cases when the integer is odd and even. This is a remnant of the more general case when x is permitted to assume complex values, where this distinction is necessary; it also neatly divides the solutions between maxima and minima:

In[23]:= **Reduce[f '[x] == 0, x, Reals] // Simplify**

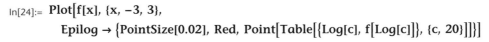

Out[23]= $C[1] \in$ Integers && $\big((C[1] \geq 1$ && $x == \mathrm{Log}[2\, C[1]]) \,\|\, (C[1] \geq 0$ && $x == \mathrm{Log}[1 + 2\, C[1]]) \big)$

Recall from Chapter 4 that $C[1] \in$ **Integers** means that $C[1]$ is an element of the set of integers. The symbol **&&** means "and" and the symbol **||** means "or." Note that **Reduce** finds every solution. The output may seem a bit difficult to read, but this is necessary. After all, there are infinitely many solutions; a careful description is necessary. In this case, however, a more concise description is possible: every solution to the equation $f'(x) = 0$ is of the form $x = \ln(c)$ where c is a positive integer. A plot confirms this:

In[24]:= **Plot[f[x], {x, −3, 3},**
    Epilog → {PointSize[0.02], Red, Point[Table[{Log[c], f[Log[c]]}, {c, 20}]]}]

Out[24]=

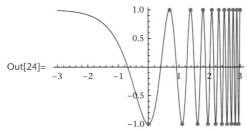

The moral of this example is that the process of finding extrema is not one that can be completely automated. Rather, you must have a clear grasp of the underlying mathematical ideas, and the flexibility to combine abstract mathematical thinking with the tools that *Mathematica* provides.

That said, however, *Mathematica* does have two built-in commands that go a long way toward automating the process of finding extrema. The commands are called **Maximize** and **Minimize**. But be careful, these commands will return only global (a.k.a. absolute) minima and maxima, not local extrema. For example, recall the first function discussed in this section.

In[25]:= **Clear[f, x];**
f[x_] := x³ − 9 x + 5;
Maximize[f[x], x]

Maximize::natt : The maximum is not attained at any point satisfying the given constraints. ≫

Out[27]= $\{\infty, \{x \to \infty\}\}$

We saw in the graph that this function does not attain a global maximum on its full domain. But we can add constraints on the values to be considered by **Maximize** as follows:

In[28]:= **Maximize[{f[x], −4 ≤ x ≤ 0}, x]**

Out[28]= $\left\{5 + 6\sqrt{3}, \left\{x \to -\sqrt{3}\right\}\right\}$

The output is a list of two items. The first gives the maximum value of the function, while the second gives a replacement rule that indicates the point in the domain where the maximum occurs. On the same interval the minimum occurs at the left endpoint.

In[29]:= **Minimize[{f[x], −4 ≤ x ≤ 0}, x]**

Out[29]= $\{-23, \{x \to -4\}\}$

Constraints can be inequalities or equations. When entering equations be sure you use double equals (==). These commands can be very useful when you want to find global extrema. Be warned that in the case of finding extreme values for transcendental functions, they may not find all solutions (this is the case for the previous example where $f(x) = \cos(\pi e^x)$; see Exercise 1). But for polynomial equations, they are bulletproof. For instance, here is an optimization word problem of the type frequently encountered in a calculus course:

> *A rectangular field is to be enclosed by a fence on three sides and by a straight stream on the fourth side. Find the dimensions of the field with maximum area that can be enclosed with 1000 ft of fence.*

We want to maximize the area, $A = xy$, subject to the constraint $2x + y = 1000$.

In[30]:= **Maximize[{x * y, 2 x + y == 1000}, {x, y}]**

Out[30]= $\{125\,000, \{x \to 250, y \to 500\}\}$

It is always a good idea to check any solution found with **Maximize** or **Minimize** by looking at a graph. As always, don't trust—verify! Here is a somewhat intricate **Manipulate** that provides a graphical confirmation by showing the rectangular field on the left and its area on the right:

In[31]:= Manipulate[Module[{y},
    y := 1000 − 2 x;
    GraphicsRow[{
        Plot[y, {x, 0, 500}, AspectRatio → .5,
            Epilog → {Gray, EdgeForm[Black], Polygon[{{0, 0}, {x, 0}, {x, y}, {0, y}}]},
            AxesLabel → {"x", "y"}, Ticks → {{0, 250, 500}, Automatic}],
        Plot[x y, {x, 0, 500}, AspectRatio → .5,
            Epilog → {PointSize[.04], Red, Point[{x, x y}]},
            AxesLabel → {"x", "Area of Rectangle"}]}, ImageSize → 400]],
    {{x, 250}, 0, 500}]

Out[31]=

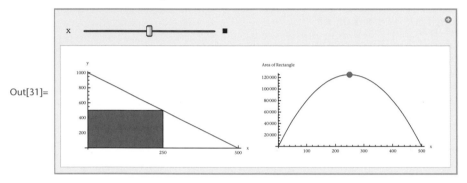

⚠ A **Module** was used in the **Manipulate** above. While not strictly necessary, it is convenient. If the line beginning with **Module** were eliminated (along with its closing square bracket on the second-to-last input line), one would simply have to replace all occurrences of **y** with $1000 − 2 x$. In fact, that was how we first made the **Manipulate**. But it was annoying having to type $1000 − 2 x$ in five different places, and it made the code more difficult to read. **Module** is a "scoping construct"; it allows one to define *local variables*. It is much like the command **With**, (first seen in Section 3.2) but it is more flexible in that delayed assignments can be made. The first argument is a list of all such variables (here there is only one, namely **y**). Then **y** is defined using the **SetDelayed** operator :=. That's it. The rest is simply a **GraphicsRow** containing the two plots. Outside of this **Module**, the symbol **y** has no assigned value. Note also that switching to a different example, such as $y = 1500 − 3 x$, would mean only having to change one line of code. **Module** is discussed in Section 8.6.

Exercises 5.6

1. Read the example concerning the function $f(x) = \cos(\pi\, e^x)$ in this section. Use **Maximize** to find extreme values of f on the domain $−3 \le x \le 3$. Compare the output to the graph in the text, and comment on what you find.

2. Use **Minimize** to find the x-coordinate of the third occurrence of the y-value $−1$ for the function

$\sin(5\,x)$ to the right of the y-axis.

3. Find the dimensions of the right circular cylinder of largest volume that can be inscribed in a right circular cone with radius r and height h.

4. Find the minimum value of the function $f(x) = x^{2/3}$.

5.7 Inflection Points

In[1]:= **Clear[f, x];**

$$f[x\_] := \frac{\text{Sin}[\pi\,x]}{x}$$

The procedure for finding points of inflection mirrors that for finding relative extrema outlined in the last section, except that second derivatives are used. A glance at the graph of f in the preceding section on page 210, suggests that f has an inflection point near $x = 2$. Let's zero in on it with **FindRoot**:

In[3]:= **FindRoot[f''[x] == 0, {x, 2}]**

Out[3]= {x → 1.89088}

In[4]:= **infpt = {x, f[x]} /. %**

Out[4]= {1.89088, −0.177769}

In[5]:= **Plot[f[x], {x, 1, 3},**
   Epilog → {PointSize[.02], Red, Point[infpt]}]

Out[5]=

The plot confirms that f has an inflection point at approximately $x = 1.89088$.

You may find it instructive to study the graph of a function and its derivatives on the same set of axes. Here is the graph of f, and the graph of its derivative with filling added. Note that f is decreasing on those intervals where f' is negative, and increasing when f' is positive. The zeros of f' correspond to the relative extrema of f.

In[6]:= **Plot[{f[x], f'[x]}, {x, 0, 3}, Filling → {2 → Axis}]**

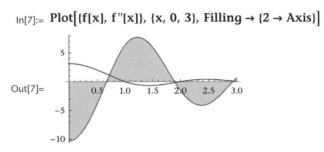

Out[6]=

And below we see f and f'' plotted together, where f'' has filling added. Note that f is concave down on those intervals where f'' is negative, and concave up where f'' is positive. The zeros of f'' correspond to the inflection points of f.

In[7]:= **Plot[{f[x], f''[x]}, {x, 0, 3}, Filling → {2 → Axis}]**

Out[7]=

Exercises 5.7

1. **Plot** the function $f(x) = \frac{\sin(\pi x)}{x}$ on the domain $-3 \le x \le 3$, then make a **ContourPlot** of the curve $f'(x) == 0$, and superimpose the two graphics using **Show**. Describe what you see.

2. **Plot** the function $f(x) = \frac{\sin(\pi x)}{x}$ on the domain $-3 \le x \le 3$, then make a **ContourPlot** of the curve $f''(x) == 0$, and superimpose the two graphics using **Show**. Describe what you see.

3. Repeat the first two exercises, but modify the **ContourPlot** input so that the first argument is not an equation but instead simply **f'[x]** or **f''[x]**. Add the option settings **Contours→ {0}** and **Color·. Function → "LightTerrain"**. This will have the effect of adding color to the vertical bands. Within the **Show** command, list the **ContourPlot** first (otherwise the colored bands will be on top of, and hence obscure, the **Plot** of f).

5.8 Implicit Differentiation

For an implicitly defined function described by a simple equation, it is probably easier to work by hand than to use a computer algebra system to differentiate. However, it is satisfying to have *Mathematica* verify your work. For complicated expressions, on the other hand, the computer will help you maintain your sanity. (To produce plots of implicitly defined functions, see Section 3.7 on page 97.)

Here's how to find $\frac{dy}{dx}$ for the implicit equation $\cos(x^2) = \sin(y^2)$. First, rewrite the equation with every nonzero term on the left-hand side, so that it is of the form *expression* = 0. In this case we get $\cos(x^2) - \sin(y^2) = 0$. The key to implicit differentiation is to tell *Mathematica* that y is to be regarded as a function of x. This is accomplished by typing **y[x]** in place of **y**. We can now differentiate the expression on the left-hand side with respect to x. For convenience, we name it **lhs**:

In[1]:= **Clear[x, y];**
$$\textbf{lhs} = \textbf{D}\left[\textbf{Cos}[\textbf{x}^2] - \textbf{Sin}\left[(\textbf{y}[\textbf{x}])^2\right], \textbf{x}\right]$$

Out[2]= $-2\, x\, \text{Sin}[x^2] - 2\, \text{Cos}[y[x]^2]\, y[x]\, y'[x]$

It is important to remember that this derivative is equal to the derivative of 0 (the right-hand side of our implicit equation), which is also 0. We can get an expression for $\frac{dy}{dx}$ by solving this equation:

In[3]:= **Solve[lhs == 0, y'[x]]**

Out[3]= $\left\{\left\{y'[x] \to -\dfrac{x\, \text{Sec}[y[x]^2]\, \text{Sin}[x^2]}{y[x]}\right\}\right\}$

In traditional notation we replace $y[x]$ by y, yielding $\frac{dy}{dx} = \frac{x\sec(y^2)\sin(x^2)}{y}$.

In some instances, you may be asked to differentiate an equation such as $\cos(x^2) = \sin(y^2)$ with respect to a third variable, such as t. In this case we assume that each of x and y are functions of t, and type **x[t]** and **y[t]** in place of **x** and **y**, respectively. The differentiation is carried out with respect to t:

In[4]:= **Clear[x, y, t];**
$$\textbf{lhs} = \textbf{D}\left[\textbf{Cos}[(\textbf{x}[\textbf{t}])^2] - \textbf{Sin}\left[(\textbf{y}[\textbf{t}])^2\right], \textbf{t}\right]$$

Out[5]= $-2\, \text{Sin}[x[t]^2]\, x[t]\, x'[t] - 2\, \text{Cos}[y[t]^2]\, y[t]\, y'[t]$

Since this expression is equal to 0, we can find $\frac{dx}{dt}$ and $\frac{dy}{dt}$ as in the previous example:

In[6]:= **Solve[lhs == 0, x'[t]]**

Out[6]= $\left\{\left\{x'[t] \to -\dfrac{Cos[y[t]^2] Csc[x[t]^2] y[t] y'[t]}{x[t]}\right\}\right\}$

In[7]:= **Solve[lhs == 0, y'[t]]**

Out[7]= $\left\{\left\{y'[t] \to -\dfrac{Sec[y[t]^2] Sin[x[t]^2] x[t] x'[t]}{y[t]}\right\}\right\}$

Exercises 5.8

1. Find $\frac{dx}{dy}$ for the implicitly defined function $\cos(x^2) = \sin(y^2)$.

2. Find $\frac{d^2 y}{dx^2}$ for the implicitly defined function $xy + y^2 = 3$ as a function of x and y.

3. A ten foot ladder is leaning against a wall. The base of the ladder is sliding away from the wall at 3 feet per second when it is one foot from the wall. How fast is the top of the ladder sliding down the wall?

4. Use **Manipulate** to make a movie of a tangent line rolling around a unit circle.

5.9 Differential Equations

There are many applied settings in which you can observe a relationship between a function and one or more of its derivatives, even when an explicit algebraic expression for the function is unknown. In such situations, it is often possible to find the algebraic expression for the function in question by solving the *differential equation* that relates the function to its derivative(s). For instance, suppose there is a function $y(t)$ whose derivative is equal to $\frac{1}{3}$ times $y(t)$ for each value of t. This sort of situation can exist, for instance, in modeling population growth: the population at time t is denoted by $y(t)$, and the rate of growth $y'(t)$ is proportional to the population at time t. As the population gets larger, it grows faster, since there are more people available to reproduce. What kind of function is $y(t)$? What is its algebraic formula? You can solve a differential equation such as this with the **DSolve** command:

In[1]:= **Clear[y, t];**

$$\textbf{DSolve}\left[\textbf{y '[t]} == \frac{1}{3}\, \textbf{y[t], y[t], t}\right]$$

Out[2]= $\{\{y[t] \to e^{t/3}\, C[1]\}\}$

The **DSolve** command takes three arguments. The first is a differential equation, an equation that includes a derivative. The second is the function whose algebraic expression you wish to find, and the third is the name of the independent variable. The second and third arguments appear redundant in an example like this one, but in more complex situations they are needed to avoid ambiguity. In any event, you need to use them, always.

The output to **DSolve** is a list of replacement rules, exactly like those produced by the **Solve** command (see Section 4.2 in the previous chapter for a detailed description of the **Solve** command and replacement rules). The **C[1]** in the output represents a constant. It can be replaced by any number to produce an explicit solution. In applied settings, some other information is usually given that will enable you to find the value of such a constant. For instance, if we use our population growth model, we might have been told that initially, at time $t = 0$, the population was 400. Then we see that $400 = y(0) = e^0 C[1] = C[1]$. Thus we conclude that the algebraic expression for $y(t)$ is $y(t) = 400\, e^{t/3}$.

In[3]:= **y[t] /. %[[1]] /. C[1] → 400**

Out[3]= $400\, e^{t/3}$

You can also use **DSolve** by giving a list of equations as the first argument. You can, for instance, put the differential equation *and* an initial condition in the list. This makes life very easy indeed:

In[4]:= **Clear[y, t];**

$$\textbf{DSolve}\left[\left\{\textbf{y '[t]} == \frac{1}{3}\, \textbf{y[t], y[0] == 400}\right\}, \textbf{y[t], t}\right]$$

Out[5]= $\{\{y[t] \to 400\, e^{t/3}\}\}$

In[6]:= **Plot[y[t] /. %, {t, 0, 10}]**

Out[6]=

Here's another example:

In[7]:= **Clear[y, t];**

$$\textbf{DSolve}\left[\left\{\textbf{y '[t]} == -\frac{1}{5}\, \textbf{y[t] + 100}\right\}, \textbf{y[t], t}\right]$$

Out[8]= $\{\{y[t] \to 500 + e^{-t/5}\, C[1]\}\}$

Here we have a family of solutions, with individual solutions determined by the values of the constant **C[1]**. For instance, here are several solutions for values of **C[1]** ranging from -500 to 500 in increments of 50:

In[9]:= **sols = Table[y[t] /. %⟦1⟧ /. C[1] → n, {n, −500, 500, 50}]**

Out[9]= $\{500 - 500\,e^{-t/5},\ 500 - 450\,e^{-t/5},\ 500 - 400\,e^{-t/5},\ 500 - 350\,e^{-t/5},\ 500 - 300\,e^{-t/5},$
$500 - 250\,e^{-t/5},\ 500 - 200\,e^{-t/5},\ 500 - 150\,e^{-t/5},\ 500 - 100\,e^{-t/5},\ 500 - 50\,e^{-t/5},\ 500,$
$500 + 50\,e^{-t/5},\ 500 + 100\,e^{-t/5},\ 500 + 150\,e^{-t/5},\ 500 + 200\,e^{-t/5},\ 500 + 250\,e^{-t/5},$
$500 + 300\,e^{-t/5},\ 500 + 350\,e^{-t/5},\ 500 + 400\,e^{-t/5},\ 500 + 450\,e^{-t/5},\ 500 + 500\,e^{-t/5}\}$

We now have a list consisting of twenty-one functions, each a solution of our differential equation, and each corresponding to a different numerical value of **C[1]**. Let's plot these functions on the same set of axes.

In[10]:= **Plot[sols, {t, 0, 15}]**

Out[10]=

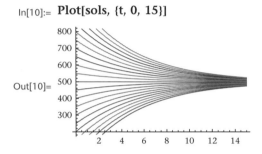

Just as there is the **NSolve** command to complement the **Solve** command, there is the **NDSolve** command to complement the **DSolve** command. Use **NDSolve** in situations where the **DSolve** command is unable to provide an exact algebraic solution (or if **DSolve** seems to be taking all day). Choose Abort Evaluation in the Evaluation menu to get *Mathematica* to stop a computation.

To use **NDSolve**, you need to specify both a differential equation *and* an initial condition in a list for the first argument. The second argument is the function to be solved for, as with **DSolve**. The third argument is an iterator, specifying the name of the independent variable and the range of values it is to assume. As for the output, you will not get an explicit algebraic formula—only **DSolve** can provide that. Rather, you get a nebulous object known as an *interpolating function*. It is a numerical approximation to the true solution of the differential equation on the specified domain. It behaves like an ordinary function in that it can be plotted, and can be used in calculations:

In[11]:= **sol = NDSolve[{y '[t] == 0.05 y[t] − 0.0001 y[t]², y[0] == 10}, y[t], {t, 0, 200}]**

Out[11]= $\{\{y[t] \to \text{InterpolatingFunction}[\{\{0.,\ 200.\}\},\ <>][t]\}\}$

In[12]:= $\mathbf{Plot[y[t] /. sol[\![1]\!], \{t, 0, 200\}]}$

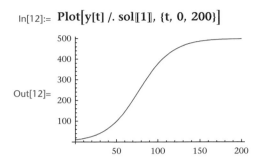

Out[12]=

You can also produce a table of values for such a function:

In[13]:= $\mathbf{data = Table[\{t, y[t] /. sol[\![1]\!]\}, \{t, 0, 200, 20\}];}$
$\mathbf{Text @ Grid[Prepend[data, \{"t", "y(t)"\}], Alignment \rightarrow ".", Dividers \rightarrow Gray]}$

Out[14]=

t	$y(t)$
0	10.
20	26.2797
40	65.5185
60	145.367
80	263.509
100	375.895
120	445.848
140	478.614
160	491.914
180	496.995
200	498.89

Exercises 5.9

1. Find the general solution to the differential equation $\frac{dy}{dx} = -4xy^2$ and then plot several solutions by choosing specific values of the constant.

2. Find the general solution for the second order differential equation $\frac{d^2y}{dx^2} + \frac{dy}{dx} = \cos(x)$ and then plot solutions for several values of the constants.

3. Use **NDSolve** to find the solution of $\frac{d^2y}{dx^2} + \frac{dy}{dx} = \cos(x)$ subject to the initial conditions $y(0) = -1$ and $y'(0) = .4$ and then plot this solution.

5.10 Integration

If you haven't been impressed thus far, this is where *Mathematica* really pays for itself. Unlike differentiation, which with perseverance can always be completed by hand, integration can be exceedingly difficult. In most cases, however, if a function has a known antiderivative, *Mathematica* can find it:

In[1]:= $\int \dfrac{1}{1-x^3} \, d\,\mathrm{x}$

Out[1]= $\dfrac{\mathrm{ArcTan}\left[\frac{1+2\,\mathrm{x}}{\sqrt{3}}\right]}{\sqrt{3}} - \dfrac{1}{3}\,\mathrm{Log}[-1+\mathrm{x}] + \dfrac{1}{6}\,\mathrm{Log}\left[1+\mathrm{x}+\mathrm{x}^2\right]$

The integration button can be found on the BasicMathInput palette. First type a function ($\frac{1}{1-x^3}$ in the example above), then highlight it with your mouse. Now press the $\int \blacksquare d\square$ button on the BasicMathIn-put palette. Your function will be pasted inside the integral at the position of the black square, and the cursor will be at the second placeholder. Here you type the variable with respect to which the integration will be performed (**x** in the example above). Now enter the cell.

If the function you wish to integrate is already on your screen (in an output cell for instance), highlight it using the mouse, then push the integration button. It will be pasted inside the integral in a new input cell. You then enter the variable with respect to which the integration is to be performed and enter the cell.

Some people find it more natural to use the palette in a slightly different way, *first* pushing the integral button, and *then* typing the function in the position delimited by the first placeholder. This is okay, but be careful. If the expression you want to integrate is a sum, you need to put grouping parentheses around the whole thing. Here's what happens if you don't:

In[2]:= $\int 1 - \mathrm{x}^2 \, d\,\mathrm{x}$

Integrate::nodiffd :

$\int 1$ cannot be interpreted. Integrals are entered in the form $\int f \, d\,x$, where d is entered as ⌐ESC⌐dd⌐ESC⌐ . »

You can probably make sense of this message: *Mathematica* sees the incomplete expression $\int 1$ from which it is supposed to subtract $x^2 \, d\,x$. That's nonsense. With the parentheses things work fine:

In[2]:= $\int \left(1 - \mathrm{x}^2\right) d\,\mathrm{x}$

Out[2]= $\mathrm{x} - \dfrac{\mathrm{x}^3}{3}$

Note also that you must be sure to **Clear** any previous assignment made to the integration variable.

Here's what to expect if you do not:

In[3]:= **x = 3**

Out[3]= 3

In[4]:= $\int 2\,x\,d\,x$

    Integrate::ilim : Invalid integration variable or limit(s) in 3. ≫

Out[4]= $\int 6\,d\,3$

Clearing *x* is the remedy here:

In[5]:= **Clear[x]**

In[6]:= $\int 2\,x\,d\,x$

Out[6]= x^2

You can produce the $\int$ symbol without the palette by typing ⎋ **int** ⎋, and you can produce the *d* symbol by typing ⎋ **dd** ⎋. This will allow you to type an integral entirely from the keyboard. Alternatively, you can use the **Integrate** command. It does the same thing as the palette button described above; in fact the palette button provides a means of utilizing the standard syntax for integrals, but when evaluated it simply calls the **Integrate** command. The standard *Mathematica* syntax leaves no ambiguity as to the necessity of grouping parentheses; the integrand is simply the first argument. The integration variable is the second.

In[7]:= **Integrate[ArcTan[x], x]**

Out[7]= $x\,\text{ArcTan}[x] - \dfrac{1}{2}\,\text{Log}\!\left[1 + x^2\right]$

It is important to remember that if a function has one antiderivative, it has infinitely many others. But given one, any other can be obtained by adding a constant to it. *Mathematica* always gives the most simple antiderivative, the one whose constant term is zero.

One may also use **Integrate** to produce a general formula by using an integrand that includes one or more symbolic parameters. Here, for instance, is the first integration formula one typically learns in a calculus course:

In[8]:= **Clear[n, x];**

    $\int x^n\,d\,x$

Out[9]= $\dfrac{x^{1+n}}{1+n}$

Note that this formula holds for *almost* all n (it fails if $n = -1$). It is an intentional design feature to not specify such special cases, like this one where there is a single exception to the general formula provided. This means it's left to you, the user, to critically contemplate the output, cognizant that there may be exceptions. However it is also possible to get a *piecewise* function as the value of an integral. This will occur when there are two or more measurable regions on which the integral assumes different values. A typical example of this behavior is when the integrand is itself a piecewise function.

$$\text{In[10]:=} \quad \int \begin{cases} \sqrt{nx} + 1 & x \geq 0 \\ e^{-nx} & x < 0 \end{cases} dx$$

$$\text{Out[10]=} \quad \begin{cases} -\dfrac{e^{-nx}}{n} & x \leq 0 \\ -\dfrac{1}{n} + x + \dfrac{2}{3} x \sqrt{nx} & \text{True} \end{cases}$$

All of the familiar integration formulae are at your fingertips. Here we see the chain rule, which is the basis for the technique of substitution:

$$\text{In[11]:=} \quad \textbf{Clear[F, u, x];}$$
$$\int F'[u[x]] \, u'[x] \, dx$$

$$\text{Out[12]=} \quad F[u[x]]$$

A more subtle feature of the **Integrate** command is the manner in which real variables are handled. By default, it is assumed that the integrand is a function that may assume complex values, and that may accept complex input. In most cases this creates no issue whatever. But there are exceptions, so it is important to know how to restrict the values of parameters to the field of real numbers. To do so, follow the syntax of this example:

$$\text{In[13]:=} \quad \textbf{Assuming}\left[t \in \textbf{Reals}, \int \sqrt{t^4 + 2t^2 + 1} \, dt\right]$$

$$\text{Out[13]=} \quad t + \frac{t^3}{3}$$

This input reads pretty much as one would say it out loud: assuming that t is an element of the reals, integrate the function that follows with respect to t. Equivalently, you may add an **Assump·. tions** option to the **Integrate** command:

$$\text{In[14]:=} \quad \textbf{Integrate}\left[\sqrt{t^4 + 2t^2 + 1}, t, \textbf{Assumptions} \rightarrow t \in \textbf{Reals}\right]$$

$$\text{Out[14]=} \quad t + \frac{t^3}{3}$$

The outputs above are simpler than that produced by a straight integration:

In[15]:= $\int \sqrt{t^4 + 2t^2 + 1} \, dt$

Out[15]= $\dfrac{t \sqrt{(1 + t^2)^2 \, (3 + t^2)}}{3 (1 + t^2)}$

This output is different since $\sqrt{(1 + t^2)^2}$ does not necessarily simplify to $1 + t^2$ when t is a complex number. Every complex number has two square roots, and the radical indicates the *principal* square root (see Exercise 2). More examples that make use of **Assumptions** are provided in the next section.

It is also worth noting that there are numerous "special" functions that cannot be defined in terms of such elementary functions as polynomials, trigonometric functions, inverse trigonometric functions, logarithms, or exponential functions, but that can be described in terms of antiderivatives of such functions. If you use *Mathematica* to integrate a function and see in the output something you've never heard of, chances are that *Mathematica* is expressing the integral in terms of one of these special functions. Here's an example:

In[16]:= $\int \cos\left[x^2\right] dx$

Out[16]= $\sqrt{\dfrac{\pi}{2}} \ \text{FresnelC}\left[\sqrt{\dfrac{2}{\pi}} \ x\right]$

Let's inquire about **FresnelC**:

In[17]:= ? **FresnelC**

FresnelC[z] gives the Fresnel integral C(z). ≫

Don't be intimidated by such output. It simply says the integral you asked for cannot be expressed in terms of elementary functions. It expresses the answer in terms of another such integral, one so famous that it has its own name (like **FresnelC**). Augustin Fresnel (1788–1827) was a French mathematical physicist who studied this and similar integrals extensively. There is a **FresnelS** integral as well, it uses sine in place of cosine.

There is also the possibility that *Mathematica* will evaluate an integral producing an expression that involves complex numbers. Such numbers can be recognized by the presence of the character *i* in the output, which denotes $\sqrt{-1}$. In cases such as this, the **Assumptions** option that we mentioned earlier will not eliminate the appearance of complex numbers. Rather, they are necessary (even in the real case) to express the antiderivative.

In[18]:= $\int \left(\sqrt{x + x^3} \right) dx$

Out[18]= $\dfrac{2\sqrt{x+x^3}\left(x^{3/2} + \dfrac{2(-1)^{3/4}\left(-\text{EllipticE}\left[i\,\text{ArcSinh}\left[(-1)^{1/4}\sqrt{x}\right],-1\right]+\text{EllipticF}\left[i\,\text{ArcSinh}\left[(-1)^{1/4}\sqrt{x}\right],-1\right]\right)}{\sqrt{1+x^2}}\right)}{5\sqrt{x}}$

In this example we also have an appearance by the special function **EllipticE**. What's that?

In[19]:= **? EllipticE**

EllipticE[*m*] gives the complete elliptic integral E(m).

EllipticE[*ϕ, m*] gives the elliptic integral of the second kind E(ϕ | m). ≫

If that's not helpful, don't worry about it. Suffice it to say that there is a whole universe of special functions out there, and you've just caught a glimpse of a small piece of it. The bottom line is that integration is difficult by nature. *Mathematica* doesn't know whether or not you hold a Ph.D. in mathematics. It does the best it can. You shouldn't be surprised or discouraged if you occasionally get a bit more back than you expected.

Another possibility when integrating is that *Mathematica* simply won't be able to arrive at an answer. Alas, some integrals are just that way. In such situations, the output will match the input exactly:

In[20]:= $\int \sqrt{\text{ArcTan}[t]}\ dt$

Out[20]= $\int \sqrt{\text{ArcTan}[t]}\ dt$

Exercises 5.10

1. Evaluate the following integrals. Note that in many cases a constant *a* appears in the integrand, and that in all cases the integration is with respect to the variable *u*. The results mimic many standard integral tables (such as those found on the inside jackets of calculus textbooks).

a. $\int \sqrt{a^2 + u^2}\ du$

b. $\int \sqrt{a^2 - u^2}\ du$

c. $\int \left(a^2 + u^2\right)^{3/2} du$

d. $\int u \sqrt{2au - u^2}\ du$

e. $\int \sec(u)\,du$

2. Show that for $c = (-1 + i)$ it is not the case that $\sqrt{c^2} = c$, then find another complex number c for which the equation does not hold.

3. Consider the family of functions $\ln x$, $(\ln x)^2$, $(\ln x)^3$, $(\ln x)^4$, etc.

   a. Integrate $(\ln x)^n$ for integers $n = 1$ through 5, identify the pattern, and propose a general formula for $\int (\ln x)^n\,dx$ for any positive integer n.

   b. Using pencil and paper, *prove* that the derivative (with respect to x) of the expression in your formula reduces to $(\ln x)^n$. You will then have proved that your formula is correct. Congratulations—you have just discovered and proved a mathematical theorem!

4. Integrate the following functions, and display the results in a table. Can you find a pattern (among the latter outputs) that will enable you to predict the value of the next integral?

$$x,\ \sqrt{x+1}\,,\ \sqrt{\sqrt{x+1}+1}\,,\ \sqrt{\sqrt{\sqrt{x+1}+1}+1}\,,$$

$$\sqrt{\sqrt{\sqrt{\sqrt{x+1}+1}+1}+1}\,,\ \sqrt{\sqrt{\sqrt{\sqrt{\sqrt{x+1}+1}+1}+1}+1}$$

5.11 Definite and Improper Integrals

Computing Definite Integrals

You've probably already found the $\int_{\square}^{\square} \blacksquare\,d\square$ button on the BasicMathInput palette. Use the $\boxed{\text{TAB}}$ key to move from one placeholder to the next:

In[1]:= $\int_{-2}^{2} (1 - x^2)\,dx$

Out[1]= $-\dfrac{4}{3}$

The same comments made in the last section with regard to grouping parentheses apply here as well; in particular, if you push the palette button *before* typing the expression you wish to integrate, it may be necessary to put grouping parentheses around that expression when you type it. If you prefer typing to palettes, the command you need is **Integrate**. It works as it did in the last section, but the second argument is now an iterator giving the name of the variable and the bounds of integration.

In[2]:= **Integrate$\left[1 - x^2, \{x, -2, 2\}\right]$**

Out[2]= $-\dfrac{4}{3}$

Here is a plot where the value of the definite integral corresponds to the *signed area* of the shaded region—the area of the portion above the x axis minus the area of the portion below it:

In[3]:= **Plot$\left[1 - x^2, \{x, -2, 2\}, \text{Filling} \rightarrow \text{Axis}\right]$**

Out[3]=

As in the previous section, the option setting **Assumptions** may be used, or equivalently an integral created using the palette may be placed as the second argument to the **Assuming** command. Here's an example:

In[4]:= **Clear[x, n];**

$$\int_{-n}^{n} \text{Abs}[x]\, d\,x$$

Out[5]= $n\,\text{Abs}[n]$

In[6]:= **Assuming$\left[n > 0, \displaystyle\int_{-n}^{n} \text{Abs}[x]\, d\,x\right]$**

Out[6]= n^2

A little thought will reveal that the first output above is exactly right; if n is a negative number the absolute value is an absolute necessity.

There is a special class of function that needs discussion. We saw in Sections 3.2 and 4.4 that *Mathematica*'s cube root function $x^{1/3}$ (internally this is **Power[x, 1/3]**) differs from the elementary cube root function found in most calculus texts when x is negative. For instance, most calculus texts use the real cube root function, for which $(-8)^{1/3} = -2$. In *Mathematica*, the principal cube root function is used instead, so that $(-8)^{1/3} = 1 + \sqrt{3}\; i$, a complex number. In Section 3.2 an alternate power command called **realPower** was defined that can be used to emulate the real-valued power functions commonly encountered in such a course. We restate that definition here for convenience:

In[7]:= **realPower[x_, p_] := If[x < 0 && Element[p, Rationals],**
  If[OddQ[Denominator[p]], If[OddQ[Numerator[p]],
    −Power[−x, p], Power[−x, p]], Power[x, p]], Power[x, p]]

If you need to integrate a power function where the power is a rational number with odd denominator, *and* the bounds of integration include negative numbers, you need to know which power function to use. If you wish to use the real-valued power function (the one typically used in calculus courses), you will want to use this **realPower** command rather than *Mathematica*'s default **Power** command. The following example illustrates the difference (note that the antiderivative of $x^{-2/3}$ is $3 x^{1/3}$):

In[8]:= **Integrate[$x^{-2/3}$, {x, −4, 0}] // ComplexExpand**

Out[8]= $-\dfrac{3}{2^{1/3}} - \dfrac{3 i \sqrt{3}}{2^{1/3}}$

In[9]:= **Integrate[realPower[x, −2/3], {x, −4, 0}]**

Out[9]= $3 \, 2^{2/3}$

Note also that with complex numbers lingering just below the surface, it should be a comfort to know that in many cases they simply cannot arise. For instance, if one has real numbers for both upper and lower bounds (so that one is integrating over a real interval), and in addition the integrand is a real-valued function on this interval, then the definite integral, if it converges, must evaluate to a *real* number. Even if *Mathematica* produces complex output (the symbol i can be seen), you can be assured that the expression is using complex numbers to represent a real number. For example, the following output must be a real number, as the integrand is real—it's the square root of a positive real number throughout the interval [0, 1]. In the next section we discuss how to approximate such knotty numbers as the output below.

In[10]:= $\displaystyle\int_0^1 \sqrt{t^4 + 2 t^2 + 2} \; dt$

Out[10]= $\dfrac{1}{3}\left(\sqrt{5} - 2\sqrt{-1+i} \; \text{EllipticE}\left[i \, \text{ArcSinh}\left[\sqrt{\dfrac{1}{2} - \dfrac{i}{2}}\right], i\right] + \right.$

$\left. 2\sqrt{1-i} \; \text{EllipticF}\left[i \, \text{ArcSinh}\left[\sqrt{\dfrac{1}{2} - \dfrac{i}{2}}\right], i\right]\right)$

Riemann Sums

Mathematica makes the computation of Riemann sums easy with the **Sum** command. **Sum** works very much like **Table**, but rather than producing a list of the specified items, it adds them:

In[11]:= **Sum[i², {i, 1, 4}]**

Out[11]= 30

This is the same as adding $1 + 4 + 9 + 16$. The advantage of using the **Sum** command for such additions can be seen when you want to add lots of numbers:

In[12]:= **Sum[i², {i, 1, 100}]**

Out[12]= 338 350

There is a palette version of the **Sum** command on the BasicMathInput palette that allows you to employ the traditional summation notation. Use the $\sum_{\square=\square}^{\square} \blacksquare$ button, and then use the [TAB] key to move from one placeholder to the next:

In[13]:= $\displaystyle\sum_{i=1}^{100} i^2$

Out[13]= 338 350

The cells below provide an example of a Riemann sum computation for a function f over the interval from a to b, with n rectangles and f evaluated at the left endpoint of each subinterval. The first cell sets the values of f, a, and b. It needs to be edited every time you move from one example to the next:

In[14]:= **Clear[f, a, b, n, x, Δx, i];**
f[x_] := Cos[x];
a = 0;
b = 2;

The following cell makes use of the values above and defines the appropriate Riemann sum as a function of n. It does not need to be edited as you move from one example to the next:

In[18]:= $\Delta x[n\_] := \dfrac{b - a}{n};$

$x[i\_, n\_] := a + i * \Delta x[n];$

$\text{leftRsum}[n\_] := \displaystyle\sum_{i=0}^{n-1} f[x[i, n]] * \Delta x[n] \,// \, N$

The function **Δx** returns the width of an individual rectangle—it is a function of n because its value depends on the number of subintervals between a and b. The function **x** returns the right endpoint of the ith subinterval. It is a function of both i and n. Lastly, **leftRsum** returns the Riemann sum for your function between a and b, with the function evaluated at the left endpoint of each subinterval. It is a function of n, for its value depends on the number of rectangles used. Here is the Riemann sum for $\cos(x)$ on the interval $[0, 2]$ with 50 rectangles:

In[21]:= **leftRsum[50]**

Out[21]= 0.937499

Note that the values of i in the summation (from 0 to $n - 1$) dictate that f be evaluated at the *left* endpoint of each subinterval. To compute a Riemann sum with f evaluated at the *right* endpoint of each subinterval you can change the bounds of the summation to 1 and n:

In[22]:= **rightRsum[n_] :=** $\sum_{i=1}^{n}$ **f[x[i, n]] * Δx[n] // N**

In[23]:= **rightRsum[50]**

Out[23]= 0.880853

Either sum can be viewed as an approximation to the definite integral of f over the interval from a to b. It is not hard to modify the process to generate other approximations such as those employing the trapezoidal rule or Simpson's rule. The approximations tend to get better as the value of n increases, as the following table shows:

In[24]:= **data = Table[{n, rightRsum[n]}, {n, 50, 400, 50}];**
dataWithHeadings = Prepend[data, {"n", "Riemann Sum"}];
Text@Grid[dataWithHeadings, Alignment → Left, Dividers → {Center, 2 → True}]

n	Riemann Sum
50	0.880853
100	0.895106
150	0.899843
200	0.902209
250	0.903628
300	0.904574
350	0.905249
400	0.905755

Out[25]= (appears beside the row for 200)

Curious about the actual value of the integral?

In[26]:= $\int_0^2 \mathbf{f[x]} \, d\mathbf{x} \,/\!/ \, \mathbf{N}$

Out[26]= 0.909297

Here is a plot where the value of the definite integral corresponds to the signed area of the shaded region:

In[27]:= $\mathbf{Plot\big[f[x], \{x, 0, 2\}, Filling \to Axis\big]}$

Out[27]=

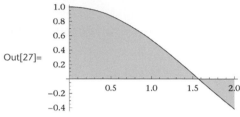

Computing Improper Integrals

Just use ∞ as a bound of integration. You may use the ∞ button on the BasicMathInput palette, or type ⎡ESC⎤ **inf** ⎡ESC⎤, or type the word **Infinity**:

In[28]:= $\int_{-\infty}^{\infty} e^{-x^2} \, d\mathbf{x}$

Out[28]= $\sqrt{\pi}$

In[29]:= $\mathbf{Integrate\Big[\dfrac{1}{x^3}, \{x, 1, \infty\}\Big]}$

Out[29]= $\dfrac{1}{2}$

Of course there is the possibility that an improper integral will fail to converge. *Mathematica* will warn you in such circumstances:

In[30]:= $\int_1^{\infty} \dfrac{1}{x} \, d\mathbf{x}$

Integrate::idiv : Integral of $\dfrac{1}{x}$ *does not converge on* {1, ∞}. ≫

In[31]:= $\int_1^\infty \frac{1}{x} \, d\mathbf{x}$

Integrate::idiv : Integral of $\dfrac{1}{x}$ does not converge on {1, ∞}. ≫

Out[31]= $\int_1^\infty \frac{1}{x} \, d\mathbf{x}$

Other improper integrals occur when a function has a vertical asymptote between the upper and lower bounds. It is dangerous to evaluate these integrals by hand using the Fundamental Theorem of Calculus without carefully considering the behavior of the function at the asymptotes. Luckily, *Mathematica* is very careful and will tell you when these integrals do and do not converge.

In[32]:= $\int_{-2}^{2} \frac{1}{x^2} \, d\mathbf{x}$

Integrate::idiv : Integral of $\dfrac{1}{x^2}$ does not converge on {−2, 2}. ≫

Out[32]= $\int_{-2}^{2} \frac{1}{x^2} \, d\mathbf{x}$

In[33]:= $\mathbf{Plot}\left[\dfrac{1}{\mathbf{x}^2}, \, \{\mathbf{x}, \, -2, \, 2\}, \, \mathbf{PlotRange} \rightarrow \{0, \, 500\}, \, \mathbf{Filling} \rightarrow \mathbf{Axis}\right]$

Out[33]=

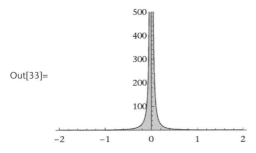

Mathematica is rightly reporting that the shaded area (were it not cut off at $y = 500$) is infinite. Here is another example:

In[34]:= $\int_{-\frac{\pi}{2}}^{\frac{\pi}{2}} \text{Csc}[x]\, d\,x$

Integrate::idiv : Integral of Csc[x] does not converge on $\left\{-\dfrac{\pi}{2}, \dfrac{\pi}{2}\right\}$. »

Out[34]= $\int_{-\frac{\pi}{2}}^{\frac{\pi}{2}} \text{Csc}[x]\, d\,x$

In[35]:= $\text{Plot}\left[\text{Csc}[x], \left\{x, -\dfrac{\pi}{2}, \dfrac{\pi}{2}\right\}, \text{PlotRange} \to 100, \text{Filling} \to \text{Axis}\right]$

Out[35]=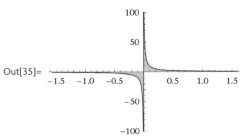

Students frequently argue that this integral should be zero due to the symmetry apparent in the graph. But *Mathematica* is returning the correct answer. Since the area to the left of $x = 0$ is not convergent the entire integral is divergent.

In[35]:= **Clear[b];**
$\text{Limit}\left[\int_{-\frac{\pi}{2}}^{b} \text{Csc}[x]\, d\,x, b \to 0, \text{Direction} \to 1\right]$

Out[36]= $-\infty$

In the previous examples the functions had asymptotes at $x = 0$. In the next example the interval also contains a vertical asymptote but the integral converges.

In[37]:= $\int_{3}^{5} \dfrac{1}{\sqrt{x - 3}}\, d\,x$

Out[37]= $2\sqrt{2}$

In[38]:= $\text{Plot}\left[\dfrac{1}{\sqrt{x-3}}, \{x, 3, 5\}, \text{PlotRange} \rightarrow \{0, 10\}, \text{Filling} \rightarrow \text{Axis}\right]$

Out[38]=

Defining Functions with Integrals

It is possible to define functions by integrating dummy variables:

In[39]:= $\text{Clear}[a, t, v, s]$
$a[t\_] := -32$

In[41]:= $v[t\_] := \displaystyle\int_0^t a[u]\,du + 20$

In[42]:= $s[t\_] := \displaystyle\int_0^t v[u]\,du + 4$

In[43]:= $s[t]$

Out[43]= $4 + 20\,t - 16\,t^2$

You simply need to remember that **Integrate** always returns the antiderivative whose constant term is equal to zero, so constants need to be included in such definitions. The function $v(t)$ above satisfies the condition that $v(0) = 20$, while the function $s(t)$ satisfies $s(0) = 4$. In the example above, $s(t)$ represents the height in feet above ground level of an object after t seconds if it is thrown vertically upward at an initial velocity of 20 feet per second and from an initial height of 4 feet; $v(t)$ is the velocity of the object at time t, and $a(t)$ is the object's acceleration. Air resistance is ignored.

Some Integrals Are Bad

And as is the case with indefinite integrals, there are functions for which there is no way to express an antiderivative in closed form, and consequently no way to evaluate the definite integral exactly:

In[44]:= $\displaystyle\int_0^1 \left(\sqrt{\text{ArcTan}[t]}\,\right) dt$

Out[44]= $\displaystyle\int_0^1 \sqrt{\text{ArcTan}[t]}\,\, dt$

Even in cases like this, you will often be able to get numerical approximations:

In[45]:= **N[%]**

Out[45]= 0.629823

The next section explores a better way to get numerical approximations of definite integrals.

Exercises 5.11

1. Make the following sketch of the graph of $f(x) = \frac{1}{x^2}$, and evaluate the definite integral of f from $x = 1$ to $x = 3$.

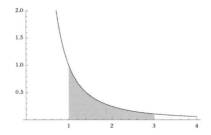

2. Evaluate the following definite integrals.

a. $\displaystyle\int_0^1 \sqrt{t^4 + 2t^2 + 1} \; dt$

b. $\displaystyle\int_0^1 \sqrt{t^4 + 2t^2 + 2} \; dt$

c. $\displaystyle\int_0^\pi \cos(t)^{10} \, dt$

3. Use a Riemann sum to approximate the second of the three integrals in the previous exercise.

a. Use $n = 100$ subintervals and left endpoints.

b. Use $n = 100$ subintervals and right endpoints.

c. Use $n = 100$ subintervals and midpoints.

d. Make a **Plot** of $f(x) = \sqrt{x^4 + 2x^2 + 2}$ and use it to decide which of the three approximations is best.

4. Your opponent chooses a number p strictly between 0 and 1. Your opponent then chooses a second number q strictly between $\sqrt{2}$ and 2. To defeat your opponent, find a strictly increasing function on the domain $[0, 1]$ passing through $(0, 0)$ and $(1, 1)$ whose arc length exceeds q, and whose integral over $[0, 1]$ is

   a. smaller than p.

   b. greater than p.

   Hint: Enter the following input:

   Manipulate$\Big[$

   $\quad$ **Plot**$\Big[\Big\{\begin{array}{ll} \frac{1-a}{a}\,x & 0 \le x \le a \\ \frac{a}{1-a}\,x + \frac{1-2a}{1-a} & a < x \le 1 \end{array}$, **{x, 0, 1}, PlotRange** $\to$ **{{0, 1}, {0, 1}},**

   $\quad$ **AspectRatio** $\to$ **Automatic, Filling** $\to$ **Axis**$\Big]$, **{{a, .75}, 0, 1}**$\Big]$

5. Under what conditions on a real number n does the integral $\int_0^1 x^n\,dx$ converge?

6. Assuming that a and b are real numbers, under what specific conditions on a and b can the integral $\int_a^b \sqrt{-t}\,dt$ be evaluated? What is does it evaluate to in this case?

7. Use **Integrate** to illustrate the two parts of the fundamental theorem of calculus.

8. Use **D** and **Integrate** to calculate a formula for $\frac{d}{dx}\int_a^{g(x)} f(t)\,dt$.

9. Sometimes **Integrate** will return output involving **Root** objects. Enter $\int_0^1 \sqrt{t^3 + 3t + 1}\,dt$ into *Mathematica*, and regardless of the output, explain why this integral *must* converge to a real (as opposed to a complex) number.

5.12 Numerical Integration

Mathematica has a numerical integration command, **NIntegrate**, which is extremely effective at providing numerical approximations to the values of definite integrals, even those (indeed, especially those) that the **Integrate** command can't handle:

In[1]:= **Integrate**$\Big[\sqrt{\text{ArcTan[t]}}\,, \text{ {t, 0, 1}}\Big]$

Out[1]= $\int_0^1 \sqrt{\text{ArcTan[t]}}\,dt$

In[2]:= **NIntegrate**$\left[\sqrt{\text{ArcTan[t]}}\, , \{t, 0, 1\}\right]$

Out[2]= 0.629823

Here's an example where using **Integrate** followed by **N** gives a different result than **NIntegrate**. That can happen! In almost all cases, **NIntegrate** will provide a better result. Here, the antiderivative provided by **Integrate** involves complex numbers, and when approximated by **N** a very small imaginary component (at the threshold of machine precision) persists.

In[3]:= $\int_0^1 \sqrt{t^4 + 2\,t^2 + 2}\ dt$

Out[3]= $\dfrac{1}{3}\left(\sqrt{5}\ -2\sqrt{-1+i}\ \text{EllipticE}\left[i\,\text{ArcSinh}\left[\sqrt{\dfrac{1}{2} - \dfrac{i}{2}}\ \right], i\right] +$

$2\sqrt{1-i}\ \text{EllipticF}\left[i\,\text{ArcSinh}\left[\sqrt{\dfrac{1}{2} - \dfrac{i}{2}}\ \right], i\right]\right)$

In[4]:= **N[%]**

Out[4]= $1.67571 - 7.40149 \times 10^{-17}\,i$

NIntegrate does a better job:

In[5]:= **NIntegrate**$\left[\sqrt{t^4 + 2\,t^2 + 2}\, , \{t, 0, 1\}\right]$

Out[5]= 1.67571

NIntegrate accepts arguments exactly as **Integrate** does for handling definite integrals. There is no palette version of **NIntegrate**. It is important to understand that **NIntegrate** works in an entirely different way from **Integrate**. Rather than attempt symbolic manipulation, **NIntegrate** produces a sequence of numerical values for the integrand over the specified interval, and uses these values to produce a numerical estimate for the integral. Although the algorithm used is quite sophisticated, you can think of **NIntegrate** as producing something analogous to a Riemann sum. The good news is that you now have at your disposal a means for estimating some very messy integrals. The bad news is that **NIntegrate** can occasionally produce poor estimates. Just as the **Plot** command can miss features of the graph of a function that are "narrow" relative to the domain over which it is plotted, **NIntegrate** can miss such features also. Problems arise if points near the narrow feature are not sampled (for a discussion of the **Plot** command in this context, see Section 3.2 on page 55). Here is an example:

In[6]:= $\mathbf{Plot}\left[e^{-(x-2)^2}, \{x, -5, 5\}, \mathbf{PlotRange} \to \{0, 1\}, \mathbf{Filling} \to \mathbf{Axis}\right]$

Out[6]=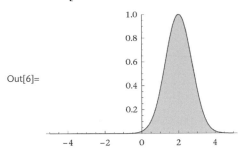

Here is the same function plotted over a much larger domain, so much larger that the bump disappears from view:

In[7]:= $\mathbf{Plot}\left[e^{-(x-2)^2}, \{x, -5000, 5000\}, \mathbf{PlotRange} \to \{0, 1\}, \mathbf{Filling} \to \mathbf{Axis}\right]$

Out[7]=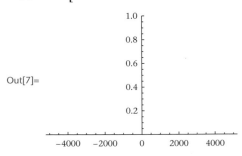

In[8]:= $\mathbf{NIntegrate}\left[e^{-(x-2)^2}, \{x, -5, 5\}\right]$

Out[8]= 1.77243

When **NIntegrate** is applied to this function over the larger domain, it also misses the bump:

In[9]:= $\mathbf{NIntegrate}\left[e^{-(x-2)^2}, \{x, -5000, 5000\}\right]$

NIntegrate::slwcon :
  Numerical integration converging too slowly; suspect one of the following: singularity, value
    of the integration is 0, highly oscillatory integrand, or WorkingPrecision too small. ≫

NIntegrate::ncvb :
  NIntegrate failed to converge to prescribed accuracy after 9 recursive bisections in x near {x}
    = {19.3758}. NIntegrate obtained 1.9195034084772933` and
    1.1959812980962528` for the integral and error estimates. ≫

Out[9]= 1.9195

The warning messages provide a hint that something might not be right, yet an incorrect output is generated. This phenomenon can be even worse if the integrand has discontinuities, for in such situations the actual definite integral may not have a real value, yet **NIntegrate** may report one. The following integral, for example, does not converge:

In[10]:= **NIntegrate** $\left[\dfrac{1}{(x-1)(x-2)}, \{x, 0, 3\}\right]$

> NIntegrate::slwcon :
>> Numerical integration converging too slowly; suspect one of the following: singularity, value of the integration is 0, highly oscillatory integrand, or WorkingPrecision too small. ≫

> NIntegrate::ncvb :
>> NIntegrate failed to converge to prescribed accuracy after 9 recursive bisections in x near {x} = {1.99809}. NIntegrate obtained 7.353131720000712` and 10.725954889917318` for the integral and error estimates. ≫

Out[10]= $0. \times 10^1$

Taking the right and left limits of the exact integral as the upper and lower bounds, respectively, approach 1 demonstrates nonconvergence:

In[11]:= **Limit** $\left[\int_0^b \dfrac{1}{(x-1)(x-2)}\, d\,x, b \to 1, \text{Direction} \to 1\right]$

Out[11]= ∞

In[12]:= **Limit** $\left[\int_a^{3/2} \dfrac{1}{(x-1)(x-2)}\, d\,x, a \to 1, \text{Direction} \to -1\right]$

Out[12]= $-\infty$

If you know that the integrand has discontinuities in the interval over which you are integrating (vertical asymptotes in the graph are a giveaway), you can instruct **NIntegrate** to look out for them by replacing the iterator {x,xmin,xmax} with {x,xmin,x_1,x_2,x_3,...,xmax}, where x_1, x_2, x_3, ... are the points of discontinuity. Sometimes this won't help, certainly not in those cases when the integral does not have a real value:

In[13]:= $\textbf{NIntegrate}\left[\dfrac{1}{(x-1)(x-2)}, \{x, 0, 1, 2, 3\}\right]$

NIntegrate::slwcon :

Numerical integration converging too slowly; suspect one of the following: singularity, value
of the integration is 0, highly oscillatory integrand, or WorkingPrecision too small. ≫

NIntegrate::ncvb :

NIntegrate failed to converge to prescribed accuracy after 9 recursive bisections in x near {x} = {≪83≫}.
NIntegrate obtained −146.633 and 28.765504119209318` for the integral and error estimates. ≫

Out[13]= -146.633

But if the integral has a value, **NIntegrate** will usually produce a very good approximation to it:

In[14]:= $\textbf{NIntegrate}\left[\dfrac{1}{\sqrt[4]{(x-1)^2}}, \{x, 0, 1, 3\}\right]$

Out[14]= 4.82843

In[15]:= $\textbf{Plot}\left[\dfrac{1}{\sqrt[4]{(x-1)^2}}, \{x, 0, 3\}, \textbf{PlotRange} \rightarrow \{0, 14\}, \textbf{Filling} \rightarrow \textbf{Axis}\right]$

Out[15]=

One strategy to help you determine if **NIntegrate** is providing an accurate answer is to examine carefully the plot of the integrand. If the numerical value provided by **NIntegrate** appears consistent with the area in the plot, but you still have your doubts, you might try breaking up your integral as a sum of integrals over various disjoint intervals whose union is the interval over which you are integrating. Place short intervals around any discontinuities:

In[16]:= $\textbf{Assuming}\left[b < 1, \displaystyle\int_0^b \dfrac{1}{\sqrt[4]{(x-1)^2}}\, dx\right]$

Out[16]= $2 - 2\sqrt{1-b}$

In[17]:= **Limit[%, b → 1, Direction → 1]**

Out[17]= 2

In[18]:= $\int_{1}^{3} \dfrac{1}{\sqrt[4]{(x-1)^2}}\, dx$

Out[18]= $2\sqrt{2}$

In[19]:= **Assuming$\left[a > 1, \int_{a}^{3} \dfrac{1}{\sqrt[4]{(x-1)^2}}\, dx\right]$**

Out[19]= $2\left(\sqrt{2} - \sqrt{-1+a}\right)$

In[20]:= **Limit[%, a → 1, Direction → -1]**

Out[20]= $2\sqrt{2}$

In[21]:= **NIntegrate$\left[\dfrac{1}{\sqrt[4]{(x-1)^2}}, \{x, 0, 0.9\}\right]$ +**

NIntegrate$\left[\dfrac{1}{\sqrt[4]{(x-1)^2}}, \{x, 0.9, 1, 1.1\}\right]$ + NIntegrate$\left[\dfrac{1}{\sqrt[4]{(x-1)^2}}, \{x, 1.1, 3\}\right]$

Out[21]= 4.82843

Good. This is consistent with the previous output. As usual, it is up to you to test and decide on the efficacy of results produced with the computer.

Exercises 5.12

1. Use **NIntegrate** to produce a numerical approximation to $\int_{0}^{1} \sqrt{t^3 + 3t + 1}\; dt$.

5.13 Surfaces of Revolution

Surfaces of revolution are often difficult for calculus students to visualize. The command **Revolution‑ Plot3D** makes this easy once you understand how it works. **RevolutionPlot3D** always rotates the curve about the vertical axis. A student in single variable calculus can interpret this as rotation about the y-axis. The plot below shows $y = x^2$, for the x values 0 through 2, rotated about the y-axis a full 360 degrees.

In[1]:= **RevolutionPlot3D$\left[x^2, \{x, 0, 2\}\right]$**

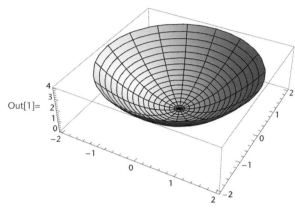

Out[1]=

Once you have generated a plot you can grab it with your mouse and rotate it to view it from any angle. With a little work you can use this feature to display a curve as if it has been rotated about the x-axis. To do this it helps to fully understand the command **RevolutionPlot3D**. The basic syntax for this command is **RevolutionPlot3D[$f(t)$,{$t,tmin,tmax$}]**. This generates a surface with height $f(t)$ at radius t rotated about the vertical axis. To get a plot of the surface generated by revolving $y = x^2$ for the x values 0 through 2 about the x-axis you must first generate the graph below:

In[2]:= **RevolutionPlot3D$\left[\sqrt{y}\,, \{y, 0, 4\}\right]$**

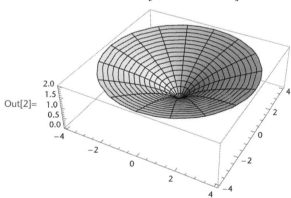

Out[2]=

Now use your mouse to orient the surface so that it appears to be a revolution about the x-axis as below:

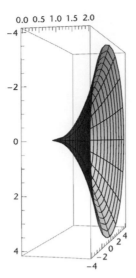

We used $\sqrt{y}$ above since it is the inverse of x^2. As x goes from 0 to 2, y goes from 0 to 4.

Sometimes it can be easier to visualize a surface by cutting it open and peering inside. You can do this by plotting it on less than a full revolution. The plot below shows the revolution of both x^2 and $\sqrt{x}$ about the y-axis through only 270 degrees. Note that we need to use radians to indicate our angle of revolution.

In[3]:= **RevolutionPlot3D** $\left[\left\{\left\{\sqrt{x}\right\}, \left\{x^2\right\}\right\}, \{x, 0, 1\}, \left\{\theta, 0, \dfrac{3\pi}{2}\right\}, \textbf{ViewPoint} \to \{4, -5, .5\}\right]$

Out[3]=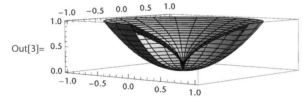

Consider the region shaded below.

In[4]:= **Plot** $\left[\{2 - x^2, x\}, \{x, 0, 1\}, \textbf{Filling} \to \{1 \to \{2\}\}\right]$

Out[4]=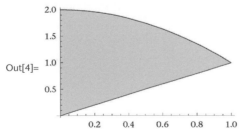

To display the surface formed when this region is revolved about the y-axis enter:

In[5]:= **RevolutionPlot3D** $\left[\{\{2-x^2\},\ \{x\}\},\ \{x,\ 0,\ 1\},\ \left\{\theta,\ -\dfrac{\pi}{4},\ \dfrac{3\pi}{2}\right\}\right]$

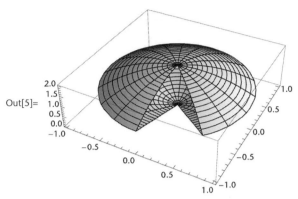

Out[5]=

To display the surface formed when this region is revolved about the x-axis enter the command below, and then maneuver the plot appropriately with your mouse.

In[6]:= **RevolutionPlot3D** $\left[\left\{\begin{array}{ll} y & 0 \le y \le 1 \\ \sqrt{2-y} & 1 < y < 2 \end{array}\right.,\ \{y,\ 0,\ 2\},\ \left\{\theta,\ 0,\ \dfrac{3\pi}{2}\right\},\ \textbf{BoxRatios} \rightarrow 1\right]$

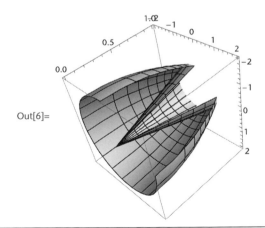

Out[6]=

Exercises 5.13

1. Use **RevolutionPlot3D** to plot $y = \sin(x)$ on the interval 0 to 4π and revolve the surface through 330 degrees.

2. Use **RevolutionPlot3D** to plot a sphere of radius 6.

5.14 Sequences and Series

Convergent sequences can be investigated with the **Limit** command (discussed in Section 5.1 on page 196). To type ∞ you can either type **Infinity** or find the symbol ∞ in the BasicMathInput palette, or just type ESC inf ESC.

In[1]:= $\mathbf{Limit}\left[\dfrac{\mathbf{n!}}{\mathbf{n^n}}, \mathbf{n} \to \infty\right]$

Out[1]= 0

In[2]:= $\mathbf{Limit[n\,Sin[\pi\,/\,n],\ n} \to \infty]$

Out[2]= π

There are several powerful commands for dealing with series. The first and most simple is the **Sum** command, discussed earlier in this chapter—see the subsection "Riemann Sums" in Section 5.11 on page 230. If you haven't yet used this command (to compute a Riemann sum, for instance), it's not hard. It works like the **Table** command, but rather than creating a list of the specified items, it adds them.

The really amazing thing about this command is that it can accept ∞ as a bound, meaning that it can find the value of an infinite series.

In[3]:= $\displaystyle\sum_{n=1}^{\infty} \dfrac{1}{n^2}$

Out[3]= $\dfrac{\pi^2}{6}$

In[4]:= $\mathbf{N[\%]}$

Out[4]= 1.64493

Of course some series fail to converge, and others have solutions that *Mathematica* will not be able to find. Solutions to the latter type can be approximated by summing a large number of terms. Here is a series that doesn't converge:

In[5]:= $\displaystyle\sum_{n=1}^{\infty} \mathbf{Cos[n]}$

Sum::div : Sum does not converge. »

Out[5]= $\displaystyle\sum_{n=1}^{\infty} Cos[n]$

Here is an example of a series involving an independent variable x. Note that the nonpalette version of the **Sum** command is more flexible than its palette counterpart in that the iterator can be adjusted to skip certain terms. Here is the sum $1 + x^2 + x^4 + \cdots$:

In[6]:= **Clear[x];**
Sum$\left[x^n, \{n, 0, \infty, 2\}\right]$

Out[7]= $\dfrac{1}{1 - x^2}$

In this example *Mathematica* reported a solution, but did not specify which values of the independent variable x are acceptable. In particular, note that if $x = \pm 1$ the denominator will be zero, and the solution makes no sense. *Mathematica* reports the solution you most probably need in such situations, but it is up to you to determine the *region of convergence*, those values of the independent variable for which the solution is valid. In the example above, x must fall strictly between -1 and 1 for the solution to be valid.

The *Mathematica* command that more or less undoes what the **Sum** command does is the **Series** command. Here are the first few terms (those with degree not exceeding five) of the Taylor series expansion of $1/(1 - x^2)$:

In[8]:= **Series$\left[\dfrac{1}{1 - x^2}, \{x, 0, 5\}\right]$**

Out[8]= $1 + x^2 + x^4 + O[x]^6$

The **Series** command requires two arguments. The first is the function for which you wish to find a power series expansion. The second is a special iterator, one whose form is {*variable*, x_0, *power*}, where *variable* names the independent variable, x_0 is the point about which the series is produced, and *power* specifies the highest power of the variable to be included in the output. The output includes a *big O* term, indicating that there are more terms in the series than those being shown. To get rid of the big O term, use the **Normal** command:

In[9]:= **Normal[%]**

Out[9]= $1 + x^2 + x^4$

You can produce a plot of this polynomial and the function. Note that the polynomial provides a good approximation to the function when x is near x_0 ($x_0 = 0$ in this example):

In[10]:= $\textbf{Plot}\left[\left\{\%, \dfrac{1}{1-x^2}\right\}, \{x, -1, 1\}\right]$

Out[10]=

Note that you can get the formula for a Taylor series expansion for an arbitrary function (such as *f*) about an arbitrary point (such as *a*). Here are the first four terms of such a series:

In[11]:= $\textbf{Clear[a, f]};$
$\textbf{Normal[Series[f[x], \{x, a, 3\}]]}$

Out[12]= $f[a] + (-a + x)\,f'[a] + \dfrac{1}{2}\,(-a + x)^2\,f''[a] + \dfrac{1}{6}\,(-a + x)^3\,f^{(3)}[a]$

In fact it is a simple matter to design a custom command for generating Taylor polynomials of degree *n* for the function *f* about the point x_0:

In[13]:= $\textbf{taylor[f\_, \{x\_, x0\_\}, n\_] := Normal[Series[f[x], \{x, x0, n\}]]}$

For example, we can now easily compute the eleventh-degree Taylor polynomial for the sine function, expanded around the point $x = 0$:

In[14]:= $\textbf{taylor[Sin, \{x, 0\}, 11]}$

Out[14]= $x - \dfrac{x^3}{6} + \dfrac{x^5}{120} - \dfrac{x^7}{5040} + \dfrac{x^9}{362880} - \dfrac{x^{11}}{39916800}$

Here is another example. The fourth-degree Taylor polynomial for cos(*x*), expanded about the point $x = \frac{\pi}{4}$, is given below:

In[15]:= $\textbf{taylor}\left[\textbf{Cos}, \left\{x, \dfrac{\pi}{4}\right\}, 4\right]$

Out[15]= $\dfrac{1}{\sqrt{2}} - \dfrac{-\frac{\pi}{4}+x}{\sqrt{2}} - \dfrac{\left(-\frac{\pi}{4}+x\right)^2}{2\sqrt{2}} + \dfrac{\left(-\frac{\pi}{4}+x\right)^3}{6\sqrt{2}} + \dfrac{\left(-\frac{\pi}{4}+x\right)^4}{24\sqrt{2}}$

And here is a list of the first five Taylor polynomials for cos(*x*), again expanded about the point $x = \frac{\pi}{4}$:

In[16]:= $\mathbf{Table}\Big[\mathbf{taylor}\Big[\mathbf{Cos},\ \Big\{x,\ \dfrac{\pi}{4}\Big\},\ n\Big],\ \{n,\ 5\}\Big]\ //\ \mathbf{Column}$

Out[16]=

$$\frac{1}{\sqrt{2}}-\frac{-\frac{\pi}{4}+x}{\sqrt{2}}$$

$$\frac{1}{\sqrt{2}}-\frac{-\frac{\pi}{4}+x}{\sqrt{2}}-\frac{\left(-\frac{\pi}{4}+x\right)^2}{2\sqrt{2}}$$

$$\frac{1}{\sqrt{2}}-\frac{-\frac{\pi}{4}+x}{\sqrt{2}}-\frac{\left(-\frac{\pi}{4}+x\right)^2}{2\sqrt{2}}+\frac{\left(-\frac{\pi}{4}+x\right)^3}{6\sqrt{2}}$$

$$\frac{1}{\sqrt{2}}-\frac{-\frac{\pi}{4}+x}{\sqrt{2}}-\frac{\left(-\frac{\pi}{4}+x\right)^2}{2\sqrt{2}}+\frac{\left(-\frac{\pi}{4}+x\right)^3}{6\sqrt{2}}+\frac{\left(-\frac{\pi}{4}+x\right)^4}{24\sqrt{2}}$$

$$\frac{1}{\sqrt{2}}-\frac{-\frac{\pi}{4}+x}{\sqrt{2}}-\frac{\left(-\frac{\pi}{4}+x\right)^2}{2\sqrt{2}}+\frac{\left(-\frac{\pi}{4}+x\right)^3}{6\sqrt{2}}+\frac{\left(-\frac{\pi}{4}+x\right)^4}{24\sqrt{2}}-\frac{\left(-\frac{\pi}{4}+x\right)^5}{120\sqrt{2}}$$

Finally, let's produce a sequence of graphics, one for each of the first twelve Taylor polynomials for the cosine function, expanded about the point $\frac{\pi}{4}$. Each plot will show the cosine function in light gray, with the Taylor polynomial in black, and with the point $\left(\frac{\pi}{4},\ \cos\!\left(\frac{\pi}{4}\right)\right)=\left(\frac{\pi}{4},\ \dfrac{1}{\sqrt{2}}\right)$, highlighted.

The individual frames are displayed in a **Grid** below, and should be read sequentially from left to right across the rows to increase the degree of the Taylor polynomial.

In[17]:= $\mathbf{tlist=Table}\Big[\mathbf{taylor}\Big[\mathbf{Cos},\ \Big\{x,\ \dfrac{\pi}{4}\Big\},\ n\Big],\ \{n,\ 12\}\Big];$

In[18]:= $\mathbf{plots=Table}\Big[\mathbf{Plot}\Big[\{f,\ \mathbf{Cos[x]}\},\ \{x,\ -2\pi,\ 2\pi\},$

   $\mathbf{PlotRange}\rightarrow 3,\ \mathbf{Ticks}\rightarrow \mathbf{None},\ \mathbf{PlotStyle}\rightarrow\{\mathbf{Black},\ \mathbf{Darker[Gray]}\},$

   $\mathbf{Epilog}\rightarrow\Big\{\mathbf{PointSize[.02]},\ \mathbf{Point}\Big[\Big\{\dfrac{\pi}{4},\ \dfrac{1}{\sqrt{2}}\Big\}\Big]\Big\}\Big],\ \{f,\ \mathbf{tlist}\}\Big];$

In[19]:= $\mathbf{GraphicsGrid[Partition[plots,\ 3]]}$

Out[19]=

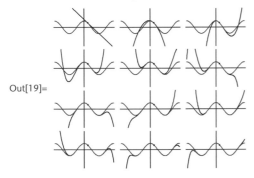

In a live session the following command is fun. Simply click on a tab to see the Taylor polynomial of that degree.

In[23]:= **TabView**[**Table**[k → plots[[k]], {k, 12}], **ImageSize** → **Automatic**]

Out[23]=

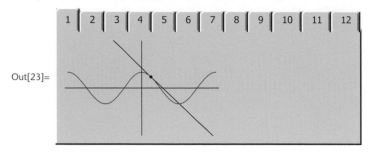

Exercise 3 below shows how to use the **Thread** command to construct this **TabView**.

Exercises 5.14

1. Find the limit of the sequence: $\frac{2}{1}, \left(\frac{3}{2}\right)^2, \left(\frac{4}{3}\right)^3, \left(\frac{5}{4}\right)^4, \ldots$

2. Find the limit of the sequence: $\frac{1}{1}\left(\frac{1}{2}\right), \frac{1}{2}\left(\frac{2}{3} + \frac{2}{4}\right), \frac{1}{3}\left(\frac{3}{4} + \frac{3}{5} + \frac{3}{6}\right), \frac{1}{4}\left(\frac{4}{5} + \frac{4}{6} + \frac{4}{7} + \frac{4}{8}\right), \ldots$

3. The **Thread** command can be used to take two lists such as {1,2,3} and {a,b,c}, and *thread* some command f through them to produce the list {f[1,a],f[2,b],f[3,c]}. It is particularly handy when constructing a **TabView** object, where the syntax requires a list of the form {*label1* → *item1*,*label2* → *item2*,*label3* → *item3*,...}. In this case, f is the command **Rule** (the **FullForm** of 1 → a is **Rule[1,a]**). **Thread** is discussed in greater detail in Section 8.4 on page 403.

   a. Enter the following inputs to see **Thread** in action.

   Thread[exampleFunction[{1, 2, 3}, {a, b, c}]]

   Thread[Rule[{1, 2, 3}, {a, b, c}]]

   Thread[{1, 2, 3} → {a, b, c}]

   b. Use **Thread** rather than **Table** to create the **TabView** shown at the end of this section.

4. Create a **TabView** that displays the first 10 distinct Taylor polynomials for sin(x) expanded about $x_0 = 0$.

6

Multivariable Calculus

6.1 Vectors

A standard notation for a vector in the plane is a coordinate pair, such as ⟨2, 5⟩. This represents the vector that has its tail at the origin and its head at the point with x coordinate 2 and y coordinate 5.

Another standard notation for this vector is $2\vec{i} + 5\vec{j}$. Here $\vec{i}$ and $\vec{j}$ denote the unit vectors in the x and y directions, respectively.

In *Mathematica*, a vector in the plane is expressed as a *list* of length two, such as {2, 5}. Vector addition and scalar multiplication work exactly as you would expect:

```
In[1]:= {2, 5} + {17, −4}
```

```
Out[1]= {19, 1}
```

```
In[2]:= −4 {2, 5}
```

```
Out[2]= {−8, −20}
```

```
In[3]:= i = {1, 0};
        j = {0, 1};
        2 i + 5 j
```

```
Out[5]= {2, 5}
```

Higher-dimensional vectors are simply given as longer lists. Here is the sum of two vectors in three-space:

```
In[6]:= {3, −57, 8} + {57, −3, π/4}
```

$$Out[6]= \left\{60, -60, 8 + \frac{\pi}{4}\right\}$$

The Dot Product and the Norm

The *dot product* of the vectors $\langle u_1, u_2, \ldots, u_n \rangle$ and $\langle v_1, v_2, \ldots, v_n \rangle$ is the scalar $u_1 v_1 + u_2 v_2 + \cdots + u_n v_n$. You can compute the dot product of vectors with *Mathematica* by placing a dot (a period) between them:

In[7]:= **{u₁, u₂}.{v₁, v₂}**

Out[7]= $u_1 v_1 + u_2 v_2$

In[8]:= **{3, 4}.{4, 5}**

Out[8]= 32

You can calculate the *norm* (i.e., the length or magnitude) of a vector using the **Norm** command.

In[9]:= **Norm[{3, 4}]**

Out[9]= 5

In[10]:= **Norm[{u₁, u₂}]**

Out[10]= $\sqrt{\mathrm{Abs}[u_1]^2 + \mathrm{Abs}[u_2]^2}$

For real vectors, this is equivalent to the square root of the dot product of the vector with itself.

In[11]:= **Simplify[Norm[{u₁, u₂}], {u₁, u₂} ∈ Reals]**

Out[11]= $\sqrt{u_1^2 + u_2^2}$

In[12]:= **$\sqrt{\text{\{u₁, u₂\}.\{u₁, u₂\}}}$**

Out[12]= $\sqrt{u_1^2 + u_2^2}$

> ⚠ We have made use of subscripts to display general vectors. This looks very nice. However, it can get you into trouble if you try to give such a vector a name. You should *never* enter input such as **u = {u₁, u₂}**. This will throw *Mathematica* into an infinite loop. See Exercise 4.

The dot product can also be employed to find the angle between a pair of vectors. You may recall that the cosine of the angle θ between vectors $\vec{u}$ and $\vec{v}$ is given by the formula:

$$\cos \theta = \frac{\vec{u} \cdot \vec{v}}{\|\vec{u}\| \, \|\vec{v}\|}$$

where $\|\vec{u}\|$ denotes the norm of $\vec{u}$. You can find the angle (in radians) between vectors like this:

In[13]:= **u = {2, 4}; v = {9, −13};**

$$\mathbf{ArcCos}\left[\frac{\mathbf{u.v}}{\mathbf{Norm[u]\,Norm[v]}}\right] \mathbf{// N}$$

Out[14]= 2.0724

Conversion to degrees requires multiplying by the conversion factor $\frac{180}{\pi}$, or dividing by the built-in constant **Degree**:

In[15]:= **% / Degree**

Out[15]= 118.74

Rendering Vectors in the Plane

One can display vectors using the graphics primitive **Arrow**.

In[16]:= **Graphics[{Arrow[{{0, 0}, {1, 1}}], Arrow[{{0, 0}, {2, 1}}]}, Axes → True]**

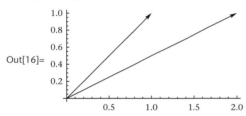

Out[16]=

Arrow accepts as its argument a list of two ordered-pairs. These represent the coordinates of the tail and head of the arrow, respectively. Note, however, that you can double click on any arrow in a graphic, then drag either end of the arrow to a new location. Or you can drag the middle portion of the arrow and move the entire thing to a new location, preserving its length and direction.

But working programmatically (rather than grabbing and dragging) is advantageous for attaining precise positioning. Here we illustrate a vector sum:

In[17]:= Graphics[{
        Arrow[{{0, 0}, {1, 2}}], Arrow[{{0, 0}, {2, 1}}],
            {Gray, Arrow[{{1, 2}, {3, 3}}], Arrow[{{2, 1}, {3, 3}}]},
            {Red, Arrow[{{0, 0}, {3, 3}}]}
        }, PlotRange → {{0, 3}, {0, 3}}, Axes → True]

Out[17]=

And why not drop it into a **Manipulate**? This has a **Locator** at the head of each of the two component vectors in the sum, so that you can drag either of those vectors by the head to move them. It's actually easier to make sense of the structure of the input when it's written in this general form:

In[18]:= Manipulate[Graphics[{
        Arrow[{{0, 0}, u}], Arrow[{{0, 0}, v}],
            {Gray, Arrow[{u, u + v}], Arrow[{v, u + v}]},
            {Red, Arrow[{{0, 0}, u + v}]}
        }, PlotRange → 3, Axes → True, Ticks → None],
        {{u, {1, 2}}, Locator, Appearance → None},
        {{v, {2, 1}}, Locator, Appearance → None}]

Out[18]=

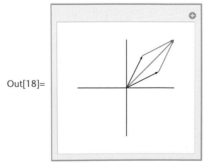

⚠ There is no primitive **Arrow** object available for 3D graphics, although the **VectorFieldPlot** package has a command called **VectorFieldPlot3D** which will draw 3D arrows for vector fields. This is discussed in Section 6.5 on page 327. The issue with 3D arrows is the arrowheads, which should be cones, and as of version 6 of *Mathematica*, there is no primitive for cones.

The Cross Product

Imagine a pair of vectors $\vec{u}$ and $\vec{v}$ in three-space drawn with their tails at the same point. The *cross product* of $\vec{u}$ and $\vec{v}$ is a normal vector to the plane determined by $\vec{u}$ and $\vec{v}$, whose magnitude is equal to the area of the parallelogram determined by $\vec{u}$ and $\vec{v}$.

You can harness *Mathematica* to take the cross product of a pair of vectors with the command **Cross**. Here that command is used to give the general formula for the cross product:

In[19]:= **Cross[{u_1, u_2, u_3}, {v_1, v_2, v_3}]**

Out[19]= {$-u_3 v_2 + u_2 v_3$, $u_3 v_1 - u_1 v_3$, $-u_2 v_1 + u_1 v_2$}

And here it is used to find the cross product of a specific pair of vectors:

In[20]:= **Cross[{1, 3, 5}, {7, 9, 11}]**

Out[20]= {-12, 24, -12}

You can also use the small ⊠ button on the BasicMathInput palette to calculate cross products. It's the button under the i near the middle of the palette. Don't confuse it with the larger ⊠ button to its left; that one is used for ordinary (component-wise) multiplication.

In[21]:= **{1, 3, 5}×{7, 9, 11}**

Out[21]= {-12, 24, -12}

Exercises 6.1

1. Find an exact expression for the sine of the angle between the vectors $\langle 2, -1, 1 \rangle$ and $\langle 3, 2, 1 \rangle$.

2. Look up the **Sign** command in the Documentation Center. Explain how to use it with the dot product to determine whether the angle between a pair of vectors is acute, right, or obtuse.

3. The dot product, we learned in this section, is implemented in *Mathematica* in infix form by placing a period between a pair of vectors. There is (as always) a "square bracket" version of this command. It is called **Dot**.

   a. Use **Dot** to take the dot product of {u1, u2, u3} with {v1, v2, v3}.

   b. The dot product is the most common example of an *inner product*. *Mathematica* has another command called **Inner** that can be used to create alternate inner products. Verify that the input **Inner[Times, {u1, u2, u3}, {v1, v2, v3}, Plus]** gives the same output as that produced in part **a.**

4. Near the beginning of this section, we did several computations using general vectors of the form $\{u_1, u_2\}$. The subscripts are obtained from the keyboard by typing, for instance, u [CTRL]-[_] 1. The **FullForm** of the resulting expression is **Subscript[u,1]**. Many textbooks will (in the course of a proof, for instance) write, "Let $\vec{u} = \langle u_1, u_2 \rangle$." While this is a convenient notation, it cannot be replicated in *Mathematica*. If you were to enter the input u = $\{u_1, u_2\}$, what would happen? The same bad thing will happen if you enter the more simple input u = u_1. Try it, then explain what's going on. As the blues singer Kelly Joe Phelps put it, "It's not so far to go to find trouble."

5. Use *Mathematica* to verify the parallelogram law in $\mathbb{R}^3$: For any pair of vectors $\vec{u}$ and $\vec{v}$,
$$\|\vec{u} + \vec{v}\|^2 + \|\vec{u} - \vec{v}\|^2 = 2\,\|\vec{u}\|^2 + 2\,\|\vec{v}\|^2 \ .$$

6.2   Real-Valued Functions of Two or More Variables

One certainly may define a real-valued function with two or more variables exactly as we did in Chapter 5, but with an additional variable, like this:

In[1]:= $f[x\_,\ y\_] := Sin[x^2 - y^2]$

However, we will generally find it more convenient (for reasons that will come to light shortly) to make a simple assignment like this instead:

In[2]:= **Clear**$[f,\ x,\ y];$
$f = Sin[x^2 - y^2];$

A function of three variables is dealt with similarly. Note that it is important to **Clear** any variables that have previously been assigned values.

In[4]:= **Clear**$[g,\ x,\ y,\ z];$
$g = x^2\,y^3 - 3\,x\,z;$

Multiletter variable names

When defining a function, remember to leave a space (or to use a *) between variables that you intend to multiply, otherwise *Mathematica* will interpret the multiletter combination as a *single* variable. For example, note the space between the **x** and the **z** in the definition of the function *g* above. Said another way, one may use multiletter variable names when defining a function; for example, names such as **x1**, **x2**, and so on.

To evaluate a function defined in this fashion, one uses replacement rules. For instance, here is $f\left(0,\ \sqrt{\pi/4}\ \right)$:

In[6]:= $f \,/. \left\{x \to 0, \, y \to \sqrt{\pi/4}\,\right\}$

Out[6]= $-\dfrac{1}{\sqrt{2}}$

It may be useful to **Simplify** the output on some occasions. Here is $f(1 - \pi, \, 1 + \pi)$:

In[7]:= $f \,/. \left\{x \to 1 - \pi, \, y \to 1 + \pi\right\}$

Out[7]= $\mathrm{Sin}\!\left[(1 - \pi)^2 - (1 + \pi)^2\right]$

In[8]:= **Simplify[%]**

Out[8]= 0

Plotting Functions of Two Variables with Plot3D

The plotting of functions of two variables can be performed with the command **Plot3D**. It works pretty much like **Plot**, but you will need an iterator specifying the span of values assumed by each of *two* variables. The plot will be shown over the rectangular domain in the plane determined by the two iterators. When first evaluated, the positive *x* direction is to the right along the front of the plot, the positive *y* direction is to the back along the side of the plot, and the positive *z* direction is up:

In[9]:= $\mathbf{Plot3D}\big[\mathbf{f, \{x, -2, 2\}, \{y, -1, 1\}}\big]$

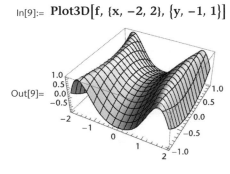

Out[9]=

Grab such a plot with your mouse and drag. This will rotate the image so that you can see it from any vantage point you like. Hold down the [OPTION] key while you drag and you can zoom in and out. It's a beautiful thing.

Note that it is a simple matter to produce a sketch of any vertical *cross-section* (sometimes called a trace) for such a plot in either the *x* or *y* direction. Simply set one of the two variables to a numerical value and make a **Plot** using the other as the independent variable.

In[10]:= **Plot[f /. y → 0, {x, −2, 2}, AxesLabel → {x, z}]**

Out[10]=

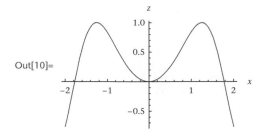

In[11]:= **Plot[f /. x → 0, {y, −1, 1}, AxesLabel → {y, z}]**

Out[11]=

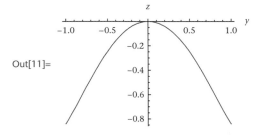

We'll discuss how one can use the **Mesh** option to superimpose these traces onto the original **Plot3D** of f in the subsection "Controlling the Mesh Lines" on page 265. See Exercise 6 for more on cross-sections.

Options for 3D Plotting Commands

The information in this section applies to any plotting command that generates a three-dimensional graphic. Such commands include **Plot3D**, **ContourPlot3D**, **ParametricPlot3D**, **SphericalPlot3D**, and **RevolutionPlot3D**.

There are a host of options available that will allow you to tweak the output of these plotting commands in some incredible ways. Among the options that are essentially the same as the familiar options for **Plot** (see Section 3.3, see page 59) are such common settings as **AxesLabel**, **PlotLabel**, **PlotPoints**, **MaxRecursion** and **PlotRange**. Other options, such as **Mesh** and **MeshFunctions**, work in a similar manner as they do in **Plot**, but now everything is one dimension higher. In short, they will take some getting used to.

PlotPoints, MaxRecursion, and Toggling Mesh to None or All

Note first that the simple setting **Mesh → None** will make the mesh lines disappear, while the setting **Mesh → All** will display all of the polygons produced by **Plot3D** to render the image. While the former is a popular setting that produces a beautiful image (especially when **PlotPoints** is bumped up from its default value, usually 15), the latter provides a window into the means by which **Plot3D** does its stuff:

In[12]:= $\text{Table}\big[\text{Plot3D}\big[e^{\text{Sin}[x\,y]},\ \{x,\ -\pi,\ \pi\},\ \{y,\ -\pi,\ \pi\},\ \text{Mesh} \rightarrow m,\ \text{MaxRecursion} \rightarrow 4\big],$
$\{m,\ \{\text{None},\ \text{All}\}\}\big]$

Out[12]=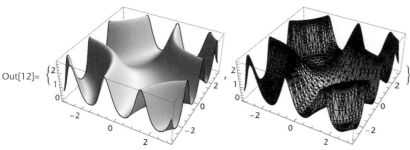

Note that like **Plot**, **Plot3D** uses an adaptive algorithm that recursively subdivides the surface into smaller polygons in areas where the surface bends more sharply. **PlotPoints** settings control how many equally spaced points are initially sampled in each direction (so a setting of 50 will force *Mathematica* to sample $50 \times 50 = 2500$ points in the domain). **MaxRecursion** controls the number of recursive subdivisions permitted to fine-tune the image. Large settings for these options produce beautiful images, but may result in perceptibly slower rendering times, and will definitely produce larger file sizes when the notebook is saved. See Exercise 2.

Adjusting the PlotRange and BoxRatios

As is the case with the **Plot** command, **Plot3D** will sometimes clip the highest peaks and lowest valleys in a plot in order to render the middle portions with greater detail. The option setting **ClippingStyle → None** will remove the default horizontal planes placed into the clipped areas. **ClippingStyle** may also be set to a **Graphics** directive such as **Opacity[.5]**.

In[13]:= $\text{Table}\Big[\text{Plot3D}\Big[\dfrac{x^2\,y^5 - x^5\,y^2}{100} + e^{-(x^2+y^2)},\ \{x,\ -3,\ 3\},\ \{y,\ -3,\ 3\},\ \text{ClippingStyle} \rightarrow k\Big],$
$\{k,\ \{\text{Automatic},\ \text{None}\}\}\Big]$

Out[13]= {image}

The setting **PlotRange → All** will force *Mathematica* to show the entire graph. Notice, however, that the bump in the middle of the plot vanishes from view due to the compression of the vertical axis:

In[14]:= $\text{Plot3D}\left[\dfrac{x^2\,y^5 - x^5\,y^2}{100} + e^{-(x^2+y^2)},\ \{x,\ -3,\ 3\},\ \{y,\ -3,\ 3\},\ \text{PlotRange} \to \text{All}\right]$

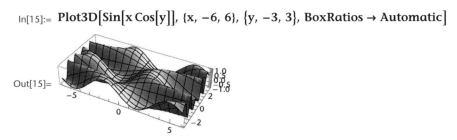

Out[14]=

The option **BoxRatios** determines the relative dimensions of the bounding box. The simple setting **BoxRatios → 1** will produce a cubical bounding box, while the setting **BoxRatios → Automatic** will scale the bounding box so that all axes have the same scale; it is analogous to the option **AspectRatio** used in two-dimensional plots. Be careful to not use this setting in cases such as the one above where one axis would be dramatically longer than the others. A setting such as **BoxRatios → {1, 1, 2}** will produce a bounding box whose horizontal sides are the same length, but whose vertical dimension is twice as long.

In[15]:= $\text{Plot3D}\big[\text{Sin}[x\,\text{Cos}[y]],\ \{x,\ -6,\ 6\},\ \{y,\ -3,\ 3\},\ \text{BoxRatios} \to \text{Automatic}\big]$

Out[15]=

The Bounding Box, Axes, and ViewPoint

The options **Boxed** and **Axes** can be used to modify the appearance of the bounding box and the tick marks that appear on three of its sides. By default, both options are set to **True**. To remove the bounding box entirely, set both to **False**. **Axes** can also be set to a list, as in the input below, to display only selected axes. The option **AxesEdge** controls in each of the three coordinate directions which of the four parallel sides of the bounding box in that direction are to be used as an axis. Each coordinate direction is specified by an ordered pair. For example, if the vertical or z axis is given the specification {-1, -1}, that means that the z axis will be placed on the left (negative x side) and front (negative y side).

In[16]:= **Plot3D[Sin[x Cos[y]], {x, −6, 6}, {y, −3, 3}, BoxRatios → Automatic, Boxed → False, Axes → {False, False, True}, AxesEdge → {Automatic, Automatic, {−1, −1}}]**

Out[16]=

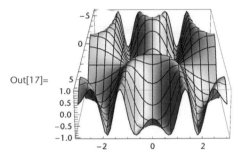

ViewPoint specifies the position in space (relative to the center of the graphic) from which it is seen. The setting {0, 0, 4}, for instance, will give a view from above, while the setting {3, 0, 1} will yield a vantage point that is three units from the origin along the positive x axis, and one unit up.

In[17]:= **Plot3D[Sin[x Cos[y]], {x, −6, 6}, {y, −3, 3}, BoxRatios → Automatic, ViewPoint → {3, 0, 1}]**

Out[17]=

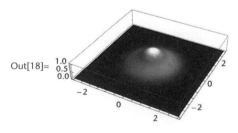

The ColorFunction

The option **ColorFunction** controls the coloring of the graph. Any of the color gradients available in the **ColorData** archive may be used to color a plot. Type and enter **ColorData["Gradients"]** for a listing of available gradients. For instance, here we color a plot using a color gradient reminiscent of that used in topographical maps, where low regions are colored dark blue, middle regions are shaded with greens and browns, and peaks are white.

In[18]:= **Plot3D[$e^{-(x^2+y^2)}$, {x, −3, 3}, {y, −3, 3}, BoxRatios → Automatic, ColorFunction → "DarkTerrain", PlotRange → All, Mesh → None]**

Out[18]=

ColorFunction allows you to assume complete control over the manner in which color is applied to a surface. With a bit of work, the graph of a function may be colored (using any color gradient you like) according to the values of any other function. See Exercise 1.

PlotStyle and Lighting

The **PlotStyle** and **Lighting** options provide another means of adjusting the appearance of the plot. In *Mathematica*, three-dimensional graphics are colored according to a physical lighting model that includes intrinsic surface color, the diffusive and reflective properties of the surface, and lighting (you may control the position, direction, and color of as many light sources as you like). By default, the polygons used to construct a **Plot3D** are all white; the lighting is responsible for all the color you see. You have total control over the output, and the possibilities are truly staggering.

PlotStyle is used to set the intrinsic surface color, and to specify the surface's diffusive and reflective properties. Several settings may be simultaneously given by wrapping them within the **Directive** command. There are three potential specifications. A straight color or opacity setting like **Blue** and/or **Opacity[.5]** can be given to set the intrinsic surface color or transparency. This color will interact with the lighting. A **Glow** setting, such as **Glow[Red]**, will emanate from the surface irrespective of the color of the lighting. Finally, a **Specularity** setting determines the diffusive and reflective properties of the surface. **Specularity** can accept two arguments. The first determines the color and amount of diffusion added to reflected light. A numerical value of 1 is equivalent to a color setting of **White**; in this case 100% of the light is reflected back, with no alteration to its color other than that determined by the surface's color. The second argument controls the shininess of the surface. Typical values range from 1 (dull) to 50 (shiny). The setting **Specularity[White, 20]** is good for creating the appearance of an anodized metallic surface:

In[19]:= **Plot3D[x Cos[x y], {x, −3, 3}, {y, −2, 2}, Mesh → None, MaxRecursion → 4,**
         PlotStyle → Directive[Lighter[Red], Specularity[White, 20]]]

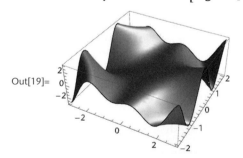

Out[19]=

Lighting can be adjusted in numerous ways. The default setting includes both ambient light and four colored light sources (although if an explicit **ColorFunction** is specified, white light from these same sources will be used instead). The simple setting **Lighting → "Neutral"** will force the use of white rather than colored lights.

In[20]:= **Plot3D[x Cos[x y], {x, −3, 3}, {y, −2, 2}, Mesh → None, MaxRecursion → 4,**
          PlotStyle → Directive[Lighter[Red], Specularity[White, 20]], Lighting → "Neutral"]

Out[20]=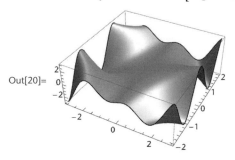

The Documentation Center page for **Lighting** gives information on setting ambient, spot, and directional light sources. We note here that the setting **Lighting → {{"Ambient", White}}** is similar to the setting **Lighting → "Neutral"**, but the latter includes point light sources and the shadows they create, and so is better at giving the illusion of depth. The former may be appropriate when a special **ColorFunction** is used and shadows would interfere with the information that the color provides.

Plotting over Nonrectangular Regions

The option **RegionFunction** can be used to specify the precise region over which a function is plotted. For instance, you may wish to plot a function over a circular domain for purely aesthetic reasons. The cone provides a classic example; it simply looks better with a circular domain:

In[21]:= **GraphicsRow[**
          {Plot3D[−$\sqrt{x^2 + y^2}$, {x, −1, 1}, {y, −1, 1}], Plot3D[−$\sqrt{x^2 + y^2}$, {x, −1, 1}, {y, −1, 1},
          RegionFunction → Function[{x, y}, x² + y² ≤ 1]]}, ImageSize → 280]

Out[21]=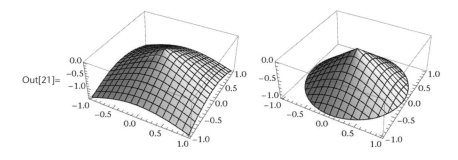

The setting **Function[{x, y}, x² + y² ≤ 1]** is a pure function. It takes a coordinate pair (x, y) as input, and returns **True** precisely if that coordinate pair lies within the unit circle. In the resulting plot, the domain is restricted to the region where this region function returns **True**. The setting in the second plot above could also have been given in the shorter form **RegionFunction** $\rightarrow$ $(\#1^2 + \#2^2 \le 1 \,\&)$. Pure functions are discussed in Section 8.4.

RegionFunction also provides an excellent means of plotting over a punctured domain. A classic example is the function $f(x, y) = \frac{x^2 y}{x^4 + y^2}$, which is not defined at the origin, and which has an essential discontinuity there. We remove a small disk from the center of the domain, and get a beautiful image:

In[22]:= **Plot3D**$\left[\dfrac{x^2\, y}{x^4 + y^2},\, \{x,\, -1,\, 1\},\, \{y,\, -1,\, 1\},\right.$

$\quad$ **RegionFunction** $\rightarrow$ **Function**$\left[\{x,\, y\},\, .1 \le \sqrt{x^2 + y^2}\,\right],$

$\quad$ **Mesh** $\rightarrow$ **None, MaxRecursion** $\rightarrow$ $\left.4\right]$

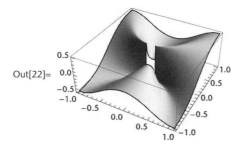

Out[22]=

Another approach to controlling the domain is by defining a function whose value outside a desired region is 0. This is easily accomplished using a **Piecewise** function. The **Exclusions** option is useful for specifying discontinuities; note how easy it is to specify the locus of discontinuities as an equation.

In[23]:= $f = \begin{cases} \sqrt{x^2 + y^2} & x^2 + y^2 < 1 \\ 0 & x^2 + y^2 \ge 1 \end{cases};$

In[24]:= **Plot3D**$\left[f,\, \{x,\, -1,\, 1\},\, \{y,\, -1,\, 1\},\, \textbf{Exclusions} \rightarrow \{x^2 + y^2 == 1\}\right]$

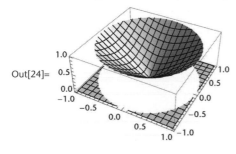

Out[24]=

Controlling the Mesh Lines

We've already discussed the two most common settings for the **Mesh** option, namely **None** and **All**. But much more is possible. Set **Mesh** to a positive integer, say 20, and there will be 20 mesh lines displayed (rather than the default 15) in each direction. Set **Mesh** to a list of two numbers, say {5, 30}, and there will be five mesh lines (bounding six regions) corresponding to fixed x values, and 30 mesh lines corresponding to fixed y values.

In[25]:= $\mathbf{Plot3D}\Big[\dfrac{x^2\,y}{x^2+y^2},\ \{x,\,-3,\,3\},\ \{y,\,-3,\,3\},\ \mathbf{Mesh}\to\{5,\,30\}\Big]$

Out[25]=

You may also specify *lists* of specific x and y values through which mesh lines should be drawn. A **Mesh** setting of {{−2}, {1}} will place one line at $x = -2$ and another at $y = 1$. This is useful for visually approximating the partial derivatives at the point (−2, 1). See Exercise 6.

In[26]:= $\mathbf{Plot3D}\Big[\dfrac{x^2\,y}{x^2+y^2},\ \{x,\,-3,\,3\},\ \{y,\,-3,\,3\},\ \mathbf{Mesh}\to\{\{-2\},\,\{1\}\}\Big]$

Out[26]=

The **MeshFunctions** option gives you even more control over the rendering of the mesh lines on a plot. The price of this versatility is that it will take a bit of practice to master. Your efforts here will be well rewarded, so read on.

By default there are two mesh functions, one for all the mesh lines corresponding to fixed x values, and one for the perpendicular collection of mesh lines corresponding to fixed y values. Together they form the familiar grid pattern that graces your **Plot3D** outputs. This default specification, if you were to manually type it, would read:

MeshFunctions → {Function[{x, y, z}, x], Function[{x, y, z}, y]}

It is a list of two pure functions, where each takes three arguments (one for each coordinate position in three-space). Equivalently, this default setting could be entered using the common shorthand notation: **MeshFunctions → {#1 &, #2 &}**. Pure functions are discussed in Section 8.4. In any event, mesh lines will be drawn where the mesh functions assume constant values; by default 15 evenly spaced values will be displayed.

Perhaps the most common non-default setting is the following, which places *level curves* on your plot. That is, the third variable (we usually call it *z*) is set to 15 evenly spaced values within the plot range, and a mesh curve is added to the surface at each of these values.

In[27]:= **Plot3D$\left[x^2 y^3 + (x - 1)^2 y, \{x, -2, 2\}, \{y, -2, 2\}, \textbf{MeshFunctions} \rightarrow \{\#3 \&\}\right]$**

Out[27]=
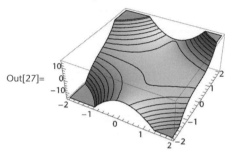

But of course you may define any mesh function you like. Here we place mesh lines according to distance from the origin. In other words, each mesh line lies on the surface of an invisible sphere centered at the origin.

In[28]:= **Plot3D$\left[x^2 y^3 + (x - 1)^2 y, \{x, -2, 2\}, \{y, -2, 2\},\right.$**
            $\textbf{MeshFunctions} \rightarrow \{\textbf{Norm}[\{\#1, \#2, \#3\}] \&\}, \textbf{PlotRange} \rightarrow 2, \textbf{BoxRatios} \rightarrow 1\right]$

Out[28]=
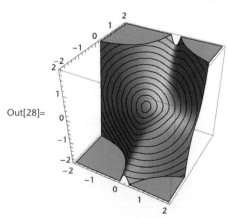

MeshShading

The **MeshShading** option allows the regions between mesh lines to receive specific color directives. The setting for this option has the same list structure as **MeshFunctions**; if there is a list of two mesh functions, you should have a list of two **MeshShading** settings. Each such setting is itself a list of directives that will by used cyclically (if this list is shorter than the number of mesh regions). Setting the **Lighting** to "Neutral" will replace the default colored lighting with white lights, so that the colors specified in the **MeshShading** are accurately rendered. For instance:

In[29]:= **Plot3D**$\left[x^2 y^3 + (x - 1)^2 y, \{x, -3, 3\}, \{y, -3, 3\}, \text{BoxRatios} \to 1, \text{MeshFunctions} \to \{\#3 \&\},\right.$
    Mesh $\to 20$, **MeshShading** $\to$ {**Red**, **Green**}, **Lighting** $\to$ "**Neutral**"$\left.\right]$

Out[29]=
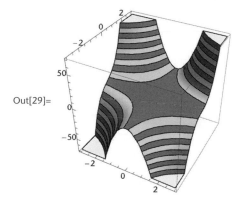

Set it to a list whose length matches the **Mesh** setting, and you will cycle precisely once through the list of directives. To utilize an entire color gradient, keep in mind that each color gradient function (such as **ColorData**["**StarryNightColors**"]) is defined on the domain $0 \le t \le 1$.

In[30]:= **Plot3D**$\left[x^2 y^3 + (x - 1)^2 y, \{x, -3, 3\}, \{y, -3, 3\}, \text{BoxRatios} \to 1,\right.$
    MeshFunctions $\to \{\#3 \&\}$, **Mesh** $\to 20$, **MeshShading** $\to$
      Table$\left[\text{ColorData}\left["\text{StarryNightColors}"\right][t], \{t, 0, 1, 1/20\}\right]$, **Lighting** $\to$ "**Neutral**"$\left.\right]$

Out[30]=
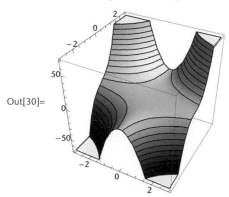

The output above is very similar to that produced with the setting **ColorFunction** $\to$ "**StarryNightColors**" (and no **MeshShading** or **Lighting** specifications). When **MeshShading** is used, each band between mesh lines is uniformly shaded. When **ColorFunction** is used, the shading varies continuously. When there are multiple **MeshFunctions**, the colors will criss-cross like a woven basket. Below we use the default **MeshFunctions** setting {#1&,#2&}:

In[31]:= **Plot3D$\left[x^2 y^3 + (x-1)^2 y, \{x, -3, 3\}, \{y, -3, 3\}$, BoxRatios → 1, Mesh → 20,**
  MeshShading → {{Yellow, Green}, {Black, White}}, Lighting → "Neutral"$\right]$

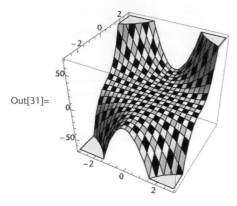

Out[31]=

Plotting Functions of Two Variables with ContourPlot

Another commonly used command for visualizing a real-valued function of two variables is **Contour-Plot**. A contour plot is a two-dimensional rendering of a three-dimensional surface. Imagine looking at the surface from above and placing contour lines (also called level curves) on the surface, each one a curve that is level in the sense that its height above (or below) the x-y plane is constant. The contour plot is much like a topographical map—it consists of the vertical projections of the contour lines onto the x-y plane. By default, **ContourPlot** will produce ten regions separated by nine contour lines. The regions will be shaded according their relative height above (or below) the x-y plane; darker regions are lower and lighter regions are higher.

We've previously used **ContourPlot** to plot solutions of *equations* (such as $\sin(x \cos y) = 0$). This solution curve can be regarded as a single contour line for the function $f(x, y) = \sin(x \cos y)$. To produce a full contour plot, use **ContourPlot** in a manner identical to that of **Plot3D**. Here we see a **ContourPlot** and a **Plot3D** of the same function, showing the same level curves and using similar shading:

In[32]:= {ContourPlot[Sin[x Cos[y]], {x, -3, 3}, {y, -3, 3}],
    Plot3D[Sin[x Cos[y]], {x, -3, 3}, {y, -3, 3}, MeshFunctions → {#3 &},
        Mesh → 9, ColorFunction → "LakeColors", ViewPoint → {0, -1, 2},
        Boxed → False, Axes → {True, True, False}]}

Out[32]=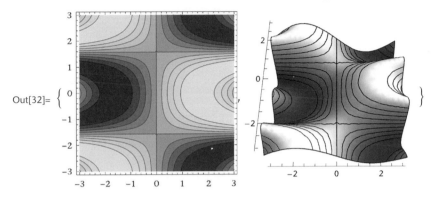

Perhaps the most commonly used option setting is **Contours**. Set it to a positive integer, say 20, and you will see 20 contour lines in the resulting plot. Set it to a specific list of values and you will see the contour lines through precisely those *z* values. If this list has a single value (as in the second plot below), you will essentially be viewing the set of solutions to an equation in two variables.

In[33]:= GraphicsRow @ {ContourPlot[(1 + x²) (1 + y²), {x, -2, 2}, {y, -2, 2}, Contours → 20],
        ContourPlot[(1 + x²) (1 + y²), {x, -2, 2}, {y, -2, 2}, Contours → {4}],
        ContourPlot[(1 + x²) (1 + y²) == 4, {x, -2, 2}, {y, -2, 2}]}

Out[33]=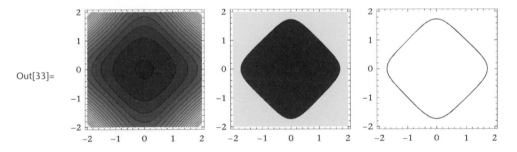

The **ContourShading** option works much like the **MeshShading** option for **Plot3D**. Note that you may set this option to **None**. As was the case with **Plot3D**, the **ColorFunction** may be set to any named color gradient.

In[34]:= **GraphicsRow @**
{ContourPlot[$(1 + x^2)(1 + y^2)$, {x, −2, 2}, {y, −2, 2}, ContourShading → {Red, Blue}],
   ContourPlot[$(1 + x^2)(1 + y^2)$, {x, −2, 2}, {y, −2, 2}, ContourShading → None],
   ContourPlot[$(1 + x^2)(1 + y^2)$, {x, −2, 2},
      {y, −2, 2}, ColorFunction → "IslandColors"]}

Out[34]=
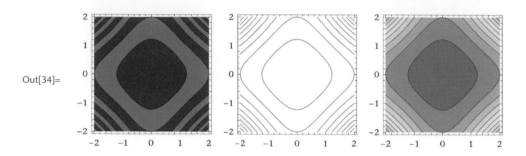

Also important are **PlotPoints** and **MaxRecursion**, which (as you might expect) can be employed to improve image quality. The function $\frac{x^2}{1-x+y}$ is not defined along the line $y = x − 1$, and **ContourPlot** with its default settings has difficulty in the vicinity of this line. The **Exclusions** option provides another means of dealing with such discontinuities.

In[35]:= **GraphicsRow @** {ContourPlot[$\dfrac{x^2}{1 - x + y}$, {x, −2, 2}, {y, −2, 2}],

   ContourPlot[$\dfrac{x^2}{1 - x + y}$, {x, −2, 2}, {y, −2, 2}, PlotPoints → 30, MaxRecursion → 3],

   ContourPlot[$\dfrac{x^2}{1 - x + y}$, {x, −2, 2}, {y, −2, 2}, Exclusions → {y == x − 1}]}

Out[35]=
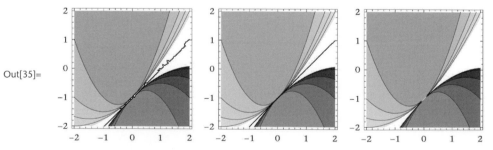

ContourPlot accepts many of the same options as **Plot3D**. Exceptions are those options that are specific to two-dimensional graphics. For instance, one uses **AspectRatio** rather than **BoxRatios** to

adjust the relative dimensions of a graphic produced by **ContourPlot**. Note that by default, a **ContourPlot** will be square.

In[36]:= **GraphicsRow @ {ContourPlot[Sin[x Cos[y]], {x, −6, 6}, {y, −3, 3}],**
    ContourPlot[Sin[x Cos[y]], {x, −6, 6}, {y, −3, 3}, AspectRatio → Automatic]}

Out[36]=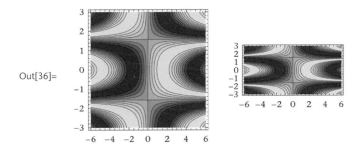

ContourPlot will embed tooltips into its output. Position the tip of the cursor along a level curve to see the value of the z coordinate for all points on that curve. The option setting **ContourLabels →** **Automatic** can be used to place these values directly onto the graphic.

In[37]:= **ContourPlot[Sin[x Cos[y]], {x, −1, 1}, {y, −1, 1}, ContourLabels → Automatic]**

Out[37]=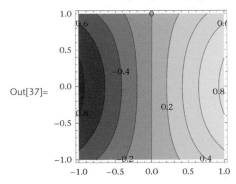

While the placement of these labels on the graphic is handled automatically, the appearance and indeed the function used to calculate each label can be adjusted. Below we use the default function value (displaying the z coordinate at the point (x, y)), but make the text gray in a six point font. We also use the **ColorData["LightTerrain"]** color gradient.

In[38]:= ContourPlot[Sin[x Cos[y]], {x, −1, 1}, {y, −1, 1},
        ContourLabels → (Style[Text[#3, {#1, #2}], GrayLevel[.3], 6] &),
        ColorFunction → "LightTerrain"]

Out[38]=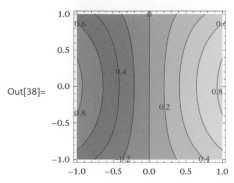

It is not difficult to write a command that will place a key next to a **ContourPlot**, as in the example below. See Exercise 5.

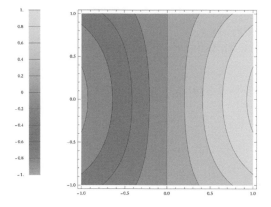

If **MeshFunctions** are specified along with specific **Mesh** values, the curves where these functions are equal to the respective **Mesh** values will be displayed. By default, there are no **MeshFunctions** displayed in a **ContourPlot** (this is different from **Plot3D**, where the default **MeshFunctions** are {#1&, #2&}, which produces the familiar grid pattern). **Mesh** curves will be superimposed on top of the level curves. Here, for instance, we display the ellipse $x^2 + 2y^2 = 1$ in yellow on the plot:

In[39]:= $\text{ContourPlot}\left[x^2 - \dfrac{4\,x\,y}{y^2 + 1}, \{x, -2, 2\}, \{y, -2, 2\}, \text{MeshFunctions} \rightarrow \{\#1^2 + 2\,\#2^2 \,\&\},\right.$

$\text{Mesh} \rightarrow \{\{1\}\}, \text{MeshStyle} \rightarrow \text{Directive[Thick, Yellow]}\Big]$

Out[39]=

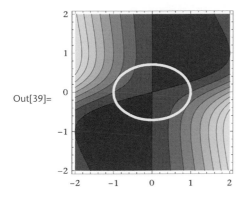

And here we display in dashed red the curve where the partial derivative with respect to x is zero, and in yellow the curves (lines in this case) where the partial derivative with respect to y is equal to zero. The critical points (and hence all maxima and minima for the function being plotted) occur at the intersection points of these curves.

In[40]:= $\text{ContourPlot}\left[x^2 - \dfrac{4\,x\,y}{y^2 + 1}, \{x, -2, 2\}, \{y, -2, 2\},\right.$

$\qquad \text{MeshFunctions} \rightarrow \left\{\text{Function}\left[\{x, y, z\}, 2\,x - \dfrac{4\,y}{1 + y^2}\right],\right.$

$\qquad\qquad \left.\text{Function}\left[\{x, y, z\}, \dfrac{8\,x\,y^2}{\left(1 + y^2\right)^2} - \dfrac{4\,x}{1 + y^2}\right]\right\}, \text{Mesh} \rightarrow \{\{0\}, \{0\}\},$

$\qquad \text{MeshStyle} \rightarrow \{\text{Directive[Thick, Dashed, Red]}, \text{Directive[Thick, Yellow]}\}\Big]$

Out[40]=

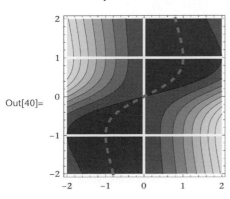

In general, it's not a bad idea when including multiple **MeshFunctions** to use **MeshStyle** to make the first one **Dashed** or **Dotted**. That way, if two curves happen to coincide, the top curve won't completely obscure the bottom one.

Plotting Level Surfaces with ContourPlot3D

Just as **ContourPlot** may be used to plot a curve defined by an equation in two variables (such as the circle $x^2 + y^2 = 1$, as outlined in Section 3.7 on page 97) by using an equation as its first argument, the **ContourPlot3D** command may be used to plot a surface defined by an equation in three variables. Behold:

In[41]:= **ContourPlot3D$\left[x^2 + y^2 + z^2 == 1, \{x, -1, 1\}, \{y, -1, 1\}, \{z, -1, 1\}\right]$**

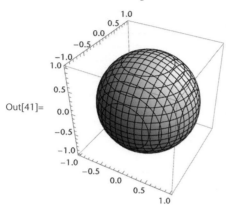

Out[41]=

And just as **ContourPlot** may be used to render a collection of level curves for a function of two variables (as discussed in the previous subsection of this chapter), **ContourPlot3D** may be used to render a collection of level surfaces for a function of three variables:

In[42]:= **ContourPlot3D$\left[x^2 + y^2 + z^2, \{x, -1, 1\}, \{y, -1, 1\},\right.$**
        $\left.\{z, -1, 0\}, BoxRatios \rightarrow \{2, 2, 1\}, Contours \rightarrow 5, Mesh \rightarrow None\right]$

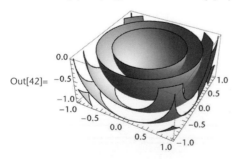

Out[42]=

Note that three iterators are needed, one for each of the three coordinate variables. Virtually all options are either identical to those of **Plot3D**, or can be surmised from those of **ContourPlot**. For instance, the **Contours** option works just as it does in **ContourPlot**. The **ContourStyle** option can be used to assign style directives to each level surface. The **ColorFunction** option can also be used for this purpose; the plot on the right uses a **ColorData** gradient specified by **ColorFunction**.

In[43]:= **GraphicsRow @ {ContourPlot3D[$x^2 + y^2 + z^2$, {x, −1, 1}, {y, −1, 1},**
 {z, −1, 0}, BoxRatios → {2, 2, 1}, Contours → 5, Mesh → None,
 Axes → False, ContourStyle → {Red, Orange, Yellow, Green, Blue}],
 ContourPlot3D[$x^2 + y^2 + z^2$, {x, −1, 1}, {y, −1, 1}, {z, −1, 0}, BoxRatios → {2, 2, 1},
 Contours → 5, Mesh → None, Axes → False, ColorFunction → "Pastel"]}

Out[43]=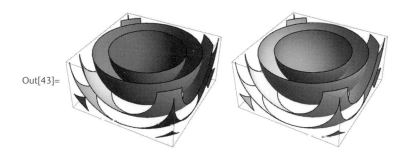

Here is a plot of the surface $\cos^2 x + \sin^2 y = 1 + \sin z$:

In[44]:= **ContourPlot3D[$\text{Cos}[x]^2 + \text{Sin}[y]^2 == 1 + \text{Sin}[z]$, {x, 0, 2$\pi$}, $\left\{y, \dfrac{\pi}{2}, \dfrac{5\pi}{2}\right\}$, {z, 0, 2$\pi$},**

 Mesh → None, ContourStyle → Directive[Brown, Specularity[White, 10]]]

Out[44]=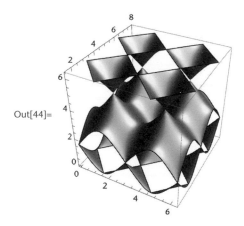

Constructing 3D plots of *solids* (rather than surfaces) can be accomplished with **RegionPlot3D**. This command is discussed in the subsection "Finding Bounds of Integration and Plotting Regions in the Plane and in Space" on page 294.

Graphics3D Primitives

Just as one can use the **Graphics** command to "manually" construct a two-dimensional graphic from primitive **Point**, **Line**, **Polygon**, and **Text** objects, one can use the **Graphics3D** command to build three-dimensional graphics. The **Graphics** command was discussed in Section 3.9 on page 114. In most cases you will use higher level commands such as **Plot3D** to generate 3D images. But there may come a time when you want to create a graphic from scratch, or to add a simple sphere or cylinder to the output of a command such as **Plot3D**. This section provides a basic introduction to such endeavors.

The primitive 3D objects that can be used to build a **Graphics3D** are many. They include familiar objects such as **Point**, **Line**, **Polygon**, and **Text**, and new ones such as **Cuboid**, **Cylinder**, and **Sphere**. Here are a few simple examples to get you started:

In[45]:= **Graphics3D[Sphere[{0, 0, 0}, 3]]**

Out[45]=

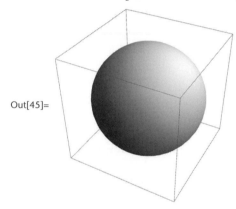

In[46]:= **Graphics3D[{Sphere[{0, 0, 0}, 3], Sphere[{0, 0, 4}, 2]}]**

Out[46]=

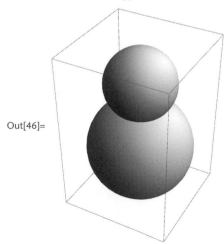

In[47]:= **Graphics3D[{**
     Sphere[{0, 0, 0}, 3],
     Sphere[{0, 0, 4}, 2],
     Sphere[{0, 0, 6.5}, 1],
     Cylinder[{{0, 0, 7.5}, {0, .5, 9}}, .8],
     Cylinder[{{0, 0, 7.5}, {0, .03, 7.6}}, 1.5],
     Cylinder[{{2, 0, 4}, {4, 0, 5}}, .2],
     Cylinder[{{−2, 0, 4}, {−4, 0, 5}}, .2]
   }, Boxed → False]

Out[47]=

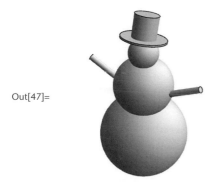

The overall situation is completely analogous to that for building **Graphics**. The single argument given to **Graphics3D** is (most simply) a primitive or a list of primitives. Here we've used only **Sphere** and **Cylinder** primitives. **Sphere** takes two arguments: the coordinates of its center, and its radius. **Cylinder** also takes two arguments. The first is a list of two points: the endpoints of its central axis. The second is its radius.

As is the case with **Graphics**, one can also apply one or more *directives* to each primitive. Directives are used to customize the appearance of the individual primitive elements, and may include color, opacity, and/or specularity settings. To apply a directive to any primitive object, replace the primitive with the list {*directive, primitive*}. If more than one directive is to be applied, wrap them in the **Directive** command, as in **Directive[Red, Opacity[.8]]**.

In[48]:= **Graphics3D[{**
    {Directive[Red, Opacity[.7]], Sphere[{0, 0, 0}, 3]},
    {Opacity[.5], Sphere[{0, 0, 4}, 2]}
    }]

Out[48]=

One may also include **Graphics3D** option settings, such as **Boxed→False**. Many of these have been discussed in Section 6.2. In particular, the setting **Lighting→ "Neutral"** can be used to turn off the colored lights that are used by default when rendering a **Graphics3D**. This will provide a more honest rendering of any colors you introduce. Note that by default, surface primitives will be white (they appear colored because of the colored lights). Here, for instance, we make a white snowman with black hat and arms:

In[49]:= **Graphics3D[{**
    Sphere[{0, 0, 0}, 3],
    Sphere[{0, 0, 4}, 2],
    Sphere[{0, 0, 6.5}, 1],
    {Lighter[Black],
       Cylinder[{{0, 0, 7.5}, {0, .5, 9}}, .8],
       Cylinder[{{0, 0, 7.5}, {0, .03, 7.6}}, 1.5],
       Cylinder[{{2, 0, 4}, {4, 0, 5}}, .2],
       Cylinder[{{−2, 0, 4}, {−4, 0, 5}}, .2]}
    }, Boxed → False, Lighting → "Neutral"]

Out[49]=

It is common to combine a **Graphics3D** with the output from one of the plotting commands. Here we use **Plot3D** to render the function $f(x, y) = xy$ with **MeshFunctions** set to measure distance on the surface to the point $(0, 0, 3)$. The plot is colored according to this distance using **MeshShading**. We use **Graphics3D** to place a small green sphere at the point $(0, 0, 3)$. We put the two images together with **Show**:

In[50]:= $\text{Show}\Big[\text{Plot3D}\Big[x\,y,\ \{x,\ -3,\ 3\},\ \{y,\ -3,\ 3\},\ \text{PlotRange} \rightarrow \{-4,\ 4\},$

   $\text{Lighting} \rightarrow \text{"Neutral"},\ \text{BoxRatios} \rightarrow 1,\ \text{Mesh} \rightarrow 15,$

   $\text{MeshFunctions} \rightarrow \Big\{\text{Function}\Big[\{x,\ y,\ z\},\ \sqrt{x^2 + y^2 + (z-3)^2}\ \Big]\Big\},$

   $\text{MeshShading} \rightarrow \text{Table}\Big[\text{ColorData}\big[\text{"TemperatureMap"}\big][1-k],\ \{k,\ 0,\ 1,\ 1./15\}\Big]\Big],$

   $\text{Graphics3D}\Big[\{\text{Darker[Green]},\ \text{Sphere}[\{0,\ 0,\ 3\},\ .15]\}\Big]\Big]$

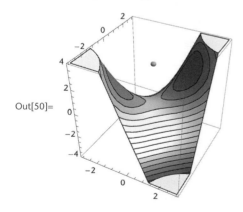

Out[50]=

⚠ When using commands such as **Plot** that produce **Graphics** (as opposed to **Graphics3D**) output, it is common to add an **Epilog** option to place **Graphics** primitives directly on the image. This makes the use of **Show** unnecessary. While **Epilog** may also be used with commands such as **Plot3D**, it cannot be used to place 3D primitives on the plot (such as the **Sphere** above). So in a 3D setting, **Show** is the best way to add primitive **Graphics3D** objects to an image.

Differentiation of Functions of Two or More Variables

Calculating Partial Derivatives

You can calculate the partial derivatives of a function of two or more variables with the **D** command. This works just as in Chapter 5:

In[51]:= **Clear[f, x, y];**
      f = Sin[x² − y²];

In[53]:= **D[f, x]**

Out[53]= $2 \, x \, Cos[x^2 - y^2]$

In[54]:= **D[f, y]**

Out[54]= $-2 \, y \, Cos[x^2 - y^2]$

Use replacement rules to evaluate a derivative at a particular point:

In[55]:= **% /. $\left\{ x \rightarrow 0, \, y \rightarrow \sqrt{\pi} \right\}$**

Out[55]= $2 \sqrt{\pi}$

Alternatively, you can calculate partial derivatives with the palette version of the **D** command by using the $\boxed{\partial_{\square} \, \blacksquare}$ button on the BasicMathInput palette. The subscript indicates the variable with respect to which the derivative should be taken. Move from one placeholder to the next with the ⎵TAB⎵ key.

In[56]:= ∂_x **f**

Out[56]= $2 \, x \, Cos[x^2 - y^2]$

If you use the palette version of **D** directly on a function such as $x^2 + 2 \, xy$, it is best to first type the function expression, then highlight it, and *then* push the palette button. If you deviate from this convention by pushing the palette button *first*, be sure to put grouping parentheses around the function expression so that you don't end up only differentiating the first summand:

In[57]:= ∂_x x² + 2 x y

Out[57]= 2 x + 2 x y

In[58]:= ∂_x (x² + 2 x y)

Out[58]= 2 x + 2 y

To find the second partial derivative $\frac{\partial^2 f}{\partial x^2}$, you can use the **D** command exactly as in Chapter 5:

In[59]:= **D[f, {x, 2}]**

Out[59]= $2 \cos[x^2 - y^2] - 4 x^2 \sin[x^2 - y^2]$

To find the mixed second partial derivative $\frac{\partial^2 f}{\partial x \partial y}$, simply do this:

In[60]:= **D[f, x, y]**

Out[60]= $4 x y \sin[x^2 - y^2]$

Alternatively, you may use the $\boxed{\partial_{\square,\square} \blacksquare}$ key on the BasicMathInput palette:

In[61]:= $\partial_{x,x}$ **f**

Out[61]= $2 \cos[x^2 - y^2] - 4 x^2 \sin[x^2 - y^2]$

In[62]:= $\partial_{x,y}$ **f**

Out[62]= $4 x y \sin[x^2 - y^2]$

Derivatives beyond the second require the **D** command:

In[63]:= **D[f, {x, 3}, {y, 4}]**

Out[63]= $-8 x^3 \left(-12 \cos[x^2 - y^2] + 16 y^4 \cos[x^2 - y^2] - 48 y^2 \sin[x^2 - y^2]\right) -$
$12 x \left(48 y^2 \cos[x^2 - y^2] - 12 \sin[x^2 - y^2] + 16 y^4 \sin[x^2 - y^2]\right)$

The Gradient

The gradient of a function of two or more variables is a vector whose components are the various partial derivatives of the function. For instance, for a function f of two variables, the gradient is the vector $\langle \partial_x f, \partial_y f \rangle$. In *Mathematica* one can simply do this:

In[64]:= $\{\partial_x$ **f**, ∂_y **f**$\}$

Out[64]= $\{2 x \cos[x^2 - y^2], -2 y \cos[x^2 - y^2]\}$

There is no built-in command for producing gradients, but if you need to make extensive use of them it is not hard to create your own:

In[65]:= $\text{grad}[f\_, \text{vars\_List}] := \text{Table}[\partial_v\, f, \{v, \text{vars}\}]$

This command takes two arguments. The first is the function whose gradient you wish to compute. The second is the list of variables used in defining the function. For example:

In[66]:= $\text{grad}\left[x^2\, y^3, \{x, y\}\right]$

Out[66]= $\left\{2\, x\, y^3,\ 3\, x^2\, y^2\right\}$

In[67]:= $\text{grad}\left[\dfrac{x_1{}^2\, x_2{}^3\, x_4{}^4}{x_3{}^5}, \{x_1, x_2, x_3, x_4\}\right]$

Out[67]= $\left\{\dfrac{2\, x_1\, x_2^3\, x_4^4}{x_3^5},\ \dfrac{3\, x_1^2\, x_2^2\, x_4^4}{x_3^5},\ -\dfrac{5\, x_1^2\, x_2^3\, x_4^4}{x_3^6},\ \dfrac{4\, x_1^2\, x_2^3\, x_4^3}{x_3^5}\right\}$

You can evaluate the gradient at a specific point in the domain using replacement rules.

In[68]:= $\left\{\partial_x\, f,\ \partial_y\, f\right\} /.\ \left\{x \to 0,\ y \to \sqrt{\pi}\,\right\}$

Out[68]= $\left\{0,\ 2\sqrt{\pi}\,\right\}$

The following **Manipulate** will sketch a gradient vector directly on the **ContourPlot** for a function. Initially it shows the gradient evaluated at the point $\left(\frac{1}{2}, \frac{1}{2}\right)$. The tail of the gradient vector is a **Locator**; you can simply click on the graphic to move it to a new position, or you can drag it around. The geometric properties of the gradient quickly become apparent: it is perpendicular to the level curve through its tail, and it points uphill.

In[69]:= $\text{Manipulate}\Big[\text{Module}\big[\{x, y\},$

$\qquad \text{ContourPlot}\left[e^{-(x^2+y^2)} + x\, y,\ \{x, -1, 1\},\ \{y, -1, 1\},\ \text{Contours} \to 20,\right.$

$\qquad\quad \text{Epilog} \to \text{Dynamic}\Big[\Big\{\text{Arrow}\Big[$

$\qquad\qquad \left\{\text{pt},\ \text{pt} + \left\{y - 2\, e^{-x^2-y^2}\, x,\ x - 2\, e^{-x^2-y^2}\, y\right\} /.\ \{x \to \text{pt}[\![1]\!],\ y \to \text{pt}[\![2]\!]\}\right\}\Big]\Big\}\Big]\Big]\Big],$

$\qquad \{\{\text{pt}, \{.5, .5\}\},\ \text{Locator},$

$\qquad\quad \text{Appearance} \to \text{Graphics}[\{\text{Red}, \text{Disk}[]\},\ \text{ImageSize} \to 5]\}\Big]$

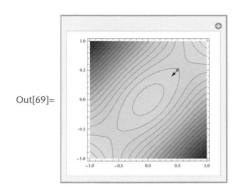

Out[69]=

⚠ There are several interesting features in this **Manipulate**. Notice that the first argument (the thing we are manipulating) is a **Module**. **Module** is used to localize variables. In this case, the variables x and y are insulated from any assignments made to them elsewhere in the session.

Module and other scoping commands are discussed in Section 8.6 on page 424. Secondly, note that the **Epilog** to the **ContourPlot** is wrapped in **Dynamic**. While not strictly necessary, this has the beneficial effect of forcing only the arrow to update as the **Locator** is moved, rather than having the **ContourPlot** itself (which does not change) get re-rendered every time the **Locator** is moved. This makes the action more "zippy." For more information, search for "Advanced Manipulate Functionality" in the Documentation Center and follow the link to the tutorial of that name. Finally, note that we use the **Appearance** option to change the appearance of the **Locator** from its default crosshair icon to a simple red dot. This option allows you to make any **Locator** look exactly the way you like.

Given a function of two variables, there is a simple means for simultaneously plotting an array of its gradient vectors over a rectangular domain, and for superimposing such a plot with a **ContourPlot** of the function. See the subsection "Plotting a Two-Dimensional Vector Field" in Section 6.5, page 325, for a discussion of the **GradientFieldPlot** command.

You can take a *directional derivative* by taking the dot product of the gradient with a unit vector in the indicated direction. Here, for example, is an expression representing the directional derivative of the function $f(x, y) = x^2 y^3$ in the direction of the vector $3\,\vec{i} - \vec{j}$:

In[70]:= $\mathbf{grad}[\mathbf{x^2\,y^3},\ \{\mathbf{x,\ y}\}].\dfrac{\{3,\ -1\}}{\mathbf{Norm}[\{3,\ -1\}]}$

Out[70]= $-\dfrac{3\,x^2\,y^2}{\sqrt{10}} + 3\sqrt{\dfrac{2}{5}}\ x\,y^3$

To evaluate the directional derivative at a specific point in the domain, use replacement rules:

In[71]:= $\% \, /. \, \{x \to 2, \, y \to 3\}$

Out[71]= $108 \sqrt{\dfrac{2}{5}}$

Optimization

There are numerous methods for finding extreme values of multivariate functions. It is certainly possible to mimic the basic techniques presented in a standard calculus course, with *Mathematica* doing the heavy lifting when the algebra gets tough. We outline such an approach in this section. There are also the built-in commands **Maximize**, **Minimize**, **NMaximize**, **NMinimize**, **FindMaximum**, and **FindMinimum**, which can be extremely useful, but which also have inherent limitations. We'll begin with these built-in commands, and then discuss the traditional approach using critical points and second derivatives.

The commands **Maximize**, **Minimize**, **NMaximize**, and **NMinimize** (first introduced in Section 5.6 on page 212) all use the same syntax; understand one and you understand them all. In the most simple setting, where your function is not overly complicated and happens to have a single extremum in its largest natural domain, these commands make light work of optimization:

In[72]:= $\textbf{Maximize}\left[-85 + 16\,x - 4\,x^2 - 4\,y - 4\,y^2 + 40\,z - 4\,z^2, \, \{x, \, y, \, z\}\right]$

Out[72]= $\left\{32, \, \left\{x \to 2, \, y \to -\dfrac{1}{2}, \, z \to 5\right\}\right\}$

If an extreme value does not exist, you can expect to see this sort of thing:

In[73]:= $\textbf{Minimize}\left[-85 + 16\,x - 4\,x^2 - 4\,y - 4\,y^2 + 40\,z - 4\,z^2, \, \{x, \, y, \, z\}\right]$

Minimize::natt : The minimum is not attained at any point satisfying the given constraints. »

Out[73]= $\left\{-\infty, \, \left\{x \to -\infty, \, y \to \dfrac{33}{10}, \, z \to \dfrac{8}{5}\right\}\right\}$

These commands attempt to find *global* extrema. They can be adapted to hunt for *local* extrema by adding constraints. Simply use a *list* as the first argument, where the second member of the list is an equation or inequality (or any logical combination of these):

In[74]:= $\textbf{f} = 12\,y^3 + 4\,x^2 - 10\,x\,y;$
$\textbf{Minimize}\left[\{f, \, -1 \le x \le 1 \, \&\& \, -1 \le y \le 1\}, \, \{x, \, y\}\right]$

Out[75]= $\{-18, \, \{x \to -1, \, y \to -1\}\}$

Here the minimum occurs at a corner of the square region. Below we search in two concentric circular regions centered at the origin. Since the *same* answer is reached in two *different* concentric regions, we are assured that the minimum occurs in the interior of each region (not on the boundary). We have found, or at least approximated, a local minimum for f:

In[76]:= **NMinimize$[\{f, x^2 + y^2 \le 1\}, \{x, y\}]$**

Out[76]= $\{-0.251173, \{x \to 0.434028, y \to 0.347222\}\}$

In[77]:= **NMinimize$[\{f, x^2 + y^2 \le 1/2\}, \{x, y\}]$**

Out[77]= $\{-0.251173, \{x \to 0.434028, y \to 0.347222\}\}$

Unfortunately, **Minimize** is unable to give us an exact numerical solution. Rather, it presents the three numbers in the output as roots of sixth degree polynomials.

In[78]:= **Minimize$[\{f, x^2 + y^2 \le 1/2\}, \{x, y\}]$**

Out[78]= $\{$Root$[76\,902\,125 + 319\,355\,960\,\#1 - 238\,172\,822\,\#1^2 +$
$46\,171\,432\,\#1^3 + 3\,783\,476\,\#1^4 - 2\,441\,664\,\#1^5 + 236\,196\,\#1^6\ \&,\ 1],$
$\{x \to$ Root$[25 + 180\,\#1 + 92\,\#1^2 - 1080\,\#1^3 - 832\,\#1^4 + 1440\,\#1^5 + 1296\,\#1^6\ \&,\ 2],$
$y \to$ Root$[25 - 232\,\#1^2 + 288\,\#1^3 - 184\,\#1^4 - 576\,\#1^5 + 1296\,\#1^6\ \&,\ 1]\}\}$

We'll see shortly that traditional methods can be used to determine that the actual local minimum occurs at $\left(\frac{125}{288}, \frac{25}{72}\right)$. Our point here is to state plainly that while commands such as **Minimize** may *sound* like a panacea for any optimization exercise, they can in fact be subtle to use and produce output that is difficult to interpret. Worse yet, they can fail completely:

In[79]:= **Minimize$[\{\mathrm{Sin}[x*y], x^2 + y^2 \le 1\}, \{x, y\}]$**

Out[79]= Minimize$[\{\mathrm{Sin}[x\,y], x^2 + y^2 \le 1\}, \{x, y\}]$

They also return only one extremum even in cases where there are two or more:

In[80]:= **Minimize$[\{x*y, x^2 + y^2 \le 1\}, \{x, y\}]$**

Out[80]= $\left\{-\dfrac{1}{2}, \left\{x \to \dfrac{1}{\sqrt{2}}, y \to -\dfrac{1}{\sqrt{2}}\right\}\right\}$

In[81]:= **x*y /. $\left\{x \to -\dfrac{1}{\sqrt{2}}, y \to \dfrac{1}{\sqrt{2}}\right\}$**

Out[81]= $-\dfrac{1}{2}$

It is for these reasons that you must always be ready with plan B. Now don't misunderstand us; **Minimize** and **NMinimize** are powerful and versatile tools. In fact, they border on the amazing. But they simply cannot be expected to work flawlessly in every situation; such is the variety and richness of the universe of mathematical functions. There are option settings for **NMinimize** that allow you to specify the method it uses. Subtle details of this sort are essential if you plan to make extensive use of these commands.

If your goal is to find *all* extrema for a differentiable function (as it often is in a calculus course), your first line of defense in constructing plan B comes right out of your calculus textbook. The *critical points* for a function are those points where the first partials are both zero (i.e., the gradient of the function is the zero vector), or where one or both partials do not exist. If a function assumes a relative minimum or maximum value in the interior of its domain, it does so at a critical point.

It is often possible to find critical points with **Solve**, **NSolve**, or **Reduce**. The setting here is just as it was in Section 4.9, where we used these commands to solve systems of equations. Recall that **Solve** and **NSolve** are designed primarily to solve polynomial equations, while **Reduce** can sometimes solve more general classes of equations. Here's an example where we use **Solve** to find the critical points of a polynomial:

In[82]:= **f = 12 y³ + 4 x² − 10 x y;**
      crPts = Solve[{∂ₓ f == 0, ∂ᵧ f == 0}, {x, y}]

Out[83]= $\left\{\{x \to 0, y \to 0\}, \left\{x \to \dfrac{125}{288}, y \to \dfrac{25}{72}\right\}\right\}$

In any of these solving commands you may use as the first argument either a list of equations, or an equation of lists. For instance, this input will also work:

In[84]:= **Solve[{∂ₓ f, ∂ᵧ f} == {0, 0}, {x, y}]**

Out[84]= $\left\{\{x \to 0, y \to 0\}, \left\{x \to \dfrac{125}{288}, y \to \dfrac{25}{72}\right\}\right\}$

You may be able to determine whether *f* has a relative minimum or maximum or saddle at a particular critical point in a purely algebraic fashion by examining the *discriminant* and the second partials evaluated at this critical point. Recall that the discriminant of *f* is the expression

$$\Delta_f = \left(\partial_{x,x} f\right)\left(\partial_{y,y} f\right) - \left(\partial_{x,y} f\right)^2.$$

The standard test to determine the status of the critical point (x, y) is as follows:

- If $\Delta_f > 0$ and $\partial_{x,x} f > 0$, then (x, y) is a relative minimum.
- If $\Delta_f > 0$ and $\partial_{x,x} f < 0$, then (x, y) is a relative maximum.
- If $\Delta_f < 0$, then (x, y) is a saddle point.
- If $\Delta_f = 0$, then the test is inconclusive.

Let's carry out this test for the two critical points found in our previous example.

In[85]:= $(\partial_{x,x} f)(\partial_{y,y} f) - (\partial_{x,y} f)^2$ /. crPts // N

Out[85]= {−100., 100.}

The first critical point, (0, 0), is therefore a saddle point, while the second is either a maximum or minimum. Which is it?

In[86]:= $\partial_{x,x} f$ /. crPts[[2]] // N

Out[86]= 8.

The positive value indicates that there is upward concavity in the *x* direction at this point. Since this point is an extreme value, it must be a minimum. A **ContourPlot** shows both critical points clearly, confirming this analysis:

In[87]:= ContourPlot[f, {x, −1, 1}, {y, −1, 1},
         Epilog → {PointSize[.02], Red, Point[{x, y} /. crPts]}]

Out[87]=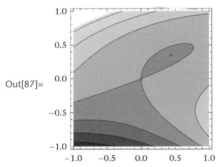

Finally, we can evaluate *f* at the critical points as follows:

In[88]:= f /. crPts

Out[88]= $\left\{0, -\dfrac{15\,625}{62\,208}\right\}$

In this example we used **Solve** to find the critical points, but **Reduce** could have been used instead:

In[89]:= Reduce[{$\partial_x f, \partial_y f$} == {0, 0}, {x, y}]

Out[89]= $\left(x == 0 \,\|\, x == \dfrac{125}{288}\right) \&\& \, y == \dfrac{4\,x}{5}$

A word about **Reduce** is in order. It is very convenient to use **Reduce** in cases where you are only interested in *real* (as opposed to complex) solutions to equations; simply add the third argument **Reals**. As this is usually the situation in calculus courses, **Reduce** may be your first choice as a solver. On the flip side, **Reduce** does not (indeed, in general it cannot, as we will see in the next example) return output in the form of replacement rules. And we like replacement rules. They are enormously convenient when they are produced programmatically, so you do not have to type them. In cases where **Reduce** produces reasonably simple output, a call to **ToRules** will convert the output into replacement rules. Just beware that an equation such as $y == \frac{4x}{5}$ will be converted to the rule $y \to \frac{4x}{5}$, which means that replacements should be made with **ReplaceRepeated** (//.) rather than **ReplaceAll** (/.):

In[90]:= **{ToRules[%]}**

Out[90]= $\left\{\left\{x \to 0, y \to \dfrac{4x}{5}\right\}, \left\{x \to \dfrac{125}{288}, y \to \dfrac{4x}{5}\right\}\right\}$

In[91]:= **{x, y} /. %**

Out[91]= $\left\{\left\{0, \dfrac{4x}{5}\right\}, \left\{\dfrac{125}{288}, \dfrac{4x}{5}\right\}\right\}$

In[92]:= **{x, y} //. %%**

Out[92]= $\left\{\{0, 0\}, \left\{\dfrac{125}{288}, \dfrac{25}{72}\right\}\right\}$

Here is a second example. We identify critical points using **Reduce** rather than **Solve**, as **Solve** simply will not work in this case. It is important to point out something that is rarely emphasized in calculus texts: the set of critical points may be *far* more complex than a few isolated points (like the two critical points we found in the previous example). For instance:

In[93]:= **f = Sin[x Cos[y]];**
Short[Reduce[{∂_x f == 0, ∂_y f == 0}, {x, y}, Reals], 10]

Out[94]//Short=

$$\left(C[1] \in \text{Integers} \;\&\&\; x == 0 \;\&\&\; \left(y == -\frac{\pi}{2} + 2\pi C[1] \;\|\; y == \frac{\pi}{2} + 2\pi C[1]\right)\right) \|$$

$$(\ll 1 \gg) \;\|\; \ll 1 \gg \;\|\; (\ll 1 \gg) \;\|\; \left(C[1] \geq 0 \;\&\&\; (C[1] \,|\, C[2]) \in \text{Integers} \;\&\&\right.$$

$$\left(\left(x \leq \frac{1}{2}(-\pi - 4\pi C[1]) \;\&\&\; \left(y == -\text{ArcCos}\left[\frac{\pi + 4\pi C[1]}{2x}\right] + 2\pi C[2] \;\|\right.\right.\right.$$

$$\left.y == \text{ArcCos}\left[\frac{\pi + 4\pi C[1]}{2x}\right] + 2\pi C[2]\right)\right) \;\|\; \left(x \geq \frac{1}{2}(\pi + 4\pi C[1]) \;\&\&\right.$$

$$\left.\left.\left.\left(y == -\text{ArcCos}\left[\frac{\pi + 4\pi C[1]}{2x}\right] + 2\pi C[2] \;\|\; y == \text{ArcCos}\left[\frac{\pi + 4\pi C[1]}{2x}\right] + 2\pi C[2]\right)\right)\right)\right)$$

There are five solutions, and only the first and last are shown (since we wrapped the input above in **Short** each of the middle three are indicated by <<1>>). Even the abbreviated output is a bit intimidating. Note that there are two constants, **C[1]** and **C[2]**, that are permitted to assume integer values. **Reduce** has found an infinite family of points and curves, parameterized by these two constants. If you are only concerned with critical points within a *bounded* domain the output can be greatly simplified, often with such parameters removed. Below we include in the list of equations the *bounds* on both x and y. The constants are no longer needed.

In[95]:= **f = Sin[x Cos[y]];**
Reduce[$\{\partial_x$ f == 0, ∂_y f == 0, $-6 \le x \le 6$, $-3 \le y \le 3\}$, $\{x, y\}$, Reals]

Out[96]= $\left(-6 \le x \le -\frac{\pi}{2} \,\&\&\, \left(y == -\text{ArcCos}\left[-\frac{\pi}{2x}\right] || y == \text{ArcCos}\left[-\frac{\pi}{2x}\right]\right)\right) ||$

$\left(-6 \le x \le \frac{1}{2}\pi\,\text{Sec[3]} \,\&\&\, \left(y == -\text{ArcCos}\left[\frac{\pi}{2x}\right] || y == \text{ArcCos}\left[\frac{\pi}{2x}\right]\right)\right) ||$

$\left(-\frac{1}{2}\pi\,\text{Sec[3]} \le x \le 6 \,\&\&\, \left(y == -\text{ArcCos}\left[-\frac{\pi}{2x}\right] || y == \text{ArcCos}\left[-\frac{\pi}{2x}\right]\right)\right) ||$

$\left(\frac{\pi}{2} \le x \le 6 \,\&\&\, \left(y == -\text{ArcCos}\left[\frac{\pi}{2x}\right] || y == \text{ArcCos}\left[\frac{\pi}{2x}\right]\right)\right) ||$

$\left(-6 \le x \le \frac{3}{2}\pi\,\text{Sec[3]} \,\&\&\, \left(y == -\text{ArcCos}\left[\frac{3\pi}{2x}\right] || y == \text{ArcCos}\left[\frac{3\pi}{2x}\right]\right)\right) ||$

$\left(-6 \le x \le -\frac{3\pi}{2} \,\&\&\, \left(y == -\text{ArcCos}\left[-\frac{3\pi}{2x}\right] || y == \text{ArcCos}\left[-\frac{3\pi}{2x}\right]\right)\right) ||$

$\left(\frac{3\pi}{2} \le x \le 6 \,\&\&\, \left(y == -\text{ArcCos}\left[\frac{3\pi}{2x}\right] || y == \text{ArcCos}\left[\frac{3\pi}{2x}\right]\right)\right) ||$

$\left(-\frac{3}{2}\pi\,\text{Sec[3]} \le x \le 6 \,\&\&\, \left(y == -\text{ArcCos}\left[-\frac{3\pi}{2x}\right] || y == \text{ArcCos}\left[-\frac{3\pi}{2x}\right]\right)\right) ||$

$\left(x == 0 \,\&\&\, \left(y == -\frac{\pi}{2} || y == \frac{\pi}{2}\right)\right)$

Okay, this is still rather intimidating. But be patient; the output rewards careful reading. Recall that && means "and" and || means "or." The very last line shows two discrete critical points, at $(0, \frac{\pi}{2})$ and $(0, -\frac{\pi}{2})$. Everything else shows a bounded domain on x, and y as a function of x on this domain. In other words, the other critical points are comprised of *curves*.

Let's embark on a brief visual investigation. In the following graphic, the solid mesh lines are curves where the partial derivative with respect to x is zero, and dashed mesh lines are curves where the partial derivative with respect to y is zero. Critical points are points where both partials are simultaneously zero. These can be discrete *points* (where the solid and dashed lines cross), or *curves* (where they coincide). This function has both types.

In[97]:= $\{fx, fy\} = \{\partial_x f, \partial_y f\};$

In[98]:= $Plot3D[Sin[x\ Cos[y]], \{x, -6, 6\}, \{y, -3, 3\}, BoxRatios \rightarrow Automatic,$
$MeshFunctions \rightarrow \{Function[\{x, y\}, fx], Function[\{x, y\}, fy]\},$
$MeshStyle \rightarrow \{Blue, Directive[Thick, Dotted]\}, Mesh \rightarrow \{\{0\}, \{0\}\}, MaxRecursion \rightarrow 3,$
$Boxed \rightarrow False, Axes \rightarrow \{True, True, False\}, ViewPoint \rightarrow \{.1, -1, 3\}]$

Out[98]=

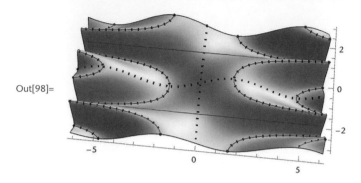

Do you see the two discrete critical points that we identified earlier? They appear to be saddles. We confirm this below:

In[99]:= $(\partial_{x,x} f) (\partial_{y,y} f) - (\partial_{x,y} f)^2 /. \{\{x \rightarrow 0, y \rightarrow -\pi/2\}, \{x \rightarrow 0, y \rightarrow \pi/2\}\}$

Out[99]= $\{-1, -1\}$

We note that for this function, **Maximize** does not produce any output, while **NMaximize** reports, as always, one maximum (even though there are in fact infinitely many on this domain). Clearly, the approach we applied here using **Reduce** is far more comprehensive.

In cases where even **Reduce** cannot find a critical point, one has the commands **FindMaximum** and **FindMinimum**. Like the command **FindRoot** (introduced in Section 4.7 on page 184), these are your weapons of last resort. They require an initial guess for each variable, and using those as starting values they hone in on a single extremum. Moreover, they are numerical tools; the solution they provide is only approximate.

Despite these limitations **FindMaximum** and **FindMinimum** can be highly effective at refining an approximate guess. They are also fast and extremely robust. Use them when other methods fail. One simple means of using these commands is to start with a **ContourPlot**, and use it to identify a local extremum. Then, using the approximate coordinates of the extremum as your initial guess, invoke **FindMaximum** or **FindMinimum**. Here's an example where we use this technique to approximate some relative extrema for a rather nasty function:

In[100]:= **Clear[f];**

$$f = e^{Sin[x\,y]} + Cos\left[\frac{5\,x}{y^2 + 1}\right] Sin\left[\frac{3\,y}{x^2 + 1}\right];$$

ContourPlot$\left[f, \{x, -2, 2\}, \{y, -2, 2\}\right]$

Out[102]=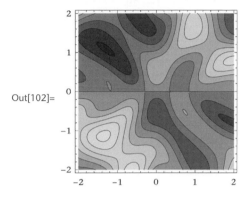

There appears to be a tiny island near $(1, -1)$, suggesting that f assumes a relative maximum value there. Now that we have it in our sights, let's zero in on it:

In[103]:= **FindMaximum$\left[f, \{x, 1\}, \{y, -1\}\right]$**

Out[103]= $\{1.51106, \{x \to 0.740375, y \to -0.529412\}\}$

Similarly, there appears to be a relative minimum near $(-1, 1)$; let's zero in on it:

In[104]:= **FindMinimum$\left[f, \{x, -1\}, \{y, 1\}\right]$**

Out[104]= $\{-0.551724, \{x \to -1.30697, y \to 1.09308\}\}$

Outstanding!

Constrained Optimization

The technique of Lagrange multipliers is easily implemented in *Mathematica*. Set things up so that the function you wish to optimize is called f, while the constraint is of the form $g = 0$. We wish to solve the system $\nabla f = \lambda \nabla g$, for some real constant λ, together with the constraint equation $g = 0$. This is easily accomplished using the **grad** command defined on page 282. Here's a simple example: maximize the quantity $4\,xy$ under the constraint that $4\,x^2 + y^2 = 8$.

In[105]:= **Clear$\left[f, g, x, y, \lambda\right];$**
f = 4 x * y;
g = 4 x^2 + y^2 − 8;

In[108]:= **Reduce[grad[f − λ ∗ g, {x, y, λ}] == {0, 0, 0}, {x, y, λ}, Reals]**

Out[108]= $((x == 1 \,\&\&\, (y == -2 \,||\, y == 2)) \,||\, (x == -1 \,\&\&\, (y == -2 \,||\, y == 2))) \,\&\&\, \lambda == \dfrac{y}{2\,x}$

This single **Reduce** input solves the system, as the three partial derivatives of the function $L(x, y, \lambda) = f(x, y) - \lambda g(x, y)$ are zero precisely when $\nabla f = \lambda \nabla g$ and $g = 0$. We next convert this solution to replacement rules, and evaluate the function at the solution:

In[109]:= **sols = {ToRules[%]}**

Out[109]= $\left\{\left\{x \to 1,\, y \to -2,\, \lambda \to \dfrac{y}{2\,x}\right\},\, \left\{x \to 1,\, y \to 2,\, \lambda \to \dfrac{y}{2\,x}\right\},\right.$

$\left.\left\{x \to -1,\, y \to -2,\, \lambda \to \dfrac{y}{2\,x}\right\},\, \left\{x \to -1,\, y \to 2,\, \lambda \to \dfrac{y}{2\,x}\right\}\right\}$

In[110]:= **{x, y} /. sols**

Out[110]= {{1, −2}, {1, 2}, {−1, −2}, {−1, 2}}

In[111]:= **f /. sols**

Out[111]= {−8, 8, 8, −8}

Note that the **Maximize**, **Minimize**, **NMaximize**, and **NMinimize** commands will do this all in one go, but they will only find a single solution. If that's all you need, there is no easier way to get there:

In[112]:= **Maximize[{f, g == 0}, {x, y}]**

Out[112]= $\{8,\, \{x \to -1,\, y \to -2\}\}$

Regardless which approach is taken, a **ContourPlot** provides a visual verification. One could make a **ContourPlot** of f, and a second **ContourPlot** with the first argument $g == 0$, then display them together with **Show**. Below we take a different approach, making a single plot with a mesh line to display the constraint curve. The solutions are shown as red dots:

In[113]:= **ContourPlot[f, {x, −2, 2}, {y, −3, 3}, Mesh → {{0}},**
     MeshFunctions → {Function[{x, y}, g]}, MeshStyle → Directive[Thick, Yellow],
     Epilog → {Red, PointSize[.02], Point[{x, y} /. sols]}]

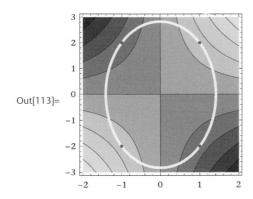

Out[113]=

Integration of Functions of Two or More Variables

In practice double, triple, in fact all multiple integrals are evaluated as *iterated* integrals. Evaluating iterated integrals is easy; you use the same **Integrate** command (from Section 5.10), adding another iterator (for definite integrals) or another variable (for indefinite integrals):

In[114]:= **Integrate[5 − x² y², {y, 1, 3}, {x, 0, 2}]**

Out[114]= $-\dfrac{28}{9}$

In[115]:= **Integrate[5 − x² y², y, x]**

Out[115]= $5\,x\,y - \dfrac{x^3\,y^3}{9}$

In the examples above we integrated first with respect to x, then with respect to y. That is, the variables are specified within **Integrate** in the same order that the integral *signs* are written in standard mathematical notation. The palette version of the **Integrate** command makes the order of integration more transparent. First type and highlight the function you wish to integrate, then push the appropriate integration button on the BasicMathInput palette and fill in the placeholders for the *innermost* integral, using the TAB key to move from one placeholder to the next. Now highlight the entire expression and push the integration button a second time, fill in the placeholders, and enter:

In[116]:= $\displaystyle\int_1^3\left(\int_0^2 (5 - x^2\,y^2)\,d\,x\right)d\,y$

Out[116]= $-\dfrac{28}{9}$

In[117]:= $\int \left(\int \left(5 - x^2 y^2\right) dx \right) dy$

Out[117]= $5xy - \dfrac{x^3 y^3}{9}$

It is perfectly acceptable to use as bounds in an inner integral expressions involving variables appearing in an outer integral. For double integrals, this allows integration over nonrectangular regions in the plane. Here we integrate over the region bounded by the circle of radius two centered at the origin:

In[118]:= $\int_{-2}^{2} \left(\int_{-\sqrt{4-y^2}}^{\sqrt{4-y^2}} \left(5 - x^2 y^2\right) dx \right) dy$

Out[118]= $\dfrac{52\pi}{3}$

And here we integrate the function $f(x, y, z) = y - z^2$ over the region bounded by a sphere of radius two centered at the origin:

In[119]:= $\int_{-2}^{2} \left(\int_{-\sqrt{4-z^2}}^{\sqrt{4-z^2}} \left(\int_{-\sqrt{4-y^2-z^2}}^{\sqrt{4-y^2-z^2}} \left(y - z^2\right) dx \right) dy \right) dz$

Out[119]= $-\dfrac{128\pi}{15}$

This last integral may take a minute or so to evaluate. A more sensible approach, even with a tool as powerful as *Mathematica*, is to use a spherical coordinate system. See the subsection "Integration in Other Coordinate Systems" in Section 6.4, page 322, for details.

Finding Bounds of Integration and Plotting Regions in the Plane and in Space

While *Mathematica* makes the evaluation of most integrals a snap, you still have to set up those integrals in the first place. And when the region over which the integration takes place is non-rectangular, this can be a subtle and challenging enterprise in itself. However, if the region in question is defined by one or more inequalities, the command **CylindricalDecomposition** will do this work for you. For instance, to find the bounds used in the last example for integration over a spherical region of radius 2 centered at the origin, one may simply do this:

In[120]:= **CylindricalDecomposition**$\left[x^2 + y^2 + z^2 < 4, \{z, y, x\}\right]$

Out[120]= $-2 < z < 2 \;\&\&\; -\sqrt{4-z^2} < y < \sqrt{4-z^2} \;\&\&\; -\sqrt{4-y^2-z^2} < x < \sqrt{4-y^2-z^2}$

Similarly, the circular region in the example preceding this one can be decomposed as follows:

In[121]:= **CylindricalDecomposition**$\left[x^2 + y^2 < 4, \{y, x\}\right]$

Out[121]= $-2 < y < 2 \,\&\&\, -\sqrt{4 - y^2} < x < \sqrt{4 - y^2}$

The second argument to **CylindricalDecomposition** is a list of the coordinate variables, and the order in which they are listed is very important. It should match the order in which the integral *signs* appear. To decompose complex regions, you may wish to experiment with the ordering to find the one that leads to the most simple decomposition. Also, use strict inequalities when describing regions of integration, as this will often simplify the output.

As useful as **CylindricalDecomposition** is, it may not be able to decompose a region defined by inequalities involving transcendental functions. For instance, if the first argument is $\sin x < y < 1 - x^2$, it will not be able to find the numerical bounds for x. See Exercise 13.

You can also make a plot of the region determined by your bounds of integration. This provides a visual confirmation for your choice of bounds. One produces the plots using **RegionPlot** for planar regions, and **RegionPlot3D** for regions in space. Here, for instance is the circular region used in the double integral above. Note that the first argument uses the bounds of the inner integral, and is presented as an inequality (it makes no difference whether strict or non-strict inequalities are used). The bounds of the outer integral are given implicitly via the iterator for y:

In[122]:= **RegionPlot**$\left[-\sqrt{4 - y^2} \le x \le \sqrt{4 - y^2}, \{x, -2, 2\}, \{y, -2, 2\}\right]$

Out[122]=

And here is a view of the volume that this double integral represents. We use **Plot3D** with both a **RegionFunction** setting (to show the plot of the integrand over the circular region) and a **Filling** setting (to show a translucent solid region under the graph of the integrand). Note also that **Plot·. Range** is needed to extend the image all the way down to the *x-y* plane.

In[123]:= $\text{Plot3D}\Big[5 - x^2 y^2, \{x, -2, 2\}, \{y, -2, 2\}, \text{Mesh} \to \text{None}, \text{PlotRange} \to \{0, 5\},$

$\text{Filling} \to \text{Axis}, \text{RegionFunction} \to \text{Function}\Big[\{x, y\}, -\sqrt{4 - y^2} \le x \le \sqrt{4 - y^2}\Big]\Big]$

Out[123]=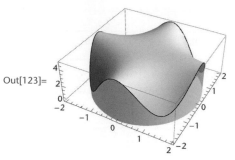

The setting for **RegionFunction** could be stated more simply as **Function[{x,y},Norm[{x,y}] ≤ 2]**. Similarly, the inequality used as the first argument to **RegionPlot** in the earlier input could be **Norm[{x,y}] ≤ 2**. We stuck here with the inequality suggested by the bounds of integration, precisely to make sure those bounds produce an appropriate image.

Both **RegionPlot** and **RegionPlot3D** expect an inequality, or a logical combination of inequalities, as their first argument. **RegionPlot3D** demands three iterators, one for each coordinate variable. Here we use **RegionPlot3D** to view the solid spherical region used for the *triple* integral example given just prior to the start of this subsection. Note how we use a logical combination of the inequalities corresponding to the bounds of the two inner integrals:

In[124]:= $\text{RegionPlot3D}\Big[-\sqrt{4 - z^2} \le y \le \sqrt{4 - z^2} \,\&\&\, -\sqrt{4 - y^2 - z^2} \le x \le \sqrt{4 - y^2 - z^2},$

$\{x, -2, 2\}, \{y, -2, 2\}, \{z, -2, 2\}\Big]$

Out[124]=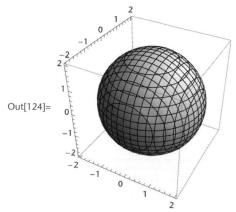

Here the first argument to **RegionPlot3D** could be stated more simply as **Norm[{x,y,z}] ≤ 2**. We stuck here with the inequalities suggested by the bounds of integration, precisely to test that these bounds produce an appropriate image.

Below we construct multiple cut-away views of this solid ball, with **MeshFunction** and **MeshShad**⋅.
ing settings applied to color the ball according the value of the integrand $y - z^2$. If this function
gives the density of the ball at the point (x, y, z), for instance, then the triple integral gives the ball's
mass. Note that the setting **BoxRatios → Automatic** is needed to give all axes the same scale (by
default **RegionPlot3D** will scale the axes in order to create a cubical bounding box).

In[125]:= **GraphicsRow[Table[RegionPlot3D[Norm[{x, y, z}] ≤ 2,**
{x, −2, rightSide}, {y, −2, 2}, {z, −2, 2}, BoxRatios → Automatic,
MeshFunctions → {Function[{x, y, z}, y − z²]}, Mesh → 10,
MeshShading → Table[ColorData["TemperatureMap"][k], {k, 0, 1, .1}],
Lighting → "Neutral", Axes → False], {rightSide, {2, 1, 0}}], ImageSize → 300]

Out[125]=

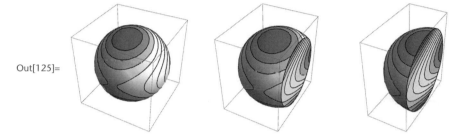

Exercises 6.2

1. In this exercise you will explore the **ColorFunction** option for **Plot3D**. **ColorFunction** may be
   set to any pure function with three variables (one for each coordinate position). Pure functions
   are discussed in Section 8.4. By default, each of the input values for this function are scaled from
   the actual coordinate values to span the range from 0 to 1. In order to use the actual coordinate
   values, the additional option setting **ColorFunctionScaling → False** must be added. Moreover
   the output of the **ColorFunction** must be a **Hue**, **RGBColor**, or other color directive (such as a
   named gradient like **ColorData["StarryNightColors"]**). The inputs to functions such as **Hue**
   should span the values from 0 to 1. In practice, this means that most "interesting" color functions will have to be **Rescale**d before being suitable for input to **Hue** or whichever color rendering function you plan to use.

   a. Make a **Plot3D** of the function $e^{\sin(x y)}$ on the domain $-2 \leq x \leq 2$, $-2 \leq y \leq 2$ with the option
      setting **ColorFunction → (#1&)**. Repeat for **(#2&)** and **(#3&)**. Note that by setting an explicit
      color function, the default **Lighting** setting switches to using white light only, so as not to
      interfere with your choice of color.

   b. Make a **Plot3D** of the function $e^{\sin(x y)} \sqrt{(x \cos(x y))^2 + (y \cos(x y))^2}$ on the domain $-2 \leq x \leq 2$,
      $-2 \leq y \leq 2$ with the option setting **PlotRange → All**. Estimate the minimum and maximum
      values obtained by the function on this domain.

c. Repeat the previous part, but this time plot the function

$$\textbf{Rescale}[e^{\textbf{Sin}[x\,y]}\sqrt{(x\,\textbf{Cos}[x\,y])^2+(y\,\textbf{Cos}[x\,y])^2}\,,\{0,4\}].$$ What do you notice about its minimum and maximum values?

d. The function above is suitable for input into a color rendering command such as **Hue** or **ColorData["StarryNightColors"]**. Let's do it; enter the following input, and comment on the coloring. What this shows is that (with a little work) the graph of one function can be colored in according to the values of any other function.

In[126]:= $\textbf{Plot3D}\Big[e^{\textbf{Sin}[x\,y]},\,\{x,\,-2,\,2\},\,\{y,\,-2,\,2\},\,\textbf{ColorFunctionScaling}\to\textbf{False},$

$\textbf{ColorFunction}\to\textbf{Function}\Big[\{x,\,y,\,z\},\,\textbf{ColorData}\big[\text{"StarryNightColors"}\big]\Big[$

$\textbf{Rescale}\Big[e^{\textbf{Sin}[x\,y]}\sqrt{(x\,\textbf{Cos}[x\,y])^2+(y\,\textbf{Cos}[x\,y])^2}\,,\,\{0,\,4\}\Big]\Big]\Big],\,\textbf{Mesh}\to\textbf{None}\Big]$

Out[126]=
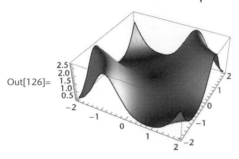

e. The following output wraps the color rendering function in **Glow**, which means that it will not react with any **Lighting**. Can you see any difference from the last input?

In[127]:= $\textbf{Plot3D}\Big[e^{\textbf{Sin}[x\,y]},\,\{x,\,-2,\,2\},\,\{y,\,-2,\,2\},\,\textbf{ColorFunctionScaling}\to\textbf{False},$

$\textbf{ColorFunction}\to\textbf{Function}\Big[\{x,\,y,\,z\},\,\textbf{Glow}@\textbf{ColorData}\big[\text{"StarryNightColors"}\big]\Big[$

$\textbf{Rescale}\Big[e^{\textbf{Sin}[x\,y]}\sqrt{(x\,\textbf{Cos}[x\,y])^2+(y\,\textbf{Cos}[x\,y])^2}\,,\,\{0,\,4\}\Big]\Big]\Big],\,\textbf{Mesh}\to\textbf{None}\Big]$

Out[127]=
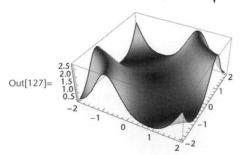

2. Use **TabView** to construct a dynamic display of a **Plot3D** object like the one shown below where **MaxRecursion** may be set to any of the values 0 to 3.

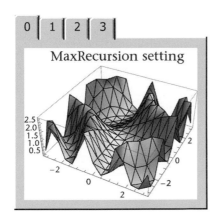

3. Make a plot of the function $f(x, y) = \frac{xy}{x^2+y^2}$ over the annular domain $.1 \le \sqrt{x^2 + y^2} \le 1$. Add

Filling to the bottom of the bounding box. Repeat for $f(x, y) = \frac{xy^2}{x^2+y^2}$. Comment on the behavior of these functions near the origin.

4. Make two images side by side, one showing a **ContourPlot** of your favorite function, and the other a **Plot3D** of that same function on the same domain. Use **MeshFunctions** to display level curves in the **Plot3D**. Use a specific **Range** of values for the **Contours** settings on the **Contour**. **Plot**, and use that same collection of values for **Mesh** settings on the **Plot3D**. This way you will synchronize the level curves being shown in each plot. Use a **ColorFunction** or **MeshShading** to apply "**LakeColors**" to your **Plot3D**.

5. Write a command called **key** that will make a graphical gradient key for a **ContourPlot** as shown on page 272. It should have the syntax structure **key[{*min,max*},*contours*]**, where *min* and *max* denote the minimum and maximum function values in the plot, and *contours* is the number of contour regions in the plot.

6. Consider the function $f(x, y) = \sin(x^2 - y^2)$ on the domain $-2 \le x \le 2$, $-1 \le y \le 1$. In this exercise you will explore several methods of illustrating *cross-sections* for this function. That is, you will set one of the coordinate variables equal to a constant. For instance, if $x = 1$ this means geometrically that you slice the graph of f with the vertical plane $x = 1$.

a. Make a **Manipulate** that will display a **Plot** of the cross-section $y = c$ for f, as c ranges from -1 to 1. For those familiar with medical imaging, this is a bit like an MRI scan of the 3D plot of f.

b. Make a **Manipulate** that will display a **Plot** of the cross-section $x = c$ for f, as c ranges from -2 to 2.

c. Make the **Manipulate** shown below that shows both of the cross-sections together with a **Plot3D** of f with appropriate **Mesh** lines.

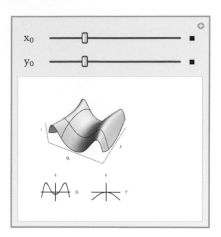

7. Describe the set of critical points for the function $f(x, y) = \sin(x^2 - y^2)$ on the domain $-2 \le x \le 2$ and $-1 \le y \le 1$. Use **Reduce** with the second argument set to **{y,x}** and again with the second argument set to **{x,y}**. Is one output easier to interpret?

8. Consider the function $f(x, y) = x \cos(xy)$.

   a. Show that f has no critical points. Make a **ContourPlot** with **MeshFunctions** and **Mesh** settings to display the curves where the partial derivative with respect to x is zero, and those where the partial derivative with respect to y is zero. Confirm visually that these two sets of curves never cross.

   b. Show that for any direction measured by the polar angle θ, and any real number $r > 0$, the function f has a point (x_0, y_0) in its domain where the directional derivative in the direction of θ exceeds r, and another point (x_1, y_1) where the directional derivative in the direction of θ is less than $-r$. Essentially, the steepness of this function is unbounded in *every* direction, despite being defined on the entire plane, and having no relative minima, maxima, or saddle points.

9. Explain how to use **ContourPlot3D** to view the graph of any real-valued function of two variables, such as $f(x, y) = 2xy$ on the domain $-1 \le x \le 1$, $-1 \le y \le 1$. How does this differ from using the **Plot3D** command to produce such a graph?

10. Maximize the quantity $x^{1/3} y^{2/3}$ under the constraint that $40x + 50y = 10\,000$.

11. Find *all* point(s) on the surface $z = xy$ closest to the point $(0, 0, 3)$. Make a **ContourPlot3D** of this surface, colored (via **MeshShading**) according to how close points are to $(0, 0, 3)$.

12. Consider the function $f(x, y) = 2\sqrt{1 - x^2}$ defined over the unit disk in the x-y plane centered at the origin.

   a. Make a **Plot3D** of f over this circular region, and use **Filling** to display the solid under the graph of f and above the x-y plane.

   b. Find the volume of this solid.

c. Make the following **Manipulate**, showing the graph from part **a** together with a movable square cross-section. If one first integrates with respect to y, the inner integral is equal to the area of this square cross-section.

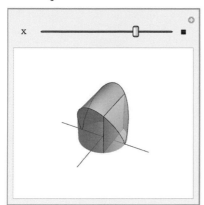

13. Find the *approximate* value of the double integral of the function $f(x, y) = 2x - y$ over the region R in the *x-y* plane bounded by $y = \sin x$ and $y = 1 - x^2$. Make a three-dimensional sketch of the signed volume that this integral represents.

14. Use **RegionPlot3D** to view the solid torus $z^2 + \left(\sqrt{x^2 + y^2} - 3\right)^2 \leq 1$. Use **MeshShading** to color the torus according to distance from the origin, with points closest to the origin appearing red, and the most distant points appearing blue. (The **ColorData["TemperatureMap"]** gradient is perfect for this.) Finally, display that portion of the surface with $-2 \leq x \leq 4$ and $0 \leq y \leq 4$.

6.3 Parametric Curves and Surfaces

Parametric Curves in the Plane

A parametric representation of a curve is a continuous vector-valued function of one variable; for each value of a variable t, the function returns a vector $\langle x(t), y(t) \rangle$ in the plane. As t varies continuously through an interval, the vectors trace out a curve. Since a vector in *Mathematica* is represented as a **List**, a parametric curve can be defined as a **List** of two or more real-valued functions. The first function represents the x coordinate, the second the y coordinate. Since there is only one variable, we revert to the paradigm for defining functions used in Chapters 3 through 5, with an underscore after the independent variable on the left side, and using **SetDelayed** (:=).

In[1]:= **s[t_] := {Cos[t] + t, Sin[t]}**

You can now find your position in the plane for any value of t:

In[2]:= $s\left[\dfrac{\pi}{4}\right]$

Out[2]= $\left\{\dfrac{1}{\sqrt{2}} + \dfrac{\pi}{4}, \dfrac{1}{\sqrt{2}}\right\}$

To plot a parametric function, use the command **ParametricPlot**:

In[3]:= **ParametricPlot**$\left[s[t], \{t, 0, 10\,\pi\}, \text{AspectRatio} \to 1/2\right]$

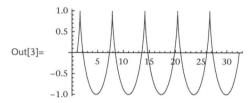

Out[3]=

ParametricPlot takes two arguments. The first is the function you wish to plot, and the second is an iterator for the independent variable (**t** in this example). **ParametricPlot** will tend to give both axes the same scale unless you explicitly tell it not to. Many curves, circles for instance, look better that way, so that's what happens by default. Be aware that in plots like the one above where one axis is far longer than the other, an **AspectRatio** setting will be in order.

You need not restrict yourself to simple functions. **ParametricPlot** works well on **Piecewise** functions, and even on interesting curves like this:

In[4]:= $c[t\_] = \left\{\displaystyle\int_0^t \text{Sin}\left[u^2\right] d\,u, \int_0^t \text{Cos}\left[u^2\right] d\,u\right\};$

In[5]:= **ParametricPlot**$[c[t], \{t, -10, 10\}]$

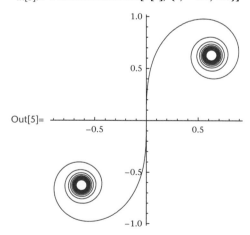

Out[5]=

⚠ Note that the definition of $c(t)$ above uses **Set** (=) rather than **SetDelayed** (:=). This causes the two integrals on the right side of the definition to be evaluated *once*, when the **c[t_]=** cell is entered. It is the expressions that are the *values* of these integrals (they happen to be Fresnel functions) that are assigned to *c*(*t*), and that are then plotted. If **SetDelayed** had been used in defining *c*(*t*), then the integrals would have to be worked out anew for each input value *t* used to create the plot (and there are several hundred such values). It would have slowed the process of plotting by several orders of magnitude.

While a **ParametricPlot** shows the set of points of the form $(x(t), y(t))$ as *t* runs through all values in an interval, it does not give any indication of which point goes with which input. **Manipulate** can be harnessed to trace out a parametric curve, with a slider to control the independent variable. Here, for instance, is a standard parameterization of the unit circle. Note the **PlotRange** setting (which keeps the plot range fixed as *t* varies), and the small but positive starting value 0.01 for the endpoint **t** (one needs *distinct* starting and ending values for the independent variable in any **ParametricPlot**).

In[6]:= **Manipulate[Show[**
ParametricPlot[{Cos[t0], Sin[t0]}, {t0, 0, t}, PlotRange → 1],
Graphics[Arrow[{{0, 0}, {Cos[t], Sin[t]}}]]
],
{{t, 1.}, 0.01, 2π}]

Out[6]=

One can also define a custom parametric plotting command that will apply a color gradient to the curve, so that it will, for instance, start in green and gradually progress through the color gradient to end in red (green for go, red for stop). Here's a simple implementation, but you'll need to try it in order to see the colors on your monitor.

In[7]:= **ParametricPlot[{Cos[t], Sin[3 t]}, {t, 0, 2 π}, ColorFunction → (Hue[.7 #3 + .3] &)]**

Out[7]=

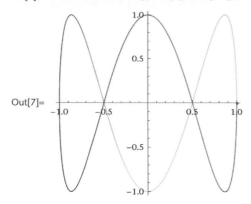

⚠ The **ColorFunction** accepts any or all of three arguments. The first two are the x and y coordinates of the parametric curve. The third (**#3** used above) is the independent variable t. By default, the values of t will be scaled to run from 0 to 1 before being input to the **ColorFunc·tion**, regardless of the domain you choose. Hence the option setting above produces a color gradient that starts at **Hue[.3]** (green) and ends at **Hue[1.]** (red). This same setting may be used to color any **ParametricPlot** according to this gradient. Exercise 4 shows how to color a parametric curve according to its *curvature*.

We note that **ParametricPlot** accepts most of the options accepted by other two-dimensional plotting commands such as **Plot**. The **PlotPoints** option, for example, can be set to a numerical value (such as 100) if you see jagged segments where you suspect they should not be. However, the adaptive algorithm employed by **ParametricPlot** is both speedy and robust; it is rare to find cases where it does anything less than an excellent job. The following **Manipulate** may help to convince you of this:

In[8]:= **Manipulate[**

$$\text{ParametricPlot}\left[\left\{\text{Cos[t]} + \frac{1}{2}\,\text{Cos[7 t]} + \frac{1}{2}\,\text{Sin[a t]},\ \text{Sin[t]} + \frac{1}{2}\,\text{Sin[7 t]} + \frac{1}{2}\,\text{Cos[b t]}\right\},\right.$$

$$\left.\{t, 0, 2\pi\},\ \text{Axes} \rightarrow \text{False},\ \text{PlotRange} \rightarrow 2\right],\ \{\{a, 17\}, 5, 25\},\ \{\{b, 12\}, 5, 25\}\right]$$

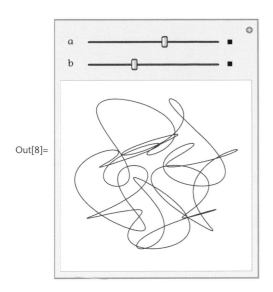

Out[8]=

The derivative of the parametric function $\langle x(t), y(t) \rangle$ is $\langle x'(t), y'(t) \rangle$. You can differentiate a parametric function just as you did a single-variable function in Chapter 5, or like we did for multivariable functions in the previous section of this chapter, using ∂:

In[9]:= **D[s[t], t]**

Out[9]= $\{1 - Sin[t], Cos[t]\}$

In[10]:= **s'[t]**

Out[10]= $\{1 - Sin[t], Cos[t]\}$

In[11]:= ∂_t **s[t]**

Out[11]= $\{1 - Sin[t], Cos[t]\}$

Note that while the **ParametricPlot** of $\vec{s}(t)$ has sharp corners (it is the first plot shown at the beginning of this section), its derivative is defined everywhere. This can happen. The **Manipulate** below shows the derivative vector $\vec{s}'(t)$ with its tail at the point $s(t)$, as t varies. When t is $\pi/2$ or $5\pi/2$, $\sin t = 1$ and $\cos t = 0$, and so the derivative is the zero vector. This happens at the top of each sharp corner in the plot.

```
In[12]:= Module[{s},
        s[t_] = {t + Cos[t], Sin[t]};
        Manipulate[Show[
            ParametricPlot[s[t0], {t0, 0, 10}, PlotRange → {{0, 10}, {−2, 2}}],
            Graphics[Arrow[{s[t], s[t] + s'[t]}]]]
        ],
        {{t, 4.8}, 0, 10}]]
```

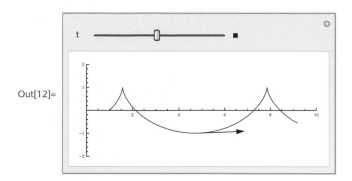

Out[12]=

If $\vec{s}(t)$ represents the position of a particle at time t, then its *velocity* vector is $\vec{s}\,'(t)$, and its *speed* is the magnitude of this vector. To compute speed, say at time $t = 3$, you can do this:

In[13]:= **Norm[s'[3]] // N**

Out[13]= 1.31063

You can even get a formula for speed as a function of t. Here we produce and **Simplify** the formula, using the optional second argument for **Simplify** in order to specify that t is permitted to assume only real values (as opposed to complex values). We could have given the second argument as **Element[t,Reals]**. The infix form of the **Element** command is invoked with the $\in$ symbol, which can be found on the third row of small buttons on the BasicMathInput palette.

In[14]:= **Simplify[Norm[s'[t]], t $\in$ Reals]**

Out[14]= $\sqrt{2 - 2\,\text{Sin}[t]}$

Note that this is consistent with the **Manipulate** above; speed is zero precisely when t is $\pi/2$, $5\pi/2$, etc.

Unit tangent vectors are constructed exactly as you would expect. The use of **Simplify** as above will generally serve you well.

In[15]:= **unitTangent[s_, t_] := Simplify$\left[\dfrac{\text{D[s, t]}}{\text{Norm[D[s, t]]}}, t \in \text{Reals}\right]$**

In[16]:= **s[t_] = {t + Cos[t], Sin[t]};**
unitTangent[s[t], t]

Out[17]= $\left\{\dfrac{\sqrt{1 - \text{Sin}[t]}}{\sqrt{2}}, \dfrac{\text{Cos}[t]}{\sqrt{2 - 2\,\text{Sin}[t]}}\right\}$

The unit tangent vector at a specific value of t can then be obtained via a simple replacement:

In[18]:= **unitTangent[s[t], t] /. t → 1.2**

Out[18]= {0.184338, 0.982863}

Unit normal vectors can be formed in a similar way (although **FullSimplify** does a better job than **Simplify** in this case):

In[19]:= **unitNormal[s_, t_] := FullSimplify$\left[\dfrac{D[unitTangent[s, t], t]}{Norm[D[unitTangent[s, t], t]]}, t \in Reals\right]$**

In[20]:= **unitNormal[s[t], t]**

Out[20]= $\left\{-\dfrac{Cos[t]}{\sqrt{2 - 2\,Sin[t]}}, \dfrac{\sqrt{1 - Sin[t]}}{\sqrt{2}}\right\}$

Even though neither the unit tangent nor the unit normal is defined when $t = \pi/2$ or $t = 5\pi/2$, the following **Manipulate** works fine, as it is unlikely to sample these precise values. We define auxiliary commands **ut** and **un** so that **unitTangent** and **unitNormal** only need to be called once (they are slow, after all, since they use **Simplify** and **FullSimplify**, respectively, each time they are called). The auxiliary commands **ut** and **un** are defined using **Set** (=). So they use the *formulas* generated by **unitTangent** and **unitNormal**, and simply replace the variable t by whatever argument x is specified. They are speedy!

In[21]:= **Module$\big[$**{s, ut, un, t},
       s[t_] = {t + Cos[t], Sin[t]};
       ut[x_] = unitTangent[s[t], t] /. t → x;
       un[x_] = unitNormal[s[t], t] /. t → x;
       Manipulate$\big[$Show$\big[$
           ParametricPlot$\big[$s[t], {t, 0, 10}, PlotRange → {{0, 10}, {−2, 2}}$\big]$,
           Graphics[{Blue, Arrow[{s[t0], s[t0] + ut[t0]}]}],
           Graphics[{Red, Arrow[{s[t0], s[t0] + un[t0]}]}]
         ],
         {{t0, 6.8}, 0, 10}$\big]\big]$

Out[21]=

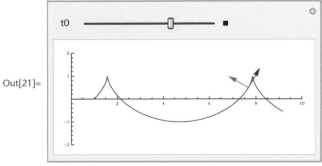

Curvature is also a simple calculation. We use the Greek letter κ (kappa) to denote this quantity. Find κ on the BasicMathInput palette, or type ⎋ k ⎋.

In[22]:= κ[s_, t_] := FullSimplify$\left[\dfrac{\text{Norm}\big[D[\text{unitTangent}[s, t], t]\big]}{\text{Norm}[D[s, t]]}, t \in \text{Reals}\right]$

In[23]:= κ[s[t], t]

Out[23]= $\dfrac{1}{2\sqrt{2 - 2\,\text{Sin}[t]}}$

And so the *radius of curvature* is the reciprocal of this quantity, $2\sqrt{2 - 2\sin t}$. At the sharp corners (when t is $\pi/2$, $5\pi/2$, etc.) the curvature is undefined, and the radius of curvature approaches zero. The **Manipulate** below shows the *osculating circle* for any value of t. This illustrates that the radius of curvature approaches zero very rapidly as t approaches $5\pi/2$.

In[24]:= Module$\Big[${s, un, curv, t},

  s[t_] = {t + Cos[t], Sin[t]};
  un[x_] = unitNormal[s[t], t] /. t → x;
  curv[x_] = κ[s[t], t] /. t → x;
  Manipulate$\Big[$Show$\Big[$ParametricPlot$\big[$s[t], {t, 0, 10}, PlotRange → {{−4, 12}, {−2, 6}}$\big]$,

    Graphics$\Big[\Big\{$Gray, Circle$\Big[$s[t0] + $\dfrac{1}{\text{curv}[t0]}$ un[t0], $\dfrac{1}{\text{curv}[t0]}\Big]\Big\}\Big]$,

    Graphics$\Big[\Big\{$Red, Arrow$\Big[\Big\{$s[t0] + $\dfrac{1}{\text{curv}[t0]}$ un[t0], s[t0]$\Big\}\Big]\Big\}\Big]\Big]$

  $\Big]$, {{t0, 6.5}, 0, 10}$\Big]\Big]$

Out[24]=

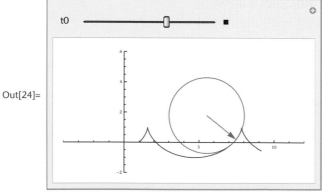

Parametric Curves in Space

Parametric curves in three-space are just like parametric curves in the plane, except that they are constructed as a list of *three* real-valued functions. The first function represents the x coordinate, the second represents the y coordinate, and the third represents the z coordinate.

In[25]:= $s[t\_] := \left\{ \dfrac{t^2}{50} Sin[t], \dfrac{t^2}{50} Cos[t], t \right\}$

To plot a parametric function in space, use the command **ParametricPlot3D**:

In[26]:= $\textbf{ParametricPlot3D}\big[s[t], \{t, 0, 8\pi\}, \textbf{AxesLabel} \to \{x, y, z\}\big]$

Out[26]=
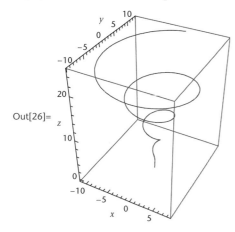

ParametricPlot3D takes two arguments. The first is the function you wish to plot (a **List** of three coordinate functions), and the second is an iterator for the independent variable. We added an **AxesLabel** option to make it easy to identify which direction is which after you rotate the figure with your mouse. Many of the other options for the other 3D plotting commands are applicable here; see the subsection of Section 6.2 called "Options for 3D Plotting Commands" on page 258. One can also use **MeshShading** or **ColorFunction** settings in exactly the same manner as for 2D parametric plots. For example, here we color a curve according to the value of the independent variable:

In[27]:= **ParametricPlot3D**$\big[$**s[t]**, {**t, 0, 8π**},
AxesLabel → {**x, y, z**}, ColorFunction → (Hue[.3 + .7 #3] &)$\big]$

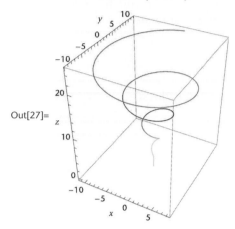

Out[27]=

Differentiation, integration, unit tangents, unit normals, and curvature work exactly as for 2D parametric functions (see the previous subsection). In the case of three-space, however, there is a well known alternate formula for curvature based on the cross-product. It is a simple matter to program a command based on this formula:

In[28]:= **curvature[r_, t_] := FullSimplify**$\left[\dfrac{\text{Norm[Cross[r'[t], r''[t]]]}}{\text{Norm[r'[t]]}^3}, \text{t} \in \text{Reals}\right]$

We may now calculate curvature for any function, at any point t in its domain:

In[29]:= **curvature[s, π]**

Out[29]= $\dfrac{50\sqrt{10\,000 + 30\,000\,\pi^2 + 2536\,\pi^4 + 12\,\pi^6 + \pi^8}}{\left(2500 + 4\,\pi^2 + \pi^4\right)^{3/2}}$

In[30]:= **curvature[s, t]**

Out[30]= $50\sqrt{\dfrac{10\,000 + 30\,000\,t^2 + 2536\,t^4 + 12\,t^6 + t^8}{\left(2500 + 4\,t^2 + t^4\right)^3}}$

Parametric Surfaces in Space

A surface in space can be parameterized much like a curve in space, but rather than using a single independent variable t, we use a pair of independent variables u and v. Whereas a parameterization of a curve in space is a continuous function from an *interval* of the real line to three-space, a parameterization of a surface is a continuous function from a *rectangle* in the plane to three-space. The image of each coordinate pair (u, v) is a point in space, a 3-tuple $\big(x(u, v), y(u, v), z(u, v)\big)$, where x, y, and z are real-valued coordinate functions.

Mathematica is instrumental in visualizing the amazing spectrum of surfaces that can be constructed in this manner. Here is an example. It illustrates that just as a parametrically defined curve can intersect itself (if the coordinate functions assume the same values at two or more distinct values of t), so too can a parametrically defined surface intersect itself. This surface is known as the Whitney umbrella, named after the American mathematician Hassler Whitney (1907–1989).

```
In[31]:= Clear[Φ, u, v];
        Φ = {u v, u, v²}

Out[32]= {u v, u, v²}

In[33]:= ParametricPlot3D[Φ, {u, −3, 3}, {v, −2, 2}]
```

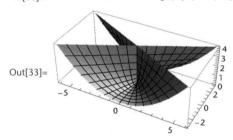

Out[33]=

The rectangular region in the *u-v* plane with $-3 \le u \le 3$ and $-2 \le v \le 2$ is mapped continuously via Φ to the surface in $\mathbb{R}^3$ shown above. As with parametric curves, the plot does not show the domain, but only the image of the domain after the parametric function is applied.

Here's another example. We map a rectangle in the *u-v* plane to a torus:

```
In[34]:= Φ = {Cos[u] (2 + Cos[v]), Sin[u] (2 + Cos[v]), Sin[v]};
```

In[35]:= **ParametricPlot3D[Φ, {u, 0, 2π}, {v, 0, 2π}]**

Out[35]=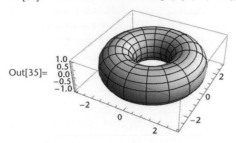

For parametric surfaces, a mesh function can accept up to five arguments. In order, the arguments are x, y, z, u, and v. The first three are the coordinates in space of the surface, while the last two are the independent variables. The default setting for the **MeshFunctions** option is {#4 &, #5 &}, meaning that the image under Φ of uniformly spaced rectangular grid lines on the domain rectangle are shown. More information can be gained by using **Mesh**, **MeshFunctions**, and **MeshShading** to apply a color gradient according to increasing values of one of the independent variables. This is accomplished in exactly the same way as described in the subsection of Section 6.2 called "Options for 3D Plotting Commands" on page 258. Below we do this for the first independent variable, u, used in the torus. The "seam" is easily visible (on a color monitor) as the sharp boundary between red and blue.

In[36]:= **ParametricPlot3D[Φ, {u, 0, 2π}, {v, 0, 2π}, Mesh → 10, MeshFunctions → {#4 &},**
    MeshShading → Table[ColorData["TemperatureMap"][k], {k, 0, 1, .1}],
    Lighting → "Neutral"]

Out[36]=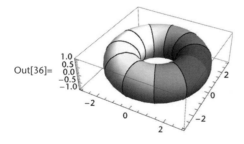

Differentiation works just as with parameterized curves. Here is the partial derivative with respect to v:

In[37]:= ∂_v **Φ**

Out[37]= $\{-\text{Cos}[u]\,\text{Sin}[v], -\text{Sin}[u]\,\text{Sin}[v], \text{Cos}[v]\}$

It is easy to use the concept of a parametric surface to generate a *surface of revolution*. You may recall surfaces of revolution from single-variable calculus; indeed, in Section 5.13 on page 242 we discussed the built-in command **RevolutionPlot3D**, which will plot the surface of revolution obtained from revolving the function $z = f(x)$ about the z axis. However, this command cannot be used to rotate the graph of such a function about the x axis. One may easily create a custom command for this purpose as follows:

In[38]:= **xRevolutionPlot3D[f_, {x_, xmin_, xmax_}] :=**
        ParametricPlot3D[{x, f Cos[θ], f Sin[θ]}, {x, xmin, xmax}, {θ, 0, 2π}]

For example, here we rotate a parabola about the x axis:

In[39]:= **f[x_] := 1 − x²;**
        GraphicsRow[{Plot[f[x], {x, −1, 1}], xRevolutionPlot3D[f[x], {x, −1, 1}]}]

Out[40]=

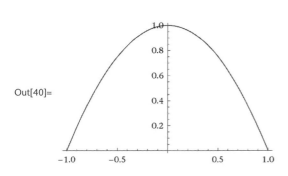
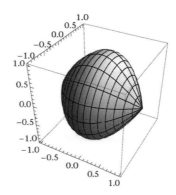

Exercises 6.3

1. Explain how to use **ParametricPlot** to view the graph of any real-valued function of a single variable, such as $f(x) = x^2 − 1$. How does this differ from using the **Plot** command to produce such a graph?

2. There are many different parameterizations of the same curve. A standard parameterization of the unit circle is $\langle \cos t, \sin t \rangle$, where $0 \le t \le 2\pi$. Verify that the parametric function $\left\langle \frac{\sin(4t)+\sin(6t)}{2\sin(5t)}, \frac{\cos(4t)-\cos(6t)}{2\sin(5t)} \right\rangle$, where $0 < t < 2\pi$, also parameterizes the unit circle for those values of t where it is defined (e.g. it is not defined at integer multiples of $t = \pi/5$).

3. Consider the vector-valued function $\vec{r}(t) = \langle 2\sin(t), \cos(t), \sin(2t) \rangle$.

   a. Superimpose a **ParametricPlot3D** of $\vec{r}(t)$ with a **ContourPlot3D** of the surface $z = xy$. Use the option **Mesh → None** in your plot of the surface. What do you find?

   b. Explain why the curve lies on the surface. Hint: you will need the double-angle formula for the sine function. If you have forgotten it, type **TrigExpand[Sin[2t]]**.

4. Use **ColorFunction** to color a **ParametricPlot** of the function $\left\langle t, e^{-t^2} \right\rangle$ on the domain $-2 \le t \le 2$ according to its *curvature* with the **"TemperatureMap"** color gradient. While this method pro-

duces continuous color transitions (as opposed to the discrete color values produced when using **MeshFunctions** for this purpose), it requires your knowing the maximum and minimum curvature values for your specific function on your specific domain.

5. Use **MeshShading** to shade a **ParametricPlot3D** of the torus,

$$\Phi(u, v) = \langle \cos(u)(\cos(v) + 2), \sin(u)(\cos(v) + 2), \sin(v)\rangle$$

where each independent variable ranges from 0 to 2π, according to values of the independent variable v. Use the color gradient **ColorData["TemperatureMap"]** with ten gradations. Use the resulting graphic to identify the "seam" in the torus created by this variable.

6.4 Other Coordinate Systems

Polar Coordinates

Conversion to and from Polar Coordinates

A point in polar coordinates is represented as an ordered pair (r, θ), where r is the distance from the point to the origin, and the angle θ is measured in radians, counterclockwise, from the positive x axis to the segment connecting the origin to the point.

To convert between polar and Cartesian coordinates, one makes use of the following triangle and some basic trigonometry:

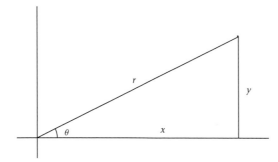

So in converting from polar to Cartesian coordinates, one uses the formulas $x = r\cos\theta$ and $y = r\sin\theta$.

In converting from Cartesian to polar coordinates, one uses the formulas $r = \sqrt{x^2 + y^2}$, and so long as $x \neq 0$, $\tan\theta = y/x$. This last equation, when solved for θ, can be expressed as follows:

$$\theta = \begin{cases} \arctan(y/x) & x > 0 \\ \arctan(y/x) + \pi & x < 0 \text{ and } y \geq 0 \\ \arctan(y/x) - \pi & x < 0 \text{ and } y < 0 \\ \pi/2 & x = 0 \text{ and } y > 0 \\ -\pi/2 & x = 0 \text{ and } y < 0 \end{cases}$$

This expression for θ is clearly a bit messy. The formula above will produce a value of θ with $-\pi < \theta \le \pi$. *Mathematica* makes the calculation of θ much easier with its **ArcTan** command. The **ArcTan** command usually takes a single number as its argument, and returns a value between $-\pi/2$ and $\pi/2$, the arc tangent of that number. But you can also feed it an x-y pair. **ArcTan[x, y]** will return the polar angle θ for the point with Cartesian coordinates (x, y), with $-\pi < \theta \le \pi$. That is, it will essentially invoke the complex formula above. So life is easy after all: in converting from Cartesian to polar coordinates, $\theta = $ **ArcTan[x, y]**. For instance:

In[1]:= **{ArcTan[1, 1], ArcTan[0, 1], ArcTan[−1, 1], ArcTan[−1, −1]}**

Out[1]= $\left\{ \dfrac{\pi}{4}, \dfrac{\pi}{2}, \dfrac{3\pi}{4}, -\dfrac{3\pi}{4} \right\}$

It is now a simple matter to automate the conversion process by creating the following commands. Note that you can type θ from the keyboard via the key sequence ⎋ th ⎋. It is also available on the BasicMathInput palette.

In[2]:= **toPolar[x_, y_] := {Norm[{x, y}], ArcTan[x, y]} // Simplify**

In[3]:= **toCartesian[r_, θ_] := {r ∗ Cos[θ], r ∗ Sin[θ]} // Simplify**

Here are some examples:

In[4]:= **toPolar$\left[-1, \sqrt{3} \right]$**

Out[4]= $\left\{ 2, \dfrac{2\pi}{3} \right\}$

In[5]:= **toCartesian$\left[10, \dfrac{\pi}{12} \right]$**

Out[5]= $\left\{ \dfrac{5\left(1 + \sqrt{3}\right)}{\sqrt{2}}, \dfrac{5\left(-1 + \sqrt{3}\right)}{\sqrt{2}} \right\}$

Plotting in Polar Coordinates

The built-in command **PolarPlot** can be used to view the graph of the polar function $r = f(\theta)$. For example:

In[6]:= PolarPlot$\left[\dfrac{1}{1 - \text{Sin}[\theta]}, \left\{\theta, \dfrac{-5\pi}{4}, \dfrac{\pi}{4}\right\}\right]$

Out[6]=

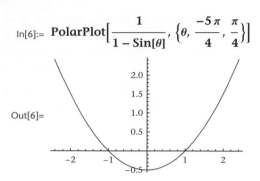

In[7]:= PolarPlot$\left[\theta + \text{Sin}[\theta^2], \{\theta, 0, 10\pi\}, \text{Axes} \rightarrow \text{False}\right]$

Out[7]=

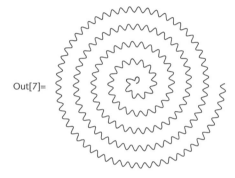

Like **Plot**, **PolarPlot** will accept a *list* of functions as its first argument (so that multiple functions can be simultaneously plotted). It accepts most of the same options accepted by **Plot**, so you will be pleased to find that you're already an expert in its usage. For example:

In[8]:= PolarPlot$\left[\left\{\sqrt{\theta}, -\sqrt{\theta}\right\}, \{\theta, 0, 4\pi\}, \text{Axes} \rightarrow \text{False},\right.$

   $\left.\text{PlotStyle} \rightarrow \{\text{Orange}, \text{Directive}[\text{Blue}, \text{Dashed}]\}\right]$

Out[8]=

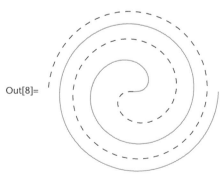

Parametric Plotting in Polar Coordinates

There's no built-in command for this, but it's easy to write the command yourself. If r and θ are each functions of the parameter t, then $x = r \cos \theta$ and $y = r \sin \theta$ are also functions of t, and so can be plotted using **ParametricPlot**. Here's how we formalize this:

In[9]:= **polarParametricPlot$\left[\{r\_, \theta\_\}, \text{args}\_\_\right]$:= ParametricPlot$\left[\{r * \text{Cos}[\theta], r * \text{Sin}[\theta]\}, \text{args}\right]$**

Put *two* underscores after **args** on the left side of the definition (two underscores means that **args** represents one *or more* arguments, separated by commas). In this case args stands for the required iterator for the independent variable *and* for any options that might be added. Here's an example:

In[10]:= **Clear[r, θ, t];**
r[t_] := t Sin[t];
θ[t_] := e^t

In[13]:= **polarParametricPlot[{r[t], θ[t]}, {t, 0, π}, Axes → False]**

Out[13]=

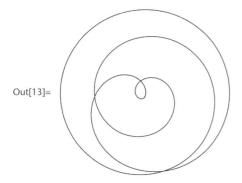

Cylindrical and Spherical Coordinates

Conversion to and from Cartesian Coordinates

When translating from one coordinate system to another it is imperative that you understand the geometry and trigonometry underlying the translation. Otherwise, you will be placing your faith entirely in the computer, never a good idea. However, it would be nice to be able to automate the process, or to be able to ask *Mathematica* for a conversion formula that you might have forgotten. To automate the translation process, you will need to load a package:

In[14]:= **Needs["VectorAnalysis`"]**

Now you will have access to the commands **CoordinatesToCartesian** and **CoordinatesFromCarte**.
sian. Each of these commands takes two arguments. The first is the point whose coordinates you want to translate, and the second is the name of the coordinate system to or from which the translation should occur:

In[15]:= **CoordinatesFromCartesian$\left[\{-\sqrt{2}, \sqrt{2}, 3\}, \text{Cylindrical}\right]$**

Out[15]= $\left\{2, \dfrac{3\pi}{4}, 3\right\}$

In[16]:= **CoordinatesToCartesian$\left[\left\{2, \dfrac{3\pi}{4}, 3\right\}, \text{Cylindrical}\right]$**

Out[16]= $\left\{-\sqrt{2}, \sqrt{2}, 3\right\}$

Working with spherical coordinates in this package demands that you pay careful attention to *Mathematica*'s conventions for this coordinate system. By default, nonzero points expressed in spherical coordinates are of the form $\{\rho, \phi, \theta\}$, where ρ is the distance from the point to the origin, ϕ is the angle from the vector determined by the point to the positive z axis, and θ is the angle used in polar and cylindrical coordinates. The second and third coordinate positions are transposed in many standard calculus texts, so beware!

In[17]:= **CoordinatesFromCartesian$\left[\{1, 0, 1\}, \text{Spherical}\right]$**

Out[17]= $\left\{\sqrt{2}, \dfrac{\pi}{4}, 0\right\}$

Best of all, you can use these conversion commands to help you remember the conversion formulas:

In[18]:= **Clear[ρ, ϕ, θ];**
CoordinatesToCartesian$\left[\{\rho, \phi, \theta\}, \text{Spherical}\right]$

Out[19]= $\{\rho \, \text{Cos}[\theta] \, \text{Sin}[\phi], \, \rho \, \text{Sin}[\theta] \, \text{Sin}[\phi], \, \rho \, \text{Cos}[\phi]\}$

In[20]:= **Clear[x, y, z];**
CoordinatesFromCartesian$\left[\{x, y, z\}, \text{Spherical}\right]$

Out[21]= $\left\{\sqrt{x^2 + y^2 + z^2}, \, \text{ArcCos}\left[\dfrac{z}{\sqrt{x^2 + y^2 + z^2}}\right], \, \text{ArcTan}[x, y]\right\}$

If you are not familiar with the **ArcTan[x, y]** convention, see the subsection "Polar Coordinates" at the beginning of this section on page 314.

⚠ It is worth noting that the **VectorAnalysis** package supports more than a dozen coordinate systems. Cartesian, cylindrical, and spherical are simply the most common. For more information, type "vector analysis package" into the search field in the Documentation Center.

Plotting in Cylindrical Coordinates

Suppose you have a function given in cylindrical coordinates, that is, where z is expressed as a function of the radius r and polar angle θ. The command **RevolutionPlot3D** can be used to produce the graph of such a function. It works much like **Plot3D**: the first argument is the expression for z in the variables r and θ, and the second and third arguments are iterators for r and θ, respectively.

In[22]:= **RevolutionPlot3D[θ, {r, 0, 3}, {θ, 0, 2π}, BoxRatios $\to$ 1]**

Out[22]=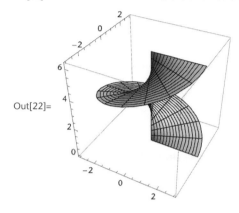

Here we plot the paraboloid $f(x, y) = x^2 + y^2$, shown over a circular domain of radius 2, with polar angle θ between 0 and $3\pi/2$:

In[23]:= **RevolutionPlot3D[r^2, {r, 0, 2}, {θ, 0, 3π/2},**
        BoxRatios $\to$ {1, 1, 2}, Boxed $\to$ False, Axes $\to$ False]

Out[23]=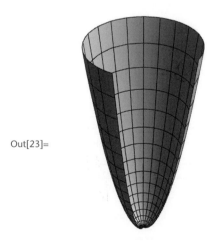

Parametric Plotting in Cylindrical Coordinates

If r, θ, and z are each parameterized by a variable such as t, you may wish to plot the curve that results from the parameterization. While there is no built-in command for this, you can create the command **parametricCylindricalPlot3D** as follows:

In[24]:= **parametricCylindricalPlot3D[{r_, θ_, z_}, args__] :=**
   ParametricPlot3D[{r * Cos[θ], r * Sin[θ], z}, args]

This command simply invokes **ParametricPlot3D** after converting the arguments from cylindrical to Cartesian coordinates. Be sure to put two underscores after **args** on the left side of the defining equation; two underscores mean that **args** stands for a sequence of one *or more* arguments. In this case, **args** represents the required iterator for the independent variable *t and* any options you might add—this will allow you to use any of the options allowed by **ParametricPlot3D**.

Here is an example of a curve that resides along the cylinder whose equation in cylindrical coordinates is $r = 1$:

In[25]:= **parametricCylindricalPlot3D[{1, t, Cos[20 t]}, {t, 0, 2π}, Boxed → False, Axes → False]**

Out[25]=

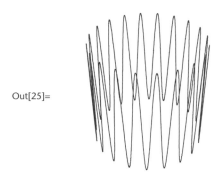

Plotting in Spherical Coordinates

If, in spherical coordinates, ρ is a function of ϕ and θ, you can produce a plot of this function with the command **SphericalPlot3D**. Using this command is much like using **Plot3D**—the first argument is the expression for the radius ρ given in terms of ϕ and θ. The second and third arguments are iterators for ϕ and θ, respectively (note that ϕ, the angle from the positive z axis, comes *first*). Here are two hemispheres, each with the equation $\rho = 2$:

In[26]:= **SphericalPlot3D[2, {φ, 0, π / 2}, {θ, 0, 2 π}]**

Out[26]=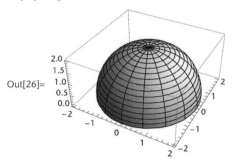

In[27]:= **SphericalPlot3D[2, {φ, 0, π}, {θ, 0, π}]**

Out[27]=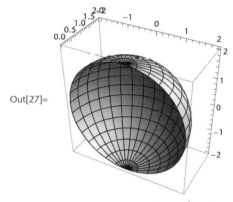

And here is a plot of the surface with the simple equation $\rho = \theta$:

In[28]:= **SphericalPlot3D[θ, {φ, 0, π}, {θ, 0, 7 π / 2}, Boxed → False, Axes → False]**

Out[28]=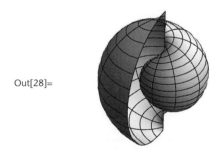

Most of the options that can be used with the command **Plot3D** will also work for **SphericalPlot3D**. A discussion of these options can be found in the subsection "Options for 3D Plotting Commands" of Section 6.2 on page 258.

Parametric Plotting in Spherical Coordinates

If ρ and ϕ and θ are each parameterized by a variable such as t, you may wish to plot the curve that results from this parameterization. While there is no built-in command for this, you can create the command **parametricSphericalPlot3D** as follows:

In[29]:= **parametricSphericalPlot3D**$\left[\{\rho\_, \phi\_, \theta\_\}, \text{args}\_\_\right] :=$
ParametricPlot3D$\left[\{\rho * \text{Sin}[\phi] * \text{Cos}[\theta], \rho * \text{Sin}[\phi] * \text{Sin}[\theta], \rho * \text{Cos}[\phi]\}, \text{args}\right]$

This command simply invokes **ParametricPlot3D** after converting the arguments from spherical to Cartesian coordinates. Be sure to put two underscores after **args** on the left side of the defining equation; two underscores mean that **args** stands for a sequence of one *or more* arguments. In this case, **args** represents the required iterator for the independent variable *t and* any options you might add—this will allow you to use any of the options allowed by **ParametricPlot3D**.

Here is an example of a curve that resides on the sphere whose equation in spherical coordinates is $\rho = 1$:

In[30]:= **parametricSphericalPlot3D[{1, t, 20 t}, {t, 0, π}, Boxed $\rightarrow$ False, Axes $\rightarrow$ False]**

Out[30]=

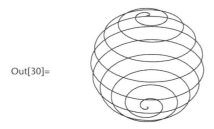

Integration in Other Coordinate Systems

No new *Mathematica* commands are needed to evaluate integrals in other coordinate systems. You simply need to know the underlying conversion formulas in order to set up such an integral.

For example, we evaluated the double integral of the function $f(x, y) = 5 - x^2 y^2$ over the disk of radius 2 centered at the origin back in the subsection "Integration of Functions of Two or More Variables" of Section 6.2 on page 293. This is more easily handled in polar coordinates. We convert the integrand into polar coordinates as follows:

In[31]:= **Clear[x, y, r, θ];**
$5 - x^2 y^2$ /. {x $\rightarrow$ r $*$ Cos[θ], y $\rightarrow$ r $*$ Sin[θ]}

Out[32]= $5 - r^4 \text{Cos}[\theta]^2 \text{Sin}[\theta]^2$

We can now integrate, replacing $dx\,dy$ with $r\,dr\,d\theta$. Since the region of integration is a disk, the bounds of integration are easily described in polar coordinates: $0 \le r \le 2$ and $0 \le \theta \le 2\pi$.

In[33]:= $\int_0^{2\pi} \left(\int_0^2 \%\, r \, dr \right) d\theta$

Out[33]= $\dfrac{52\pi}{3}$

And how about the triple integral of the function $f(x, y, z) = y - z^2$ over the region bounded by a sphere of radius two centered at the origin? We did this one in Cartesian coordinates earlier as well. We accomplish the same result in spherical coordinates as follows. We first convert the integrand into spherical coordinates. Now what were those conversion formulas?

In[34]:= **Needs["VectorAnalysis`"]**

In[35]:= **Clear[x, y, z, ρ, ϕ, θ];**
CoordinatesToCartesian[{ρ, ϕ, θ}, Spherical]

Out[36]= $\{\rho\, \text{Cos}[\theta]\, \text{Sin}[\phi],\ \rho\, \text{Sin}[\theta]\, \text{Sin}[\phi],\ \rho\, \text{Cos}[\phi]\}$

We can make replacement rules from these conversions like so:

In[37]:= **Thread[{x, y, z} $\rightarrow$ %]**

Out[37]= $\{x \rightarrow \rho\, \text{Cos}[\theta]\, \text{Sin}[\phi],\ y \rightarrow \rho\, \text{Sin}[\theta]\, \text{Sin}[\phi],\ z \rightarrow \rho\, \text{Cos}[\phi]\}$

> △ The **Thread** command is used here to "thread" **Rule** ($\rightarrow$) over the lists of variables and conversion expressions. The **FullForm** of the input above is **Thread[Rule[List[x, y, z], List[···]]]**. **Thread** has the effect of distributing **Rule** over the lists, producing a list of rules rather than a rule of lists. So the output has the form **List[Rule[x,···], Rule[y,···],Rule[z,···]]**. **Thread** is discussed in Section 8.4 on page 410.

Here is the converted integrand:

In[38]:= **y $- z^2$ /. %**

Out[38]= $-\rho^2\, \text{Cos}[\phi]^2 + \rho\, \text{Sin}[\theta]\, \text{Sin}[\phi]$

And now we integrate, replacing $dx\,dy\,dz$ with $\rho^2 \sin(\phi)\,d\rho\,d\phi\,d\theta$. Since we wish to integrate over a sphere of radius 2 centered at the origin, we choose as our bounds of integration $0 \le \rho \le 2$, $0 \le \phi \le \pi$, and $0 \le \theta \le 2\pi$. The result agrees with our earlier output, but it evaluates far more quickly due to the more simple bounds of integration.

$$\text{In[39]:=} \int_0^{2\pi}\left(\int_0^{\pi}\left(\int_0^2 \% * \rho^2 \, \text{Sin}[\phi]\, d\rho\right)d\phi\right)d\theta$$

$$\text{Out[39]=} \quad -\frac{128\,\pi}{15}$$

Exercises 6.4

1. Make a **Manipulate** with two controllers that displays a graph of the polar function $r = f(\theta) = \sin(n\,\theta)$, where n is allowed to vary from .01 to 3, and the variable θ assumes values from 0 to *length*, where *length* is permitted to vary from 2π to $100\,\pi$. The resulting curves are known as *roses*.

2. Explain how to use **ParametricPlot** to produce the same output as that produced by **PolarPlot** to view the graph of the polar function $r = f(\theta)$. Test your solution on the function $f(\theta) = \theta$.

3. Explain how to use **ParametricPlot** to produce the graph of the inverse polar function $\theta = f(r)$. Carry this out on the function $f(r) = r^2 - 2r + 1$ as r goes from 0 to 2.

4. Make a **Manipulate** to view various **PolarPlot**s of the *superformula* with polar equation
$r(\theta) = \left(\left|\cos\left(\frac{m\theta}{4}\right)\right|^{n_2} + \left|\sin\left(\frac{m\theta}{4}\right)\right|^{n_3}\right)^{\frac{-1}{n_1}}$. Use sliders that allow m, n_1, n_2, and n_3 to range from 1 to 20. Restrict m to assume only integer values in this range.

5. A *homotopy* between two surfaces is a smooth deformation from one surface to the other governed by a single real parameter t ranging from 0 to 1. Make a **Manipulate** that illustrates the homotopy from the Roman surface ($t = 0$) to the Boy surface ($t = 1$) given by:

$$x = \frac{\sqrt{2}\,\cos(2u)\cos^2 v + \cos u \sin(2v)}{2 - t\sqrt{2}\,\sin(3u)\sin(2v)},$$

$$y = \frac{\sqrt{2}\,\sin(2u)\cos^2 v - \sin u \sin(2v)}{2 - t\sqrt{2}\,\sin(3u)\sin(2v)},$$

$$z = \frac{3\cos^2 v}{2 - t\sqrt{2}\,\sin(3u)\sin(2v)},$$

where $-\frac{\pi}{2} \le u \le \frac{\pi}{2}$ and $0 \le v \le \pi$.

6.5 Vector Fields

Defining a Vector Field

Recall that a parameterized curve is a vector-valued function of one variable. That is, it's a function taking $\mathbb{R} \to \mathbb{R}^2$ or $\mathbb{R} \to \mathbb{R}^3$. A *vector field* is a vector-valued function of two or more variables. It is a function taking $\mathbb{R}^2 \to \mathbb{R}^2$ or $\mathbb{R}^3 \to \mathbb{R}^3$ (or in general: $\mathbb{R}^n \to \mathbb{R}^n$). You define a vector field exactly as you might expect:

In[1]:= **Clear[f, x, y];**
$$f = \{x^4 + y^4 - 6 x^2 y^2 - 1, \, 4 x^3 y - 4 x y^3\}$$

Out[2]= $\{-1 + x^4 - 6 x^2 y^2 + y^4, \, 4 x^3 y - 4 x y^3\}$

A three-dimensional vector field has three coordinate functions:

In[3]:= **Clear[g, x, y, z];**
$$g = \{y - z, \, z - x, \, x - y\}$$

Out[4]= $\{y - z, \, -x + z, \, x - y\}$

Plotting a Two-Dimensional Vector Field

You will need to load the **VectorFieldPlots** package:

In[5]:= **Needs["VectorFieldPlots`"]**

You now have access to the commands **VectorFieldPlot** and **VectorFieldPlot3D**:

In[6]:= **VectorFieldPlot[{y, x}, {x, −1, 1}, {y, −1, 1}]**

Out[6]=

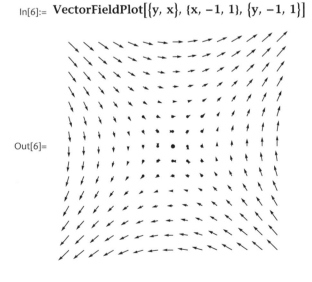

The first argument to **VectorFieldPlot** is the vector field to be plotted. It is followed by two iterators, one for each of the two coordinate variables. Each side of the rectangular domain is subdivided into 15 equal pieces, and at each of the $15 \times 15 = 225$ points of the resulting grid the tail of a vector is placed, the value of the vector field at that point. The lengths of the vectors are scaled so that even the longest vectors will not overlap one another. You can change the number of vectors displayed with the **PlotPoints** option. Set it to a positive integer such as 10 to view a 10×10 display. Set it to a list of two such integers such as $\{10, 5\}$ to view ten columns and five rows of vectors. Lower **Plot·. Points** settings will speed up the evaluation time, and in some cases, they can produce a more readable image. Note that by default the same scale is given to each axis.

In[7]:= **GraphicsRow**[{
    VectorFieldPlot[{y, x}, {x, −1, 1}, {y, 0, 1}, **PlotPoints** → 10],
    VectorFieldPlot[{y, x}, {x, −1, 1}, {y, 0, 1}, **PlotPoints** → {10, 5}]
}, **Dividers** → **All**]

Out[7]=

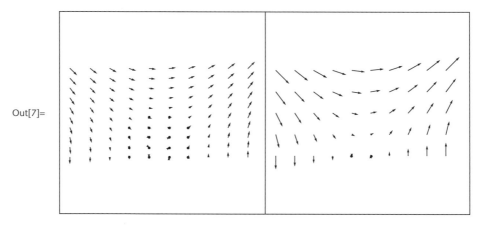

A related and sometimes useful command is **GradientFieldPlot**. The syntax for this command is identical to that of **Plot3D** and **ContourPlot**. It will essentially apply **VectorFieldPlot** to the *gradient* of the function given as the first argument. Below we superimpose a **ContourPlot** with a **Gradient·. FieldPlot** for the function $f(x, y) = xy$. The gradient of this function is $\langle y, x \rangle$, precisely the field we plotted earlier. Note that the gradient vector for any point is orthogonal to the level curve through that point. The gradient points in the direction of steepest ascent.

In[8]:= **Show[**
ContourPlot[x∗y, {x, −1, 1}, {y, −1, 1}, Contours → 20],
GradientFieldPlot[x∗y, {x, −1, 1}, {y, −1, 1}, PlotPoints → 10]]

Out[8]=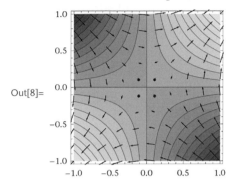

Note also that it is important to list the **ContourPlot** first to create this graphic. Had it been listed second, the contour plot would be overlaid on *top* of the vector field plot, and so would obscure it.

The command **VectorFieldPlot3D** is used to plot three-dimensional vector fields. By default, arrowheads are not drawn. The option setting **VectorHeads → True** can be used to add arrowheads.

In[9]:= **GraphicsRow[{**
VectorFieldPlot3D[{x, y, z}, {x, −1, 1}, {y, −1, 1}, {z, −1, 1}],
VectorFieldPlot3D[{x, y, z},
{x, −1, 1}, {y, −1, 1}, {z, −1, 1}, VectorHeads → True]
}, ImageSize → 260]

Out[9]=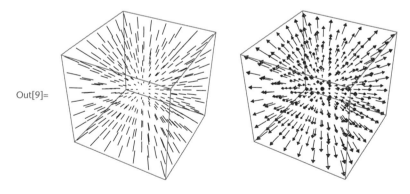

By default, there are seven vectors drawn in each coordinate direction, for a total of $7^3 = 343$ vectors in the plot. As before, this behavior can be modified via the **PlotPoints** option. And as you might expect, there is a **GradientFieldPlot3D** command, whose syntax precisely matches that of **Contour‧ Plot3D**. It can be used to plot the gradient field for a real-valued function of three variables. Below we show the gradient field for the function $f(x, y, z) = x^2 y − z$, and on the right we add three level surfaces for this function as well. Again, the gradient vectors are orthogonal to the level surfaces, and point in the direction of steepest ascent.

In[10]:= **GraphicsRow[{**
  GradientFieldPlot3D[$x^2 y - z$, {x, 0, 1},
    {y, 0, 1}, {z, 0, 1}, PlotPoints → 4, VectorHeads → True],
  Show[
    GradientFieldPlot3D[$x^2 y - z$, {x, 0, 1}, {y, 0, 1}, {z, 0, 1}, PlotPoints → 4],
    ContourPlot3D[$x^2 y - z$, {x, 0, 1}, {y, 0, 1}, {z, 0, 1},
      Contours → 3, Mesh → None, ContourStyle → Opacity[.8]]
  ]}, ImageSize → 260]

Out[10]=

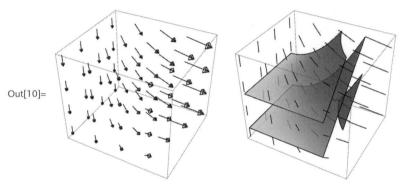

Divergence and Curl of a Three-Dimensional Vector Field

The *divergence* of a three-dimensional vector field $f(x, y, z) = f_1(x, y, z)\vec{i} + f_2(x, y, z)\vec{j} + f_3(x, y, z)\vec{k}$ is the real-valued function

$$\text{div}\, f(x, y, z) = \partial_x f_1 + \partial_y f_2 + \partial_z f_3.$$

The *curl* of f is the three-dimensional vector field

$$\text{curl}\, f(x, y, z) = \left(\partial_y f_3 - \partial_z f_2\right)\vec{i} + \left(\partial_z f_1 - \partial_x f_3\right)\vec{j} + \left(\partial_x f_2 - \partial_y f_1\right)\vec{k}.$$

The easiest way to compute divergence and curl with *Mathematica* is to load the **VectorAnalysis** package, which gives you access to the **Div** and **Curl** commands.

In[11]:= **Needs["VectorAnalysis`"]**

If you will be working in a single coordinate system, say in Cartesian coordinates, go ahead and set the coordinate system and name the coordinate variables. This should be done once. The default coordinate system is **Cartesian**, but the default coordinate variable names are **Xx**, **Yy**, and **Zz**, which may not be your first choice. Here we set the coordinate variable names to be **x**, **y**, and **z**:

In[12]:= **SetCoordinates[Cartesian[x, y, z]]**

Out[12]= Cartesian$[x, y, z]$

You are now ready to calculate:

In[13]:= **Div[{$x^2 y$, z, x y z}]**

Out[13]= $3 x y$

In[14]:= **Curl[{$x^2 y$, z, x y z}]**

Out[14]= $\{-1 + x z, -y z, -x^2\}$

If you will be doing calculations in other coordinate systems, you simply set the coordinate system and the coordinate variable names you would like to use. Typical choices are **Cartesian[x, y, z]**, as we used above, or **Cylindrical[r, θ, z]**, or **Spherical[ρ, ϕ, θ]**. The commands **Div** and **Curl** will accept a coordinate system specification as an optional second argument.

In[15]:= **Div[{r^2 z, $-\theta$, z}, Cylindrical[r, θ, z]]**

Out[15]= $\dfrac{-1 + r + 3 r^2 z}{r}$

In[16]:= **Curl[{r^2 z, $-\theta$, z}, Cylindrical[r, θ, z]]**

Out[16]= $\left\{0, r^2, -\dfrac{\theta}{r}\right\}$

Exercises 6.5

1. The option setting **ScaleFactor → None** may be added to **VectorFieldPlot** input to turn off the automatic scaling of vectors. While the vector fields are then drawn with perfect accuracy, the vectors may overlap one another. This exercise will illustrate that overlapping vectors can be confusing to view. This is why the default settings include vector scaling that prevents overlapping vectors.

   a. Sketch the vector field $F(x, y) = \langle y, x \rangle$, without vector scaling.

   b. Show that for this field, the head of *every* vector lies on the line $y = x$.

2. Use *Mathematica* to verify that the divergence of the curl of *any* vector field is zero.

6.6 Line Integrals and Surface Integrals

Line Integrals

Here is a parameterization of a curve $\vec{r}(t)$ that joins the point $(-1, -1)$ to the point $(2, 2)$ as t runs from -1 to 2:

In[1]:= **Clear[r, x, y, t];**
x[t_] := t;
y[t_] := $t^3 - t^2 - t$;
r[t_] := {x[t], y[t]}

In[5]:= **curve = ParametricPlot[r[t], {t, -1, 2}]**

Out[5]=

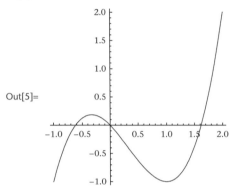

Here is a vector field in the plane:

In[6]:= **Clear[f];**
f[x_, y_] := $\{x^4 + y^4 - 6x^2y^2 - 1, 4x^3y - 4xy^3\}$

And here we superimpose a plot of the vector field with a plot of the curve:

In[8]:= **Needs["VectorFieldPlots`"]**

In[9]:= **Show[VectorFieldPlot[f[x, y], {x, -1, 2}, {y, -1, 2}, PlotPoints → 10], curve]**

Out[9]=

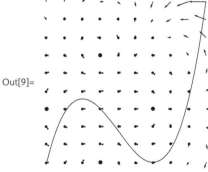

The calculation of the line integral $\int \vec{f} \cdot d\vec{r}$ is straightforward. Here is the integrand:

In[10]:= $\mathbf{f[x[t], y[t]].r'[t] // Simplify}$

Out[10]= $-1 - 4\,t^4 - 16\,t^5 - 12\,t^6 + 40\,t^7 + 41\,t^8 - 64\,t^9 - 18\,t^{10} + 40\,t^{11} - 11\,t^{12}$

And here is the integral:

In[11]:= $\displaystyle\int_{-1}^{2} \% \, d\mathbf{t}$

Out[11]= $\dfrac{54\,102}{5005}$

In[12]:= $\mathbf{N[\%]}$

Out[12]= 10.8096

Line integrals in three or more dimensions are just as easy to evaluate. Plots for three dimensions will require the commands **ParametricPlot3D** and **VectorFieldPlot3D**.

Surface Integrals

Here is a surface:

In[13]:= $\mathbf{Clear[\Phi, u, v, x, y, z]};$
$\mathbf{x[u\_, v\_] := \left(1 - v^2\right) Sin[u]};$
$\mathbf{y[u\_, v\_] := \left(1 - v^2\right) Sin[2\,u]};$
$\mathbf{z[u\_, v\_] := v};$
$\mathbf{\Phi[u\_, v\_] := \{x[u, v], y[u, v], z[u, v]\}}$

In[18]:= $\mathbf{surface = ParametricPlot3D\big[\Phi[u, v], \{u, 0, 2\,\pi\},}$
$\mathbf{\{v, -1, 1\}, Mesh \rightarrow None, PlotStyle \rightarrow Opacity[.8]\big]}$

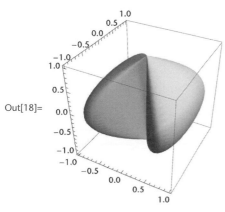

Out[18]=

And here is a three-dimensional vector field:

In[19]:= **Clear[f];**

$$f[x\_, y\_, z\_] := \left\{2\,x,\, 2\,x\,y,\, \frac{1}{z}\right\}$$

In[21]:= **Needs["VectorFieldPlots`"]**

In[22]:= **Show$\left[\text{VectorFieldPlot3D}[f[x, y, z],\right.$**
$\{x, -1, 1\},\, \{y, -1, 1\},\, \{z, -1, 1\},\, \text{PlotPoints} \to 8],\, \text{surface}\big]$

Out[22]=

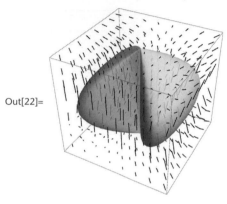

The surface integral can be evaluated with ease. Here is the integrand. Be sure to use the cross product (×) and not the (larger) multiplication operator (×) when pulling that symbol from the BasicMathInput palette.

In[23]:= **$f[x[u, v], y[u, v], z[u, v]].(\partial_u\, \Phi[u, v] \times \partial_v\, \Phi[u, v])$**

Out[23]= $2\left(1 - v^2\right)\left(2\,\text{Cos}[2\,u] - 2\,v^2\,\text{Cos}[2\,u]\right)\text{Sin}[u] + 2\left(1 - v^2\right)^2\left(-\text{Cos}[u] + v^2\,\text{Cos}[u]\right)\text{Sin}[u]\,\text{Sin}[2\,u] +$
$\dfrac{1}{v}\left(4\,v\,\text{Cos}[2\,u]\,\text{Sin}[u] - 4\,v^3\,\text{Cos}[2\,u]\,\text{Sin}[u] - 2\,v\,\text{Cos}[u]\,\text{Sin}[2\,u] + 2\,v^3\,\text{Cos}[u]\,\text{Sin}[2\,u]\right)$

In[24]:= **Simplify[%]**

Out[24]= $\left(-1 + v^2\right)\text{Sin}[u]$
$\left(2 + \left(-6 + 4\,v^2\right)\text{Cos}[2\,u] + \left(-1 + v^2\right)^2\,\text{Sin}[u] + \text{Sin}[3\,u] - 2\,v^2\,\text{Sin}[3\,u] + v^4\,\text{Sin}[3\,u]\right)$

And here we evaluate the integral:

In[25]:= $\displaystyle\int_{-1}^{1}\left(\int_{0}^{2\pi} \% \, d\mathbf{u}\right)d\mathbf{v}$

Out[25]= $-\dfrac{32\,\pi}{35}$

Exercises 6.6

1. Consider the vector field $\vec{F}(x, y) = \frac{\langle -y,x \rangle}{\sqrt{x^2+y^2}}$.

    a. Plot this vector field on the domain $-2 \le x \le 2$, $-2 \le y \le 2$.

    b. Let $r(t) = \langle t, t \rangle$. Sketch this curve for $0 \le t \le 2$, and superimpose it with the plot above.

    c. Evaluate the line integral $\int \vec{F} \cdot d\vec{r}$ for $0 \le t \le 2$.

    d. Let $r(t) = \langle t, t^3 - t^2 - t \rangle$. Sketch this curve for $0 \le t \le 2$, and superimpose it with the plot from part a.

    e. Evaluate the line integral $\int \vec{F} \cdot d\vec{r}$ for $0 \le t \le 2$.

2. Consider the vector field $\vec{F}(x, y) = \langle \cos(y) \cos(x \cos(y)), -x \cos(x \cos(y)) \sin(y) \rangle$.

    a. Show that this is a gradient field, and superimpose its plot with a contour plot of its potential function on the domain $-2 \le x \le 2, -2 \le y \le 2$.

    b. Evaluate the line integral $\int \vec{F} \cdot d\vec{r}$ for any curve $\vec{r}(t)$ from $(-\pi/2, 0)$ to $(\pi/2, 0)$.

7
Linear Algebra

7.1 Matrices

Entering Matrices

Traditionally, matrices are denoted by capital letters, but in *Mathematica* you will want to use lowercase letters, since capitals are reserved for built-in functions. If you really can't live in a world where matrices are denoted by lowercase letters, you can use uppercase letters provided you do *not* use those letters that are the names of built-in commands or constants: C, D, E, I, K, N, and O.

To enter a matrix in *Mathematica* first type the name of your matrix followed by an equal sign. Then select Table/Matrix ▷ New... in the Insert menu. A dialogue box will appear. Select Matrix and enter the correct number of rows and columns, then click OK. A matrix of the appropriate dimensions will appear in a fresh input cell with a placeholder for each entry. Click on the first placeholder and type a value, and then use the ⏀ key to move to the next entry. Enter the cell when you have finished:

$$\text{In[1]:= } \mathbf{mat1} = \begin{pmatrix} 2 & 3 & 4 & 5 & 6 & 7 \\ 1 & 1 & 1 & 1 & 1 & 1 \\ 4 & 5 & 4 & 5 & 4 & 5 \\ 11 & 2 & 2 & 2 & 2 & 2 \\ 0 & 0 & 0 & 0 & 0 & 1 \end{pmatrix}$$

Out[1]= {{2, 3, 4, 5, 6, 7}, {1, 1, 1, 1, 1, 1}, {4, 5, 4, 5, 4, 5}, {11, 2, 2, 2, 2, 2}, {0, 0, 0, 0, 0, 1}}

Look carefully at the output above. *Mathematica* thinks of a matrix as a list of lists. Each row is enclosed in curly brackets with entries separated by commas, the rows are separated by commas, and the entire matrix is enclosed in curly brackets. You can enter a matrix in this form also, but it can be a little messy:

In[2]:= **mat2 = {{1, 2, 3}, {3, 4, 5}, {5, 6, 7}}**

Out[2]= {{1, 2, 3}, {3, 4, 5}, {5, 6, 7}}

The command **MatrixForm** will produce a nicely formatted rectangular array with brackets on the sides. It is best not to use the **MatrixForm** command when defining a matrix, as it would then be impossible to perform some operations. It is better to simply request that the output be in **Matrix·Form** whenever you want a nice look at your matrix:

In[3]:= **mat2 // MatrixForm**

Out[3]//MatrixForm=

$$\begin{pmatrix} 1 & 2 & 3 \\ 3 & 4 & 5 \\ 5 & 6 & 7 \end{pmatrix}$$

You can request that *Mathematica* output every matrix in **MatrixForm** by typing the following command at the beginning of a session:

In[4]:= **$Post := If[MatrixQ[#], MatrixForm[#], #] &**

In[5]:= **mat1**

Out[5]//MatrixForm=

$$\begin{pmatrix} 2 & 3 & 4 & 5 & 6 & 7 \\ 1 & 1 & 1 & 1 & 1 & 1 \\ 4 & 5 & 4 & 5 & 4 & 5 \\ 11 & 2 & 2 & 2 & 2 & 2 \\ 0 & 0 & 0 & 0 & 0 & 1 \end{pmatrix}$$

In order to avoid confusion we will continue to affix //**MatrixForm** to all our inputs in this chapter.

⚠ **$Post** is a global variable whose value, if set, is a function that will be applied to every output generated in the current session. The simplest setting would be something like **$Post:=MatrixForm**, which would put *every* output cell into **MatrixForm**. This would work if every output were a matrix, but it would produce unwanted behavior if nonmatrix output were generated. Hence the rather intimidating setting above.

The command **If[MatrixQ[#], MatrixForm[#], #]&** is an example of something called a *pure function*. It looks rather fancy and cryptic, but the idea of a pure function is quite simple, and from the perspective of programming, is also quite elegant. In order to understand the working of a pure function, you need to understand the two symbols # and &. The symbol # represents the argument of the function, and the symbol & is used to separate the definition of the function from the argument. So, for instance, the input #^{2}&[3] would produce the output **9**. In essence, we have created a function whose name #^{2}& reveals precisely what it does. See Section 8.4 for a discussion of pure functions.

In the **If[MatrixQ[#], MatrixForm[#], #]&** example above, things are only a little more complicated. Understand first that the argument # will represent an output generated in the current session. The effect of the function will be to put matrix output into **MatrixForm**, but to leave nonmatrix output alone. This is accomplished with the **If** command, which takes three arguments. The first is a condition. The second is what is returned if the condition is true. The third is what is returned if the condition is false. The condition is checked with the

> **MatrixQ** command. **MatrixQ[x]** returns **True** if x is a matrix and **False** otherwise.

Mathematica is happy to report the dimensions of your matrix. When fed a matrix as input, the **Dimensions** command returns a list containing the number of rows and columns in the matrix, respectively:

In[6]:= **Dimensions[mat1]**

Out[6]= {5, 6}

There are several commands that produce matrices quickly. To get a 3×5 matrix with random integer entries between 0 and 50, type:

In[7]:= **RandomInteger[50, {3, 5}] // MatrixForm**

Out[7]//MatrixForm=

$$\begin{pmatrix} 40 & 2 & 41 & 39 & 33 \\ 19 & 44 & 44 & 1 & 10 \\ 30 & 36 & 8 & 42 & 21 \end{pmatrix}$$

The familiar **Table** command is easy to use. The next command gives a 5×5 matrix whose i, jth entry is $i + 2j$:

In[8]:= **Table[i + 2 j, {i, 5}, {j, 5}] // MatrixForm**

Out[8]//MatrixForm=

$$\begin{pmatrix} 3 & 5 & 7 & 9 & 11 \\ 4 & 6 & 8 & 10 & 12 \\ 5 & 7 & 9 & 11 & 13 \\ 6 & 8 & 10 & 12 & 14 \\ 7 & 9 & 11 & 13 & 15 \end{pmatrix}$$

The iterators can be set to start at values other than 1:

In[9]:= **Table[i + 2 j, {i, −2, 3}, {j, 0, 2}] // MatrixForm**

Out[9]//MatrixForm=

$$\begin{pmatrix} -2 & 0 & 2 \\ -1 & 1 & 3 \\ 0 & 2 & 4 \\ 1 & 3 & 5 \\ 2 & 4 & 6 \\ 3 & 5 & 7 \end{pmatrix}$$

To get a 3×4 zero matrix you can type this:

In[10]:= **Table[0, {3}, {4}] // MatrixForm**

Out[10]//MatrixForm=

$$\begin{pmatrix} 0 & 0 & 0 & 0 \\ 0 & 0 & 0 & 0 \\ 0 & 0 & 0 & 0 \end{pmatrix}$$

You can also produce a zero matrix by using Table/Matrix ▷ New... in the Insert menu. Just check the Fill with 0 box. Yet another way is to use the command **ConstantArray**, like this:

In[11]:= **ConstantArray[π, {3, 5}] // MatrixForm**

Out[11]//MatrixForm=

$$\begin{pmatrix} \pi & \pi & \pi & \pi & \pi \\ \pi & \pi & \pi & \pi & \pi \\ \pi & \pi & \pi & \pi & \pi \end{pmatrix}$$

We can produce a 4×4 lower triangular matrix with entries on and below the diagonal equal to $i + 2j$, and above the diagonal equal to 0, by typing:

In[12]:= **Table$\left[\text{If}\left[i \geq j, i + 2j, 0\right], \{i, 4\}, \{j, 4\}\right]$ // MatrixForm**

Out[12]//MatrixForm=

$$\begin{pmatrix} 3 & 0 & 0 & 0 \\ 4 & 6 & 0 & 0 \\ 5 & 7 & 9 & 0 \\ 6 & 8 & 10 & 12 \end{pmatrix}$$

The **If** command takes three arguments. The first is a condition or predicate, i.e., an expression that evaluates to either **True** or **False**. The second is the expression to evaluate if the condition is true. The third is the expression to evaluate if the condition is false. **If** is discussed in Section 8.5.

The **Array** command works much like the **Table** command but uses a function (either built-in or user-defined) rather than an expression to compute the entries. For a function f that takes two arguments, the command **Array[f, {m, n}]** gives the $m \times n$ matrix whose i, jth entry is $f(i, j)$. For example, using the built-in function **Min** for f produces a matrix where each entry is the minimum of the row number and column number of that entry's position:

In[13]:= **Array[Min, {4, 5}] // MatrixForm**

Out[13]//MatrixForm=

$$\begin{pmatrix} 1 & 1 & 1 & 1 & 1 \\ 1 & 2 & 2 & 2 & 2 \\ 1 & 2 & 3 & 3 & 3 \\ 1 & 2 & 3 & 4 & 4 \end{pmatrix}$$

Here is a second example, this time with a user-defined function:

In[14]:= **Clear[f];**
f[i_, j_] := i³ + j²;
Array[f, {2, 3}] // MatrixForm

Out[16]//MatrixForm=
$$\begin{pmatrix} 2 & 5 & 10 \\ 9 & 12 & 17 \end{pmatrix}$$

We can use the **Array** command to produce a general 3×4 matrix whose i, jth entry (the entry in row i and column j) is a_{ij}.

In[17]:= **Clear[a, mat];**
mat = Array[a_{##} &, {3, 4}]; mat // MatrixForm

Out[18]//MatrixForm=
$$\begin{pmatrix} a_{1,1} & a_{1,2} & a_{1,3} & a_{1,4} \\ a_{2,1} & a_{2,2} & a_{2,3} & a_{2,4} \\ a_{3,1} & a_{3,2} & a_{3,3} & a_{3,4} \end{pmatrix}$$

The command below gives the identity matrix.

In[19]:= **IdentityMatrix[4] // MatrixForm**

Out[19]//MatrixForm=
$$\begin{pmatrix} 1 & 0 & 0 & 0 \\ 0 & 1 & 0 & 0 \\ 0 & 0 & 1 & 0 \\ 0 & 0 & 0 & 1 \end{pmatrix}$$

This can also be accomplished using Table/Matrix ▷ New… in the Insert menu by checking the Fill with 0 and Fill Diagonal with 1 boxes.

The following command gives a diagonal matrix with the enclosed list on the diagonal:

In[20]:= **DiagonalMatrix[{a, b, c, d}] // MatrixForm**

Out[20]//MatrixForm=
$$\begin{pmatrix} a & 0 & 0 & 0 \\ 0 & b & 0 & 0 \\ 0 & 0 & c & 0 \\ 0 & 0 & 0 & d \end{pmatrix}$$

We can also use **DiagonalMatrix** to create a superdiagonal matrix.

In[21]:= **DiagonalMatrix[{a, b, c}, 1] // MatrixForm**

Out[21]//MatrixForm=

$$\begin{pmatrix} 0 & a & 0 & 0 \\ 0 & 0 & b & 0 \\ 0 & 0 & 0 & c \\ 0 & 0 & 0 & 0 \end{pmatrix}$$

Or a subdiagonal matrix:

In[22]:= **DiagonalMatrix[{a, b, c}, −1] // MatrixForm**

Out[22]//MatrixForm=

$$\begin{pmatrix} 0 & 0 & 0 & 0 \\ a & 0 & 0 & 0 \\ 0 & b & 0 & 0 \\ 0 & 0 & c & 0 \end{pmatrix}$$

Editing Matrices

It is a simple matter to add another row or column to an existing matrix. Start with either a matrix generated by the Table/Matrix ▷ New... dialogue box, or any **MatrixForm** output. To add a row, click on the matrix just above where you want a new row to appear and press the key combination ⃞CTRL⃞⏎. A row of placeholders will appear. To add a new column, click on the matrix where you want the new column to appear. Press the key combination ⃞CTRL⃞, and a column of placeholders will appear. If the original matrix appeared in a **MatrixForm** output cell, the modified matrix will appear in a new input cell. You can also use the Table/Matrix menu for these tasks: look in the submenu for Add Row and Add Column:

In[23]:= **mat1 =** $\begin{pmatrix} 2 & 3 & 4 & 5 & \square & 6 & 7 \\ 1 & 1 & 1 & 1 & \square & 1 & 1 \\ \square & \square & \square & \square & \square & \square & \square \\ 4 & 5 & 4 & 5 & \square & 4 & 5 \\ 11 & 2 & 2 & 2 & \square & 2 & 2 \\ 0 & 0 & 0 & 0 & \square & 0 & 1 \end{pmatrix}$ **;**

To form a new matrix from existing matrices we use the command **ArrayFlatten**. This command allows us to use entire matrices as if they are individual entries in a matrix. Thus the following command will stack the matrices **mat1** and **mat2** on top of each other. We use curly brackets, {}, to indicate that each matrix should be treated as a row in the new matrix and then "flattened" into a single matrix. This command will only return a matrix if the input matrices have the same number of columns.

In[24]:= **mat1 = RandomInteger[9, {3, 4}];**
mat1 // MatrixForm

Out[25]//MatrixForm=
$$\begin{pmatrix} 8 & 1 & 7 & 7 \\ 6 & 9 & 5 & 6 \\ 0 & 8 & 0 & 7 \end{pmatrix}$$

In[26]:= **mat2 = RandomInteger[9, {3, 4}];**
mat2 // MatrixForm

Out[27]//MatrixForm=
$$\begin{pmatrix} 0 & 3 & 3 & 6 \\ 9 & 2 & 8 & 1 \\ 7 & 7 & 8 & 9 \end{pmatrix}$$

In[28]:= **ArrayFlatten[{{mat1}, {mat2}}] // MatrixForm**

Out[28]//MatrixForm=
$$\begin{pmatrix} 8 & 1 & 7 & 7 \\ 6 & 9 & 5 & 6 \\ 0 & 8 & 0 & 7 \\ 0 & 3 & 3 & 6 \\ 9 & 2 & 8 & 1 \\ 7 & 7 & 8 & 9 \end{pmatrix}$$

To form the matrix consisting of **mat1** and **mat2** side by side we use curly brackets to indicate that the individual matrices should form a single row.

In[29]:= **ArrayFlatten[{{mat1, mat2}}] // MatrixForm**

Out[29]//MatrixForm=
$$\begin{pmatrix} 8 & 1 & 7 & 7 & 0 & 3 & 3 & 6 \\ 6 & 9 & 5 & 6 & 9 & 2 & 8 & 1 \\ 0 & 8 & 0 & 7 & 7 & 7 & 8 & 9 \end{pmatrix}$$

One can also form a *block matrix*. Below we have a matrix comprised of four blocks, where **mat1** appears in the upper left position, and **mat2** appears in the lower right position. The remaining positions are comprised entirely of zeros.

In[30]:= **bm = ArrayFlatten[{{mat1, 0}, {0, mat2}}];**
bm // MatrixForm

Out[31]//MatrixForm=

$$\begin{pmatrix} 8 & 1 & 7 & 7 & 0 & 0 & 0 & 0 \\ 6 & 9 & 5 & 6 & 0 & 0 & 0 & 0 \\ 0 & 8 & 0 & 7 & 0 & 0 & 0 & 0 \\ 0 & 0 & 0 & 0 & 0 & 3 & 3 & 6 \\ 0 & 0 & 0 & 0 & 9 & 2 & 8 & 1 \\ 0 & 0 & 0 & 0 & 7 & 7 & 8 & 9 \end{pmatrix}$$

Using **Grid** instead of **MatrixForm**, we can make the blocks easily visible:

In[32]:= **Grid[bm, Dividers → {{5 → True}, {4 → True}}, Frame → True]**

Out[32]=

8	1	7	7	0	0	0	0
6	9	5	6	0	0	0	0
0	8	0	7	0	0	0	0
0	0	0	0	0	3	3	6
0	0	0	0	9	2	8	1
0	0	0	0	7	7	8	9

The **Take** command can be used to extract submatrices of a given matrix. We'll use a general 5×5 matrix to get a good look at what is happening:

In[33]:= **Clear[a, mat];**
mat = Array[a## &, {5, 5}]; mat // MatrixForm

Out[34]//MatrixForm=

$$\begin{pmatrix} a_{1,1} & a_{1,2} & a_{1,3} & a_{1,4} & a_{1,5} \\ a_{2,1} & a_{2,2} & a_{2,3} & a_{2,4} & a_{2,5} \\ a_{3,1} & a_{3,2} & a_{3,3} & a_{3,4} & a_{3,5} \\ a_{4,1} & a_{4,2} & a_{4,3} & a_{4,4} & a_{4,5} \\ a_{5,1} & a_{5,2} & a_{5,3} & a_{5,4} & a_{5,5} \end{pmatrix}$$

Take can be used with 2 or 3 arguments. The first argument is the matrix name, the second indicates which rows are desired, the optional third argument indicates the columns. The following command will return the first three rows of the matrix **mat**:

In[35]:= **Take[mat, 3] // MatrixForm**

Out[35]//MatrixForm=

$$\begin{pmatrix} a_{1,1} & a_{1,2} & a_{1,3} & a_{1,4} & a_{1,5} \\ a_{2,1} & a_{2,2} & a_{2,3} & a_{2,4} & a_{2,5} \\ a_{3,1} & a_{3,2} & a_{3,3} & a_{3,4} & a_{3,5} \end{pmatrix}$$

This command will return the last two rows:

In[36]:= **Take[mat, −2] // MatrixForm**

Out[36]//MatrixForm=

$$\begin{pmatrix} a_{4,1} & a_{4,2} & a_{4,3} & a_{4,4} & a_{4,5} \\ a_{5,1} & a_{5,2} & a_{5,3} & a_{5,4} & a_{5,5} \end{pmatrix}$$

To get rows 2 through 4 we use a list:

In[37]:= **Take[mat, {2, 4}] // MatrixForm**

Out[37]//MatrixForm=

$$\begin{pmatrix} a_{2,1} & a_{2,2} & a_{2,3} & a_{2,4} & a_{2,5} \\ a_{3,1} & a_{3,2} & a_{3,3} & a_{3,4} & a_{3,5} \\ a_{4,1} & a_{4,2} & a_{4,3} & a_{4,4} & a_{4,5} \end{pmatrix}$$

If we want every other row we can enter:

In[38]:= **Take[mat, {1, −1, 2}] // MatrixForm**

Out[38]//MatrixForm=

$$\begin{pmatrix} a_{1,1} & a_{1,2} & a_{1,3} & a_{1,4} & a_{1,5} \\ a_{3,1} & a_{3,2} & a_{3,3} & a_{3,4} & a_{3,5} \\ a_{5,1} & a_{5,2} & a_{5,3} & a_{5,4} & a_{5,5} \end{pmatrix}$$

The list $\{1, -1, 2\}$ above indicates that we want to start at the first row, end at the last row, and increase the index of the selected rows by 2. In a matrix with 5 rows you could equivalently use the list $\{1, 5, 2\}$.

If we use 3 arguments we can select rows and columns.

In[39]:= **Take[mat, 2, −4] // MatrixForm**

Out[39]//MatrixForm=

$$\begin{pmatrix} a_{1,2} & a_{1,3} & a_{1,4} & a_{1,5} \\ a_{2,2} & a_{2,3} & a_{2,4} & a_{2,5} \end{pmatrix}$$

So to extract columns we use **All** for the second entry. To get the last 3 columns enter:

In[40]:= **Take[mat, All, −3] // MatrixForm**

Out[40]//MatrixForm=

$$\begin{pmatrix} a_{1,3} & a_{1,4} & a_{1,5} \\ a_{2,3} & a_{2,4} & a_{2,5} \\ a_{3,3} & a_{3,4} & a_{3,5} \\ a_{4,3} & a_{4,4} & a_{4,5} \\ a_{5,3} & a_{5,4} & a_{5,5} \end{pmatrix}$$

We can extract a submatrix by indicating a range of values for the rows and columns in lists,

In[41]:= **Take[mat, {2, 4}, {3, 5}] // MatrixForm**

Out[41]//MatrixForm=

$$\begin{pmatrix} a_{2,3} & a_{2,4} & a_{2,5} \\ a_{3,3} & a_{3,4} & a_{3,5} \\ a_{4,3} & a_{4,4} & a_{4,5} \end{pmatrix}$$

Or we could ask for the submatrix consisting of only the first and fourth rows and the second and fourth columns.

In[42]:= **Take[mat, {1, 4, 3}, {2, 4, 2}] // MatrixForm**

Out[42]//MatrixForm=

$$\begin{pmatrix} a_{1,2} & a_{1,4} \\ a_{4,2} & a_{4,4} \end{pmatrix}$$

The **Span** command is an alternative to **Take**. The notation is similar and slightly more efficient. A **Span** is indicated by the ;; symbol. The name of the command is not needed. The previous **Take** command is equivalent to the following using **Span**:

In[43]:= **mat〚1 ;; 4 ;; 3, 2 ;; 4 ;; 2〛 // MatrixForm**

Out[43]//MatrixForm=

$$\begin{pmatrix} a_{1,2} & a_{1,4} \\ a_{4,2} & a_{4,4} \end{pmatrix}$$

Exercises 7.1

1. Use the **Table** command to enter a matrix with the integers 1 through 10 on the diagonal, 0 below the diagonal, and 1 above the diagonal.

2. Consider the block matrix shown below. Write a custom command **blockMatrix** that will generate matrices of any size of this form. For instance, the output below should result from **blockMatrix[5]//MatrixForm**.

$$\begin{pmatrix}
1 & 0 & 0 & 0 & 0 & 0 & 0 & 0 & 0 & 0 & 0 & 0 & 0 & 0 & 0 \\
0 & 2 & 2 & 0 & 0 & 0 & 0 & 0 & 0 & 0 & 0 & 0 & 0 & 0 & 0 \\
0 & 2 & 2 & 0 & 0 & 0 & 0 & 0 & 0 & 0 & 0 & 0 & 0 & 0 & 0 \\
0 & 0 & 0 & 3 & 3 & 3 & 0 & 0 & 0 & 0 & 0 & 0 & 0 & 0 & 0 \\
0 & 0 & 0 & 3 & 3 & 3 & 0 & 0 & 0 & 0 & 0 & 0 & 0 & 0 & 0 \\
0 & 0 & 0 & 3 & 3 & 3 & 0 & 0 & 0 & 0 & 0 & 0 & 0 & 0 & 0 \\
0 & 0 & 0 & 0 & 0 & 0 & 4 & 4 & 4 & 4 & 0 & 0 & 0 & 0 & 0 \\
0 & 0 & 0 & 0 & 0 & 0 & 4 & 4 & 4 & 4 & 0 & 0 & 0 & 0 & 0 \\
0 & 0 & 0 & 0 & 0 & 0 & 4 & 4 & 4 & 4 & 0 & 0 & 0 & 0 & 0 \\
0 & 0 & 0 & 0 & 0 & 0 & 4 & 4 & 4 & 4 & 0 & 0 & 0 & 0 & 0 \\
0 & 0 & 0 & 0 & 0 & 0 & 0 & 0 & 0 & 0 & 5 & 5 & 5 & 5 & 5 \\
0 & 0 & 0 & 0 & 0 & 0 & 0 & 0 & 0 & 0 & 5 & 5 & 5 & 5 & 5 \\
0 & 0 & 0 & 0 & 0 & 0 & 0 & 0 & 0 & 0 & 5 & 5 & 5 & 5 & 5 \\
0 & 0 & 0 & 0 & 0 & 0 & 0 & 0 & 0 & 0 & 5 & 5 & 5 & 5 & 5 \\
0 & 0 & 0 & 0 & 0 & 0 & 0 & 0 & 0 & 0 & 5 & 5 & 5 & 5 & 5
\end{pmatrix}$$

7.2 Performing Gaussian Elimination

Referring to Parts of Matrices

Always remember that internally, *Mathematica* thinks of a matrix as a list of lists. So to refer to a part of a matrix we use the same notation discussed in Section 3.11 on page 126. The basic rule is that you use double square brackets to refer to individual items in a list:

In[1]:= **mat1 // MatrixForm**

Out[1]//MatrixForm=

$$\begin{pmatrix}
8 & 1 & 7 & 7 \\
6 & 9 & 5 & 6 \\
0 & 8 & 0 & 7
\end{pmatrix}$$

To get the second row, type:

In[2]:= **mat1[[2]]**

Out[2]= {6, 9, 5, 6}

Or use the ▪ button found on the BasicMathInput palette. We'll do this for the remainder of the chapter, since it looks a bit nicer:

In[3]:= **mat1[[2]]**

Out[3]= {6, 9, 5, 6}

To retrieve the entry in row 3, column 4, type:

In[4]:= $\mathbf{mat1}_{[3,4]}$

Out[4]= 7

To extract a single column indicate that you want all rows. For example, to get the third column type:

In[5]:= $\mathbf{mat1}_{[All,3]}$

Out[5]= {7, 5, 0}

Gaussian Elimination

A matrix is in *reduced row echelon form* if the first nonzero entry in each row is a 1 with only 0s above and beneath it. Furthermore, the rows must be arranged so that if one row begins with more 0s than another, then that row appears beneath the other. Any matrix can be put into reduced row echelon form by performing successive elementary row operations: multiplying a row by a nonzero constant, replacing a row by its sum with a multiple of another row, or interchanging two rows.

You can ask *Mathematica* to find the reduced row echelon form of a matrix by using the command **RowReduce**:

In[6]:= **Clear[mat];**

$$mat = \begin{pmatrix} 1 & 1 & 4 & 25 \\ 2 & 1 & 0 & 7 \\ -3 & 0 & 1 & -1 \end{pmatrix};$$

RowReduce[mat] // MatrixForm

Out[8]//MatrixForm=

$$\begin{pmatrix} 1 & 0 & 0 & 2 \\ 0 & 1 & 0 & 3 \\ 0 & 0 & 1 & 5 \end{pmatrix}$$

You can also perform "manual" row reduction. Use $\mathbf{mat}_{[i]}$ to refer to the ith row of the matrix **mat**. To replace the second row with the sum of the second row and −2 times the first row, type:

In[9]:= $\mathbf{mat}_{[2]} = \mathbf{mat}_{[2]} - 2\,\mathbf{mat}_{[1]};$
    mat // MatrixForm

Out[10]//MatrixForm=

$$\begin{pmatrix} 1 & 1 & 4 & 25 \\ 0 & -1 & -8 & -43 \\ -3 & 0 & 1 & -1 \end{pmatrix}$$

The first line performed the operation, and the semicolon suppressed the output; the second line asked *Mathematica* to display the revised matrix in **MatrixForm**. Next we can add 3 times the first row to the third row, and the second row to the first row:

In[11]:= $\mathbf{mat}_{[\![3]\!]} = \mathbf{mat}_{[\![3]\!]} + 3\,\mathbf{mat}_{[\![1]\!]};$
$\mathbf{mat}_{[\![1]\!]} = \mathbf{mat}_{[\![1]\!]} + \mathbf{mat}_{[\![2]\!]};$
$\mathbf{mat}\,/\!/\,\mathbf{MatrixForm}$

Out[13]//MatrixForm=
$$\begin{pmatrix} 1 & 0 & -4 & -18 \\ 0 & -1 & -8 & -43 \\ 0 & 3 & 13 & 74 \end{pmatrix}$$

Now add 3 times the second row to the third row:

In[14]:= $\mathbf{mat}_{[\![3]\!]} = \mathbf{mat}_{[\![3]\!]} + 3\,\mathbf{mat}_{[\![2]\!]};$
$\mathbf{mat}\,/\!/\,\mathbf{MatrixForm}$

Out[15]//MatrixForm=
$$\begin{pmatrix} 1 & 0 & -4 & -18 \\ 0 & -1 & -8 & -43 \\ 0 & 0 & -11 & -55 \end{pmatrix}$$

Finally, we can multiply the third row by $-\frac{1}{11}$, multiply the second row by -1, add -8 times the third row to the second row, and add 4 times the third row to the first row:

In[16]:= $\mathbf{mat}_{[\![3]\!]} = \left(-\dfrac{1}{11}\right)\mathbf{mat}_{[\![3]\!]};$

$\mathbf{mat}_{[\![2]\!]} = -1\,\mathbf{mat}_{[\![2]\!]};$
$\mathbf{mat}_{[\![2]\!]} = \mathbf{mat}_{[\![2]\!]} - 8\,\mathbf{mat}_{[\![3]\!]};$
$\mathbf{mat}_{[\![1]\!]} = \mathbf{mat}_{[\![1]\!]} + 4\,\mathbf{mat}_{[\![3]\!]};$
$\mathbf{mat}\,/\!/\,\mathbf{MatrixForm}$

Out[20]//MatrixForm=
$$\begin{pmatrix} 1 & 0 & 0 & 2 \\ 0 & 1 & 0 & 3 \\ 0 & 0 & 1 & 5 \end{pmatrix}$$

Exercises 7.2

1. Use row operations to write the matrix $\begin{pmatrix} 1 & 2 \\ 3 & 4 \end{pmatrix}$ as the product of an upper triangular matrix and an *elementary matrix*. An elementary matrix is a matrix that differs from the identity matrix by a single row operation.

7.3 Matrix Operations

If two matrices have the same dimensions, we can compute their sum by adding the corresponding entries of the two matrices. In *Mathematica*, as in ordinary mathematical notation, we use the + operator for matrix sums:

In[1]:= **mat3** = $\begin{pmatrix} 1 & 0 & 0 \\ 2 & 3 & 4 \\ -1 & 5 & -1 \end{pmatrix}$; **mat4** = $\begin{pmatrix} 2 & 2 & 3 \\ 0 & 0 & 1 \\ 5 & 5 & 5 \end{pmatrix}$;

mat3 + mat4 // MatrixForm

Out[2]//MatrixForm=

$$\begin{pmatrix} 3 & 2 & 3 \\ 2 & 3 & 5 \\ 4 & 10 & 4 \end{pmatrix}$$

We can also find their difference:

In[3]:= **mat3 − mat4 // MatrixForm**

Out[3]//MatrixForm=

$$\begin{pmatrix} -1 & -2 & -3 \\ 2 & 3 & 3 \\ -6 & 0 & -6 \end{pmatrix}$$

We can perform scalar multiplication:

In[4]:= **7 ∗ mat3 // MatrixForm**

Out[4]//MatrixForm=

$$\begin{pmatrix} 7 & 0 & 0 \\ 14 & 21 & 28 \\ -7 & 35 & -7 \end{pmatrix}$$

And we can multiply matrices. The *i, j*th entry of the *product* of the matrix **a** with the matrix **b** is the dot product of the *i*th row of **a** with the *j*th column of **b**. Multiplication is only possible if the number of columns of **a** is equal to the number of rows of **b**.

In *Mathematica*, use the dot (i.e., the period) as the multiplication operator for matrices:

In[5]:= **mat3.mat4 // MatrixForm**

Out[5]//MatrixForm=

$$\begin{pmatrix} 2 & 2 & 3 \\ 24 & 24 & 29 \\ -7 & -7 & -3 \end{pmatrix}$$

Be careful to use the dot to perform matrix multiplication. The symbol * will simply multiply corresponding entries in the two matrices (not a standard matrix operation):

In[6]:= **mat3 * mat4 // MatrixForm**

Out[6]//MatrixForm=

$$\begin{pmatrix} 2 & 0 & 0 \\ 0 & 0 & 4 \\ -5 & 25 & -5 \end{pmatrix}$$

The **Transpose** command will produce the transpose of a matrix, the matrix obtained by switching the rows and columns of that matrix:

In[7]:= **Transpose[mat3] // MatrixForm**

Out[7]//MatrixForm=

$$\begin{pmatrix} 1 & 2 & -1 \\ 0 & 3 & 5 \\ 0 & 4 & -1 \end{pmatrix}$$

To find a power of a matrix use the command **MatrixPower**. The first argument is the matrix, and the second argument is the desired power:

In[8]:= **MatrixPower[mat3, 10] // MatrixForm**

Out[8]//MatrixForm=

$$\begin{pmatrix} 1 & 0 & 0 \\ 10\,249\,364 & 36\,166\,989 & 20\,498\,728 \\ 7\,834\,130 & 25\,623\,410 & 15\,668\,261 \end{pmatrix}$$

The *inverse* of a square matrix, if it exists, is the matrix whose product with the original matrix is the identity matrix. A matrix that has an inverse is said to be *nonsingular*. You can find the inverse of a nonsingular matrix with the **Inverse** command:

In[9]:= **Inverse[mat3] // MatrixForm**

Out[9]//MatrixForm=

$$\begin{pmatrix} 1 & 0 & 0 \\ \frac{2}{23} & \frac{1}{23} & \frac{4}{23} \\ -\frac{13}{23} & \frac{5}{23} & -\frac{3}{23} \end{pmatrix}$$

It is a simple matter to check that the product of a matrix with its inverse is the identity:

In[10]:= **%.mat3 // MatrixForm**

Out[10]//MatrixForm=

$$\begin{pmatrix} 1 & 0 & 0 \\ 0 & 1 & 0 \\ 0 & 0 & 1 \end{pmatrix}$$

⚠ Note that the **%** in the last input represents the inverse of **mat3** rather than the **MatrixForm** of that inverse. This is the reason for the cell tag Out[73]//MatrixForm=. If you refer to any such output cell (with **%** or **%%**, for instance), *Mathematica* will use the output generated *before* **MatrixForm** was applied. In other words, the output is a matrix, it is only *displayed* in **MatrixForm**. This makes it easy to incorporate **MatrixForm** output into new input.

The *determinant* of a square matrix is a number that is nonzero if and only if the matrix is nonsingular. Determinants are notoriously painful to compute by hand, but are a snap with *Mathematica*'s **Det** command:

In[11]:= **Det[mat3]**

Out[11]= -23

Any matrix operation can be performed either on a matrix whose entries are numeric, or on a matrix whose entries are purely symbolic. For example, you can find the formula for the determinant of a general 3×3 matrix:

In[12]:= **Clear[a]; mat5 = Array[a## &, {3, 3}]; mat5 // MatrixForm**

Out[12]//MatrixForm=

$$\begin{pmatrix} a_{1,1} & a_{1,2} & a_{1,3} \\ a_{2,1} & a_{2,2} & a_{2,3} \\ a_{3,1} & a_{3,2} & a_{3,3} \end{pmatrix}$$

In[13]:= **Det[mat5]**

Out[13]= $-a_{1,3} a_{2,2} a_{3,1} + a_{1,2} a_{2,3} a_{3,1} + a_{1,3} a_{2,1} a_{3,2} - a_{1,1} a_{2,3} a_{3,2} - a_{1,2} a_{2,1} a_{3,3} + a_{1,1} a_{2,2} a_{3,3}$

Notice how the determinant arises naturally in the inverse of a matrix. Here is the entry in the first row and first column of the inverse of **mat5**:

In[14]:= **Inverse[mat5]₍₁,₁₎**

Out[14]= $\left(-a_{2,3} a_{3,2} + a_{2,2} a_{3,3} \right) \Big/$
$\left(-a_{1,3} a_{2,2} a_{3,1} + a_{1,2} a_{2,3} a_{3,1} + a_{1,3} a_{2,1} a_{3,2} - a_{1,1} a_{2,3} a_{3,2} - a_{1,2} a_{2,1} a_{3,3} + a_{1,1} a_{2,2} a_{3,3} \right)$

Here is the same entry with the determinant replaced by the symbol **det**:

In[15]:= **Inverse[mat5]₍₁,₁₎ /. Det[mat5] → det**

Out[15]= $\dfrac{-a_{2,3} a_{3,2} + a_{2,2} a_{3,3}}{det}$

The *trace* of a matrix is the sum of the entries along the main diagonal. The trace of a matrix may be calculated with the command **Tr**:

In[16]:= **Tr[mat5]**

Out[16]= $a_{1,1} + a_{2,2} + a_{3,3}$

Be careful, there is a command whose name is **Trace**, but it has nothing to do with linear algebra; don't use it to compute the trace of a matrix.

Exercises 7.3

1. Using the **Dividers** option to the **Grid** command, find a way to format a matrix with vertical bars on the sides instead of parentheses. It is handy to be able to do this when typesetting, as vertical bars are traditionally used to denote the determinant of the matrix they enclose. Use your result to typeset the following equation:

$$\begin{vmatrix} 1 & 2 \\ 3 & 4 \end{vmatrix} = -2.$$

2. Find the inverse of the matrix $\begin{pmatrix} 1 & 7 & 5 & 0 \\ 5 & 8 & 6 & 9 \\ 2 & 1 & 6 & 4 \\ 8 & 1 & 2 & 4 \end{pmatrix}$ by appending the identity matrix to this matrix and

then using Gaussian elimination to find the inverse.

7.4 Minors and Cofactors

Another command to be wary of is **Minors**. This command computes determinants of submatrices but not according to the traditional definition of minors. Traditionally, if A is a square matrix then the *minor* M_{ij} of entry a_{ij} is the determinant of the submatrix that remains after the ith row and jth column are deleted from A. $M = (M_{ij})$ is the matrix of minors. But the command **Minors** will return a matrix whose ijth entry is the determinant of the submatrix that remains after the $(n - i + 1)$st row and $(n - j + 1)$st column are deleted from A. Yes, this is really confusing, but see if you can see the difference in the examples below.

In[1]:= **Clear[a]; mat5 = Array[a## &, {3, 3}]; mat5 // MatrixForm**

Out[1]//MatrixForm=
$$\begin{pmatrix} a_{1,1} & a_{1,2} & a_{1,3} \\ a_{2,1} & a_{2,2} & a_{2,3} \\ a_{3,1} & a_{3,2} & a_{3,3} \end{pmatrix}$$

This is the matrix returned by the built in **Minors** command:

In[2]:= **Minors[mat5] // MatrixForm**

Out[2]//MatrixForm=

$$
\begin{pmatrix}
-a_{1,2}\,a_{2,1} + a_{1,1}\,a_{2,2} & -a_{1,3}\,a_{2,1} + a_{1,1}\,a_{2,3} & -a_{1,3}\,a_{2,2} + a_{1,2}\,a_{2,3} \\
-a_{1,2}\,a_{3,1} + a_{1,1}\,a_{3,2} & -a_{1,3}\,a_{3,1} + a_{1,1}\,a_{3,3} & -a_{1,3}\,a_{3,2} + a_{1,2}\,a_{3,3} \\
-a_{2,2}\,a_{3,1} + a_{2,1}\,a_{3,2} & -a_{2,3}\,a_{3,1} + a_{2,1}\,a_{3,3} & -a_{2,3}\,a_{3,2} + a_{2,2}\,a_{3,3}
\end{pmatrix}
$$

The custom command below will give us the traditional matrix of minors. Notice that the entries are the "reverse" of the entries above. The **Map** command is discussed in Section 8.4.

In[3]:= **minorsMatrix[m_List ? MatrixQ] := Map[Reverse, Minors[m], {0, 1}]**

In[4]:= **minorsMatrix[mat5] // MatrixForm**

Out[4]//MatrixForm=

$$
\begin{pmatrix}
-a_{2,3}\,a_{3,2} + a_{2,2}\,a_{3,3} & -a_{2,3}\,a_{3,1} + a_{2,1}\,a_{3,3} & -a_{2,2}\,a_{3,1} + a_{2,1}\,a_{3,2} \\
-a_{1,3}\,a_{3,2} + a_{1,2}\,a_{3,3} & -a_{1,3}\,a_{3,1} + a_{1,1}\,a_{3,3} & -a_{1,2}\,a_{3,1} + a_{1,1}\,a_{3,2} \\
-a_{1,3}\,a_{2,2} + a_{1,2}\,a_{2,3} & -a_{1,3}\,a_{2,1} + a_{1,1}\,a_{2,3} & -a_{1,2}\,a_{2,1} + a_{1,1}\,a_{2,2}
\end{pmatrix}
$$

To get a single minor, say M_{23} we can simply ask for that entry from the output of the **minorsMa⋅trix** command.

In[5]:= **minorsMatrix[mat5]⟦2,3⟧**

Out[5]= $-a_{1,2}\,a_{3,1} + a_{1,1}\,a_{3,2}$

The *matrix of cofactors* is the matrix whose *ij*th entry is $(-1)^{i+j}\,M_{ij}$. We can use our **minorsMatrix** command to compute a matrix of cofactors.

In[6]:= **cofactorsMatrix[m_List ? MatrixQ] :=**
   Table[(-1)^{i+j}, {i, Length[m]}, {j, Length[m]}] * minorsMatrix[m]

Notice that the * above will multiply the corresponding entries of the two matrices.

In[7]:= **cofactorsMatrix[mat5] // MatrixForm**

Out[7]//MatrixForm=

$$
\begin{pmatrix}
-a_{2,3}\,a_{3,2} + a_{2,2}\,a_{3,3} & a_{2,3}\,a_{3,1} - a_{2,1}\,a_{3,3} & -a_{2,2}\,a_{3,1} + a_{2,1}\,a_{3,2} \\
a_{1,3}\,a_{3,2} - a_{1,2}\,a_{3,3} & -a_{1,3}\,a_{3,1} + a_{1,1}\,a_{3,3} & a_{1,2}\,a_{3,1} - a_{1,1}\,a_{3,2} \\
-a_{1,3}\,a_{2,2} + a_{1,2}\,a_{2,3} & a_{1,3}\,a_{2,1} - a_{1,1}\,a_{2,3} & -a_{1,2}\,a_{2,1} + a_{1,1}\,a_{2,2}
\end{pmatrix}
$$

Finally, recall that the *adjoint* of a matrix is the transpose of its matrix of cofactors. There is a lovely relationship between the inverse of a matrix and its adjoint: $A^{-1} = \frac{1}{\det(A)}\,\mathrm{adj}(A)$. Let's use an example to illustrate this fact.

In[8]:= **Clear[mat];**
mat = RandomInteger[9, {4, 4}];
mat // MatrixForm

Out[10]//MatrixForm=

$$\begin{pmatrix} 8 & 1 & 2 & 9 \\ 6 & 0 & 9 & 8 \\ 7 & 9 & 5 & 7 \\ 8 & 0 & 2 & 6 \end{pmatrix}$$

In[11]:= $\left(\dfrac{1}{\text{Det[mat]}} \right)$ **Transpose[cofactorsMatrix[mat]] // MatrixForm**

Out[11]//MatrixForm=

$$\begin{pmatrix} -\dfrac{171}{803} & -\dfrac{35}{803} & \dfrac{19}{803} & \dfrac{281}{803} \\ -\dfrac{7}{803} & -\dfrac{39}{803} & \dfrac{90}{803} & -\dfrac{85}{1606} \\ -\dfrac{126}{803} & \dfrac{101}{803} & \dfrac{14}{803} & \dfrac{38}{803} \\ \dfrac{270}{803} & \dfrac{13}{803} & -\dfrac{30}{803} & -\dfrac{507}{1606} \end{pmatrix}$$

Did we get the correct inverse?

In[12]:= **%.mat // MatrixForm**

Out[12]//MatrixForm=

$$\begin{pmatrix} 1 & 0 & 0 & 0 \\ 0 & 1 & 0 & 0 \\ 0 & 0 & 1 & 0 \\ 0 & 0 & 0 & 1 \end{pmatrix}$$

We did indeed!

Exercises 7.4

1. Find the adjoint of $A = \begin{pmatrix} 8 & 0 & 3 & 7 \\ 9 & 4 & 2 & 9 \\ 2 & 8 & 0 & 7 \\ 8 & 9 & 7 & 0 \end{pmatrix}$ using the determinant and the inverse of A, then check your

answer using the **cofactorsMatrix** command.

2. Write a command to find the determinant of a matrix by cofactor expansion along the first row.

7.5 Working with Large Matrices

If you have a large matrix with only a few nonzero entries you can use the **SparseArray** command to enter, store, and work with the matrix efficiently. To create a **SparseArray** simply give the position and value for each nonzero entry of the matrix as follows:

In[1]:= **s1 = SparseArray[{{1, 1} → a, {2, 3} → b, {5, 2} → c, {6, 7} → d}]**

Out[1]= SparseArray[<4>, {6, 7}]

The output from the **SparseArray** command gives us the number of nonzero entries and then the dimensions of the matrix we've created. We can use **MatrixForm** to get a look at this matrix.

In[2]:= **s1 // MatrixForm**

Out[2]//MatrixForm=

$$\begin{pmatrix} a & 0 & 0 & 0 & 0 & 0 & 0 \\ 0 & 0 & b & 0 & 0 & 0 & 0 \\ 0 & 0 & 0 & 0 & 0 & 0 & 0 \\ 0 & 0 & 0 & 0 & 0 & 0 & 0 \\ 0 & c & 0 & 0 & 0 & 0 & 0 \\ 0 & 0 & 0 & 0 & 0 & 0 & d \end{pmatrix}$$

Equivalently, we can enter a list of positions and a list of corresponding values.

In[3]:= **s2 = SparseArray[{{1, 1}, {2, 3}, {5, 2}, {6, 7}} → {a, b, c, d}]**

Out[3]= SparseArray[<4>, {6, 7}]

In[4]:= **s2 // MatrixForm**

Out[4]//MatrixForm=

$$\begin{pmatrix} a & 0 & 0 & 0 & 0 & 0 & 0 \\ 0 & 0 & b & 0 & 0 & 0 & 0 \\ 0 & 0 & 0 & 0 & 0 & 0 & 0 \\ 0 & 0 & 0 & 0 & 0 & 0 & 0 \\ 0 & c & 0 & 0 & 0 & 0 & 0 \\ 0 & 0 & 0 & 0 & 0 & 0 & d \end{pmatrix}$$

SparseArray will create a matrix that fits all the nonzero entries we specify. We can also specify a matrix of a different size.

In[5]:= **s3 = SparseArray[{{1, 1}, {2, 3}, {5, 2}, {6, 7}} → {a, b, c, d}, {8, 10}]**

Out[5]= SparseArray[<4>, {8, 10}]

In[6]:= **s3 // MatrixForm**

Out[6]//MatrixForm=

$$\begin{pmatrix} a & 0 & 0 & 0 & 0 & 0 & 0 & 0 & 0 & 0 \\ 0 & 0 & b & 0 & 0 & 0 & 0 & 0 & 0 & 0 \\ 0 & 0 & 0 & 0 & 0 & 0 & 0 & 0 & 0 & 0 \\ 0 & 0 & 0 & 0 & 0 & 0 & 0 & 0 & 0 & 0 \\ 0 & c & 0 & 0 & 0 & 0 & 0 & 0 & 0 & 0 \\ 0 & 0 & 0 & 0 & 0 & 0 & d & 0 & 0 & 0 \\ 0 & 0 & 0 & 0 & 0 & 0 & 0 & 0 & 0 & 0 \\ 0 & 0 & 0 & 0 & 0 & 0 & 0 & 0 & 0 & 0 \end{pmatrix}$$

We can create a **SparseArray** in which the unspecified entries have a value other than zero.

In[7]:= **s4 = SparseArray[{{1, 1} → a, {2, 3} → b, {5, 2} → c}, {5, 5}, 2]**

Out[7]= SparseArray[<3>, {5, 5}, 2]

In[8]:= **s4 // MatrixForm**

Out[8]//MatrixForm=

$$\begin{pmatrix} a & 2 & 2 & 2 & 2 \\ 2 & 2 & b & 2 & 2 \\ 2 & 2 & 2 & 2 & 2 \\ 2 & 2 & 2 & 2 & 2 \\ 2 & c & 2 & 2 & 2 \end{pmatrix}$$

The **Normal** command will convert the output of **SparseArray** to the list form of a matrix.

In[9]:= **Normal[s4]**

Out[9]= {{a, 2, 2, 2, 2}, {2, 2, b, 2, 2}, {2, 2, 2, 2, 2}, {2, 2, 2, 2, 2}, {2, c, 2, 2, 2}}

We can use **Table** to help us list the nonzero entries of a large matrix. For example the command below creates a 16 by 12 matrix with 1s in positions (2, 3), (4, 6), (8, 9), and (16, 12).

In[10]:= **s5 = SparseArray[Table[{2^i, 3 i} → 1, {i, 4}]]**

Out[10]= SparseArray[<4>, {16, 12}]

This large matrix makes a mess if we ask for a numerical output, but a picture can tell us a lot about our matrix.

In[11]:= **MatrixPlot[s5]**

Out[11]=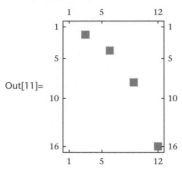

These plots will automatically color entries with larger values in a darker color.

In[12]:= **s6 = SparseArray$\left[\text{Table}\left[\{2^i, 3\,i\} \to i, \{i, 4\}\right]\right]$**

Out[12]= SparseArray[<4>, {16, 12}]

In[13]:= **MatrixPlot[s6]**

Out[13]=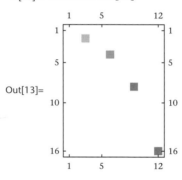

Sparse arrays can have more than two dimensions.

In[14]:= **s7 = SparseArray$\left[\text{Table}\left[\{2^i, 3\,i, i+1\} \to i, \{i, 4\}\right]\right]$**

Out[14]= SparseArray[<4>, {16, 12, 5}]

ArrayRules will return the positions and values we gave for a sparse array.

In[15]:= **ArrayRules[s7]**

Out[15]= {{2, 3, 2} → 1, {4, 6, 3} → 2, {8, 9, 4} → 3, {16, 12, 5} → 4, {_, _, _} → 0}

Band can be used with **SparseArray** to give a matrix in which a single value is present in each position on a diagonal beginning at the given starting position.

In[16]:=   **Clear[b];**
          SparseArray[{Band[{3, 2}] → 3, Band[{1, 4}] → b}, {6, 6}]

Out[17]=   SparseArray[<7>, {6, 6}]

In[18]:=   **% // MatrixForm**

Out[18]//MatrixForm=

$$
\begin{pmatrix}
0 & 0 & 0 & b & 0 & 0 \\
0 & 0 & 0 & 0 & b & 0 \\
0 & 3 & 0 & 0 & 0 & b \\
0 & 0 & 3 & 0 & 0 & 0 \\
0 & 0 & 0 & 3 & 0 & 0 \\
0 & 0 & 0 & 0 & 3 & 0
\end{pmatrix}
$$

Or a band can be a list of values.

In[19]:=   **SparseArray[Band[{3, 2}] → {2, 4, 6, 8}, {6, 6}]**

Out[19]=   SparseArray[<4>, {6, 6}]

In[20]:=   **% // MatrixForm**

Out[20]//MatrixForm=

$$
\begin{pmatrix}
0 & 0 & 0 & 0 & 0 & 0 \\
0 & 0 & 0 & 0 & 0 & 0 \\
0 & 2 & 0 & 0 & 0 & 0 \\
0 & 0 & 4 & 0 & 0 & 0 \\
0 & 0 & 0 & 6 & 0 & 0 \\
0 & 0 & 0 & 0 & 8 & 0
\end{pmatrix}
$$

Exercises 7.5

1. Use **SparseArray** to create the following picture:

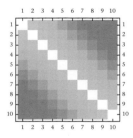

2. Use **SparseArray** to create the following matrix:

$$\begin{pmatrix} 1 & 2 & 0 & 0 & 0 & 0 & 0 & 0 & 0 & 0 & 0 & 0 \\ 3 & 4 & 0 & 0 & 0 & 0 & 0 & 0 & 0 & 0 & 0 & 0 \\ 0 & 0 & 1 & 2 & 0 & 0 & 0 & 0 & 0 & 0 & 0 & 0 \\ 0 & 0 & 3 & 4 & 0 & 0 & 0 & 0 & 0 & 0 & 0 & 0 \\ 0 & 0 & 0 & 0 & 1 & 2 & 0 & 0 & 0 & 0 & 0 & 0 \\ 0 & 0 & 0 & 0 & 3 & 4 & 0 & 0 & 0 & 0 & 0 & 0 \\ 0 & 0 & 0 & 0 & 0 & 0 & 1 & 2 & 0 & 0 & 0 & 0 \\ 0 & 0 & 0 & 0 & 0 & 0 & 3 & 4 & 0 & 0 & 0 & 0 \\ 0 & 0 & 0 & 0 & 0 & 0 & 0 & 0 & 1 & 2 & 0 & 0 \\ 0 & 0 & 0 & 0 & 0 & 0 & 0 & 0 & 3 & 4 & 0 & 0 \\ 0 & 0 & 0 & 0 & 0 & 0 & 0 & 0 & 0 & 0 & 1 & 2 \\ 0 & 0 & 0 & 0 & 0 & 0 & 0 & 0 & 0 & 0 & 3 & 4 \end{pmatrix}$$

7.6 Solving Systems of Linear Equations

Nonhomogeneous Systems of Linear Equations

Suppose we want to solve a system of linear equations in the form $mx = b$, where m is the coefficient matrix, x is a column vector of variables, and b is a column vector. Such a system is called *nonhomogeneous* when b is a vector with at least one nonzero entry. *Mathematica* offers several options for solving such a system, and we will explore each in turn. In this first example m is a nonsingular matrix and the system has a unique solution. Enter the equation $mx = b$ by typing **m.x==b**. Note how *Mathematica* interprets this equation:

In[1]:= **Clear[m, x, x1, x2, x3, x4, b];**

$$m = \begin{pmatrix} 1 & 5 & -4 & 1 \\ 3 & 4 & -1 & 2 \\ 3 & 2 & 1 & 5 \\ 0 & -6 & 7 & 1 \end{pmatrix}; \ x = \begin{pmatrix} x1 \\ x2 \\ x3 \\ x4 \end{pmatrix}; \ b = \begin{pmatrix} 1 \\ 2 \\ 3 \\ 4 \end{pmatrix};$$

m.x == b

Out[3]= {{x1 + 5 x2 − 4 x3 + x4}, {3 x1 + 4 x2 − x3 + 2 x4},
     {3 x1 + 2 x2 + x3 + 5 x4}, {−6 x2 + 7 x3 + x4}} == {{1}, {2}, {3}, {4}}

We can interpret this as a list of four linear equations, each in four variables.

Just to be sure let's check that m is nonsingular:

In[4]:= **Det[m]**

Out[4]= 35

We now use the command **ArrayFlatten** to form the augmented matrix, and the command **RowRe**·. **duce** to find the reduced row echelon form of the matrix.

In[5]:= **ArrayFlatten[{{m, b}}] // MatrixForm**

Out[5]//MatrixForm=

$$\begin{pmatrix} 1 & 5 & -4 & 1 & 1 \\ 3 & 4 & -1 & 2 & 2 \\ 3 & 2 & 1 & 5 & 3 \\ 0 & -6 & 7 & 1 & 4 \end{pmatrix}$$

In[6]:= **RowReduce[%] // MatrixForm**

Out[6]//MatrixForm=

$$\begin{pmatrix} 1 & 0 & 0 & 0 & -\frac{127}{35} \\ 0 & 1 & 0 & 0 & \frac{141}{35} \\ 0 & 0 & 1 & 0 & \frac{139}{35} \\ 0 & 0 & 0 & 1 & \frac{13}{35} \end{pmatrix}$$

We conclude that $x_1 = -\frac{127}{35}$, $x_2 = \frac{141}{35}$, $x_3 = \frac{139}{35}$, $x_4 = \frac{13}{35}$.

The command **LinearSolve** provides a quick means for solving systems that have a single solution:

In[7]:= **LinearSolve[m, b]**

Out[7]= $\left\{ \left\{ -\frac{127}{35} \right\}, \left\{ \frac{141}{35} \right\}, \left\{ \frac{139}{35} \right\}, \left\{ \frac{13}{35} \right\} \right\}$

We can also use the **LinearSolve** command to form a function for matrix m that can be applied to any vector b.

In[8]:= **Clear[f]; f = LinearSolve[m]**

Out[8]= LinearSolveFunction[{4, 4}, <>]

In[9]:= **f[b]**

Out[9]= $\left\{ \left\{ -\frac{127}{35} \right\}, \left\{ \frac{141}{35} \right\}, \left\{ \frac{139}{35} \right\}, \left\{ \frac{13}{35} \right\} \right\}$

Or we can solve the system $m x = b$ for x by multiplying both sides on the left by m^{-1}, to get $x = m^{-1} b$.

In[10]:= **Inverse[m].b**

Out[10]= $\left\{\left\{-\dfrac{127}{35}\right\}, \left\{\dfrac{141}{35}\right\}, \left\{\dfrac{139}{35}\right\}, \left\{\dfrac{13}{35}\right\}\right\}$

Finally, we can use the command **Solve** to solve this system, just as in Section 4.9 on page 191. But we have to be careful using **Solve**. When we use the Table/Matrix ▷ New... dialogue box to create *m*, *x*, and *b*, both *m x* and *b* are lists of lists. The **Solve** command takes a list of equations as its first argument and a list of variables as its second argument—it unfortunately cannot accept lists of lists. There is a simple solution: We will have to re-enter *x* and *b* without using the Table/Matrix ▷ New... dialogue box, expressing each as a single list. If we do this, the equation **m.x == b** is acceptable as input to the **Solve** command. Note how *Mathematica* interprets the equation **m.x == b** as a single list of equations when *x* and *b* are entered this way:

In[11]:= **Clear[x, b]; x = {x1, x2, x3, x4}; b = {1, 2, 3, 4}; m.x == b**

Out[11]= $\{x1 + 5\,x2 - 4\,x3 + x4, \ 3\,x1 + 4\,x2 - x3 + 2\,x4,$
$\qquad 3\,x1 + 2\,x2 + x3 + 5\,x4, \ -6\,x2 + 7\,x3 + x4\} == \{1, 2, 3, 4\}$

In[12]:= **Solve[m.x == b, x]**

Out[12]= $\left\{\left\{x1 \rightarrow -\dfrac{127}{35}, \ x2 \rightarrow \dfrac{141}{35}, \ x3 \rightarrow \dfrac{139}{35}, \ x4 \rightarrow \dfrac{13}{35}\right\}\right\}$

An *inconsistent* system of equations has no solutions. If we use the **Solve** command on such a system, the output will be an empty set of curly brackets:

In[13]:= **Clear[m, x, b];**

$m = \begin{pmatrix} 1 & 1 & 1 \\ 1 & 1 & 1 \\ 1 & -1 & -1 \end{pmatrix}; \ x = \{x1, x2, x3\}; \ b = \{1, 2, -1\};$

Solve[m.x == b, x]

Out[15]= {}

However, if we row-reduce, we can see the inconsistency in the system:

In[16]:= **ArrayFlatten[{{m, Transpose[{b}]}}]**

Out[16]= {{1, 1, 1, 1}, {1, 1, 1, 2}, {1, −1, −1, −1}}

In[17]:= **RowReduce[%] // MatrixForm**

Out[17]//MatrixForm=
$\begin{pmatrix} 1 & 0 & 0 & 0 \\ 0 & 1 & 1 & 0 \\ 0 & 0 & 0 & 1 \end{pmatrix}$

The last row represents the impossible equation $0 = 1$.

If you use the **LinearSolve** command with an inconsistent system you will be told off:

In[18]:= **LinearSolve[m, b]**

> *LinearSolve::nosol : Linear equation encountered that has no solution.* ≫

Out[18]= LinearSolve[{{1, 1, 1}, {1, 1, 1}, {1, −1, −1}}, {1, 2, −1}]

And if you try to find the inverse of **m** you will be told off again:

In[19]:= **Inverse[m].b**

> *Inverse::sing : Matrix {{1, 1, 1}, {1, 1, 1}, {1, −1, −1}} is singular.* ≫

Out[19]= Inverse[{{1, 1, 1}, {1, 1, 1}, {1, −1, −1}}].{1, 2, −1}

The remaining possibility for a system of equations is that there are an infinite number of solutions. The **Solve** command nicely displays the solution set in this situation. The warning message can be safely ignored in this case:

In[20]:= **Clear[m, x, b];**

$$m = \begin{pmatrix} 2 & 3 & -4 \\ 4 & 6 & -8 \\ 1 & -1 & -1 \end{pmatrix}; x = \{x1, x2, x3\}; b = \{8, 16, 1\};$$

Solve[m.x == b, x]

> *Solve::svars : Equations may not give solutions for all "solve" variables.* ≫

Out[22]= $\left\{\left\{x1 \rightarrow \dfrac{11}{5} + \dfrac{7\,x3}{5},\ x2 \rightarrow \dfrac{6}{5} + \dfrac{2\,x3}{5}\right\}\right\}$

Be very careful when using the **LinearSolve** command. In a system having an infinite number of solutions it will return only one of them, giving no warning that there are others. In this example it returns only the solution where $x_3 = 0$:

In[23]:= **LinearSolve[m, b]**

Out[23]= $\left\{\dfrac{11}{5}, \dfrac{6}{5}, 0\right\}$

Row reduction gives the solution with little possibility for confusion:

In[24]:= **ArrayFlatten$\left[\{\{m, \text{Transpose}[\{b\}]\}\}\right]$**

Out[24]= {{2, 3, −4, 8}, {4, 6, −8, 16}, {1, −1, −1, 1}}

In[25]:= **RowReduce[%] // MatrixForm**

Out[25]//MatrixForm=

$$\begin{pmatrix} 1 & 0 & -\frac{7}{5} & \frac{11}{5} \\ 0 & 1 & -\frac{2}{5} & \frac{6}{5} \\ 0 & 0 & 0 & 0 \end{pmatrix}$$

Thus, for each real value assumed by x_3, there is a solution with $x_1 = \frac{11}{5} + \frac{7}{5} x_3$, and $x_2 = \frac{6}{5} + \frac{2}{5} x_3$.

The moral is that you should be very careful using the command **LinearSolve** unless you know you have a nonsingular matrix and hence a single solution. To check this, you can use the **Det** command, keeping in mind that a singular matrix has determinant zero. When in doubt it is best to use row reduction and your knowledge of linear algebra to find the solution vectors.

Homogeneous Systems of Equations

A system of equations of the form $mx = 0$, where m is the coefficient matrix, x is a column vector of variables, and 0 is the zero vector, is called *homogeneous*. Note that $x = 0$ is a solution to any homogeneous system. Now suppose m is a square matrix. Recall that such a system of linear equations has a unique solution if and only if m is nonsingular. Hence, we see that if m is nonsingular, a homogeneous system will have only the *trivial* solution $x = 0$, while if m is singular the system will have an infinite number of solutions. The set of all solutions to a homogeneous system is called the *null space* of m:

In[26]:= **Clear[m, x, b];**

$$m = \begin{pmatrix} 0 & 2 & 2 & 4 \\ 1 & 0 & -1 & -3 \\ 2 & 3 & 1 & 1 \\ -2 & 1 & 3 & -2 \end{pmatrix}; x = \begin{pmatrix} x1 \\ x2 \\ x3 \\ x4 \end{pmatrix}; b = \begin{pmatrix} 0 \\ 0 \\ 0 \\ 0 \end{pmatrix}; \text{Det[m]}$$

Out[27]= **0**

In[28]:= **RowReduce$\left[$ArrayFlatten[{{m, b}}]$\right]$ // MatrixForm**

Out[28]//MatrixForm=

$$\begin{pmatrix} 1 & 0 & -1 & 0 & 0 \\ 0 & 1 & 1 & 0 & 0 \\ 0 & 0 & 0 & 1 & 0 \\ 0 & 0 & 0 & 0 & 0 \end{pmatrix}$$

This reduced form of the augmented matrix tells us that $x_1 = x_3$, $x_2 = -x_3$, and $x_4 = 0$. That is, any vector of the form $(t, -t, t, 0)$, where t is a real number, is a solution, and the vector $(1, -1, 1, 0)$ forms a *basis* for the solution space. Bases are discussed in the next section of this chapter.

The command **NullSpace** gives a set of basis vectors for the solution space of the homogeneous equation $m\,x = 0$:

In[29]:= **NullSpace[m]**

Out[29]= {{1, −1, 1, 0}}

Using LinearSolve and NullSpace to Solve Nonhomogeneous Systems

We have seen that the **LinearSolve** command will only return one solution when a matrix equation $m\,x = b$ has an infinite number of solutions. This can be confusing at first, but you should understand that there is a reason for its behavior. If you were to take the sum of the solution vector provided by **LinearSolve** with any vector in the null space of m, you would get another solution vector. Moreover, every solution vector is of this form. Here's an example:

In[30]:= **Clear[m, b];**

$$m = \begin{pmatrix} 0 & 2 & 2 & 4 \\ 1 & 0 & -1 & -3 \\ 2 & 3 & 1 & 1 \end{pmatrix}; b = \begin{pmatrix} 2 \\ 0 \\ 0 \end{pmatrix};$$

In[32]:= **LinearSolve[m, b]**

Out[32]= {{−9}, {7}, {0}, {−3}}

In[33]:= **NullSpace[m]**

Out[33]= {{1, −1, 1, 0}}

This tells us that there are an infinite number of solutions. For each real number t, there is a solution $(-9, 7, 0, -3) + t\,(1, -1, 1, 0)$. In other words, $x_1 = -9 + t$, $x_2 = 7 - t$, $x_3 = t$, and $x_4 = -3$. This is exactly what row reduction tells us, in slightly different language:

In[34]:= **RowReduce[ArrayFlatten[{{m, b}}]] // MatrixForm**

Out[34]//MatrixForm=

$$\begin{pmatrix} 1 & 0 & -1 & 0 & -9 \\ 0 & 1 & 1 & 0 & 7 \\ 0 & 0 & 0 & 1 & -3 \end{pmatrix}$$

Exercises 7.6

1. For which values of a will the following system of linear equations have no solutions, one solution, or an infinite number of solutions?

$$\begin{aligned} x + 2\,y - 3\,z &= 4 \\ 2\,x - y + 5\,z &= 2 \\ 4\,x + 3\,y + a^2\,z &= a + 3 \end{aligned}$$

2. Find the equation of the circle that contains the points $(4, -3)$, $(-4, 5)$, and $(-2, 7)$.

7.7 Vector Spaces

Span and Linear Independence

Suppose we are given a set $\{v_1, v_2, v_3, \ldots, v_n\}$ of vectors. Any vector that can be expressed in the form $a_1 v_1 + a_2 v_2 + a_3 v_3 + \cdots + a_n v_n$ is said to be in the *span* of the vectors $v_1, v_2, v_3, \ldots, v_n$, where the coefficients a_i are scalars.

We can determine whether a given vector b is in the span of the vectors $v_1, v_2, v_3, \ldots, v_n$ by letting m be the matrix whose columns are $v_1, v_2, v_3, \ldots, v_n$, and then determining whether the equation $m x = b$ has a solution. A solution x, if it exists, provides values for the scalars a_i.

For example, in real three-space, is the vector $b = (1, 2, 3)$ in the span of the vectors $v_1 = (10, 4, 5)$, $v_2 = (4, 4, 7)$, and $v_3 = (8, 1, 0)$?

```
In[1]:= Clear[v1, v2, v, b, m, c];
        v1 = {10, 4, 5};
        v2 = {4, 4, 7};
        v3 = {8, 1, 0};
        b = {1, 2, 3};
        m = Transpose[{v1, v2, v3}];
        c = LinearSolve[m, b]
```

$$Out[7]= \left\{ \frac{3}{2}, -\frac{9}{14}, -\frac{10}{7} \right\}$$

We can check that $\frac{3}{2} v_1 - \frac{9}{14} v_2 - \frac{10}{7} v_3 = b$.

```
In[8]:= c[[1]] v1 + c[[2]] v2 + c[[3]] v3
```

```
Out[8]= {1, 2, 3}
```

A set of vectors $\{v_1, v_2, v_3, \ldots, v_n\}$ is said to be *linearly independent* if every vector in their span can be expressed in a unique way as a linear combination $a_1 v_1 + a_2 v_2 + a_3 v_3 + \cdots + a_n v_n$. Put another way, this means that the only way to express the zero vector as such a linear combination is to have each coefficient $a_i = 0$. If it is possible to write $a_1 v_1 + a_2 v_2 + a_3 v_3 + \cdots + a_n v_n = 0$ with at least one of the $a_i \neq 0$, then the set of vectors $\{v_1, v_2, v_3, \ldots, v_n\}$ is linearly *dependent*.

To check whether a set of vectors $\{v_1, v_2, v_3, \ldots, v_n\}$ is linearly independent, let m be the matrix whose columns are $v_1, v_2, v_3, \ldots, v_n$, and check that the equation $m x = 0$ has only the trivial solution:

In[9]:= **NullSpace[m]**

Out[9]= {}

Yes, these are linearly independent vectors. Alternatively, we could check that the matrix whose rows (or columns) are v_1, v_2, v_3, ..., v_n, is nonsingular:

In[10]:= **Det[{v1, v2, v3}]**

Out[10]= 14

Bases

A *basis* for a vector space is a set of linearly independent vectors whose span includes every vector in the vector space. Given a spanning set of vectors $\{v_1, v_2, v_3, ..., v_n\}$ for a vector space we can easily obtain a basis for that space. Form a matrix whose rows are the vectors v_1, v_2, v_3, ..., v_n, and row-reduce:

In[11]:= **Clear[v1, v2, v3, v4, m, a, b, c];**
v1 = {2, 1, 15, 10, 6};
v2 = {2, −5, −3, −2, 6};
v3 = {0, 5, 15, 10, 0};
v4 = {2, 6, 18, 8, 6};
m = {v1, v2, v3, v4};
RowReduce[m] // MatrixForm

Out[17]//MatrixForm=

$$\begin{pmatrix} 1 & 0 & 0 & -2 & 3 \\ 0 & 1 & 0 & -1 & 0 \\ 0 & 0 & 1 & 1 & 0 \\ 0 & 0 & 0 & 0 & 0 \end{pmatrix}$$

The nonzero rows of this matrix form a basis for the space spanned by the set $\{v_1, v_2, v_3, v_4\}$. This space is also called the *row space* of the matrix *m*.

We can also find a basis consisting of a subset of the original vectors. If we row-reduce the matrix whose columns are the vectors v_1, v_2, v_3, ..., v_n, then the columns containing the *leading 1*s will form a basis for the column space, and the corresponding columns from the original matrix will also form a basis for the column space. (An entry in a row-reduced matrix is called a leading 1 if the entry is a 1 and it has only zeros to its left.)

In[18]:= **Clear[v1, v2, v3, v4, m];**
v1 = {2, 1, 15, 10, 6};
v2 = {2, −5, −3, −2, 6};
v3 = {0, 5, 15, 10, 0};
v4 = {2, 6, 18, 8, 6};
m = Transpose[{v1, v2, v3, v4}];
RowReduce[m] // MatrixForm

Out[24]//MatrixForm=

$$\begin{pmatrix} 1 & 0 & \frac{5}{6} & 0 \\ 0 & 1 & -\frac{5}{6} & 0 \\ 0 & 0 & 0 & 1 \\ 0 & 0 & 0 & 0 \\ 0 & 0 & 0 & 0 \end{pmatrix}$$

The vectors $(1, 0, 0, 0, 0)$, $(0, 1, 0, 0, 0)$, and $(0, 0, 1, 0, 0)$ form a basis for the column space of *m*. The vectors from the same columns in *m* will also form a basis for the column space. Hence v_1, v_2, and v_4 will form a basis for the space spanned by the set $\{v_1, v_2, v_3, v_4\}$. We can confirm that $\{v_1, v_2, v_4\}$ is a linearly independent set:

In[25]:= **NullSpace[Transpose[{v1, v2, v4}]]**

Out[25]= {}

We see here an example of a general truth: a vector space may have many distinct bases. The number of vectors in any basis for that vector space, however, will always be the same. This number is called the *dimension* of the vector space.

Rank and Nullity

The dimension of the null space of a matrix is called the *nullity* of the matrix. We can find the nullity by using the **Length** command to count the vectors in a basis for the null space:

In[26]:= **Length[NullSpace[m]]**

Out[26]= 1

The *rank* of a matrix is the common dimension of the row space and the column space. The rank plus the nullity must equal the number of columns in a matrix.

In[27]:= **MatrixRank[m]**

Out[27]= 3

Orthonormal Bases and the Gram–Schmidt Process

Given a set of vectors it is frequently desirable to find a collection of vectors with the same span that have some special properties.

```
In[28]:= Clear[v1, v2, v3, u1, w1, w2, w3];
         v1 = {2, 3, −4, 1, 0};
         v2 = {1, 5, −6, 10, −3};
         v3 = {7, −2, 1, 1, 1};
```

It is easy to find a *unit vector*, a vector whose length or norm is 1, in the same direction as a given vector. We simply need to divide each component by the norm of the vector. The command **Normalize** does this automatically.

```
In[32]:= Norm[v1]
```

$$Out[32]= \sqrt{30}$$

```
In[33]:= u1 = Normalize[v1]
```

$$Out[33]= \left\{ \sqrt{\frac{2}{15}}, \sqrt{\frac{3}{10}}, -2\sqrt{\frac{2}{15}}, \frac{1}{\sqrt{30}}, 0 \right\}$$

```
In[34]:= Norm[u1]
```

$$Out[34]= 1$$

A collection of vectors is *orthogonal* if the vectors are mutually perpendicular, i.e., if the dot product of every pair is 0. The set is *orthonormal* if in addition each vector has norm 1. Given a basis for a vector space, we can use the **Orthogonalize** command to find an orthonormal basis. **Orthogonalize** uses the Gram–Schmidt process unless another method is specified using the **Method** option. The argument for the command **Orthogonalize** is a list of linearly independent vectors. The output is a list of mutually orthogonal unit vectors with the same span:

Before we apply **Orthogonalize** let's check that our vectors are linearly independent:

```
In[35]:= NullSpace[Transpose[{v1, v2, v3}]]
```

$$Out[35]= \{\}$$

Good, we are free to proceed.

In[36]:= **{w1, w2, w3} = Orthogonalize[{v1, v2, v3}];**
{w1, w2, w3} // MatrixForm

Out[37]//MatrixForm=

$$
\begin{pmatrix}
\sqrt{\dfrac{2}{15}} & \sqrt{\dfrac{3}{10}} & -2\sqrt{\dfrac{2}{15}} & \dfrac{1}{\sqrt{30}} & 0 \\[2ex]
-4\sqrt{\dfrac{6}{1405}} & -\dfrac{1}{\sqrt{8430}} & 4\sqrt{\dfrac{2}{4215}} & \dfrac{83}{\sqrt{8430}} & -\sqrt{\dfrac{30}{281}} \\[2ex]
\dfrac{5368}{\sqrt{38\,274\,729}} & -706\sqrt{\dfrac{3}{12\,758\,243}} & \dfrac{1489}{\sqrt{38\,274\,729}} & \dfrac{1574}{\sqrt{38\,274\,729}} & 176\sqrt{\dfrac{3}{12\,758\,243}}
\end{pmatrix}
$$

It is easy to check that any pair of these vectors is orthogonal. Just enter a list whose items are dot products of every possible pair of distinct vectors. The output will be a list of zeros if the vectors in each pair are orthogonal:

In[38]:= **{w1.w2, w2.w3, w3.w1}**

Out[38]= {0, 0, 0}

And here we check that they are all unit vectors:

In[39]:= **{Norm[w1], Norm[w2], Norm[w3]}**

Out[39]= {1, 1, 1}

The familiar concepts of vector length and the angle between pairs of vectors in Euclidean vector spaces can be generalized to other vector spaces that admit an *inner product*—a generalization of the dot product. As with the dot product, two vectors whose inner product is zero are said to be orthogonal. And a vector whose inner product with itself is 1 is said to be a unit vector.

For example, consider the vector space P_3 of polynomials in the variable x of degree at most three with real coefficients. Given 2 polynomials p and q in P_3 we can form their inner product using the function f defined below:

In[40]:= **Clear[f, p, q]**

In[41]:= $\mathbf{f[p\_,\ q\_] := \displaystyle\int_{-1}^{1} p * q\, dx}$

Applying f to the vector w_1 below we see that $w_1 = \dfrac{1}{\sqrt{2}}$ is a unit vector in the inner product space P_3.

In[42]:= **Clear[x, w1, w2, w3, w4];**
$\mathbf{w1 = \dfrac{1}{\sqrt{2}}; \ w2 = x; \ w3 = x^2; \ w4 = x^3;}$

In[44]:= **f[w1, w1]**

Out[44]= 1

And we can see that the vectors w_1 and w_2 are orthogonal.

In[45]:= **f[w1, w2]**

Out[45]= 0

The **Orthogonalize** command can be applied in any inner-product space. The default inner product for **Orthogonalize** is the dot product but a different inner product function can be specified as an optional second argument.

In[46]:= **{v1, v2, v3, v4} = Orthogonalize[{w1, w2, w3, w4}, f]**

Out[46]= $\left\{ \dfrac{1}{\sqrt{2}}, \ \sqrt{\dfrac{3}{2}}\, x, \ \dfrac{3}{2}\sqrt{\dfrac{5}{2}} \left(-\dfrac{1}{3} + x^2 \right), \ \dfrac{5}{2}\sqrt{\dfrac{7}{2}} \left(-\dfrac{3x}{5} + x^3 \right) \right\}$

We can apply the inner product to these vectors to check that they are pairwise orthogonal unit vectors.

In[47]:= **f[v3, v3]**

Out[47]= 1

In[48]:= **f[v2, v3]**

Out[48]= 0

QR-Decomposition

The QR-Decomposition of a matrix is a factorization of a matrix with linearly independent column vectors, into a product of a matrix Q that has orthonormal column vectors and a matrix R that is invertible and upper triangular. The matrix Q is obtained by applying the Gram–Schmidt process to the column vectors of the matrix. The matrix R is then uniquely determined.

Consider the matrix m.

In[49]:= $m = \begin{pmatrix} 1 & 0 & 0 \\ -1 & 2 & 0 \\ 0 & 1 & 3 \end{pmatrix};$

In[50]:= **Det[m]**

Out[50]= 6

In[51]:= $\mathbf{q = Transpose\big[Orthogonalize\big[Transpose[m]\big]\big];}$
$\mathbf{MatrixForm\big[q\big]}$

Out[52]//MatrixForm=

$$\begin{pmatrix} \dfrac{1}{\sqrt{2}} & \dfrac{1}{\sqrt{3}} & -\dfrac{1}{\sqrt{6}} \\[2mm] -\dfrac{1}{\sqrt{2}} & \dfrac{1}{\sqrt{3}} & -\dfrac{1}{\sqrt{6}} \\[2mm] 0 & \dfrac{1}{\sqrt{3}} & \sqrt{\dfrac{2}{3}} \end{pmatrix}$$

In[53]:= $\mathbf{r = Inverse\big[q\big].m;}$
$\mathbf{MatrixForm[r]}$

Out[54]//MatrixForm=

$$\begin{pmatrix} \sqrt{2} & -\sqrt{2} & 0 \\[1mm] 0 & \sqrt{3} & \sqrt{3} \\[1mm] 0 & 0 & \sqrt{6} \end{pmatrix}$$

In[55]:= $\mathbf{q.r \; // \; MatrixForm}$

Out[55]//MatrixForm=

$$\begin{pmatrix} 1 & 0 & 0 \\ -1 & 2 & 0 \\ 0 & 1 & 3 \end{pmatrix}$$

The command **QRDecomposition** automates the process.

In[56]:= $\mathbf{qr = QRDecomposition[m]}$

Out[56]= $\left\{\left\{\left\{\dfrac{1}{\sqrt{2}}, -\dfrac{1}{\sqrt{2}}, 0\right\}, \left\{\dfrac{1}{\sqrt{3}}, \dfrac{1}{\sqrt{3}}, \dfrac{1}{\sqrt{3}}\right\}, \left\{-\dfrac{1}{\sqrt{6}}, -\dfrac{1}{\sqrt{6}}, \sqrt{\dfrac{2}{3}}\right\}\right\},\right.$
$\left.\left\{\left\{\sqrt{2}, -\sqrt{2}, 0\right\}, \left\{0, \sqrt{3}, \sqrt{3}\right\}, \left\{0, 0, \sqrt{6}\right\}\right\}\right\}$

In[57]:= $\mathbf{Map\big[MatrixForm, \; qr\big]}$

Out[57]= $\left\{ \begin{pmatrix} \dfrac{1}{\sqrt{2}} & -\dfrac{1}{\sqrt{2}} & 0 \\[2mm] \dfrac{1}{\sqrt{3}} & \dfrac{1}{\sqrt{3}} & \dfrac{1}{\sqrt{3}} \\[2mm] -\dfrac{1}{\sqrt{6}} & -\dfrac{1}{\sqrt{6}} & \sqrt{\dfrac{2}{3}} \end{pmatrix}, \begin{pmatrix} \sqrt{2} & -\sqrt{2} & 0 \\[1mm] 0 & \sqrt{3} & \sqrt{3} \\[1mm] 0 & 0 & \sqrt{6} \end{pmatrix} \right\}$

The command **QRDecomposition** returns 2 matrices, q and r, where $q^t r$ is equal to the original matrix. Notice that the first matrix in this list is the transpose of our matrix q above.

In[58]:= **Transpose[qr[[1]]].qr[[2]]**

Out[58]= {{1, 0, 0}, {−1, 2, 0}, {0, 1, 3}}

Exercises 7.7

1.a Find an orthonormal basis for the vector space spanned by the vectors $v_1 = (1, 2, 3)$, $v_2 = (4, 5, 6)$, $v_3 = (7, 7, 8)$ and use the result to show that the product of an orthonormal matrix with its transpose is the identity matrix.

b. Explain why this makes sense.

7.8 Eigenvalues and Eigenvectors

Given an $n \times n$ matrix m, the nonzero vectors v_i such that $m\,v_i = \lambda_i v_i$ are the *eigenvectors* of m, and the scalars λ_i are the *eigenvalues* of m. There are at most n eigenvalues. First we will use the commands **Eigenvalues**, **Eigenvectors**, and **Eigensystem** to find eigenvalues and eigenvectors. Then we will walk through the process "manually."

Finding Eigenvalues and Eigenvectors Automatically

Here is a simple matrix:

In[1]:= **Clear[m];**
m = Array[Min, {2, 2}]; m // MatrixForm

Out[2]//MatrixForm=
$$\begin{pmatrix} 1 & 1 \\ 1 & 2 \end{pmatrix}$$

To get the eigenvalues, type the following command (look for λ in the BasicMathInput palette):

In[3]:= **{λ1, λ2} = Eigenvalues[m]**

Out[3]= $\left\{ \dfrac{1}{2}\left(3 + \sqrt{5}\right), \dfrac{1}{2}\left(3 - \sqrt{5}\right) \right\}$

For the eigenvectors, type:

In[4]:= **{v1, v2} = Eigenvectors[m]**

Out[4]= $\left\{\left\{-2 + \frac{1}{2}\left(3 + \sqrt{5}\right), 1\right\}, \left\{-2 + \frac{1}{2}\left(3 - \sqrt{5}\right), 1\right\}\right\}$

We find two eigenvalues and two eigenvectors. Let's check that $m\,v_1 = \lambda_1\,v_1$:

In[5]:= **m.v1 // Simplify**

Out[5]= $\left\{\frac{1}{2}\left(1 + \sqrt{5}\right), \frac{1}{2}\left(3 + \sqrt{5}\right)\right\}$

In[6]:= **λ1 ∗ v1 // Simplify**

Out[6]= $\left\{\frac{1}{2}\left(1 + \sqrt{5}\right), \frac{1}{2}\left(3 + \sqrt{5}\right)\right\}$

In[7]:= **m.v1 == λ1 ∗ v1**

Out[7]= True

You can easily check that $m\,v_2 = \lambda_2\,v_2$ as well.

The command **Eigensystem** gives both the eigenvalues and the eigenvectors. The output is a list whose first item is a list of eigenvalues and whose second item is a list of corresponding eigenvectors:

In[8]:= **Eigensystem[m]**

Out[8]= $\left\{\left\{\frac{1}{2}\left(3 + \sqrt{5}\right), \frac{1}{2}\left(3 - \sqrt{5}\right)\right\}, \left\{\left\{-2 + \frac{1}{2}\left(3 + \sqrt{5}\right), 1\right\}, \left\{-2 + \frac{1}{2}\left(3 - \sqrt{5}\right), 1\right\}\right\}\right\}$

We can ask that the output of any of these commands be numerical approximations by replacing **m** with **N[m]**:

In[9]:= **Eigensystem[N[m]]**

Out[9]= {{2.61803, 0.381966}, {{0.525731, 0.850651}, {0.850651, −0.525731}}}

Even for a simple matrix with integer entries the eigenvalues can be quite complicated and involve complex numbers:

In[10]:= **Clear[m];**
m = Array[Min, {3, 3}]; m // MatrixForm

Out[11]//MatrixForm=

$$\begin{pmatrix} 1 & 1 & 1 \\ 1 & 2 & 2 \\ 1 & 2 & 3 \end{pmatrix}$$

In[12]:= **Eigenvalues[m]**

Out[12]= $\{\text{Root}[-1 + 5\#1 - 6\#1^2 + \#1^3 \;\&, 3],$

$\qquad \text{Root}[-1 + 5\#1 - 6\#1^2 + \#1^3 \;\&, 2], \text{Root}[-1 + 5\#1 - 6\#1^2 + \#1^3 \;\&, 1]\}$

The eigenvalues here are returned as **Root** objects, in this case the three roots of the characteristic polynomial $-1 + 5x - 6x^2 + x^3$. The option setting **Cubics → True** will permit the display of such roots in terms of radicals.

In[13]:= **Eigenvalues[m, Cubics → True]**

Out[13]= $\left\{ 2 + \dfrac{7^{2/3}}{\left(\frac{3}{2}\left(9 + i\sqrt{3}\right)\right)^{1/3}} + \dfrac{\left(\frac{7}{2}\left(9 + i\sqrt{3}\right)\right)^{1/3}}{3^{2/3}} \right.,$

$\qquad 2 - \dfrac{\left(\frac{7}{2}\right)^{2/3}\left(1 - i\sqrt{3}\right)}{\left(3\left(9 + i\sqrt{3}\right)\right)^{1/3}} - \dfrac{\left(1 + i\sqrt{3}\right)\left(\frac{7}{2}\left(9 + i\sqrt{3}\right)\right)^{1/3}}{2 \cdot 3^{2/3}},$

$\qquad 2 - \dfrac{\left(\frac{7}{2}\right)^{2/3}\left(1 + i\sqrt{3}\right)}{\left(3\left(9 + i\sqrt{3}\right)\right)^{1/3}} - \dfrac{\left(1 - i\sqrt{3}\right)\left(\frac{7}{2}\left(9 + i\sqrt{3}\right)\right)^{1/3}}{2 \cdot 3^{2/3}} \left. \right\}$

There is a similar option setting for quartics. One may also get a numerical approximation of the eigenvalues as follows:

In[14]:= **Eigenvalues[m] // N**

Out[14]= {5.04892, 0.643104, 0.307979}

For an $n \times n$ matrix *Mathematica* will always return n eigenvalues even if they are not all distinct. The eigenvalues will occur in the same frequency as the roots of the characteristic polynomial (as explained in the next subsection). *Mathematica* will also output n eigenvectors. If there are fewer than n linearly independent eigenvectors, the output may contain one or more zero vectors. These zero vectors are there for bookkeeping only; actual eigenvectors are nonzero by definition:

In[15]:= **Clear[m];**

$$m = \begin{pmatrix} 2 & 1 & 0 \\ 0 & 2 & 0 \\ 0 & 0 & 0 \end{pmatrix};$$

Eigensystem[m]

Out[17]= {{2, 2, 0}, {{1, 0, 0}, {0, 0, 0}, {0, 0, 1}}}

Finding Eigenvalues and Eigenvectors Manually

Even though *Mathematica* can produce eigenvalues and eigenvectors very quickly, it is still sometimes enlightening to go through the process "manually." To find the eigenvalues we first form the *characteristic polynomial*, which is the determinant of the matrix $\lambda I - m$, where m is a square matrix, λ is an indeterminate, and I is the identity matrix of the same dimensions as m:

In[18]:= **Clear[m];**

$$m = \begin{pmatrix} 2 & -1 & 0 \\ -1 & 2 & 0 \\ 0 & 0 & 3 \end{pmatrix};$$

$$c = \text{Det}\big[\lambda\, \text{IdentityMatrix}[3] - m\big]$$

Out[20]= $-9 + 15\lambda - 7\lambda^2 + \lambda^3$

Then we find the roots of the characteristic polynomial:

In[21]:= **Solve[c == 0, λ]**

Out[21]= {{λ → 1}, {λ → 3}, {λ → 3}}

There are two eigenvalues $\lambda = 1$ and $\lambda = 3$. The eigenvalue 3 is reported twice because it occurs twice as a root of the characteristic polynomial c. We can see this clearly by factoring c:

In[22]:= **Factor[c]**

Out[22]= $(-3 + \lambda)^2 (-1 + \lambda)$

Of course, most characteristic polynomials will not factor so nicely. To find the eigenspace of each eigenvalue λ_i we will find the null space of the matrix $\lambda_i I - m$:

In[23]:= **NullSpace$\big[1 * \text{IdentityMatrix}[3] - m\big]$**

Out[23]= {{1, 1, 0}}

In[24]:= **NullSpace$\big[3 * \text{IdentityMatrix}[3] - m\big]$**

Out[24]= {{0, 0, 1}, {−1, 1, 0}}

The eigenspace for the eigenvalue $\lambda = 1$ has one basis vector: (1, 1, 0). The eigenspace for the eigenvalue $\lambda = 3$ has two basis vectors: $(0,\ 0,\ 1)$ and $(-1,\ 1,\ 0)$.

Let's have *Mathematica* check our work:

In[25]:= **Eigensystem[m]**

Out[25]= $\{\{3,\ 3,\ 1\},\ \{\{0,\ 0,\ 1\},\ \{-1,\ 1,\ 0\},\ \{1,\ 1,\ 0\}\}\}$

Diagonalization

A square matrix **m** is *diagonalizable* if there exists a diagonal matrix **d** and an invertible matrix **p** such that $m = p\,d\,p^{-1}$. In this case, the expression on the right hand side is called a *Jordan decomposition* or *diagonalization* of **m**. An $n \times n$ matrix is diagonalizable if and only if it has n linearly independent eigenvectors. In this case the matrix **p** will be the matrix whose columns are the eigenvectors of **m** and the matrix **d** will have the eigenvalues of **m** along the diagonal (and zeros everywhere else):

We can use **Eigensystem** to find the eigenvalues and eigenvectors and then form the matrices **p** and **d** ourselves or use **JordanDecomposition** and have *Mathematica* compute the matrices **p** and **d**. Notice that the matrices we get by each method are slightly different. The order in which the eigenvalues and eigenvectors are listed causes this difference.

In[26]:= $\mathbf{Clear\big[m,\ p,\ c,\ d\big];}$

$$m = \begin{pmatrix} 2 & -1 & 0 \\ -1 & 2 & 0 \\ 0 & 0 & 3 \end{pmatrix};$$

In[28]:= **{evals, evecs} = Eigensystem[m]**

Out[28]= $\{\{3,\ 3,\ 1\},\ \{\{0,\ 0,\ 1\},\ \{-1,\ 1,\ 0\},\ \{1,\ 1,\ 0\}\}\}$

In[29]:= **d = DiagonalMatrix[evals];**
        d // MatrixForm

Out[30]//MatrixForm=
$$\begin{pmatrix} 3 & 0 & 0 \\ 0 & 3 & 0 \\ 0 & 0 & 1 \end{pmatrix}$$

In[31]:= **p = Transpose[evecs];**
        p // MatrixForm

Out[32]//MatrixForm=
$$\begin{pmatrix} 0 & -1 & 1 \\ 0 & 1 & 1 \\ 1 & 0 & 0 \end{pmatrix}$$

In[33]:= **p.d.Inverse[p] // MatrixForm**

Out[33]//MatrixForm=
$$\begin{pmatrix} 2 & -1 & 0 \\ -1 & 2 & 0 \\ 0 & 0 & 3 \end{pmatrix}$$

In[34]:= **Clear[p, d];**
{p, d} = JordanDecomposition[m]

Out[35]= {{{1, 0, −1}, {1, 0, 1}, {0, 1, 0}}, {{1, 0, 0}, {0, 3, 0}, {0, 0, 3}}}

In[36]:= **Map[MatrixForm, %]**

Out[36]= $\left\{ \begin{pmatrix} 1 & 0 & -1 \\ 1 & 0 & 1 \\ 0 & 1 & 0 \end{pmatrix}, \begin{pmatrix} 1 & 0 & 0 \\ 0 & 3 & 0 \\ 0 & 0 & 3 \end{pmatrix} \right\}$

In[37]:= **p.d.Inverse[p] // MatrixForm**

Out[37]//MatrixForm=
$$\begin{pmatrix} 2 & -1 & 0 \\ -1 & 2 & 0 \\ 0 & 0 & 3 \end{pmatrix}$$

Exercises 7.8

1. Form the LU-decomposition of the matrix $m = \begin{pmatrix} 2 & -1 & 0 \\ -1 & 2 & 0 \\ 0 & 0 & 3 \end{pmatrix}$.

7.9 Visualizing Linear Transformations

A *linear transformation F* is a function from one vector space to another such that for all vectors u and v in the domain, $F(u + v) = F(u) + F(v)$, and such that for all scalars k, $F(k v) = k F(v)$. Once bases have been specified for each vector space, a linear transformation F can be represented as multiplication by a matrix m, so that $F(v) = m.v$ for all vectors v in the domain of F.

We can better understand a linear transformation by studying the effect it has on geometric figures in its domain. *Mathematica* can be used to visualize the effect of a linear transformation from $\mathbb{R}^2$ to $\mathbb{R}^2$ on a geometric object in the plane. We first produce a polygonal shape by specifying the coordinates of its vertices. We can then apply a linear transformation to each of these points and see where they land. Examining the geometric changes tells us how the linear transformation behaves.

To produce a figure on which to demonstrate transformations, go to the Graphics menu and select New Graphic. Next, bring up the drawing tools via Graphics ▷ Drawing Tools, and select the line segments tool (push the appropriate button, or type the letter s). Now click on the graphic repeatedly to draw a picture, being careful not to click on any previous points (to close the loop) until you are done. Don't get too fancy; just a single closed loop is all that is needed. For instance, here is a stunning portrait of our dog, Zoe:

Now click on the graphic so that the orange border is showing, copy it to the clipboard (Edit ▷ Copy) and paste it into the following command:

In[1]:= **dog = First @ Cases**[, **Line**[**pts_**] → **pts**, **Infinity**]

Out[1]= {{0, 0}, {0.237841, 0.700376}, {0.145025, 0.981963}, {0.145025, 1.30109},
{0.087015, 1.54514}, {0.063811, 2.08954}, {0.145025, 2.31481},
{0.353861, 2.37112}, {0.214637, 2.1834}, {0.168229, 1.92058},
{0.249443, 1.639}, {0.841145, 1.73286}, {1.32843, 1.67654}, {1.51406, 1.73286},
{1.63008, 2.05199}, {1.7113, 2.22094}, {1.7113, 1.75163}, {1.7345, 1.65777},
{1.83892, 1.65777}, {1.81571, 1.52636}, {2.03615, 1.24478}, {1.89693, 0.906873},
{1.59528, 1.15091}, {1.60688, 0.3437}, {1.7461, 0.118431}, {1.7461, 0.00579624},
{1.38644, 0.00579624}, {1.34003, 0.625287}, {0.643911, 0.644059},
{0.400269, 0.212293}, {0.609105, 0.118431}, {0.620707, 0.00579624}, {0, 0}}

The details of how the **Cases** command works are discussed in Section 8.8. But what it produces is simply the list of Zoe's coordinates. Her picture is easily recovered from this coordinate list, either as a **Line** or **Polygon** object:

In[2]:= {Graphics[Line[dog]], Graphics[{Brown, Polygon[dog]}]}

Out[2]= {  }

⚠ If when constructing a graphic you invoke the line segments tool *more than once*, you will produce a graphic with more than one **Line** object in it. Things are a bit more complicated here. In such cases do not apply **First** to the **Cases** input above. **Cases** will produce a list containing *multiple* lists of points. Give this master list a name (such as **dog**). To display this list, instead of **Graphics[Line[dog]]**, use **Graphics[Map[Line,dog]]** (or equivalently: **Graphics[Table[Line[s],{s,dog}]]**). To multiply the matrix **m** by each vertex in the dog lists, we use **Map[m.#&,dog,{2}]**. This "maps" the **Function[v,m.v]** over the dog list at the second level. **Map** and **Function** are described in detail in Section 8.4 on page 403. Finally, to display the transformed image, put this all together to get:

Graphics[{Brown, Map[Line, Map[m.#&, dog, {2}]]}]

You will probably not want to use **Polygon** to render an image made from multiple **Line** objects.

We can reflect Zoe about the y-axis using the matrix $\begin{pmatrix} -1 & 0 \\ 0 & 1 \end{pmatrix}$. We simply multiply each of Zoe's coordinates by this matrix, then make a **Polygon** from the transformed coordinates. Both the original and transformed figures are shown below:

In[3]:= Graphics$\left[\left\{\left\{\text{Brown, Polygon}\left[\text{Table}\left[\begin{pmatrix} -1 & 0 \\ 0 & 1 \end{pmatrix}.v, \{v, \text{dog}\}\right]\right]\right\}, \text{Line}[\text{dog}]\right\}, \right.$

Axes → True$\Big]$

Out[3]=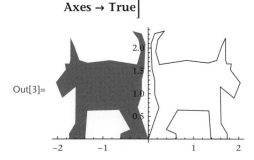

Here Zoe is reflected about the line $y = x$, using the matrix $\begin{pmatrix} 0 & 1 \\ 1 & 0 \end{pmatrix}$:

In[4]:= Graphics$\Big[\Big\{\Big\{$Brown, Polygon$\Big[$Table$\Big[\begin{pmatrix} 0 & 1 \\ 1 & 0 \end{pmatrix}$.v, {v, dog}$\Big]\Big]\Big\}$, Line[dog]$\Big\}$,

Axes $\to$ True, PlotRange $\to 3\Big]$

Out[4]=

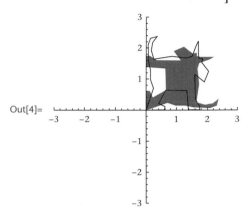

The most simple type of linear transformation is a dilation or contraction. The standard matrix for this type of transformation is $\begin{pmatrix} c & 0 \\ 0 & c \end{pmatrix}$. If $0 < c < 1$ we have a contraction, while if $c > 1$, we have a dilation. Using **Manipulate** we allow c to vary dynamically. Below we display the dilation matrix together with the graphical output. Toward this end, we introduce a **displayMatrix** command that will round all matrix entries to two decimal places, leave room in front of each entry for a minus sign, and generally make the matrix entries easy to read as the parameter c is manipulated.

In[5]:= **displayMatrix[m_] := MatrixForm @**
Map[NumberForm$\big[$Chop[N[#], 10^{-3}], {3, 2}, NumberSigns $\to$ {"−", " "}$\big]$ &, m, {2}]

⚠ The **displayMatrix** command utilizes both **Map** and **Function**, which are discussed in Section 8.4 on page 403, in order to operate individually on each matrix entry. It also makes use of **NumberForm**, which is used to regulate the display of numbers, and **Chop**, which is used to round sufficiently small numbers to zero. **NumberForm** is discussed in Section 8.3.

In[6]:= Manipulate$\Big[$

Labeled$\Big[$Graphics$\Big[\Big\{\Big\{$Brown, Polygon$\Big[$Table$\Big[\begin{pmatrix} c & 0 \\ 0 & c \end{pmatrix}$.v, {v, dog}$\Big]\Big]\Big\}$, Line[dog]$\Big\}$,

Axes → True, PlotRange → 10$\Big]$, (∗ the label ∗)

$\begin{pmatrix} c & 0 \\ 0 & c \end{pmatrix}$ // displayMatrix, {{Right, Top}}$\Big]$,

{{c, 2.75}, .2, 5}$\Big]$

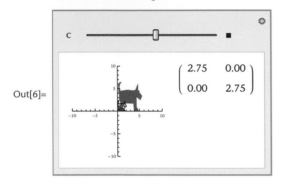

Out[6]=

We can rotate a figure in two dimensions through an angle θ using the standard rotation matrix.

In[7]:= RotationMatrix[θ] // MatrixForm

Out[7]//MatrixForm=
$\begin{pmatrix} \text{Cos}[\theta] & -\text{Sin}[\theta] \\ \text{Sin}[\theta] & \text{Cos}[\theta] \end{pmatrix}$

In[8]:= Manipulate$\Big[$

Labeled$\Big[$Graphics$\Big[\{\{$Brown, Polygon[Table[RotationMatrix[θ].v, {v, dog}]]$\}$,

Line[dog]}, Axes → True, PlotRange → 4, PlotLabel → "Bad Dog"],

(∗ the label ∗)RotationMatrix[θ] // displayMatrix, {{Right, Top}}$\Big]$, {{θ, .8}, 0, 2 π}$\Big]$

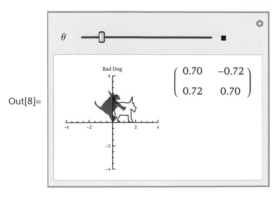

Out[8]=

We can compose linear transformations by multiplying the individual matrices for the transformations. Below we've combined a reflection about the *x*-axis with a dilation and a rotation.

In[9]:= $\text{Manipulate}\Big[\text{With}\Big[\Big\{m = \begin{pmatrix} 1 & 0 \\ 0 & -1 \end{pmatrix} . \begin{pmatrix} c & 0 \\ 0 & c \end{pmatrix} . \text{RotationMatrix}[\theta]\Big\},$

$\quad \text{Labeled}\Big[\text{Graphics}[\{\{\text{Brown, Polygon}[\text{Table}[m.v, \{v, \text{dog}\}]]\},$

$\quad\quad \text{Line}[\text{dog}]\}, \text{Axes} \rightarrow \text{True, PlotRange} \rightarrow 10],$

$\quad\quad (* \text{ the label } *) \text{Row}\Big[\Big\{\text{MatrixForm}\Big[\begin{pmatrix} 1 & 0 \\ 0 & -1 \end{pmatrix}\Big], \text{".", displayMatrix}\Big[\begin{pmatrix} c & 0 \\ 0 & c \end{pmatrix}\Big],$

$\quad\quad \text{".", displayMatrix}[\text{RotationMatrix}[\theta]], \text{"=", displayMatrix}[m]\Big\}\Big],$

$\quad\quad \text{Top}\Big]\Big], \{\{\theta, 2\}, 0, 2\pi\}, \{\{c, 2.5\}, 1, 4\}\Big]$

Out[9]=

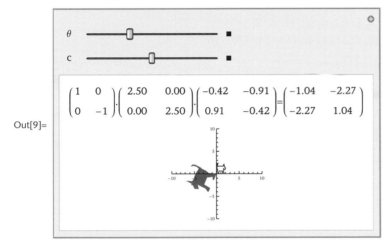

In 3-dimensions, we can easily access any of the dozens of polyhedra available in the **Polyhedron Data** collection, or any of the **Geometry3D** objects in the **ExampleData** collection. Here, for instance, is the *space shuttle*:

In[10]:= **ExampleData[{"Geometry3D", "SpaceShuttle"}]**

Out[10]=

We can easily extract its vertex coordinates as follows (to save space we display only the first few):

In[11]:= **vertices = N @ ExampleData[{"Geometry3D", "SpaceShuttle"}, "VertexData"];**
        Take[vertices, 10]

Out[12]= {{−4.99949, −0.68171, 0.569242}, {−4.99976, −0.491153, 0.805206},
        {−5.34948, −0.470935, 0.566062}, {−4.99976, 0.491153, 0.805206},
        {−4.90671, 0.620194, 0.686502}, {−4.99949, 0.68171, 0.569242},
        {−5.29975, −0.147914, 0.811038}, {−5.56803, −0.1192, 0.568687},
        {−4.90671, −0.620194, 0.686502}, {−5.56803, 0.1192, 0.568687}}

Collections of these vertices are assembled to make the polygonal faces. The first face, for instance, is a triangle comprised of the first, second, and third vertices in the above list.

In[13]:= **faces = ExampleData[{"Geometry3D", "SpaceShuttle"}, "PolygonData"];**
        Take[faces, 10]

Out[14]= {{1, 2, 3}, {4, 5, 6}, {3, 7, 8}, {1, 9, 2}, {7, 3, 2},
        {10, 11, 12}, {12, 4, 6}, {12, 11, 4}, {13, 14, 15}, {16, 17, 18}}

In total there are 310 vertices and 393 faces:

In[15]:= **{Length[vertices], Length[faces]}**

Out[15]= {310, 393}

We can reassemble this information into a three-dimensional graphic using **GraphicsComplex**, like this:

In[16]:= **Graphics3D[{EdgeForm[], GraphicsComplex[vertices, Polygon[faces]]}]**

Out[16]=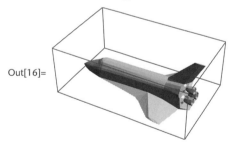

So, proceeding as in the two-dimensional case, we dynamically display the figure resulting from the application of a linear transformation to each of the vertices of the figure above. For instance, below we show the effect of composing rotations about each of the three coordinate axes, respectively:

In[17]:= Manipulate[
    With[{m = RotationMatrix[θ, {1, 0, 0}].
            RotationMatrix[φ, {0, 1, 0}].RotationMatrix[φ, {0, 0, 1}],
        vertices = N @ ExampleData[{"Geometry3D", "SpaceShuttle"}, "VertexData"],
        faces = ExampleData[{"Geometry3D", "SpaceShuttle"}, "PolygonData"]},
      Labeled[
        Graphics3D[
          {EdgeForm[], GraphicsComplex[Table[m.v, {v, vertices}], Polygon[faces]]},
          PlotRange → 8], displayMatrix[m], {{Right, Top}}]],
    {{θ, .5}, 0, 2 π}, {φ, 0, 2 π}, {φ, 0, 2 π}]

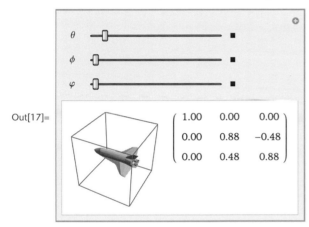

Out[17]=
$$\begin{pmatrix} 1.00 & 0.00 & 0.00 \\ 0.00 & 0.88 & -0.48 \\ 0.00 & 0.48 & 0.88 \end{pmatrix}$$

Exercises 7.9

1. Draw a simple line drawing and construct a graph that demonstrates its reflection about the *x*-axis.

2. One can apply matrix transformations to each vertex in any of the objects in the **Polyhedron‐ Data** collection.

   a. Enter the input below to render a *square gyrobicupola*:

      PolyhedronData["SquareGyrobicupola"]

   b. Extract the vertices and face indices for this polyhedron. Hint: A similar extraction was carried out in the text for the *space shuttle*. The syntax is slightly different here, however. The relevant properties are now called **"VertexCoordinates"** and **"FaceIndices"**. Type **PolyhedronData["‐ SquareGyrobicupola","Properties"]** for a listing of *all* available properties.

   c. How many vertices and faces are there in this example?

   d. Construct a **Manipulate** that will enable you to rotate the polyhedron about any of the three coordinate axes.

8

Programming

8.1 Introduction

When you put several commands together to accomplish some purpose beyond the capacity of any one individually, you are *programming*. *Mathematica* is intentionally designed for this purpose. Like anything else, getting good at programming takes practice. But it is also exceedingly handy to have familiarity with commands that lend themselves to such greater enterprises. We've seen plenty of *Mathematica* in the first seven chapters; in this chapter we'll discuss commands that are especially useful for programming. Keep in mind that we only have room here for a brief introduction to these concepts. Entire books, much longer than this one, have been written on this subject. Think of this chapter as a gentle introduction.

We begin in Section 8.2 with some important background material, a consideration of the *internal* form of any and every *Mathematica* expression. Every expression, input, output (or a cell, or an entire notebook) is highly structured. Before it is possible to operate on any such expression, you simply have to know what you are dealing with. You have to understand its *structure*.

Some of the most fundamental structures in *Mathematica* are the various types of numbers. These are addressed in Section 8.3. The internal forms of the various types of numbers are discussed, along with notions such as precision and accuracy. *Mathematica* has the capacity to carry out calculations to arbitrarily high precision. In this section we also discuss a myriad of possibilities for the display of numbers.

Section 8.4 introduces the workhorses of *functional programming*, commands like **Map** and **Function** and **MapThread**. Section 8.5 introduces the staples of procedural programming, with predicate commands (that return **True** or **False**), and control structures and looping commands such as **If**, **Do**, **While**, and **For**. These commands instruct *Mathematica* to carry out a sequence of instructions, and similar commands are often among the first encountered when one learns an elementary programming language.

Section 8.6 discusses commands that limit the scope of auxiliary functions and symbols that are sometimes needed in programming. These *scoping commands* are essential to insulate local definitions from any global assignments that a user might make. Section 8.7 introduces the essential commands that facilitate iteration, such as **NestList**, **NestWhileList**, **FoldList**, and **FixedPointList**.

Finally, section 8.8 discusses patterns and pattern matching in the context of defining commands, making replacements, and for use in specific commands like **Cases**.

8.2 FullForm: What the Kernel Sees

Every *Mathematica* expression is either an *atom* or a *nested expression*. An atom is the most simple type of expression: a number, a symbol, a string. It is an expression that cannot be decomposed into simpler component pieces. The **AtomQ** command will tell you if an expression is atomic. Here are a few examples:

In[1]:= **Clear[a, x];**
Grid[Table[{exp, AtomQ[exp]}, {exp,
{2, 2.0, 2/3, 2 + 3 i, π, a, Plot3D, Sin, "a string", 2 + a, a[x]}}], Dividers → Gray]

Out[2]=

2	True
2.	True
$\frac{2}{3}$	True
$2 + 3\,i$	True
π	True
a	True
Plot3D	True
Sin	True
a string	True
2 + a	False
a[x]	False

A nested expression has the form **head**[*arg1, arg2, ...*]. The head is typically atomic (it is usually a command name, although it may itself be a nested expression), and the arguments are either nested expressions or atoms. The arguments are enclosed in square brackets (typically there are one or more arguments, but zero arguments are permitted). The command **Head** will display the head of any nested expression. Here are a few examples (for each expression in the left column, its head appears in the right column):

In[3]:= **Clear[a, b, c, g, x, y, myCommand];**
Grid[Table[{exp, Head[exp]}, {exp, {myCommand[x], g[x, y], a[b[x, y], c], a[b][c]}}],
Dividers → Gray]

Out[3]=

myCommand[x]	myCommand
$g[x, y]$	g
$a[b[x, y], c]$	a
$a[b][c]$	$a[b]$

Even the expression **a[b][c]** qualifies as a legitimate nested expression. The head is the nested expression **a[b]**.

Every non-atomic *Mathematica* expression has this form, a head followed by square brackets enclosing zero or more arguments.

That last statement should give you pause. Consider the expression **2 + a**. It is not atomic (we saw this in the second to last output above), so what is the head? Where are the square brackets? What are the arguments? It does not appear to have the form **head[*arg1*, *arg2*, …]**. What gives?

In[4]:= **Head[2 + a]**

Out[4]= Plus

What's going on is that the internal or **FullForm** of this expression is not revealed when we type **2 + a**. These paltry three characters are parsed into the following before being sent to the kernel for evaluation:

In[5]:= **2 + a // FullForm**

Out[5]//FullForm=
          Plus[2, a]

Ah, so this expression *does* have the form of a nested expression after all, and the head is indeed **Plus**. *Mathematica* allows you to type **2+a** because you're a human, and that's what you're used to (this is called the *infix form* of the **Plus** command). In this and in dozens of other cases you are permitted to create expressions that do not look like proper nested expressions. This flexibility is granted simply to make your interactions with *Mathematica* more natural, and to make the typing as simple as possible. But in each of these cases your input is parsed into a properly structured nested expression before being sent to the kernel. It is crucial to understand this fact if you are to program effectively in *Mathematica*. **FullForm** is a great tool for peeking under the hood to view the internal form of any *Mathematica* expression. Here are some other examples (for each expression in the left column we show its **FullForm** in the right column):

In[6]:= Grid[Table[{exp, FullForm[exp]},

$\{$exp, $\{2 + a, 2*a, -a, 2\wedge a, \sqrt{a}\,, 2/a, \pi, e, \{2, a\}, \_, a\_, a\_\_, a[[1]],$

$a \,\&\&\, b, a \,||\, b, !\, a, a \rightarrow 2, a \,/.\, b, a \,//.\, b, a == b, a \neq b, a < b, a \leq b,$

$a \in \text{Reals}, a \sim\sim b, a'[x], \int a[x]\, dx\}\}\big], \text{Dividers} \rightarrow \text{Gray}\big]$ // Quiet

Out[6]=

$2 + a$	Plus[2, a]
$2\,a$	Times[2, a]
$-a$	Times[-1, a]
2^a	Power[2, a]
$\sqrt{a}$	Power[a, Rational[1, 2]]
$\dfrac{2}{a}$	Times[2, Power[a, -1]]
π	Pi
e	E
$\{2, a\}$	List[2, a]
$\_$	Blank[]
$a\_$	Pattern[a, Blank[]]
$a\_\_$	Pattern[a, BlankSequence[]]
$a[[1]]$	Part[a, 1]
$a \,\&\&\, b$	And[a, b]
$a \,||\, b$	Or[a, b]
$!\, a$	Not[a]
$a \rightarrow 2$	Rule[a, 2]
$a \,/.\, b$	ReplaceAll[a, b]
$a \,//.\, b$	ReplaceRepeated[a, b]
$a == b$	Equal[a, b]
$a \neq b$	Unequal[a, b]
$a < b$	Less[a, b]
$a \leq b$	LessEqual[a, b]
$a \in \text{Reals}$	Element[a, Reals]
$a \sim\sim b$	StringExpression[a, b]
$a'[x]$	Derivative[1][a][x]
$\int a[x]\, dx$	Integrate[a[x], x]

⚠ Note that **Quiet** has been applied (in postfix form) in the previous input. This suppresses all warning messages. In this case, for instance, the **a/.b** input generates a warning message that **b** is neither a replacement rule nor a list of replacement rules.

Note that **FullForm** can be subtle to use in some cases, as an expression may evaluate before **Full·
Form** is applied. If one enters **FullForm[a=b]**, for instance, the expression **a=b** evaluates and
returns **b**, and then the **FullForm** of **b** (which is simply **b**) is displayed. In fact, the **FullForm** of **a=b**
is **Set[a, b]**. In such cases, wrapping the expression in **Defer** will prevent this sort of premature
evaluation.

In[7]:= **FullForm[a = b]**

Out[7]//FullForm=

    b

In[8]:= **Defer[FullForm[a = b]]**

Out[8]= Set[a, b]

In[9]:= **Defer[FullForm[a := b]]**

Out[9]= SetDelayed[a, b]

Understanding the structure of the *Mathematica* language allows you to do many things. One clearly
sees at this point, for instance, the internal distinctions between the symbols =, :=, and ==. They
correspond respectively to the commands **Set**, **SetDelayed**, and **Equal**. You will soon be able to
harness your knowledge of the structure of expressions to operate in interesting ways on complex
expressions. This is the essence of programming in *Mathematica*.

One last symbol deserves our attention in this context: the semicolon. We have used this symbol to
suppress output on many occasions. It also allows us to evaluate several commands in a single input
cell, like this:

In[10]:= **a = 3; 2 a**

Out[10]= 6

The **FullForm** of the input above can be seen via **Defer**:

In[11]:= **Defer[FullForm[a = 3; 2 a]]**

Out[11]= CompoundExpression [Set[a, 3], Times[2, a]]

And here is the **FullForm** of an expression that *ends* in a semicolon:

In[12]:= **Defer[FullForm[a = 3;]]**

Out[12]= CompoundExpression [Set[a, 3], Null]

The command is **CompoundExpression**, and each argument is itself an expression. The arguments
are evaluated in turn, but only the output associated with the expression in the final argument is
displayed. **CompoundExpression** is an invaluable tool in writing *Mathematica* programs, for it
allows several inputs to be evaluated in turn, one after the other, with only the output of the last
input displayed.

Here's one more example that may be revealing. Copy any graphic you like into an input cell, and ask for its **FullForm** or **InputForm** to see its underlying structure. In this case we used the Drawing Tools palette to create a simple image with the Line Segments tool.

In[13]:=   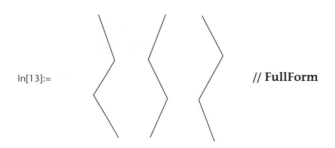   **// FullForm**

Out[13]//FullForm=

Graphics[List[Line[List[List[0.21111111111111117`, 0.8333333333333334`],
    List[0.2972222222222223`, 0.5972222222222223`],
    List[0.18611111111111114`, 0.41666666666666674`],
    List[0.31666666666666665`, 0.1972222222222222`]]],
  Line[List[List[0.5611111111111111`, 0.8361111111111111`],
    List[0.4722222222222222`, 0.6027777777777779`],
    List[0.5722222222222222`, 0.40000000000000013`],
    List[0.4833333333333334`, 0.19999999999999996`]]],
  Line[List[List[0.7527777777777778`, 0.8305555555555556`],
    List[0.8611111111111112`, 0.6222222222222222`],
    List[0.7361111111111112`, 0.3944444444444444`],
    List[0.8166666666666667`, 0.18055555555555558`]]]],
  Rule[PlotRange, List[List[0, 1], List[0, 1]]]]]

⚠ In fact, *Mathematica* notebooks are themselves valid nested expressions. If you were to open a *Mathematica* notebook in a text editor, you would see a plain text file with the structure **Notebook[*arg1*, *arg2*, ...]**. The individual arguments in a notebook are cells, and every cell is nested expression in its own right of the form **Cell[*arg1*, *arg2*, ...]**, and so on. This state of affairs is most definitely intentional, and is even a little bit devious. It is devious in that the FrontEnd does not reveal the highly structured nature of the underlying document, just as it does not reveal the **FullForm** of expressions such as $\sqrt{a}$, unless you ask for it. But underneath, the structure is there. The benefit (and a distinguishing feature of *Mathematica*) is that you have *access* to this underlying form. Because cells and even entire notebooks have the structure of a valid expression, it is possible to program *Mathematica* to operate on an entire notebook. This was done, for example, in the writing of this book. Each chapter in this book is a *Mathematica* notebook. The entire notebook expressions for all of the chapter files were sent to the kernel to programmatically generate the table of contents. They were sent again to make the index, and so on. While the details of these specific techniques lie beyond the scope of this book, it is important to understand the potential for operating programmatically on an entire notebook.

Exercises 8.2

1. Find the **Head** of each of the following expressions:

   a. $x \rightarrow 2$

   b. $\sqrt{2}$

   c. {1, 2, 3}

   d. $\# + 1 \,\&$

2. Find the **FullForm** of each of the following expressions:

   a. $x \rightarrow 2$

   b. 1/2

   c. $\sqrt{2}$

   d. {1, 2, 3}

3. What is the head of the expression $a'[x]$? Find its **FullForm**, and base your answer on what you see. Check your answer with **Head**.

4. What is the **FullForm** of the expression $2x + 1 /. x \rightarrow 3$? Use **Defer** and **FullForm** to find out.

5. What is the **FullForm** of the expression $x = 3; 2x$? Use **Defer** and **FullForm** to find out.

6. The command **TreeForm** produces a visual representation of the **FullForm** of any expression. Find the **TreeForm** of the expression $2x + 1 /. x \rightarrow 3$.

7. The **Part** command was introduced in Chapter 3 to extract a part of a list. It is typically invoked via typing double square brackets. For instance the input $\{a, b, c\}[[2]]$ will produce the output **b**. But **Part** can also be used to extract parts of compound *Mathematica* expressions.

   a. Apply **TreeForm** to the input $a * b + c * d^2$.

   b. Extract the zeroth, first, and second parts of this same input.

   c. Find parts $[[2,1]]$ and $[[2,2]]$.

   d. Find parts $[[2,2,1]]$ and $[[2,2,2]]$.

8. Go to the Graphics menu, create a new graphic, bring up the Drawing Tools palette, and draw an arrow. Copy the arrow graphic into a new input cell, and apply **TreeForm** to the result.

9. A **String** in *Mathematica* is any collection of characters or symbols enclosed in double quotations. Strings are atomic expressions. There are many commands available to operate on strings, but one of the most basic is **StringExpression**. **StringExpression**[*string1*, *string2*] will concatenate the

two strings *string1* and *string2* into a single string. The infix form of **StringExpression** is ~~. That is, one may invoke **StringExpression** by typing *string1~~string2*.

a. Type and enter a string. What do you see? What do you see if you apply **FullForm** to the input?

b. Apply **FullForm** to the input "**I am**"~~" **putting strings together.**"

c. Apply **Defer** to the input **FullForm["a"~~"b"]**.

d. The command **ToString** will take any expression and convert it to a string. It is often used in conjunction with **StringExpression** to create a string that depends on some external input. Use **ToString** and **StringExpression** to create a command that will take a numerical input *n* and return the string "*n* **is my favorite number.**"

10. A notebook is comprised of cells. Each cell expression in a notebook has the head **Cell**. To see the underlying form of a **Cell** expression requires a special technique, as the FrontEnd will display **Cell** expressions nicely, that is, in a manner which hides the underlying structure of the expression.

a. Click anywhere in any cell in any notebook, and in the menus go to Cell ▷ ShowExpression. The underlying cell structure will be revealed. In this state, you can edit it directly if you like. Then toggle it back to normal with the same technique. Try this on several different cells in one of your notebooks.

b. A **Cell** is a versatile structure, capable of many forms, from input to output to text to graphics. So it may not be surprising to learn that **Cell** accepts a myriad of options. How many options would you guess **Cell** can accept? Test your answer using the **Options** command.

8.3 Numbers

Types of Numbers: Integer, Rational, Real, and Complex

When working with a calculator or spreadsheet, one is typically not concerned with whether one enters a whole number (such as 12) or a decimal number (such as 12.0). These are, after all, the same number. In *Mathematica*, however, they are treated very differently, and for a good reason. Decimal numbers are cursed with an inherent ambiguity stemming from the fact that while there are an infinite number of decimal places, we cannot possibly write them all. There are two distinct situations in which one would write a decimal number with finitely many places. In one, we write such a number when we are rounding it, such as when writing $\pi \approx 3.14159$. In the other, we agree to stop writing decimal digits if beyond a certain point all the digits are known to be zero, such as when writing $1/4 = .25$. Unfortunately, when one gives a computer a decimal number such as 3.14159 or .25, there is no way for the computer to know which situation you are in. When you type .25, should the computer interpret that to mean $1/4$, or should it instead read it as the first two digits of some potentially longer number, whose other decimal places are not known? *Mathematica* chooses the latter: it treats all decimal numbers as *approximations*, where only the given decimal digits are known, and where all additional decimal digits are treated as unknown. *Mathematica* refers to such numbers as **Real** numbers.

By contrast, an **Integer**, or whole number, is exact. There is no ambiguity. Likewise, fractions with integer numerator and denominator are also exact. Such fractions are called **Rational** numbers. While any kind of number is an atomic expression in *Mathematica*, the **Head** command (introduced in the last section) can be used to identify the type of any number.

In[1]:= **Head[12.0]**

Out[1]= Real

In[2]:= **Head[12]**

Out[2]= Integer

In[3]:= **Head[12 / 7]**

Out[3]= Rational

It is often a shock for new *Mathematica* users to encounter output such as the following:

In[4]:= $\dfrac{22}{7}$

Out[4]= $\dfrac{22}{7}$

Mathematica simply will not convert an **Integer** or **Rational** number to a **Real** unless instructed to do so. In cases where you seek a decimal output, either enter at least one **Real** number in the input, or use the **N** command to convert it for you. Note that typing **22.** is the same as writing **22.0**.

In[5]:= $\dfrac{22.}{7}$

Out[5]= 3.14286

In[6]:= $\dfrac{22}{7}$ **// N**

Out[6]= 3.14286

In addition to **Integer**, **Rational**, and **Real** numbers, there are also complex numbers, such as $2+3i$, where i represents the square root of -1. Regardless of which type of numbers comprise the individual real and imaginary components of such a number, *Mathematica* treats the entire expression as a **Complex** number.

In[7]:= **Head[2 + 3 i]**

Out[7]= Complex

In[8]:= **Head[2.0 + 3.0 *i*]**

Out[8]= Complex

Displaying Numbers

It is important to understand that while real (decimal) numbers are *displayed* with six significant digits, internally they are stored to at least machine precision (usually 16 significant digits). Perhaps you have already discovered this; if you copy a real number from an output cell and then paste it into a new input cell you will see the "full" machine representation of the number. Alternately, you can use the command **InputForm** to display all the digits of a real number.

In[9]:= **N[π]**

Out[9]= 3.14159

In[10]:= **N[π] // InputForm**

Out[10]//InputForm=
    3.141592653589793

Note *Mathematica*'s **InputForm** for scientific notation:

In[11]:= **N[$\pi * 10^{20}$] // InputForm**

Out[11]//InputForm=
    3.1415926535897933*^20

It is possible to display all the digits of a real number in any format you can imagine. While *Mathematica*'s **InputForm** is handy for peeking under the hood, a more practical command for displaying numbers is **NumberForm**. Here, for example, we see the first 12 digits of π (including the digit to the left of the decimal point).

In[12]:= **NumberForm[N[π], 12]**

Out[12]//NumberForm=
    3.14159265359

This is not too exciting, as it looks like the output for **N[π,12]**. However, if the second argument to **NumberForm** is a list of *two* positive integers, the first number specifies the total number of digits to be displayed and the second specifies the number of digits to the *right of the decimal*. This can be very useful. Here we see the first ten decimal places of π (compare the output carefully with the output above; **NumberForm** displays the number *rounded* to the correct number of specified digits):

In[13]:= **NumberForm[N[π], {11, 10}]**

Out[13]//NumberForm=
    3.1415926536

If you ask for more total digits than needed, they will not be displayed.

In[14]:= **NumberForm[1.0, {10, 5}]**

Out[14]//NumberForm=
    1.00000

However the option **NumberPadding** allows you to specify characters to pad the areas to the left and right of the displayed digits.

In[15]:= **NumberForm[1.0, {10, 5}, NumberPadding → {"▫", "0"}]**

Out[15]//NumberForm=
   ▫▫▫▫▫1.00000

The padding on the left in the output above appears to have one extra character; this is the space reserved for the sign character in the case of negative numbers:

In[16]:= **NumberForm[−1.0, {10, 5}, NumberPadding → {"▫", "0"}]**

Out[16]//NumberForm=
   ▫▫▫▫−1.00000

A similar command is **PaddedForm**, which works essentially the same way as **NumberForm**, but it will also "pad" the number with white space on the left, leaving room to accommodate all the requested digits (and the sign character). Using **PaddedForm** will often free you from having to add a **NumberPadding** option to **NumberForm**.

In[17]:= **NumberForm[1.0, {10, 5}]**
       NumberForm[1.0, {10, 5}, NumberPadding → {" ", "0"}]
       PaddedForm[1.0, {10, 5}]

Out[17]//NumberForm=
    1.00000

Out[18]//NumberForm=
      1.00000

Out[19]//PaddedForm=
      1.00000

PaddedForm is useful for displaying numbers in a table so that numbers in a column are all displayed with the same number of places to the right of the decimal, and with decimal points aligned.

In[20]:= **Table[{n, PaddedForm[N[n * π], {5, 2}]}, {n, 0, 6}] // Grid**

Out[20]=
0	0.00
1	3.14
2	6.28
3	9.42
4	12.57
5	15.71
6	18.85

Numbers that are very small or very large, however, will disturb the neat display above. Such numbers will (sensibly enough) be displayed in scientific notation (with the requested 2 places shown to the right of the decimal):

In[21]:= **PaddedForm[.000001234, {12, 2}]**

Out[21]//PaddedForm=

$$1.23 \times 10^{-6}$$

In[22]:= **PaddedForm[1 001 234.5678, {12, 2}]**

Out[22]//PaddedForm=

$$1.00 \times 10^{6}$$

If you do not want such numbers represented in scientific notation (for instance, if you are displaying monetary values and want your answer in dollars and cents), both **NumberForm** and **Padded·. Form** accept the option setting **ExponentFunction → (Null&)**, which prohibits the display of exponents.

In[23]:= **PaddedForm[.000001234, {12, 2}, ExponentFunction → (Null &)]**

Out[23]//PaddedForm=

0.00

In[24]:= **PaddedForm[1 001 234.5678, {12, 2}, ExponentFunction → (Null &)]**

Out[24]//PaddedForm=

1001234.57

This mechanism provides a sensible means of representing quantities such as money, where precisely two decimal places should be displayed. The following command could be used whenever a monetary value x is to be shown. This particular implementation allows for at most ten digits to the left of the decimal (so don't use it to display the national debt).

In[25]:= **Clear[dollar];**
dollar[x_] := PaddedForm[N[x], {12, 2}, ExponentFunction → (Null &)]

In[27]:= {dollar[0.0049], dollar[0.0050], dollar[π], dollar[$10^9 \pi$]} // Column

Out[27]=
0.00
0.01
3.14
3141592653.59

Suppose you have one dollar, and it loses $1/3$ of its value each year. Here's what happens to your dollar over time. The second column shows the numerical value to the default six significant digits, while the third column displays this same value rounded to the nearest penny:

In[28]:= Grid[Table[{n, N[$(2/3)^n$], dollar[$(2/3)^n$]}, {n, 0, 15}],
        Alignment → ".", Dividers → Gray]

Out[28]=

0	1.	1.00
1	0.666667	0.67
2	0.444444	0.44
3	0.296296	0.30
4	0.197531	0.20
5	0.131687	0.13
6	0.0877915	0.09
7	0.0585277	0.06
8	0.0390184	0.04
9	0.0260123	0.03
10	0.0173415	0.02
11	0.011561	0.01
12	0.00770735	0.01
13	0.00513823	0.01
14	0.00342549	0.00
15	0.00228366	0.00

More complex structures such as loan amortization tables can be built in a similar fashion.

If the number we wish to display is an *exact* integer (no decimal point) we need not specify digits of precision, and scientific notation will not be used.

In[29]:= NumberForm[10^{30}]

Out[29]//NumberForm=
1000000000000000000000000000000

But very large numbers are easier for humans to read if the digits are blocked in, say, groups of three. **NumberForm** and **PaddedForm** have an option called **DigitBlock** to allow for this sort of display.

In fact there are a host of options that allow you full control over the display of numbers. Look up **NumberForm** in the Documentation Center for more information.

In[30]:= **NumberForm$\left[10^{30}$, DigitBlock $\rightarrow$ 3$\right]$**

NumberForm$\left[10^{30}$, DigitBlock $\rightarrow$ 5, NumberSeparator $\rightarrow$ " "$\right]$

Out[30]//NumberForm=
1,000,000,000,000,000,000,000,000,000,000

Out[31]//NumberForm=
1 00000 00000 00000 00000 00000 00000

Note that you can go into *Mathematica*'s Preferences panel, and make global adjustments to these settings. In the Preferences panel, look under Appearance ▷ Numbers ▷ Formatting, and tweak to your heart's content. This will invoke your display preferences for every session.

In this example we modify the command **dollar** to use 3-digit blocks:

In[32]:= **Clear[dollar];**

dollar[x_] :=

PaddedForm$\left[$N[x], {12, 2}, ExponentFunction $\rightarrow$ (Null &), DigitBlock $\rightarrow$ 3$\right]$

In[34]:= **dollar$\left[10^9\right]$**

Out[34]//PaddedForm=
1,000,000,000.00

NumberForm and its cousin **PaddedForm** have several other close relatives including **Scientific-Form**, **EngineeringForm**, and **AccountingForm**. These work much the same way, but have different default settings. Information can be had in the Documentation Center.

Precision and Accuracy

Here's an experiment. Find another program on your computer that is capable of doing arithmetic, for instance a calculator program or a spreadsheet. Ask that program to evaluate 2^{1023} and 2^{1024}. Now try it in *Mathematica*. As with any calculation, with *Mathematica* you can ask for a numerical approximation or an exact answer:

In[35]:= **N$\left[2^{1023}$, 10$\right]$**

Out[35]= $8.988465674 \times 10^{307}$

In[36]:= 2^{1024}

Out[36]= 179 769 313 486 231 590 772 930 519 078 902 473 361 797 697 894 230 657 273 430 081 157 ˙.
732 675 805 500 963 132 708 477 322 407 536 021 120 113 879 871 393 357 658 789 768 ˙.
814 416 622 492 847 430 639 474 124 377 767 893 424 865 485 276 302 219 601 246 094 ˙.
119 453 082 952 085 005 768 838 150 682 342 462 881 473 913 110 540 827 237 163 350 ˙.
510 684 586 298 239 947 245 938 479 716 304 835 356 329 624 224 137 216

In most cases you'll find that other programs will give an answer like the output above for 2^{1023}, but they will choke on 2^{1024}, and fail to produce an answer. This is because most programs rely on your computer's hardware, in particular on its floating point unit (FPU), to carry out arithmetic operations. And this number is simply too big for most floating point units commonly in use at the time of this writing. It's a matter that most of us rarely think about, but while the real number system is infinite, the number system utilized by most FPU's (commonly IEEE double–precision floating point arithmetic) is finite. That is, there is a finite quantity of numbers available in this system, and so there is necessarily a *largest* number. In most systems it happens to be just under 2^{1024}. The boundary occurs at a power of two since the FPU converts numbers to base 2 before operating on them. You can have *Mathematica* query your hardware and determine the largest number supported by the FPU on your machine by entering the following:

In[37]:= **$MaxMachineNumber**

Out[37]= 1.79769×10^{308}

In[38]:= **N$[2^{1024}]$**

Out[38]= $1.797693134862316 \times 10^{308}$

Mathematica handles numbers differently than most other programs. It will make use of your computer's FPU whenever possible in order to save time, since hardware is generally several orders of magnitude faster than software. But when you input a real number too large, too small, or too precise for the FPU to handle, or if the result of evaluating your input produces such a number, *Mathematica* will seamlessly switch into high precision mode, abandoning the FPU and carrying out the calculation itself. In one sense you never need to worry about it, for it happens automatically. In another sense, it is useful to understand just how *Mathematica* interprets real numbers so that you can better understand its output, and so that you can manually switch to high precision arithmetic should you desire to do so.

For instance, enter the following input. Then select the output with your mouse, copy it, and paste it into a new input cell. This is what you will see:

In[39]:= **N$[\pi]$**

Out[39]= 3.14159

3.141592653589793`

This procedure causes *Mathematica* to give you a peek under the hood at how it views this number. You can also force *Mathematica* to show it to you with the command **FullForm** (the command **InputForm** will also display all the digits of the number, but it does not display the backquote character `` ` ``).

> In[40]:= **N[π] // FullForm**

> Out[40]//FullForm=
>   3.141592653589793`

We already know that the **N** command will by default display only six significant digits of a number, while internally there is a machine number lurking underneath. Machine numbers, that is, numbers accessible to your computer's FPU, never have more than a fixed number of significant digits, usually 16. We will use the term *precision* to indicate how many significant digits a real number has, and hence we say that machine numbers generally have a precision of 16. Machine numbers are identified (in **FullForm**) by the backquote `` ` `` appearing as the final character. If you ever copy and paste a number, revealing its internal structure as a machine number, don't worry. Numbers can be input in this form and the output is no different than it would otherwise be.

> In[41]:= **100 ∗ 3.141592653589793`**

> Out[41]= 314.159

One way to input a high precision number is to type a decimal number with a total of more than 16 digits. Another is to use **N** specifying (with the second argument) more than 16 digits of precision.

> In[42]:= **N[2, 40]**

> Out[42]= 2.000000000000000000000000000000000000000

If you copy and paste the output above, or apply **FullForm** to it, you will see the internal structure of a high precision number:

> In[43]:= **N[2, 40] // FullForm**

> Out[43]//FullForm=
>   2.`40.

The **FullForm** of a high precision number is the number itself followed by the backquote character `` ` `` followed by the number's precision. High precision numbers may also be entered directly this way:

> In[44]:= **2`40**

> Out[44]= 2.000000000000000000000000000000000000000

In order to understand *Mathematica*'s internal form for *any* high precision number, we just combine the notation above with the internal form for scientific notation (discussed in the previous subsection). For example:

In[45]:= $N[2 * 10^{100}, 40]$ // **FullForm**

Out[45]//FullForm=
            2.`40.*^100

A simple way to force *Mathematica* to jump into high precision mode when evaluating an input is to make sure *every* number appearing in the input is a high precision number. If any single number in the input has only machine precision, the answer can be no more precise. The **Precision** command displays the precision of any quantity.

In[46]:= **Precision[2`40]**

Out[46]= 40.

In[47]:= **Precision[N[2, 40]]**

Out[47]= 40.

In[48].– **Precision[2.]**

Out[48]= MachinePrecision

When high precision numbers are combined arithmetically, the precision is no greater than that of the least precise number in the input.

In[49]:= **N[2, 40] * N[2, 30]**

Out[49]= 4.00000000000000000000000000000

In[50]:= **Precision[%]**

Out[50]= 30.

However, with some operations the precision can decrease below that of the least precise number in the input. In the following example it is useful to think of each number as an infinite decimal number, the first few digits of which are 2 followed by 29 or 39 zeros. When subtracted, their difference begins 0.000000 ... (with 29 zeros after the decimal point), but beyond that nothing is known. No *significant* digits of the difference can be surmised. The precision is 0.

In[51]:= **N[2, 30] – N[2, 40]**

Out[51]= $0. \times 10^{-30}$

In[52]:= **Precision[%]**

Out[52]= 0.

This may seem unfair. However, we do know that the result is zero to 29 decimal places, even though we don't know any of the actual nonzero digits of the difference. The command **Accuracy** will tell you (roughly) how many digits to the right of the decimal point are known to be correct.

In[53]:= **Accuracy[%%]**

Out[53]= 29.699

The following won't give a high precision number, since the machine precision number 2.0 appears in the input. You cannot take a machine precision real number and increase its precision. In fact, you cannot do any operation involving a machine precision number and end up with high precision output.

In[54]:= **N[2., 40]**

Out[54]= 2.

In[55]:= **Precision[%]**

Out[55]= MachinePrecision

Finally, note that exact numbers have infinite precision:

In[56]:= **Precision[2]**

Out[56]= ∞

In[57]:= **Precision[π]**

Out[57]= ∞

Exercises 8.3

1. You may be familiar with the parable about the peasant who is to be rewarded by the king with many sacks of rice. The peasant says, "Why don't you simply give me one grain of rice the first day, 2 the second day, 4 the third day, and so on, each day giving me twice the quantity of the previous day, and do this for one month?" The King, thinking this will cost less, agrees. Make a table showing how many grains of rice the King owes each day, from day one to day 31. Use **DigitBlock**s of length three to make the numbers easy to read.

2. In this section we advocate the use of **PaddedForm** to display numbers in a table or column, each with the same number of decimal places and with the decimal points aligned. Another technique for accomplishing such alignment without necessarily restricting the number of decimal places is with the **Alignment** option in the **Grid** and **Column** commands. Look up this option in the Documentation Center, and use it to display the **Table** below in a column. You may also wish to consult Exercise 7 in Section 3.5.

In[58]:= **Table[$10^n * N[\pi]$, {n, 0, 5}]**

Out[58]= {3.14159, 31.4159, 314.159, 3141.59, 31415.9, 314159.}

8.4   Map and Function

Two fundamental *Mathematica* programming commands, **Map** and **Function**, are introduced in this section. An understanding of these commands is something that distinguishes a *Mathematica* power user from a casual user. They will facilitate your being able to do powerful list manipulations, and expand your capability to do interesting tasks with great efficiency. We'll tackle them one at a time, then show how they can be used together.

Map is a command for applying a function to each member of a list. For instance, we can test a list of numbers to see which of the numbers are primes:

In[1]:= **Map[PrimeQ, {2, 3, 4, 5, 6}]**

Out[1]= {True, True, False, True, False}

Or we can apply an undefined function to a list of undefined quantities:

In[2]:= **Clear[f, a, b, c];**
      Map[f, {a, b, c}]

Out[3]= {f[a], f[b], f[c]}

The first argument of **Map** is a function or command. The second argument is a list. The members of the list are fed to the function, one by one, and the resulting list of values is returned.

There is a commonly used infix syntax for **Map**. Instead of typing **Map[***f, list***]**, one can instead type *f* **/@** *list*. Effectively, one can **Map** a function over a list with just two keystrokes:

In[4]:= **f /@ {a, b, c}**

Out[4]= {f[a], f[b], f[c]}

This will seem strange at first, but it is akin to typing $2 + 3$ instead of the more formal **Plus[2, 3]**. It departs from the standard "square bracket" notation employed by most *Mathematica* commands. With a bit of practice, however, it's quite natural.

We now turn our attention to a second command, **Function**, that is typically used to construct functions to be used only once (for instance, functions to be **Map**ped over a list). In order to create a function that squares its argument, for example, and apply it to every item in a list, either of these inputs will do:

In[5]:= $\text{Map}\big[\text{Function}\big[\text{x, x}^2\big], \{\text{a, b, c}\}\big]$

Out[5]= $\big\{\text{a}^2, \text{b}^2, \text{c}^2\big\}$

In[6]:= $\text{Function}\big[\text{x, x}^2\big] \text{/@ \{a, b, c\}}$

Out[6]= $\big\{\text{a}^2, \text{b}^2, \text{c}^2\big\}$

This may seem like overkill; we've typed more input than the output we produced. But the idea is extremely powerful, as we can now map *any* function over *any* list. We'll explore more interesting examples shortly.

In general, to create a function one types **Function**[*input,output*]. The input variable *x* above could be replaced by any symbol; it's simply a dummy variable. An alternate syntax is commonly used that both minimizes typing and standardizes the name of the dummy variable to be the **Slot** character **#**. To give a **Function** using this syntax, use only one argument: the output expression (using the **#** for the variable):

In[7]:= $\text{Map}\big[\text{Function}\big[\text{#}^2\big], \{\text{a, b, c}\}\big]$

Out[7]= $\big\{\text{a}^2, \text{b}^2, \text{c}^2\big\}$

Even more brevity in typing can be attained by disposing entirely of the **Function** command name. One may simply type the output expression (again using only **#** for the variable) and then type the ampersand character **&** to mark the end of the function. It's a bit odd at first, but you'll pick up on it quickly. Instead of **Function**$\big[\text{#}^2\big]$, for example, one instead may type a paltry three characters: **#^{2} &**. For instance:

In[8]:= $\text{Map}\big[\text{#}^2 \text{ \&, \{a, b, c\}}\big]$

Out[8]= $\big\{\text{a}^2, \text{b}^2, \text{c}^2\big\}$

Or even better:

In[9]:= $\text{#}^2 \text{ \& /@ \{a, b, c\}}$

Out[9]= $\big\{\text{a}^2, \text{b}^2, \text{c}^2\big\}$

This last form is the most cryptic, but it is also the quickest to type, and is by far the most commonly encountered syntax convention for mapping a function over a list. You will see it frequently in examples in the Documentation Center. Here are a few examples. Remember the **Slot** character **#** is simply a stand-in for each member of the list that follows.

In[10]:= **Column[N[π, #] & /@ Range[20]]**

Out[10]=
3.
3.1
3.14
3.142
3.1416
3.14159
3.141593
3.1415927
3.14159265
3.141592654
3.1415926536
3.14159265359
3.141592653590
3.1415926535898
3.14159265358979
3.141592653589793
3.1415926535897932
3.14159265358979324
3.141592653589793238
3.1415926535897932385

In[11]:= **GraphicsRow[Plot[Sin[x⁴], {x, 0, 2}, PlotStyle → #] & /@ {Dashed, Dotted, Thick}]**

Out[11]=
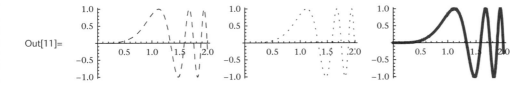

In[12]:= $\mathtt{Plot}\big[x^\# \text{ \& /@ } \{1/6, 1/5, 1/4, 1/3, 1/2, 1, 2, 3, 4, 5, 6\},$
$\{x, 0, 1\}, \text{Ticks} \to \text{None}, \text{AspectRatio} \to 1\big]$

Out[12]=

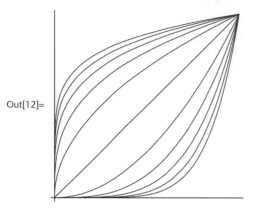

In[13]:= $\mathtt{GraphicsRow}\big[$
$\mathtt{Plot}\big[x^\#, \{x, 0, 1\}, \text{Ticks} \to \text{None}, \text{AspectRatio} \to 1, \text{AxesOrigin} \to \{0, 0\}\big] \text{ \& /@}$
$\{1/6, 1/5, 1/4, 1/3, 1/2, 1, 2, 3, 4, 5, 6\}\big]$

Out[13]=

In[14]:= $\mathtt{Text} @ \mathtt{Style}\big[\mathtt{Grid}\big[\{\#, \text{"= "}, \mathtt{Expand}[\#]\} \text{ \& /@ } \mathtt{Table}\big[(1 + x)^n, \{n, 9\}\big], \text{Alignment} \to \text{Left}\big],$
$\text{"TraditionalForm"}\big]$

$$1 + x \quad = \quad 1 + x$$
$$(1 + x)^2 \quad = \quad 1 + 2x + x^2$$
$$(1 + x)^3 \quad = \quad 1 + 3x + 3x^2 + x^3$$
$$(1 + x)^4 \quad = \quad 1 + 4x + 6x^2 + 4x^3 + x^4$$

Out[14]= $(1 + x)^5 \quad = \quad 1 + 5x + 10x^2 + 10x^3 + 5x^4 + x^5$
$$(1 + x)^6 \quad = \quad 1 + 6x + 15x^2 + 20x^3 + 15x^4 + 6x^5 + x^6$$
$$(1 + x)^7 \quad = \quad 1 + 7x + 21x^2 + 35x^3 + 35x^4 + 21x^5 + 7x^6 + x^7$$
$$(1 + x)^8 \quad = \quad 1 + 8x + 28x^2 + 56x^3 + 70x^4 + 56x^5 + 28x^6 + 8x^7 + x^8$$
$$(1 + x)^9 \quad = \quad 1 + 9x + 36x^2 + 84x^3 + 126x^4 + 126x^5 + 84x^6 + 36x^7 + 9x^8 + x^9$$

Note that it is possible to **Map** a **Function** over a list without using either command. Beginning in *Mathematica* 6, one may use the special iterator form $\{x, list\}$ in a **Table** to accomplish the same thing. In fact, this idea has been used repeatedly throughout this book. For instance:

In[15]:= **Table[x², {x, {a, b, c}}]**

Out[15]= $\{a^2, b^2, c^2\}$

In[16]:= **GraphicsRow[**
Table[Plot[Sin[x⁴], {x, 0, 2}, PlotStyle → sty], {sty, {Dashed, Dotted, Thick}}]]

Out[16]=

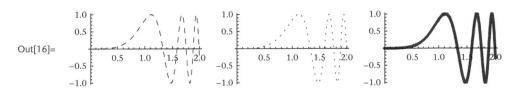

Keep in mind, however, that *Mathematica* has been around since the late 1980s. Prior to version 6, the **Map-Function** combo was ubiquitous. Its use still pervades examples in the Documentation Center, and is found in much of the code you are likely to see. And it's more than a relic. It is, with a little practice, very easy both to type and to read. It avoids the use of a dummy variable (like the **sty** variable in the example above). And in cases where the list being mapped over is generated by **Table**, the **Map-Function** combo negates the need to nest one **Table** inside another.

It should also be noted that both **Function** and **Map** are widely used independently of each other. In short, both are essential programming tools.

A **Function** can be given multiple arguments. This form is required by the **Sort** command, which is used to sort a given list. For instance:

In[17]:= **myList = RandomInteger[100, 15]**

Out[17]= $\{40, 1, 79, 47, 51, 68, 45, 12, 19, 18, 64, 100, 91, 5, 11\}$

In[18]:= **Sort[myList]**

Out[18]= $\{1, 5, 11, 12, 18, 19, 40, 45, 47, 51, 64, 68, 79, 91, 100\}$

The sorting may be accomplished via a sorting function which returns **True** precisely when its two arguments are given in the desired order. Each of the notations below accomplish the same thing: they put the list in reverse order:

In[19]:= **Sort[myList, Function[{x, y}, x > y]]**

Out[19]= $\{100, 91, 79, 68, 64, 51, 47, 45, 40, 19, 18, 12, 11, 5, 1\}$

In[20]:= **Sort[myList, Function[#1 > #2]]**

Out[20]= $\{100, 91, 79, 68, 64, 51, 47, 45, 40, 19, 18, 12, 11, 5, 1\}$

In[21]:= **Sort[myList, #1 > #2 &]**

Out[21]= {100, 91, 79, 68, 64, 51, 47, 45, 40, 19, 18, 12, 11, 5, 1}

Note that there are many other ways to accomplish this. For instance, one could **Reverse** the list after it is sorted in ascending order, or one could call the built-in **Greater** command, which accomplishes the same thing as our **Function** above:

In[22]:= **Reverse[Sort[myList]]**

Out[22]= {100, 91, 79, 68, 64, 51, 47, 45, 40, 19, 18, 12, 11, 5, 1}

In[23]:= **Sort[myList, Greater]**

Out[23]= {100, 91, 79, 68, 64, 51, 47, 45, 40, 19, 18, 12, 11, 5, 1}

But here we sort a list of vectors according to their **Norm**. There is no better way to accomplish this feat than with a sorting **Function**:

In[24]:= **myList = RandomInteger[100, {10, 3}]**

Out[24]= {{82, 7, 96}, {97, 10, 6}, {13, 96, 6}, {28, 63, 42}, {45, 75, 17}, {87, 98, 40}, {84, 86, 58}, {62, 0, 6}, {59, 35, 65}, {2, 97, 35}}

In[25]:= **Sort[myList, Norm[#1] < Norm[#2] &]**

Out[25]= {{62, 0, 6}, {28, 63, 42}, {45, 75, 17}, {59, 35, 65}, {13, 96, 6}, {97, 10, 6}, {2, 97, 35}, {82, 7, 96}, {84, 86, 58}, {87, 98, 40}}

And here we sort the same list of vectors according to the value of the third coordinate:

In[26]:= **Sort[myList, #1[[3]] < #2[[3]] &]**

Out[26]= {{62, 0, 6}, {13, 96, 6}, {97, 10, 6}, {45, 75, 17}, {2, 97, 35}, {87, 98, 40}, {28, 63, 42}, {84, 86, 58}, {59, 35, 65}, {82, 7, 96}}

In[27]:= **Clear[myList]**

RegionFunction and **MeshFunctions** specifications in 3D plotting commands are typically each given as a **Function** with multiple arguments. In this setting the **Slot** values **#1**, **#2**, and **#3** stand for the coordinate values x, y, and z respectively. Below the **RegionFunction** setting specifies that the domain is the interior of the circle of radius 2 centered at the origin, while the **MeshFunctions** setting specifies that **Mesh** lines will be drawn at equally spaced z values.

In[28]:= Plot3D$\left[e^{-(x^2+y^2)}, \{x, -2, 2\}, \{y, -2, 2\}, \textbf{RegionFunction} \rightarrow (\textbf{Norm}[\{\#1, \#2\}] < 2 \,\&),\right.$

$\left.\textbf{MeshFunctions} \rightarrow \{\#3 \,\&\}, \textbf{PlotPoints} \rightarrow 30\right]$

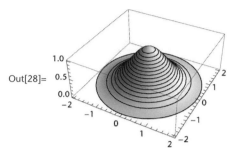

Out[28]=

Functional Programming

Mathematica is a *functional programming* language. That is, unlike languages such as BASIC and C, *Mathematica* commands can operate not only on specific types of numbers and data structures, but on arbitrary expressions. In particular, the argument to one function may be another function. This provides a powerful and elegant paradigm for programming. While we will not provide a philosophical discussion on the advantages and nature of functional programming, suffice it to say that if you've read and followed this section to this point you're already doing it. **Map** and **Function** are your point of entry. Commands such as **Apply**, **Thread**, and **MapThread** (introduced below) will expand your horizons, while **Nest**, **Fold**, replacement rules and pattern matching (introduced later in the chapter) will take you to the next level.

A useful command that is similar to **Map** is **Apply**. Like **Map**, **Apply** takes two arguments: a function and an expression (often a list). The output is the second argument, with its head *replaced* by the function in the first argument. That's it; **Apply** will pluck the head off of any expression and replace it with something else. For example, **Apply[Times, List[a, b, c]]** will return **Times[a, b, c]**:

In[1]:= **Apply[Times, {a, b, c}]**

Out[1]= a b c

Apply can be given in infix form via **@@**.

In[2]:= **Times @@ {a, b, c}**

Out[2]= a b c

Here's another example. We randomly generate 40 points in the plane (ordered pairs of numbers, with each coordinate between −1 and 1), then replace **Point** by **Line** to connect the individual points with line segments, and by **Polygon** to fill the resulting regions. Finally, we display all three together.

In[3]:= **pts = Point[RandomReal[{−1, 1}, {40, 2}]];**
Graphics[pts]

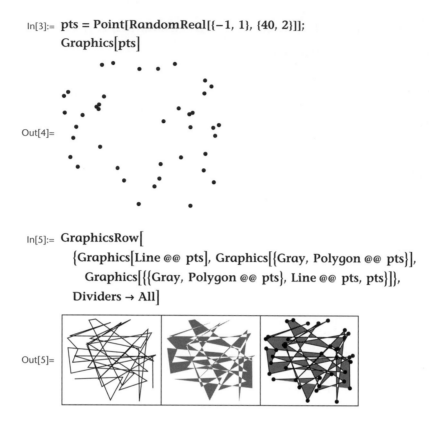

Out[4]=

In[5]:= **GraphicsRow[**
  {Graphics[Line @@ pts], Graphics[{Gray, Polygon @@ pts}],
  Graphics[{{Gray, Polygon @@ pts}, Line @@ pts, pts}]},
  Dividers → All]

Out[5]=

In[6]:= **Clear[pts]**

The command **Thread** can be used to "thread" a function over several lists. In the example below, the (undefined) function is called **f**. It is called with two arguments, each of which is a list. Wrapping this expression in **Thread** causes f to be called on corresponding members of the two lists, with the output being a list of the results:

In[7]:= **Thread[f[{a, b, c}, {1, 2, 3}]]**

Out[7]= {f[a, 1], f[b, 2], f[c, 3]}

Here are two applications. The first shows how to use **Thread** to programmatically create a list of rules from a list of left-side values and a list of right-side values. In this case, the command **Rule** plays the role of the function **f** above. The second example illustrates that **Thread** has the same effect as **Transpose** on a list of lists (i.e., on a matrix). In this case **List** plays the role of the function **f** above.

In[8]:= **Thread[{a, b, c} → {1, 2, 3}]**

Out[8]= {a → 1, b → 2, c → 3}

In[9]:= **Thread[{{a, b, c}, {1, 2, 3}}]**

Out[9]= {{a, 1}, {b, 2}, {c, 3}}

The command **MapThread** combines the functionality of **Map** and **Thread**. The example below illustrates a typical implementation. It essentially does what **Thread** does, but there are two arguments, with the function (in this case **f**) being given alone as the first argument.

In[10]:= **MapThread[f, {{a, b, c}, {1, 2, 3}}]**

Out[10]= {f[a, 1], f[b, 2], f[c, 3]}

An example that illustrates the utility of **MapThread** follows. Suppose you wish to construct a 3D graphic of a right cylinder whose top and bottom are regular polygons. These polygons are easily constructed (we utilize **Map** to add the third coordinate to each vertex):

In[11]:= **n = 10;**

$$\textbf{pts = Table}\Big[\textbf{\{Cos[t], Sin[t]\}}, \Big\{\textbf{t, 0, 2}\pi, \frac{\textbf{2}\pi}{\textbf{n}}\Big\}\Big];$$

bottom = Map[Append[#, 0] &, pts];

top = Map[Append[#, 1] &, pts];

Graphics3D[Map[Polygon, {top, bottom}]]

Out[15]=
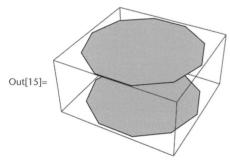

The rub is constructing the *n* rectangles that make up the sides. Suppose that $\{b_1, b_2\}$ is a list of two adjacent vertices on the bottom polygon, and that $\{t_1, t_2\}$ are the vertices on the top polygon directly above these. The side of the cylinder with these four vertices will have the form **Polygon[$\{b_1, b_2, t_2, t_1\}$]**. To get this, we will **Partition** the top and bottom vertices into sublists of length 2 with an offset (or overlap) of 1, and **Reverse** each ordered pair of vertices on the top. We'll then use **MapThread** to **Join** the corresponding lists. Here's an illustration of the idea:

In[16]:= **Partition[{b1, b2, b3}, 2, 1]**

Out[16]= {{b1, b2}, {b2, b3}}

In[17]:= **Reverse /@ Partition[{t1, t2, t3}, 2, 1]**

Out[17]= {{t2, t1}, {t3, t2}}

In[18]:= **MapThread[Join, {%%, %}]**

Out[18]= {{b1, b2, t2, t1}, {b2, b3, t3, t2}}

Here's the finished product:

In[19]:= **sides = MapThread[Join, {Partition[bottom, 2, 1], Reverse /@ Partition[top, 2, 1]}];**
Graphics3D[Polygon /@ Join[{top, bottom}, sides]]

Out[20]=

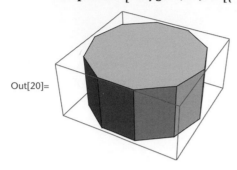

In[21]:= **Clear[n, pts, top, bottom, sides]**

Exercises 8.4

1. The command **First**, when applied to a list, will return the first item in the list. More generally, **First[f[a,b,c]]** will return the first argument **a** for any command **f**. Compare the outputs of the commands **Options[NSolve]** and **First/@ Options[NSolve]**. What is the command **f** to which **First** is being applied in this case?

2. Use **Function** to define a command which when given an integer argument *n* between 1 and 26 will return the *n*th letter of the alphabet. Use it to find the 19th letter of the alphabet.

3. What is the **FullForm** of the pure function $\#^2$ &?

4. What is the **FullForm** of the pure function **Norm[{#1, #2}] < 3**?

5. One could have, back at the beginning of Chapter 3, taken a different approach to defining a function such as $f(x) = x^2 + 3x - 1$ in *Mathematica*. Back then we advocated the following convention to define this function: **f[x_] := $x^2 + 3x - 1$**. In this exercise we'll consider an alternate approach: **f = Function[x, $x^2 + 3x - 1$]**.

   a. Define *f* using **Function**, then make a **Plot** of *f* on the domain $-5 \le x \le 2$.

   b. Use *Mathematica* to differentiate and integrate *f*.

6. How would you use **Function** to define the multivariable real-valued function $f(x, y) = x^2 y - x + 3y$?

7. How would you use **Function** to define the vector field $f(x, y) = \langle x^2 y - x + 3y, \cos x\rangle$?

8. Map, Function, and **Apply** can be used to transform a simple **Table** into a stunning display. In this exercise you will work with the table below, where each row holds the left and right sides of a trigonometric identity.

$$t = \text{Table}[\{\text{Tan}[k\,a], \text{Together}[\text{TrigExpand}[\text{Tan}[k\,a]]]\}, \{k, 2, 9\}];$$

a. Use **Map, Function, Apply** and **Equal** on **t**, and display the result with **Column** and **Tradition·. alForm** to produce the output below:

$$\tan(2\,a) = \frac{2\cos(a)\sin(a)}{\cos^2(a)-\sin^2(a)}$$

$$\tan(3\,a) = \frac{\sec(a)\left(3\cos^2(a)\sin(a)-\sin^3(a)\right)}{\cos^2(a)-3\sin^2(a)}$$

$$\tan(4\,a) = \frac{4\left(\cos^3(a)\sin(a)-\cos(a)\sin^3(a)\right)}{\cos^4(a)-6\sin^2(a)\cos^2(a)+\sin^4(a)}$$

$$\tan(5\,a) = \frac{\sec(a)\left(\sin^5(a)-10\cos^2(a)\sin^3(a)+5\cos^4(a)\sin(a)\right)}{\cos^4(a)-10\sin^2(a)\cos^2(a)+5\sin^4(a)}$$

$$\tan(6\,a) = \frac{2\left(3\sin(a)\cos^5(a)-10\sin^3(a)\cos^3(a)+3\sin^5(a)\cos(a)\right)}{\cos^6(a)-15\sin^2(a)\cos^4(a)+15\sin^4(a)\cos^2(a)-\sin^6(a)}$$

$$\tan(7\,a) = \frac{\sec(a)\left(-\sin^7(a)+21\cos^2(a)\sin^5(a)-35\cos^4(a)\sin^3(a)+7\cos^6(a)\sin(a)\right)}{\cos^6(a)-21\sin^2(a)\cos^4(a)+35\sin^4(a)\cos^2(a)-7\sin^6(a)}$$

$$\tan(8\,a) = \frac{8\left(\sin(a)\cos^7(a)-7\sin^3(a)\cos^5(a)+7\sin^5(a)\cos^3(a)-\sin^7(a)\cos(a)\right)}{\cos^8(a)-28\sin^2(a)\cos^6(a)+70\sin^4(a)\cos^4(a)-28\sin^6(a)\cos^2(a)+\sin^8(a)}$$

$$\tan(9\,a) = \frac{\sec(a)\left(\sin^9(a)-36\cos^2(a)\sin^7(a)+126\cos^4(a)\sin^5(a)-84\cos^6(a)\sin^3(a)+9\cos^8(a)\sin(a)\right)}{\cos^8(a)-36\sin^2(a)\cos^6(a)+126\sin^4(a)\cos^4(a)-84\sin^6(a)\cos^2(a)+9\sin^8(a)}$$

b. Use **Map, Function, Apply** and **Rule** on **t**, and display the result with **TabView** and **Tradition·. alForm** to produce the output below:

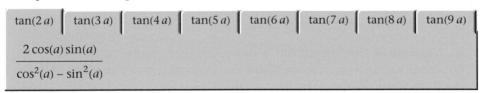

| $\tan(2\,a)$ | $\tan(3\,a)$ | $\tan(4\,a)$ | $\tan(5\,a)$ | $\tan(6\,a)$ | $\tan(7\,a)$ | $\tan(8\,a)$ | $\tan(9\,a)$ |

$$\frac{2\cos(a)\sin(a)}{\cos^2(a)-\sin^2(a)}$$

9. Look up the term *functional programming* in Wikipedia, and contrast it with *procedural programming*.

10. A *cipher* is an encryption scheme whereby each individual character in the message is replaced by some other character or symbol. For instance, one could encode a message by replacing every *a* with *b*, every *b* with *c*, and in general replacing each letter with the next letter, except for *z* which is replaced with *a*. A cipher such as this that is based on a simple shift (replacing each letter with the letter a fixed number of characters to its right) is called a *Caesar cipher*.

a. Use **StringReplace, CharacterRange, Thread**, and **RotateLeft** to build a command **encode**

that will implement this cipher on any **String** comprised of lowercase letters.

  b. Create a **decode** command to decode an encrypted message (you may wish to use **RotateRight**).

11. Modify the commands in the previous exercise so that a second argument controls the number of places that each character is shifted to the left in the encryption process.

8.5 Control Structures and Looping

In contrast to the techniques introduced in the previous section, *procedural programming* is a paradigm in which one gives step by step instructions to the computer. This is often the first type of programming one encounters, using a language such as BASIC or C. *Mathematica* supports this style of programming with looping commands such as **Do**, **For**, and **While**, and control structures such as **If** and **Which**. In this section we'll discuss the use of these commands.

The most simple looping command is **Do**. Its syntax is like that of **Table**; the first argument is an expression, and additional arguments are iterators. The expression is evaluated once for each value assumed by the iterated variable. For example:

In[1]:= **myList = {};**
    Do[PrependTo[myList, k], {k, 10}];
    myList

Out[3]= {10, 9, 8, 7, 6, 5, 4, 3, 2, 1}

Above we begin with an empty list **myList**, and then **PrependTo** (put at the beginning of) this list each of the first ten whole numbers in turn, beginning with 1. While effective, this procedural code is certainly not the easiest way to produce this list. Here's another way:

In[4]:= **Reverse[Range[10]]**

Out[4]= {10, 9, 8, 7, 6, 5, 4, 3, 2, 1}

As a second example, we use **Do** to write a procedural program for calculating the factorial of any integer. Yes, there is a built-in command **Factorial** (!) that does this already; the point is simply to illustrate how **Do** works. We begin by having **Do** calculate 4 factorial. First the dummy variable **x** is set to 1. Then as k assumes the integer values 1 to 4 in turn, **x** is set to k times its current value. So first **x** becomes $1 \times 1 = 1$, then $2 \times 1 = 2$, then $3 \times 2 = 6$, then $4 \times 6 = 24$.

In[5]:= **x = 1;**
    Do[x = k * x, {k, 4}];
    x

Out[7]= 24

We use this idea to create a command **fac** to calculate the factorial of any positive integer n. We use **SetDelayed** (:=) for we do not want to evaluate the right side until **fac** is called.

In[8]:= **fac[n_] := (x = 1; Do[x = k * x, {k, n}]; x)**

For example:

In[9]:= **TabView[Table[ToString[n] ~~ "!" → fac[n], {n, 15}], 13]**

Out[9]=

| 1! | 2! | 3! | 4! | 5! | 6! | 7! | 8! | 9! | 10! | 11! | 12! | 13! | 14! | 15! |

6 227 020 800

In[10]:= **Clear[fac, x]**

Note that the first argument to **Do** can be a **CompoundExpression** (a sequence of commands separated by semicolons). This allows you to **Do** more than one thing, or to organize your code into simple steps. For instance, below we get serious and harness **Do** to implement the *secant method* for approximating the root of an equation $f(x) = 0$. You may recall that this method begins with two points x_0 and x_1 near the root in question. One then builds a sequence of values $x_1, x_2, x_3,...$ that (one hopes) will be successively better approximations to the actual root. The sequence is constructed recursively via the second-order difference equation

$$x_{n+1} = x_n - \frac{x_n - x_{n-1}}{f(x_n) - f(x_{n-1})} f(x_n).$$

Below we harness **Do** to carry out nine steps of this process on the cubic $f(x) = x^3 - 2x + 2$ (you can check that f has only one real root), starting at $x_0 = -1$ and $x_1 = -3/2$. In this implementation we use **x0** and **x1** to represent the current values of x_{n-1} and x_n, respectively, in the equation above. We use **xtemp** to temporarily hold the value of x_n so that x_{n-1} may assume this value in the next iteration. Note also that the iterator for **Do** in this case is the ultra-simple {9}, which simply means, "do this nine times."

In[11]:= **f[x_] := x³ - 2 x + 2**

In[12]:= **x0 = -1;**
x1 = -3/2;
Do[xtemp = x1;

$$x1 = x1 - \frac{x1 - x0}{f[x1] - f[x0]} f[x1];$$

x0 = xtemp;
Print[N[x1, 40]], {9}]

$$-2.0909090909090909090909090909090909090909091$$

$$-1.7094540612516644474034620505992 01065246$$

$$-1.7572059088653598309817648685407 67091628$$

$$-1.7698322573735966862953097269129 82898092$$

$$-1.7692876392216070755478015705362 91382136$$

$$-1.7692923524110248601104785537089 65415028$$

$$-1.7692923542386376035746646973481 16397970$$

$$-1.7692923542386314152404013423314 42514107$$

$$-1.7692923542386314152404094643350 33492634$$

In this case we obtain 38 digit precision, for the actual real root (to forty digit precision) looks like this:

In[15]:= **N[Reduce[f[x] == 0, x, Reals], 40]**

Out[15]= $x == -1.7692923542386314152404094643350 33492671$

While **Do** is effective, the secant method and the Newton-Raphson method for approximating roots can be implemented more efficiently using **NestList**. Implementations can be found in Section 8.7. See page 437 for Newton-Raphson, and Exercise 5 on page 442 for the secant method.

Do can also accept more than one iterator. Below **k** assumes integer values from 0 to 3, while **m** assumes the values **a**, **b**, and **c**.

In[16]:= **myList = {};**
        Do[AppendTo[myList, k + m], {k, 0, 3}, {m, {a, b, c}}];
        myList

Out[18]= {a, b, c, 1 + a, 1 + b, 1 + c, 2 + a, 2 + b, 2 + c, 3 + a, 3 + b, 3 + c}

In[19]:= **Clear[myList]**

Predicates

Many control structures rely on conditions that are either true or false. If a condition is true, a certain set of instructions are given, while if the condition is false, an alternate set of instructions are given. In logic, a statement that is either true or false is called a *predicate*. In computer science, a command that returns one of the values true or false is sometimes referred to as a *query*. *Mathematica* has many predicate commands, which often end in the letter Q (for query). These commands return either the symbol **True** or the symbol **False**.

In[20]:= **PrimeQ$\left[2^{16} + 1\right]$**

Out[20]= True

In[21]:= **Table[EvenQ[n], {n, 10}]**

Out[21]= {False, True, False, True, False, True, False, True, False, True}

Another useful predicate command is **FreeQ**, which will return **True** if the expression appearing in its first argument is completely free of the pattern or expression in its second argument. Note that for atomic expressions (such as numbers), one can use their **Head** (e.g., **Integer**, **Rational**, **Real**, **Complex**) for the second argument.

In[22]:= **FreeQ$\left[\{2, 3, 4\}, \text{Complex}\right]$**

Out[22]= True

In[23]:= **FreeQ$\left[\{2, 3, 4 + 2\,i\}, \text{Complex}\right]$**

Out[23]= False

In[24]:= **FreeQ$\left[\text{Solve}\left[x^3 + 34\,x^2 - 9\,x + 1 == 0, x\right], \text{Complex}\right]$**

Out[24]= False

An equation can be a useful predicate.

In[25]:= **2 == 3**

Out[25]= False

In[26]:= **N$[\pi]$ == 1.0 $* \pi$**

Out[26]= True

Note also that one can reverse the output of a predicate command by wrapping it in **Not**. The prefix form of **Not[*expr*]** is !*expr*.

In[27]:= **! False**

Out[27]= True

In[28]:= **! PrimeQ[8]**

Out[28]= True

In the case of equations, one may type != for **Unequal**, or use the ≠ button on the BasicMathInput palette.

In[29]:= $2 \neq 3$

Out[29]= True

Here's an application that requires predicates: the **Select** command is used to select those items from a list that satisfy a condition. More precisely, a predicate command is applied to each member of the given list, and **Select** returns those items in the list for which the predicate is **True**. Here we **Select** all integers from 1 to 30 that are prime:

In[30]:= **Select[Range[30], PrimeQ]**

Out[30]= {2, 3, 5, 7, 11, 13, 17, 19, 23, 29}

It is common to use a **Function** to create a specialized predicate. Here we select those items in the given list whose value is at least 4:

In[31]:= **Select[{1, 2, 3, 4, 5, 6}, # ≥ 4 &]**

Out[31]= {4, 5, 6}

Here are all integers from 1 to 1000 with more than 3 distinct prime factors:

In[32]:= **Select[Range[1000], Length[FactorInteger[#]] > 3 &]**

Out[32]= {210, 330, 390, 420, 462, 510, 546, 570, 630, 660, 690,
          714, 770, 780, 798, 840, 858, 870, 910, 924, 930, 966, 990}

Select is useful for extracting numerical items from long lists. For instance, a few of the countries listed in **CountryData** do not currently have oil consumption figures available.

In[33]:= **CountryData["Andorra", "OilConsumption"]**

Out[33]= Missing[NotAvailable]

Recalling that **CountryData[]** returns a list of all countries in the data set, the input and output below reveals that (at the time of this writing) there are 237 countries in the world, and there are *numerical* oil consumption values known for 211 of these, while these data are missing for the remaining 26.

In[34]:= **Length /@ {CountryData[], Select[CountryData[],**
          NumericQ[CountryData[#, "OilConsumption"]] &], Select[CountryData[],
          CountryData[#, "OilConsumption"] == Missing["NotAvailable"] &]}

Out[34]= {237, 211, 26}

Control Structures: If, Which, Piecewise

The most basic control structure is the **If** command. Its usage is straightforward: it accepts three arguments. The first is a predicate. The second is what is to be evaluated if the predicate is **True**, and the third is what is to be evaluated if the predicate is **False**. Here, for example, we test a few nearby numbers for primality, and display the results in a table:

In[36]:= **Text @ Grid[**
    Table[{k, If[PrimeQ[k], "prime", "composite"]}, {k, 101, 117, 2}],
    Dividers → Gray]

Out[36]=

101	prime
103	prime
105	composite
107	prime
109	prime
111	composite
113	prime
115	composite
117	composite

Here's an example in which we combine an **If** control structure with a **Do** loop to investigate a conjecture made by Leibniz himself in the field of number theory. Leibniz observed that:

$$2^2 - 1 \text{ is divisible by 3,}$$
$$2^4 - 1 \text{ is divisible by 5,}$$
$$2^6 - 1 \text{ is divisible by 7,}$$
$$2^8 - 1 \text{ is NOT divisible by 9,}$$
$$2^{10} - 1 \text{ is divisible by 11,}$$
$$2^{12} - 1 \text{ is divisible by 13,}$$
$$2^{14} - 1 \text{ is NOT divisible by 15,}$$
$$2^{16} - 1 \text{ is divisible by 17, and so on.}$$

He conjectured that $2^n - 1$ will be evenly divisible by $n + 1$ if and only if $n + 1$ is an odd prime. The numbers on the right in these examples, after all, are primes precisely in those cases where divisibility occurs. One can restate this conjecture as follows: $\frac{2^n - 1}{n+1}$ will be an integer precisely when $n + 1$ is an odd prime. Here we check it for the values of n up to 200. It would appear that Leibniz was on to something!

In[37]:= $\text{Table}\left[\text{If}\left[\text{PrimeQ}[n + 1] == \text{IntegerQ}\left[\frac{2^n - 1}{n + 1}\right], \text{True}, \text{False}\right], \{n, 2, 200, 2\}\right]$

Out[37]= {True, True, True, True, True, True, True, True, True, True, True, True, True, True, True,
  True, True, True, True, True, True, True, True, True, True, True, True, True, True, True,
  True, True, True, True, True, True, True, True, True, True, True, True, True, True,
  True, True, True, True, True, True, True, True, True, True, True, True, True, True,
  True, True, True, True, True, True, True, True, True, True, True, True, True, True,
  True, True, True, True, True, True, True, True, True, True, True, True, True, True,
  True, True, True, True, True, True, True, True, True, True, True, True, True, True}

The predicate above (the first argument in the **If** command) in this case is an equation with one of **True** or **False** appearing on each side. It will be **True** if and only if the two symbols agree. For instance:

In[38]:= {True == True, True == False, False == True, False == False}

Out[38]= {True, False, False, True}

A quick way to make sure a long list (such as the **Table** above) contains only the symbol **True** is to **Apply** the **And** command to it. **And** gives **True** only if each of its arguments is **True**. We see, for instance, that Leibniz was correct up through $n = 338$:

In[39]:= $\text{And } @@ \text{Table}\left[\text{If}\left[\text{PrimeQ}[n + 1] == \text{IntegerQ}\left[\frac{2^n - 1}{n + 1}\right], \text{True}, \text{False}\right], \{n, 2, 338, 2\}\right]$

Out[39]= True

But, unfortunately, when $n = 340$ the conjecture fails. And it fails for several larger values of n as well. Here are the values of $n + 1$ for which it fails up through $10\,000$:

In[40]:= **counterExamples = {};**

$\text{Do}\left[\text{If}\left[\text{PrimeQ}[n + 1] \text{ != } \text{IntegerQ}\left[\frac{2^n - 1}{n + 1}\right],\right.$

$\left.\text{AppendTo}[\text{counterExamples}, n + 1]\right], \{n, 2, 10\,000, 2\}\right];$

counterExamples

Out[42]= {341, 561, 645, 1105, 1387, 1729, 1905, 2047, 2465, 2701, 2821,
  3277, 4033, 4369, 4371, 4681, 5461, 6601, 7957, 8321, 8481, 8911}

So the conjecture, despite its promising start, is most definitely false. How exactly does it fail? Either 341 is not prime while $\frac{2^{340}-1}{341}$ is an integer, *or* 341 is prime while $\frac{2^{34}-1}{341}$ is not an integer. It turns out to be the former:

In[43]:= **PrimeQ[341]**

Out[43]= False

In[44]:= **IntegerQ$\left[\dfrac{2^n - 1}{n + 1} \; /. \; n \to 340\right]$**

Out[44]= True

All of our counterexamples fail this way:

In[45]:= **PrimeQ /@ counterExamples**

Out[45]= {False, False, False, False, False, False, False, False, False, False, False,
    False, False, False, False, False, False, False, False, False, False, False}

Does it never fail the other way round? That is, if p is an odd prime, must it be the case that $\dfrac{2^{p-1} - 1}{p}$ is an integer? The answer is *yes*. This is a consequence of Fermat's little theorem (which you can look up online at MathWorld). So to his credit, Leibniz was half right. If he had a copy of *Mathematica*, he certainly would have been able to see the folly of his original conjecture. Given that the first counterexample occurs at $n = 340$, and involves checking that $2^{340} - 1$ is divisible by 341, it is understandable that he believed this conjecture. And given that you have access to *Mathematica*, it is a reasonably simple matter for you to make investigations of this nature to peer deeply into the world of numbers.

Which is similar to **If**. The arguments come in pairs. The first argument in each pair is a predicate, and the second is an expression to evaluate if that predicate is **True**. **Which** will return the output associated with the *first* predicate that is **True**. For instance:

In[47]:= **Text @ Grid[Table[{n, Which[n == 1, "is a unit", PrimeQ[n], "is a prime",**
        EvenQ[n], "is an even composite", OddQ[n], "is an odd composite"]},
      {n, 10}], Alignment → {{Right, Left}}]

Out[47]=
1	is a unit
2	is a prime
3	is a prime
4	is an even composite
5	is a prime
6	is an even composite
7	is a prime
8	is an even composite
9	is an odd composite
10	is an even composite

The number $n = 1$ satisfies the first and last predicate, but it is the expression corresponding to the first that is evaluated.

Similar to **Which** is the **Piecewise** command, introduced in Section 3.6. It has the advantage of reading very nicely when its infix form is utilized. Type ⎋**pw**⎋ followed by one or more ⌃⏎ (Mac OS) or ⎈⏎ (Windows), one for each additional line.

$$\text{In[48]:= } \textbf{Text} @ \textbf{Grid}\left[\textbf{Table}\left[\left\{n, \begin{cases} \text{"is a unit"} & n == 1 \\ \text{"is a prime"} & \text{PrimeQ[n]} \\ \text{"is an even composite"} & \text{EvenQ[n]} \\ \text{"is an odd composite"} & \text{OddQ[n]} \end{cases}\right\}, \{n, 10\}\right],\right.$$

$$\left. \textbf{Alignment} \rightarrow \{\{\textbf{Right, Left}\}\}\right]$$

Out[48]=

1	is a unit
2	is a prime
3	is a prime
4	is an even composite
5	is a prime
6	is an even composite
7	is a prime
8	is an even composite
9	is an odd composite
10	is an even composite

Looping with While and For

The most basic looping command is **Do**. The commands **While** and **For** also allow you to repeat a procedure, but rather than using an iterator to control the body of the loop, a predicate is utilized instead. Each of these procedural commands closely mirrors its counterpart in the C language.

The **While** command takes two arguments. The first is a predicate. The second is the body, which will be evaluated repeatedly until the predicate returns **False**. Here we use a **While** loop to find the first prime number greater than 1000. We **Set** a dummy variable k to be 1000, and then **Increment** k (increase its value by 1) until it is a prime. The value of this prime (the current value of k) is then returned.

```
In[49]:= k = 1000;
        While[ ! PrimeQ[k], Increment[k]];
        k
```

Out[51]= 1009

Note that the **Increment** command has the alternate postfix syntax ++. That is, **Increment[k]** can be typed as **k++**. Here, for instance, we use the same technique to find the first prime greater than one million:

In[52]:= **k = 1 000 000;**
　　　　While[! PrimeQ[k], k++];
　　　　k

Out[54]= 1 000 003

The **For** command accepts four arguments (no pun intended), although three will suffice if the body is empty. You can, for instance, use **For** to write a procedure like those above to find the first prime number exceeding 1000: for k starting at 1000, and as long as k is not a prime, continue incrementing k by one. At this point, return the value of k. Here is how to implement this program:

In[55]:= **For[k = 1000, ! PrimeQ[k], k++]; k**

Out[55]= 1009

The general syntax takes the form **For[***start, test, increment, body***]**. Upon entry, *start* is evaluated, and then the *increment* and *body* are evaluated repeatedly until the *test* returns **False**. In the example below, we take a starting number and repeatedly divide it by 2 until the result is no longer an integer. The body makes use of the **Print** command, which forces the value of k to be printed at each step.

In[56]:= **For[k = 1296, IntegerQ[k], k = k/2, Print[k]]**

1296

648

324

162

81

Exercises 8.5

1. Enter the input **?*Q** to get a listing of all commands that end with a capital Q. Here you will find many of the basic predicate commands that will output one of the symbols **True** or **False**.

2. The great French mathematician Pierre de Fermat (1601–1665) postulated that every number exceeding by one the quantity two raised to a power of two must be a prime number. That is, every number of the form $2^{(2^n)} + 1$ is prime according to Fermat. It was about a century later that he was proved wrong, by none other than Leonard Euler. Find the first counterexample to Fermat's famous conjecture.

3. The two most commonly used methods for incrementing a dummy variable are **Increment** (*postfix* form ++), described in this section, and **PreIncrement** (*prefix* form ++). Enter the commands **j = 1; j++** and **k = 1; ++k**, and describe the difference.

4. Find the smallest positive integer n with the property that $\int_0^{21/20-1/n} x^n\, dx > \frac{1}{10}$.

5. Write a **For** loop to carry out the following procedure: Beginning with the number 1, keep adding a random integer chosen between 1 and 100 to the current value until such time as the result is a prime.

   a. Write the loop so that all intermediate results are displayed.

   b. Write the loop so that a *list* of all intermediate values, including the last, is displayed.

   c. Write the loop so that only the number of iterations required is displayed.

   d. Run the procedure from part **c** 1000 times (using **Table**), and **Tally** the results.

8.6 Scoping Constructs: With and Module

When writing a program it is common to make one or more intermediate assignments. See, for instance, the example at the end of Section 8.4 on page 411, where we wrote a program to display a 3D graphic of a right cylinder whose base is a regular n-gon. In that example assignments were made to the symbols **n**, **pts**, **top**, **bottom**, and **sides**. These assignments were only used to create the image, and were not needed afterward. Another example appears below. It provides a means of drawing a regular n-gon for any integer $n > 2$.

In[1]:= **n = 10;**

$$\textbf{Graphics}\Big[\textbf{Line}\Big[\textbf{Table}\Big[\{\textbf{Cos[t], Sin[t]}\}, \Big\{\textbf{t, 0, 2}\pi, \frac{2\pi}{\textbf{n}}\Big\}\Big]\Big]\Big]$$

Out[2]=

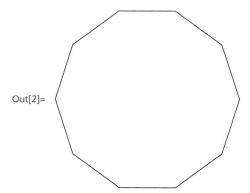

The only potentially bad consequence of this construction is that the symbol **n** has been **Set** to the value 10. This has the potential to interfere with other evaluations involving this symbol that you might try to make. For instance, if after entering the input above, you try to **Solve** an equation for n you will run into trouble:

In[3]:= **Solve[3 n + 1 == 22, n]**

General::ivar : 10 is not a valid variable. ≫

Out[3]= Solve[False, 10]

Essentially, you must be diligent in **Clear**ing all such assignments before using these symbols in another setting. A better practice is to make assignments *locally*. This is easily accomplished by putting them inside of a *scoping* command, such as **With** or **Module**. Whatever is assigned in a scoping command *stays* in the scoping command.

In[4]:= **Clear[n];**

$$\textbf{With}\left[\{n = 5\}, \textbf{Graphics}\left[\textbf{Line}\left[\textbf{Table}\left[\{Cos[t], Sin[t]\}, \left\{t, 0, 2\pi, \frac{2\pi}{n}\right\}\right]\right]\right]\right]$$

Out[5]=

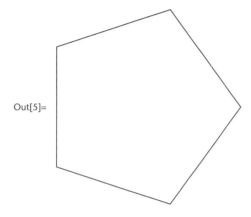

In this case, **n** has not been assigned a value in the **Global`** context (where one typically works):

In[6]:= **n**

Out[6]= n

This means that the local assignment made to the symbol **n** will not interfere with subsequent evaluations:

In[7]:= **Solve[3 n + 1 == 22, n]**

Out[7]= {{n → 7}}

With accepts two arguments. Its first argument is a list of assignments. Its second argument is an expression. The assignments given in the first argument only work in the expression appearing in the second argument. Their scope is local; they do not persist afterward, nor do they affect any previous assignments. The command name **With** suggests its use; you can read the input code like a sentence that begins, "With *n* = 10, do the following...." Here's another example. Note how the

With statement does not affect the earlier assignment **n = 3**, and how this assignment does not affect the **n** appearing within the **With** statement.

In[8]:= **n = 3;**
   With[{n = 10}, n²]

Out[9]= 100

In[10]:= **n**

Out[10]= 3

Another useful scoping construct, and indeed a more general one, is **Module**. It works much like **With**, insulating any symbols you have already defined from its own local variables, and vice-versa. The main difference between **Module** and **With** (from the user's perspective) is that the local variables in a **Module** do not need to be assigned in the first argument (although they do have to be listed there). Delayed assignments (:=) may also be used in a **Module**, while only immediate assignments (=) can be used in **With**. Here's a simple example:

We're going to draw a star shape. We'll begin with a list of $2n$ points equally spaced around the unit circle. We then multiply every second point (as we move clockwise around the circle) by a scalar, to move it farther from the origin along its radial axis. Finally, we connect the resulting list of points with line segments. Let's do this step by step with $n = 5$:

In[11]:= **n = 5;**

$$\mathbf{pts = Table\left[\{Sin[t], Cos[t]\}, \left\{t, 0, 2\pi, \frac{2\pi}{2n}\right\}\right]}$$

Out[12]= $\left\{\{0, 1\}, \left\{\sqrt{\frac{5}{8} - \frac{\sqrt{5}}{8}}, \frac{1}{4}\left(1 + \sqrt{5}\right)\right\}, \left\{\sqrt{\frac{5}{8} + \frac{\sqrt{5}}{8}}, \frac{1}{4}\left(-1 + \sqrt{5}\right)\right\}, \right.$

$\left\{\sqrt{\frac{5}{8} + \frac{\sqrt{5}}{8}}, \frac{1}{4}\left(1 - \sqrt{5}\right)\right\}, \left\{\sqrt{\frac{5}{8} - \frac{\sqrt{5}}{8}}, \frac{1}{4}\left(-1 - \sqrt{5}\right)\right\}, \{0, -1\},$

$\left\{-\sqrt{\frac{5}{8} - \frac{\sqrt{5}}{8}}, \frac{1}{4}\left(-1 - \sqrt{5}\right)\right\}, \left\{-\sqrt{\frac{5}{8} + \frac{\sqrt{5}}{8}}, \frac{1}{4}\left(1 - \sqrt{5}\right)\right\},$

$\left.\left\{-\sqrt{\frac{5}{8} + \frac{\sqrt{5}}{8}}, \frac{1}{4}\left(-1 + \sqrt{5}\right)\right\}, \left\{-\sqrt{\frac{5}{8} - \frac{\sqrt{5}}{8}}, \frac{1}{4}\left(1 + \sqrt{5}\right)\right\}, \{0, 1\}\right\}$

Note how our list has $2n + 1 = 11$ points, with the first equal to the last. To get a corresponding list of scale factors for each of these points, we utilize the **Riffle** command to intersperse a scale-factor of 2.5 at every second position in a list of $n + 1 = 6$ ones. The resulting list has length $2n + 1$ to match our list of points.

In[13]:= **scaleList = Riffle[Table[1, {n + 1}], 2.5]**

Out[13]= {1, 2.5, 1, 2.5, 1, 2.5, 1, 2.5, 1, 2.5, 1}

The final picture is obtained by multiplying the two lists (which multiplies their corresponding members), and wrapping the resulting list of points in the **Line** command:

In[14]:= **Graphics[Line[scaleList * pts]]**

Out[14]=

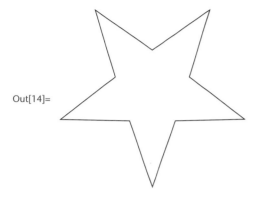

In[15]:= **Clear[n, pts, scaleList]**

Here is how we could organize the individual commands above into a coherent piece of code, all in a single input cell, and in such a way that none of the local variables interferes with a global symbol of the same name. Note that while **n** and **scaleFactor** are assigned in the first argument, the other local variables **pts** and **scaleList** are listed but not assigned there. Rather, they are assigned in the body of the **Module**. This body (the second argument to **Module**) is a **CompoundExpression** (expressions separated by semicolons). The first two such expressions define the local variables **pts** and **scaleList**, and the third creates the **Graphics**. Note also that the values assigned to **pts** and **scaleList** depend on the values of **n** and **scaleFactor**. This would be impossible using **With**, where all local variables must be assigned in the first argument, and independently of one another.

In[454]:= $\text{Module}\big[\{n = 5, \text{scaleFactor} = 2.5, \text{pts}, \text{scaleList}\},$

$\text{pts} = \text{Table}\big[\{\text{Sin[t]}, \text{Cos[t]}\}, \big\{t, 0, 2\pi, \frac{2\pi}{2n}\big\}\big];$

$\text{scaleList} = \text{Riffle[Table[1, \{n + 1\}], scaleFactor]};$

$\text{Graphics}\big[\text{Line}[\text{scaleList} * \text{pts}]\big]\big]$

Finally, we can use this code to create a command for sketching stars, letting the user select values for *n* and the scale factor.

In[16]:= $\text{star}[n\_, \text{scaleFactor\_}] := \text{Module}\Big[\{\text{pts, scaleList}\},$

$\qquad \text{pts} = \text{Table}\Big[\{\text{Sin}[t], \text{Cos}[t]\}, \Big\{t, 0, 2\pi, \dfrac{2\pi}{2n}\Big\}\Big];$

$\qquad \text{scaleList} = \text{Riffle}[\text{Table}[1, \{n + 1\}], \text{scaleFactor}];$

$\qquad \text{Graphics}\big[\text{Line}\big[\text{scaleList} * \text{pts}\big]\big]$

$\Big]$

For instance:

In[17]:= $\text{GraphicsGrid}[\text{Table}[\text{star}[n, k], \{n, 5, 7\}, \{k, 1, 4, .5\}]]$

Out[17]=

Note that it is not *necessary* to use any local variables in the definition above, and hence not necessary to use a **Module** at all. One could just do the following:

In[18]:= $\text{star}[n\_, \text{scale\_}] :=$

$\qquad \text{Graphics}\Big[$

$\qquad\qquad \text{Line}\Big[\text{Riffle}[\text{Table}[1, \{n + 1\}], \text{scale}] * \text{Table}\Big[\{\text{Sin}[t], \text{Cos}[t]\}, \Big\{t, 0, 2\pi, \dfrac{2\pi}{2n}\Big\}\Big]\Big]\Big]$

This is essentially just the last line of code in the earlier **Module**, with local variables **pts** and **scale·List** replaced by their definitions. While more elegant in one sense, some would find the code here more difficult to read. A **Module** allows you to break a complex set of instructions into smaller pieces, with each one easy to read and understand. In more complex settings, a **Module** is actually a more efficient way to code. For instance, if a single large **Table** appears more than once in a program, it is generally more efficient to assign a local variable to represent it (so the **Table** is evaluated only once), and then use that local variable every time the **Table** is needed.

This happens in the example provided below, where the local variable **circlePts** is used twice. This example shows code to produce illustrations of a *circular frustum* (loosely speaking, a cone with its tip cut off). The output is a **Manipulate** in which the user controls the top and bottom radii and the height *h* between them. The code is based on the example given at the end of Section 8.4 on page 411. In this case the top and bottom circles are approximated by many-sided polygons. The number of sides for these polygons is determined by the step size (.05) in the **Table** that defines **circlePts**.

In[19]:= Manipulate[

Module[{circlePts, bottomPts, topPts},

  circlePts = Table[{Cos[t], Sin[t]}, {t, 0, 2 π, .05}];

  bottomPts = Map[Append[#, −h / 2.] &, r2 * circlePts];

  topPts = Map[Append[#, h / 2.] &, r1 * circlePts];

  Graphics3D[{EdgeForm[], Polygon /@ MapThread[Join,

      {Partition[bottomPts, 2, 1, 1], Reverse /@ Partition[topPts, 2, 1, 1]}]},

    PlotRange → 1, Boxed → False, ImageSize → {200},

    PlotLabel → Style["surface area =\n $\pi(r_1+r_2)\sqrt{h^2 + (r_1 - r_2)^2}$ =" ~~

      ToString[PaddedForm[$\pi (r1 + r2) \sqrt{h^2 + (r1 − r2)^2}$, {4, 2}]]]]]

],

{{r1, .6, "r_1"}, .01, 1, Appearance → "Labeled"},

{{r2, 1., "r_2"}, .01, 1, Appearance → "Labeled"},

{{h, 1.}, 0, 2, Appearance → "Labeled"}, Alignment → Center]

Out[19]=

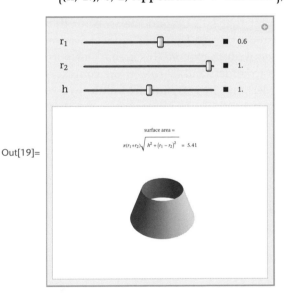

Scoping and Dynamic Elements

Most of the dynamic interfaces and controls that we have seen, such as sliders and buttons, have been generated by the **Manipulate** command. But, as you would expect, **Manipulate** makes calls to a host of lower-level commands that do the real magic, and you have access to these commands as well. The fundamental command at the heart of all such live interactive interfaces is **Dynamic**. Wrap an expression in **Dynamic** and the front end will automatically update it whenever its value changes. Below, for example, we make a **Slider** that ranges from 0 to 3, and that is used to control the values assumed by the symbol **x**.

In[20]:= {Slider[Dynamic[x], {0, 3}], Dynamic[x]}

Out[20]= {⟨————————————————————[ ]—————————————⟩, 1.78}

Note that moving the slider (we moved the one above to 1.78) will actually make an assignment to the symbol **x**:

In[21]:= x

Out[21]= 1.78

The construction of dynamic interfaces with *Mathematica*, while remarkably simple compared with most other programming languages, is a vast subject that falls beyond the scope of this book. The tutorials in the Documentation Center titled "Introduction to Dynamic" and "Advanced Dynamic Functionality" are excellent resources for those who wish to explore this arena. Our purpose here is to introduce the **DynamicModule** command, and to understand its role in the context of the other scoping commands. Like **Module**, any symbols declared in a **DynamicModule** will be insulated from assignments made elsewhere. Below, for instance, we duplicate the input above within a **DynamicModule**.

In[22]:= DynamicModule[{x = 2.5},
         {Slider[Dynamic[x], {0, 3}], Dynamic[x]}]

Out[22]= {⟨——————————————————————[ ]—————————⟩, 2.5}

The dynamic content is now completely insulated from the global variable **x**, whose value is still 1.78:

In[23]:= x

Out[23]= 1.78

Here's a simple but more interesting example. Below we take a thick, orange **PolarPlot** whose independent variable tops out at the dynamically controlled quantity **u**, and superimpose it with the same (but thin) **PolarPlot** on the full domain $0 \le \theta \le 2\pi$. A slider allows you to adjust **u**, so that you can follow the parameterization from 0 to 2π.

In[24]:= **DynamicModule[{u = 4.5},**
    Column[{Slider[Dynamic[u], {.01, 2π}],
        Dynamic @ Show[PolarPlot[Cos[θ] − 2 Cos[4 θ] + 3 Sin[5 θ], {θ, 0, 2π}],
            PolarPlot[Cos[θ] − 2 Cos[4 θ] + 3 Sin[5 θ], {θ, 0, u},
                PlotStyle → Directive[Thick, Orange]]]}, Frame → Gray]]

Out[24]=

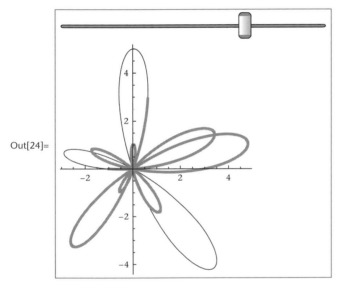

This example illustrates once again the powerful implications of working in a functional programming environment. The **Dynamic** command accepts general *Mathematica* expressions (such as the **Show** expression above), and permits them to be dynamically updated.

The interface and input code above is nearly identical to what one could produce using **Manipu·. late**. The *real* benefit of using dynamic programming constructions (instead of **Manipulate**) is the precise control that is afforded regarding which quantities get dynamically updated and which do not. This is controlled by careful placement of **Dynamic** elements. Above, *both* the static polar plot and the dynamic orange plot are re-evaluated whenever the slider is moved. This is a consequence of wrapping the entire **Show** expression in **Dynamic**. An alternate and slightly more sophisticated input that produces the same output follows. In this case, the static plot is evaluated only once. Only the thick orange plot is dynamically updated by the controller.

In[25]:= **DynamicModule**[{u = 4.5, dynamicPlt},

      dynamicPlt = **Dynamic** @ **First** @ **PolarPlot**[Cos[θ] − 2 Cos[4 θ] + 3 Sin[5 θ],

          {θ, 0, u}, **PlotStyle** → **Directive**[Thick, Orange]];

      Column[{**Slider**[**Dynamic**[u], {.01, 2 π}],

          Show[PolarPlot[Cos[θ] − 2 Cos[4 θ] + 3 Sin[5 θ], {θ, 0, 2 π}], **Graphics**[dynamicPlt]]},

        Frame → **Gray**]]

Out[25]=

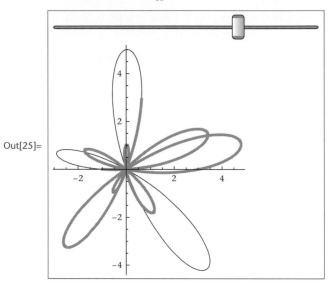

In the input above we applied **First** to the thick, orange **PolarPlot**. This returns the first argument of the **Graphics** generated by **PolarPlot** (essentially a **Line** object with dozens or hundreds of points). **Dynamic** is applied to this quantity, and it is later displayed (by wrapping it in **Graphics**) together with the static plot. The behavior of this output and the previous one are essentially the same, but in principle this latter one is zippier and more responsive as the slider is moved, as fewer items need to be dynamically updated. If you were to add a static but complicated **ContourPlot** to the **Show** argument in each of the last two inputs, the relative zippiness provided by this latter approach would be obvious.

A **DynamicModule**, unlike a **Module**, stores its information in the Front End. If you save a notebook with the output cell above included and re-open it later, it will display properly and the slider will still work, even if you do not re-evaluate the input. Moreover, you could copy the output above and paste it in several different places. Each pasted copy would work independently of the others. In essence, the **DynamicModule** can be thought of as providing insulation in such a way that it stakes out specific real estate in a notebook in which the localizations take place.

Exercises 8.6

1. Here is one way to generate the nth partial sum $1 + \frac{1}{2} + \frac{1}{3} + \cdots + \frac{1}{n}$ of the harmonic series. Explain how it works, and use it to calculate the 100th partial sum of the harmonic series. Compare the output with that of the built-in command **HarmonicNumber**. See also Section 8.7 on page 439 for an alternate definition using **Fold**.

$$\textbf{harmonicNumber}[\textbf{n\_}] := \textbf{Module}\left[\{s = 0\}, \textbf{For}\left[i = 1, i \le n, i++, s = s + \frac{1}{i}\right]; s\right]$$

2. A local variable named **x** within a **Module** creates a symbol with a name such as **x\$30075**, where the stuff to the right of the local variable name is the current value of the system variable **\$Mod·. uleNumber**. This variable is incremented each time any **Module** is called. Create a **Do** loop that will evaluate the expression **Module[{x}, Print[x]]** ten times.

3. In addition to **With** and **Module**, there is a third scoping command called **Block**, whose syntax and purpose matches that of **Module**. **Block** uses a slightly different approach to insulate its local variables. To illustrate how it works, suppose that you have entered **x = 3** in a session, and then create a **Block** with the local assignment **x = 2**. No new symbols will be created. Rather, when the **Block** is evaluated the value of **x** will be temporarily cleared and the local assignment will be utilized. After **Block** is finished the old value of **x** will be restored.

   a. Enter the input below to see **Block** in action.

      x = 3; Block[{x = 2}, Print[x]]; x

   b. Enter the inputs below and explain the different outputs.

      Clear[x]; expr = x + 1
      Block[{x = 2}, x + expr]
      Module[{x = 2}, x + expr]
      Clear[expr]

8.7 Iterations: Nest and Fold

Consider the following input:

In[1]:= **Clear[f, x];**
        NestList[f, x, 3]

Out[2]= {x, f[x], f[f[x]], f[f[f[x]]]}

The command **NestList** is a fundamental tool for iterating a function. When one enters **Nest· List[**command, start, n**]**, a list of length $n + 1$ is created with *start* as the first entry. This is followed by the result of applying *command* to *start* and then the result of applying *command* to this result, and so on, up through *n* applications of *command*. The command **Nest** is similar, and will output only the last item in this list.

In[3]:= **Nest[f, x, 3]**

Out[3]= f[f[f[x]]]

Here's a famous example of the type of problem that is especially amenable to computer exploration using iterations. It is known as the reverse-add problem, or sometimes as the *versum* problem (this being a derivative of "reverse sum"). Take a positive integer and add it to the integer obtained by writing the original number backwards. For instance, if the original number is 29, one adds $29 + 92 = 121$. The result in this case is a *palindrome*, a number that reads the same forward and backward. If you start with 39 and carry out this procedure you get $39 + 93 = 132$ which is not a palindrome. However, apply the procedure to 132 and you get the palindrome 363. It was conjectured long ago that no matter what the starting number a palindrome will eventually result when this procedure is iterated.

Here is a means of using *Mathematica* to carry out the reverse-add procedure. Each step of the procedure can be accomplished by extracting the digits of the input number (**IntegerDigits**), reversing this list of digits (**Reverse**), then converting the reversed digit list back to a number (**FromDigits**) and finally adding it to the original.

In[4]:= **Clear[step];**
step[n_] := n + FromDigits[Reverse[IntegerDigits[n]]]

For example:

In[6]:= **{39, step[39], step[step[39]]}**

Out[6]= {39, 132, 363}

In[7]:= **NestList[step, 39, 2]**

Out[7]= {39, 132, 363}

To explore the conjecture (that every input will lead eventually to a palindrome), let's make a command that will identify palindromes. The command **palStyle** accepts an integer as input and outputs that integer with a frame around it if it is a palindrome and in black otherwise.

In[8]:= **palStyle[n_] := If[IntegerDigits[n] == Reverse[IntegerDigits[n]], Framed[n], n]**

For example, starting with 79 we see three palindromes in the first 20 iterations:

In[9]:= **palStyle /@ NestList[step, 79, 20]**

Out[9]= $\{$79, 176, 847, 1595, 7546, 14 003, $\boxed{44\,044}$, $\boxed{88\,088}$, 176 176, 847 847,

1 596 595, 7 553 546, 14 007 103, $\boxed{44\,177\,144}$, 88 354 288, 176 599 676,

853 595 347, 1 597 190 705, 6 668 108 656, 13 236 127 322, 35 608 290 553 $\}$

For this particular application it would be nice to have a mechanism whereby the iterations would stop as soon as a palindrome is produced, for it is simply not clear how many iterations may be required. The command **NestWhileList** (or **NestWhile** if only the last item is to be output) is the ticket. The syntax is like that of **NestList**, but instead of using a positive integer for the third argument to indicate the number of iterations, use a predicate instead. The iterations will continue as long as the predicate returns **True**. Here, for instance, we set up a pure function for this purpose:

In[10]:= **NestWhileList[step, 79, IntegerDigits[#] ≠ Reverse[IntegerDigits[#]] &]**

Out[10]= {79, 176, 847, 1595, 7546, 14 003, 44 044}

And here we see the number of iterations required to reach a palindrome for each of the first 195 integers. That is, above each integer n on the horizontal axis we see a vertical bar indicating the minimal number of iterations required to reach a palindrome. Integers n that are palindromes appear directly on the horizontal axis:

In[11]:= **ListPlot[Table[{n,**

Length[NestWhileList[step, n, IntegerDigits[#] ≠ Reverse[IntegerDigits[#]] &]] −

1}, {n, 195}], Filling → Axis, PlotStyle → PointSize[.002],

PlotRange → All, AspectRatio → 1 / 3, AxesOrigin → {0, 0}]

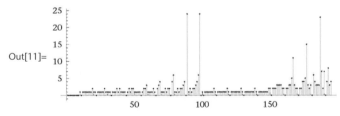

We stopped at 195 here for a very good reason. The number 196 will not produce a palindrome even after *millions* of iterations. For this reason it is strongly suspected that the original conjecture is false, although at the time of this writing this has not been proved. In other words, no one really knows if after enough iterations of this procedure starting at 196 a palindrome will be produced. All that is known is that a palindrome will not be produced quickly. If you were to call our **NestWhileList** input with 196 as the starting value, it would run (if you let it) for days, weeks, maybe years. Suffice it to say that you might get bored waiting. For this reason it is possible to add an escape mechanism to **NestWhileList** so that after a certain number of iterations it will stop, regardless of whether the predicate is **True** or not. The following input accomplishes this. The fourth argument (1) indicates that the predicate needs only one argument (the last result). The final argument (50) specifies the maximal number of iterations to allow. Here we see that there are no palindromes in the first 50 iterations when one starts with 196:

In[12]:= **palStyle** /@
     NestWhileList[step, 196, IntegerDigits[#] ≠ Reverse[IntegerDigits[#]] &, 1, 50]

Out[12]= {196, 887, 1675, 7436, 13 783, 52 514, 94 039, 187 088, 1 067 869, 10 755 470, 18 211 171,
     35 322 452, 60 744 805, 111 589 511, 227 574 622, 454 050 344, 897 100 798,
     1 794 102 596, 8 746 117 567, 16 403 234 045, 70 446 464 506, 130 992 928 913,
     450 822 227 944, 900 544 455 998, 1 800 098 901 007, 8 801 197 801 088,
     17 602 285 712 176, 84 724 043 932 847, 159 547 977 975 595, 755 127 757 721 546,
     1 400 255 515 443 103, 4 413 700 670 963 144, 8 827 391 431 036 288,
     17 653 692 772 973 576, 85 191 620 502 609 247, 159 482 241 005 228 405,
     664 304 741 147 513 356, 1 317 620 482 294 916 822, 3 603 815 405 135 183 953,
     7 197 630 720 180 367 016, 13 305 261 530 450 734 933, 47 248 966 933 966 985 264,
     93 507 933 867 933 969 538, 177 104 867 844 767 940 077, 947 154 635 293 536 341 848,
     1 795 298 270 686 072 793 597, 9 749 270 977 546 801 719 568,
     18 408 442 064 004 592 449 047, 92 502 871 604 050 616 929 528,
     175 095 833 209 091 234 750 057, 925 153 265 399 993 573 340 628 }

Let's apply this procedure to each of the first thousand numbers and make a list of the results:

In[13]:= **data = Table[NestWhileList[step, n,**
     IntegerDigits[#] ≠ Reverse[IntegerDigits[#]] &, 1, 50], {n, 1000}];

For example:

In[14]:= **palStyle** /@ **data[[485]]**

Out[14]= {485, 1069, 10 670, 18 271, 35 552, 61 105, 111 221, ⎡233 332⎤}

Here is a **ListPlot** like that produced earlier, but with a **Tooltip** added which will display the coordinates of a data point as you mouseover it.

In[15]:= **ListPlot[Tooltip @ {First[#], Length[#] − 1} & /@ data,**
     Filling → Axis, PlotStyle → PointSize[.002],
     AspectRatio → 1 / 3, PlotRange → All, AxesOrigin → {0, 0}]

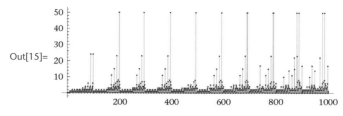

Below are all numbers between 1 and 1000 that, like 196, do not produce a palindrome after 50

iterations. In fact, even with many more iterations none of these numbers have ever produced a palindrome. See Exercise 2.

In[16]:= **First /@ Select[data, Length[#] == 51 &]**

Out[16]= {196, 295, 394, 493, 592, 689, 691, 788, 790, 879, 887, 978, 986}

In[17]:= **Clear[data]**

For a second example of programming iteratively, consider the Newton-Raphson method for approximating a root of an equation $f(x) = 0$, where f is a differentiable function. The technique, you may recall, entails making an initial guess x_0 for the root, and then calculating a sequence of (what we hope will be) successively better approximations $x_1, x_2, x_3, \ldots$ via the iterative formula

$$x_{n+1} = x_n - \frac{f(x_n)}{f'(x_n)}$$

Here is a command **newtonStep** that can be iterated with **NestList**. In order that it may be iterated, it needs to accept a *single* numerical input. But we would also like to be able to specify the function f whose root we wish to approximate. We accommodate both of these demands by using the syntax below:

In[18]:= **Clear[newtonStep, f, x];**

$$\textbf{newtonStep[f\_] = Function}\left[\textbf{x, Simplify}\left[\textbf{x} - \frac{\textbf{f[x]}}{\textbf{f'[x]}}\right]\right];$$

We can now specify a function f explicitly like this:

In[20]:= **f[x_] := 2 – x²;**
newtonStep[f][x]

Out[21]= $\dfrac{1}{x} + \dfrac{x}{2}$

Or as a pure function, like this:

In[22]:= **newtonStep[2 – #² &][x]**

Out[22]= $\dfrac{1}{x} + \dfrac{x}{2}$

Either way, we know that the function $f(x) = 2 - x^2$ has a positive root at $x = \sqrt{2}$. Here we use the Newton-Raphson technique to approximate this root, using the initial value of **N[1,40]**:

In[23]:= **NestList[newtonStep[f], N[1, 40], 8] // Column**

> 1.00000000000000000000000000000000000000
> 1.50000000000000000000000000000000000000
> 1.41666666666666666666666666666666666667
> 1.41421568627450980392156862745098039216
Out[23]= 1.41421356237468991062629557889013491012
> 1.41421356237309504880169623502530243361
> 1.41421356237309504880168872420969807857
> 1.41421356237309504880168872420969807857
> 1.41421356237309504880168872420969807857

We see that seven iterations are sufficient to give 38 digit accuracy in this case (since the last two rows—the seventh and eight iterates—agree at every digit, and since two digits of precision were lost during the iteration process). This agrees with our knowledge of the root:

In[24]:= $N\left[\sqrt{2}, 38\right]$

Out[24]= 1.41421356237309504880168872420969807857

It may be worth recalling that the built-in command **FindRoot** is designed to be used in cases such as this, where a good approximation to the root of a function is desired. Programming the Newton-Raphson method is intended to shed light on the behavior of this algorithm. We don't mean to imply that it is the best and only tool for this purpose.

In[25]:= **FindRoot[$2 - x^2 == 0$, {x, 1}, WorkingPrecision → 40]**

Out[25]= {x → 1.414213562373095048801688724209698078570}

There are several other iteration commands available beyond **Nest** and **NestList**. One of the most useful is **FixedPointList**. This is a special case of **NestWhileList** that halts when the outputs become indisinguishable from one another. That is, it provides a simpler means of doing what the **NestWhile List** input below does:

In[26]:= **NestWhileList[newtonStep[f], N[1, 40], UnsameQ, 2] // Column**

> 1.00000000000000000000000000000000000000
> 1.50000000000000000000000000000000000000
> 1.41666666666666666666666666666666666667
> 1.41421568627450980392156862745098039216
Out[26]= 1.41421356237468991062629557889013491012
> 1.41421356237309504880169623502530243361
> 1.41421356237309504880168872420969807857
> 1.41421356237309504880168872420969807857

In[27]:= FixedPointList[newtonStep[f], N[1, 40]] // Column

Out[27]=
1.0000000000000000000000000000000000000000
1.5000000000000000000000000000000000000000
1.4166666666666666666666666666666666666667
1.4142156862745098039215686274509803921 6
1.4142135623746899106262955788901349101 2
1.4142135623730950488016896235025302436 1
1.4142135623730950488016887242096980785 7
1.4142135623730950488016887242096980786

And, as you would expect, there is a **FixedPoint** command that simply returns the final value:

In[28]:= FixedPoint[newtonStep[f], N[1, 40]]

Out[28]= 1.4142135623730950488016887242096980786

Here we use Newton's method to give an approximation of $\pi/4$ (i.e., as a root of $f(x) = \sin x - \cos x$).

In[29]:= FixedPoint[newtonStep[Sin[#] − Cos[#] &], N[1, 40]]

Out[29]= 0.78539816339744830961566084581987572105

In[30]:= N[π/4, 38]

Out[30]= 0.78539816339744830961566084581987572105

Note that **FixedPoint** and **FixedPointList** can accept a third argument, which specifies the maximal number of iterations. This is useful when it is not clear in advance that the iteration will converge.

The commands **Fold** and **FoldList** are used to iterate a function of two variables over its first variable, while the second variable assumes successive values in a given list. That sounds worse than it is. The input below illustrates the idea. The first argument is the function to be iterated, the second argument is the starting value for this function's first variable, and the third argument is the list of values for the function's second variable. The length of this list controls the number of iterations to perform:

In[31]:= Clear[f, a];
FoldList[f, a, {1, 2, 3}]

Out[32]= {a, f[a, 1], f[f[a, 1], 2], f[f[f[a, 1], 2], 3]}

In[33]:= Fold[f, a, {1, 2, 3}]

Out[33]= f[f[f[a, 1], 2], 3]

Here is how to use **FoldList** to create a list whose nth member is the nth partial sum $1 + \frac{1}{2} + \frac{1}{3} + \cdots + \frac{1}{n}$ of the harmonic series:

In[34]:= $\text{FoldList}\left[\#1 + \dfrac{1}{\#2} \ \&, \ 1, \ \text{Range}[2, \ 10]\right]$

Out[34]= $\left\{1, \ \dfrac{3}{2}, \ \dfrac{11}{6}, \ \dfrac{25}{12}, \ \dfrac{137}{60}, \ \dfrac{49}{20}, \ \dfrac{363}{140}, \ \dfrac{761}{280}, \ \dfrac{7129}{2520}, \ \dfrac{7381}{2520}\right\}$

Notice that changing the initial value from **1** to **1.** causes numerical approximations to be used throughout. This increases the speed of computation and produces results sufficient for plotting:

In[35]:= $\text{FoldList}\left[\#1 + \dfrac{1}{\#2} \ \&, \ 1., \ \text{Range}[2, \ 10]\right]$

Out[35]= {1., 1.5, 1.83333, 2.08333, 2.28333, 2.45, 2.59286, 2.71786, 2.82897, 2.92897}

In[36]:= $\text{ListPlot} @ \text{FoldList}\left[\#1 + \dfrac{1}{\#2} \ \&, \ 1., \ \text{Range}[2, \ 200]\right]$

Out[36]=

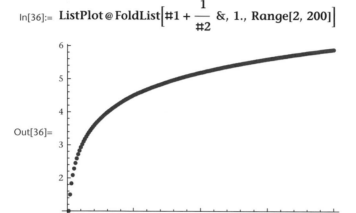

An even simpler means of calculating partial sums is via the **Accumulate** command. Given a finite list {a, b, c,...}, **Accumulate** will return a list of the partial sums: {a, a+b, a+b+c,...}.

In[37]:= $\text{Accumulate}[\text{Table}[1 / n, \ \{n, \ 10\}]]$

Out[37]= $\left\{1, \ \dfrac{3}{2}, \ \dfrac{11}{6}, \ \dfrac{25}{12}, \ \dfrac{137}{60}, \ \dfrac{49}{20}, \ \dfrac{363}{140}, \ \dfrac{761}{280}, \ \dfrac{7129}{2520}, \ \dfrac{7381}{2520}\right\}$

Another useful iteration command is **Differences**, which will return the differences between successive members in a list.

In[38]:= $\text{Differences}[\{1, \ 4, \ 9, \ 16\}]$

Out[38]= {3, 5, 7}

Whereas one could use **Nest** to iterate this command, it will accept a second argument (specifying the number of iterations desired) to save you the trouble:

In[39]:= **Differences[Range[10]²]**

Out[39]= {3, 5, 7, 9, 11, 13, 15, 17, 19}

In[40]:= **Differences[Range[10]², 2]**

Out[40]= {2, 2, 2, 2, 2, 2, 2, 2}

In[41]:= **Differences[Range[10]², 3]**

Out[41]= {0, 0, 0, 0, 0, 0, 0}

The input below shows a means of displaying successive differences for the first ten terms in the harmonic sequence, where each row after the first represents the differences for the row above. The display is a **Column** with each row aligned at its center. Individual rows are **Grid**s (each with only one row), where the **ItemSize** option is utilized to guarantee a fixed width for each item. It is this fixed width that is needed to produce an easy-to-read display. Exercise 10 in Section 8.8 will have you build a command to automate this procedure for any initial list.

In[43]:= **Column[Table[Grid[{Differences[Table[1/n, {n, 10}], k]}, ItemSize → 3.25], {k, 0, 9}], Alignment → Center]**

Out[43]=

$$1 \quad \frac{1}{2} \quad \frac{1}{3} \quad \frac{1}{4} \quad \frac{1}{5} \quad \frac{1}{6} \quad \frac{1}{7} \quad \frac{1}{8} \quad \frac{1}{9} \quad \frac{1}{10}$$

$$-\frac{1}{2} \quad -\frac{1}{6} \quad -\frac{1}{12} \quad -\frac{1}{20} \quad -\frac{1}{30} \quad -\frac{1}{42} \quad -\frac{1}{56} \quad -\frac{1}{72} \quad -\frac{1}{90}$$

$$\frac{1}{3} \quad \frac{1}{12} \quad \frac{1}{30} \quad \frac{1}{60} \quad \frac{1}{105} \quad \frac{1}{168} \quad \frac{1}{252} \quad \frac{1}{360}$$

$$-\frac{1}{4} \quad -\frac{1}{20} \quad -\frac{1}{60} \quad -\frac{1}{140} \quad -\frac{1}{280} \quad -\frac{1}{504} \quad -\frac{1}{840}$$

$$\frac{1}{5} \quad \frac{1}{30} \quad \frac{1}{105} \quad \frac{1}{280} \quad \frac{1}{630} \quad \frac{1}{1260}$$

$$-\frac{1}{6} \quad -\frac{1}{42} \quad -\frac{1}{168} \quad -\frac{1}{504} \quad -\frac{1}{1260}$$

$$\frac{1}{7} \quad \frac{1}{56} \quad \frac{1}{252} \quad \frac{1}{840}$$

$$-\frac{1}{8} \quad -\frac{1}{72} \quad -\frac{1}{360}$$

$$\frac{1}{9} \quad \frac{1}{90}$$

$$-\frac{1}{10}$$

Exercises 8.7

1. If one were to set **f = Function[x, 2x]**, then the input **Nest[f, x, 4]** would produce the output **16x**. Give the definition of a Function called **f** so that **Nest[f, x, 4]** produces the outputs below. Be sure to check your answers.

    a. 10000 x

b. x^{16}

c. $\sqrt{1 + \sqrt{1 + \sqrt{1 + \sqrt{1 + x}}}}$

d. $\cfrac{1}{1 + \cfrac{1}{1 + \cfrac{1}{1 + \cfrac{1}{1+x}}}}$

2. When the reverse-add procedure is applied to some numbers, a palindrome is not produced even after millions of iterations. It is suspected (although it has not yet been proved) that a palindrome will *never* result with these numbers. The numbers in this class are known as the *Lychrel numbers* (do an internet search for A023108 and follow the link to the Online Encyclopedia of Integer Sequences for more information). Carry out an investigation of the orbit of the number 196 under ten thousand iterations of the reverse-add procedure, and confirm that no palindrome is produced.

3. When an iteration scheme has a fixed point, it is often a matter of interest to understand how quickly the fixed point is approached. Does it take many iterations to get (for instance) 100 digits of precision, or just a few? A very simple means for garnering a qualitative assessment of the rate of convergence for an iterative sequence of real numbers can be had as follows: Make an **Array`.` Plot** where each row represents an iterate, and where each digit is represented by a different tonal value. When a particular decimal position stabilizes to its final value, the column in the array representing that position will be monotone from that point on down. This concept is illustrated below:

a. Use **NestList** to iterate the function $f(x) = \frac{1}{x} + \frac{x}{2}$ ten times, with a starting value of **N[1,20]**.

b. **Map** the function **First[RealDigits[#]]&** over the output above to convert each number into a list of its digits.

c. Wrap the output above with **ArrayPlot** to produce a visual representation.

d. Repeat parts **a** through **c** in a single input, but where the initial value is **N[1,100]**.

e. Repeat part **d**, where the function to be iterated is $f(x) = \frac{1}{x} + \frac{x}{3}$, and where there are 200 (as opposed to 10) iterations in total. Contrast the results to those of part **d**.

4. Add the option setting **ColorFunction → "Rainbow"** to your favorite **ArrayPlot** and see what happens.

5. The secant method for finding a real root of an equation $f(x) = 0$ was discussed in Section 8.5 on page 415, where it was implemented via a **Do** loop. If you go online and visit *MathWorld* (www.mathworld.com) and lookup "secant method," you will find the *Mathematica* code shown below for implementing the secant method using **NestList**. Explain how the code works, and run nine iterations on the function $f(x) = x^3 - 2x + 2$ with starting values $x_0 = -1$ and $x_1 = -3/2$. Does it give the same result as the implementation using **Do**? (We did exactly this example on page 415.)

In[43]:= **secantMethodList[f_, {x_, x0_, x1_}, n_] :=**
    NestList[Last[#] – {0, (Function[x, f][Last[#]] * Subtract @@ #)/
        Subtract @@ Function[x, f] /@ #} &, {x0, x1}, n]

6. When a function f is iterated and converges to a fixed point x^*, it must be the case that $f(x^*) = x^*$ (why?). Geometrically, this means that the point (x^*, x^*) is the intersection of the graphs of $y = f(x)$ and $y = x$. One often illustrates the convergence of the iteration from a particular starting value x_0 by making a *cobweb* diagram. This is comprised of the graphs of $y = f(x)$ and $y = x$, together with line segments joining the points (x_0, x_0), $(x_0, f(x_0))$, $(f(x_0), f(x_0))$, $(f(x_0), f(f(x_0)))$, and so on, with alternating vertical and horizontal segments heading ever deeper into the iteration scheme. An illustration is provided below for the function $f(x) = 2.9\,x(1 - x)$ and starting point $x_0 = 0.5$. Program *Mathematica* to produce such a diagram.

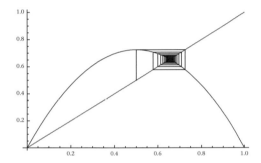

7. Make a **Manipulate** showing cobweb diagrams (like that of the previous exercise) for the family of functions $f(x) = a\,x(1 - x)$, with a slider for a ranging from 2.5 to 3.7, and a second slider for the starting point x_0 ranging from 0.1 to 0.9.

8. The command **ContinuedFraction** will accept a real number as input and will output a list of integers that specifies the *simple continued fraction* form of the input (provided a finite or repeating continued fraction exists). The output {1,2,3}, for example, represents the continued fraction
$1 + \dfrac{1}{2+\frac{1}{3}}$.

  a. Enter **ContinuedFraction[10/7]**, and check that $\frac{10}{7} = 1 + \dfrac{1}{2+\frac{1}{3}}$.

  b. Use **Fold** and **Defer** to write a command named **displayCF** that will accept a (finite) digit list as input and will display the simple continued fraction corresponding to that digit list. For instance, **displayCF[{1,2,3}]** should return $1 + \dfrac{1}{2+\frac{1}{3}}$. Moreover (by using **Defer**), you will be able to click on and then enter the output to evaluate it.

  c. Use **displayCF** to display a continued fraction that approximates π to within 10^{-20}. You can use **ContinuedFraction[Rationalize[π, 10^{-20}]]**, for instance, to find a continued fraction sequence for a rational number close to π.

9. Use **Accumulate** to find the first ten partial sums of the series $1 + \frac{1}{4} + \frac{1}{9} + \frac{1}{16} + \frac{1}{25} + \cdots$. Euler showed this series converges to $\frac{\pi^2}{6}$ in 1735, solving a decades old problem (known as the *Basel problem*) and securing fame for himself in the process. Make a **ListPlot** of the first thousand partial sums together with a horizontal line at height $\frac{\pi^2}{6}$. Comment on the rate of convergence.

8.8 Patterns

For those who wish to program with *Mathematica*, patterns are often the most inaccessible aspect of the language. They are the last frontier to be conquered. For those who "get it" on the other hand, patterns are most definitely a source of power. With an understanding of the fundamentals of patterns, there is the possibility of developing toward power-user status. Without such an understanding, there is little hope.

The first thing to recognize is that you have been using patterns for quite a while.   The most typical instance is in a function definition that includes an underscore (_) on the left hand side, like the first input shown below. While the subject of patterns is far too vast to adequately cover here, our hope is to be able to convey enough basic knowledge and some illustrative examples so that you will be able to recognize the power of patterns and replacement rules as you go about your work.

A *pattern* is a structure that can be used to represent an entire class of expressions. *Mathematica* has extensive tools for building sophisticated patterns, for detecting when a particular expression matches a given pattern, and for making replacements according to criteria given as patterns. We have already used the most basic type of pattern when defining functions. The **x_** on the left side of the definition below, for example, is a pattern.

In[1]:= **Clear[f, g, u]**;
     f[x_] := x + 1

Here is the **FullForm** of this definition:

In[3]:= **Defer[FullForm[f[x_] := x + 1]]**

Out[3]= SetDelayed[f[Pattern[x, Blank[]]], Plus[x, 1]]

The pattern itself, **x_**, is show below:

In[4]:= **FullForm[x_]**

Out[4]//FullForm=
          Pattern[x, Blank[]]

We already have a pretty clear sense that this means **x** is the independent variable. If the function **f** above is called with a numerical argument, say for instance that the user enters **f[2]**, then the expression on the right side of the definition will be evaluated with 2 replacing the **x** and the result is 3. In the broader context of *Mathematica* itself, the pattern **x_** can represent *any* structurally valid expression (either an atom or a nested expression, as discussed in Section 8.2). For instance:

In[5]:= **f[g[u]]**

Out[5]= $1 + g[u]$

One important use of patterns is to restrict the class of expressions that will match the left side of a definition. If, for instance, one wanted to define a function **f** that would only work with numeric arguments, this structure would do the trick:

In[6]:= **Clear[f];**
      f[x_?NumericQ] := x + 1

In[8]:= **f[24]**

Out[8]= 25

Non-numeric input does not match the pattern **x_?NumericQ**, and so the definition given above is not applied; rather the expression is returned unevaluated:

In[9]:= **f[g[u]]**

Out[9]= $f[g[u]]$

There is much to say here. First note the structure of the pattern. The name of the pattern (we used **x**) can be, of course, whatever you like. It is simply the name used to refer to the pattern on the right side of the definition. The underscore is essential; we'll discuss this soon. The **?** can be followed by any predicate command. An expression matches the pattern if and only if the predicate returns **True** for that expression. A handy way to explore this idea is with the command **MatchQ**. The first argument is an expression and the second is a pattern.

In[10]:= **MatchQ[g[u], x_?NumericQ]**

Out[10]= False

In[11]:= **MatchQ[24, x_?NumericQ]**

Out[11]= True

For the purpose of matching the name **x** is not even necessary. The underscore (**Blank[]**) suffices:

In[12]:= **MatchQ[24, _?NumericQ]**

Out[12]= True

Next, note that the same symbol **f** may be given a different definition for a different form of input. Recall that the function **f** was defined above for numeric input *x* as $x + 1$. We can add another definition for an input that is a string; **f** will then return an output corresponding to *either* type of input.

In[13]:= **f[x_ ? StringQ] := "YOUR INPUT WAS: " ~~ x**

In[14]:= **f["blah blah blah"]**

Out[14]= YOUR INPUT WAS: blah blah blah

In[15]:= **f[3]**

Out[15]= 4

In[16]:= **f[apple]**

Out[16]= f[apple]

Since **apple** is neither a string nor numeric (its head is **Symbol**), **f** returns unevaluated.

This notion of multiple definitions, one for each of several forms of input, can be useful. For example, consider the famous *Collatz conjecture* (for Lothar Collatz, who proposed it in 1937): start with a positive integer n. If n is even, return $n/2$. If n is odd, return $3n + 1$. Iterate this process while the result is not 1. The conjecture states that regardless of the starting number, the process will eventually lead to the number 1. The conjecture has been tested extensively, and while it appears to be true, it has not been proven. But programming the function to be iterated is a snap:

In[17]:= **Clear[f];**
f[n_ ? EvenQ] := n / 2;
f[n_ ? OddQ] := 3 n + 1

Here, for example, is the orbit of the starting number 342. It takes a while, but it eventually gets to 1. See Exercise 5 to further explore this conjecture.

In[20]:= **NestWhileList[f, 342, # ≠ 1 &]**

Out[20]= {342, 171, 514, 257, 772, 386, 193, 580, 290, 145, 436, 218, 109, 328, 164, 82, 41, 124, 62, 31, 94, 47, 142, 71, 214, 107, 322, 161, 484, 242, 121, 364, 182, 91, 274, 137, 412, 206, 103, 310, 155, 466, 233, 700, 350, 175, 526, 263, 790, 395, 1186, 593, 1780, 890, 445, 1336, 668, 334, 167, 502, 251, 754, 377, 1132, 566, 283, 850, 425, 1276, 638, 319, 958, 479, 1438, 719, 2158, 1079, 3238, 1619, 4858, 2429, 7288, 3644, 1822, 911, 2734, 1367, 4102, 2051, 6154, 3077, 9232, 4616, 2308, 1154, 577, 1732, 866, 433, 1300, 650, 325, 976, 488, 244, 122, 61, 184, 92, 46, 23, 70, 35, 106, 53, 160, 80, 40, 20, 10, 5, 16, 8, 4, 2, 1}

Now the function **f** above could also effectively be defined as a **Piecewise** function. Patterns in this case provide an alternate approach. There are other cases where patterns provide a uniquely elegant means of identifying a pertinent class of expression. In order to see such examples it is necessary to broaden our knowledge of pattern structures. The next fundamental pattern structure we introduce is a _ (**Blank[]**) followed immediately by a symbol, typically a command name. Any expression having that symbol as its **Head** will match this pattern. It is the internal **FullForm** of the expression (discussed in Section 8.2) that determines a match.

In[21]:= **MatchQ[{1, 2, 3}, _List]**

Out[21]= True

In[22]:= **MatchQ[{1, 2, 3}, _Times]**

Out[22]= False

If a particular expression (such as {**1,2,3**} below) matches two patterns, the more specific will generally be used first:

In[23]:= **Clear[f];**
　　　　　f[x_List] := Apply[Times, x];
　　　　　f[x_] := x

In[26]:= **f[{1, 2, 3}]**

Out[26]= 6

In[27]:= **f[g[u]]**

Out[27]= g[u]

Note that the evaluation sequence is important. Structurally, the input 23^2 is represented as **Power[23, 2]** before evaluation. Its head is **Power**. After evaluation it becomes 529, and its head is **Integer**. Expressions will be evaluated *before* being matched to a pattern.

In[28]:= **Defer[FullForm[23^2]]**

Out[28]= Power[23, 2]

In[29]:= **MatchQ[#, _Integer] & /@ $\left\{23, 23^2, \int_0^1 2t\,dt, \int_0^1 t\,dt\right\}$**

Out[29]= {True, True, True, False}

One may combine the two pattern structures discussed above. Suppose, for instance, you wish to create a function which will only accept a positive integer as its argument. This can be accomplished with the pattern **_Integer?Positive**. It will only match an expression that evaluates to an **Integer**, and which returns **True** when the predicate command **Positive** is applied.

In[30]:= `MatchQ[#, _Integer?Positive] & /@ {23, -23, 23.}`

Out[30]= {True, False, False}

In[31]:= `Clear[f];`
`f[x_Integer?Positive] := 3 x + 1`

In[33]:= `f /@ {23, -23, 23.}`

Out[33]= {70, f[-23], f[23.]}

In case you were wondering, yes, this could also be accomplished via the slightly more cumbersome pattern **_?(Positive[#]&&IntegerQ[#]&)**.

In[34]:= `MatchQ[#, _?(Positive[#] && IntegerQ[#] &)] & /@ {23, -23, 23.}`

Out[34]= {True, False, False}

Now let's consider those pesky underscores. While a single underscore _ (**Blank[]**) will match any expression, a double underscore __ (two underscores back-to-back, full name **BlankSequence[]**) is an object that will match any *sequence* of one or more expressions (i.e., expressions separated by commas). Just as with the single underscore, it can be preceded by a name (e.g., **x__**) and it can be followed by either a question mark and predicate, or by a command name. For instance, consider the following definition. The pattern **x__Integer** will be matched by a sequence of one or more integers. Every argument in the sequence must be an integer in order for there to be a match. The name **x** refers to the entire sequence.

In[35]:= `Clear[f, a];`
`f[x__Integer] := Times[x]`

In[37]:= `f[1, 2, 3]`

Out[37]= 6

In[38]:= `f[3]`

Out[38]= 3

In[39]:= `f[1, 2, a]`

Out[39]= f[1, 2, a]

Using the double underscore, you can easily create a command that is based on a built-in command. For instance, below we create a command **f** that simply invokes **ParametricPlot3D** with the same arguments. It produces two versions of the same image. The pattern **args__** represents the *entire* sequence of arguments.

In[40]:= **Clear[f, t];**
f[args__] := GraphicsRow[{ParametricPlot3D[args],
ParametricPlot3D[args, PlotStyle → Dotted]}, ImageSize → 280]

In[42]:= **f[{Sin[t] Cos[50 t], Sin[t] Sin[50 t], t}, {t, 0, π},**
BoxRatios → 1, Boxed → False, Axes → False]

Out[42]=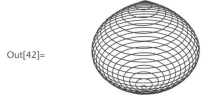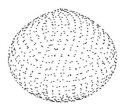

Finally, there is the *triple* underscore ___ (**BlankNullSequence[]**), which will match any sequence of *zero* or more expressions. This is especially useful for adding optional arguments to a user-defined command. For example, the command **myPlot** will call the **Plot** command with some specific option settings, including a **PlotLabel** and **AxesLabel** that are based on the values of the requisite arguments. In the definition below, **f** and **iter** represent the requisite arguments for the **Plot** command, while **opts** represents any additional option settings the user wishes to add. Since such settings have the head **Rule**, we demand this via the pattern **opts___Rule**. The triple underscore is appropriate here since **myPlot** might be called without any options.

In[43]:= **Clear[myPlot];**
myPlot[f_, iter_List, opts___Rule] := Plot[f, iter, opts, PlotStyle → Thick,
PlotLabel → "y = " ~~ ToString[TraditionalForm[f]], AxesLabel → {iter[[1]], "y"}]

In[45]:= **myPlot[1 − x², {x, −1, 1}]**

Out[45]=

$y = 1 - x^2$

Note that the **PlotLabel** and **AxesLabel**s are based on the values provided to the myPlot command's requisite arguments (in the example below, for instance, the variable t is used instead of x). Note also that because **opts** appears on the right side of the **myPlot** definition *before* the specific option settings (e.g., **PlotStyle → Thick**), any user-supplied option settings will override these defaults. For instance, here a different **PlotStyle** is specified:

In[46]:= **myPlot$\left[e^t, \{t, 0, 3\}, \text{PlotStyle} \to \text{Dashed}\right]$**

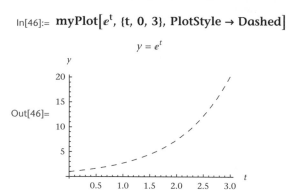

The three types of underscores can also be used in a **StringExpression** (~~). The inputs below demonstrate their use in this setting. Given several strings, **StringExpression** will concatenate them into a single string, as in the **PlotLabel** setting for **myPlot** above. Below the command **Dictionary·Lookup** is used to scour the dictionary for words that begin with "angle." In the first case it finds all such words that have a single additional character (there are three). In the second case it finds all such words with one or more additional letters (there are seven, including the three from the first output). In the last it finds all such words with zero or more additional letters. The output is the same as the second case with one exception: the word "angle" itself is also present.

In[47]:= **DictionaryLookup["angle" ~~ _]**

Out[47]= {angled, angler, angles}

In[48]:= **DictionaryLookup["angle" ~~ __]**

Out[48]= {angled, anglepoise, angler, anglers, angles, angleworm, angleworms}

In[49]:= **DictionaryLookup["angle" ~~ ___]**

Out[49]= {angle, angled, anglepoise, angler, anglers, angles, angleworm, angleworms}

So far we have discussed the three types of underscores, that it is permissible to name a pattern by preceding any type of underscore with a symbol (e.g., **x_**), and that it is possible to restrict the type of expression that will match a pattern in one of two ways: by following the underscore with either a command name (such as **x_Integer**), or with a question mark followed by a predicate command (such as **x_?NonNegative**). When defining your own commands this knowledge will get you a long way, as patterns like these are very common on the left side of definitions. But patterns have *many* other uses, and there are countless cases where more sophisticated pattern objects are needed. The next order of business will be to explain how such objects are constructed.

We will do this by introducing the **Cases** command. Like **Select**, this command is used to extract items from a list. Unlike **Select** (which applies a predicate command to the list items and returns those for which the predicate is **True**), **Cases** returns those items from the list that match a pattern. For instance:

In[50]:= **Cases**[{0, 2, −2, 4, −4, 6, −6}, _?**NonNegative**]

Out[50]= {0, 2, 4, 6}

For the most basic use of **Cases**, the first argument is the list, and the second is a pattern object. It is the multitude of possible variations for this second argument we wish to address. Here are some illustrative examples:

In[51]:= **Clear**[x, g, a, b, c];
Cases[x /. **NSolve**[3 x^4 − x^3 + 5 x^2 + 7 x + 1, x], _**Real**]

Out[52]= {−0.758966, −0.162674}

In[53]:= **Cases**[**NSolve**[3 x^4 − x^3 + 5 x^2 + 7 x + 1, x], {x → _**Real**}]

Out[53]= {{x → −0.758966}, {x → −0.162674}}

In[54]:= **Cases**[{1, a, a^2, a^3, a^π, a^4}, **Power**[a, _]]

Out[54]= {a^2, a^3, a^π, a^4}

In[55]:= **Cases**[{1, a, a^2, a^3, a^π, a^4}, a^{−?(#>3&)}]

Out[55]= {a^π, a^4}

In[56]:= **Cases**[{1, a, a^2, a^3, a^π, a^4}, a^{−Integer}]

Out[56]= {a^2, a^3, a^4}

In[57]:= **Cases**[{g[1], g[a], g[a, b], g[a, b, c]}, g[_]]

Out[57]= {g[1], g[a]}

In[58]:= **Cases**[{g[1], g[a], g[a, b], g[a, b, c]}, g[_**Symbol**]]

Out[58]= {g[a]}

In[59]:= **Cases**[{g[1], g[a], g[a, b], g[a, b, c]}, g[__**Symbol**]]

Out[59]= {g[a], g[a, b], g[a, b, c]}

In[60]:= **Cases**[{g[1], g[a], g[a, b], g[a, b, c]}, g[___, b, ___]]

Out[60]= {g[a, b], g[a, b, c]}

The point here is that a pattern object can be any ordinary expression, but typically it will contain one or more of the various underscores.

Pattern objects can also make use of a number of special commands. For instance, **Except[***pattern***]** is a pattern object that will match any expression except those that match *pattern*. It is useful in cases when it is more convenient to say what something isn't rather than what it is. The input below is a simplified example of a list where some members have the form **Missing["Not Available"]**. For instance, many of the curated data commands such as **CountryData** will use this symbol when there is missing data. **Cases** and **Except** can be used to extract those data values that are not missing.

In[61]:= **Cases[{1, 2, Missing["Not Available"]}, Except[Missing[_]]]**

Out[61]= {1, 2}

The **Repeated** (..) command is useful for matching repeating sequences of objects. In the first input below we find all cases of a list comprised of the same expression *a* repeated multiple times. In the next input we find all cases of a list comprised only of integers.

In[62]:= **Cases[{{.12, 2, 3}, {2, 2, 2}, {3, 2, 3}}, {(a_)..}]**

Out[62]= {{2, 2, 2}}

In[63]:= **Cases[{{.12, 2, 3}, {2, 2, 2}, {3, 2, 3}}, {_Integer ..}]**

Out[63]= {{2, 2, 2}, {3, 2, 3}}

Other such pattern commands include **Longest**, **Shortest**, **Condition**, and **PatternSequence**.

Most of the pattern objects used in the **Cases** examples above were not named. Another setting that often makes use of pattern objects is that of making replacements, and this enterprise generally requires that patterns be named. Here are two simple examples. In the first, no patterns are used. In the second, a simple named pattern is used to make the replacements:

In[64]:= $1 + x + x^2 + x^3 \,/. \, x \to x^2$

Out[64]= $1 + x^2 + x^4 + x^6$

In[65]:= $1 + x + x^2 + x^3 \,/. \, a\_Integer \to a + 1$

Out[65]= $2 + x + x^3 + x^4$

In the second example every integer in the expression is increased by 1. It is important to make clear that the **x** in the expression does not get transformed to x^2 under this replacement (even though x is mathematically equivalent to x^1). Rather, patterns are matched to the underlying **FullForm** of the expression in question.

Now imagine that in the last example you wish to increase by 1 only the *exponents* (not the 1 at the far left). The pattern object **Power[x, n_]** will match the exponents, or equivalently x^{n}-. Note that you need to name the pattern (in this case **n**) in order to refer to it on the right side of the rule.

In[66]:= $1 + x + x^2 + x^3 \;/.\; x^{n-} \to x^{n+1}$

Out[66]= $1 + x + x^3 + x^4$

⚠ If you want to increase the exponents on *all* of the *x*'s, the simplest means of doing so is with the pattern object **Power[x, n_.]**. Note the dot (a simple period) after the underscore. The **n_.** represents an *optional* argument to a function, and it will assume a default value if it is omitted. For the **Power** command, the default value is 1. In other words, **MatchQ[x, Power[x, n_.]]** will return **True**. So the rule **Power[x, n_.] → Power[x, n+1]** will do the trick.

In the example below, a simple replacement rule is used to turn an integer into a row of a table:

In[67]:= $\mathbf{Grid[Range[10] \;/.\; n\_Integer \to \{Defer[n\,!],\; "=",\; n\,!\},\; Alignment \to Right]\;//}$
TraditionalForm

Out[67]//TraditionalForm=

1!	=	1
2!	=	2
3!	=	6
4!	=	24
5!	=	120
6!	=	720
7!	=	5040
8!	=	40 320
9!	=	362 880
10!	=	3 628 800

Here's yet another example of named patterns being used in the context of making replacements. We begin with a table, where on any row you will find two mathematically equivalent trigonometric expressions.

In[68]:= **Clear[a, k, n];**
Grid[
    Table[{Cos[k a], TrigExpand[Cos[k a]]}, {k, 2, 9}],
    Alignment → Left, Dividers → Gray
    ] // TraditionalForm

Out[69]//TraditionalForm=

$\cos(2a)$	$\cos^2(a) - \sin^2(a)$
$\cos(3a)$	$\cos^3(a) - 3\cos(a)\sin^2(a)$
$\cos(4a)$	$\cos^4(a) - 6\sin^2(a)\cos^2(a) + \sin^4(a)$
$\cos(5a)$	$\cos^5(a) - 10\sin^2(a)\cos^3(a) + 5\sin^4(a)\cos(a)$
$\cos(6a)$	$\cos^6(a) - 15\sin^2(a)\cos^4(a) + 15\sin^4(a)\cos^2(a) - \sin^6(a)$
$\cos(7a)$	$\cos^7(a) - 21\sin^2(a)\cos^5(a) + 35\sin^4(a)\cos^3(a) - 7\sin^6(a)\cos(a)$
$\cos(8a)$	$\cos^8(a) - 28\sin^2(a)\cos^6(a) + 70\sin^4(a)\cos^4(a) - 28\sin^6(a)\cos^2(a) + \sin^8(a)$
$\cos(9a)$	$\cos^9(a) - 36\sin^2(a)\cos^7(a) +$ $126\sin^4(a)\cos^5(a) - 84\sin^6(a)\cos^3(a) + 9\sin^8(a)\cos(a)$

Looking carefully at the expanded expressions in the right column, we observe that the sine function only occurs with an even exponent. This means we can easily eliminate all sine functions from the expressions on the right: use the fact that $\sin^2(a) = 1 - \cos^2(a)$. Or raising each side of this identity to an arbitrary integer power n, we have $\sin^{2n}(a) = \left(1 - \cos^2(a)\right)^n$. Here is how one could make such a replacement:

In[70]:= **TrigExpand[Cos[7 a]] /. Sin[a]$^{\text{n\_?EvenQ}}$ $\to$ $\left(1 - \text{Cos[a]}^2\right)^{\text{n/2}}$**

Out[70]= $\text{Cos[a]}^7 - 21\,\text{Cos[a]}^5\left(1 - \text{Cos[a]}^2\right) + 35\,\text{Cos[a]}^3\left(1 - \text{Cos[a]}^2\right)^2 - 7\,\text{Cos[a]}\left(1 - \text{Cos[a]}^2\right)^3$

Finally, we **Expand** this to get a nice expression for $\cos(7a)$ as a polynomial in $\cos(a)$:

In[71]:= **Expand[%]**

Out[71]= $-7\,\text{Cos[a]} + 56\,\text{Cos[a]}^3 - 112\,\text{Cos[a]}^5 + 64\,\text{Cos[a]}^7$

Here is the table that results from this procedure:

In[72]:= **Grid[**
    Table[{Cos[k a],
        TrigExpand[Cos[k a]] /. Sin[a]$^{\text{n\_?EvenQ}}$ $\to$ $\left(1 - \text{Cos[a]}^2\right)^{\text{n/2}}$ // Expand}, {k, 2, 9}],
    Alignment $\to$ Left, Dividers $\to$ Gray
    ] // TraditionalForm

Out[72]//TraditionalForm=

$\cos(2\,a)$	$2\cos^2(a) - 1$
$\cos(3\,a)$	$4\cos^3(a) - 3\cos(a)$
$\cos(4\,a)$	$8\cos^4(a) - 8\cos^2(a) + 1$
$\cos(5\,a)$	$16\cos^5(a) - 20\cos^3(a) + 5\cos(a)$
$\cos(6\,a)$	$32\cos^6(a) - 48\cos^4(a) + 18\cos^2(a) - 1$
$\cos(7\,a)$	$64\cos^7(a) - 112\cos^5(a) + 56\cos^3(a) - 7\cos(a)$
$\cos(8\,a)$	$128\cos^8(a) - 256\cos^6(a) + 160\cos^4(a) - 32\cos^2(a) + 1$
$\cos(9\,a)$	$256\cos^9(a) - 576\cos^7(a) + 432\cos^5(a) - 120\cos^3(a) + 9\cos(a)$

Exercise 6 asks you to use this table to prove that $\cos(\pi/21)$ is a root of the polynomial $f(x) = 1 + 16\,x + 32\,x^2 - 48\,x^3 - 96\,x^4 + 32\,x^5 + 64\,x^6$.

The **Cases** command discussed earlier in this section can also make replacements. That is, one can find all cases within a list (or indeed any expression) of subexpressions that match a particular pattern, and replace each of these by something else. It sounds a bit far fetched, but it's actually incredibly powerful and useful. There was an example in Section 7.9, for instance, where we extracted all **Line** objects from a graphic and replaced each with the underlying list of points. Let's recreate an example like that one:

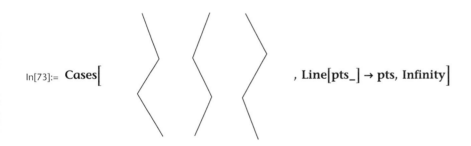

In[73]:= **Cases**[⟨⟨⟩⟩ , **Line[pts_]** → **pts**, **Infinity**]

Out[73]= {{{0.211111, 0.833333}, {0.297222, 0.597222},
    {0.186111, 0.416667}, {0.316667, 0.197222}},
    {{0.561111, 0.836111}, {0.472222, 0.602778}, {0.572222, 0.4}, {0.483333, 0.2}},
    {{0.752778, 0.830556}, {0.861111, 0.622222},
    {0.736111, 0.394444}, {0.816667, 0.180556}}}

The first argument to **Cases** here is not a list, but rather a **Graphics** that was produced with the Drawing Tools palette. Note the third argument to **Cases** is **Infinity**. **Cases** goes into the **FullForm** of the **Graphics** and searches at *every* level (since the third argument is **Infinity**) for subexpressions matching the pattern object **Line[pts_]**. Each matching expression is replaced by **pts**, and a list of all such matching expressions is returned. The result in this case is three lists of points (or more precisely, a *list* of three lists of points).

When making replacements, it is often desirable to assign a name to an entire pattern object. The **Pattern** command is used for this purpose. The infix form of this command is the colon (:). An expression of the form *name:pattern* is used to associate *name* with *pattern*. In the (simple but common) setting where the pattern object is a simple underscore, the colon can be eliminated altogether. That is the expression **x_** (that is so commonly seen) is equivalent to **x:_**. The colon is essential when naming a more intricate pattern object. Consider, for instance, the example below in which every row that begins with 1 in a matrix gets replaced with that same row multiplied by 3:

In[74]:= $\begin{pmatrix} 1 & 3 & 5 & 7 \\ 7 & 9 & 1 & 8 \\ 1 & 2 & 3 & 4 \\ 2 & 5 & 9 & 1 \end{pmatrix}$ /. a : {1, __} → 3 a // **MatrixForm**

Out[74]//MatrixForm=

$\begin{pmatrix} 3 & 9 & 15 & 21 \\ 7 & 9 & 1 & 8 \\ 3 & 6 & 9 & 12 \\ 2 & 5 & 9 & 1 \end{pmatrix}$

The name **a** is associated with the pattern object {1, _}. So **3a** represents the scalar 3 times this list, which has the effect of multiplying every member of the list by 3.

Note that when you make a replacement via **ReplaceAll** (/.), the very first item in the evaluation sequence will be the right side of the **Rule**. That is, when you enter the cell containing a replacement, the right side of the **Rule** is evaluated first. In the example below (which is just like the previous example, except here we **Reverse** each row in the matrix that begins with 1) this is problematic. The input **Reverse[a]** generates an error message (because **a** is a **Symbol**, not a **List**). The output, however, is correct.

In[75]:= $\begin{pmatrix} 1 & 3 & 5 & 7 \\ 7 & 9 & 1 & 8 \\ 1 & 2 & 3 & 4 \\ 2 & 5 & 9 & 1 \end{pmatrix}$ /. a : {1, __} → **Reverse[a] // MatrixForm**

Reverse::normal : Nonatomic expression expected at position 1 in Reverse[a]. ≫

Out[75]//MatrixForm=

$\begin{pmatrix} 7 & 5 & 3 & 1 \\ 7 & 9 & 1 & 8 \\ 4 & 3 & 2 & 1 \\ 2 & 5 & 9 & 1 \end{pmatrix}$

In a case such as this, it is better to *delay* evaluation of the right side of the **Rule** until *after* the replacements have been made. Then **Reverse** will be applied only to an actual list, and all is fine.

The key to doing this is to use **RuleDelayed** (:> or :→) instead of **Rule**:

$$\text{In[76]:=} \begin{pmatrix} 1 & 3 & 5 & 7 \\ 7 & 9 & 1 & 8 \\ 1 & 2 & 3 & 4 \\ 2 & 5 & 9 & 1 \end{pmatrix} /. \, a : \{1, \_\_\} :\to \text{Reverse}[a] \, // \, \text{MatrixForm}$$

Out[76]//MatrixForm=

$$\begin{pmatrix} 7 & 5 & 3 & 1 \\ 7 & 9 & 1 & 8 \\ 4 & 3 & 2 & 1 \\ 2 & 5 & 9 & 1 \end{pmatrix}$$

Another example may help to clarify the distinction between **Rule** and **RuleDelayed**. In the first input below, the right side of **Rule** is evaluated prior to making the replacements. Hence every replacement receives the same random integer. In the second input, the right side of **RuleDelayed** is not evaluated until after the replacements have been made. Hence **RandomInteger[100]** is evaluated three times.

In[77]:= {a, a, a} /. a → RandomInteger[100]

Out[77]= {94, 94, 94}

In[78]:= {a, a, a} /. a :→ RandomInteger[100]

Out[78]= {31, 74, 22}

⚠ In order to understand the evaluation sequence upon entering a particular expression, wrap the expression with **Trace**. The result will be a list of every expression that is encountered during the evaluation process, with the final item being the output. In the case of an expression with head **ReplaceAll** whose second argument is a **Rule**, the right side of the **Rule** will be the first thing evaluated.

The final pattern command that we will introduce is called **Optional**. This allows you to build a command with an optional argument. Optional accepts a pattern object as its first argument, and the default value to be used if that pattern is omitted as its second argument. For instance, this command will draw a random sample from the list **x**. If a second argument is given, that will be the size of the sample. If no second argument is given, a random sample of size three will be generated.

In[79]:= **Clear[f];**
randomSample[x_List, Optional[y_, 3]] := RandomChoice[x, y]

In[81]:= **randomSample[Range[100], 5]**

Out[81]= {3, 6, 58, 85, 23}

In[82]:= **randomSample[Range[100]]**

Out[82]= {49, 68, 13}

> ⚠ The infix form of **Optional** is a colon (:). There are *two* distinct commands whose infix form is given by a colon (:). For an expression matching the form *symbol:pattern*, the meaning is **Pattern[***symbol, pattern***]**. On the other hand, for an expression matching the form *pattern:expression*, the meaning is **Optional[***pattern, expression***]**. So the left side of the definition above could have been entered as **randomSample[x_List, y_:3]**. This can be confusing to someone trying to learn about patterns, but it never leads to syntactic ambiguity, for the first argument to **Pattern** must be symbol, while the first argument to **Optional** should be a pattern object. Mercifully, this dual use of a single symbol is exceedingly rare (another example is !, which is used for both **Factorial** and the logical negation command **Not**).

Exercises 8.8

1. Define a function **f** with a single argument. The function will return unevaluated unless

   a. the argument is an even integer greater than 10. In this case the function returns the string "**success**".

   b. the argument is either an even integer, or is greater than 10. In this case the function returns the string "**success**".

2. Explain the following output. Doesn't **x_1** represent a pattern that will only match the number 1?

   In[83]:= **Clear[f];**
   f[x_ 1] := "success";
   f /@ {1, 2, 2., "donkey"}

   Out[85]= {success, success, success, success}

3. Find a word that contains the five letters "angle," (contiguous, and in that order) and which begins with the letter "q" and ends with the letter "s."

4. A DNA molecule is comprised of two *complementary* strands twisted into a double helix, where each strand may be represented as an ordered sequence of the letters A, C, G, and T. The complementary strand is built from a given strand by replacing every A by T, every T by A, every G by C, and every C by G. In other words, A is swapped with T, and C is swapped with G. Define a command **complementaryDNA** that will take a list of character strings from the four-letter alphabet "A","C","G", and "T" (which is how we will represent a strand of DNA) and return the complementary strand, in which all As and Ts are switched, and in which all Gs and Cs are switched.

5. This exercise concerns the Collatz conjecture, which was discussed in this section.

   a. Write a command **collatz**, that when given a positive integer will return the orbit of that integer under the iterated Collatz process. The conjecture states that every orbit ends at 1, so use **NestWhileList** with iterations occurring as long as the iterated function does not return 1. To be safe, put a cap on it so that it will never carry out more than 1000 iterations.

b. Run the **collatz** command on each of the first 20 integers, and make a **Table** of the results. **Map** the command **Length** over this table to see how many iterations were carried out for each input. Make a **ListPlot** of the results. Did any number require all 1000 possible iterations? If not, we can be confident that every orbit ends in 1.

c. **Map** the **Partition** command over your data table to replace an orbit such as {5,16,8,4,2,1} with a list of pairs of successive numbers, like this: {{5,16},{16,8},{8,4},{4,2},{2,1}}.

d. **Flatten** the result at level 1 to produce a single list of pairs, then feed that list of pairs to the **Union** command (to eliminate duplicate pairs). The list should end like this:
{...{88,44},{106,53},{160,80}}.

e. Use **Map** to **Apply** the command **Rule** to each pair from part c to obtain an amalgamated list of all orbits. It should end like this: {..., 88 → 44, 106 → 53, 160 → 80}. Now feed the result to the command **GraphPlot** to get a visualization of the orbit space for the Collatz process.

f. Repeat the entire exercise for the first 100 integers (rather than just the first twenty). Do it yet again for the first thousand.

6. Use the trigonometric example from page 454 to prove that $\cos(\pi/21)$ is a root of the polynomial $f(x) = 1 + 16\,x + 32\,x^2 - 48\,x^3 - 96\,x^4 + 32\,x^5 + 64\,x^6$. You may wish to take a look at the example from Section 4.6 on page 180.

7. Make a replacement to **Range[15]** and wrap the result in **TabView** to produce the output shown below.

8. Make a command **scaleRuns** that will take a list $\mathcal{L}$ of zeros and ones, and return a list in which every run of k consecutive ones in $\mathcal{L}$ is replaced with k consecutive ks. For instance, the input {1,1,0,1,1,1,0,0} should produce the output {2,2,0,3,3,3,0,0}. You may want to make use of the **Split** command and the **Repeated** command.

9. Use the **scaleRuns** command of the previous exercise to build a command that will take a list of zeros and ones and display it using an **ArrayPlot** with a single row (with one item in the array for each member of the list), and where each consecutive run of ones is shaded according to the length of the run. Use **Partition** to modify this command so that it will break a long sequence (say with more than 50 elements) into several rows.

10. Make a command **differenceTable** that will accept two arguments. The first is a list. The second is an optional argument (with default value 3) that specifies the **ItemSize** for each item in a **Grid**. The output will be a difference table display like the one appearing at the end of Section 8.7 on page 441. You can model the command on the input for the example given there.

Index

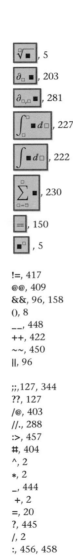

The Student's Introduction
to *Mathematica*®

Second edition

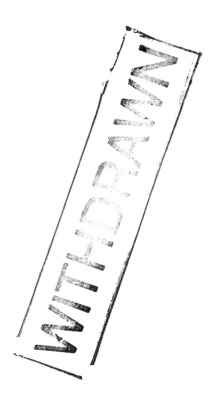

The unique feature of this compact student's
introduction is that it presents concepts in an
order that closely follows a standard mathematics curriculum, rather than structured along
features of the software. As a result, the book
provides a brief introduction to those aspects
of the *Mathematica*® software program most
useful to students. The second edition of this
well-loved book is completely rewritten for
Mathematica® 6, including coverage of the
new dynamic interface elements, several hundred exercises, and a new chapter on programming. This book can be used in a variety
of courses, from precalculus to linear algebra. Used as a supplementary text it will aid
in bridging the gap between the mathematics
in the course and *Mathematica*®. In addition to its course use, this book will serve as
an excellent tutorial for those wishing to learn
Mathematica® and brush up on their mathematics at the same time.

Bruce F. Torrence and Eve A. Torrence are both
Professors in the Department of Mathematics at
Randolph-Macon College, Virginia.